PUBLIC HEALTH

IN THE VICTORIAN AGE

VICTORIAN SOCIAL CONSCIENCE

A series of facsimile reprints of selected articles from
*The Edinburgh Review, The Westminster Review, The Quarterly
Review, Blackwood's Magazine* and *Fraser's Magazine*
1802–1870

THE SERIES INCLUDES:

Poverty 4 vols.
Urban Problems 2 vols.
The Working Classes 4 vols.
Prostitution
Emigration
Population Problems 2 vols.
Trade Unions 4 vols.
Working Conditions
Public Health 2 vols.

PUBLIC HEALTH IN THE VICTORIAN AGE

Debates on the issue from

19th century critical journals

With an introduction

by

Ruth Hodgkinson

Volume I

1973

GREGG INTERNATIONAL PUBLISHERS LIMITED

Publisher's Note.
Articles entitled 'Mal 'aria' *Quarterly Review* Vol 30 1823
and 'Public Health and Mortality' *Quarterly Review* Vol 66
1840 have been abridged

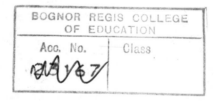

ISBN 0 576 53263 0

Republished in 1973 by Gregg International Publishers Limited
Westmead, Farnborough, Hants, England

Printed in Germany

CONTENTS

Dr Haygarth on Infectious Fevers — Edinburgh Review Vol 1 1802 pp 245–252

Willan and others on Vaccination — Edinburgh Review Vol 9 1806 pp 32–66

Pamphlets on Vaccination — Edinburgh Review Vol 15 1809 pp 322–351

On the Causes, Cure and Prevention of Contagious Fever — Edinburgh Review Vol 31 1818 pp 413–440

Vaccination and Small-pox — Edinburgh Review Vol 37 1822 pp 325–337

Sanitary Reform — Edinburgh Review Vol 91 1849 pp 210–228

Supply of Water to the Metropolis — Edinburgh Review Vol 91 1849 pp 377–408

Cholera and Quarantine — Edinburgh Review Vol 96 1852 pp 403–435

History of Small-Pox and Vaccination — Quarterly Review Vol 19 1818 pp 357–375

Contagion and Quarantine — Quarterly Review Vol 27 1822 p. 524–553

Mal 'aria — Quarterly Review Vol 30 1823 pp 133–140

Plague, a Contagious Disease — Quarterly Review Vol 33 1825 pp 218–257

Vaccination — Quarterly Review Vol 33 1825 pp 550–560

Directions of the Privy Council — Quarterly Review Vol 46 1831 pp 264–273

Public Health and Mortality — Quarterly Review Vol 66 1840 pp 115–130

Report on the Sanitary Condition of the Labouring Classes — Quarterly Review Vol 71 1842 pp 417–453

Sanitary Consolidation — Quarterly Review Vol 88 1850 pp 435–492

INTRODUCTION

Consideration of the health of the people on its present scale and complexity has been another product of the Industrial Revolution. If becoming 'the workshop of the world' worsened living conditions, it also gradually made amelioration possible. An increase in national wealth meant a rise in the standard of living; and the great technological and scientific advances played their part. Later came the dependence on progress in scientific medicine.

With acceleration in industrialisation, urbanisation and the increase in population, the problems of the public health, in the widest connotation, assumed an urgency never known before in history. The need for a pure water supply, sewage disposal, street paving and cleansing, for instance, had been recognised in antiquity. Overcrowding and insanitary dwellings had always existed, but not to the degree reached in the nineteenth century. Not only did the population double during the first fifty years from an estimated 9 m. to 18 m., but the imbalance of the distribution reached disturbing dimensions. As the mobility of labour increased, the settling and integration of migrants became difficult. This was augmented by the immigration of starving Irish, and later, political refugees from continental Europe. The social upheaval of the Industrial Revolution with its psychological and physical ill effects, the unhealthy environmental and working conditions, poverty, disease, epidemics, were all interrelated problems.

Agricultural areas and decaying centres of domestic industry had their health hazards. But it was in the new urban industrial areas, or extended old ones, that the most blatant abuses arose. Cheap shelter was provided in conglomerations of shoddy back-to-back houses devoid of any amenities, or in decrepit old houses in the town centre, where frequently whole families would share a room without water, sanitation or refuse disposal. Cellar dwellings, insanitary, airless and damp were common. Dark alleys and courts received all the filth and refuse thrown out, not only from private homes but from the innumerable small businesses such as bone or tripe boilers, tanneries or slaughterhouses. Blood, offal, excrement was left to decompose, until sufficiently large heaps had accumulated to make removal a profitable business proposition. A nauseating stench hung permanently over whole neighbourhoods. Domestic smoke was added to the palls of industrial smoke; air pollution was early recognised as a danger to health.

Water was obtained from a pump or standpipe serving dozens, and sometimes hundreds of people. The supply was available for only a few hours a day and not infrequently was drawn from rivers into which sewers emptied, or from wells where the surface water was contaminated. For rich and poor, lack of adequate and efficient sanitation was a serious danger awaiting not only local and central government action but also technological innovations. Indoor privies of the wealthy drained into cesspits, often in their own cellar, and emptied rarely. Outdoor privies or a 'necessary' (a tub) were shared by many families of poor. Besides the filth, stench, contaminated water and insalubrious homes, the health of the labouring classes was undermined by the poor quality and quantity of food. Malnutrition was a by-product of low wages, casual labour and unemployment. Food adulteration was common, extending even to poisonous additives.

Closely allied to the degradation of domestic life in the first half of the nineteenth century were the conditions of work. Factories subjected operatives to an intensity, speed and depersonalisation of work to which the labour force had been unaccustomed. The psychological ill-effects were matched by the physical degeneration. Long, unbroken hours of work in humid, ill-ventilated and dust-laden environment (a worker could be fined if he opened a window or was caught wasting time washing himself) impaired the health of the 'Hands' and also affected succeeding generations. Outbreaks of 'fevers' and debilitating complaints were common. In addition there was much maiming and mutilation through the dangerous and unfenced machinery. Many masters were very brutal especially with their child workers.

Conditions in the coalmines were equally inhuman. In 1840, 3,000 women and girls were still working underground, hauling tubs of hewn coal by means of belts and chains attached to their bodies. Mills and mines received the greatest notoriety, but for the longest part of the nineteenth century the largest number of work people were employed in small workshops or in their own homes. In the mid-sixties three quarters of a million were engaged in the clothing, laundry and carpet industries alone. Confined twelve to sixteen hours in overcrowded, overheated rooms with their vitiated atmosphere, workers were prone to contracting lung diseases and fevers. In the sweated trades a whole family might live and work in a single room. Health and lives were gravely wasted. Government interference did not come until late, and once again, improvement was aided by technological advances in industry. It was similar with the unhealthy trades, where occupational diseases such as lead poisoning and lung affections were common almost until the end of the century.

The expectation of life is a good index of the health of the people. In industrial areas in mid-century it was 18 to 25, and 40 for the country as a whole. The general mortality rate was 22 per 1,000; this did not begin to fall until the last quarter of the century to reach 16 per 1,000 in 1900. But such statistics do not give the complete picture. A large proportion of people suffered permanently from subnormal health or some form of physical disability as a result of environmental and working conditions or undernourishment. Succeeding generations were born weakly. The 'submerged masses' of the politician had a far deeper and wider connotation. Closely interrelated with immediate health problems were the causes and the consequences of widespread promiscuity, a high illegitimacy rate, early childbearing, infanticide, orphanage, crime, brutality and alcoholism.

Obviously a great deal of medical care was required. But little was available for the underprivileged. Quacks flourished well into the second half of the nineteenth century. Countless poor could not afford treatment or medicines of any kind. After the new Poor Law of 1834 the destitute sick came under the Poor Law medical service, and this grew to great dimensions by the end of the century. But how effective was personal medical care or curative medicine? Modern medical science was still in its infancy. Medical training, practice and organization had to undergo radical improvement before the profession could cope with the increasing demands upon it. Institutional medical treatment was unpopular. It was also inadequate. Hospital hygiene, amenities and nursing were generally scandalous during the first half of the nineteenth century. This held for the workhouse sick wards, and the voluntary hospital founded to cater for the poorer classes.

Although there was dire necessity for improving curative medicine this was less vital at the time than preventing the infectious crowd diseases and epidemics. 'Environmental' disease had to be tackled by 'sanitary' measures. Preventive medicine had to combat smallpox, the fevers, cholera and tuberculosis, the greatest killer of the time, before there could be an effective scientific medical revolution in the twentieth century. The public health movement was continuous but it was fear of epidemics, particularly cholera, that immediately roused the apathetic or shook the government into legislation. The first outbreak of asiatic cholera occurred in 1831–2 and took over 50,000 lives. A Central Board of Health and ineffectual local health boards were formed. All were disbanded when the scare was over. The second epidemic came in 1848, and again there were 50,000 deaths. Between 1848 and 1854 cholera claimed a quarter of a million victims, and the third epidemic in 1854, 20,000. The fourth and last epidemic broke out in 1866 when there were 14,000 deaths.

By the 1860s there had also been four epidemics of typhoid, but the disease was endemic and accounted for about 20,000 deaths a year. Typhus, confused so long with typhoid, took 4,000 lives a year. The epidemic of scarlet fever in 1840 saw 20,000 deaths. Smallpox was one of the most dreaded diseases. It was endemic in urban areas, and throughout the nineteenth century there was an average of 6,000 deaths a year. During the epidemic of the late thirties 31,000 people succumbed, and 44,000 in that of 1871–3.

All the problems which beset Britain as she emerged as an industrial country were accentuated by the depression which followed the long Napoleonic War. Inevitably an increase in disease correlated with an increase in poverty. Large-scale government measures were imperative. But effective reforms were long delayed for many reasons. The British had no experience of state paternalism. Public action for public welfare had few champions. Neither did the people feel that the state had any obligation for improving health and welfare. Parliament, composed of a landed aristocracy, was ill-tuned to the needs of a new age. The fear of revolution, which lasted for decades, restrained many purposeful philanthropists who would have been concerned with ameliorating the lot of the labouring classes. The chaos of local administration militated against local improvement. Local authorities and private utility companies jealously guarded their rights from central interference. Vested interests were powerful opponents for generations to public health or welfare measures. The Treasury kept a tight rein on civil expenditure, and two-thirds of the national budget was allocated to military departments.

So improvement came only after much controversy and many heated battles. Local Improvement Commissioners existed in the eighteenth century but these could not cope with rapid urbanisation. Overlapping of functions and inefficiency could only be met by government intervention on a national scale. Gradually the prevailing philosophy of *laissez-faire* was undermined from many sides, for industrial expansion depended on a healthy labour force. The nineteenth century also witnessed a powerful re-surgence of humanitarianism. It also spawned whole new classes of men: doctors who became familiar with the lives of the poor, educationalists, and administrators in new public services, such as the Poor Law, Public Health and Factory. There arose many new professions directly or indirectly connected with improving health and welfare. And regularly, the outbreak of an epidemic, especially of cholera, was the catalyst in getting action out of a recalcitrant or procrastinating administration.

Everything depended on central and local government reform. Improvement in the lives of the working classes only began after the Parliamentary Reform Act of 1832, and the Municipal Corporations Act of 1835. Civil Service reform started after the middle of the century, as did the increasing use of inspectors and special bodies for implementing legislation. Also by this time it was recognised that self-interest and self-help could not cope with the ever increasing problems of health and working conditions. So the ruling upper and middle classes, long before the lower classes, became aware of the need for government responsibility and obligation in matters affecting the public health.

Most of our welfare services stem from measures for combating poverty. The architect of the new Poor Law of 1834 was Edwin Chadwick. He early recognised the close connection between poverty and sickness, and his transference in 1848 from Poor Law to Public Health is significant. In 1838–39 he instigated Poor Law investigations into the worst slums of London, following these with a monumental inquiry covering huge sections of Great Britain. The lesson still being learned from Chadwick's Sanitary Report of 1842 is that the prevention of sickness is not only a question of humanity but also of economy. This was a forceful weapon in his long struggle to convert public opinion. Chadwick was also responsible for the organisation of the Royal Commission on the Health of Towns, and although not a member, drafted almost the entire first report of 1844.

But few giants have succeeded alone or begun *de novo*. Chadwick had a few able allies and dedicated lieutenants. The progenitors of the nineteenth century public health movement were a small group of doctors in Manchester who voluntarily formed a short-lived local Board of Health in 1795 headed by Dr. Percival and his 'Resolutions'. By the time Chadwick came to power Dr. J. P. Kay (later Sir James Kay-Shuttleworth) had produced a survey on *The Moral and Physical Conditions of the Working Classes employed in the Cotton manufacture of Manchester* (1833) and Dr. Southwood Smith, had in 1825, launched the Sanitary Idea in its new nineteenth century concept with his long essay on Fevers. This was extended into a book in 1830.

As with other areas of welfare the success of the public health movement depended on the growing number of societies. Most effective were the Health of Towns Association founded in 1844, and the Epidemiological Society in 1850. The Literary and Philosophical, and the Statistical Societies of large towns, such as Liverpool, Manchester and Leeds contained large numbers of doctors and reformers who could enlighten business men and local dignitaries. The published Transactions of all societies contributed to informing public opinion and pressurising the government. And essential to every aspect of health improvement was Dr. William Farr, Compiler of Abstracts at the Registrar General's Office. For forty years, from 1840 to 1880, he appended long detailed essays to the statistical reports, not only analysing facts and figures, but also including his many ideas on reforms.

The first really effective Public Health measure was introduced in 1848. The General Board of Health was instituted for a trial period of five years and local Boards of Health could be formed as single health authorities and appoint medical officers. But the Act was only mandatory where the death rate exceeded 22 per 1,000, or if one tenth of the ratepayers petitioned. There was great delay in implementing every section of the statute, but some drainage and sanitation schemes got underway. There was unusual procrastination in the appointment of Medical Officers of Health, and these like the Poor Law Medical Officers worked only part-time. The special qualification of the Diploma in Public Health was not introduced until 1875.

The General Board of Health came to an end in 1854. It was renewed on an annual basis until 1858 when it was replaced by the Medical Office of the Privy Council. Personal opposition to Chadwick was the primary reason for the fall of the Board, and his public career ended prematurely in 1854. Chadwick's unpopularity and his genius lay in his unflinching determination to introduce strong central control and to drive an unwilling government and country into efficient rationalised administration. Further, he insisted on rigid conformity to a principle.

Chadwick's mantle fell on John Simon, the second giant in the public health movement. He instituted inquiries into every aspect of health, hygiene and living and working conditions, employing special investigators and inspectors. For a generation he published massive annual reports on the health of the country. Although he felt his work frustrated, public health interest and activity moved on a larger plane. They also gradually amended the purely Sanitary Idea and became more medically orientated. And from the fifties, whilst medical science and practice were still largely ineffective, government activity was accelerated to improve health and living standards. There were many Nuisances Removal and Diseases Prevention Acts, Lodging Houses Acts, Factory Acts. Food adulteration began to be investigated, and measures for better water supplies and sanitation were implemented, if slowly. Personal medical care was being steadily improved for the destitute by the many Orders of the Poor Law Board. The effects were cumulative and interrelated. After mid-century, the rise in the standard of living and acceleration in technological advances in many directions contributed to slow improvement in national health and welfare.

The Sanitary Idea lingered on, but the new science of bacteriology was emerging. This was to usher in additional concepts for public health. The miasmatic theory which predominated during the first half of the nineteenth century was old. Disease was regarded as originating directly from filth and excrement. The effluvia or miasma in the air had to be removed or prevented by sanitary improvement. This was linked with the battle between contagionists who believed in infection, and the anti-contagionists who doubted whether any disease could be transmitted by direct infection (The demarcation was not as strict as has been supposed; this will become evident from the reviews). Just before mid-century, John Snow with his scientific inquiries into cholera, and William Budd into typhoid, produced evidence that the cause of infection was some specific organism which was passed by intestinal discharges into sewage, and then through defective sanitation into water supplies. Although the annihilation of the organism was their primary target, they regarded the cleanliness, pure water supply and efficient sewage disposal advocated by the sanitarians as very important.

In 1849 another significant development in the medical aspect of public health occurred. Typhoid and typhus fever were differentiated. Other infectious diseases were also being described.

It was just a generation after Southwood Smith, in *The Edinburgh Review* of 1825, had published his monumental paper which marked the turning point in the theory and practice of preventive medicine from simple quarantine measures to 'sanitary science'. He had helped to launch modern public health concepts. Yet within a few decades the miasmatic theory was proved wrong and his sanitary reform ideas insufficient.

It is in the context of current medical theories, and not only the practical manifestations of the public health movement, that the texts of the journals which follow must be viewed.

The press at any time is an index of what is uppermost in the public mind. The fear of epidemics, particularly of cholera, was in the forefront in non-medical as well as medical circles. So was smallpox and vaccination. Jenner had won great acclaim at the end of the eighteenth century, but until the mid-nineteenth century his discovery aroused serious controversy. The many and very long articles in numerous journals are therefore a good indication of how much thought was devoted to the theories and practice of combating infectious diseases, either by the old quarantine regulations or by more comprehensive sanitary improvement. Further, reformers are dependent first on the public being made aware of problems and, second, on creating interest in their amelioration. The periodicals of the nineteenth century played a leading part in enlightening the middle and upper classes, those sections of the community which controlled the destiny of the whole. They must take their place alongside the Transactions and Reports of specialist and learned societies as aiding the public health movement and indirectly bringing pressure to bear on the government.

The Journals*

The nineteenth century was the great age of journals. They were generally quarterlies of prodigious size. For us they provide an index of the issues which predominated at any particular moment. Current thoughts, particular theories, and the arguments in the major controversies are made available in great detail. We can trace the evolution of ideas in politics, economics and medicine and in social reform. We learn not only more of the men known to us, but also of the lesser known who were involved in important issues. The generalisations with which we are familiar are elucidated and substantiated.

The journals were published with a dual purpose: education and entertainment. The author of *Cholera Gossip*, Dr. W. A. Guy (*Fraser's*, vol. 40, 1849), pointed out that he was writing for readers who would open the pages of the magazine for relaxation, not mere amusement. He therefore wished to speak with seriousness, but not weary the reader with formidable tables and sustained discussion. That so many authors produced both, gives us an insight into the demand, standards and stamina of the nineteenth-century reading public. It is also an indication of the earnest desire for enlightenment in every field.

As those who governed the journals held particular principles on politics or social and economic policies, contributors were chosen carefully. But articles were frequently published presenting opposing points of view, of service to contemporaries, and researchers now. *The Edinburgh Review* claimed that its reviewers were free to speak their minds, and did so in no uncertain terms. Editors and authors kept a close watch on each others' publications. In 1853 (vol. 47) *Fraser's* pointed out that the fifth and sixth numbers of *The Westminster Review* of 1825, on contagion and quarantine, had attracted a great deal of attention, but accused the writer (Southwood Smith) of bias. He had 'ignored facts propounded by experienced men who held opposite opinions'. The reviewer (unidentified) had done his homework, for he quoted the *Quarterly* (vol. 33, 1825) which came out in direct refutation of the *Westminster*, and the *Edinburgh* of September 1826 'which closed

---

* I am greatly indebted to the *Wellesley Index to Victorian Periodicals, 1824–1900*, vols. 1 & 2, ed. Walter E. Houghton. This gives the identity of most contributors, short general notes on the journals and a bibliography of articles. Vol. 3 of the *Wellesley Index* has not yet been published, so we have to await information regarding *The Westminster Review*.

the contest'. He concluded with a recapitulation on quarantine from the 1852 October issue of the *Edinburgh*.

It was often politic for authors to remain anonymous. But it was also the policy of the journals until the mid-sixties for their articles to remain unsigned. Ninety per cent remained so for the century as a whole, and always in the *Edinburgh* and *Quarterly*. The writers were all men of erudition and of high standing in a particular profession. Many wrote with great knowledge about a remarkable variety of subjects. All showed literary ability. One author maintained that the general reading public 'derive knowledge and form opinions exclusively from the laudatory articles'. (*Fraser's*, vol. 47, 1853)

The Edinburgh Review was founded in 1802 by Francis Jeffrey, later Lord Jeffrey, Sydney Smith and Francis Horner. Jeffrey was a celebrated Scottish judge and staunch Whig politician. He was editor from 1803 to 1829. His own contributions to the journal were collected into four volumes in the 1840s. Smith was a divine and a reformer, but also a well-known author and wit. Horner, a barrister and politician, was the brother of Leonard, the geologist and educationalist who became chief factory inspector. Lord Brougham, the radical reformer, was closely connected with these three, and was responsible for many outspoken reviews. Although the *Edinburgh* stood out for social and political reform, it tried to steer a moderate course.

The Quarterly Review was launched in 1809 by the High Tories to counter the *Edinburgh*'s opposition to the government. The founders: Lord Canning, the statesman, John Murray, the publisher, and Sir Walter Scott were, however, not reactionaries, but believed in a 'humane paternalism'. They were not apathetic to social reform, for they included essays by Lord Shaftesbury for example, on factories, child labour and ragged schools. *The Quarterly* like *The Edinburgh Review* enlisted a small group of regular contributors who wrote on an extraordinary wide range of topics.

Fraser's Magazine for Town and Country appeared in London monthly. For over fifty years it represented 'progressive thought', chiefly on politics, but also on religion and social conditions. It was the brainchild of William Maginn who was the first editor, from 1830 to 1847. He was an extremely versatile Irish wit whose work had been too outspoken for *Blackwood's*. Four of the six articles reproduced from *Fraser's* are by Dr. W. A. Guy, a pioneer nineteenth-century medical statistician and a leading sanitary reformer. Altogether Guy wrote thirteen lengthy essays on public health questions for *Fraser's*.

Probably the greatest influence of any journal on social and health issues was that of *The Westminster Review*. It came into being in 1825 and it is significant that Southwood Smith, the outstanding public health reformer, was one of the founders. He used it as his airing ground, and in it Chadwick also published many of his ideas.

In the public health field all these journals followed a similar pattern presenting much the same subjects. Thereby they illustrated which were the predominant issues at any particular time. Foremost in the early nineteenth century were the conflicting theories on the etiology of infectious diseases, contagion, quarantine and isolation, and vaccination. The 'fevers' and cholera were rightly an obsession. From the 1840s interest in public health measures was demonstrated by the emphasis being shifted to an analysis of books and reports on the health of towns, and to scientific studies on water supplies and the need for state action on a national scale. Further, it is of interest to note how many reviews gave extensive coverage to overseas experiences and developments. The international aspect was very strong.

We must remember that these were not medical journals, nor were many writers on medical subjects doctors. But as was said in *The Edinburgh Review* (vol. 6, 1806) on smallpox and vaccination, medical questions ought in general to be left to medical journals, but the topics were of such importance that they were of great interest to everyone. All the reviews were written with great knowledge and skill. To be able to amass so many facts and statistics, and to sustain arguments to such a degree was an amazing tribute to the learning and capacity for hard work of the authors. It was no less to the readers. Rarely were the articles restricted to analysing the books before them. They were generally full-scale essays embodying the reviewer's own research and opinions.

The early public health movement owed a debt to Edinburgh. Its medical school was alone in Great Britain in interesting its students in public health problems. In 1807 it appointed the first Professor of Medical Jurisprudence and Medical Police, Andrew Duncan. From 1820 to 1856 William Alison, a great public health reform enthusiast, was Professor of Medicine. Owing to the restrictions placed on medical education in England up to the 1830s, many Englishmen went for their training to western Europe or Scotland. Southwood Smith, Kay and Percival were only three of many, who returned home influenced by what they had learned in Edinburgh on the importance of viewing medicine in a broader social context.

It is therefore significant that the first volume of *The Edinburgh Review* published a study on the prevention of infectious fevers. The author of the book discussed was John Haygarth, who had pioneered the treatment of fever by isolation in 1783, and had also written on smallpox and inoculation. Haygarth addressed his work to Dr. Percival, founder of the voluntary Manchester Board of Health and one of the pioneer public health reformers. The study was first presented to the Bath Literary and Philosophical Society. (We have noted the importance of learned societies as providing a meeting place for doctors.) John Thomson, the reviewer, was one of the early influential writers of *The Edinburgh Review* group. He was a surgeon and expert on military medicine. He agreed with Haygarth's ideas on fever being contagious and that victims should be isolated to prevent its spread. Isolation wards were to be well-ventilated and cleanliness was stressed. (Such improvements were very necessary in institutions at the time.) In 1818 the *Edinburgh* published another review on fevers. It was written by either Thomson or

Dr. A. J. G. Marcet of Guy's Hospital. As all reviews, it was not only an analysis of eight publications, but a prodigious work embracing the history of fevers, and the ideas on their causes and cure in the light of medical knowledge of the time. The prevention of fevers should no longer be left to physicians but should be taken up by the politicians and philanthropists. Typhus, it was pointed out, was of several varieties (typhus and typhoid had not yet been differentiated) ' but all arise from specific contagion' and fatigue and subnormal health made people susceptible to the disease. Again, isolation, fumigation and cleanliness were prescribed, and the setting up of fever hospitals.

In 1825 Dr. Southwood Smith countered in *The Westminster Review*. As physician to the only special fever hospital in London, he spoke with wide experience of fevers. With his two long essays he has been attributed with founding the whole new concept of sanitary science which had hitherto meant quarantine regulations only. Ostensibly he was reviewing thirteen works including two books by Charles MacLean, the much travelled medical and political writer, who utterly repudiated the idea of contagion and was regarded as leader of the anti-contagionists. Southwood Smith gave a clear definition of contagious disease and the theories. With detailed accounts of yellow fever and other fevers abroad he tried to prove that fevers were non-contagious. He elaborated his own thesis of the miasmatic theory of the etiology of disease and championed the anti-contagionists. By stressing the connection between sanitary conditions and disease, he became one of the pioneers of the sanitary reform movement. He came out strongly against the absurd and ineffective quarantine regulations: he did not, as others, demand total abolition, but rather that they should form part of a sanitary code. This, he concluded, deserved the serious attention of the physician, the merchant, the statesman and the philanthropist. He succeeded.

Five years later he published an extension of these reviews in his book *A Treatise on Fever* and emphasised preventive measures. This book in turn received an exciting review in the *Westminster* (vol. 12, 1830). Apart from giving an excellent synopsis of Smith's Treatise, Smith's tenets on the pathology of fevers were compared with William Stoker's *Pathological Observations on Continued Fever*. The author presented the conflicting arguments to the general public, as well as the medical profession, for the ' controversy which now agitates this country upon the subject of Fever, is of equal importance to every class of society'. Because of the ' great national distress', it was of the utmost urgency to find means of prevention and treatment.

By this time the threat of an invasion of asiatic cholera loomed large. *The Westminster*, true to its altered title, *The Westminster and Foreign Quarterly Review*, published a long work on the incidence of cholera overseas (vol. 15, 1831). The panic was beginning and measures for prevention were sought desperately. New and old disinfectants were among the suggestions. The author deplored the dissension in the medical profession regarding the many forms of treatment, which included bleeding and opium.

Fraser's published a review on John Webster's *Essay on Epidemic Cholera* (vol. 6, 1832). Webster repudiated the contagious character of the disease and the asiatic origin of the epidemic. He believed the new form was only a more severe strain of the bilious cholera which was always present. Dr. D. M. Moir, an authority on cholera, attacked these assertions in his survey, but proposed that the truth probably lay between the contagionist and anti-contagionist theories.

The Quarterly (vol. 27, 1822) had produced a long article analysing the controversy over contagion and epidemic diseases. As on so many occasions the plague entered into the discussion. Quarantine was also rarely omitted, and here again the restrictive, expensive system was criticised. Economic reasons were always included. In 1825 Robert Gooch, an Edinburgh physician, continued on the same theme, and in 1831 Robert Ferguson published a review on cholera. The versatility of medical men at this time is noteworthy. Ferguson was an obstetrician, later becoming accoucheur to Queen Victoria, but he wrote many well-informed papers for the *Quarterly* on a wide variety of subjects, including prisons and public health. In volume 46 he reviewed seven works on cholera, devoting forty pages to discussing the disease abroad. He then criticised the regulations of the Privy Council for combating the epidemics: 'the government of this country neither has done, nor are doing, nor even as yet contemplate doing, what we conceive to be their duty in relation to that pestilence which hovers at our doors'. After attacking the government's inertia he gave suggestions adding 'notes' for private families.

The second cholera epidemic of 1848 brought panic once again. From the journals we learn that public health-wise, little had been achieved since 1831–32. Medical ideas had also altered little. But John Snow, through the observations he made of the incidence of cholera, was enabled to present his new theories in 1849. In the same year, the *Westminster* published a review which focussed first on the great early epidemics such as the Black Death and the Great Plague. Then the startling observation followed: that asiatic cholera was not a new disease in 1817 in India, but already existed in the seventeenth and eighteenth centuries. Turning to the General Board of Health reports on quarantine, the author pointed out that this proved conclusively that quarantine establishments were useless as a means of prevention and that isolating the sick was inhuman, a relic of medieval superstition.

A new aid was by this time beginning to make significant contributions to combating disease. This was the official collection and publication of statistics. *Fraser's* (vol. 40, 1849) printed an excellent article entitled 'Cholera Gossip' in which W. A. Guy praised the facts and figures offered by the Registrar General. Well qualified to do so as a medical statistician, Guy analysed the information on the incidence and deaths from cholera. He insisted that as the places and classes of people attacked were known, something could be done by sanitary measures to prevent further epidemics.

With a third outbreak of cholera threatening in 1853, the Board of Health reports on quarantine and on the 1848–49 epidemic were closely scrutinised.

The Board was attacked in *Fraser's* (vol. 47) for its non-contagionist attitude and for relying solely on sanitary measures for the prevention of disease. The quarantine issue was still open, so was the contagionist theory. *The Edinburgh Review* (vol. 96, 1852) also published a paper on the Board's reports. James Howell, possibly an army medical officer, praised the sanitary movement, and in recapitulating public health progress, drew attention particularly to the reports made to the Poor Law Commission in 1838–39 by Doctors Southwood Smith, Arnott and Kay, as being the first to attract the attention of Parliament to the causes of sickness among the poor.

Smallpox, another scourge of the nineteenth century, was not involved in contagion theories. It had always been recognised as contagious, but controversy was aroused by vaccination. It must be remembered that Jenner lived until 1823, so probably read the tremendous amount written for and against his discovery. *The Edinburgh Review* (vol. 9, 1806) published an article exceedingly informative at the time, and interesting to the historian. On the dispute over vaccination and inoculation, it purported to survey a tract of Robert Willan, an Edinburgh graduate and well known physician and dermatologist. In fact it was the reviewer's own thesis, normal procedure in the journals. Frequently, books or reports for review were not even mentioned. The article is attributed to Andrew Duncan, the younger. He was an eminent physician of Edinburgh who had several professorships at the medical school and there held the first chair in Medical Jurisprudence and Medical Police in Britain, 1807 to 1819. He presented all arguments, including the original quotations which reveal the strength of feeling aroused. The vituperate language, not uncommon in the nineteenth century, would scarcely be regarded as ethical today!

Much of the controversy arose because vaccination was still new. The vaccine was sometimes impure, despite the National Vaccine Establishment. Re-vaccination was not known and the dosage was unsure. When vaccination became compulsory in 1853 conscientious objectors joined the medically orientated anti-vaccinationists.

In 1810 *The Edinburgh Review* (vol. 15) produced a long list of material published on vaccination, with comments by Frances Jeffrey. This, he said, was just a small portion of the literature on 'acrimonious controversy'. We learn that 'this disgraceful warfare' had, until 1809 been confined to the Metropolis and had only just crossed the Tweed. Eight years later, the *Quarterly* (vol. 19) produced a good history of smallpox in antiquity, and in other countries with their ideas for prevention and treatment. In 1825 (vol. 33) Robert Gooch, the Edinburgh physician, discussed the pamphlet of Robert Ferguson in which he lamented that in the native country of Jenner's incalculable discovery, crowds of poor went unvaccinated. In many other European countries vaccination was compulsory and mortality from the disease had greatly decreased. Gooch gave statistics and compared records with those of towns in Britain. He believed immunity was for life, but drew attention to the conjecture that the influence of vaccination might wear off.

For mitigating the severity of the disease Ferguson proposed first vaccinate, and a few days later inoculate with smallpox.

In addition to covering the medical aspects of public health, the theories and controversies and the terrible incidence of infectious disease, the journals were alive to the activity and practical aspirations of reformers. Evidence that sanitary reform was arousing wide attention in the country from the 1840s is provided by the reviews. The subject now predominated over those which we have noted. A public health policy had been established.

In 1840 Ferguson had deplored that 'England is the only country devoid of a medical police (state health policy and administration) and into which the public health has been allowed to shift for itself' (*Quarterly* vol. 66). Chadwick was just beginning. His monumental Sanitary Report was admirably summarised and discussed in the *Quarterly* (vol. 71, 1842) by Sir Francis B. Head, an author and colonial governor. He emphasised Chadwick's point: that the health of the nation was nearly synonymous with its wealth. It was the duty as well as the interest of the state to protect its 'labouring power'. The public health movement was furthered by the reports of the Health of Towns, and the Metropolitan Sanitary Commissions. W. A. Guy not only analysed these in *Fraser's* (vol. 36, 1847) but compared London with other European capitals, once again making use of his statistical knowledge. He eulogised on the sanitary reform movement and re-iterated its objectives very clearly.

The first real success of the reformers came with the Public Health Act of 1848, which understandably raised tremendous interest – and concern – in the country. The Bill had been emaciated and many very necessary improvements omitted. Whilst deploring the shortcomings of the statute, Guy called it 'An Act which, in honest, firm and willing hands, is capable of working a complete physical revolution in the disease-smitten towns of England' (*Fraser's*, vol. 38, 1848). He praised Chadwick but warned him that England 'will not suffer even an enlightened and benevolent despotism'. He was right. In 1854 Chadwick was sacked. Guy, once again in *Fraser's* (vol. 50, 1854), eulogised on the achievements of the Board of Health but outlined all the work which still remained to be done. He condemned the House of Commons for murdering eight or nine public health measures which had recently been launched and also the local opposition. As a portent for the distant future he mentiond John Simon's suggestion of a Ministry of Health.

A characteristic of Chadwick's administration was his dependence on civil engineers. For his sanitary science they were more important to him than doctors. It is therefore significant to remember the development of the engineering profession and how several branches aided public health. This was reflected in the choice of contributors to the journals by mid-century, and their subjects. The *Edinburgh* published one of its best reviews in vol. 91, 1850; the author was William O'Brien, an engineer. He was also an excellent historian of public health progress. As a disciple of Chadwick he pointed out the high cost of medical care for the poor, an expense to the parish which was to a great extent preventable. True to his training, he gave a critical account of London water supplies. A more technical study on water supply was provided in *The Westminster Review* in 1856. The ideas of Josiah Parks, the civil engineer and inventor of deep drainage, were discussed, and the experiments of Dr. Arthur Hassall, one of the pioneers of purer food and water, were criticised. Hassall was the most important figure in the *Lancet* inquiries of the early fifties into food adulteration, and again in similar subsequent government investigations. *The Quarterly Review* (vol. 88, 1850) also printed a paper by a sanitary engineer. F. O. Ward had earlier published an article on London water supplies, but in 1850 he produced 58 pages which included not only a survey of public health statutes and government reports, but in the main, advocated very emphatically the need for strong administrative centralisation and consolidation of responsible local bodies, in the interest of efficiency and economy. He was a true follower of Chadwick, but the principles were not realised until the closing decades of the century.

However necessary, the sanitary movement was too narrowly conceived for some reformers, who desired a more comprehensive approach. The *prevention* of disease was not enough. The promotion of the health of the people as a more complete policy was envisaged under a system of *medical police* – in the German connotation. The term was anathema in England and rarely used. In 1846 *The Westminster Review* dared to entitle an extensive essay: *The Medical Police of the United Kingdom*. This advocated the reorganisation of the medical profession and medical education, the appointment of full-time medical officers, public provision of medical care, and the closer relation of medicine to political economy. The *Westminster* was always a pioneer in social and health reforms.

The reviews chosen from these journals are but a selection. There are many more on closely related subjects. And there are many more journals. The mine of information presented in periodicals was essential to creating an awareness of problems and for soliciting sympathy and action. In this they succeeded. They were intended for a wider spectrum of society, and if they aimed at entertainment and relaxation, we must today marvel at the intelligence of the reader and wonder at his seriousness. It is hard for us to imagine anyone save the dedicated reformer, or reactionary opponent, appreciating the length and depth of the articles.

These reprints are not for the casually interested. They are for the researcher or for scholars who wish to fill in the gaps left in conventional histories. They must come with a sound knowledge of public health history, and their lengthy study will be amply rewarded by exciting new discoveries. They will be able to survey the domestic scene more closely and also make valuable comparisons with other countries. (It is for researchers that I have given names and a little information on authors, but the *Wellesley Index* should be consulted in conjunction with these periodicals. This would provide fuller perspective.)

For the historian, for whom it is essential that he view his special interest in broad context, the nineteenth-century journals are also a must. From the writings of the time we can recapture events, character and ideas. They are not only valuable source material but help us to live in that period and feel and think as people did then.

We must be grateful for these reproductions for making these records readily available. Even more so, when we are told that 'Victorian periodicals are doomed to rapid destruction due to chemical reactions in the pulp paper on which they are printed'.†

Ruth G. Hodgkinson
February 1973

† George W. Cook, The Victorian Periodicals Newsletter, 10, 1970, p. 37.

Art. XXIX. *A Letter to Dr Percival on the Prevention of Infectious Fevers; and an Address to the College of Physicians at Philadelphia, on the Prevention of the American Pestilence.* By John Haygarth, M. D. Cadell & Davis. London, 1801. 8vo. pp. 188.

THE author of this letter has been long favourably known to the public, by his valuable writings on small-pox ; and though the discoveries of Dr Jenner, with regard to the vaccine inoculation, may have, in some degree, superseded his former labours, we are happy to perceive he still continues, with undiminished ardour, to carry on the warfare he had commenced ; and to meditate, in the present work, a new, and, we hope, not unsuccessful blow, at that many-headed monster *contagion*. From this letter it appears, that, while Morveau was engaged in an attempt to subdue the malignity of all pestilential exhalations, by the short and efficacious methods which chymistry affords, this intelligent physician was no less usefully employed, in investigating the nature of febrile contagion, in so far as regards the laws by which it is communicated, and the means by which it may be prevented. Such of our readers as are already acquainted with the outlines of Dr Haygarth's Inquiry with regard to the small-pox, and of his Plan to exterminate that disorder, will enter readily into the train of investigation which he has pursued in the present publication.

This letter is divided into two parts. In the first, the author lays down, and endeavours to illustrate, certain preliminary principles, from which, in the second part, he deduces a number of practical conclusions.

The facts, or cases, upon which the whole of the reasoning in this letter is founded, are exhibited in the form of tables. In these tables the number of families infected, the patient's name, the date when attacked by fever, the date when fever began after being exposed to infection, the number in the family infected, and the number which remained uninfected, are marked in separate columns. This synoptical mode of recording and exhibiting cases in an inquiry of this sort, is attended with many advantages: While it abridges the labour of the observer, it brings within a narrower and more distinct field of view the numerous facts, which, in narration, must have extended over many pages. The facts, which these tables contain, appear to have been observed with great accuracy,; but we are doubtful whether they are sufficiently numerous, to warrant conclusions so very general, as those which our author has deduced from them.

In this inquiry, Dr Haygarth, very properly, in our opinion, takes it for granted, that fever is an infectious disease. In the present state of medical knowledge, indeed, it would not, we conceive, be at all more absurd to deny the existence of fever altogether, than to maintain that it is not propagated by contagion.

The proportion of persons susceptible of febrile infection, as calculated from the *data* contained in the tables, is much greater than, we believe, had been commonly suspected. From the facts there recorded, it would seem that not more than one person in twenty-three escape, of those who have been sufficiently exposed to the action of the contagion.

‘ The same mode of reasoning (p. 33.) as was successfully employed in the inquiry, how to prevent the small-pox, may be equally applicable to the present question. It was there calculated upon the *datum*, that only one person in twenty is naturally exempted from the distemper: that if two together have escaped, the probability that they were never both exposed to an infectious quantity of the poison, is above 400 to 1 ; if three in a family have escaped, above 8000 to 1.’—‘ If all the cases (p. 35.) in succession, where persons have breathed the air of a chamber of a patient ill of a contagious fever, and yet have escaped infection, were estimated in this mode of calculation, the chances would be, not only of thousands, but of millions, indeed many *millions* to one, that such persons had not been exposed to an infectious dose of the poison. ’

In proposing to ascertain the quantity of febrile poison necessary to produce infection, Dr Haygarth remarks, p. 36—

‘ In this whole investigation, you will, I am certain, keep in mind one medical truth—it cannot be called a theory, a term often applied to doubtful disquisitions : the larger the dose of a poison or drug, the greater, in general, is the effect which it produces. ’ &c.

The illustration is ingenious, we confess ; but we are ignorant how far we may safely trust to it, in explaining the operation of contagious poisons. If the principle contended for by Dr Haygarth were admitted, would it not follow, that the violence of an infectious disease must always be in proportion to the quantity of the poison introduced into the system ? Would not, for

instance, the malignity of the casual small-pox always correspond
with the quantity of the poison applied? and, would not the
number of pustules, in the inoculated small-pox, bear always a
definite proportion to the number and size of the punctures
which had been made, and the quantity of inoculating matter
introduced? In reasoning from analogy, we are frequently exposed to many unknown sources of fallacy; and we are never
more in danger of being deceived, than when we attempt to explain one obscure subject by another.

The sphere of infection appears to extend only to a very small
distance from the body of a patient affected with fever.

' In 1777, I began (p. 8.) to ascertain, by clinical observations,
according to what law the variolous infection, and, in 1780 and 1781,
according to what law the febrile infection, is propagated. I found,
that the pernicious effects of the variolous miasm were limited to a
very narrow sphere. In the open air, and in moderate cases, I discovered that the infectious distance does not exceed half a yard.—
Hence, it is probable, that even when the distemper is malignant,
the infectious influence extends but to a few yards from the poison.
I soon also discovered, that the contagion of fevers was confined to
a much narrower sphere. Upon these principles, which it is the main
purpose of this letter to explain and establish, I discerned the safety
and wisdom of admitting fever patients into separate wards of the
Chester Infirmary itself, instead of an adjoining building, as I had
proposed in 1774. '

This is a principle which we should be glad to see fully established, as it would save ourselves and others from many anxieties, which perhaps are groundless, and dangers which exist only in imagination. We must regret, therefore, that the author
has not given a more ample detail of the facts upon which an o-
pinion of so much practical importance is founded; as it does
not seem to follow from the facts stated in the tables, nor indeed
to be directly deducible from any thing contained in the other
parts of the letter.

The infection communicated to several persons at the Old
Bailey in May 1750, by prisoners who had not the fever themselves, and who were placed, during the whole time they were
in court, at a considerable distance from those who received the
infection, seems to have occurred to Dr Haygarth, as an objection
to the opinion, that febrile contagion operates only within a very
narrow sphere: But he endeavours to evade the force of this objection, by supposing, that the febrile poison is infectious at a
greater distance than usual, in air which has been vitiated by the
respiration of a number of persons crowded together. The
production of fever, in these cases, therefore, he regards as an
exception to the law usually followed by nature in the propagation

of contagion. We are not prepared to controvert the hypothesis by which Dr Haygarth solves the difficulty ; but, upon a subject so obscure in its own nature, as the propagation of contagion, we should feel more indebted to the Doctor for an accumulation of new facts, than for any hypothetical explanations,
however ingenious.

We confess we were a little surprised to find Dr Haygarth denying (at p. 54.), in so positive and unqualified a manner, that
the clothes of visitors, &c. exposed to febrile miasms, can ever
acquire a pestilential quality, so as to communicate infection.
He refers, in proof of this opinion, to his Inquiry and Sketch.
We have perused the passages to which he refers, but without
obtaining any additional information on the subject of febrile contagion. We happen indeed to have ovserved, very lately, two
unequivocal instances, in which fever was communicated from one
person to another, through the intervention of a third, who himself never had any symptom of the disease ; and we are at a loss
to conjecture in what way the poison could be conveyed, unless
by the clothes. In one of the instances to which we refer, it
was conveyed to a distance of more than three miles.

From the invisibility of febrile contagion, our author argues,
that it must be dissolved in, and not merely diffused through, the
air ; and he deduces, from that opinion, the following very important conclusion.

' If the febrile miasms (p. 57.) be dissolved in air, and attracted
from it by clothes, they could not, *in the same circumstances*, on any
known principle, be again attracted from clothes by air. This would
be contrary to the law of elective attraction, which is as well founded as any in natural philosophy.

This argument, which is intended as a kind of demonstration
of the impossibility of infection being conveyed from air to
clothes, and from clothes to air again, seems to be somewhat inconsistent with a suggestion contained in page 46—

' It may be a subject of consideration, whether the mischief produced by the contagion of prisoners in a court of justice, may not be
ascribed to the increase of malignity in the febrile poison, when it
has long lodged and *putrefied* in dirty clothes and confined air. '

The proposition, however, as stated by our author, is undoubtedly true ; but there seems to be an unintentional *equivocation* in
the words ' *in the same circumstances.* ' The laws of elective attraction, we allow to be as well founded as any in natural philosophy ; but we deny that they operate in the manner described by
our author. Air and clothes have both, by hypothesis, an affinity for the matter of febrile contagion. If clothes, therefore, be

immersed in air impregnated with this substance, they will imbibe a quantity of the poison, greater, or less indeed, according to the respective affinities of the clothes and the air. But it will not follow, from any law of elective attraction with which we are acquainted, that if clothes, thus impregnated, be carried into a fresh portion of air, this air will not absorb from them a greater or less portion of the poison. On the contrary, we maintain, that the poison will pass from the air to the clothes, and from the clothes to the air again, till the affinities between these substances are brought to an equilibrium. Water and common air, Dr Haygarth must allow, have both an affinity for carbonic acid ; but, because water absorbs a portion of this acid from air which contains it in abundance, are we warranted, either by experiment or observation, to maintain, that the water will not, in any circumstances, impart a portion of the acid to the air ? We are ignorant of the affinities of the different articles of dress for febrile contagion. There may be some among them, for any thing we know, which imbibe in it a large quantity, though it may exist in them in a state of very loose combination. We submit to Dr Haygarth, whether the number of those who, in the common intercourse of society, catch febrile infection, without ever coming into contact with a person ill of fever, or without being able to trace the way in which the infection had been communicated, ought not to induce a belief that the contagion is often conveyed, by clothes, to a considerable distance from the source from which it originates.

We were somewhat amused with finding, in p. 58, a paragraph bearing this very singular title—*Contagion dangerous at a greater distance than fermenting liquors or fire ;* nor could we well conceive what the principle was which the author meant to lay down and illustrate, till we came to the following passages.

' But there is another theoretical opinion, delivered on the credit of a physician whose memory I shall ever hold in the highest reverence, which appears to me so erroneous and so dangerous, as to require a full refutation.

' I received the following intelligence from undoubted authority. A celebrated professor, when treating upon the cause of fever, in his lectures on the practice of medicine, expressed himself in the following manner—" Contagion is a matter always deriving its origin from the human body. It has been imagined, that contagions have been widely diffused in the atmosphere; but it has been proved, that when they are diffused, and at a distance from their source, they are rendered harmless. This is similar to vapours of fermenting liquors, and of fire; which, near to their source, are destructive of animal life,

but, at a small distance, become innocent, either by mixture or diffusion. This appears to be the case in contagion. " To refute this
very dangerous and erroneous doctrine, it will be sufficient to remark,
that, in a small, close, dirty room, neither a common fire, nor the fermentation of beer, has any fatal or even pernicious effect. Whereas,
in a situation exactly similar, the febrile poison infects all who are exposed, except about one in twenty-three, or a still less proportion. '

We apprehend that our author has in some degree misunderstood the meaning of the professor ; for if the principles which
he himself has adopted be just, surely there can be nothing either
very erroneous or dangerous in the doctrine delivered in the
passages we have now quoted. The fermenting liquors and fire
are obviously mentioned by way of illustration only; and the
celebrated professor (Dr Cullen, we presume) coincides entirely
in opinion with our author—that where contagions are widely
diffused, and at a distance from their source, they are rendered
harmless.

Dr Haygarth is of opinion, that fever is not contagious before the fourth day from the commencement of the attack. It
were to be wished he had pointed out the facts upon which
this principle rests; for, at present, it appears as if it were derived rather from the analogy which subsists between fever and
small-pox, than from any well authenticated and decisive observations.

One of the most curious, and, to us, certainly one of the most
original parts of the publication, is that in which our author
endeavours to discover how long the poison of fever may remain
latent in the constitution. From the tables it appears, that the
period which elapses from the reception of the poison, till the
commencement of the fever, varies from a few days to two
months. We are doubtful whether the whole of the calculations
with regard to this point rest on a foundation sufficiently solid,
as we know of no way in which it is possible to determine when
a person, living in a contagious atmosphere, has breathed an
infectious dose of the poison. Perhaps this point can be determined, only, by observing when the fever appears in those who
have had but a single, and, as it were, but casual intercourse
with an infected person.

Few objections occur to us, to be made to the practical conclusions contained in the *second* part of this letter, which have
not, in some measure, been already anticipated in our remarks
on the principles from which they are derived. Most of these
conclusions are of so consolatory a nature, that we wish to see
them established beyond the possibility of doubt or of cavil. For

the gratification of such of our readers as may not have seen the letter, we shall give them in our author's own words.

' 1. Medical, clerical, and other visitors of patients in infectious fevers, may fully perform their important duties, with safety to themselves.

' 2. In any house with spacious apartments, the whole family, even the nurses of a patient ill of a typhous fever, may be preserved from infection.

' 3. Schools may be preserved from febrile infection.

' 4. In an hospital, infectious fevers ought never to be admitted into the same wards with patients ill of other diseases.

' 5. When an infectious fever is in a small house, the family cannot be preserved from it, unless the patients are removed into a separate building.

' 6. In like manner, infectious fevers may be prevented in the army and navy. '

The fourth conclusion has not, hitherto, received that attention from those who are entrusted with the management of the sick in infirmaries, which its importance seems so obviously to demand. To introduce, with our knowledge, a patient ill of a fever into any ward, among those who have not the disease, appears to us to be no less culpable than ' wittingly to allow the admixture of a small proportion of a poisonous ingredient, as arsenic, into the diet of an hospital. '

The proposal, to have a large room set apart, in boarding-schools, hospitals, &c. for the reception of those who may be occasionally attacked by fever, or any other infectious disorder, has our most hearty approbation. It must, were it carried into execution, prove the means of saving many from falling victims to contagion.

We concur also with the author, in thinking that the establishment of fever wards in infirmaries, next to a perpetual attention to cleanliness, and a free ventilation in private dwellings, is the means, of all others, best calculated to arrest the progress, and diminish the number of contagious diseases.

In the course of this letter, Dr Haygarth alludes to the practice of acid fumigations; but as he does not particularly recommend them, we infer that he places no very great dependence upon their use. We are, however, inclined to think, that though a due attention to cleanliness may render them, for the most part, unnecessary in private houses; yet that there are many situations in which their use ought not to be dispensed with. They cannot fail to be of advantage in fever wards, in jails, in hospitals, and in ships; in short, wherever the febrile poison may be supposed to exist in a concentrated state.

There is a caution of great national importance, suggested by our author, which seems to be highly deserving of the attention of those who are entrusted with the management of the Navy—‘ Prisoners, taken out of an infectious jail, should never be mixed with the crew of a ship, till a sufficient time had elapsed to discover whether any latent poison had infected them. ’

In the address to the College of Physicians at Philadelphia, Dr Haygarth adduces very solid reasons for believing the yellow fever to be contagious ; and proposes that measures, similar to those he has suggested with regard to fever in general, should be adopted for its extermination.

We cannot take leave of this benevolent and intelligent author, without expressing to him our grateful acknowledgments for the pleasure and instruction we have received from the perusal of his letter; and insinuating, at the same time, our persuasion, that this letter is intended merely as a prelude to a fuller investigation, and more enlarged discussion of the subject of febrile contagion.

ART. III.   *On Vaccine Inoculation.*   By Robert Willan, M.D.
F. A. S.   4to.   pp. 160.   London, 1806.

Commentaries on the Lues Bovilla, or Cow-Pox.   By Benjamin
Moseley M.D., Author of a Treatise on Tropical Diseases, &c.
and of a Treatise on Lues Bovilla, or Cow-Pox; Physician to
the Royal Military College at Chelsea, Member of the College
of Physicians of London, &c. &c.   Second Edition.   8vo.
pp. 260.   London, 1806.

A Reply to the Antivaccinists.   By James Moore, Fellow of the
Royal College of Surgeons, London.   8vo.   pp. 70.   London,
1806.

*Observations on the pernicious Consequences of Cow-Pox Inocula-
tion, containing many well authenticated Cases, proving its in-
security against the Small-Pox.*   By Robert Squirrel, M.D.
Second Edition.   12mo.   pp. 74.   London, 1806.

MEDICAL subjects ought in general, we think, to be left to the
Medical Journals; but the question as to the efficacy of
vaccination is of such incalculable importance, and of such universal interest, as to excuse a little breach of privilege.   We let
our lawyers manage actions of debt and of trespass as they think
proper, without our interference; but, when the case touches
life or reputation, we insist upon being made parties to the consultation, and naturally endeavour at least to understand the
grounds of the discussion.   The question now before us is nothing less than, whether a discovery has actually been made, by
which the lives of *forty thousand* persons may be annually saved
in the British islands alone, and double that number protected
from lengthened suffering, deformity, mutilation and incurable
infirmity.   This is not a question, therefore, which is interesting only to the physiologist or the medical practitioner: it concerns nearly every community in the universe, and comes home
to the condition of almost every individual of the human race;
since it is difficult to conceive, that there should be one being
who would not be affected by its decision, either in his own person, or in those of his nearest connexions.   To the bulk of mankind, wars and revolutions are things of infinitely less importance; and even to those who busy themselves in the tumult of
public affairs, it may be doubted whether any thing can occur
that will command so powerful and permanent an interest, since
there are few to whom fame or freedom can be so intimately and
constantly precious, as personal safety and domestic affection.

I

Every body knows, that ever since Dr Jenner proposed the practice of vaccination as a preventive of small-pox, a controversy has been maintained as to the safety and efficacy of that new inoculation. This controversy has now lasted for upwards of eight years; in the course of which it has not only given birth to an infinite number of publications of all descriptions, but has been illustrated by a vast multitude of instances and experiments, from which both parties have attempted to draw conclusions in favour of their own opinions. Although the subject is not perhaps entirely exhausted, and the zeal of the disputants assures us that it will not be prematurely abandoned, yet it appears to us, that there is evidence enough already produced to determine the opinion of all impartial judges; and, at all events, we think it right, that the import of that evidence should be fairly laid before the public, in a popular and concise form. It is among the first duties of those who conduct a work that has obtained an extensive circulation, to diffuse the knowledge of every thing that may be serviceable to mankind, and to consider the amusement of their readers, or the formation of their taste, as very subordinate objects to the communication of useful intelligence. We have, therefore, placed at the head of this article, the names of the most recent publications on both sides of the question; and propose, after giving a short view of the discovery itself, and of the evils to which it professed to be a remedy, to lay before our readers the result of the reasonings and investigations that have hitherto been made public with regard to it.

It is fortunately no longer necessary to cast a glance on the state of the original and natural small-pox, before any thing had been devised for the mitigation of the horrors with which it was attended. A pestilence it was, more desolating and destructive than that which now engrosses the name; and, after repeatedly laying waste some of the fairest provinces of the old world, proceeded to depopulate extensive regions in the new. With all the advantages of our long experience, and improved medical skill, the natural small-pox is still fatal, in the most favourable situations in Great Britain, to more than one in every six who are infected. *

Inoculation was brought into use nearly one hundred years ago; and a most noble and blessed discovery it certainly was, as it put it in the power of every one to diminish the hazard to which he was formerly subjected, in a most important degree. Of those who have the disorder naturally, we have already said, that one is

---

* See Dr Sim's evidence before the Committee of the House of Commons, and the papers delivered in by him.

found to die in six.   Of inoculated patients, only one dies in 250.
This at least is Dr Willan's calculation; and we are persuaded
that it is very near the truth.   In London, where it ought to be
best ascertained, some eminent practitioners have stated the proportion to be so high as 1 in 100.   The zealous antivaccinists have
denied it to be greater, under judicious treatment, than 1 in 1000.
It cannot be denied, however, that besides this risk to life, the disease, even under this mitigated form, has frequently proved an exciting cause to scrophula, and other dreadful distempers, and has
often been attended with blindness and deformity.

In this situation, it was not perhaps to be wondered at, that many individuals hesitated to expose their children spontaneously to
a risk of such magnitude, and flattered themselves that, by carefully secluding them from occasions of infection, the danger might
be smaller on the whole than that which they would certainly encounter in inoculation.   The consequence of these impressions,
independent of many superstitious antipathies, was, inevitably,
that inoculation could never be *universally* adopted ; and the result, however extraordinary it may at first appear, has been
clearly proved to have been *an increased mortality* upon the whole,
in consequence of its partial adoption.

To explain this, it is only necessary to recollect, that the inoculated small-pox is an *infectious* disease, as well as the natural
small-pox ; and that those who take it naturally from an inoculated patient, uniformly have it as violently as if they had been infected from a case of spontaneous disease : it is to all intents and
purposes the natural small-pox again in them.   Now, if it be
considered that several hundred thousand persons have been annually inoculated in these kingdoms for the last fifty years, it
will be easy to calculate the immense addition that must have
been made in that period to the cases of actual disease, and
the increase of natural small-pox that may be supposed to have
arisen from this constant multiplication of the sources and centres of infection.   From a calculation made by Dr Heberden,
without any view to this question, it appears accordingly, that
for the last thirty years of last century, there were ninety-five
persons died of small-pox in London, out of every thousand reported in the bills of mortality ; while the average number, before the introduction of inoculation, was only seventy in every
thousand.   Another calculation, made upon two periods of
forty years before and after inoculation was adopted, makes the
proportion only as eighty-nine to seventy-two ; but, whichever
of these we adopt, the increase of the total mortality must appear
to be very formidable ; more especially if it be considered that
these calculations are made for the case of the metropolis, where
the risk of infection, even before the use of inoculation, must at

all times have been greater than in the less crowded districts of the country. In a general view, we may safely set down the additional mortality produced by the partial use of this admirable remedy, at little less than one fourth of the whole. Inoculation, therefore, though in itself a most precious and beneficent invention has not hitherto been of any essential benefit to the community. Though many individuals have profited by it, it has destroyed more lives, upon the whole, than it has preserved, and has aggravated the sufferings of those who have refused to employ it, in a greater degree, than it has relieved those who have availed themselves of its protection. What sort of an evil the small-pox still is, in spite of the vaunted palliative of inoculation, may be judged of from the fact, that forty thousand persons are supposed to die of it every year in Great Britain, and that it actually kills one out of every ten who enter the bills of mortality.

In such a situation, it will be allowed that there was a sufficient motive to seek for some further improvement in our mode of managing this disease; and that it was natural to prosecute with enthusiasm every suggestion which held out a prospect of finally disarming this cruel depredator on the lives and happiness of the community. This is what Dr Jenner professes to have done by the introduction of the cow-pox. The best and most authentic account of his discovery is to be found in the evidence delivered by him when examined in 1802 before a Committee of the House of Commons. For the sake of such readers as may not have that publication at hand, we shall now give a short abstract of this simple and interesting narrative. The first part may be given in Dr Jenner's own words.

' My inquiry into the nature of the cow-pox commenced upwards of twenty-five years ago. My attention to this singular disease was first excited by observing, that among those whom in the country I was frequently called upon to inoculate, many resisted every effort to give them the small-pox. These patients I found had undergone a disease they called the Cow-pox, contracted by milking cows affected with a peculiar eruption on their teats. On inquiry, it appeared that it had been known among the dairies time immemorial, and that a vague opinion prevailed that it was a preventive of the small-pox. This opinion I found was, comparatively, new among them ; for all the older farmers declared they had no such idea in their early days : a circumstance that seemed easily to be accounted for, from my knowing that the common people were very rarely inoculated for the small-pox, till that practice was rendered general by the improved method introduced by the Suttons : so that the working people in the dairies were seldom put to the test of the preventive powers of the cow-pox. '

Upon inquiry at the medical practitioners in the country, Dr Jenner then tells us he was at first mortified to find that they all agreed in holding, that cow-pox was not to be relied on as a certain preventive of small-pox; and their report seemed to be confirmed by the actual occurrence of small-pox in several persons who were said to have had the cow-pox. Dr Jenner, however, was not willing to abandon the pleasing prospect that had opened to him, and resolved to inquire into the matter more carefully than any one seemed previously to have thought of doing. The first discovery he made was, that the cow was subject to a variety of distinct eruptions upon her teats, all of which were capable of producing ulceration on the hands of the milkers, and passed in the dairies by the indiscriminate appellation of cow-pox. After a short course of observation, he was easily able to distinguish the true cow-pox from other accidental eruptions, and flattered himself that he had thus discovered the true cause of the apparent uncertainty of a preventive, the powers of which were universally admitted to a certain extent. His hopes, however, were damped a second time, when he found that some persons who had been infected from the genuine cow-pox, had, nevertheless, proved liable to variolous infection, and that one was sometimes effectually protected, when another infected from the same sore, proved liable to after contagion. By diligent and continued observation, however, he was fortunately enabled to explain this anomaly also. He ascertained, by repeated experiments, that when the matter was taken from the ulcer or sore on the cow, after a certain stage of its progress, it produced a sore in the human body of a character altogether different from that which resulted from an earlier infection, and that it was only the disorder communicated in the earlier stages of the case, and before the matter originally secreted had undergone any change or decomposition, that had the power of shielding the patient from the infection of small-pox.

Having brought his observations so far to maturity, it occurred to him to try the experiment of propagating the disease by inoculation, first from the animal, and afterwards from one human creature to another. In the year 1796, he accordingly inoculated a young man from the hand of a milker, who had the distinctive symptoms of the genuine cow-pox, and had the pleasure of finding that, when inoculated for the small-pox, at the distance of some months, he completely resisted the contagion. The experiment was afterwards enlarged ; and, after inoculating some hundred children, and putting them, at different intervals, to the test of a subsequent inoculation for small-pox without effect, he ventured to communicate his discovery to the world in a treatise published in 1798, which was followed up the year after, by a still longer list of experiments and observations. In these works, Dr Jenner suggested, that the disease itself probably was not original in the animal from which it took its name, and that several circumstances led him to believe that it originated from the distemper called the *grease* in the heels of *horses*, and was communicated to the cow by being milked by persons employed in dressing such horses. The cow-pox was uniformly unknown in those dairies where the milking was performed by women ; and in all the instances in which Dr Jenner could trace its introduction, he found that the milkers had been recently before in the habit of handling horses affected with the grease. This conjecture, it is said, has since been verified, by inoculating the cow from the grease directly, which produced the genuine form of the cow-pox.

The first public opposition that was made to this discovery, was in a publication of Dr Moseley's in 1798. In this work, which was entitled, a Dissertation on Sugar, the Doctor ingeniously contrived to introduce a violent philippic against the new practice of vaccination, in which, as he had no experience or observation to found upon, he contents himself with pouring out an immense quantity of abuse, in a style of which we shall by and by indulge our readers with a specimen, and summing up his argument in the following alarming interrogations. ' Can any person say what may be the consequence of introducing a *bestial* humour into the human frame after a long lapse of years ? Who knows, besides, what *ideas* may rise in the course of time from a *brutal* fever having excited its incongruous impressions on the brain ? Who knows, also, but that the human *character* may undergo strange mutations from *quadrupedan* sympathy, and that some modern Pasiphae may rival the fables of old ? '

This delectable diatribe was republished three times, in different forms, before it attracted any general notice ; but the enemies of the practice having been extremely active in spreading alarming reports as to its consequences among the lower people, the following advertisement was published in July 1800.

' Many unfounded reports having been circulated, which have a tendency to prejudice the mind of the Public against the Inoculation of the Cow-Pox, we, the undersigned Physicians and Surgeons, think it our duty to declare our opinion, that *those persons who have had the Cow-Pox are perfectly secure from the infection of the Small-Pox.*—We also declare, that *the inoculated Cow-Pox is a much milder and safer disease than the inoculated Small-Pox.* '

This certificate was signed with the respectable names of Drs Baillie, Lettsom, Garthshore, Willan, Lister, Vaughan, and Thornton ; and by those of Messrs Cline, Abernethy, Ashley Cooper, Moore, and by five and twenty other physicians and surgeons of the first reputation in the metropolis. Some candid and interesting discussion, as to the symptoms and effects of the disease, took place about the same time, between Dr Jenner and Drs Woodville and Pearson, under whose superintendance the practice was prosecuted to a great extent. In 1801, Mr Ring published one thousand and forty chaotic pages in defence of the new practice ; and in 1802, the subject was submitted to the consideration of a Committee of the House of Commons, who, after taking the evidence of Drs Ash, Sir W. Farquhar, Blane, Woodville, Baillie, Pearson, Heberden, and thirty-two other practitioners of the first eminence in London, gave a report decidedly favourable to the new system. Out of the forty persons examined upon this occasion, indeed, there were only three, viz. Dr Moseley, Dr Rowley, and Mr Birch, who expressed any doubts of its efficacy ; and at this time, it is remarkable, that neither of these gentlemen went beyond the expression of doubt; all the rest were decided and confident in their testimony ; and Dr Woodville stated, in particular, that, in the last six months, he had vaccined, at the Small-Pox Hospital, 7,500 patients, the half of whom had been since inoculated with the small-pox matter, without the smallest effect being produced in any one instance.

This ample and public testimony seemed for a while to set the question at rest ; and, except in a few obscure pamphlets, and communications to the medical journals, little was heard in opposition to it, till 1804, when Mr Goldson of Portsmouth published six cases of small-pox occurring after vaccination, accompanied with observations calculated to shake the confidence which was now very generally placed in the security of the Jennerian inoculation.   These were answered by Mr Ring and others, who endeavoured to show that, in some of his cases, Mr Goldson's patients had not had the genuine cow-pox in the first instance, and that in others, they had not had the genuine small-pox thereafter.   This part of the controversy was conducted with temper, and with a reasonable degree of candour.   In the end of the same year, however, Dr Moseley published his treatise on the cow-pox, in which the ravings of Bedlam seemed to be blended with the tropes of Billingsgate.   Dr Rowley followed on the same side, and in the same temper, with 500 cases of ' the beastly new diseases produced from cow-pox, ' and attracted customers, by two coloured engravings at the head of his work, of ' the cow-poxed, ox-faced boy, ' and ' the cow-poxed, mangy girl. '   The battle now became general.   The Reverend Rowland Hill thundered in defence of vaccination—Dr Squirrel leaped from his cage upon the whole herd of vaccinators—Mr Birch insisted upon stating his serious reasons for objecting to cow-pox—Drs Thornton and Lettsom chanted pæans in its praise—Mr Lipscomb strutted forward with a ponderous, wordy dissertation on its fail-

ure and mischiefs ; and Messrs Ring, Merriman, and Blair, answered every body,—and exasperated all their opponents, by their
intemperance and personality. Charges of murder and falsehood
were interchanged among the disputants, without the smallest
ceremony; the medical journals foamed with the violence of their
contention; it raged in hospitals and sick-chambers ; and polluted, with its malignity, the sanctity of the pulpit, and the harmony of convivial philanthropy.

In the whole course of our censorial labours, we have never
had occasion to contemplate a scene so disgusting and humiliating
as is presented by the greater part of this controversy ; nor do we
believe that the virulence of political animosity or personal rivalry or revenge ever gave rise, among the lowest and most prosti-
tuted scribblers, to so much coarseness, illiberality, violence, and
absurdity, as is here exhibited by gentlemen of sense and education, discussing a point of professional science with a view to the
good of mankind. At one time, indeed, we were so overpowered and confounded by the rude clamour and vehement contradic-
tions of the combatants, that we were tempted to abandon the
task we had undertaken, and leave it to some more athletic critic
to collect the few facts and the little reasoning which could be
discerned in this tempest of the medical world. We were encouraged, however, to proceed by the excellent pamphlet of Mr
Moore, of which we have perfixed the title to this article ; and,
after refreshing ourselves with the sober sense and accurate information of Dr Willan, we at last found courage to go through Dr
Moseley's commentaries, and the exquisite observations of Dr
Squirrel.

Before entering into the particulars of the controversy which
has been thus warmly maintained, or endeavouring to lead our
readers to form any opinion from the evidence produced in th
course of it, we think it proper to make one or two general remarks, on what may be called the external character of the debate,
and on the circumstances which may impress us with a favourable
or unfavourable opinion of the respective disputants, independent
of the intrinsic weight of their proofs and reasonings. There are
some cases which cannot be reached by argument or evidence, in
which we must trust to the decision of authority; and there are
others, still more numerous, in which the preponderance of conflicting authorities must be determined by what we can learn of
the character and motives of those who bring them forward.

Now, the first circumstance which seems calculated to make
an indelible impression upon an ordinary mind, in a question of
any difficulty, is where there is a decided majority of competent judges in favour of one side of it. In any disputable point

of law or medicine, most people would be pretty well satisfied
with an opinion adhered to by nine tenths of the profession; and,
imputing the dissentient of a small minority to caprice or ignorance, would probably never think it worth while to make any
further inquiry. Now, the bitterest enemies of vaccination will
not deny, that more than nine tenths of the medical world are decidedly and zealously in favour of it; and that all their demonstrations of its dangers and terrors have been insufficient to convert a single one of their brethren from so damnable and dangerous a heresy.

But testimonies, it may be said, should be weighed, and not
numbered; and a few judicious voices should outweigh ' a whole
theatre ' of others. Here, again, we are afraid the vaccinators
will have a splendid and indisputable triumph. The only physicians, we think, that have publicly combated the doctrines of Dr
Jenner, are Drs Moseley, Rowley, and Squirrel. Now, without
intending the least disparagement to those three ingenious gentlemen, we certainly may be permitted to doubt, whether they stand
quite so high in the public opinion as some of those to whom
they have opposed themselves, or even whether an opinion signed by all three would have so much weight, with competent judges, as the single judgement of Baillie, Heberden, Willan, Farquhar, Pearson, or Vaughan. As for the authority due to Messrs
Birch, Rogers, and Lipscomb, we should humbly conceive that
it might be fully balanced by that of Cline, Abernethy, Ashley
Cooper, and Home. If the mere mention of these names were
not sufficient to decide the question of authority, it would be easy
for us to match each of the antivaccinists with at least ten London
practitioners of higher name than himself, and of learning and
opportunities as unquestionably superior. We confine the parallel to London, to give the antivaccinists all the advantage in our
power; for, in the country at large, we believe, they have not
one respectable practitioner on their side in five hundred. In this
great seat and school of medicine, we are assured, they are without
a single public adherent. If the question is to be settled by authority, therefore,—by the number or the respectability of those who
have taken part in it, the antivaccinists can have no pretension to
be listened to. If a clear opinion be given by all the leading
counsel at the Bar, and an unanimous judgment be pronounced in
conformity to it by the twelve Judges of the land, what should
we say of a few Old Bailey pleaders and jobbing attorneys, who
should appeal to the public in behalf of an opposite conclusion ?

But eminent men may have interests and passions as well as
other persons, and these may bias their judgments, or suborn their
testimony; and it is right that a popular appeal should be allow-

ed, to control or expose those who might otherwise overbear every thing by their combination. This, no doubt, is a very important consideration; and it may help to explain some things that would otherwise appear very unaccountable in this controversy; though, we are afraid, not much to the advantage of the antivaccinists. It is a fact universally admitted, that the smallpox has, for a very long period, been the most lucrative of all diseases to the medical faculty in general, and that, whatever benefit the world at large might derive from its extirpation, the consequences, in a pecuniary point of view, would be extremely unfavourable to them. This has not escaped the sagacity of Dr Willan, when, probably with a view to abate the rancour of the antivaccinists, he recommends that the inoculation and subsequent cure of the patient should always be left to a regular practitioner; and adds, ' that indeed they deserve their reward, since, by adopting and encouraging the new practice, they abandon what has for centuries been the most lucrative part of their profession.' Of the light which this observation throws upon the management of the controversy, and of the influence which it ought to have with us in judging of the argument before us, we think it better to speak in Mr Moore's words, than in our own.

' It must be owned, indeed,' he observes, ' that, on this occasion, there was superadded to the general tendency of doctors to differ, a particular motive, which rarely fails of having that effect upon all mankind. Small-pox was the source of no inconsiderable portion of the income of every medical practitioner; insomuch, that neither physicians nor surgeons would abandon this disease to the management of the other. The physician claimed it as a contagious fever, and therefore a medical case; but as the surgeon was the inoculator, he did not choose to relinquish the profits of the subsequent treatment. While each was eager for the whole, it was hardly to be expected, that a plan to take it from both, would be kindly received by either.

' Jenner's discovery was a touchstone, to detect what proportion of selfishness alloyed the human heart. It was calculated to make known, whether the scenes of misery, which medical men are compelled to witness, blunt their feelings. The result has certainly reflected distinguished honour on the Faculty; for the plan to exterminate the small pox, has been zealously adopted by the medical men of every part of the world which it has reached. There are, however, and I acknowledge it with reluctance, a few practitioners, who must be excluded from participating in the praise thus acquired by the majority.' p. 4. 5.

It appears, then, that the great multitude of learned and judicious men, who have given their sanction to this practice, have done so in direct opposition to their own pecuniary interest, to their known dislike of rashness and innovation, and to that natu-

ral jealousy with which they must at first have regarded a discovery so simple and important, in the merit of which they could
claim no share. The few who have opposed vaccination, have
acted, it must be admitted, exactly as those principles, with which
the others had to struggle, would have induced them to act; and,
in estimating their comparative authority, it is impossible not to
impute something to the operation of such powerful agents. We
are unwilling to urge this consideration very far; but it cannot
be forgotten, when prejudice and bias are spoken of, that the medical advocates for vaccination give their testimony in opposition
to their own interest and vanity, and that its opponents give
theirs in conformity to the dictates of those principles.

There is still one general observation to be made on the history
and complexion of this debate, which we are afraid will go as far
to discredit the arguments of the antivaccinists, as any which have
now been suggested. Almost all those who now oppose the practice of vaccination, and insist upon the proofs of its failure and
mischievous effects, opposed it with equal vehemence and confidence, before they pretended to have heard of its failure or bad
consequences at all. Dr Moseley, of whose language on the subject, in 1798, the reader has already had a specimen, has himself stated that his opposition to it was founded at that time ‘ on
the basis of theory ; ’ and, two years after he had three times re-
printed that miserable specimen of scurrilous buffoonery, he informed the Committee of the House of Commons, that he did
not himself know of any instance in which it had either failed to
prevent small-pox, or been followed by constitutional diseases, although he had heard of some such things from persons, none
of whom he could then recollect, or mention to the Committee.
Mr Birch makes very nearly the same statement. Thus, we find
Dr Moseley, in 1798, as full of contempt and abhorrence for vaccination, as he is at this moment, though it is certain that at that
time he had neither read nor seen any thing that was not decidedly in its favour. It must be allowed that this disposition to oppose, before there were any grounds for opposition, does not indicate a very liberal or impartial disposition in an observer; and naturally disposes us to regard with some suspicion the evidence
which he may afterwards bring forward in support of his preconceived antipathies. An avowed enemy is rejected as a witness in
every court of law; but if it appears that he is not only hostile,
but necessarily ignorant, we may well ask what weight can be
given to his testimony in opposition to that of impartial persons
who must have known much more of the circumstances. We
are glad, upon this subject, to avail ourselves once more of Mr
Moore's excellent observations.

' If vaccination frequently fails, and occasions miserable consequences, these disappointments and disasters ought naturally to occur most frequently to those who have vaccinated the greatest numbers; and repeated mortifications and reproaches would naturally excite so much vexation, as to induce them to abandon the practice. But, so far from this being the case, those who have vaccinated the most extensively, persist in recommending it with the same zeal as ever; their infatuation continues, though in other respects they are men of distinguished good sense, and good nature.

' Who then are those, who meet with the unlucky failures, and wretched effects of vaccination? The very persons who opposed the practice before any failures could have existed; and when every known fact was favourable. They decried vaccination, from its commencement, among all their acquaintances; they never adopted it, and consequently have seen little of the practice; yet it unaccountably happens, that all the unsuccessful cases fall under their observation. ' p. 15, 16.

There is but one other criterion to which we wish to appeal, before entering with our readers upon the precise points that are at issue between these disputants. All the presumptions are against Dr Moseley and his adherents. His opponents are confessedly many, and learned, and judicious; and as he differs from their concurring opinion, the natural inference is, that he is not judicious and learned, and that he cannot be safely relied on as an accurate observer, a sagacious expounder, or a correct reporter of the phenomena. It is possible, however, that this inference may be erroneous;—Dr Moseley and his friends may be persons of transcendent genius and exemplary candour. Reputation may be unmerited, and multitudes may be deceived. If the opposers of vaccination give indisputable proofs of superior talents and better temper than their adversaries, there will be a certain presumption in favour of their conclusions, from the admitted character of the men, independent of the reasons which they may urge in their support. On the other hand, if, from their writings, it be manifest that they are men of weak and uncultivated understanding; that their passions are vehement, and their judgment infirm; that they are ignorant or negligent of the first rules of reasoning, and incapable of stating their opinions in intelligible language, it probably will not appear too much to affirm, that they are entitled to little credit, in a controversy which confessedly requires much accuracy of discrimination, much nice observation, and patient and persevering research. It would not be fair to the reader to lay the statements of the parties before him without making him in some degree acquainted with their character. We shall venture, therefore, to present him with a few extracts from the most recent and most vaunted compositions of the antivaccinists, that he may judge for himself what manner of men they

arc that have set themselves thus boldly against the opinion of
their most celebrated brethren.

Of this sect, Dr Moseley is the great champion, and perhaps
the founder.   Our readers may take the following specimen of
this learned person's temper, modesty, and taste in composition.

' It is a lamentable reflection, that men of learning should have
joined in this *diabolical conspiracy.*   But much more lamentable is the
reflection, that such men should persevere in it ;—wish to remain in
mental bondage;—and be as eager in retaining this slavery of thought,
as those illiterate and ignorant cow-pox pamphleteers are, who have
so pestered the public.

' Driven from post to post, they still struggle for existence ; and,
with worm-like tenacity of life, they seem determined to expire in the
last expedient.

' From this cow-pox medley of weak philosophers, and *strong fools,*
the world will form some estimate of the state of physic in England.

' The medical tribe in London, must be viewed in an extraordinary
light by people of understanding, when they see what havock Dr
Jenner and his cow have made in their intellects.

' Their wild rhapsodies, and devotions for these authors of their
distraction, were never equalled without the walls of a Pagan temple.

' One bewildered soul, starting in his phrenzy, vows that " the
sweet influence of the Pleiades, and the bands of Orion, " are nothing
but Jennerian pustules ;—then decorates Vaccina with moons and
stars,—worships the divine Beast in Pythagorean relationship,—sends
her to the Heavens as a Constellation,—and swears he will have a
Cow instead of a Bull in the Zodiac.

' Another *cut-throat*, *Smithfield scelerat*, drags Vaccina to the slaughter-house ; and in carnivorous hymns, sings the praises of her divisibility on the shambles, in beef-steaks, rounds, and surloins,— like a
savage of New Zealand.

' But these ravers are not the men who alone have carried the
cow-pox disastrous practice into its widely extended effect.   Nor are
these the only men, from whom the public will, in due time, expect
retribution.

' The *culprits* who keep out of sight, and prompt the mischief, and
have not honour enough to renounce, nor courage enough openly to defend their conduct, will not be forgotten. '   Moseley's Pref. p. xiii. xiv.

It will be remembered, that Dr Benjamin Moseley is here
speaking of such men as Baillie, Farquhar, Heberden, Cline,
Cooper, and Abernethy, and, in fact, of the whole practising
physicians in London, with the exception of his facetious friend
Dr Squirrel.   After this, it can excite no surprise to find him exclaiming, that, ' the evasions and base subterfuges which have been
resorted to, to support this wicked project, equal in depravity the
blackest page in the history of man. '   Of his pleasantry and rea-

soning powers, we meet with the following example at the second page of his commentary.

' The public can now discern the " darkness visible " in which they have been enveloped. They can discover a Cow Poxer from another man ; and can determine that, though a Cow Poxer may be an human being, it does not follow that he should be rational.

' Cow Poxers have gone a great way, to prove that man is not endowed with reason ; and that, though he may be capable of performing, and sometimes addicted to, rational pursuits, yet the source thereof is not radical, nor always present in his composition.

' It appears by their philosophy, that the brain of man is not the proper bed of that numen in which reflection and forethought repose, and cogitate on the fitness, and consequence of his actions.

' Reason, it seems, is only a momentary right way of thinking ; which, in the absence of caprice, comes and passes away like a thief ; or a shadow ; or a lucid interval of sense in the head of a Cow Poxer.

' Reason, they say, and say rightly, gives no pleasure to its possessor ; and generally pain to others. Besides, they find it is destitute of the comfortable sodality of folly ;—that contagious felicity, in which one fool makes many.

' The public have admitted, since this new light has " purged their visual ray "—that I had a *genuine,* and not a *spurious* paroxysm of reason, about the autumnal equinox of the year 1798 :—brought on by reading Dr Jenner's first publication on the Cow Pox.

' In this paroxysm, I denounced the people of England, *en masse,* for being Cow Pox mad.

' Part of its effects are known ; and part to be related ;—which is the purport of this dissertation. ' p. 2, 3.

After narrating a nonsensical and despicable story of a patient vaccinated by the Reverend Rowland Hill, who is said to have broken out afterwards into ulcers, which were followed by patches of hair, " some of it very like cows' hair ! " he breaks out into the following rhapsody of low and miserable buffoonery, which we really believe is unequalled for dulness and vulgarity by any thing that ever issued from Grub-Street.

' Rowland Hill may tell people there is no harm in a shaggy skin ; and may say the heart of Aristomenes was hairy ; and that he was not the worse for it. So the fact certainly was. But then he never had the Cow Pox. Besides, the case is not similar in other respects. Aristomenes was an Athenian general ; this poor child is not an Athenian general.

' Rowland Hill may also say, Esau was hairy all over, and that he was not the worse for it. Here again Rowland Hill will be wrong. For it is well known to people who read the Scriptures, that it was from the circumstance of Esau's having an hairy skin, that his cunning mother was enabled to make his brother Jacob cheat him out of his father's blessing.

' Perhaps Rowland Hill thinks there is no blessing but his own worth
a farthing. I think differently. Let him consider the loss of power
and property which Esau sustained from his hairy skin, and ask himself if he should have liked it.

' This is not all the above child's misery. He has had a constant
vaccine diarrhœa upon him ever since he had the Cow-Pox; and his
food runs through him involuntarily. ' p. 55, 56.

This is sufficiently commiserable ; but if we would ' sound the
very base string of humility, ' we must turn to the Doctor's separate chapters addressed to the said Reverend Rowland Hill ;
the first of which begins in this manner.

' Rowland,—I bought your phamphlet, entitled, " *Cow-pock Inoculation Vindicated ;* " dated the 25th of March 1806.

' I paid a shilling for it. Rowland,—it is not dear. The same
quantity of folly, falsehood, and impudence, could not have been
bought for twice the money of any other cow-poxer,—from the
Ganges to the Mississippi. ' p. 189.

We are almost ashamed to pollute our page with the trash
that follows ; but Dr Moseley is cried up by the antivaccinists as
a man of infinite wit and genius ; and it is our duty to make his
pretensions public. After introducing a paltry piece of buffoonery in a supposed dialogue between Mr Hill and a Lady, the reverend vaccinator is made to conclude as follows.

' Rowland. " And well you may. Madam, I tell you her very
dung is a fine poultice for horses' feet, and *greasy heels.* Kings and
princes eat it, by way of *mustard*; and Dr Moseley knows it, if he
were candid enough to confess it. "

' Rowland,—I do confess it. You are very right. Truth sometimes surprises me, but never offends me. I have seen many kings
and princes eat voraciously of this cow-pox mustard. Try it, Rowland ; and you will never eat Durham mustard again. I will give you
the receipt for making it, from a work of the highest authority.

' Mind, Rowland.

" Take the finest part of the filth in the guts of the cow, and season it with salt and pepper. Mix the ingredients well together. "

' I know my credit has long stood very low with cow-poxers ; but
I hope this will raise it ; and, as a further confirmation of your cor-
rectness, I refer scrupulous readers to the learned work itself ; where
they will not only find the above receipt, but the following interesting
remarks on it.

' This *Mustard*, made with cow-dung, is reckoned a most curious
sauce by the Æthiopians,—mind, Rowland—by the Æthiopians ;—
and they call it *Manta*. But only princes, and very great persons,
can attain this royal dish ; because it requires much pepper, which
all men have not.

' Mind, Rowland. It requires *much* pepper ; an article, luckily
for Cow-Poxers, not dear in England. ' p. 198—200.

Poor Dr Moseley!—Yet this is the gentleman who complains (p. 182. 3.) of ' the rude expressions ' of Dr Thornton, and of those ' violations of decorum which communicate so much asperity to discussion, ' and who thinks it necessary to tell Mr Hill (p. 225.) that ' his language is licentious, gross, ungentlemanlike, and highly reprehensible. '

Dr Rowley writes worse, if possible, than Dr Moseley ; and does not reason any better. He agrees with him in thinking all the advocates for vaccination ' raving mad ; ' and is almost as eloquent in descanting on ' the horrid, filthy, *beastly* diseases which they have nefariously introduced among mankind. ' He is pleased also to say, that ' small-pox is a visitation of God; but the cow-pox is produced by presumptuous and impious man. The former, heaven ordained ; the latter is, perhaps, a daring and profane violation of our holy religion ; and heaven seems daily to justify this supposition, from the dreadful calamities cow-pox has occasioned. ' He afterwards quotes a text in support of this pious opinion, which is too indelicate even to be referred to ; and then seriously proposes it ' as a question to be considered by the learned ministers of the gospel of Christ, Whether it be not impious and profane, *to wrest out of the hands of the Almighty the divine dispensations of Providence ? '* That these passages are not culled, with any malignant skill, from the Doctor's publication, but are really taken at random, as fair specimens of his writing, our readers may perhaps be more inclined to believe, after perusing the following entire paragraph, which contains the whole of his argument against the possibility of exterminating small-pox. It appears at the 16th page of his book, with this regular title.

' *Small-pox not exterminated, but at this moment epidemic, and never can be exterminated by vain man.*

' The small-pox, in 1805, is, at the moment I am writing this work, *epidemic* in various parts of London, and it must be always epidemic at certain seasons, unless the vaccinators have *more* power than the Almighty God himself; unless they be blasphemous enough to suppose human weakness can oppose the divine ordinance of God, the Creator of man, and all beings. I have lately had under my care some of the worst species of malignant small-pox ever seen, even after *vaccination,* in our small-pox wards at the *St Mary le-Bone Infirmary,* which many of the faculty have seen. The mode of treatment, by mixtures of bark and vitriolic acid, with the comparative view of cow-pox and small-pox inoculation, was read by me before the Honourable Committee of the House of Commons, deputed to examine cow-pox inoculation; the paper was delivered to the Honourable Committee, and, as I understood, was to form part of the Report, but, for what reason I cannot pretend to say, never appeared. This requires some future explanation ; for, what I did read and say, is for the most part suppressed ; and what it was impossible for me to say, has been, through some error, published, as the original paper in my possession fully proves. *It appears then, that extermination is impossible.* ' p. 16.

In this exquisite piece of ratiocination, Dr Rowley first of all asserts, that God Almighty cannot prevent the small pox ; he next alleges, that the House of Commons garbled his evidence ; and from these curious premises, he draws this logical conclusion, that the extermination of the small-pox is impossible! We can safely assure our readers that the rest of his reasonings are constructed in the very same manner.

Dr Squirrel's book, however, is the most entertaining of the whole. We will venture to say, though we know it to be a bold assertion, that there never was any thing so ill-written, or so vulgar and absurd, produced before, by a person entitling himself a Doctor of Medicine. There is a certain nimbleness and agility about him, however, which keeps us in good humour, and he whisks about with such a self-satisfied springiness and activity, that it is really enlivening to look on him. In an unauthorised address to the King, he assures him that the practice of vaccination ' has undermined the health, and destroyed *more lives of the most innocent and infantile part of his Majesty's dominions* than can well be imagined.' He then proceeds to the display of his reasoning faculties in the following profound and eloquent paragraph.

' The cow-pox is unnatural to the human frame ; and whatever operates contrary to the law of nature, can seldom boast of long inheritance ; for nature detests an enemy as well as abhors a vacuum, and she endeavours with as strong efforts to destroy the one as to fill up the other. Providence never intended that the vaccine disease should affect the human race, else why had it not, before this time, visited the inhabitants of the globe ? Notwithstanding this, the vaccine virus has been forced into the blood by the *manufacturing hand* of man, and supported, not by science or reason, but by conjecture and folly only, with a pretence of its exterminating the small-pox, from the face of the earth, and producing a much milder disease than the variolous inoculation ; yet, after these bold and unqualified assertions, the natural infection has exerted its own right, and the small-pox, subsequent to vaccination, has made its appearance ; for " nature will be nature still : " hence the puerility and the impropriety of such a conduct, viz. of introducing vaccination, with a boasted intention not only to supplant, but also to change and alter, and, in short, to pervert the established law of nature. The law of God prohibits the practice; the law of man, and the law of nature, loudly exclaim against it. ' p. iii. iv.

After this, he complains bitterly of Parliament for voting a reward to Dr Jenner ' for introducing the cow-pox virus into the vital fluid of the helpless infants of his Majesty's subjects ; ' and ends with supplicating that exalted personage ' to *prohibit* the

1

destructive practice of vaccine inoculation throughout his dominions. '

In the book itself, we have the old cry about horrid, filthy,
beastly diseases ; a positive assertion, that the grease in horses is
the scrophula ; a proposal to put all the infants that have been
vaccinated through a course of mercury ; and an earnest recommendation of a book called ' Maxims of Health, ' and a medicine called ' Tonic Powders;' both compounded by, and sold for
the benefit of, the said Dr Squirrel.   He also threatens to prosecute Mr Moore for having written contemptuously of him ; and
very wittily recommends his powders to another antagonist, in the
following smart sentence.

' They lessen irritability, correct and evacuate vitiated humours,
and have a great tendency to cool and diminish the fury of the brain,
by which means they will induce a conduct of reason and consisten-
cy; and, as they have a power to remove nervous symptoms, especially deception and cowardice, they come particularly well recommended to Aculeus. '

Such are the three graduated champions who have openly taken
the field against the patrons of vaccination, and boldly challenged
the rest of the medical world to defend that abominable practice
against them.   It would be injustice to Messrs Goldson and Birch
to confound them with this triad of Doctors, whom they have
submitted to follow in this contest.   They both write, especially
the former, like men of some sense and moderation ; and we entertain good hopes of seeing them converted from their present
heresy to the faith of the majority of their brethren.   They neither of them join in the absurd clamours of the genuine antivaccinists ; but, admitting the greater part of what the advocates for
the new practice have asserted, they think it necessary to enlarge
upon difficulties and discouragements to which we shall proceed
to say something immediately.   In the mean time, we may surely be permitted to observe, that from the specimens we have already seen of the talents and disposition of the antivaccinists,
there would be some reason to wonder if it should turn out that
they had discovered a truth which had escaped the researches of
the rest of the medical world.

The controversy which has engendered all this virulence and
absurdity, resolves itself, when strictly considered, into a few
distinct points of inquiry.   The practical question is, simply,
Whether vaccination ought to be adopted in preference to inoculation with small-pox ? and this question can only be decided,
it is evident, by taking a comparative view of the advantages
and disadvantages of vaccination and small-pox inoculation.

The great advantage of small-pox inoculation is, that it prevents certainly, or almost certainly, the recurrence of that dis-

order, and that it is, in general, infinitely milder than the natural
form of the disease. Its disadvantages are, partly, that it is attended with considerable hazard, both to life and to the general
constitution; and that, being an infectious disease, its partial adoption exposes greater numbers to the natural malady, than
would otherwise fall in the way of it. In consequence of this
circumstance, we have already seen that the total mortality by
small-pox has increased nearly one fourth since the practice of
inoculation became general.

The advantages of vaccination, according to the report of its
advocates, are, 1. That the disease which it communicates is not
in any degree infectious; 2. That it is as effectual a preventive
of small-pox as the old inoculation; and, 3. That it produces a
disease infinitely milder, and less hazardous, than arose from the
former practice.

Of these three invaluable properties ascribed to cow-pox by its
admirers, the *first* is unequivocally admitted by its opponents:—
the disease is universally allowed not to be infectious. If there
be any ground for ascribing the other properties to it, this alone
must be admitted to give it an immense advantage. If it be but
nearly as safe a disease as inoculated small-pox, or *nearly* as effectual a preventive, it must be incalculably preferable to it, with a
view to the interests of society. By inoculating small-pox, the
hazard of the community is inevitably increased; and as the disease is extremely infectious, it is evidently quite impossible to aim
at its extirpation by the continuance of the practice. By vaccination, no malady can be propagated beyond the person of the patient; and if he be effectually withdrawn from the risk of small-
pox contagion, it is evident that a prospect is held out, of finally
extirpating that tremendous distemper altogether. In inoculation,
we only hunt the wild tygers with the tame ones, and therefore
never can exterminate the breed. In vaccination we run them
down with other animals, and, with due exertions, may clear
the country of them entirely.

The other two points, however, are the most material; and it is
with regard to them chiefly that the debate has been all along maintained. The opposers of vaccination deny, positively, that it will
effectually prevent the small-pox; and they allege that it is more
dangerous to life, and more prejudicial to health, than the inoculation of small-pox. We shall consider these two positions as shortly as possible, in the order in which they have been mentioned.

The most determined enimies to vaccination do not pretend
to deny that it prevents small-pox for a certain time, or to a certain degree. The unquestionable facts that have been accumulated by its admirers, have established that general point in the most

complete and satisfactory manner. Dr Woodville, alone, subjected near 4000 vaccinated patients to the small-pox inoculation,
in the course of six months, and found that every one of them
resisted the infection.   That experiment has since been repeated,
probably not less than a million of times, with the very same result.   Cow-pox, therefore, is confessedly a preventive of small-
pox ; and the only question is, whether it be an infallible and a
permanent preventive.

   Upon this question, it is rather unfortunate for its opponents,
that their little phalanx has been divided into a number of ir-
reconcileable interests.   Mr Goldson acknowledges that the natural or original cow-pox, received directly from the animal,
does appear to afford a perfect security from small-pox ; but
that the operation of the inoculated disease is more precarious and uncertain.   The rest of the antivaccinists, we believe,
reject this distinction.   Dr Moseley rather seems to admit, that
inoculated cow-pox will render the constitution incapable of small-
pox infection for a certain period ; but that its virtue wears out in
the course of time, and leaves the unsuspecting patient to a more
dangerous attack of the malady.   Dr Rowley, and we rather
think Dr Squirrel, though we would not rashly pretend to have
ascertained the meaning of that eloquent person, appear to deny it even this limited efficacy, and contend, that it affords no security against small-pox infection for any period whatsoever.
Differing thus from each other in every essential particular, they
agree in nothing but the vehemence with which they clamour a-
gainst all who oppose themselves to their practical conclusions.

   Mr Goldson's theory need not detain us very long.   It exhibits,
we think, as perverse an application of scepticism and credulity,
as we have ever met with.   There are perhaps one hundred authenticated cases of natural cow-pox, in which the patients have
been found to resist variolous infection ; and upon this scanty testimony, Mr Goldson implicitly believes that natural cow-pox is an
infallible preventive of small-pox.   There are more than one hundred thousand cases of inoculated cow-pox, in which the patients
have equally resisted all subsequent infection ; and yet he refuses
to believe that the inoculated cow-pox can be depended upon as a
preventive ! This is almost as absurd, as it is in Mr Birch first to
tell us that cow-pox is nothing but small-pox transmitted through
a cow, and then to maintain that it is in the highest degree hazardous
and improper to substitute the cow-pox inoculation for that of small-
pox.   Yet these are the two most rational antagonists of vaccination.

   Dr Moseley's notion, however, we believe, has had more cur-
rency ; and certain timid persons, we are afraid, have been induced to suspect, that the security afforded by vaccination is not

of a permanent nature, but is liable to be exhausted by time. It
is certain, however, that there is nothing either in Dr Moseley's
reasonings, or in the analogy of other physiological facts, to justify such an observation.   Dr Moseley says, that there are many
eruptive diseases which render the constitution for the time incapable of variolous infection, though they were never understood
to impart any permanent security; and that ' cow-pox possesses
no more specific power to resist the small-pox, than scald-head,
or itch, or the yaws, or leprosy, or the *pustule maligne,* or the bites
of venomous insects, or other eruptive and cutaneous disorders. '

Now, we admit the premises upon which this reasoning is founded ; but we utterly deny the conclusion.   We believe it to be perfectly well established, that certain violent cases of eruption will
often indispose the body to receive the infection of small-pox, and
enable it indeed for the time to resist every species of cutaneous infection ; but it is most material to observe, that this effect is only
produced during the actual presence and continuance of the eruptive distemper.   It was never pretended by any body, not even
by Dr Moseley, that a person who had been completely cured of
scald-head, or itch, or leprosy, would resist the infection of small-
pox, merely because he had been affected with these distempers
some months or years before.   If the cow-pox, therefore, have
no other preventive virtue than these disorders, then it ought only
to resist small-pox during the fifteen or twenty days that the vesicle continues ; and the patient must we liable to contagion again in
less than a month at the farthest.   The fact, however, is indisputable, that out of the hundred thousand vaccinated patients
who have resisted variolous infection, no one was ever put to the
test of it, till after he had been for many months recovered of the
cow-pox, and free from any symptom of distemper.

Dr Moseley's argument, therefore, is founded upon a false analogy; but the facts to which he alludes evidently furnish ground, when
properly considered, for the very contrary conclusion.   When infection is prevented by the active subsistence of a previous and sensible disease, we naturally ascribe our immunity to the disordered
or suspended action of those organs by which infection is communicated ; and reasonably infer, that, as soon as they are restored to their functions by the return of health, the infection will
take place as before.   There is here a visible change, to which we
can impute the restoration of our susceptibility; or, rather, there
is the removal of a visible obstacle which stood for a while in the
way of it.   But if, in consequence of any preceding operation,
we find that we are enabled to resist contagion *in a state of perfect health,* and while all our organs appear to perform their offices with perfect vigour and regularity, we naturally infer that

this immunity will prove permanent, as we feel that it does not
depend upon any extraordinary state of the system, or the action
of any occasional cause that may afterwards be withdrawn.
There is no event, in this case, to which we can look forward as
likely to deprive us of this immunity, because it does not depend,
as in the other, on an unnatural and accidental state of the body,
which must speedily come to an end. The power of resisting
small-pox is, in the one case, the symptom of a disease, and may
be expected to disappear along with it;—in the other it is a constitutional property, which there is no reason to think will be altered by the mere lapse of time. A patient affected with itch,
is prevented from taking small-pox, only as a man is prevented
from seeing by the swelling of his eyelids ; when the itch is cured, and the swelling subsides, he is infected, and sees as before.
A vaccinated patient is prevented from taking small-pox, as a
man is prevented from seeing by having the optic nerve destroyed,—he can never see again. In the one case, the enemy is resisted by our own superior force, and, of course, may be resisted always. In the other, he is only repelled by the accidental interference of strangers, and, of course, may overpower us as soon
as they turn their backs.

It seems contrary, therefore, to all analogy, and all rules of
reasoning, to suppose, *à priori*, that an immunity which is found
to subsist for a certain time in the usual and healthful state of the
system, will gradually and insensibly wear away without any apparent cause, or any sensible change to indicate its extinction ;
and the facts which bear at all upon the question, so far from suggesting or supporting such a supposition, seem, in our apprehension, completely to refute and discredit it. In the first place, the
natural and inoculated small-pox,—the measles, and the hooping-
cough,—which are the only other cases in which a preceding disease is found to bestow an immunity after its own cessation, are
allowed to confer a permanent immunity, and not one that is
gradually and silently destroyed by the lapse of time. In the
second place, the matter seems experimentally settled, by the
case of the *natural* cow-pox, in which the security has been
found unimpaired and entire after the lapse of twenty, thirty,
forty, and fifty years. Lastly, even if we were to admit the
whole of the cases of small-pox occurring after vaccination,
which the enemies of the practice have founded on, we could
never hold that the preventive virtue naturally wore out in a
certain time, because these cases are alleged to have occurred
indiscriminately at all periods after vaccination which have yet
been possible. In cases of continual exposure, they are said to
have taken small-pox at all distances, from three months to seven

years after vaccination.   It is impossible to suppose, therefore,
that the preventive power of cow-pox wears out of the human
frame in a certain period of time.   If the cases are to be admitted at all, it would be more rational to suppose that it imparted
a weak or imperfect power of resistance, which might be overcome by a powerful contagion.

But there are cases, it seems; and, whatever be the errors or
inconsistencies of the theories proposed by those who bring them
forward, the cases themselves must be decisive of the fate of vaccination.   If small-pox have repeatedly occurred after it, it must
be rash to trust to its security, and the system must eventually be
abandoned.   It is true, no doubt, that multitudes of such cases
have been alleged; and that some of them have not been explained
in a manner quite satisfactory to the sanguine admirers of vaccination; but our impression is, upon the whole, very decidedly, that
by far the greater part of them are either cases in which there
never was the genuine cow-pox at first, or cases in which there
was not genuine small-pox at last; and that the remaining list of
failures and disasters, if any remain, is neither more numerous
nor more discouraging than may be supplied from the history of
variolous inoculation.   Of the individual cases themselves, the
statement and verification of which fill many hundred pages of
the controversial volumes before us, it cannot be expected that
we should give any detailed history; but we are persuaded
we shall do much more for the satisfaction and illumination of
our readers, by laying before them the following admirable observations of Mr Moore upon the medical law of evidence.   We
make no apology for the length of the quotation, as we are persuaded that the writing and the reasoning of this passage must
afford the highest gratification, even to those readers who are not
particularly interested in its present application.

' The evidence that is requisite to prove or disprove any proposition
in the science of medicine, is of a peculiar kind.   It differs entirely from
that species of proof which satisfies a court of law.   Both direct and
circumstantial evidence, which would leave no doubt in the breasts of
judges and juries, have often not the slightest tendency to render a medical fact even probable.   The declarations, and even the oaths of the
most conscientious, disinterested, and able men, are all insufficient.

' The reason of this is, that few men, even those of considerable
capacity, distinguish accurately between opinion and fact.

' When a man asserts he has been cured of a particular disease by a
certain drug, he is apt to think he is declaring a fact which he knows
to be true; whereas this assertion includes two opinions, in both of
which he may be completely mistaken.   The first is an opinion of his
having had the disease specified; the second, that the medicine employ-

ed removed the disease. Most people are convinced that they are
acquainted with the malady they are afflicted with ; they consider it as
a mere matter of fact : and when they are cured, they have as little
doubt of the remedy that accomplished it. This belief is often strength-
ened by the confident declarations, and specious behaviour of the person who exhibits the remedy: and if the patient possesses gratitude,
this also heightens the delusion. He is thus easily prevailed upon to
swear positively, both to the disease and the remedy, as if they were
plain facts obvious to the senses ; whereas, both the one and the o-
ther are frequently beyond the reach of human knowledge.

' The cases adduced of diseases caused by vaccination, to the truth
of which the parents will often take their oath, form no stronger presumption of these facts, than the affidavits that are daily sworn to of
consumption, gout, or cancer being cured, prove that a specific for
these distempers has been discovered. This species of unintentional
perjury has been very common during the last century in every part
of Europe ; and the more improbable the fact is, the more numerous
are the affidavits, and the more respectable the signatures. Clergymen, judges, and peers, are daily swearing, that they have been
cured of incurable diseases : but the meanest apothecary smiles with
contempt, when he reads their splendid testimonials.

' If the difficulty of ascertaining the proper dose of the best medicines was fully known, it would prevent any man of sense signing a
paper to induce others to buy a nostrum. One man, for example,
can take eight or ten grains of calomel, whereas another, with the
same complaint, cannot endure more than half a grain. Hence it
appears that one man requires twenty times the dose of another :
how then can this medicine be graduated for public sale ? The most
credulous bishop, or even the most foolish gentleman, who exposes
his name on a quack bill, would laugh at a shoemaker who pretended that he could make shoes to fit all feet.

' The character of the person for whose advantage these affidavits
are taken, is little understood by the public. Reflect for a moment
what kind of man that must be, who is base enough to conceal a medicine endowed with the power of curing cancer, gout, consumption,
or any of the deplorable distempers that afflict mankind. If such a
discovery were actually made, and kept secret, the discoverer must
be both a villain, for concealing what would save thousands from
misery and death ; and a fool,—because, by this conduct, he lives
despised, and probably poor ; whereas, the disclosure of such a secret would infallibly procure him honours and riches.

' It is not with medicine alone that the cunning empiric performs
his cures. He sometimes operates more successfully by an unusual incomprehensible legerdemain trick. Mesmer convinced thousands of
the nobility, and even some men of science in Paris, that he could
cure diseases without either medicine or change of diet. He placed
his patients round a box full of broken glass, and made them pinch
each other's thumbs, while he waved a rod of steel in the air. By

employing a mysterious jargon, he even made many believe that
they were capable of doing the same; and they paid him large sums
for being taught this valuable art. De Mainaduc and Miss Pres-
cott have improved upon this plan. By moving their hands, they
could extract any disease out of a sick man's body; swallow it
themselves, and then puff it into the air. Distance did not hinder
them from operating with success. They could cure a man in India. And, though the knave De Mainaduc, with this wonderful
power, died young, the art continues to be practised and paid for
magnificently, and the cures are attested by coronets and mitres.

'After these instances, it is superfluous to speak of Perkins, though
he had a better trick than either. The other quacks commonly took
the trouble of seeing their patients, hearing their cases, and talking
to them. Perkins saved himself all this embarrassment. He solder-
ed bits of brass and iron together; which, he said, could cure gout,
rheumatism, sprains, inflammations, and twenty other diseases, and
sold them for six guineas a pair. He quickly printed, with most respectable attestations, many more cures than are now published of
the failure of Vaccination. He established a Perkinian Society of
gentlemen of consideration, who zealously, to this day, extol the
fame of the tractors. Several worthy clergymen purchased tractors,
and most patiently and charitably applied them to their poor parishioners. For a time they performed surprising cures, and thought
they rescued the afflicted from the extortion of the apothecary.
These miracles are now at an end; the gout and rheumatism rage as
formerly; but Perkins has made his fortune.

'It thus appears that lists of cases, however certified, rather de-
ceive, than enlighten. The regular physician who adopts this method of proving a medical fact, takes the very path he ought most
sedulously to shun. Yet if any one should attempt, by investigating each particular case, to refute it; he would soon discover the
impossibility of succeeding. I have been requested, on various occasions, to make such researches, and generally found that the patients were completely convinced of the truth of the attestation;
whether the remedy was physic, magnetism, or a tractor. In short,
they were ready to take the most solemn oath to what was quite
impossible to be true.

'Not aware of this, some of Dr Jenner's friends first investigated
the cases of pretended failure of Vaccination. In some instances,
they discovered, that what had been called the Small-pox, was, in
fact, the Chicken-pox; in others, a rash; and in some bug-bites.
Where the Small-pox had occurred, the patient had either never
been vaccinated at all, or the spurious inflammation alone had taken
place.

'But as soon as one case was refuted, another was rumoured. The
investigation sometimes occasioned a dispute with the medical attendant. For if any mistake was committed by him, either in vaccinating, or in the opinion he had given of the eruption, he found his

reputation at stake. This occasioned warm altercations; both parties obstinately persisted in being in the right, and neither could be
confuted nor silenced : for the question does not admit of demonstration.' p. 29—36.

Of the truth of these positions we are so perfectly convinced,
that, even if our limits admitted of it, we should decline laying
before our readers the particulars of any of these disputed cases.
It is necessary, however, to explain a little more particularly the
grounds of our scepticism as to facts so strongly asserted.

The first position is, that in all, or almost all the cases, where
small-pox have really occurred after an alleged vaccination, the
patient really never had the cox-pox, the inoculation having mis-
carried, by accident or inattention. The total number of such
cases, we believe, is considerably under an hundred out of little
less than half a million of vaccinated subjects ; and, when the
following particulars are attended to, we are persuaded that they
will appear infinitely fewer than might have been reckoned on,
from the novelty, and, in some respects, the nicety, of the practice. In the first place, it is well known that, within a short
time after the promulgation of the discovery, a multitude of individuals, of all sexes and professions, (Dr Willan says not less than
10,000), many of whom had never seen the disorder in their lives,
took upon them to practise the inoculation in all parts of the
kingdom. That some mistakes should be committed by such
practitioners, even in a matter of the utmost simplicity, could
not excite wonder ; but the truth is, that the operation was a
matter of considerable nicety, and not perfectly understood, even
by medical practitioners, till after the publication of Dr Jenner's
full directions and engravings in 1802. The causes of mistake
were various. 1st, The matter was sometimes taken from a
spurious sore, in the first instance, which, though it raised a
vesicle, and excited inflammation in the inoculated patient, could
never, of course, communicate the genuine disease. 2d, It was
still oftener taken from the true sore at too late a stage of its
progress ; in which case, though it seldom failed to produce a
very active inflammation, it could never give the true cow-pox.
3d, The matter, though taken in proper time, was sometimes decomposed or corrupted, by being too long kept, or exposed to air,
or heat or cold, or diluted in too much fluid. 4th, When all
these circumstances were attended to, it sometimes happened that,
owing to the existence of eruptive fever, or violent cutaneous disorders, the patient did not receive the full constitutional affection,
nor indicate the decided symptoms of regular vaccination. Lastly,
It was some time before even the regular practitioners were so
perfectly acquainted with those characteristic and decided appearances, as to be able to say with certainty, whether the vaccination

had actually taken effect or not. The circulation of Dr Jenner's descriptions and engravings went far to remove this uncertainty; but it was not, perhaps, completely obviated till the publication of Dr Willan's excellent observations, in which he has described all the various forms and appearances of the spurious, as well as the true vesicle, in a way which puts it in the power of any attentive reader, in the least degree acquainted with the subject, to attain perfect assurance in every case that can occur to him.

These observations apply chiefly to the earlier periods of the practice; and it is very remarkable, accordingly, that by far the greater number of instances of alleged failure occur before the year 1802, and that they occur infinitely oftener in the practice of those inexperienced persons, whom zeal had induced to usurp the functions of a profession to which they had not been educated, than of the regular practitioner, who had vaccinated to a much greater extent. No one instance of failure has occurred in the practice of Dr Jenner himself; and his relative, Mr G. Jenner, publicly states, that he has also inoculated 5000 persons, without a single miscarriage. We agree entirely with Dr Willan, in earnestly dissuading any person from practising vaccination, who has not been carefully instructed in all the necessary precautions, and has not learned, by long observation, to recognize with certainty the genuine from the spurious infection. It would be much better, indeed, that the operation should in all cases be entrusted to a regular practitioner, except where there is a difficulty in obtaining his assistance in a situation of urgency.

The circumstances that have now been mentioned would account, we conceive, for a considerable number of alleged failures, without the necessity of supposing that vaccination itself is, in its completest form, a precarious and insecure preventive of infection. By far the greater number of those alleged failures, however, are cases in which some other distemper has been mistaken or misrepresented for small-pox. The error that has been committed here is of two kinds. In the first place, by mistaking eruptions altogether of a different description, such as chicken-pox, rash, swine-pox, and even itch, and the bites of insects, for small-pox; and in the second place, by representing, as genuine and formidable small-pox, that secondary variolous affection, to which it is perfectly well known that many persons are subject, when exposed to contagion, who have formerly had the disease in the most unequivocal manner.

The first requires no explanation. A multitude of such cases have been detected and exposed by the advocates for vaccination; and a multitude have been abandoned by those who first brought them forward, as having been originally stated upon inaccurate information. The second point is of more consequence, as it has served to bring into general notice a fact in the history of the small-pox, which the patrons of the old inoculation were much disposed to keep out of observation.

The general rule certainly is, that no person has the disease twice; and in a certain sense, the exceptions to it must be allowed to be very few indeed; but it is an established fact, that very many persons who have gone through the disease, either in the natural way, or by inoculation, are liable, when inoculated a second time, or exposed to powerful contagion, to a secondary and mitigated attack of fever and eruptions, in the course of which pustules are formed, from which the genuine small-pox may be inoculated. Nurses who sleep with children in the small-pox are familiarly known to be liable to these affections; and tha., many times in the course of their lives. And a multitude of indisputable cases are cited in the volumes before us, of similar effects being produced by a second inoculation for small-pox, after the first has taken full effect; * or even after a very severe and dangerous attack of the natural disorder. In all these cases, however, the symptoms are decidedly milder than in the proper original small-pox; the fever is of shorter duration, and the pustules are smaller, and dry up and fall off much earlier than in the genuine form of the disease. There is no instance in which it has been followed by fatal or serious consequences. Now, it is apparent, even upon the face of the statements made by the anti-vaccinists themselves, that almost all the alleged cases of small-pox following vaccination were cases of this description. The fever was always shorter than usual; the pustules were smaller, and usually fewer in number; and, almost in every case without exception, they were found to dry up and disappear much sooner, than in the true and original disorder. It is the opinion of Dr Willan, therefore, (p. 70, 71), and it seems to be confirmed by the import of the whole evidence, that the vaccine inoculation bestows as great security at least as that for the small-pox; and has even this advantage over it, that imperfect vaccination has always a certain effect in modifying the subsequent attack of small-pox; whereas, an imperfect inoculation for small-pox is admitted to have no subsequent effect whatsoever, (p. 76.) It seems also to be ascertained, that the vaccine inoculation, even though not adopted till after the contagion of small-pox has been received, will modify and control the original distemper to such a degree, as to deprive it of all alarming malignity. It was for some time

* See Ring's answer to Moseley, and authorities cited, p. 194, &c. —Moore's reply, p. 55, 56, &c.—Willan, p. 65-71, &c.—Birch's Serious Reasons, p. 45.

supposed, that a sort of neutral or hybrid disease, was generated by this coincidence of the two separate ones ; but the experiments detailed by Dr Willan (p. 7.) seem to prove that each of them runs a distinct course, although modified and restrained as to the violence of the symptoms, by the presence of the other.

With these cautions and observations, we may safely leave the reader to peruse all the cases which are detailed by the enemies of vaccination, in evidence of its inefficiency as a preventive of small-pox. Of the temper and judgment with which they are selected and narrated, some conjecture may be formed from the specimens which have been already given of their writing ; but there is one sentence of Dr Rowley's which seems to render any further observation unnecessary, and to make it superfluous to hunt through the laborious and persevering detection of the vaccinists. This learned Doctor, who has collected many more cases of failure than all his brethren put together, disposes of the whole controversy in this peremptory manner.

' Indeed, no other questions are admissible in vaccination, than, Have the parties been *inoculated* for the cow-pox ? Have they been vaccinated ! *Yes.* Have they had the small-pox afterwards ? *Yes.* As to *how, when, where, whether the cow-pox took, was genuine, or spurious, or any arguments, however specious,* as pretexts for doubt or failure, they are evasive and irrelative to the question. They may confound fools, but not heighten the credit of vaccination. ' p. 34.

After such a declaration, it certainly cannot be worth while to refute Dr Rowley's cases. It would be little less absurd to tell a Jury, in a trial for murder, that the only question was, whether a pistol had been fired or not, and that it was of no consequence to inquire, whether it was loaded with ball, or whether the sufferer had died by a pistol shot.

The antivaccinists themselves seem to admit, that by such *irrelative* and *evasive* inquiries, more than nine-tenths of their cases of failure may be explained in a satisfactory manner. But still, they urge, there are a few remaining, which have been admitted by the vaccinators themselves to have exhibited the decisive symptoms of genuine cow-pox, followed by genuine small-pox. The admission to which these gentlemen allude, is contained in the first of the following paragraphs of a report given in by the Medical Council of the Jennerian Society, and signed by upwards of fifty of the most eminent practitioners in London. That Council, upon considering the Report of a Committee, declare, that it appears to them, among other things,

' That it is admitted by the Committee, that a few cases have been brought before them, of persons having the small-pox, who had *apparently* passed through the cow-pox in a regular way.

' That cases, supported by evidence equally strong, have been also brought before them, of persons who, after having once regularly
passed through the small-pox, either by inoculation or natural infection, have had that disease a second time.

' That in many cases, in which the small-pox has occurred a second time, after inoculation or the natural disease, such recurrence
has been particularly severe, and often fatal; whereas, when it has
appeared to occur after vaccination, the disease has generally been
so mild, as to lose some of its characteristic marks, and even sometimes to render its existence doubtful. '

Now, there are two ways of viewing this, equally reconcileable with the facts of the case, and with the report of the Society.
The one is, to hold that though those few persons *appeared* to have
gone through the cow-pox regularly, yet that, in reality, there had
been something imperfect in the vaccination; and that, if the
means of more exact scrutiny had been afforded, such an imper-
fection might have been made manifest.   This is the decided opinion of Mr Moore, who says, ' he can more easily believe that
an able physician should commit a mistake (or disguise one)
than that such an incongruity should occur; ' and of Dr Willan, who, after stating the result of his own most careful observation to be uniformly in favour of the claims of vaccination, says,
' If such failures do ever occur, they must occur in a very small
proportion; and I am convinced that the subjects of them will
not be found liable to take small-pox in the same manner and
form as before vaccination. '   The other view of the question is,
that these failures do really occur, but in so very small a proportion, as to furnish no objection whatsoever against the practice of
vaccination.   That practice must maintain its ground triumphantly, if it can be shown to be *as effectual* a preventive of small-pox
as the old inoculation.   Now, we think it has been demonstrated, beyond the possibility of contradiction, that the number of
authenticated cases of small-pox after the old inoculation, and
even after a former attack of the natural disease, are more numerous in proportion, than those that are alleged, with any probability, of such an occurrence after complete vaccination.

It has become a fashion among the opposers of vaccination to
assert, without ceremony, and in the most positive manner, that
no person ever had the small-pox twice,—and from this they conclude, without any more ado, that, if they can show one instance
of its occurrence after vaccination, the question is decided in favour of the old method.   We have heard the same confident assertion made in conversation; and we have therefore been at some
pains to look into the evidence of the opposite proposition, which
appears to us as clearly and completely established as any fact in
the history of diseases.   We have no longer room to insert even

an abstract of those cases; but we shall refer our readers to the places where they may be found, after stating, very shortly, the two earliest that appear on record.

The first occurred in the case of a child of Dr Croft. ' He was inoculated by Dr Steigerthal, physician to King George the First. Dr Deering was an eyewitness of the operation; and assures us, great care was taken in the choice of matter. He had the small-pox of the confluent kind, and in a severe manner, in consequence of this inoculation, and yet had it again *very full*, in the natural way, twelve months after. This, says Dr Woodville, in his History of Inoculation, p. 217, is *a striking fact, which has never been contradicted.*' A second case was published about the same time by Dr Pierce Dod: ' It occurred in a son of Mr Richards, member of parliament for Bridport, who was inoculated for the small-pox. About sixty pustules came out; which maturated, scabbed, and went off in the usual manner. Two years afterwards he had the disease again, more severely, in the natural way. This case was communicated to Dr Dod by Dr Brodrepp, a learned and experienced physician, the grand-father of the child, who attended him on both occasions,' and was much canvassed by the controversialists of that day. A third very striking case is mentioned by Mr Ring in his answer to Dr Moseley (p. 209. &c.), of a person who was much seamed and scarred by natural small-pox in his youth, who, after he was a grandfather, died of a second attack of the confluent disorder. A fourth case is mentioned at p. 211. of the same work, of the very same description, and with the same issue; a fifth is detailed at p. 213.; a sixth at p. 215.; and a seventh at p. 280.: Three others are given from a foreign publication at p. 199. Several similar facts are detailed in Mr Ring's large treatise, p. 59. 86. 946, &c.; and the case of the Earl of Westmeath's child has lately been laid before the public in a way that precludes all doubts as to its authenticity.

On the whole, we think there are not fewer than twenty distinct cases of small-pox occurring a second time in the same subject, each of them authenticated far more completely than any one that has been cited by the adversaries of vaccination. We are persuaded, indeed, that we shall be supported by every impartial person who makes himself master of the whole evidence, in saying, that there are not so many as ten cases of small-pox, after perfect vaccination, proved in such a way as to be entitled to any sort of attention. Now, the Medical Council, consisting of almost all the great practitioners in London, have reported, that ' nearly as many persons have been already vaccinated in this kingdom, as were ever inoculated for the small-pox, since the first introduction of that practice;' so that, if the two cases were exactly upon a footing, the risk of failure seems to be at least twice as great in the small-pox inoculation as in that for cow-pox.

But the cases are not by any means on a footing; and, when rightly considered, the advantage will be found to be still more decidedly on the side of vaccination. In the first place, an infinitely greater proportion of vaccinated patients have been intentionally subjected to the most violent forms of variolous infection, than of those who had been inoculated for small-pox. For fifty years back, the confidence of the country, in the efficacy of inoculation, has been so firmly established, that it was seldom put to the test, either by a second inoculation, or by voluntary exposure to infection. The anxiety, and the contest about vaccination, had the effect of making it almost a regular practice to inoculate again with variolous matter, or to put the patient in some other way to the proof. It is not too much, perhaps, to say, that one-fifth of the whole number vaccinated has been subjected to this severe ordeal; and that not more than one in five hundred of inoculated patients have undergone a similar probation. If the two operations, therefore, were only of equal virtue, the cases of failure should be an hundred times more numerous among the vaccinated than the inoculated patients. In point of fact, they are absolutely fewer. It deserves also to be considered, that cases of failure in inoculated small-pox must now be picked up, in a great measure, from old books or old people, and that it is fair to presume that a much greater number than can now be authenticated have occurred, and been forgotten in the course of the last seventy years; whereas, all the instances of failure in vaccination having happened within these six years; and while the keen eyes of so many disputants were fixed on the issue, it may be concluded, that few or none have been lost to the public, and that we are now completely aware of the full extent of the calamity.

In whatever way this part of the question be considered, therefore, we conceive it to be clearly made out, that vaccination, if it do not absolutely and certainly secure the patient from the contagion of small-pox, gives him a security, at least as effectual as could be given by the old practice of inoculation. We are conscientiously persuaded, that, to this extent, it may be relied on with the most implicit confidence.

The only other point which remains to be considered is, whether vaccination communicates as safe and mild a disease as inoculation? Upon this, however, it would be a mere waste of words to enlarge: the public knows perfectly, by experience, that the cow-pox is incomparably a milder disease than the inoculated small-pox; and there is certainly no one instance in which the fever attending it has risen to a fatal, or even to an alarming height. As to the trash that has been written to prove that it has given birth to a multitude of new and dreadful cutaneous distempers; as there is not a shadow of evidence to connect these appearances with the preceding vaccination, the only answer that can be mede to it is, that it was never pretended that the cow-pox would insure the patient, for all the rest of his life, from scrophula or itch, or tinea, or leprosy, or syphilis. The whole proof that is offered, in any of the alleged cases, is; that a person who had been vaccinated, was afterwards affected by these disorders, sometimes at the distance of years.

It was not necessary, perhaps, to make any other answer to assertions so improbable and intemperate: But Dr Willan has condescended to answer them; and has set this part of the question, it appears to us, finally to rest. Dr Willan, it is well known, is the oracle of the metropolis in all cutaneous disorders, and has more practice in that department than all the rest of his brethren put together. Now, he says, in the first place, that after a careful examination of all the cases alluded to, *no new disorders* have been introduced into the nosology since the discovery of vaccination; and that the old cutaneous complaints of the metropolis have not become either more virulent or more general. As a proof of this, he exhibits a table (p. 82.) of the number of cases of cutaneous eruption in the Public Dispensary, from 1796 to 1805; the result of which is, that their proportion to other diseases was rather greater before Dr Jenner's discovery, than in the sixth and seventh years of vaccination. In the next place, he exhibits a statement, from the senior surgeon of the Gloucester Infirmary, in which cow-pox has been familiar for the last fifty years, which purports, 1st, That there is not a more healthy race of beings, or one more free from cutaneous complaints, than the milkers at dairies, who are constantly exposed to cow-pox; and, 2d, that though many hundred patients have been under his charge for cow-pox in the last fifty years, *not one* has complained, in all that time, of any cutaneous affection as its consequence. In the last place, Dr Willan gives it as his decided opinion, that the vaccine inoculation is much less apt to produce inflammation and suppuration of the glands than inoculated small-pox; and that he has never known an instance of scrophula that could be fairly referred to it.

There are, no doubt, one or two unfortunate cases, and we believe no more, in which the wound in the arm has degenerated into a dangerous ulcer. This may be owing to the incautious use of a rusty lancet, or of one charged with matter which had run into putridity; or it may be owing to a singular and unaccountable irritability of constitution, akin to that which Dr Willan says he has known produce the most violent disorders from the appli-

1

cation of a blister, or give rise to incurable ulcerations from the bite of a leech.   It is needless to say that similar disasters may arise from common inoculation—they may arise from the scratch of a pin.

Although the arguments in favour of vaccination appear, when impartially considered, to be thus evidently triumphant, we are well aware, from the recollection of our own sentiments on the occasion, that some people, who have not leisure to enter into the merits of the controversy, may be staggered by the simple and palpable fact, that a certain number of persons, of some education and acuteness, have set themselves so outrageously against it, and may think it safer to resist novelties, as to the merit of which there is a difference of opinion, and adhere to the good old way, which every body so lately concurred in recommending.   To such persons, it may be of some use to state, that the good old way of inoculation of small-pox met, in its day, with an opposition not less virulent and persevering, than cow-pox seems destined to encounter ; and was assailed with as much bad language, and nearly as much bad argument, as is now poured out against vaccination.   Dr Wagstaffe, in 1721, published a variety of pamphlets against it, in which he maintains, with great vehemence, that it does not prevent the small-pox in future ; that it produces a variety of shocking distempers, itch, ulcers, boils, hectic, *caries,* &c. ; that it often produces an unfavourable confluent small-pox ; and, in general, that it is to the full as fatal as the natural disorder.   The same positions were maintained in a great variety of eloquent publications by Dr Hillary, and Messrs Howgrave, Sparham, and Massey.   But the most magnificent and imposing piece of composition that has been preserved upon this side of the question, is a sermon preached by the Reverend Edmond Massey, ' upon the dangerous and sinful practice of inoculation, ' in 1722.   In this performance, the reverend person maintains, that Job's distemper was the confluent small-pox, and that he had been inoculated by the Devil : he then asserts, that diseases are sent by Providence for the punishment of our sins ; and that this attempt to prevent them, is ' a diabolical operation. '   He comforts himself, however, by reflecting, that its pretensions, in this way, are utterly vain and groundless ;—he says they are mere ' forgers of lies, ' who pretend that it will prevent the small-pox ; enlarges upon the miseries and evils that inoculation threatens to introduce; and hopes that a time will come, when those preparers of poison, and spreaders of infection, will have a stigma fixed on them, and no longer be permitted to mingle with other professional men ; which, he says, indeed, is as presumptuous in them as it was in the Devil to mingle with the sons of God.

These, and similar expressions, which abound in the writings of that day, will go far, we fear, to deprive Drs Moseley and Squirrel of any claim to originality in the style of eloquence they have exerted themselves so meritoriously to revive. We beg them, however, to believe, that it was by no means for this invidious purpose that we have referred to their prototypes, but merely with a view to set the minds of those readers at rest, who might be inclined to doubt, whether men of education could possibly be so positive and so angry in support of what was certainly wrong. Drs Wagstaffe and Hillary, with their faithful squires and followers, have been effectually confuted by the experience of little less than a century ; and their forgotten cavils and rhapsodies now excite no other emotions in the reader, than those mild sensations of contempt and wonder with which the next generation will look on the lucubrations of Squirrel and Moseley, if any accident should draw them from the shelter of that oblivion to which they are rapidly descending.

We will not add to the length of this article by any general observations on the importance of the subject on which it is employed. There is only one point of practical importance which we have omitted to consider ; and that is, the propriety of continuing the practice of putting the efficacy of vaccination to the test, by subjecting the patient afterwards to repeated variolous inoculation. Most of the violent admirers of the new practice oppose this as unnecessary ; and the instances of troublesome, and even dangerous affections, resulting from such inoculation, although no genuine small-pox be produced, certainly afford an argument of some weight against it. At the same time, we believe this risk to be so small, that, in order to allay the anxiety of parents, we do not see any great harm in continuing the practice till that anxiety shall disappear from the increasing reliance on vaccination, or until the extinction of small-pox shall render it impossible to find matter for the inoculation. It is a point still less doubtful, however, that it would be advisable to institute a very strict examination into the cases of all persons vaccinated before 1802, and to repeat the operation in every case that appears in the slightest degree doubtful ; ascertaining, at the same time, the fact of the constitutional affection, by Mr Bryce's ingenious test of inoculating one arm from the vesicles formed on the other, and judging of the state of the system by the sudden maturation of the second incision. If the first vesicle be quite regular, we are inclined to think, that the success of this experiment will afford the most perfect assurance of the constitutional affection having been completely produced.

ART. V.   1. *Report of the Royal College of Physicians of London on Vaccination ; with an Appendix, containing the Opinions of the Royal Colleges of Physicians of Edinburgh and Dublin, and of the Royal Colleges of Surgeons of London, of Dublin, and of Edinburgh.* Ordered to be printed, 8th July 1807. pp. 13. Folio.

2. *Ministère de l'Interieur ; Séance Générale de la Société Centrale etablie pour l'Extinction de la Petite Verole en France, par la Propagation de la Vaccine.* pp. 130. 8vo. 12. Juin 1806.

3. *L.* 30,000 *for the Cow-Pox ! ! !   An Address (to Lord H. P, and) to the British Parliament on Vaccination, (of the greatest Importance to Mankind) ; wherein the Report of the College of Physicians is completely confuted.* Audi alteram partem—*Be candid, be just.* By Ferdinand Smyth Stuart, Efq. Second Edition ; with an Appendix and Plates. pp. 85 & xxi.   8vo. London, 1807.

4. *A Letter to the Right Honourable Spencer Perceval, Chancellor of the Exchequer, &c. &c. on the Expediency and Propriety of regulating, by Parliamentary Authority, the Practice of Variolous Inoculation,*

Inoculation, with a View to the Extermination of the Small-Pox.
pp. 36. 8vo. London, 1807.

5. *A Popular View of Vaccine Inoculation, with the Practical Mode of conducting it, showing the Analogy between the Small-Pox and Cow-Pox, and the Advantages of the Latter.* By Joseph Adams, M. D. F. L. S. Phisician to the Small-Pox and Inoculation Hospitals, &c. pp. 161. 12mo. London, 1807.

6. *The Cow-Pox Chronicle, or Medical Reporter. (Stamped Newspaper.)* Jan. 23d, 1808.

7. *The Fatal Effects of Cow-Pox Protection; manifested by a Narrative of the Occurrences which have recently happened at Ringwood in Hampshire.* 8vo. London, 1808.

8. *Report of the Royal Jennerian Society on the supposed Failures at Ringwood.* Feb. 1808.

9. *The Vaccine Scourge, in Answer to the Calumnies and Falsehoods lately circulated with great Industry by that extraordinary Surgeon Mr Birch, and other Antivaccinists.* ' A Rod for a Fool's Back.' 8vo. London, 1808.

10. *The Vaccine Phantasmagoria.* pp. 27. 4to. London. 1808.

11. *Hints for the Consideration of Parliament, in a Letter to Dr Jenner on the supposed Failures of Vaccination at Ringwood, including a Report of the Royal Jennerian Society on that Subject, after a careful Public Investigation upon the Spot ; also containing Remarks on the prevalent abuse of Variolous Inoculation, and on the dreadful Expense of Out-Patients attending at the Small-Pox Hospital.* By William Blair, Surgeon, &c. pp. 300. 8vo. London, 1808.

12. *Debates in Parliament, respecting the Jennerian Discovery, including the late Debate on the future Grant of 20,000l. to Dr Jenner ; together with the Report of the Royal College of Physicians of London, with introductory Remarks.* By Charles Murray. pp. 164. 8vo. London, 1808.

13. *A Statement of some Objections to the Bill as amended by the Committee of the House of Commons, to prevent the spreading of the Infection of the Small-Pox ; to which is subjoined, a Copy of the Bill.* By A. Highmore, Gent. pp. 32. 8vo. London, 1808.

14. *An Answer to Mr Highmore's Objections to the Bill before Parliament, to prevent the spreading of the Infection of the Small-Pox , with an Appendix, containing some interesting Communications from foreign Medical Practitioners on the Progress and Efficacy of Vaccine Inoculation.* By Charles Murray. pp. 70. 8vo. London, 1808.

15. *An Inquiry into the Laws of Epidemics ; with Remarks on the Plans lately proposed for exterminating the Small-Pox.* By Joseph Adams, M. D. &c. pp. 157. London, 1809.

16. *Practical Observations on the Inoculation of Cow-Pox, pointing out a new mode of obtaining and preserving the Infection; and also a certain Test of perfect Vaccination. Illustrated by Cases and Plates. The Second Edition; with an Appendix, containing additional Observations, together with a Plan for extinguishing the Contagion of the Small-Pox in the British Empire, and for rendering the Vaccine Inoculation general and effectual.* By James Bryce, F. R. S. Edinburgh, Member of the Royal College of Surgeons, &c. pp. 214. and Append. pp. 132. 8vo. Edinburgh, 1809.

17. *An Inquiry into the antivariolous Power of Vaccination; in which, from the State of the Phenomena, and the Occurrence of a great variety of Cases, the most serious Doubts are suggested, of the Efficacy of the whole Practice; and its Powers, at best, proved to be only Temporary; from which also will appear the Necessity of, and proper Period for, again submitting to Inoculation with variolous Virus.* By Thomas Brown, Surgeon, Musselburgh. *Magna est veritas, et prevalebit.* pp. 327. 8vo. Edinburgh, 1809.

18. *Report of the Surgeons of the Edinburgh Vaccine Institution, containing an Examination of the Opinions and Statements of Mr Brown of Musselburgh on Vaccination.* Drawn up at the Desire of the Managers, and published by their Direction, for the Benefit of the Institution. pp. 35. with Append. pp. 8. 8vo. Edinburgh, 1809.

19. *A Letter, in reply to the Report of the Surgeons of the Vaccine Institution, Edinburgh; with an Appendix, containing a variety of interesting Letters on the Subject of Vaccination, and including a Correspondence with Dr Duncan, Dr Lee, and Mr Bryce: from which also the Public will be able to appretiate the Authority of the Surgeons of the Vaccine Institution, and to form a correct Opinion of the whole Subject.* By Thomas Brown, Surgeon, Musselburgh. 8vo. Edinburgh, 1809.

O N a former occasion we entered at considerable length into the merits of Vaccination, and gave a sketch of the acrimonious controversy it had excited in the medical world. Since that time the subject has acquired still greater interest, and has given rise to various legislative projects, of no common delicacy and importance. It is very probable, we think, that these will soon be renewed and multiplied; and, in disposing of them, we are well aware, that the utmost caution will be requisite; lest, on the one hand, we prevent the adoption of safe and effectual means, for limiting the ravages of the most loathsome and destructive of our diseases—or, on the other, increase, by precipitate coercion, the evils we wish to avert.

The

The long lift of publications prefixed to this article, and which, after all, is but a fmall portion of what has lately been written on the fubject, will give our readers an idea of the keennefs with which the vaccine controverfy is ftill maintained. While the vaccinifts have been ftrengthening their pofition by parliamentary votes and collegiate reports ;—while Mr Blair has been fl gging Mr Birch, and Mr Ring has been founding a peal in the ears of Dr Mofely,—the nicknames, handbills, fquibs, and caricatures of their adverfaries, have been too fuccefsfully employed, where they were calculated to do moft mifchief—among the weak and the ignorant. This difgraceful warfare, we muft however remark, has been almoft entirely confined to the metropolis ; and, till within thefe few months, was unknown on this fide of the Tweed.

It would be both an irkfome and unprofitable tafk, to attempt to give a regular view of all that has been written for and againft cowpox, fince the fubject was formerly under our confideration. With a few praifeworthy exceptions, the difpute has been carried on with the fame violence and difregard of accuracy, either in obferving or in reafoning, which we had formerly fo much occafion to reprobate. In truth, vaccination has had to ftruggle, not only againft the indefatigable activity of avowed opponents, but alfo againft the treacherous manœuvres of pretended friends, and the mifguided zeal of injudicious partifans. While Dr Auban recommends vaccination to the followers of Mahomet as a preventive, not only of fmallpox, but alfo of the plague, Dr Gillum, in the courfe of his arguments for a *gradual* introduction of cowpox, ferioufly expreffes his fears to Lord Hawkefbury, that by relinquifhing fmallpox inoculation, we fhall have the plague again introduced among ourfelves. This fagacious conjecture is affumed as a fact in another lucubration of the fame author,— ' On the Efficacy of inoculated Smallpox *in promoting the Population of Great Britain.* '—' Inoculation, ' obferves this profound and patriotic writer, ' has fupplied mild fmallpox, and ' confequently faved to the country the multitude of inhabit- ' ants formerly deftroyed by the plague. Hence, had ino- ' culation been known, and feafonably employed, the plague ' of London in 1665 might have been prevented, and the lives ' of 100,000 of its inhabitants faved, exclufive of their off- ' fpring.

　' *Et nati natorum, et qui nascuntur ab illis.* '

But, leaving Dr Gillum to his profound meditations, it is time for us to enter upon the cardinal point of the controverfy, which is, whether vaccination be an effectual preventive of fmallpox or not. This, it is evident, is entirely a queftion of fact ; and will be more fatisfactorily anfwered, in proportion to the extent and uniformity of our actual experience and obfervation. In both refpects, we do not know almoft any difputable point, certainly not one in the whole range of medical fcience, of which the af-firmative is as decifively proved. The great majority, we may fay all the refpectable part of the profeffion, now concur in con-fidering vaccination as a fafe and perfect fecurity againft fmall-pox ; in recommending and promoting it in evident oppofition to their private intereft ; and in entrufting to it, in full confidence of its efficacy, not merely the lives of their patients, but of their children and deareft relatives. Thofe who received the firft ac-counts of it with moft fcepticifm and doubt, are now its firmeft patrons and advocates ; and, in this inftance, the young and the enthufiaftic have been ultimately fupported by the teftimony of the old and experienced. In proof of this, we need only quote the concluding paragraph of the report of the London College of Phyficians, who, under the authority of Parliament, endeavoured to collect the opinion of the profeffion at large.

‘ From the whole of the above confiderations, the College of Phy-ficians feel it their duty ftrongly to recommend the practice of vac-cination. They have been led to this conclufion by no preconceived opinion, but by the moft unbiaffed judgment, formed from an irre-fiftible weight of evidence which has been laid before them. For when the number, the refpectability, the difintereftednefs, and the extenfive experience of its advocates are compared with the feeble and imperfect teftimonies of its few oppofers ; and when it is confi-dered that many, who were once adverfe to vaccination, have been convinced by further trials, and are now to be ranked among its warmeft fupporters, the truth feems to be eftablifhed as firmly as the nature of fuch a queftion admits ; fo that the College of Phyfi-cians conceive, that the public may reafonably look forward, with fome degree of hope, to the time when all oppofition fhall ceafe, and the general concurrence of mankind fhall at length be able to put an end to the ravages at leaft, if not to the exiftence, of the fmallpox. ’

The detailed and valuable report of the Central Society to the minifter of the interior of France, is not lefs fatisfactory ; nor has any feeling of national rivalry prevented them from own-ing their obligations to this country for one of the moft unex-pected and beneficial difcoveries ever made in the art of medicine. We could eafily quote fimilar teftimonies, in favour of vaccina-tion, from every Medical Board in Europe. The remoteft cor-ners of the globe, indeed, have now experienced its efficacy. In every country into which it has been introduced, its progrefs has

been

been uniform and fteady; and no experiment, perhaps, was ever conducted on fo extenfive a fcale, nor any difcovery fo rapidly diffeminated. We have no *data* to eftimate correctly the number of individuals, of every race, and of every climate, who have been vaccinated; or to afcertain the proportion of favourable cafes: but thefe are not neceffary in order to enable us to form a decifive opinion upon the great queftions regarding vaccination. A remedy, a mode of practice, or an opinion, may become fafhionable in *one* country from adventitious circumftances; but they will not make their way in *all* countries, and under all variety of circumftances. Vaccination, however, has penetrated to the remoteft corners of the globe; and, wherever it has been introduced, the increafing experience of every year has only ferved to confirm the general confidence in its efficacy. It is impoffible to explain thefe facts upon any other principle, than that the advantages derived from it are fubftantial and permanent. Simple as the practice is, it is attended with fome trouble; and nothing but a very firm and general conviction of its utility, could induce the bulk of the population of any country, much lefs of fo many countries, to fubmit to it.

Nor is the great extent of the practice to be explained, by afcribing it to any undue influence of profeffional men. Their perfuafions might have confiderable weight within a certain circle of friends and patients; and imitation might lead a confiderable number more to follow their example: but we repeat, that nothing but a conviction of its utility could have induced fo large a proportion of the inhabitants of the world to receive and adopt it. Even the patronage it has experienced from medical men of every defcription, is conclufive in its favour. When firft promulgated, it was received with fcepticifm and diftruft; its phenomena were ftrictly inveftigated; and its reputed antivariolous powers repeatedly expofed to the fevereft tefts, until all doubts were removed. In Scotland, we know of only *one* medical man who is not fatisfied with it, and who does not recommend or practife it; and the fame gentleman is the only individual of the profeffion, in any country, who, as far as we have learned, has abandoned it, after having been fatisfied, or rather, as we fhall prefently fee, pretending to have been fatisfied of its efficacy. It muft alfo be remembered, that the general practice of vaccination is injurious to the pecuniary interefts of the profeffion; and therefore, the patronage beftowed upon it by them is a moft honourable proof of the candour and difintereftednefs of the profeffion at large. We have heard a great deal of railing about jobs and jobbing; and Mr Brown has infinuated, ' that the motives of

its

its greatest advocates are not more disinterested than those of its greatest enemies. ' But although it might be granted that a few individuals may have been actuated by the desire of notoriety,—by a sure introduction into practice,—or by the hopes of being appointed to a lucrative office in the vaccine institutions, still, the motives of the great majority of the profession, are evidently above all suspicion. The inoculator cannot expect the same remuneration for performing an apparently easy operation, for the event of which the most timid mother has not a moment's anxiety, as for conducting his patient safely through a painful, loathsome, and dangerous disease. Vaccination has even cut off entirely a very considerable source of the professional emoluments of the physician. Natural smallpox is entirely banished from the higher and middling classes of society ; and the cowpox is too insignificant a complaint to require the consultation of an extraordinary medical attendant. But, although vaccination be adopted and recommended by far the greatest and most respectable part of the profession, still it has been most obstinately opposed by a few individuals, and by means the best calculated to make an impression on the timid and ignorant. We shall now examine the grounds of their opposition, and their pretensions to our notice. They contend that vaccination does not afford sufficient security against smallpox ; that it has injurious effects on the constitution ; and that it has put an end to inoculation, without serving the same purposes.

The first is the most important objection ; not on account of its being better founded than the others, but on account of the nature of the evidence brought in support of it ; which consists in a multiplicity of statements, originating in misconception or misrepresentation, and not admitting of a general and permanent refutation. One fact is no sooner explained or contradicted, than another is invented.

The boldest and most determined antivaccinists of the present day, however, will scarcely venture to maintain, as they did once, that Cow-Pox affords no security whatever. The thousands, and tens of thousands, in every quarter of the world, whom it has enabled to resist variolous contagion,—the total extinction of that pestilence in whole countries, and the security against its importation, which they have experienced from there being no subjects for it to operate upon,—leave no doubt upon the subject. Hence, most of those who originally maintained that opinion, in the most positive and peremptory manner, have now shifted their ground ; and contend, that though vaccination must be allowed to impart security *for a time*, this security gradually decays, and is at last exhausted.

exhausted. This hypothetical objection was satisfactorily refuted long ago by Drs Willan and Stanger. The latter found, by direct experiment, that the insertion of variolous matter into the arms of twenty children, who had been vaccinated in 1801, produced exactly the same effects in 1802 and in 1804. This same opinion, however, has been lately brought forward, with much parade and pretension, by Mr Thomas Brown, surgeon in Musselburgh, as if it were something new and incontrovertible. The sensation produced by the vaunting advertisements of this gentleman's book in the public papers, induced the Managers of the Public Dispensary and Vaccine Institution, to make a strict inquiry into the cases he had referred to; and a report from the surgeons of that useful charity was drawn up and published. Mr Brown has since replied, both in a pamphlet and in the newspapers; and we shall now proceed to examine his statements and arguments a little more closely, both because they are the most recent and the most detailed that have been laid before the public, and because the reputed facts, having taken place in our immediate neighbourhood, are more easily inquired into.

Before we can admit that any instance of unsuccessful vaccination has been established, we must be satisfied of two things; *first*, that the patients were properly vaccinated; and, *secondly*, that they were afterwards affected with the small-pox.

The difficulty of ascertaining the former of these circumstances, is the chief cause of what are called cowpox failures. ' There is little doubt,' say the London College, ' that some of the failures are to be imputed to the inexperience of the early vaccinators. ' And, indeed, when we consider that, from the very nature of the cow-pox, the distinction between a mere local affection, affording no security even for a day, and a perfect constitutional affection, is so small, as to require the utmost attention on the part of the most experienced; that, at the beginning of the practice, all the necessary minutiæ were not thoroughly understood; that from the simplicity and safety of the operation, ladies and clergymen, midwives and farriers, vied with each other in multiplying their inoculations: And when we also consider that the total number of those vaccinated in Great Britain, during the few years which have elapsed since the promulgation of the discovery, is perhaps not less than those variolated since inoculation was first introduced, it is so far from being surprising that some failures have taken place, that we ought rather to wonder that they have been so few. Even now, some practitioners seem to be ignorant of what is necessary to constitute constitutional cowpox. Of this number, we cannot help suspecting, is our Scotish anti-
vaccinist,

vaccinift, who, at the fame time, difplays confiderable ignorance of the phenomena of fmallpox. ' In conformity, then,' fays he, ' both with my own experience of the phenomena of inoculation and vaccination, I contend, that if you have a veficle, attended with an areola, you may depend upon the production of whatever effects it is capable of.' Some of the other antivaccinifts go ftill farther, and reprefent every puncture by a lancet armed with vaccine virus, whatever effect it produce, or even if it fhould not produce any effect at all, as a true vaccination, for which the fupporters of the practice muft be refponfible, in cafe fmallpox fhould fupervene.

The teftimony of perfons entertaining fuch opinions cannot poffibly be admitted, as to the fact of the vaccination having been complete, even when they have had an opportunity of witneffing the progrefs of the veficle. The cafes, which they ftate on hearfay evidence, and on the authority of ignorant mothers, of courfe are ftill more fufpicious; and, in truth, there is no tale fo improbable, no ftory fo palpably abfurd, but, provided it be adverfe to vaccination, it is immediately received with open ears and willing hearts, by Drs Mofely and Squirrel, and Meffrs Birch and Lipfcomb. If it militate againft cowpox, it muft be true; and it is needlefs to inveftigate it. Mr Brown, we muft do him the juftice to fay, is honeft or hardy enough to confefs this.

' It is perhaps proper to notice, that I carefully avoided having any communication with the different practitioners by whom the children were vaccinated, being aware of the ftrong hold which fyftem has upon the human mind; more efpecially in this very important fubject; thinking it beft, for the attainment of truth, to ftate with the greateft poffible accuracy, the parents' account of the circumftances that attended the vaccination of their children, notice the appearance of the arm, and give the names of the families, whereby an opportunity is afforded to any of the practitioners to fatisfy themfelves.'

In his reply to the furgeons of the vaccine inftitution, he betrays ftill lefs referve in maintaining the fame doctrine. Some of his ftatements with regard to certain cafes of fuppofed failure at Haddington, having been contradicted by the medical gentleman who had the care of them, with a civil expreffion of his regret that Mr Brown had not applied to him *before* publifhing his book, that learned perfon moft valiantly replies—

' Far from regreting that I did not communicate with the medical gentlemen at Haddington, before I mentioned in my book that fuch cafes had occurred there, I have daily reafon to congratulate myfelf on the opinion I had formed of the extenfive and alarming effects of fyftem on the human mind; for, had I done fo, and afterwards had

had been regulated by the information I certainly would have re-ceived, undoubtedly no such opinions would have been promulgat-ed; and which, ' says Mr Brown, ' I now find many very respectable characters, both in and out of the profession, consider as entitled to attention and respect. '

Such a confession is of itself sufficient to destroy all confi-dence in Mr Brown's testimony. It proves a conviction in his own mind, that, had he communicated with *the only persons* who could possibly give satisfactory evidence with regard to these cases, it would have been adverse to his views. In the same spirit, ac-cordingly, we find him bringing forward cases, in which he ad-mits, that ' the pustules were so small, and the inflammation so trifling, as to make the practitioner in attendance suspect that he had not undergone the true form of the disease; ' and others, in which the inoculator informed the parents, at the time, that the child was *not* properly vaccinated. Nay, he gives the names of respectable practitioners, as having performed that operation to their perfect satisfaction, on patients whom, to their knowledge, they never saw. ' The oldest (of two children) was vaccinated by me, ' says Mr Brown, ' when four months old, in the arm; and the other by *Mr Keith,* surgeon of the Berwickshire militia in both, about the same age. I recollect perfectly, that the vesicle and areola were quite characteristic; and the mother describes, that the areola in both were equal to the size of half-a-crown; and that Mr Keith saw the arm in its progress, and expressed him-self satisfied of the child having passed through the disease. ' Now, the whole of this statement turns out to be incorrect; and the most charitable supposition is, that the mother imposed upon Mr Brown, by saying what she saw was agreeable to him. ' So far from having vaccinated the child in question, ' writes Mr Keith, in a letter which we are authorised to quote, ' I never, to my knowledge, *saw it;* but, on inquiry, find that it was vaccinat-ed by *my hospital serjeant,* at the request of the mother, who supplied the hospital with milk; *the first and only time* of his ever attempting the operation. He saw it *but once* at the distance of eight days after; and at present only recollects, that the vesi-cle was *smaller* than he had been in the habit of seeing in those vaccinated by me. These examples fully develop the motives of Mr Brown's conduct in carefully avoiding all communication with the gentlemen by whom these cases were said to be vaccinated; and explain why, in a pretended investigation of truths of such importance, he wilfully shut his eyes, and, when the object he ought to have drawn from nature was before him, chose to copy its reflection from a distorting mirror.

Is

It should also be remembered, that, of those vaccinated gratuitously, either at public institutions, or by individual surgeons, a great number never return to show the progress of the vesicle ; and yet, nothing was more common than for these people, in order to excuse their laziness and indifference, to report that the surgeons were well satisfied with the appearances, and had even taken matter from the arm.   This, indeed, occurred so frequently, at the Vaccine Institution of Edinburgh, that the managers were at last obliged to order, that each patient should deposit a pledge, to be forfeited, unless they attend regularly at the stated periods. This has had the best effects ; though for a time it diminished the number of applicants.

Another prolific source of alleged failures, is the mistaking chicken-pox, and other eruptive distempers, for small-pox.   That such a mistake has often been made, even by practitioners of much experience, cannot be doubted.   The diagnosis of regular consitutional small-pox, is indeed abundantly easy ; and if we were to refuse that name to every eruption which had not the nosological character, or did not correspond with the best systematic descriptions, we should hear very seldom of small-pox after vaccination.   It would be foreign to our present purpose, to inquire into the nature of all the varieties and modifications of which small-pox is said to be susceptible.   It is enough for us to prove, that, since the introduction of vaccination, eruptive diseases, of a very different nature, have been confounded with small-pox.   Mr Brown's cases are especially liable to objection on this account, because he has coupled them with a theory which sets all diagnosis at defiance.   Mr Brown contends, in direct contradiction to all analogy and observation, that before his period of security is elapsed, persons who have been vaccinated are liable to be partially affected by the small-pox ; that at an early period, it produces a slight rash ; at a more advanced period, papulæ, which disappear without suppurating ; afterwards pustules, which continue a few days ; and at length complete small-pox.   What opinion is to be formed of the professional knowledge or candour of a man, who records such cases as the following as instances of small-pox after vaccination ?   ' The oldest fell sick on ' the Wednesday following ; and, at the time I saw the other, ' was confined to bed, and had been so for two days.   He was ' extremely sick, and affected with starting, sneezing, and other ' symptoms of eruptive fever.   When I called, *three days after,* ' the sickness was gone, and *no pustular eruption followed.* ' p. 192.   This is one of Mr Brown's cases of natural small-pox. His inoculated small-pox is no less singular.   Thus, in his twelfth case, ' No *constitutional symptoms* could be detected ; a slight
                                            ' heat

' heat appeared on the fkin, but little or no alteration on the
' pulfe.' Next day, ' from the report of Mr M. and the maid,
' *she had sneezed repeatedly,* which they attributed to cold ; and
' her appetite appeared impaired.' The day after, ' fhe had
' fneezed fome the preceding night ; only drank tea to breakfaft,
' but eat no bread.' Such ftatements are truly ridiculous ; but
we muft refer our readers, for an able analyfis of the whole feries
by the furgeons of the Vaccine Inftitution, to their Report.

After fuch a refutation of Mr Brown's ftatements, his hypothefis is fcarcely worthy of any notice, in fo far as it is founded
on obfervation ; and it is obvioufly contrary to all analogy, although he has attempted to bolfter it up, by miftating the moft
univerfally received principles of pathological fcience. It is well
known, that two general conftitutional difeafes cannot exift in the
body at the fame time. But it is equally well known, that an attack of fuch a difeafe, as foon as it is over, leaves the body as fufceptible to the impreffions of any other as it was before ; nay, in
many cafes, renders it much more fo ; fince, in every elementary
writer, we find debility from preceding disease enumerated among
the caufes predifpofing the body to receive infection. Mr Brown,
however, has the merit of inventing a very different doctrine.
' Indeed, there feems to be a general principle in the laws of the
' animal economy, that after it has been influenced by any power,
' it is, for fome time, exempted not only from a repetition of its
' effects, but alfo from thofe of any other caufe ; and the dif-
' tance feems, in general, to bear a proportion to the feverity and
' extent of the power previoufly exerted.' In another paragraph,
he has ftill more luminoufly explained the principle upon which
he fuppofes this exemption to depend. ' Thefe cafes, and the
' whole phenomena and circumftances of vaccination, fhow, that
' there are juft grounds for concluding, that a fpecific action may
' exift, *minus* or *negatively,* in the conftitution ; that therefore it
' would be improper, in the event of vaccination being found in-
' adequate to maintain its antivariolous character, to reinoculate
' thofe cafes which have previoufly undergone vaccination, be-
' fore it was capable of producing a diftinct conftitutional effect.'
We really cannot perfuade ourfelves to reply to fuch arguments ;
but it is not a little fingular, that his hypothefis fhould be directly contradicted by his own experience. Mr Brown has vaccinated, in all, about 1200 ; of whom, upon his principles, and upon the fuppofition that he vaccinated nearly the fame number
every year while he continued the practice, 400 or 500 have now
recovered their original fufceptibility of fmall-pox infection, and
300 are liable to be affected by it in a mitigated form. But, of
his alleged cafes of failure in his own practice, *eight* only have
2   occurred

occurred in the former clafs, and *ten* in the latter ; fo that, were we to credit his ftatements, the antivariolous influence of cow-pox would feem to increafe, and to become almoft doubled after five years. But it is not by Mr Brown's experience that we wifh any fact or opinion on the fubject to reft ; we muft go to lefs fufpicious authority. Every practitioner is acquainted with the numerous obfervations recorded in Willan and other writers on the fubject. In addition to thefe, we have real fatisfaction in quoting the general refult of the experience of the furgeons of the Vaccine Inftitution at Edinburgh.

'With regard to the facts which have occurred in the practice of the furgeons of the Vaccine Institution, which tend to confirm or refute the doctrine of the mere temporary protection afforded by vaccination against the small-pox, the reporters beg leave to state, that the refult of their experience is in strict conformity with that of Dr Jenner, and the other advocates of vaccination. They have lately inoculated with small-pox, children who were vaccinated eight and nine years ago, and find that they completely resist the disease; they have not been able to produce on any of them more than a lo-cal inflammation, which disappeared in four or five days. They have, almost every year, visited numbers of children who were vac-cinated during the first years of this institution; and this they have again done within these three months. In this investigation, they have found a great many of those who were vaccinated in the years 1801 and 1802, that is, seven and eight years since, who have been frequently and freely exposed, and especially within these last six months, to the contagion of the natural small pox, by playing, sleep-ing, and otherwise mixing with children in all the different stages of that disease, without being infected.' p. 32, 33.

The medical attendants of the Foundling Hofpital of Dublin have alfo lately publifhed an account of fome very decifive and fatisfactory experiments made in that Inftitution, to difprove the hypothefis, that the preventive powers of vaccination diminifh in proportion to the diftance of time from inoculation. Nine child-ren, who had been vaccinated prior to July 1801, were inoculat-ed with fmall-pox matter in July 1804, and expofed to the con-tagion in every poffible way ; and all of them refifted the infec-tion. Thefe nine children, together with ten others vaccinated between July 1801 and Auguft 1802, were *again* fubmitted to fmall-pox inoculation on the 22d December 1809, (*i. e.* the firft clafs upwards of *eight*, and the fecond upwards of *seven* years after the vaccination.) 'In every inftance,' fays Mr Creighton the reporter, 'the punctures in the arm of each child, from the 'third day, inflamed, and continued until the feventh, when the 'inflammation gradually fubfided, as certified by Mr Stewart, '(furgeon-general), and marked in a table, which, in another
'publication,

' publication, will be more fully expreffed ;—which circumftance
' has proved the activity of the fmall-pox matter inferted, and
' which muft have affected the conftitution, was it in the leaft
' fufceptible of the difeafe. Fourteen days (Jan. 4. 1810) have
' now elapfed : the inflammation of the punctures is entirely gone,
' and never was attended with the flighteft *fever, sickness or erup-*
' *tion.* '

' In corroboration of the above facts,' continues Mr Creighton, ' conducted with every degree of accuracy, and which can-
' not admit of the fmalleft doubt on the minds of those gentle-
' men who have witneffed them, and hereunto fubfcribed their
' names, I can fafely affert, that I have fubmitted *upwards of*
' *five hundred infants* and children, vaccinated by me at this Infti-
' tution, and at the Difpenfary for Infant Poor and Cow-Pox In-
' oculation, as eftablifhed in the year 1800, to a like experiment,
' and *with the same result in every instance.* '

We ourfelves had lately an opportunity of witneffing an equally fatisfactory refult in regard to the duration of the antivariolous effects of vaccination, from fome trials made in a public hofpital in
this city, in which it was the practice to vaccinate, upon admis-
fion, every child which had not previoufly been vaccinated, or had
the fmall-pox. A boy admitted in 1808, concerning whom no
information was received, was erroneoufly fuppofed to have been
vaccinated, and the operation was not repeated. In the beginning of
October 1809, this boy, although not more expofed to fmall-pox
infection than an hundred other children living under the fame
roof with him, was feized with natural fmall-pox, and had a very full crop of the diftinct kind, which ran their courfe with perfect regularity. With *virus* taken from this boy on the 5th day of
the eruption, feventeen children of the hofpital were inoculated,
who had all been vaccinated at former periods, varying from five
months to *upwards of eight years.* The refult of this experiment
proved, *first,* that although a confiderable degree of fwelling and
hardnefs, or even a diftinct puftule on the arm, with furrounding inflammation, may fometimes be produced by inoculation with variolous *virus,* yet the conftitution is incapable of being affected with the
fmall-pox : *secondly,* that thefe different effects, from a flight hardnefs to a diftinct puftule with furrounding inflammation, are produced from circumftances altogether independent of the period intervening between the time of vaccination and the infertion of the
variolous virus : and, *lastly,* that the power of cow-pox, in protecting the conftitution againft the fmall-pox, is as complete at
the end of eight years, as at the end of five months; and that,
during *this* period at leaft, it is to be regarded as a perfect fecurity.

There are even facts on record which prove that the antivariolous powers of cow-pox are permanent, or, at leaft, that they fuf-
fer no diminution in the courfe of upwards of half a century.

Farmer Jefty, according to the report of the Broad-Street Vaccine Inftitution, vifited London in 1805, and ' afforded decifive
' evidence of his having vaccinated his wife and two fons in the
' year 1774, who were thereby rendered unfufceptible of the
' fmall-pox, as appears from the expofure of all the three parties
' to that diforder frequently, during the courfe of *thirty-one* years;
' and from the inoculation of the two fons for the fmall-pox fif-
' teen years ago. '

Dr Jenner has recorded cafes of perfons who had been cafu-
ally affected with the cow-pox, and had refifted fmall-pox upwards of fifty years; and, in a very excellent report of the Medical Faculty in Kiel, upon the cow-pox in the dutchies of Schles-
wig and Holftein, there is the remarkable cafe of a woman, then
alive, who had the cow-pox when a year and a half old, and had
remained fecure againft fmall-pox infection for *sixty years*.   In
another cafe, the protection had then lafted 56, and in many 40,
30, 20 years.

There is no fact, therefore, we conceive, relating to the animal economy, which can be confidered as more decifively proved, than that the antivariolous powers of cow-pox do not decreafe
or wear out by length of time.   At the fame time, it muft be
admitted, that there are fome apparently authenticated exceptions
to the univerfality of its antivariolous influence.   Within the circle of our own obfervation, none of thefe have occurred; and
it is a very remarkable thing, that they are confined almoft ex-
clufively to the lower orders of fociety, and to the practice of
certain individuals.   Mr Brown admits, and has attempted an
explanation of this fact, in which we are defired to believe, that
gentlemen, at the head of the profeffion, never hear of cafes of
fmallpox after cowpox, becaufe the poor only are expofed to
fmallpox contagion; and that thofe who have moft practice even
amongft the poor, never hear of failures, becaufe the poor never
complain when difappointed and deceived, and never feek for af-
fiftance even in the moft dangerous and loathfome maladies.

Before concluding this part of the fubject, it is abfolutely neceffary that we fhould notice the laft report from the Original
Vaccine Inftitution, Broad-Street, London, both on account of
its fingularity, and of the ufe Dr Brown has made of it in fup-
port of his hypothefis.

' The late authentic inftances of failure after vaccination, de-
' mand from this Inftitution an explicit declaration of the refults
' of their experience on this point, for ten folid years from its e-
                                                    ' ftablifhment.

' ftablifhment. During the courfe of the firft five years, the al-
' leged examples of failure not being fubftantiated by juft evi-
' dence, the Inftitution faw no facts to render queftionable the
' unqualified affertion of the promulgator, Dr Jenner, " that
" thofe who have undergone the cowpock are, *for life,* unfufcep-
" tible of fmallpox. " Each fubfequent year, however, has fur-
' nifhed cafes of failure, on conclufive evidence, progreffively in-
' creafing in number. Notwithftanding thefe adverfe occurren-
' ces, our experience juftifies the opinion, that vaccination is emi-
' nently beneficial to the community and the individual ;
 ' Firft, becaufe a very large proportion of vaccinated perfons
' have been found not fufceptible of the fmallpox, on trial of the
' moft decifive tefts.
 ' Secondly, becaufe (a very fmall proportion of cafes excepted)
' the fmallpox fubfequent to cowpock is a milder affection than
' the flighteft cafes of inoculated fmallpox.
 ' Thirdly, becaufe the chance of death is far lefs than even in
' the inoculated fmallpox.
 ' Fourthly, becaufe fecurity, equal to that of fmallpox inocula-
' tion, may be given by the harmlefs practice of a fecond vaccin-
' ation, as long ago recommended by this Inftitution.
 ' It is to be confidered, however, that the effects of the vac-
' cine infection have hitherto been but partially inveftigated ; and
' the refults of further experience and obfervation, of which re-
' cords will continue to be preferved, will not fail to be report-
' ed. '
 We agree with Mr Brown in regretting that this Inftitution has
not condefcended to be more particular as to the facts alluded to in
this report. It is, in truth, fo vague and ambiguous, that it may be
interpreted either in favour of, or againft vaccination. Accordingly, Mr Brown, while he ridicules the advice which it gives, and
defcants on the dangers to be apprehended from following it,
gladly feizes upon the admiffion, that the effects of vaccination
have been hitherto but partially inveftigated, and that authentic inftances of failure have now been collected. On the other hand,
it might be contended, that the report is decidedly in favour of
vaccination, and that the perplexities which it ftates, are to be attributed entirely to our limited knowledge of *the laws* of this difeafe, as well as of thofe of fmallpox. It ftrongly recommends
the practice of vaccination. It pofitively ftates, that fecurity, e-
qual to that of fmallpox inoculation, may be obtained from it.
And, fo far are we from confidering it of any confequence, that
the admiffions to which we have alluded fhould come from one of
the oldeft eftablifhments in the kingdom, that we are very much
difpofed to afcribe them to the known peculiarities which have al-

ways

ways diftinguifhed their opinions ;—fince it is notorious to all who
are acquainted with the hiftory of vaccination, that, though friendly to the practice in general, this Inftitution has, from the very
beginning, acted uniformly in oppofition to Dr Jenner, reprefent-
ing him as the mere promulgator of a fact known to every farmer
in Gloucefterfhire, and as having left the hiftory and character of
the difeafe to be inveftigated and afcertained by *their* experience
and obfervations.

Upon the whole, we are fatisfied that we concede more than is
neceffary, when we conclude our obfervations on the antivariolous
powers of cowpox in the terms of the Collegiate Report. ‘ The
‘ fecurity derived from vaccination, if not abfolutely perfect, is as
‘ nearly fo as can perhaps be expected from any human difcovery ;
‘ for, amongft feveral hundred thoufand cafes, with the refults of
‘ which the College have been made acquainted, the number of
‘ alleged failures has been furprifingly fmall ; fo much fo, as to
‘ form certainly no reafonable objection to the general adoption of
‘ vaccination ; for it appears, that there are not nearly fo many
‘ *failures* in a given number of vaccinated perfons, as there are
‘ *deaths* in an equal number of perfons inoculated for the fmall-
‘ pox. ’

The fecond general objection to cowpox inoculation, is, that it
produces new and unheard of difeafes.　This, we may obferve,
was firft advanced as a conjecture, prior to all experience, and upon grounds purely hypothetical ; though facts have fince been
referred to by thefe ill-auguring theorifts.　Thefe theories, it is
fcarcely neceffary to notice, as we are now in poffeffion of fufficient experience to decide the queftion.　With regard, however,
to the facts which have been referred to by the enemies of vaccination, nothing can be more vague and inconclufive.　We have
heard all the common cutaneous difeafes, which uniformly attend
on filth and poverty, attributed to the cowpox.　If, in a fcro-
phulous family, any fymptom of that difeafe fhould appear in a
child who had been vaccinated, no matter how long before, ftill
the cowpox is alone to blame for having engendered foul humours.
Nay, if meafles, or hoopingcough, or pleurify, fhould be unufu-
ally fatal, even though the fufferers were never vaccinated, ftill
the cowpox is the caufe of the mortality.　Clamorous affertions
of this kind, enforced by difgufting caricatures of mangy girls and
oxfaced boys, have done more to prevent the univerfal adoption
of vaccination, than any doubts of its efficacy.　Of thefe, the
moft ridiculous, perhaps, is the frontifpiece to a publication ‘ by
‘ Ferdinand Smyth Stuart, Efq. phyfician, barrackmafter, and
‘ great grandfon to King Charles the Second, ’ in which Dr Jenner and his coadjutors, *cornuted* and *caudated*, are reprefented feed-
ing

ing a monster with baskets full of infants; while, to poor Dr Thornton is assigned the final drudgery of shovelling them into a scavenger's cart, after being duly digested. The following is the poetical description by which this eloquent representation is illustrated.

' A mighty and horrible monster, with the horns of a bull, the hind hoofs of a horse, the jaws of the krakin, the teeth and claws of a tyger, the tail of a cow,—all the evils of Pandora's box in his belly, —plague, pestilence, leprosy, purple blotches, fœtid ulcers, and filthy running sores covering his body,—and an atmosphere of accumulated disease, pain and death around him, has made his appearance in the world, and devours mankind—especially poor helpless infants ; not by scores only,—or hundreds, or thousands,—but by hundreds of thousands. '

Dr Moseley, again has described, in technical style, a whole tribe of new cowpox diseases ; and Mr Stuart has discovered a brutal degeneration of the human species.

' The cowpox mange or farcy, cowpox ulcers, with pus, green —green *as grass*, clearly demonstrating their bovine origin ; cowpox evil or abscess, cowpox mortification, are nothing in comparison of the brutalization of the noblest work of the creation. '—' Among the numerous shocking cases of cowpox which I have heard of, I know not if the most horrible of all has yet been published, viz. of a child at Peckham, who, after being inoculated with the cowpox, had its former natural disposition absolutely changed to the *brutal;* so that it ran upon all fours like a BEAST, bellowing like a cow, and butting with its head like a bull. For my part, ' he adds, with philosophical *scepticism,* ' I can scarcely think it possible, having *had no time to as-certain the truth !* '

' O Moseley ! thy books, nightly phantasies rousing,
    Full oft make me quake for my heart's dearest treasures :
For fancy, in dreams, oft presents them all brousing
    On commons, just like little Nebuchadnezzars.
There, nibbling at thistles, stand Jem, Joe and Mary ;
    On their foreheads, oh horrible ! crumpled horns bud :
Here Tom with a tail, and poor William all hairy,
    Reclin'd in a corner, are chewing the cud. '

The diary of Dr Barrackmaster Stuart's own child's illness and death, is truly humiliating, and excites a mixed emotion of ridicule and compassion. But as if the powers of language were not sufficient to excite our sympathy with his sufferings, and our indignation at the beastly disease which occasioned them, he has elucidated the history by a very amiable representation of Mrs Stuart with the baby on her knee, the cradle on one side, and a bason of gruel on the other ;—notwithstanding all which, we should have had no doubt that the poor babe's death was owing to scrophula, had it been of less than royal extraction.

But

But to be serious.—The following appears to us to be a satisfactory answer to all this disgraceful clamour. Dr Bateman,
from the records of the Public Dispensary of London, has proved, that the proportion of cutaneous eruptions to all other diseases, was the same before the publication of Dr Jenner's Inquiry, as in the sixth and seventh year of vaccination. And the
Report of the London College states, ' The testimonies before
' the College of Physicians are very decided in declaring, that
' vaccination does less mischief to the constitution, and less fre-
' quently gives rise to other diseases, than the small-pox either
' natural or inoculated. The College feel themselves called upon
' to state this strongly, because it has been objected to vaccina-
' tion, that it produces new, unheard-of, and monstrous diseases.
' Of such assertions, *no proofs have been produced ;* and after di-
' ligent inquiry, the College believe them to have been the inven-
' tions of designing, or the mistakes of ignorant men. '
    The last important objection which we shall notice, is, that
vaccination has put an end to small-pox inoculation, without being
so extensively adopted in its stead. In this objection may be
traced the motives of many of the keenest opposers of the new
practice ; and it must be confessed, that its advocates have afforded some pretext for it, by their injudicious and unfounded complaints of want of patronage and encouragement. The truth is,
however, that when all the obstacles which vaccination has had
to encounter, are considered, its progress must appear to have
been inconceivably rapid. It has been adopted by millions who
never would have submitted to variolation. For example, in
this very city, gratuitous inoculation for smallpox had long been
offered to the poor at the Public Dispensary, but altogether in vain ;
while, at the same useful charity, no less than 10,000 have been
vaccinated since February 1801. This greater willingness on
the part of the poor to inoculate for cowpox than for smallpox,
may be ascribed partly to their conviction of its utility and superior safety, and partly to its not being opposed by the mistaken
but very powerful prejudice which prevails among the religious
sectaries in this kingdom, that the wilful inoculation of any *disease* is an impious interference with the ordinances of the Almighty ; while they do not consider the slight affection produced
by vaccination as a disease. But while it has thus become much
more general than smallpox inoculation ever was at home, the rapidity of its progress in the most remote corners of the earth, is
altogether without example It has been gratefully received by
people of the most opposite races and religions, encouraged by
governments of every description, and been the subject of publications

cations in every written language. Manuals of vaccination, in the *Chinese* and *Polish* tongues, are now before us, illustrated with coloured figures.   In our own colonies in the East Indies, its success has been astonishing; and the numbers who have been vaccinated are such, that, in the settlements of Bombay, smallpox is said to be altogether exterminated.   The reports of its progress in Ceylon are particularly interesting, on account of its insular situation so nearly resembling our own.   The following is the report made of it by a resident physician.

' The dreadful ravages which the smallpox usually commit-
' ted in Ceylon, previous to the introduction of vaccination,
' must be in the recollection of every one ; and it affords me
' infinite pleasure to observe, that, agreeably to the most cer-
' tain information I have been enabled to procure, that de-
' structive malady has not existed in any part of the British
' possessions on this island during the year 1808, except in the
' district of Galle, into which it was brought on the 31st of Ja-
' nuary by a Maldivian boat, last from Bengal.   A large propor-
' tion of the crew of this boat died; and the disease was com-
' municated by a fisherman, who visited it on its first arrival, to
' two or three inhabitants in the neighbourhood of Galle, but it
' spread no further ; which must be attributed chiefly to the fa-
' vourable influence of vaccination, which has been so extensive-
' ly diffused in that and the other districts of the island.' *Report* 809.

We have here a striking proof of the good effects of *general* vaccination Contagion may be introduced ; but it dies for want of susceptible subjects :—a firebrand may be applied ; but there is no fuel to produce a conflagration.   Even old Spain was roused from its apathy by the obvious advatages of vaccination ; and sent forth an expedition, worthy of its better days, which circumnavigated the globe for the sole purpose of carrying to all its vast possessions, and to those of several other nations, the inestimable gift of vaccination : and, in point of fact, it succeeded in disseminating it, not only through the boundless colonies of Spain, but through the vast Archipelago of the Visayan islands, and in establishing it wherever it touched in its progress.

So far as our information extends, therefore, we conceive there is no foundation whatever for this objection.   Cowpox, we verily believe, is far more generally resorted to than smallpox ever was ; and the public, of course, must have great gain by the substitution.

So much for the objections : but we cannot allow the objectors to escape quite so easily.   In a controversy as to matter of

fact, where the witnesses contradict each other, it is absolutely necessary to ascertain, as far as possible, their relative credibility; and to settle our belief by comparing the number and value of opposite experiences. We have already seen, that these are decidedly, and almost infinitely, in favour of the advocates of vaccination. Still, however, the statements of their opponents may have been candid, and their opposition sincere; and the frequent occurrence of adverse facts would have perplexed us, and left doubts upon our minds with regard to the universal safety and efficacy of the practice. Fortunately, however, the conduct of the antivaccinists themselves has set our minds at ease. Their zeal has so far overstepped their prudence, and they have given such evident proofs of want of observation and candour, and have had recourse to such mean tricks and devices to frighten the timid and mislead the ignorant, as to deprive them of all credit with the well informed and judicious. What opinion must be entertained of the fairness or judgment of a man who could affix, on the walls of the most populous streets of London, posting-bills, displaying, in gigantic letters, " *Fatal Effects of Cowpox!* " with an earnest recommendation to heads of families to peruse the treatise in which they are stated,—who employs the driver of errand-carts to distribute them indiscriminately to travellers upon the roads near London,—and could deliberately state, as one of his serious reasons for continuing the smallpox inoculation, that, ' in the populous part of the metropolis, where the abundance of ' children exceeds the means of providing food and raiment for ' them, this pestilential disease is considered as a merciful provi- ' sion on the part of Providence to lessen the burthen of a poor ' man's family!' Another device of the same gentleman, was the publication of a newspaper, for the exclusive purpose of attacking vaccination and its patrons with the lowest and most contemptible abuse.

But the most unjustifiable part of this gentleman's conduct is his wilful falsification of the report of the College of Physicians, —a public record widely distributed under the sanction of Parliament. The few passages we have already quoted from it, will enable our readers to judge, whether it be in any respect warrantable to assert, ' that the Report of the College of Physicians allows ' the evidence, produced before the committee of the House of ' Commons, to be totally overthrown; that they allow there is no ' spurious cowpox; and that failure, disorder, and death, some- ' times occur from some deviation in the genuine Jennerian cow- ' pox, which, after a precise period, fails in its security, and, if it ' does any thing, produces a new kind of eruption, tumour, or ' ulceration.'

' ulceration. '—Mr Stuart, however, improves upon this hint; and,
in his Addrefs to the Britifh Parliament, thus exprefles himfelf.
' *Patres* confcripti ! celebrated and illuftrious fenators of Britain,
' lay afide all prejudice, and receive, I entreat you, the following
' information with candour and attention, viz. That all the phy-
' ficians, furgeons and apothecaries, moft eminently diftinguifhed
' for abilities and profeffional fkill, *all to a man*, now acknow-
' ledge, that vaccination is not a certain preventive of the fmall-
' pox ; and that it fometimes produces new, dangerous, and fatal
' difeafes. Thefe *truths* are at this time univerfally granted, and
' candidly acknowledged, by ever intelligent medical gentleman ;
' and this is all I contend for. ' * Now, in thefe paffages, there
can be no mifconception or miftake, to be accounted for by ignorance ; and, therefore, we are afraid we muft fet them down as
inftances of wilful and unpardonable mifreprefentation. Mifquo-
tation, indeed, feems to be a favourite figure with the antivaccinifts ; and with none more remarkably, than with their newly-en-
lifted Scotifh auxiliary, who, we may remark by the way, wifhes
to be confidered as the firft writer, on that fide of the queftion,
entitled to any fort of attention ; and treats all his predeceffors
altogether as cavalierly as his opponents. In proof of this gentleman's extreme loofenefs, and unfairnefs of quotation, we might
refer to the greater part of his extracts from the public reports,
and the writings of Dr Jenner and Mr Bryce ; but we fhall content ourfelves with one example, in the cafe of Dr Willan, whom
he ingenioufly contrives to quote as an authority for an opinion
which he openly difavows, and that by the fimple method of
ftating a fort of caution or exception to his general opinion, as
the opinion itfelf.—' I fhall, perhaps, be afked, ' fays Dr W.,
' whether I think that the variolous eruptions, in all the cafes ad-
                                                    ' duced

---

* The reader may take this further specimen of the eloquence and
accurate reasoning of this scion of royalty.—' The *Omnipotent* GOD
' of *Nature*, the inconceivable *Creator* of *all existence*, has permitted
' *Evil, Buonaparté*, and *Vaccination* to exist,—to prosper,—and even
' to triumph for a short space of time,—perhaps as the scourge and
' punishment of mankind for their sins, and for reasons no doubt the
' best, far beyond the powers of our very circumscribed and limited
' portion of penetration and knowledge to discover.——But, are we
' to worship—to applaud—or even to submit to *Evil*,—to *Buonaparté*,
' —or to *Vaccination*,—because they have for some time been pro-
' sperous ?—No !—Never let us degrade our honour—our virtue—or
' our consciences—by such servility :—let us contend against them,
' with all our exertions and might ;—not doubting but we shall ulti-
' mately triumph, in a cause supported by *truth, humanity*, and *virtue*,
' and which therefore we well know *Heaven* itself must *approve.* '

' duced above, were the confequences of imperfect vaccination?'
This is the queftion ;—and here is the anfwer which is immediately
fubjoined ; and of which Mr Brown, when profeffing to quote both
queftion and anfwer, has *omitted* the whole which we have put in
italics. ' *Vaccine inoculators were, at first, generally satisfied with*
' *any vesicular appearance, surrounded by inflammation ; and even*
' *now, I believe, many practitioners would consider the specious ir-*
' *regular vesicle, described page* 39, *as a sufficient guarantee against*
' *the smallpox ; not being aware how frequently it denotes a temporary*
' *incapacity to be affected by either the variolous or vaccine virus.   I*
' *have had reason, on minute inquiry, to conclude, that, in a very great*
' *majority of the cases which occurred near London, the vaccination was*
' *imperfect.*   There is, *however,* great difficulty in obtaining clear
' and diftinct information on the fubject,' &c.   Willan, p. 73.—
Brown, p. 317.

In the fame manner, in quoting the admiffion of the London
College, that cafes of fmallpox have occurred, after apparently
perfect vaccination, he takes fpecial care to leave out the word
apparently ; and, at laft, makes that learned Body admit, that fuch
failures had occurred where there was ' fufficient proof of the
' moft perfect vaccination.'   Dr Willan's treatife will alfo be
fearched in vain for any thing like the defcription of chickenpox,
which Mr Brown has pretended to extract from it.   When a perfon thus ventures to falfify public records to ferve a particular
purpofe, it really is not eafy to give implicit credit to ftatements
made on his own authority, in oppofition to general experience.

The eftablifhed efficacy of vaccination as a preventive of fmall-
pox, has given rife to various legiflative projects for the utter extermination from this kingdom of that deftructive peftilence ; and
it muft be confeffed, that our infular fituation feems to give fome
encouragement to fuch a project.   Even prior to the difcovery of
vaccination, this had been ftrongly urged by Dr Haygarth in this
country, Scuderi in Sicily, and a whole tribe of enthufiafts in
Germany.   Infurmountable difficulties, however, appeared on e-
very fide ; and nothing was ever attempted.   The idea has been
again revived, and certainly with greater plaufibility, fince the antivariolous powers of cowpox have become known.   Still, however, there are very ftrong, and perhaps infurmountable, objections to every thing hitherto devifed, or which perhaps may be
devifed for carrying it into effect.   But, before we enter upon the
difcuffion of thefe, we muft notice fome opinions of Dr Adams,
phyfician to the Smallpox Hofpital, and a pretended friend to vaccination ; for if his opinion be true, viz. that cowpox is identical
with fmallpox, or that they are but varieties of the fame difeafe,
it is plain that the diffufion of the one can never lead to the extirpation

pation of the other; fince, if there be any foundation for the opinion, that fmallpox may be converted into cowpox, it is impoffible not to conclude, that cowpox will, in many circumftances, degenerate into fmallpox. Dr Adams's arguments for their identity, are derived from the near refemblance of the moft favourable kinds of fmallpox to cowpox, and ' prefumptive proofs deduced from the laws of all other morbid poifons, that the variolous and vaccine *is* the fame.' And he proceeds pofitively to ftate, that by ' continuing, with great caution, to inoculate at the hofpital from *pearl* fmallpox, (the Doctor's hobbyhorfe), we at laft fucceeded in procuring a fucceffion of virus fo nearly refembling the vaccine, that an univerfal fufpicion prevailed among the parents, that they were deceived by the fubftitution of one for the other.' The facts ftated by Dr Adams are certainly curious; but it appears that the practice faid to have been followed by him was not neceffary for their converfion, as has been fatisfactorily proved by Mr Bryce, (App. p. 70.); and, indeed, the facts and obfervations ftated by that gentleman irrefiftibly fuggeft to the mind the miftake committed, at the commencement of the practice of vaccination, in the very fame hofpital, by Dr Adams's celebrated predeceffor. Dr Woodville inoculated with variolous virus, when he believed he was ufing vaccine; and Dr Adams feems to have reverfed the matter.

His prefumptive proofs proceed upon a notoriously erroneous affumption, that if a perfon be inoculated at the fame time with the virus of two feparate diftempers, the one will remain unaltered till the other complete its progrefs, and will then take as many days to run its courfe as if it had not been inferted until the progrefs of the firft was complete. The fact is, as ftated by Mr Bryce, ' that both punctures will advance regularly, as if only one had been made during the period neceffary for the local ftage of thefe infections, and until the conftitutional affection from one of them is excited, at which time, and not before, the progrefs of the other morbid poifon, provided its local courfe be finifhed, will be arrefted, until the firft conftitutional affection has difappeared.' In the fame manner, Dr Adams miftates the fact, when he afferts, that ' if fmallpox and cowpox are inferted at the fame time, in different parts of the fame perfon, we find *no interruption whatever* in the progrefs of either. Both begin and go through their feveral courfes with the fame regularity, as if only one of them had been inferted in two different places.' Now, Mr Bryce's experiments prove inconteftably, that as foon as a conftitutional affection is produced, by fmallpox for example, the further progrefs of the vaccine affection, if its local courfe be finifhed, is arrefted until the variolous action has exhaufted itfelf on the conftitution; or it is altogether fuperfeded according to circumftances.

cumftances. Dr Adams is alfo wrong in his third pofition, that if a perfon be vaccinated for example, and in two or three days be inoculated in one place with variolous, and in another with cowpox matter, the fame confequences will follow as if both infertions had been of one matter. For the faƈt undoubtedly is, that, in fuch a cafe, the fecondary vaccination will have its progrefs accelerated, and will arrive at maturity at the fame time with the primary vaccination ; while the fmallpox puftule will *not* be accelerated, but proceed through its local ftage in the ufual manner. Thefe faƈts prove, in the moft decifive manner, that Dr Adams's opinion is erroneous, even upon his own principles ; and that fmallpox and cowpox are effentially different difeafes, not convertible, in any circumftances, into each other.

Of all the plans for exterminating fmallpox by means of cowpox, which we have feen, Mr Bryce's is the moft detailed, and will ferve us as a text for the obfervations we have to offer. This plan embraces three feveral objeƈts. 1ft, To induce parents and others to have all children vaccinated before a certain age ; 2d, To get correƈt lifts of all thofe who have not been vaccinated ; and, 3d, To put it in the power, and indeed in the way of all perfons, to get the operation performed with fkill and fafety, by diftributing corps of vaccinators up and down the country.

We fhall not go into the various details with which Mr Bryce has endeavoured to explain his projeƈt, and to obviate the objections he has anticipated. We fhall only obferve, with a view to the fecond branch of his plan, that however defirable fuch lifts might be, we are afraid the procuring of them would be attended with greater difficulties than Mr Bryce has forefeen. When we confider how inaccurately the regifters of births and marriages and the bills of mortality are kept, and how many inconveniences, both perfonal and political, have arifen from this inaccuracy, we can only exprefs our wifhes, that vaccination may furnifh a motive, fufficiently powerful, to lead to their fimplification and correction ; but we muft confefs, that we have no hopes of feeing any reform in this refpeƈt carried into effeƈt. His corps of vaccinators, too, would never be tolerated, either by the public or by the profeffion ; and would, at all events, foon degenerate into a fcene of jobbing and intrigue.

It is the firft part of Mr Bryce's plan, however, which requires moft attention, and about which there is likely to be the greateft difference of opinion. With regard to the aid which he feems to expeƈt from the private patronage and exertions of men of influence and reputation, there cannot be a doubt, that it is the duty of every fuch man to inftruƈt and enlighten the public with regard to the advantages to be derived from vaccination ; and to remove the prejudices

judices excited againſt it by thoſe intereſted in the continuance of variolation. Theſe however have hitherto had but a very inconſiderable effect; and it is well remarked by the College of Phyſicians, ' The lower orders of society can hardly be induced to adopt precautions against evils which may be at a distance; nor can it be expected from them, if these precautions are attended with expense. Unless, therefore, from the immediate dread of epidemic smallpox, neither vaccination nor inoculation appear at any time to have been general; and when the cause of terror has passed by, the public have relapsed again into a state of indifference and apathy, and the salutary practice has come to a stand. *It is not easy to suggest a remedy for an evil so deeply imprinted in human nature.*' Bryce, App. p. 37.

It is this apathy or indifference which is the moſt powerful obſtacle to the progreſs of vaccination; and we have conſidered its effects as the moſt ſerious objection to the practice. Should we, by means of it, ſucceed in baniſhing ſmallpox altogether from this iſland, or from large diſtricts of it, there is ſome danger that vaccination would ſoon be very generally neglected, and that, ſo large a proportion of the people would be left ſuſceptible of ſmallpox, that its effects, whenever it ſhould chance to be imported, would be truly calamitous. It is on this account that we have heard very judicious perſons dread the partial extinction of the ſmallpox. They would have it preſerved, for the ſame reaſon that the clergyman would not have the Devil killed, or that inſurance offices rejoice in occaſional fires. But the poſſible dangers of exterminating the ſmallpox are much too viſionary to cauſe us to relax a moment in our efforts for that purpoſe; and, if we were to ſucceed in extirpating it in any one country, the danger of importing it would probably be much diminiſhed, by the diminution of its ſource in other regions, and the encouragement which ſuch an event would hold out to proceed againſt it with ſtill greater vigour.

Are we, however, to uſe any other means than mere advice and example? Are we to reſort to any meaſures of compulſion or reſtraint? Are we to have recourſe to legiſlative meaſures? Theſe are great political queſtions, in regard to which the preſent and late rulers of the ſtate have expreſſed very different opinions; Mr Perceval conceiving that more evil than good would reſult from any meaſure of coercion; and Lord H. Petty taking a different, and, we are inclined to think, a more correct view of the ſubject.

' Though I would not interfere ' (ſaid his Lordship) ' with the freedom of an individual with regard to the mode of preſerving his own health, yet I have no difficulty in ſaying that no individual has a right to conduct himſelf, even in the purſuit of preſerving his own health according to the beſt of his judgment, ſo as to endanger the health of a great portion of the community by ſpreading an infection, which is the caſe when individuals go abroad while they are
under

under the process of inoculation under the old mode. This practice I understand to be increasing, and may be attended with dangerous effects. I know that in a country like this, where the inhabitants have been so accustomed to liberty in almost every thing, and in this practice among the rest, it must be difficult, and, without some infringement of liberty, perhaps impossible, to put an end altogether to this inconvenience. This, I am afraid, can hardly be done without some sort of compulsion ;—and that is odious to the people of this country. But although compulsion be odious, while it calls on mankind to be active against their will, yet while it goes no farther than to forbid their doing that which is hurtful to others, I think that a state has not only a right, but that it is its duty to enforce it. I would therefore say, that if persons will persist in following the old system of inoculation, they should be compelled to confine their practice within their own houses, and shall not be allowed to spread these ravages and this pest over the community at large. ’ Debates, p. 74, 75.

The professional arguments for the restriction of smallpox inoculation, are indeed very strong. Every person variolated becomes a centre of contagion, spreading disease and death around him. In addition to this obvious fact, and the instances quoted in various publications, we may state what took place in Weimar, both on account of its authenticity, and because, from its date, it cannot be suspected of exaggeration or colouring. The smallpox had not been seen in that city for about five years, when it became prevalent in the neighbouring villages. The Duke, anxious for the safety of his children, wished to protect them by inoculation, but did not think himself entitled to take a step, however interesting to himself, which might endanger the lives of his subjects, without strongly warning them by advertisement, and inviting them to follow his example. Notwithstanding these laudable and truly paternal precautions, an epidemic was the consequence, which was distinctly traced to the ducal residence, and proved fatal to above fifty individuals in that small city. Even prior to the discovery of vaccination, in many countries smallpox inoculation was not permitted except during the prevalence of an epidemic. But if such a restriction was at all tolerable then, it is surely much more so now, when it is in the power of every person to protect himself, and those under his care, without endangering the safety of others.

Mr Highmore and Dr Adams, *both of the Smallpox Hospital,* have argued in favour of smallpox inoculation on very absurd and untenable grounds. Mr Highmore, for instance, is afraid, that if variolation be prevented, we shall not be able to test our vaccinated patients ; and that the progress of vaccination will be impeded, if it be encouraged, as ‘ the flower which is forced
into

into a too early maturity has neither strength nor fragrance comparable with that which blooms by fair and regular cultivation. '
Dr Adams's arguments are still more insidious, and equally futile. This gentleman apologizes to the public, for having so long delayed to offer, in print, his opinion on a subject so immediately connected with his engagements, and on which the public, he conceives, had a right to demand the result of his inquiries. But he was afraid of having his motives impeached ; and there was a difficulty of finding any thing to oppose. At last, the letter to Mr Perceval, in which Sir Edmund Carrington, late chief justice of Ceylon, shows, from our statute books, the legality of restraining every infectious disease, even smallpox, appeared to the physician of the Smallpox Hospital worthy of refutation ; and a most singular attempt at refutation he has produced. As, on a former occasion, under the mask of a popular inquiry into vaccination, he had endeavoured to palm his *pearlpock* upon the credulity of the people ; so, now, he endeavours to obscure the question relative to restricting inoculation, under the pretence of a general inquiry into the laws of epidemics. ' To defend small-
' pox inoculation,' says he, ' is only to repeat all that was said
' fifty years ago, and has been repeated ever since, till the last ten
' years. To admit that vaccination is a most important improve-
' ment, is equally superfluous. To say that this second improve-
' ment ought not by force to supersede the first, would only lead
' to those arguments by which smallpox inoculation was first de-
' fended ; and to answer clamour and invective, requires a mind
' organized like those who use them. ' To this we can only answer, that the case is totally altered within these ten years. Till then, we had only a choice of evils, and we were not restricted in the only means offered to us of defending ourselves, lest in so doing we should injure our neighbours. But now that we possess a means of defence, equally useful to ourselves, and perfectly harmless to all around us, we are no longer entitled, either by reason or justice, to have recourse to the former. When Dr Adams talks of a law restricting variolation, operating against the conscientious, without restraining the unprincipled or unfeeling, we must confess that we do not understand him. That none but the unfeeling would now have recourse to variolation, we might perhaps be disposed to allow; but that any such restriction would operate *against* the conscientious, so long as they have vaccination in their power, is what we will not admit. The great difficulty is, to prevail upon the mass of the people to use *any* preventive. With those, who have sufficient judgment to have recourse to one, the transition to a better is easy and natural. This was strongly exemplified in a fishing village in this vicinity. The first person in Newhaven, who had the

courage

courage and prudence to have his children inoculated with small-pox, was obliged to fly, as a monster, from the fury of his igno-rant neighbours; and yet it was in that very village that vaccination first became general in Scotland,—and in that very man's family was it begun. Dr Adams's whole chapter upon the recent plans for exterminating smallpox, is one of the most extraordinary pieces of reasoning we ever met with. We cannot exterminate small-pox, it seems, because constant and indestructible sources of con-tagion may be bought from every old-clothesman in Monmouth-Street, and may be dug up in every grave! While these exist, the restriction of inoculation will not narrow its operations! We must not attempt to exterminate smallpox, because we do not know how to exterminate measles and scarlet fever; and because our ancestors never attempted any thing of the kind! And, lastly, restricting smallpox inoculation, and even forbidding the inocula-tion of outpatients at the hospitals, is compelling vaccination!

‘ The discovery of vaccination is certainly a most invaluable
‘ acquisition ; and those who are satisfied with it, do right to re-
‘ commend it to the world. Happy for themselves and others,
‘ if they had been contented to recommend it by their example,
‘ and by the facility which the practice itself offers. If they go
‘ further than this, there is only one step more they can conscien-
‘ tiously take, that is, the forcing vaccination on *all*, under certain
‘ penalties. I know there are many men, whose intentions are
‘ perfect purity and benevolence, and who would start at such an
‘ imputation ; but what else are we doing in prohibiting inocula-
‘ tion of smallpox, or even in refusing it to those who are unable
‘ to make a pecuniary return, or temporary seclusion ? If they
‘ do not submit to vaccination, are they not without the chance
‘ of escaping six years at most, many of them less than a month,
‘ in the metropolis ? Of escaping what ? A disease which is said
‘ to destroy one sixth of the sufferers,—besides maiming, blind-
‘ ing, and disfiguring many more. Do we know of any penalty
‘ heavier than an almost double decimation, and these additional
‘ torments ? ’

How far it would be prudent to forbid smallpox inoculation al-together, may admit of some doubt ; but that the managers of the Smallpox Hospital acted rightly, when they at last prohibited Dr Adams from converting it into a source of pestilence, we conceive to be undeniably established by the statement made, without con-tradiction, in the House of Commons, with regard to the effect of inoculating outpatients.

‘ There is, ’ said Mr S. Bourne, ‘ a very laudable institution in this country established for the inoculation of the smallpox. I un-derstand it is the practice now to inoculate outpatients there, to the

I　　　　　　　　　　　　amount

amount of 2000 a year ; and that it is usual for these outpatients to resort twice a week to be inspected at this hospital by the surgeon. Now, it must be quite obvious, that this is a practice of the most dangerous nature ; and that if we were to prescribe a mode of spreading the contagion, it would be difficult for human ingenuity to devise any thing better adapted for the purpose. No one would be more unwilling than myself to compel individuals to adopt any particular mode for the preservation of their health, because it is not in itself a proper subject of compulsion ; but still I must say, that however reluctant I may be to use any restraint upon such a subject, some means should be taken to prevent the dissemination of this contagious malady. I think that the Legislature would be as much justified in taking measures to prevent this evil, by restraint, as a man would be in snatching a firebrand out of the hands of a maniac, just as he was going to set fire to a city. ' Debates, p. 79.

ART. IX. 1. *Report of the Select Committee on Contagious Fever in London: Ordered by the House of Commons to be printed,* 20th *May* 1818. pp. 52. Folio.

2. *A Bill to establish Fever Hospitals, and to make other Regulations for the Relief of the Suffering Poor, and for Preventing the Increase of the Infectious Fever in Ireland: Ordered by the House of Commons to be printed,* 19th *May* 1818. pp. 12. Folio.

3. *Reports of the Practice in the Clinical Wards of the Royal Infirmary of Edinburgh, during the Months of November and December* 1817, *and January* 1818, *and May, June, and July* 1818. By ANDREW DUNCAN, junior, M. D. F. R. S. E. Fellow of the Royal College of Physicians, Professor of Medical Police, and of Medical Jurisprudence in the University of Edinburgh, and one of the Physicians to the Royal Public Dispensary and Lunatic Asylum. Edinburgh, 1818. 8vo. Constable & Co.

4. *A Succinct Account of the Contagious Fever of this Country, exemplified in the Epidemic now prevailing in London ; with the appropriate Method of Treatment as practised in the House*

of Recovery : To which are added, Observations on the Nature and Properties of Contagion, tending to correct the Popular Notions on this Subject, and pointing out the Means of Prevention. By THOMAS BATEMAN, M. D. F. L. S. &c. Physician to the Public Dispensary, and Consulting Physician to the Fever Institution in London. 8vo. pp. 177. London, 1818. Longman & Co.

5. *Medical Report of the House of Recovery and Fever Hospital in Cork-Street, Dublin.* By F. BARKER M. D. Honorary Fellow of the King's and Queen's College of Physicians; Professor of Chemistry in Trinity College, Dublin; and Senior Physician to the Hospital. 8vo. pp. 80. Dublin, 1818. Graisberry & Campbell.

6. *Observations on Contagion.* By WHITLEY STOKES M. D. Honorary Fellow of the College of Physicians; Lecturer on Natural History to the University of Dublin; late Senior Fellow of Trinity College; and late Professor of the Practice of Medicine. 8vo. Dublin, 1818.

7. *Statements relative to the present Prevalence of Epidemic Fever among the Poorer Classes of Glasgow. With some Suggestions for affording more adequate Assistance to the Sick, and for Checking the further Progress of the Contagion : in a Letter addressed to the Honourable the Lord Provost of Glasgow.* By RICHARD MILLAR M. D. Lecturer on Materia Medica in the University, one of the Physicians to the Infirmary, and to the Glasgow Lock Hospital. 8vo. Constable & Co. 1818.

8. *Practical Observations on Continued Fever, especially that Form at present existing as an Epidemic; with some Remarks on the most efficient Plan for its Suppression.* By ROBERT GRAHAM M. D. Regius Professor of Botany in the University of Glasgow; President of the Faculty of Physicians and Surgeons; and one of the Physicians to the Royal Infirmary, Glasgow. 8vo. Constable & Co. 1818.

I T may be questioned whether, in the present state of society, the epidemical visitations of a contagious disease are not productive of more misery than war itself—fertile, as it unquestionably is, in every species of calamity. The actual victims of war are not only numerically fewer, but, for the most part, belong exclusively to a class openly and almost voluntarily devoted to War horrors :—while epidemical sickness is an evil that threatens indiscriminately every class of the community; and is chiefly afflicting, from its invading that cherished sanctuary of domestic life, in which the happiness of every individual must mainly centre. The universality of the infliction; the anguish of the immediate sufferers; the distress of relatives, and often the subsequent poverty and desolation of families; conspire to fill up the measure of misfortune, and give to the destructive operations of an Epidemic, a character of the deepest gloom,—which is not, like the fatal scenes of a battle field, cheered by one spark of valour or patriotism, nor redeemed by one consoling sentiment of duty or fame.

The unhappy prevalence of Contagious Fever for the last two years, not merely amongst the poor and destitute, but amongst those whom opulence has placed far above what are generally held to be the causes of infection, forms an evil which, if not altogether novel in its nature, is at least so in its extent. Its causes, therefore, and the means of arresting its present ravages, and of preventing them in future,—are topics that should not, in circumstances like the present, be left to the discussion of Physicians, but should be taken up by the Politician and the Philanthropist: and accordingly, it is gratifying to find, that the matter has been deemed of sufficient importance to deserve Parliamentary investigation. In our humbler province, we should wish to do something in the same good cause; and have, for this purpose, selected the able tracts whose titles are prefixed to this article. Our object, however, is not to analyze the mere medical information they contain, (though that, we readily admit, is very respectable), but to convey to our readers some more practical and popular considerations on Fever in general, and particularly on the present Epidemic.

From history we learn, that, in no era of the world, has society been exempted from Epidemic Fever; but it has always committed its chief ravages at those distressing junctures when war and scarcity had been extending the dominion of evil beyond its ordinary limits. For example, after every irruption of the Goths into the Roman provinces, Epidemic sickness was sure to follow, and to thin the remains of population which the sword had spared. Indeed, on most occasions of general or local calamity, whether in ancient or modern times, contagion has made known its destructive presence; and in this way has the poison been perpetuated from age to age, and from year to year. From the remotest periods, down to the present day, it has been reproduced an infinite number of times, and in an infinite variety of constitutions, without any perceptible alteration in its character or laws. Sometimes it has extended only to a few; at other times it has spread amongst multitudes: yet, with whatever scope of operation it has appeared,—whether Epidemical, and ravaging a kingdom, or confined to a hamlet or a hut,—it has never become wholly extinct; but has lurked as a fatal spark among the neglected embers of society, ready to burst forth into a blaze at every favourable opportunity.

In the present Epidemic, the same effects have resulted from Peace, that were wont, in other times, to result from War: for it is well known, that it was not till after the return of peace, when a suspension of trade, and pecuniary embarrassments from a war of unexampled length and expenditure, began to press upon the population, by privations of unusual severity, that sickness became generally prevalent. None of our readers require to be reminded of the unprecedented stagnation of every branch of commerce and manufacture which marked the gloomy years of 1816 and 1817; and the consequent scarcity of all kinds of employment. The labouring poor who, in ordinary years, had maintained themselves and families in tolerable comfort, were thrown out of work by thousands, and abandoned not only to want, but to that heart-breaking depression of spirits, which we firmly believe to be more deleterious to the health and functions of the human frame, than inclement seasons, or any ordinary morbid causes, of a description merely physical. To poverty and mental depression, debility from insufficient nourishment was speedily joined; for the failure of the crop in 1816, superadded the inflictions of Providence to the pressure of political adversity. Had it not been for the multitude of our charitable establishments, and the unusual wide-opening of the hand of private benevolence, we verily believe that hundreds would have died of actual famine, and exhibited, in these kingdoms, a calamitous set-off against any afflicting occurrences of this sort recorded in history. Even as it was, the distress was enormous, both in extent and degree; and we have in our possession details of suffering, and of the disgusting substitutes for food to which the poor were driven, that would produce horror, as well as pity, in the minds of our readers, were we to state them: We shall therefore pass over the shocking minutiæ of this subject.

Want of fuel, and of proper clothing, were also evils of first-rate magnitude; and, with their necessary consequence—filth, rendered the wretchedness of the poor scarcely susceptible of additional aggravation. Can it be wondered at, then, that febrile contagion (which is seldom dormant in large cities) should spread widely in such a mass of apt materials,—or that, when fanned by the sigh of despair on the one hand, and of hunger on the other, it should be blown up into one of the most raging Epidemics that has appeared for many generations?

Scarcity of labour, and the misery and the privations of every sort which thence result, are but the first in a train of greater evils that, in such calamitous times, assail the poor.   Suffering, too often leads them to vice and to crime.   Their want of intellectual resources, leaves them accessible to every sort of immorality, but more especially to a degrading intemperance; for, in the temporary excitement of intoxication, they hope to assuage that gnawing canker of the mind, which is little less intolerable than hunger itself.   Again, how frequently does the poor man's conviction, that ' the world is not his friend, nor the world's law, ' goad him on to theft or robbery,—to the reckless destruction of a fellow-creature, or of himself!   And surely, if misery thus predisposes him to moral evil, we may cease to wonder that it should also render him greatly susceptible of natural disorders.

In this hasty sketch, we have touched upon the chief moral and physical causes of the Epidemic; and these are, in our view, reduced within very narrow limits; namely, an original, unextinguished Contagion—fostered by these accidental circumstances, viz. depression of mental energy from want of employment, &c.; depression of bodily vigour from want of nourishment; and, in all probability, a peculiar constitution of the atmosphere not hitherto distinctly explained.   We are aware that many able authors hold, that concomitant circumstances alone, such as foul air, filth, putrid animal effluvia, cold, wet, fatigue, and bad diet, will generate contagion, even though none previously existed.   Dr Bateman, in particular, seems still to hold this doctrine, and expressly maintains, that want of nourishment has been the great cause of the present Epidemic.   His words are—

' The history of all nations affords abundant evidence of the constant concurrence of dearth and pestilence.   The pestilence appears to have generally assumed the character of a contagious fever, modified in its form, and more or less virulent and fatal, according to the circumstances under which it occurred. ' p. 1.

' As Epidemic Fever *is unquestionably generated, in the first instance,* by defective nutriment; so we cannot doubt that it continues to *originate* in many successive individuals, during the existence of its cause, independently of any communication with each other, ' &c. p. 11.

Now, we will confess that this doctrine appears to us not only to be erroneous, but to be the very reverse of true: For we believe that deficient nutriment, (provided it do not go the length of impoverishing the blood, and thus depraving the solids), instead of being favourable to the existence of fever, is the very reverse; inasmuch as it lowers the tone of the con-

D d 2

stitution, and lessens the liability to all diseases of increased excitement. Without speculating about the relation of fever to inflammation, or stopping to inquire whether the increased action in the system which follows the application of contagion is an original part of the disease, or merely an exertion of the medical powers of nature, we are sufficiently borne out by facts when we say, that it is to this increased action, or to the exhaustion which *necessarily* follows it, that fever owes its general fatality. By consequence, it is reasonable to believe, that in those who have been scantily fed, the disease is less apt to occur, or if it does occur, the increased motion of the bloodvessels, is of a less durable and vehement character, and infinitely more manageable, than in those who had been lolling in repletion and indolence up to the moment of attack; and in whom the fibre is necessarily more rigid, the vessels more prone to engorgement, and the disposition to undue excitement more exalted. Nor is this opinion merely theoretical; we have the evidence of many facts confirming it, did our limits permit us to state them. Out of the many, however, we may mention the very striking one, that, in the present sickness, fever has been proportionally more fatal among the rich than the poor.

The general principles, therefore, which we have been explaining, remain unshaken, and are summarily these :—that exclusively of the febrile diseases attended with eruptions, such as small-pox, measles, &c. there is but one species of Contagious Fever, namely, Typhus :—that this disease admits of several varieties, but that all of them arise from specific contagion as their sole cause,—a cause, without which all other auxiliary circumstances would be inefficient. Nevertheless, we are decidedly of opinion, that such auxiliary circumstances are essential in paving the way for the operation and dissemination of the poison, by begetting a general state of predisposition. In fact, situated as we are, there is scarcely an influence or element which may not, by its excess, produce in our system the unfortunate state of preparation we allude to. Adversity may agitate, intemperance may derange, excess of study or of fatigue may exhaust, and want of food may debilitate;—thus rendering the body more liable to the power of contagion, or more easily thrown into fever by a dose of the poison so trifling as, in other circumstances, would have been harmless. Nay, further, we do not absolutely deny that a series of these predisposing circumstances constantly applied, may, by their incessant operation, excite fever in the system without the aid of contagion at all; but the malady thus excited, though often mistaken for the genuine Typhus, is only an occasional—inci-

2

dental—or (to use medical language) a sporadic disease; and
as it is not derived from contagion, so it never becomes contagious in its progress, or infects the healthy who hold intercourse with the sick, unless its original nature is changed by
crowding and deficient ventilation.   But the more ordinary
way in which these noted predisposing circumstances exert
their effects is, by rousing into action the contagious virus already received into the animal system;—or, in other words, by
becoming what physicians call ' exciting causes.'   There is
every reason to conclude, that contagion is often inhaled, without any fever being the consequence: and, we firmly believe,
this happy exemption would be more frequent, were not the
latent powers of the poison accidentally fostered and evolved
by the assisting circumstances so often referred to.

We have already seen, that these ' lædentia '—these injurious circumstances—are partly of a physical and partly of a moral nature: the chief of the former order are, want of nourishment, inebriety, fatigue, and cold; and of the latter, grief,
mental anxiety, or despair.   It would be difficult to say which
of these two are the most ruinous to health: the operation of
the former is, to be sure, more intelligible; yet the influence of
the latter on the vital functions in health and disease, is a subject of most interesting speculation to the physician and the
moralist.   Many phenomena in the history of our species lead
us to believe in the governing power of mind over matter, to
an extent, at first sight incredible.   How often have energies
purely mental, enabled men to retard the assaults of sickness,
and even the chilly approach of death !   On the other hand,
a sudden relaxation of these energies lays them open even to
the minor causes of disease, or perhaps subjects them to ideal
calamities.   It has long been remarked, that in armies, or o-
ther large bodies of men, disease makes little progress while the
mind is strongly engaged, and the exciting passions steadily
kept alive by enterprise or success; but that, as soon as great
reverses are experienced, and mental depression ensues, diseases
make very great havoc,—being increased not only in their general number, but in their individual fatality.   What takes place
after a disastrous campaign, was pretty accurately shadowed out
in that gloomy season of public adversity which reigned during
the early part of the present Epidemic, and which rendered its
mortality, as might be expected, greatest at first.

Although the predisposing circumstances already pointed out
must be highly instrumental in exciting and diffusing Typhus,
still it is evident something more must happen ere that fever
can prevail as an Epidemic.   To be convinced of this, we

have only to recollect, that at all times, in a crowded society like ours, contagion must meet with mental depression from moral causes, and exhaustion from scarcity, with all their sequelæ of filth, intemperance, and the like, ready prepared to aid its operation. But seeing that, even under this conjunction of circumstances, epidemics do not prevail at all times, nor even very frequently,—it is manifest some additional auxiliary must yet be wanting. The contagion of Measles, Scarlet-fever, or Whooping-cough, like that of Typhus, is never wholly extinct in any country; yet these diseases only prevail epidemically during particular seasons: It therefore becomes a very interesting point in Medical Physics, to determine the reason why they spread some years so much more widely than others. We cannot say that we have yet met with any very satisfactory solution of this curious and interesting question. The phenomenon, we are afraid, cannot be explained: and we must be content, in our ignorance, to refer it to the influence of what was styled by Sydenham and the older physicians, ' peculiar constitutions of the air ' during certain years, or portions of years, disposing the body to take on one kind of diseases in preference to another. What this peculiar state or constitution of the atmosphere favourable to epidemics is, we know not: yet we cannot help believing that it exists; and that the occult quality, whatever it may be, has no relation to the thermometrical or barometrical conditions of that fluid. Whether it is at all connected with its electrical states, it would be fruitless to conjecture. Sydenham conceives, upon slight enough grounds, that ' it proceeds from a secret and inexplicable alteration in the bowels of the earth, whereby the air is contaminated with such effluvia as dispose bodies to this or that disease as long as the same constitution prevails, which at length, in a certain space of time, withdraws, and gives way to another. ' For our parts, from attending to the history of health and disease during a succession of seasons, we are persuaded that changes of mighty importance take place in the air we breathe, without their being at all appreciable by either our eudiometers or hygrometers: and this we must, at present, be satisfied to receive as an ultimate fact, for which we cannot account.

The existence of a special condition in the air, as the leading cause of the spreading of various Epidemics, is by no means without close analogy in its favour. For example, every one knows that, in the East-Indies, liver-complaints are remarkably frequent; though the climate, so far as depends on heat, moisture, &c. is entirely like that of the West-Indies, where such complaints are comparatively rare. Again—it is a matter of almost daily observation, that an east wind is highly disagreable to valetudinarians, and unfavourable to the cure of some diseases : it has even been known, in the course of one. night, to change for the worse all the ulcers in a large hospital. This, however, must be attributed to some latent peculiarity in the wind that now and then blows from that quarter; for neither its cold, its dryness, nor its barometrical properties, can account for the effects it occasionally produces.

This unknown constitution of the atmosphere, then, we take to be a *sine qua non* in the production of Epidemic Fever; and that, if contagion is a prerequisite to render the spreading of the disease possible, the aërial change is also a prerequisite to render that spreading probable. When these two principal causes meet with the favouring circumstances formerly explained, all of them act and react interchangeably upon each other; and the result of such a complication and union of noxious agencies, is an epidemic such as we see it.

While on the subject of atmospheric influence, we may add a word on the received opinion, that cold is peculiarly favourable to Typhous contagion; and that atmospheric warmth extinguishes it altogether. The latter proposition, we think, may very reasonably be doubted, since there are no facts that we know of directly to confirm it; and all analogy is against it; so that we might rather expect, *a priori*, that our fevers should be aggravated by heat, as all the violent fevers of southern climates, arising from marsh exhalations, are rendered more virulent by high temperature. Plague also—the most contagious of all human diseases—rages most violently in such degrees of warmth as are more nearly allied to extreme heat than to cold. On the whole, we are rather inclined to think, that heat operates beneficially upon Typhoid contagion, only by giving occasion to its being dissipated and diluted, and thereby rendered innocuous : because, in hot weather, the abodes of disease and filth are necessarily thrown open to the winds of heaven, and due ventilation (often fruitlessly recommended by the physician), now that it becomes indispensable as a matter of common comfort, is enforced by the poor themselves.—As corroborating this opinion, we refer to Dr Barker's valuable Report; where he has shown, by a table, that the fever in Dublin went on, during the whole summer, progressively increasing.

It will not be irrelevant to add a few words on the manner in which the matter of contagion may be admitted into the body. It may be conveyed into the stomach by the saliva; or it may be absorbed by the skin, in some instances : but we are convinced, that by far the most ordinary way is inhalation by the lungs. It is in this way applied to that delicate membranous expansion which covers all the minute blood-vessels distributed with such an infinitude of branches around the air-cells of the lungs. We have little doubt but that the poison, thus applied, is absorbed by the blood, and thus finds its way into the course of the circulation. Besides its general effects on the sympathies of the nervous system, it seems to deteriorate the mass of blood itself, and render it unfit to maintain the irritability of the heart, and the excitability of the brain. Some of the most conspicuous phenomena, particularly in the last stage of fevers, are referable solely to this depravation of the blood. On this matter, however, we shall take occasion to say more hereafter.

This is all that we think it necessary to observe on the causes of the present Epidemic. We must now say a word or two on the means of cure; and in so doing we shall chiefly aim at removing popular prejudices, on points where they are most pernicious. We may remark, by the way, that the only safe rule for the treatment of Typhus is, that there should be no general rule at all. Each Epidemic varies in its character; and almost every case of the same Epidemic has circumstances peculiar to itself, which must modify the treatment. We often observe a highly malignant disease produce one of an opposite type in others, and the contrary : so that there is no judging *a priori,* or from any thing but the actual symptoms, what the precise treatment in any given case ought to be. Yet, were we bold enough to venture on any thing like a general maxim in Physic, we should certainly lean to the side of the evacuating system,— sensible that this method, invariably pursued, would do infinitely less harm than the opposite.

The symptom in Fever that first alarms a patient's friends, is Debility; and, to remove it, all their well-meant efforts are earliest directed. But it is dreadful to think with what lamentable consequences they are often attended. We firmly believe, that the fear of debility has been the destruction of thousands of lives, by the rash treatment to which it has given birth. It is quite a received axiom amongst the poor, that weakness must always be met and supported by cordials; and that strength can only be communicated to the languid frame through the medium of generous diet. How often do we see their fevers, during the first three or four days, when alone medical treatment can be of much avail, not merely neglected, but—what is infinitely worse—goaded into malignity by stimulating treatment! The unhappy patient is put to bed; warm malt liquor, or even spirits and water, are administered at intervals; and the stomach is loaded with nourishing broths or cordial panadas; and thus every thing is hurried on from bad to worse. We can scarcely conceive any thing more important to the safety of society at large, than to convince ignorant and prejudiced persons of the folly and danger of such a practice. To the admonitions of the professional man they too often turn a deaf ear; or they comply with them very imperfectly, and even, perhaps, act in direct and dogged opposition. This evil well deserves the notice of the humane and enlightened. It is only from the kind advices of those who, from their rank in society, or other causes, have influence over the minds of the lower orders, that we can expect a salutary reform in this particular.

If there is any thing true in medicine, it is, that debility, during the first days of fever, is only apparent,—and that the first stage is one of *oppression.* Instead of increasing this oppression,—instead of spurring the over-wrought vital powers by ill-omened stimulants, do not nature and reason point out that the system should be unloaded and tranquillized, and that the stomach should be relieved from the drudgery of digestion? Even admitting, for a moment, that nutritious food were required under such circumstances, it is quite obvious that it could never be digested nor assimilated: it must ly as an uneasy load, and embarrass those vital functions which it cannot sustain. As well might we screw up the barometer in order to bring fair weather, as thrust down nourishment into a powerless stomach and a feverish frame, in order to recal strength.

There is, among this class of society, another cardinal error; to wit, that of forcing a perspiration in fever, ' to carry it off, ' as their phrase is. Misled, in the first instance, by the sense of chilliness generally present, and by the sweat which Nature now and then, perhaps, employs as the means of dissolving the febrile paroxysm, they bury the unlucky patient in bed-clothes, and every refreshing access of air is carefully excluded: perhaps, to add to his torments, a fire is kindled, and the sufferer lies sweltering in clammy oleaginous perspiration, panting for breath, and rapidly becoming exhausted by the murderous kindness exercised towards him. Surely, than this, nothing can be more cruelly injudicious; for every medical man, with the least pretension to experience, must have seen cases on cases where, even after the most profuse perspirations, whether breaking out naturally or elicited by art, no permanent relief of the febrile symptoms has followed. This system of forcing perspiration, then, is useless, and worse than useless; for it is sure to do harm, by augmenting and fixing determinations of blood to the brain and other parts essential to life, and by causing an accumulation of the stimulus of morbid heat.

If perspiration be a desireable object, we know of no more likely means of bringing it out, than to take off the febrile stric-
ture of the skin by the free admission of cool air, the use of
cool drink and light bed-clothes : but, indeed, sweating is generally to be regarded rather as the effect, than the cause of the
departure of fever. This should never be forgotten.

The use of Emetics at the beginning of the disease has been
sanctioned by so many great physicians, that it has now become
a popular practice, and is often resorted to at first without any
regular medical advice. The practice in this indiscriminate way,
is certainly liable to many grave objections. The exertion of
vomiting powerfully propels the blood to the brain, and sometimes gives rise to such an irritability of stomach as all our subsequent efforts cannot allay. Surely the more obvious benefits
of emetics as evacuants, may be secured, in many cases, by purgatives, which do not expose the patient to the same dangers.
—We do not deny their great utility in many cases; for example, where, previously to fever, the stomach has been over-
loaded by indigestible food : we also admit that the succussion
their operation gives to the whole system is useful in removing
inward congestions of blood, and developing the necessary and
salutary stage of moderate reaction. What we contend for is,
that the unlimited, and therefore empirical, employment of them
in all cases, even when the cold stage is gone by, is frequently
unnecessary, and sometimes dangerous.

We next come to speak of another remedy which has been
said to possess the power of arresting fever, and which, by its
high promise of general benefit, a few years back, greatly excited the hopes of physicians and philanthropists :—we mean the
affusion of cold water on the naked body. This practice was
introduced to general notice by the late amiable Dr Currie,
whose distinguished talents, both as a physician and a man of
letters, will be long remembered. The remedy, indeed, was by
no means new : and was probably resorted to in the very infancy
of the healing art as a natural and summary cure for excess of
heat. In proof of this, we have the testimony of travellers, to
show that savage nations, both in the Eastern and Western he-
mispheres, have been in the habit, from the remotest times, of
treating their occasional fevers by ablutions with cold water;
and we think this simple expedient is very likely to have suggested itself to rude minds. (See Bancroft's Essay, p. 95.)—
We are far from saying this with any view of lessening the merit
of Dr Currie : for ' if, ' (as Malpighi observes concerning our
illustrious Harvey), ' in arts and sciences he is properly to be
deemed the discoverer who by a proper investigation unravels

Nature's perplexities, and calls in reason and experience to support, and facts to confirm, '—then truly will Dr Currie be esteemed the discoverer of this remedy.

After many patient and persevering trials of cold affusion in the fevers of all climates, it seems to be now laid aside almost by common consent. That it does not possess the power of cutting short the disease, is admitted on all hands; and the conclusion we have formed is, that its effects are beneficial, so far as they go, but transient. We have never seen it effect any premature solution of the complaint, nor have we often been so fortunate as to witness its tendency to sleep and perspiration. But though it possesses not those commanding effects which its benevolent proposer taught us to look for, and though the relief it produces is but temporary, it is a valuable auxiliary, and may often be made cooperative to the recovery of the patient. In the first place, it conduces to cleanliness,—removes, for a time, the grievous irritation of febrile heat,—and produces considerable refreshment and exhilaration; lessening that feverish anxiety, and relieving that loathing at the stomach, which are so depressing in all the stages of the disease. For these reasons we think that the practice itself, or at least a modification of it, should be adopted in most cases. At the same time we should add, that we have seen a good many instances where the affusion would have been dangerous on account of the commotion of the nervous system; and others where the mere fatigue attending its frequent administration, (for to be useful it must be frequent), would have more than counterbalanced the good to be expected. On these accounts it is generally advisable to substitute the more cautious process of sponging the body of the patient with cold or tepid water and vinegar, as he lies along at his ease. By repeating this at seasonable intervals, we shall produce all the benefit of the cold affusion, and at the same time avoid its dangers.

The administration of cold water as drink, is also a most material improvement, for which we are indebted to modern times; and in the use of it, happily, there is less need for scrupulousness than in the case of its external employment. Its free exhibition was first suggested by the Italian physicians, and Dr Cyrillus of Naples published a paper in the Philosophical Transactions (No. 410. p. 142.) expressly recommending it without any other remedy whatsoever. In our own country, also, about the beginning of last century, and previous to Dr Cyrillus's paper, Dr Hancocke published a treatise on its efficacy, under the affected title of ' Febrifugum Magnum. ' Yet it is only within the last twenty or thirty years that cold water, or even cool drinks, have become general remedies. The lower orders do not regard them with the same aversion as cold.affusion; indeed the eagerness with which nature craves them, and the exquisite refreshment they afford, are enough to subdue prejudices even the most inveterate.

The next great and radical advancement in the treatment of fever, of which modern times can justly boast, is Blood-letting. This remedy appears, from the writings of Hippocrates, to have been very freely employed in that age. Even in this country, until the middle of last century, it was generally resorted to; and had the sanction of the great Sydenham. His disciples were not silent on the merits of this practice, as is evident from some of the early medical writings of last century. * We know not well how so powerful a remedy should have fallen into disuse; but we believe it was chiefly owing to the influence of those eminent men, Fothergill, Pringle, Lind, Dr John Hunter, Cullen, and Brown, who gave the tone to medical doctrine, and spread a fear of the lancet all over Europe, by propagating, in their prelections and writings, the false notion that Typhus is a disease of direct debility. The practice, after a period of unmerited eclipse, is now happily revived, and has materially lessened the mortality of our ordinary fevers.

It is gratifying to think, that this revival has not been brought about by the caprice of fashion, but by an induction from facts. For a good number of years past, blood-letting has been a favourite remedy in the fevers of warm climates: in them it was resorted to, at first, more from necessity than choice, because their violence and rapidity were found to set at defiance the remedies ˙recommended in the schools of medicine. In fact, within the Tropics, as the products of the vegetable and animal kingdoms rush through their successive stages of growth, maturity, and decay, with greater luxuriance and rapidity, so also the phenomena of fever are more marked and terrible, and run their course with greater vehemence and celerity. The consequence is, that physicians who treated fever in such countries had, comparatively, the same advantage as those who study nature with the aid of a microscope. They could see more distinctly, and estimate more justly, the secret sources of the dan-

---

* Not many months ago, an enlightened friend showed us a rare little volume on the subject, with a quaint title, published in London by a Dr Whyte, A. D. 1712. We were surprised and gratified to observe, that the views as to the efficacy of early depletion, and the arguments used to recommend it, a century ago, are such as the present day might not blush to own.

gerous symptoms : these being exposed before them, and mag-
nified, as it were, it was to be expected that the remedies should
become more energetic and simple ; and in proportion as they
became so, they have become more successful.   This success
abroad has contributed not a little to extend more active depletion to the treatment of our fevers at home : and the practice
has been patronized by individuals of superior understanding,
who had previously convinced themselves of the unsoundness
of the reigning opinions on this disease, and had altered their
practice accordingly.

   Betwixt the publication of Dr Hamilton's † excellent work
and the revival of blood-letting, purgatives had taken a very
conspicuous part—indeed we may say the only active part—in
the treatment of Fever.   Prejudices against this class of medicines, had descended from the earliest times, and were deeply
rooted in the mind both of Physicians and of the Vulgar.   It
was formerly a favourite dogma with the advocates of the hu-
moral pathology, that a peccant matter is the cause of fever,
and that purgatives would only obstruct the fermentation, con-
coction, &c. which they conceived indispensable to the expul-
sion of this offending cause.   Though the doctrine is exploded,
the prejudices to which it gave rise are still in very considerable
force.   It is amazing with what dread people in general look
upon all sort of evacuants in this complaint.   Purgatives are
more particularly the objects of dislike, from their supposed effect of carrying away the nourishment and strength of the patient.   Yet it would be very easy to show, that cathartics, instead of debilitating, are really, in fever, the very best tonics
in the world ; and form the quickest and safest restoratives to
health and strength.

   Fevers have been judiciously divided into three stages : the
1*st* is one of oppression ; the 2*nd* of over-excitement ; and the
3*rd* of exhaustion :—the third is undoubtedly a necessary consequence of the other two, for it is a law throughout animated
nature, that excess of action is followed by fatigue or collapse.
It is chiefly in the first two stages that energetic measures of
depletion, by blood-letting and purgatives, can be considered
admissible ;—in the last, our sole aim is to support the strength
of the vital powers by cordials, taking care, at the same time,
not to over-stimulate.   Yet, even in this advanced state, some
active purgatives are indispensably required every second or
third day : though at this time there must be conjoined with

----

   † Dr Hamilton on the Utility and Administration of Purgative
Medicines.   Edinburgh, 1803.

them a prudent use of wine and other stimuli. These means are opposite in appearance, but by no means so in principle. In fact, to carry off the offensive fluids, is now, if possible, more necessary than ever. By so doing, the patient is exhilarated and refreshed; and besides, a healthy secretion of bile and of gastric juice is prompted by it. Under such circumstances, a moderate allowance of ripe porter or ale will often have all the good effects of wine: nay, there are many patients with whom they will be found to agree much better.

When we reflect how very grateful a complete change of linen is; even in the fullest health, we can readily imagine what a delicious gratification it must be to the arid and burning skin of a person in fever. Besides, it deserves to be more generally known, that clean linen acts as a spur upon the cutaneous pores, and thus either elicits perspiration, or at least causes a salutary determination of blood to the surface. Indeed we know of few means so absolutely indispensable as a change of linen daily, or even twice a day; combined with thorough ventilation, and strict cleanliness of the patient's person and apartment. Without these, the best medical treatment will be nugatory: and the professional attendant who does not make them the primary objects of his attention, degrades himself from a philanthropic physician, to a mere mixer of drugs. Yet of drugs, properly so called, how very few are really necessary in fever ! In the early stages, such as are given should be of an active nature; and towards the close, in general none, save purgatives, are necessary; as recovery will be better promoted by regulating the diet, and tempering it to the diminished powers of the stomach.

As diet is so important a subject, we should perhaps be somewhat more explicit with regard to it. Nature has wisely provided that, throughout the active part of the attack, there should be an absolute loathing of solid food—a pretty convincing proof that it would be hurtful. Nothing, then, should be offered at such times except lemonade, subacid fruits, gruels, milk and water, butter-milk, whey, and the like, so long as any unnatural heat or thirst remain. In the stage of exhaustion, panadas, Indian arrow root, nourishing broths, animal jellies, madeira mixed with milk, and a draught of brisk ale or soda-water, are highly proper. A spoonful of common yeast given at intervals, will often be serviceable at this period of the complaint. Generally on the head of diet,—it is necessary to be very circumspect, as premature indulgences always retard recovery, and often produce a serious—perhaps fatal—relapse.

It must be interesting to the general inquirer, as well as the medical scholar, to mark how very different the treatment of fever is at the present day, from what it universally was a few years back. At that time, bark, opium, camphor, wine, brandy, and other stimulants, were used from the very first; now-a-days these have given place (at least amongst the well informed of the medical community) to a series of remedies entirely opposite. Much of this difference of practice is to be attributed to a notable revolution in medical opinion; but some share of it, perhaps, must, in candour to our predecessors, be ascribed to a change in the disease itself. The character of diseases is modified by causes often wholly unknown. That every Epidemic has its own peculiar constitution, is an observation as old as Sydenham; and this accurate physician was wont to remark, that his treatment, during any given season, was never fairly successful until he had found out the *genius* of the reigning fever. It is probable, then, that, from some unknown cause, Epidemic Fevers are now more of an inflammatory nature than formerly; but, on the other hand, we think it plain, that, were our modern fevers treated by stimulants, hot regimen, and deficient ventilation, they would become sufficiently malignant; and rapidly put on those appearances of extreme debility and putrescency, which gave our forefathers such a horror at any thing like evacuation. We hold, that, in very many instances, the type of a febrile disease is completely in the hands of the attending physician; and that treatment will often alter it entirely. The mere neglect of ventilation and evacuants, will, even in simple fevers, produce an alarming prostration of the vital powers: This prostration, again, will be more readily removed by strict attention to these particulars, than by the most powerful cordials in the whole Materia Medica. Dr Bateman has stated some interesting facts on this point; and we have seen many of a similar nature.

After this explanation, the reason must be pretty apparent why our forefathers had so generally a disease of debility to encounter: The kind of treatment they adopted at first, did, indeed, render the exhibition of bark and wine requisite, as a necessary result of their total neglect of depletion. The prostration thus artificially superinduced, was gratuitously ascribed to the type of the disease. Notwithstanding all these errors, it is well known that many recovered: This shows that the stimulating plan had its share of success; (though, doubtless, not a few perished for want of those modern measures which are so much more successful.) That the same end should be attained by means diametrically opposite, is a paradox in medical science, that should teach physicians to mingle humility with the just pretensions of their art. In order to explain this paradox, apparently one of two suppositions must be true : During the reign of the antiquated practice, either nature was more compassionate than art, and so carried the day against the formidable odds of the disease and the doctor ; or else the constitution of fevers is materially changed from what it then was ; so that a malady which can now be safely combated only by blood-letting and purgatives, could then be safely treated by tonics and stimulants. We are much inclined to solve the difficulty, by adopting, *in part*, both of these opinions,—leaning, however, very much to the former.

Upon the whole, it is gratifying to think that improved views of the pathology of fever are now gaining ground so rapidly, and that men of talent are taking a leading part in prosecuting the active treatment. Their authority must, in process of time, operate a change on that herd of *practitioners* who still pursue the beaten track of former years, and hold their camphor-juleps and ether-mixtures in perpetual requisition, immediately after they are summoned to a case of fever. For our own parts, we look upon Typhus as, to all *practical* intents and purposes, an inflammatory disease ; and are satisfied that, in by far the majority of cases ending in death, there has been inflammation, acute, or sub-acute, of some vital organ: Nevertheless, we think it evident, that in the precession of causes to effects, it is the nervous system that first suffers ; and that its derangement modifies all the subsequent phenomena, so as to give inflammation a different aspect from what it has in other diseases, purely and primitively inflammatory. Of the precise nature of this disturbance we know just as little as we do about the ultimate nature of attraction, or the intimate essence of life; its effects, however, are a suppression of the energy of intellect and of volition, tremors, general pains, lassitude, coldness, and so forth. All these indicate an unknown change in the centre of the nervous influence, (the brain and spinal cord) ; and, as signs, they appear to be primary and essential,—commotion in the heart and arteries being only symptomatic.

We are further of opinion, that contagion, when inhaled by the lungs, and absorbed by the blood, effects a change upon the constitution of that fluid,—a change very different from its condition in ordinary inflammation ; *—that, in short, its mass is poisoned (to speak popularly) by this invisible virus. In this way we can, in some measure, explain the breaking out of livid

---

* Blood drawn in fever, very seldom shows the inflammatory crust, or buffy coat, which it almost constantly does in pure inflammation.

blotches, and the occurrence of hæmorrhages from the bowels, and other parts of the body, in the last stage of our worst fevers. These, we conceive, proceed from a dissolution of the blood, and from the impaired vitality of the minute vessels; allowing some of it to escape in inky spots under the skin, or in a flux of semi-putrescent gore from their unresisting mouths. Such appearances are seldom or never seen in diseases truly inflammatory.— We remark, with pleasure, that our opinions, on this interesting matter, are pretty nearly akin to those of Dr Armstrong, in his late classical work on Typhus.

We now proceed to discuss the measures of prevention :—which depend, of course, very much on what we know or believe as to the nature of the contagion. Now, contagion exists either in the state of an invisible matter, exhaling from the body of the patient; or else adhering to articles of clothes, furniture, or the like. In the latter state, it is known amongst medical men by the appellation of ' fomites ; ' and every thing concurs to prove, that its virulence is not impaired by this lurking condition; but, on the contrary, is maintained in a state of greater concentration and activity, than even when it first emanates from the patient's body.

We have already remarked, that a specific poison, capable of causing a similar disease in others, is generated in the system of a person under fever. This poison, as soon as the disease is fairly begun, continues unintermittingly to exhale from every pore, until convalescence is nearly completed. Not only the surface of the skin, but also the inner surface of the lungs, mouth, intestines, and bladder, continue to pour out the contagious vapour; consequently the very secretions and excretions are highly impregnated with it. In truth, the patient is surrounded, for two or three feet, by an atmosphere of his own, very deleterious to all persons susceptible of the disease who may happen to be exposed to it. As a matter of precaution, therefore, strict non-intercourse with the sick should be enforced; and those whom duty or inclination leads to visit the patient, should be very careful not to inhale his breath, or expose themselves to that steam of perspirable matter which rises from his body when the bed-clothes are turned down for the purpose of rendering him any offices of help. While engaged in such duties, they should hold in their breath for a time; and, if under the unavoidable necessity of inhaling the tainted atmosphere, they should, as soon afterwards as possible, blow from the nose, and wash the mouth, with a view of detaching any infectious particles that may be adhering to these passages. All the discharges

of the patient should be thrown away as soon as they are rendered, and the vessel washed with boiling water.   But the most
important precaution of all is, to maintain a perpetual circulation of air in the patient's chamber.   For this purpose, a small
chink of the window should be left open both at top and bottom,—and the opposite window, where there is one, or else the
door of the room, should also be a little opened.   When open
windows cannot be had recourse to on account of high winds,
or other inclemency of the weather, a small fire must be kindled in the grate.   Though not considerable enough to raise
the temperature of the room above a degree or two, it will have
the salutary effect of causing a current, and frequent renewal of
the air in the chamber.   For the better success of ventilation,
the bed curtains should never be drawn close around the patient, but merely one of them let down to screen him from the
irritation of the light.

It is very seldom, particularly in the abodes of the poor, that
ventilation is sufficiently attended to: this arises partly from
their natural carelessness, but more especially from their groundless apprehension of the patient's ' catching cold' from the
admission of cool air.   We call this a groundless apprehension,
because, in a uniformly low temperature, patients are little liable
to colds: it is only sudden alternations that give rise to them.
Besides, we have observed, that when the body is under fever,
it is not so susceptible, as in health, of minor diseases like catarrh.   But, even were it otherwise, precautions may easily be
taken against an occurrence of this kind, by interposing a screen
betwixt the current of air and the patient's body, more particularly when he lies asleep, or when the atmosphere is frosty.

In small, close, and filthy chambers where contagious fever
is, the air of the apartment will soon become so surcharged
with contagious effluvium, that the majority of those who inhale
it, will afterwards take the disease: but if free air be admitted,
the virus becomes so diffused that the air of the room may be
respired without danger:—just as if we dissolve an ounce of
arsenic in a bucket of water, we shall form a liquid which few
could taste with impunity; but if we throw the same quantity
into the Forth or the Thames, the poison becomes so dilute as
to be incapable of producing the smallest inconvenience.

We must agree with Dr Bateman in condemning the custom,
so frequently adopted, of sprinkling the sick-chamber with aromatic vinegar, or other perfumes.   These most assuredly have
not the smallest influence in preventing infection ; but, on the
contrary, rather tend to vitiate the air.   As they disguise offensive smells, we fear they are too often employed as a succeda-

neum for ventilation ; and in this view they are greatly o be re-
probated. The criterion of proper purity for a sick chamber
is, that it communicate no perceptible smell whatever to a stranger entering it.

With regard to camphor bags, nosegays, smelling bottles,
&c. in which many put their trust for safety, when they visit an
infected chamber, we are satisfied they can have no good effect
whatever, unless in so far as they give confidence to the mind
of those who employ them, and prevent the depressing passion
of fear,—a passion that predisposes wonderfully to the reception
of all contagious diseases.

Another very essential precaution consists in frequently changing the body and bed-linen of the patient, and occasionally
sponging his skin with tepid water and vinegar. While this,
as we before remarked, is very conducive to the recovery of the
sick, it contributes no less to the safety of the attendants. As
soon as the linen is thrown off, it should be collected in a tub
and covered over with water, into which a handful of lime or
caustic potash may be thrown, for the purpose of detaching the
animal matters with which it may be impregnated. In one
word, then, unremitting regard to ventilation, and the strictest
attention to cleanliness in all its parts, constitute the whole secret of evading contagion : and if, along with these means, the
attendants and visitors will take care never to approach their
heads so nigh the patient as to risk inhaling his breath, the
effluvium of his body, or the vapour of his evacuations, they
need not fear any contagious disease, however malignant may
be its type.

As to the sphere of the contagious effluvium, and the distance
at which it may affect persons exposed to it,—there is, we think,
the most convincing and satisfactory proof, deduced from a long
course of experiments and observation, that the exhalations ra-
diate from the body of the patient only to the distance of two
or three feet, provided the noxious vapour be not accumulated,
and condensed, in the room, for want of ventilation. This sufficiently shows how unfounded are the fears that many express
at living in a district of the town where fever is prevalent, or
in the neighbourhood of fever hospitals, and infirmaries. If
the precautions now recommended are at all attended to, we
may live with safety even in the same house where fever exists.

When mattresses, blankets, linen, clothes, or furniture, are
imbued with contagious matter, actual contact with these substances is necessary to produce infection. Yet it is frequently
surprising how slight and accidental a contact may be sufficient
to produce the effect : and when we reflect how often the dis-

ease is propagated by means of infected lodging houses, bedding, clothes, goods, &c. we ought to be on our guard; and on all occasions attend rigidly to purification of suspected articles of apparel or furniture, by fumigating, boiling, scouring, and freely exposing them to the breeze.

It will not be irrelevant to say something, in this place, about the degrees of predisposition to the disease in various persons. The liability to be affected by contagion differs greatly in different individuals; some being acted upon by very small doses of the poison, while others resist the strongest. Part of this difference of susceptibility must, perhaps, be attributed to an unknown condition of the nervous system; but, we believe, it chiefly depends on the state of the blood; for, as we before observed, contagion, in most instances, finds its way into the system through the medium of that fluid. Blood is said to be rich when the red part is considerable in proportion to the whole mass; and vice versâ. Those in whom the process of sanguification is most vigorous, have a great share of red particles in their circulating fluid; their fibre is also strong and rigid; and their complexion florid. Such persons are observed to be little liable to contagion, compared with persons of an opposite habit. Those—again—in whom the blood is impoverished, are marked by a pale exsanguious complexion, and lax fibre; arising, in all likelihood, from weakness of the sanguific powers. Such persons are observed to be very susceptible of contagion. Habit alone renders the human frame much less easily influenced by this, as well as by any other noxious cause. It is only on this principle that we can explain why physicians and nurses generally escape fevers, though it is obvious they are exposed to them in a degree, greater by a hundred-fold, than any other class of individuals. Yet to this law of habit, as to most others, there are exceptions: for whenever an Epidemic is severer than usual, the ordinary attendants by no means invariably escape. On the present occasion, many medical men, and especially hospital nurses, have fallen a sacrifice to their professional duty: the mortality, also, among clergymen and others, in the daily practice of visiting the sick, has been very considerable.

Whether the Epidemic is on the increase or decline, forms, at the present moment, a very interesting question. We are sorry to say, from all the evidence that appears, there is reason to apprehend that it has not yet attained its maximum of extension; for there are accounts of its having broken out in some parts of the empire which have hitherto escaped its ravages,— while nowhere does it show any well-marked tendency to decrease. That it would by and by decline of its own accord,

even if let alone, is probable from the history of former Epidemics, none of which, we believe, have lasted much beyond
three years, and few quite so long : but what extent of mischief
might previously be inflicted, is quite beyond the reach of calculation. It is therefore highly necessary that public measures
of prevention should be adopted with all speed and vigour.

We would recommend, then, for the general welfare (what
has already been so far done in Ireland, Glasgow and Edinburgh), that certain individuals in every town or county should
erect themselves into an Association for the Suppression of
Fever. Their number should be proportioned to the size or
populousness of the district which their exertions are meant to
protect; and, in other respects, they should be men of diligence
and intelligence. It is essential to the object of the Institution,
that the members should consist of those who, from their rank,
intellect or influence, have the confidence of the lower orders :
we have no doubt that, in every town, a sufficient number of such
individuals would be found, public-spirited enough to volunteer
their services in this benevolent cause. In fact, it is obviously
the self-interest of every one to assist, to the utmost of his power,
in extinguishing a disease that, if left to itself, must involve every
Class of Society.

This Association should comprise one or more magistrates of
the place to which it belongs, so that its suggestions may have
more weight, and its operations be aided occasionally by com-
pulsatory civil power. Above all, it should comprehend the
Clergy of all denominations; because, from their character and
station, they generally have great influence over the poor : It
should also comprehend a sufficient number of the Faculty, for
the purpose of examining the habitat of the disease, ascertaining its extent, and the means of eradication. Such an Association, it is evident, should have the power of collecting voluntary
subscriptions, or even of imposing assessments to provide funds
for executing the object of its establishment. It would be well
if government or parliamentary grants, for the latter purpose,
were given to such districts as have suffered long and extensively from the Epidemic.

These previous matters being duly arranged, every town or
county should be parted off by parishes, or other more convenient divisions.; and two inspectors, one of whom should be a
medical man, appointed to each. It should be the duty of the
inspectors to visit and minutely examine the state of health of
every family in their division once a week, or oftener, if circumstances require it : and if any cases of fever are found, they must
have them removed to a hospital as soon as possible, and after-

3

wards take upon themselves the charge of having the infected dwellings cleaned and fumigated. The poor should be required to lodge with the President of the Association, or with the inspectors of their district, information of any new case, as soon as it appears. Dr Haygarth, to whom the world is indebted for many judicious directions for the extinction of contagious diseases, has proposed that persons should be incited by some small pecuniary rewards to give the information in question : but we believe that the mere solicitude of neighbours for their own safety will be a sufficient inducement to them to make known any infected house in their quarter to the proper authority, as soon as they know that a proper authority is expressly provided for the purpose of remedying the evil.

The Association should next proceed to procure tenements to be converted into temporary Fever-hospitals. Barracks are, generally speaking, well adapted to the purpose; and at the present time, when so many of them must be unoccupied with troops, their temporary appropriation in this way would be productive of very great benefit. In Edinburgh, the grant of Queensberry barracks has greatly facilitated the disposal of the numerous cases. Prison-depôts might also be occupied for a similar purpose : but where neither these nor barracks are to be had, a warehouse, storehouse, granary, or the like, may be made to answer the intention. Architectural requisites are of no consequence, provided the premises be but large, dry, and well ventilated. Indeed their internal fitting up cannot be too simple : we have often been struck by the injudiciousness of multiplying closets and wooden partitions, which only tend to lodge contagious matter, and obstruct the free circulation of air, in large hospitals.

The number of these Receiving-houses must be multiplied according to the emergency; but if the measures are promptly pursued, and patients removed during the first days of illness, it will speedily be found that we have choked up the fountainhead of the disease, and that the necessity for multiplying hospitals is entirely obviated. If, on the other hand, we allow the mischief to get greatly ahead; or if only half measures are pursued, the consequence will be, that a treble expense will be incurred; and even then, in all probability, the object will be not accomplished.

When patients are removed to the hospital, they must be stripped, and well washed with warm water and soap; taking care to cut off their hair, and remove all their ordinary clothes. These, after being carefully washed and dried, must be put aside in a store-room for the purpose, until the patient goes out of the hospital. During his stay in the Establishment, when not confined to bed, he should be accommodated with a hospital-dress, consisting of double flannel or fleecy hosiery.

Although it be a matter of primary importance to have the sick conveyed from their own houses during the first days of fever, as it incalculably lessens the danger of diffusing the disease, still in the ulterior stages, or even in the last stage, such removal is by no means without use. But on such occasions the Inspectors must be prepared to encounter a great deal of obloquy and opposition from the relatives of the patient: for no popular prejudice is more strong than that which holds it dangerous to move a patient under such circumstances. The certainty of ' catching cold, ' and many other casualties, will be prophetically announced as the result of such an unheard-of measure. We can, nevertheless, assure our readers that such a removal, even in the last stage of fevers, may, in general, be effected with perfect safety: nay, free exposure to the air will be often salutary. The only consideration that can make the measure at all questionable is, the debility of the patient—not the risk of exposing him. That debility, for instance, may be so great as to render him unable to bear the erect posture in a sedan chair; but even then, he may be laid on a mattress, or truckle-bed, in the horizontal posture, and in this way carried to the hospital. There is most respectable authority to prove that gestation, as a remedy in fever, has been repeatedly successful in cases where the extreme prostration of the powers of life, and signs of putrescency, had defied all other means; and would, in all probability, but for this simple, though unusual expedient, have ended in death. We would, therefore, recommend this subject to the serious attention of medical men during the present epidemic. We presume almost every military surgeon that has served in the late campaigns, must have witnessed the safety—not to say utility—of gestation in all stages of Typhous Fever, and must be able to confirm what we have now brought forward.

We must also allude to another popular prejudice, which tends greatly to counteract or defeat any exertions made to exterminate an epidemic:—we mean the reluctance which many of the poorer classes evince at being sent to public hospitals. In some instances, perhaps, this repugnance arises from a manly feeling of independence, inciting them to decline the aid of charity; but, in by far the greater number, it springs from a very general, though most erroneous impression, that in public hospitals medical ' experiments are tried ' upon the patients. This charge is, of course, too absurd to deserve any serious refutation: and we are certain, from personal knowledge, that the prejudice has no foundation except in the vulgar and suspicious folly of those who entertain it—entertain it, too, against a profession which gives more gratuitous aid to the poor than any other, and which—to say nothing of it as a science—ranks at least as the noblest of the arts. Yet, however unfounded, this prejudice must be combated and argued down, as it stands materially in the way. Indeed the prejudices of the poor, no less than their diseases, will claim much attention from the Association: and here, in particular, the aid of the Clergy may be most beneficially exerted.

On the subject of these Hospitals, we have only further to remark, that all visits of relations to patients, unless in cases of approaching death, should be steadily interdicted; as contagion has very often been traced to such imprudent communications. Again,—those who have recovered should not be too speedily sent home among their friends, but should be kept in a separate ward until all danger of their infecting others is gone by. The establishment of a convalescents' ward will have a further advantage—it will prevent relapses; for most of these troublesome, and other fatal occurrences, owe their existence either to premature indulgences in diet, premature exposure to cold: or else to the patient's being exposed, while still feeble, to a strong contagion from a newly received patient, often injudiciously placed in the next bed to him.

Though the appointment of Fever Infirmaries is an object of such real consequence, the Association will find they have but half accomplished their duty if they neglect cleansing those hotbeds of contagion, the dirty and infected hovels of the poor. Too much care cannot be bestowed on this great object; because, without it, we may multiply houses of recovery to no purpose. The Inspectors, therefore, as soon as the sick are removed, should cause the house to be carefully swept; every neglected corner must be emptied, and all useless rubbish burnt or buried. Every apartment must then be fumigated with nitric or muriatic acid in a state of vapour. The next step is to wash the floor and furniture with soap and water, and to whitewash the walls with lime. After this, fires must be lighted, and the doors and windows thrown open for a few hours, so as to ensure a thorough perflation of air. Articles of bedding, after being exposed to the acid fumes, should be hung up to the breeze. The fumigation should be performed under the direction of the Medical Inspector, and repeated if he deem it necessary. With regard to the acid to be employed, we have only to remark, that the muriatic, though weaker than the nitric, has a stronger chemical affinity for animal matter : and as it is at the same time more diffusible, it should in general be preferred. Besides, it is cheaply and easily obtained ; the only necessary articles being sulphuric acid and some common kitchen-salt. By pouring the former upon the latter, a sufficient quantity of acid vapour will be speedily disengaged ; and we may increase it at pleasure by the application of moderate heat. The oxymuriatic acid gas (chlorine of Sir H. Davy) has also a remarkable power in destroying infectious matter : and is readily obtained by pouring sulphuric acid upon a mixture of pulverized per-oxyd *(black)* of manganese, water, and common salt.

There are other objects that must engage the attention of the Association, (but into the details of these our limits will not permit us to enter),—such as, the suppression of mendicity ; the establishment of general washing-houses for cleansing gratuitously the clothes of the poor, and other minute local regulations; placarding infected houses so as to guard strangers from entering them ; directing domiciliary visits to obscure and dirty lodging-houses, and placing them and their inmates under a strict surveillance of the Inspectors. The suppression of beggars is a measure of primary importance; for it is certain that this class of persons have been greatly instrumental in spreading the disease both in Ireland and in this country. Often, indeed, the breath which was expended in benedictions, and thanks to those who bestowed charity, has been found to blast with infection the persons it was meant to bless!—Dr Stokes's treatise very judiciously points out the evils of mendicity at the present crisis.

Before concluding, we may remark that contagion often lurks for a considerable time in the system before it excites fever. The length of this latent period has been variously estimated. Dr Haygarth reckons its *maximum* as high as seventy-two days, and Dr Bancroft extends it to five or six months. The latter appears to us quite an extravagant computation, and has not a single analogy in its favour, save the remote and feeble one of the hydrophobic poison. Nevertheless, there is little doubt that the seeds of fever often remain concealed for several days, and sometimes, though rarely, for two or three weeks, ere they manifest themselves in actual symptoms. The knowledge of such occurrences is valuable, not only as throwing light on the laws of contagion, but as guiding us to extend our means of precaution. These occurrences, also, explain how fever, in many instances, should break forth in isolated situations where no contagion can be traced ; because they show that, betwixt his receiving the infection and the appearance of the disease, a person might travel from the most distant parts of the empire. In this manner we can readily imagine the fever to have been first imported into Great Britain from the sister island, and subsequently carried from one place to another; because a series of facts proves, that the epidemic first began in Ireland.

We have thus once more performed an important duty, at the risk of offending many of our polite and fastidious readers :—and endeavoured to make our popularity subservient to the great cause of humanity, in spite of our consciousness that we are exposing it to hazard by the experiment. At the expense, we fear, of some disgust, and certainly of much tediousness, we have now put into the hands of many the means of doing a great deal of substantial good, and of mitigating and abridging a scene of most pitiable suffering. We trust, too, that we have also put it into the heads and the hearts of no few, to avail themselves, in practice and effect, of what has thus been suggested : and, with this view, we have purposely abstained from all ingenious theories and questionable speculations, and confined ourselves to such safe, simple, and radical directions, as all benevolent individuals of ordinary understanding can at once perfectly comprehend, and correctly apply. The good that may be done, or the misery at least that may be prevented, at such a season as this, by their resolute exertions, we verily believe to be incalculable :— and are persuaded, not only that the present scene of affliction may thus be speedily made to pass away, but that the habits and precautions to which the great body of the poor, and their immediate advisers, may thus be successfully trained, will prevent the recurrence of the same evils, on any future occasion, to nearly the same extent.

Art. II. 1. *An Account of the Varioloid Epidemic which has lately prevailed in Edinburgh, and other Parts of Scotland; with Observations on the Identity of Chicken-Pox with Modified Small-Pox: In a letter to Sir James M'Grigor, Director-General of the Army Medical Department, &c. &c.* By John Thomson, M. D. F. R. S. E. Surgeon to the Forces, Honorary Member of the Royal Medical Society of Edinburgh, Professor of Surgery to the Royal College of Surgeons, Regius Professor of Military Surgery in the University, and Consulting Physician to the Edinburgh New-Town Dispensary. London, Longman & Co. Edinburgh, Brown. 1820.

2. *Historical Sketch of the Opinions entertained by Medical Men respecting the Varieties and the Secondary Occurrence of Small-Pox; with Observations on the Nature and Extent of the Security afforded by Vaccination against Attacks of that Disease: In a Letter to Sir James M'Grigor, Director-General of the Army Medical Department, &c.* By John Thomson, M. D. F. R. S. E. Surgeon to the Forces, Honorary Member of the Royal Medical Society of Edinburgh, Regius Professor of Military Surgery in the University, and Consulting Physician to the Edinburgh New-Town Dispensary. London, Longman & Co. Edinburgh, Brown. 1822.

VACCINATION, we are perfectly persuaded, is a very great blessing to mankind; but not quite so great a blessing, nor so complete a protection, as its early defenders conceived it to be. The proof of this has been admitted with great reluctance; but it has unfortunately become too strong for denial or resistance. The first answers given to the instances of failure, with which the friends of vaccination were pressed, were, either that the disease which had occurred after vaccination was chicken-pox, and not small-pox; or that the process of vaccination had been unskilfully or imperfectly conducted; or that it was one of those very rare cases which occurred in the times of inoculation, and from which vaccination itself did not pretend to be wholly exempt. In the Report of the Vaccine Pock Institution for 1803, the Reporters observe—

' It may be useful to notice, that we have been alarmed two or three times with the intelligence of the small-pox occurring several weeks or months after our patients had undergone the cow-pox. We thought it our duty to visit and examine these patients, and also to inquire into their history among their attendants, and by these means we obtained the completest satisfaction, that the pretended small-pox was generally the chicken-pox. '—*Historical Sketch,* pp. 161, 162.

The following is an abstract of their Report for 1817.

' The continued investigation of the *failures* of vaccination which have taken place here, lead also to conclusions similar to those of the Directors of the Dublin Institution ; and it has been found, that almost all the subjects of these cases have been vaccinated by *methods less effectual* than those which have been adopted and inculcated by the Establishment, the great success of the practice of which, since its foundation in 1808, is the strongest inducement for the plan being generally followed. For which reason, the Board printed a new and correct edition of their instructions, which contain the practice of the Establishment; and they are now distributing the copies gratuitously over the whole empire. Should these be accurately followed, and every person vaccinated be thoroughly infected with the regular vaccine, the Board are fully convinced that failures would become so rare, as *hardly* to merit the public attention. '— *Historical Sketch,* pp. 246, 247.

In 1819, the Board admit that the testimonies of some of their correspondents in the country have been unfavourable; that *great numbers* of persons who had been vaccinated, have been subsequently seized with a disease presenting all the essential characters of small-pox; but that, in the great majority of such cases, the disease has been of short duration, and unattended by symptoms of danger : they add, however, that, in several of these cases, the malady has been prolonged to its ordinary period; and that in eight, it has proved fatal. They still continue, however, to refer these cases to imperfect vaccination; and they recommend that two punctures should be made in each arm, and the greatest care taken that the vesicles run their full and destined career. In 1820, there is the following melancholy admission.

' It is true that we have received accounts from different parts of the country, of numerous cases of small-pox having occurred after vaccination ; and we cannot doubt that the prejudices of the people against this preventive expedient are assignable (and not altogether unreasonably, perhaps,) to this cause. These cases the Board has been industriously employed in investigating ; and though it appears that many of them rest only on hearsay evidence, and that others seem to have undergone the vaccine process imperfectly, some years since, when it was less well understood, and practised less skilfully than it ought to be ; yet, after every reasonable deduction, we are compelled to allow, that too many still remain on undeniable proof, to leave any doubt that the pretensions of vaccination to the merit of a perfect and exclusive security in all cases against small-pox, were admitted at first rather too unreservedly.'—*Historical Sketch,* p. 273.

And then they proceed to talk of the *controlling* power of vaccination, instead of its *protecting* power. The fact in short is, that, within these six or seven years, the small-pox has broken out in many parts of Great Britain in an epidemic shape, and nearly annihilated the pretensions of cow-pox as an *absolute* security against the disorder.

In 1818–19, there broke out a violent epidemical small-pox in Edinburgh and its neighbourhood. Of this epidemic, Dr Thomson saw 836 cases. Of this number, 281 had neither passed through small-pox nor vaccination; and of these more than *one in four* died. Dr Thomson saw, in this epidemic, 41 cases of persons who had passed through small-pox; and had an accurate account of 30 others of the same sort. Of these 71 patients, three only died, giving a proportion of *one in twenty-three.* Of the 484 vaccinated individuals affected with this epidemic, *only one* died—

—' a result which, to me, ' says Dr Thomson, ' appears truly astonishing, when I reflect on the general severity of the eruptive fever, on the great diversities in the state of health, and in the constitutional tendencies of the individuals attacked by it, and on the circumstances, often so very unfavourable to recovery, in which many of these individuals have been placed.

' It has been impossible to see the general mildness of the varioloid epidemic in those who had undergone the process of vaccination, and the severity, malignity, and fatality of the same disease in the unvaccinated, and not to be convinced of the great and salutary powers of cow-pock in modifying small-pox, in those who were afterwards affected with this disease. Proofs cannot be imagined more convincing and satisfactory of the efficacy of the practice of vaccination, and of the incalculable benefits bestowed upon mankind by its discoverer, than those I have had the pleasure of witnessing. It has been very agreeable also to observe, that the terrors at first excited by the occurrence of this varioloid epidemic, in the families of those who had undergone cow-pock inoculation, have gradually given way in the progress of the disease ; and that the comparison of

small-pox, in their modified and unmodified forms, has often forced
a conviction of the advantages of cow-pock inoculation upon the
minds even of the most ignorant and prejudiced, and induced them
to seek protection for themselves and their offspring in a practice
which they had formerly neglected or despised.' pp. 42–44.

Among the unprotected, either by inoculation or vaccination, the epidemic exhibited in its progress all the varieties of
small-pox, from the mildest to the most malignant form. ' The
' mildest form in which it occurred' (says Dr Thomson), ' as
' well as the most malignant, were those of strictly vesicular
' eruptions, in which scarcely a particle of purulent matter was
' to be observed from the commencement to the termination.'
It is well known that the mortality of variolous epidemics has,
in particular years, not amounted to more than 1 in 50; whereas the mortality of this epidemic among the unprotected was 1
in 4.

Where the disease occurred in individuals who had gone
through natural or inoculated small-pox, the interval between
the two attacks varied from ten days to thirty years. The eruptive fever in the greater number was severe, but in some cases
so mild as to be scarcely perceptible. The eruption sometimes
resembled chicken-pox, either in its pustular or vesicular form;
in others it resembled that of distinct small-pox; in a third
class, small-pox of the confluent kind.

In this epidemic, the class of patients which excited the
greatest curiosity was, of course, that which had passed through
the process of vaccination; and as that process was recurred to
from the general alarm in families where small-pox was prevailing, repeated opportunities occurred of observing the co-ex-
istence of these two disorders in the same individual, and the
*wonderful power which the cow-pox appeared to possess of miti-
gating the severity of small-pox, or even sometimes, in the midst of
general contagion,* of preventing it altogether. Instances, of
course, occurred where the vaccinated individual had been so
long (previously to the operation) exposed to the virus of small-
pox, that the vaccine matter lost its controlling power. In a
great proportion of cases in this class, the eruptive fever was
severe, and frequently mistaken, at its commencement, for typhus. In many cases, however, it was so slight as to be scarcely perceptible; and, even when severe, ceased suddenly on the
appearance of the eruption, so that it was seldom necessary for
patients to remain in bed during the progress of the disease.
In a few individuals, the fever was not followed by any eruption. In some of the severer cases, a considerable degree of
secondary fever occurred, accompanied by swelling of the face,

increased inflammation of the internal fauces, hoarseness, and ptyalism; but these symptoms were almost always of short duration, and left the patient in a degree of health and vigour very different from that of those who had passed through eruptions equally copious, of natural coherent small-pox. One instance occurred of a vaccinated person who had the varioloid disease for the third time. In above forty of the vaccinated, it had occurred for the second time, after intervals, varying from a few days to several years. In some of these cases, it exhibited, in the first attack, the appearance of chicken-pox, and in the second, that of small-pox, and *vice versa.* In some, both attacks resembled chicken-pox ; in others, both resembled small-pox. Of the vaccinated, as before stated, one only died out of 484. In this disease, nothing occurred to warrant the supposition that the modifying powers of vaccination are weakened by time. On the contrary, the epidemic was observed to attack those chiefly who were under ten years of age; so that increasing years appeared rather to lessen, than increase the susceptibility of small-pox contagion.

' It is not easy to conceive ' (says Dr Thomson) ' that the efficacy of cow-pock inoculation, in protecting against the attacks and the dangers of small-pox, is likely ever to be subjected to a severer trial than that which it has experienced in the almost universal prevalence of the late very malignant epidemic. From the best information I have been able to procure, the deaths from natural small-pox in this epidemic has in general varied from one in three to one in five —a degree of fatality from small-pox which has been but seldom observed to occur, and which has not, so far as I have been able to learn, any where taken place since the introduction of vaccination. It is to the severity of this epidemic, I am convinced, that we ought to attribute the greatness of the number of the vaccinated who have been attacked by it, and not to any deterioration in the qualities of the cow-pock virus, or to any defects in the manner in which it has been employed. Had a variolous constitution of the atmosphere, similar to that which we have lately experienced, existed at the time Dr Jenner brought forward his discovery, it may be doubted whether it ever could have obtained the confidence of the public. It is to the severity also of the epidemic, I conceive, that we must attribute the very great number of acknowledged cases of secondary small-pox which have occurred during its progress—a number certainly much greater than is recorded to have occurred during any former small-pox epidemic. The modifying effects of primary on secondary small-pox, which I have had occasion to observe, lead me to believe, that had the late epidemic been of a milder character, the secondary small-pox occurring in it would have exhibited more of a varicelloid, and less of a variolous character, than they have done, and in all probability would not have been recognised either by myself or by others as cases of secondary small-pox. The same remark is, I conceive, if possible, still more applicable to the cases of small-pox which have occurred after vaccination ; for who, among the friends of this practice, would ever have allowed any varioloid eruption to be small-pox, to which he could have assigned any of the multifarious attributes of chicken-pox ? '—*Historical Sketch,* pp. 394–96.

In 1820, Mr Cross published ' A Description of the Vario-
' lous Epidemic which occurred in Norwich in the Year 1819,
' *and destroyed five hundred and thirty individuals :* With an
' Estimate of the Protection afforded by Vaccination; and a
' Review of past and present Opinions upon Chicken-pox and
' modified Small-pox.' The epidemic was introduced into that city in the end of the year 1818, and appears, from Mr Cross's description, to have produced among the vaccinated, unvaccinated, and those who had previously had the small-pox, effects in every respect similar to those described in Dr Thomson's epidemic. It is quite clear from these, and similar histories referred to by Dr Thomson, that where small-pox prevails epidemically, and with severity, vaccination cannot be depended upon as a preservative against its attacks; that such an immunity is not conferred by the natural small-pox, or by inoculation; but that all who have gone through this disorder in any of these forms, and particularly the young, are, when the disorder is very malignant and very general, liable to be reinfected. But it appears also, in such cases (though it does not prevent the disorder), that vaccination moderates it, and renders it comparatively harmless and insignificant; and that, though stript of those very high pretensions with which it first came into the world, it is still one of the most valuable presents which Science ever made to mankind.

' The disappointment I felt, in common with others, in being forced to believe that vaccination, in whatever manner it may be performed, is not in all circumstances an absolute, or even a general preventive of small-pox, has been in some measure compensated for, by the increasing conviction I have received of the wonderful power which this process possesses of modifying the phenomena, and securing against the dangers of small-pox ; and I cannot but believe, that the same gratifying conviction must irresistibly force itself upon the minds of every individual who may have an opportunity of observing the remarkable differences that exist in the appearances and fatality of natural small-pox, and of small-pox modified by vaccination. The results of my observation of this modifying power, have led me to regard every vaccination as being as perfect as it can be rendered, which bears the characters originally described by Dr Jenner ; and I must retain this conviction till evidence, different from any of which the public are yet in possession, shall be adduced of the existence of spurious vaccine vesicles, of the deterioration of cow-pock virus, and of the superiority of one mode of vaccination over another,—*hypotheses* which have been successively resorted to, in order to account for the occurrence of small-pox after vaccination. I have not been able to discover, after the most minute attention, that any difference of effect whatever in the modifying power of vaccination has depended upon the skill of the operator, or upon his peculiar mode of performing the operation. Indeed, I have often had occasion to see the small-pox mild in children who had been vaccinated by their parents, and severe in those who had been conducted through this process by the highest authorities in vaccination. '— *Historical Sketch*, pp. 397, 398.

During the prevalence of the varioloid epidemic, Dr Thomson had great occasion to doubt whether or not the chicken-pox and the small-pox were separate diseases; and his doubt has ended in a strong conviction that they both originate from one common contagion, and that chicken-pox is nothing more than a variety of small-pox.

This conjecture Dr Thomson finds M. Geoffroy to have made in his Memoires de la Société Royale Médecine, for 1777.

' A child, ' says M. Geoffroy, ' was attacked with chicken-pox (petite verole volante), which terminated in the space of four days without pitting. A few days afterwards, his eldest sister, about eight years old, and who had been constantly with her brother, was seized with the same disease, which latterly became a very abundant true small-pox, but distinct, possessing all the characters, running through all the stages, and followed by boils, as is but too frequently the case after small-pox. '—' A similar fact, ' he adds, ' if it frequently took place, would prove that the chicken-pox and the small-pox are not of so different a nature as is commonly believed, but that the one is perhaps merely a diminutive of the other. '—*Historical Sketch*, p. 121.—And Mr Ring observes, ' that the similarity of the two disorders have caused them to be mistaken for each other by *the first physicians in Europe.* '—*Ibid.* p. 164.

Dr Bateman of London appears also to admit the common origin of small-pox and chicken-pox; and Dr Henderson, who had an opportunity of witnessing a varioloid epidemic at Perth, is of the same opinion. (*Variol. Epidem.* p. 271.) Many other testimonies in support of this opinion are quoted by Dr Thomson.

In the contagion which prevailed at Edinburgh, the disorder among the vaccinated and the inoculated exhibited many of those appearances which have been regarded as characteristic of chicken-pox; but then these cases occurred in the midst of cases of coherent and confluent small-pox. They could often be distinctly traced to small-pox infection; and they gave rise to small-pox in all the various forms of that disease. In the same house, the same room, nay, in the same bed, were patients infected by a common origin, which could be traced with the utmost exactness; the one exhibiting all the appearances of chicken-pox, the second with mild small-pox, and the third with small-pox of the most malignant kind : and yet it is contended, that the chicken-pox is something essentially different from the small-pox. This is much the same as to say, that three men who had got drunk out of the same cask, were affected with various complaints, and from different causes, because one was a little drunk, the second very drunk, and the third roaring and raving with ebriety.

'In a house in the Canongate, where a child was dying of the most malignant small-pox, an infant had a scanty eruption of pure transparent vesicles, surrounded with superficial erythema, which came out without much fever, and faded into thin scales by the fifth day, without becoming pustular. In the Causewayside a child, of the name of Hardy, had a scanty eruption of transparent superficial vesicles, which became milky, and crusted by the fifth and sixth days, without becoming pustular, except under some of the crusts; and in the same room there was a boy with the crusts separating from his body, after a severe attack of confluent malignant small-pox, and another in whom distinct small-pox were going through their course in a regular manner. In Blackfriars Wynd, a child had an eruption of pure vesicles, which became somewhat milky, but shrivelled and scabbed by the fifth day ; while, in the adjoining room, another child went through a distinct small-pox, which, though at first vesicular, became pustular, and stood out for eight days.'— *Variol. Epidem.* pp. 291, 292.

The following case is still stronger, and seems to us almost irresistible. It is contained in an extract of a letter from Mr John Malloch to Dr Thomson.

' " No case of small-pox had occurred in this town for nine years till last winter, when an idle boy, who was in the habit of wandering about the country, frequenting markets, &c. happened to be at a house where some of the inmates were said to be ill of small-pox. He himself had been vaccinated some years before. On his return home, he was seized with febrile symptoms, and confined for two or three days to bed, when an eruption, similar to chicken-pox, made its appearance. Immediately the fever abated, and in a few days more he left his bed, and attended a cattle market, half a mile's distance from the town, without experiencing any bad consequences. About a week afterwards, one of his master's children was taken ill, and went through the regular stages of small pox in a mild manner ; then a second similarly ; a third suffered in a very alarming degree from the confluent kind ; a fourth one rather worse than the two first ; and the youngest, of eight months old, had what, if the other

3

cases had not occurred, I would, without hesitation, have called chicken-pox ; for there was little or no fever, the pustules were filled with a watery fluid, which was not converted into the purulent appearance of small-pox. None of these children had undergone vaccination. " '—*Variol. Epidem.* pp. 278, 279.

If these disorders are not of common origin, then two epidemics were prevalent in Edinburgh at the same time, and the same patients ought to have been infected with both ; but this was not observed to be the case either there or elsewhere; for, out of 155 patients who had passed through the small-pox, not one, says Dr Thomson, has been subsequently attacked by the vesicular disease. But if there were two epidemics at the same time, and persons were not affected with both epidemics together, or consecutively, then those epidemics were mutually guarantees against each other. Small-pox, then, is a guarantee against chicken-pox, and chicken-pox against small-pox, which has not yet been asserted by physicians, and is contrary to the fact. The boy sleeping with his varicellous brother would become varicellous. The small-pox, with common appearances, would never produce varicellous appearances,—which is also contrary to the fact. If, then, there have been two coexistent epidemics in Edinburgh, they have adjusted their mutual pretensions in a much more amicable manner than any two coexistent physicians who were watching their progress. The disease enters the *flat* perhaps in a varioloid form ; the eldest of the fourteen children who inhabit it is seized with what is commonly called chicken-pox ; but this second epidemic, unwilling to grasp at too much, leaves the next boy to the small-pox ; indulges that disorder with a third and fourth gratification, then resumes its rights on the fifth and sixth child, till both, tired with Scotch fecundity, give up the remaining members of the family to the confluent and malignant branches of the disease. To suppose this the same disorder produced by the same contagion, and modified by the particular constitution of the patients, sometimes so trifling as scarcely to be called disease, at other times rapidly hurrying its victim to a loathsome death ;—to suppose this is to make a supposition consonant to fact and to reason ; but to mistake a difference of intensity for a difference of genus, is to defeat the great object of scientific classification, and to multiply distinctions which do not differ. There are innumerable disorders, of which the slightest cases differ from the worst cases as much as any two generically different complaints can do from each other.

Much has been written upon Pus and Pimples;—many volumes have been employed upon Eruptions;—there are folios on Scabs. If any man has a breaking out on his nose, he may

334 *Vaccination and Small-pox.*   Nov.

be sure to find it in a book. If it is not in page ten, it is in page twenty. No phlegmonous variety is unpainted, unprinted, or past over in silence by the doctors. In spite, however, of the extreme accuracy with which chicken-pox and small-pox have been described, Dr Thomson contends that, in practice, no such distinction can be adhered to.

' Prepared, as I conceived myself in some measure to have been, for the observation of such a malady as the present, by the study of cutaneous affections, and by a strict attention, for a long period, to the diagnostic symptoms of eruptive diseases, it has been often to me a source of mortification to find, that I was not able to perceive in individual varioloid cases those peculiar marks or characters by which many of my professional brethren have been enabled to satisfy themselves of a difference in the phenomena of chicken-pox and modified small-pox. Indeed, while I continued to believe in the separate and independent existence of chicken-pox, I had been repeatedly informed, that cases which I was convinced, from the symptoms, were cases of chicken-pox, were not chicken-pox, but cases of modified small-pox ; and since I have begun to doubt of the independent existence of chicken-pox, I have as often been informed, that the cases which I considered to be cases of modified small-pox, were not such, but cases of chicken-pox. I have used every means in my power to acquire the information that would enable me to guess, even with tolerable certainty, at a distinction which I am told is made with little difficulty by others, but all to no purpose; for I am at this moment as far from being able to distinguish modified small pox from the eruptions which I have been accustomed, for thirty years, to consider as chicken-pox, as I was when I first began to observe the present varioloid disease. '—*Variol. Epidem.* pp. 56–57.

It appears from the Historical Researches of Dr Thomson, that, notwithstanding the opinion that chicken-pox and small-pox are different, no satisfactory proof is to be found in our medical records of their ever having prevailed separately; but, on the contrary, there are many proofs that all the varieties of the genuine, as well as the spurious small-pox, have in the same epidemic come in and gone out together, in the same manner as they have been observed to do during the period of vaccination.

The idea, that chicken-pox arises from a different contagion from that which produces small-pox, was embodied into a regular doctrine by Dr Heberden, in 1767. His arguments were, that chicken-pox attacks those who have passed through small-pox, and *vice versa*; and that the mode of attack, appearance, progress and termination, were different; and that neither of these diseases ever attack the same person a second time. This last supposition we now know to be untrue; and every pheno-

menon of the disorders admit of a much clearer and plainer
solution, by the supposition that they are both different modifications of the same contagion. Previous to the time of Dr
Heberden, indeed, this was the common opinion respecting
these diseases. They were supposed to be varieties of the
same complaint, usually accompanying each other in their progress and appearance; though sometimes the one and sometimes the other is reported to have been first observed.

Gandoger de Foigny, and many other writers on Chicken-
pox, attempt to give a very accurate diagnosis between chicken-
pox and small-pox; but, if an accurate diagnosis *could* be
given, it still would not prove the two disorders to be essentially different; but only, that the same disease was modified by some of those innumerable circumstances which ex-
asperate or mitigate the infirmities of the human body. It
should excite no surprise, that diseases so different as chicken-
pox and small-pox are said to be, should proceed from one
common origin, when we know for certain that it is quite un-
important from what sort of small-pox the inoculating matter
is taken. Mild small-pox matter may produce the confluent
small-pox; and matter taken from a confluent case may produce the mildest small-pox. The disease seems to depend
much more upon the body that receives, than the body which
communicates it.

‘ I knew one-and-twenty persons * inoculated the same day with
matter taken from one who had a confluent small-pox, and died of
it; yet these, notwithstanding, all had it in as favourable a way as
could be wished for ; and I have inoculated many more with matter
of the malignant kind, without any manner of ill effect.’—*Historical
Sketch*, p. 50.

Mr Bryce, evidently a sensible and judicious man, observes,
in his communication to Dr Thomson, that the varicellous disorder does not prevent the regular progress of the cow-pock.
But is Mr Bryce prepared to contend, that the small-pox is the
same antidote against the cow-pox that the cow-pox is against
the small-pox? And if not, how is the common origin of chicken-
pox and small-pox disproved by the admission of his fact?
Even if it were otherwise, is it absurd to suppose, that small-
pox, in one state and in one degree of intensity, may effect
changes in the body, and produce effects which, in another
state, and under a less degree of intensity, it is not able to do?
—that it may prevent cow-pox, when in its pustular, although it
cannot do so in its vesicular state? Does any body doubt, that

---

* Dr Frewen’s Essay on Inoculation, 1749.

true variolous virus may be so diluted or so putrified, that it will produce no infection at all, or an infection completely differing from small-pox in its orthodox form? If a steady diagnosis *can* be made between chicken-pox and secondary small-pox; if the characteristics of the first of these disorders are so clear and plain, let the following questions be answered: Are the vesicles preceded or not preceded by papulæ? What is the occurrence, degree, and duration of the eruptive fever? At what period do the vesicles appear to shrivel and burst? Do the vesicles ever become pustular? If pustular, can they be distinguished from modified small-pox and natural small-pox? How long do they continue fluid without scabbing? How long is it before the scabs fall off? Do they leave behind them hills or holes? All these questions are answered by Dr Heberden, Mr Bryce, Dr Alison, and Dr Abercrombie; but, unfortunately, their answers do not agree.

These are the material points and reasonings in Dr Thomson's books, written diffusely, but with that sense, diligence and penetration, which have carried him to his present medical eminence. It is probable from them that, in strong variolous epidemics, cow-pox is not a preservative to be depended upon against the small-pox; but it is equally true, that it renders that disease comparatively harmless and insignificant. The difference between Dr Thomson and his antagonists upon other points seems to be one rather of reasoning than practice; but it appears to us that he is most probably right. If a disease comes into an house in the shape of A, and breaks out in one case in the shape of B, and in another in the shape of C; or if it comes in the shape of B, and produces A and C; or if C will produce the other two letters, then it seems agreeable to common sense to suppose, that A, B, and C, are not separate disorders, but modifications of the same disorder. This probability is confirmed, if the same patient has neither the three disorders at once, nor one after the other. It is still more confirmed, if these diseases, in some cases separate and distinct, are in others so blended, that it is extremely difficult (if not impossible) to determine to which class they belong.

It is always wise to extract good from evil, when it is practicable so to do. The late varioloid epidemics have put an end for ever to that laborious, though unintentional, distortion of truth, by which all cases of secondary small-pox were either determined to be chicken-pox, or referred to imperfect vaccination. If the disorder had been more mild in this last epidemic, the same explanation would have sufficed. When a variolous epidemic shall again occur of a milder description, it is probable that the vaccinated will be more protected from its attacks, and that secondary small-pox will reassume that milder and varicellous variety of the complaint, which Dr Thomson appears to have degraded from the dignity of a separate disease to the rank and file of small-pox complaints. We are far, however, from thinking the point definitively settled; but we incline much more to the reasoning of Dr Thomson than to that of his opponents. The dispute is conducted on both sides with mutual respect, and just as we expected it would be conducted by the learned, honourable, and respectable men * whose names appear in the controversy.

* We were particularly pleased with a very sensible, well-written letter by Dr Abercrombie. We do not agree with the reasoning, but we were struck with its clearness, conciseness, and sense.

ART. VII. — 1. *Report of the General Board of Health on the Measures appointed for the Execution of the Nuisances-removal and Diseases-prevention Act, and the Public Health Act, up to July* 1849. Presented to Parliament.

2. *Report on Quarantine by the General Board of Health.* Presented to Parliament, 1849.

3. *Statement of the Course of Investigation and Results of Experiments as to the means of Removing the Refuse of Towns in Water, and applying it as Manure.* By EDWIN CHADWICK, Esq. C. B. Reynell and Weight, 1849.

SEEN through the departing shadow of a wide-wasting pestilence, the science which aims at preserving health by precautionary arrangements, now presents itself divested of the vulgar and unsightly attributes which formerly repelled public attention too much from its details; and stands forth in the true and pure light of its beneficent object — the saving of human life. In England alone, the average annual number of deaths from disease is, in round numbers, 300,000, — while that of deaths from the mere decay and exhaustion of the human frame by the progress of time, is only 35,000. In the difference between these two numbers we see the vast and vital field in which the sanitary reformer proposes to work. That disease shall ever be entirely exterminated, is of course beyond the belief or hope of the most sanguine: But every disease has somewhere its specific and efficient cause, — and that these causes can be removed, or much weakened in their action, in very many instances, is not only within the bounds of hope, but has been satisfactorily proved. When sanitary legislation gives us its successful results, they will be represented by the reduction of the number of those who die of disease, in their early days, or in the prime of

life — and in the increased number of those who have completed
their allotted course in health and been peacefully gathered to
their fathers.

Accordingly sanitary improvements have not directly in view
the extension of the *natural* period of human life, but only the
removal of influences which *artificially* curtail it.   The opinions
of Condorcet and his disciples, therefore, are widely distinct from
the inductive philosophy of those who have demonstrated the
benefit of removing from the vicinity of man those external
poisons which embitter and abridge his existence.   Their object
is not the vain one of indefinitely protracting existence by human
art.   It seems indeed a remarkable fact, whence something has
yet, we think, to be learned, that wherever the average length
of life is improved there is a tendency to equality; and that
the miraculously long livers, appear chiefly where the average
vitality is shortest, and where men subject to noxious agencies
present in general the most attenuated and degraded physical
condition, — as if it were an exceptional law of nature, that
those whose frames can for a certain time resist these deadly
influences, become, ' like him who fed on poisons,' hardened
against the common causes of mortality.   Nor, were we to suppose it in the power of art materially to enlarge the allotted
span of healthy existence, and to make extreme old age the common lot, instead of the rare privilege of a few, — must we
necessarily suppose the boon accompanied by a great increase
of human happiness.   Treatises *de senectute* have more than one
aspect.   In the general case, when a green old age has been
reached, the task of life may be considered to have been performed, and its enjoyments substantially exhausted; the journey
has been completed, and the tired body may part with the
spirit in peace, leaving the arena of life to new competitors.
The associations with which survivors surround the memory of
their aged relatives are accordingly more tender than bitter.
And such deaths, it is felt, do not so much make a chasm in
existence as a natural change, consonant with the decay and
reproduction which are the routine of the world's progress.
Young hands are strengthening their grasp to lead us forward
in our journey through life, as the elder race waxes feeble
and drop away.   It is when the opening bud is blighted, or
life is cut off in the full bloom of usefulness, — in the midst of
happiness, affection, and esteem, — that the great calamities of
mortality are exhibited.   Such are the desolate spots of human
existence, standing in the centre of its healthy fruition, waste
and arid — showing happy aims defeated, and its joys engulphed
in unfathomable sorrows.   The science that promises in some

measure to mitigate the horrors of this howling wilderness, is surely an object before which sarcasm and faction and selfishness may well be dumb.

There are some initial views connected with this subject, on which a few years ago it might have been necessary to enlarge, but which may now, thanks to the enlightened perseverance of Mr. Chadwick and his coadjutors, be taken for granted as a part of the received creed of every intelligent observer. Whatever difficulties may still haunt the speculations of economists on the increase of population, no one now doubts that it is for the interest of the public at large, no less than for the happiness of the few immediately interested in each human being, that the life once breathed should, if possible, be preserved, until it is released by the natural wearing away of its earthly tabernacle. We all know that, in the economic sense of the term, a short-lived population is generally a surplus population, — not only because those who are reckless of preserving life will be careless of all its obligations, and will be poor and vicious, but because the tendency of early deaths is chiefly, to shorten the existence of those who produce more than they consume, and to increase the number of those who must be dependent on the charity of others.   Sir W. Temple's antithesis, that we cannot care too little for life nor too much for health, must not be misunderstood.   ' A cholera widow,' is a significant expression occasionally used by the Board of Health, to indicate one who has been thrown on the parish by the death of that husband who, if he had not been prematurely cut off, might have supported her for years, and left his children old enough to earn bread for themselves.   Many communities are now thus paying, in alarmingly swollen poor-rates, for the short-sighted selfishness which made them grudge the cost of precautionary arrangements.   These are truths which have now so far found acceptance throughout the educated part of society, that it seems unnecessary to examine at length the reasons for believing in them.   Nor, while the value to the public at large of preserving every human life that can be preserved, is fully admitted, does any rational man doubt that there come into existence in all places, and especially where men are densely congregated, physical agencies destructive of life, which, though capable of being removed, are too often left to do their deadly work undisturbed.   These broad facts appearing to require nothing to be said in their support, our remarks may be more profitably confined to some of the less obvious influences likely to be exercised by sanitary reform; and to an inquiry into the sources of the apathy, the prejudices, and the other difficulties which stand in the way of this class of improvement.

One of the primary prejudices — one of those least spoken of but most felt — which sanitary reform has to encounter, is a vague apprehension of undue interference. All regulations for securing cleanliness and removing filth, are apt to be considered as invasions of the privacy of the domestic hearth and the person, and amounting to an impertinent intermeddling, in matters concerning which it is insulting even to be inquisitive. But in reality the object of sanitary reform is to free the citizen from the vile fetters with which the acts of others have actually bound him, and to leave him free to pursue the natural tendency towards civilisation and refinement, rather than to assume any arbitrary control over his actions. We believe it to be quite true that it always injures the individual to do for him what he ought, and is able, to do for himself. But the operative workman must live in the city, or starve; and if selfish wealth has made the city such that he cannot find a cell in it which is not a living tomb, saturated with corruption — then he is not left to the freedom of his own actions, but is subject to an abominable bondage caused by the conduct of others. The strength and skill of Hercules could not enable the city artisan of Glasgow to live in purity; and if legislation cleanses the Augean stable, it is not doing for him what he should have been left to do for himself, but only saving him from suffering by the selfishness of third parties beyond his reach.

In fact no nation which has made many steps forward in civilisation can be without some sort of Edile police: And the real grievance is, not that such a thing does not exist, but that it is so very imperfect and defective. Like most other great benefits, it will be better accomplished through enlightened and well weighed legislation, suggested by skilful minds devoted to the task, than by the blind chance which has hitherto ruled it; and one of its new qualities will naturally be its careful adjustment to the proper medium between obnoxious interference and fatal neglect. Hitherto such vulgarisms as sewers, drains, and other things not less important and still more vulgarly suggestive, were deemed to be the proper province of bricklayers, scavengers, and nightmen. A respectable builder or plumber might perhaps condescend to give his attention to such works — but scarcely, if he had risen to the rank of an alderman or bailie. So was it of old with the noble art of surgery, linked to the humble and almost servile craft of the barber. But the portentous influences connected with both fields of exertion, have at last dignified them, in spite of sordid and unpleasing associations. And neither is a recognition of the importance of such functions so novel as it may seem. The sanitary rules to which the Jews were subjected were part of their Religion —

as those of other Eastern nations still are ; and travellers who are acquainted with these countries, assure us that there are in Leviticus precepts still marvellously well adapted to the preservation of life. There were similar regulations both in Mexico and Peru. But the Romans were the most sagacious and extensive legislators in such matters. They were in many things masters of the practical; and have left vestiges still pregnant with the wisdom of experience. With them nothing seems to have been deemed 'common or unclean' that could protect the public health. We find Pliny writing to Trajan about a fetid stream passing through Amastris, as if it were an affair of State. The cloacæ of the Tarquins are still among the architectural wonders of the world. The censors, ediles, and curators, who at different periods had charge of the buildings, and of the apparatus for the removal of impurities, were invested with great powers for the execution of their functions, and derived a corresponding dignity from them. The arrangements for supplying the houses of Rome with water were most minute. Those for ventilation and drainage, still traceable in the several remains of Roman amphitheatres, have struck our most advanced sanitarians with surprise at their remarkable adaptation to their purpose; while Mr. Chadwick tells the Commissioners of Sewers that he has lately received from a friend in Zurich a specimen of exactly such an earthenware pipe as he is now recommending for the distribution of sewage. It had been laid down by the Romans, and 'has worked until recent times under 500 feet of pressure!' Indeed it is easy to see from Vitruvius, and from portions of the collection of Grævius, that the rules and operations for the protection of health in Rome, were of a very radical and peremptory character, and allowed no minor interests to interfere with them. It seems to have been a rule with them, that from the time when the foundation of a city was laid, to that of the summit of its greatness, no structural operation, public or private, should be permitted to take a shape which might render it a harbour either for disease or crime; and it is to this vigilant forethought that, in the absence of other organising agencies discovered only in our later times, we may attribute the success with which that remarkable people preserved social order, throughout so dense and vast a mass of human beings as the inhabitants of the imperial city in the days of its greatness.

It is not creditable to this country that, by neglecting initiatory precautions, it should have allowed so much to be done which must now be undone. In the restrictions which prevent every man from doing for his own profit or gratification that which inflicts on his neighbour a deadly injury, there is no hardship;—it is simple justice. Our law requires that the railway

company, the master of the steam boat, and the manufacturer of
gunpowder, should respectively conduct their operations so as
not to endanger the safety of the community ; and there can be
no reason why the same responsibility should not be attached to
those whose profitable occupation is building or spinning. Such
intervention on behalf of the public is not to be confounded
with the old sumptuary laws, — for it interferes with things,
not with persons ; nor can it be compared to attempts to
regulate labour and wages, or to restraints on trade, — for it is
not done to procure, by the artificial adjustment of something,
which men can best settle for themselves, some speculative
advantage, but, on the principle of *salus populi suprema lex,* to
protect one set of human beings from being the victims of
disease and death through the selfish cupidity of others. The
owner of the soil is the person who mainly profits by the
accumulation of a city population, — his, at all events, are advantages for which he neither toils nor spins ; and many of the
princely fortunes of our day have been created by the rapid
rise — often causeless and capricious, so far as the owner himself
may know — of city populations. It does not seem then to be a
very hard rule either of morality or law, that a proprietor, who
accumulates wealth by any such means, shall be compelled to
submit to regulations which, should they even in some degree
reduce the amount of his gains, may be a security, against the
lives of those who by the necessities of their position are enriching
him, from being sacrificed to his avarice or his recklessness.
While he derives a profit by letting out his square yards of the
earth's surface, it surely is not unfair that he should become
bound not to transfer it to the occupant perforated throughout
with pit-falls in which health and life may be lost.

But this is not the only form in which there is a debt due
to the more miserable classes in our cities, by the wealthy and
the well to do. The progress of wealth—and even the progress
of civilisation, in so far as the great outward manifestations
of civilisation may be held its types, — has the effect, when it
is partial, of deteriorating the class that is thrown out in
the race or lottery of life. When, through the influence of
external circumstances which they are unable to control, a
portion of the population remain as all originally were, their
position is lower than that of the first common barbarism. This
term is applied to communities who are nearly all on a level—
with habits which, as they are not directed by the lights of
civilisation, have not been formed in its shades. And accordingly we cannot attribute to the American hunter or the Arab
wanderer any of the degradation which invests the no less
savage occupant of a large town, who skulks round the corner

when he sees a policeman, and scowls at the rich man's carriage rolling over the muddy road, where he traces the impression of his children's naked feet. The two classes of barbarians are as distinct from each other as the moss-stained stream that passes through a heath-clad moor, and the continuation of the same stream, black and greasy, from having served the fifty steam engines, and received the manifold impurities, of a large manufacturing town. . Civilisation and wealth have been the causes of this degradation; and it must be their function, knowing what they now cannot fail to know, to remedy the evils they have unconsciously inflicted.

Indeed, the neglected refuse of civilisation has the faculty of nourishing social savages among mankind, just as it provides the favourite haunts of the vermin which frequent sewers and dung heaps. If the arrangements for preserving physical purity are not made for all, but only for those who can easily pay for them, not only will the poorer classes be left in their own natural debasement, but will become the recipients of all the additional filth which their richer neighbours cast off. A not uncommon occurrence where a town has rapidly increased is, that a village inhabited by the humbler classes, nestled in a pleasant dell beside a river, where the natural facility for drainage, and pure air, kept the people clean and healthy, has been changed into one of those degraded suburbs, described with dreary uniformity of misery in the sanitary reports, which the skill of Crabbe could not improve upon ; because a few gay handsome streets, inhabited by rich people, have converted the neighbouring heights into a city of palaces; and all those impurities, of the existence of which the fastidious citizens are scarcely aware, are now sent down to flood the poor inhabitants of the pristine village.

But the higher and the middle classes have, besides the obligation of plain justice, a great and palpable *interest* in making sacrifices for the purification of their degraded neighbours, so far as this can be accomplished without destroying self-dependence. We cannot separate ourselves from uncleanness and misery by mere walls and lanes, and remain safe. The way in which the Cholera pursued its career is a marked type of the common interest which all classes have in keeping each other above that Slough of Despond—utter physical degradation. Filth and vice drew it first to their favourite seats, as the loadstone draws iron; But when it was once introduced within the limits of a city community, none were wealthy or moral or wise enough to be safe from its stroke. Those who are permitted to lag far behind the onward march of their neighbours, are always dangerous as well as melancholy objects. The human being who has sunk below a certain level naturally gravitates to depths still lower; and it depends greatly on the objects with which he comes in contact, whether he is impelled forward or is arrested in this progress. Wherever the first needs of life are too easily obtained, or where the body of a people is not obliged to labour as a condition necessary to their self-respect, there is a dangerous tendency to lean on such facilities — and abandon the efforts of self-sustentation, which ennoble, or keep erect, the better races of mankind. This propensity is widely exhibited among those nations whose happy climate demands little care or labour for the mere support of animal existence; and was well illustrated by that ingenious magistrate who predicted, that if the Strand were lined with empty casks, they would all be speedily occupied by people who would rear a cask-living race. It may seem hard to deprive the wretch of the bulk-head or empty cellar, which he is content to make his idle home; but it is one of those hardships with which acts of mercy often must begin. When the frightful demoralisation of Liverpool was recently exposed, and it was shown that between thirty and forty thousand inhabitants of that fine city lived in dens called cellars, the bold resolution was taken of at once *amputating* this morbid mass, by rendering cellars illegal habitations. The operation commenced in 1842; and after about 3000 people were ejected, a more stringent method was adopted in 1847. The operation of removal — under the judicious management of Dr. Duncan, the medical officer of health — was gradual, but systematic and steady; and near the end of 1849, 4700 cellars had been cleared of 20,000 inhabitants! Time enough has not elapsed to let the full effect of this bold measure be seen; but the officer of health has already had to report the significant fact, respecting one of the districts formerly most afflicted by poverty and disease, that while the last epidemic preceding the clearance carried off 500 inhabitants, — the Cholera, which broke out during the time that the forced change of residence was in progress, slew the comparatively small number of 94.

An overflowing abundance of evidence, confirmed by the experience of every dweller in towns, shows that the unclean districts, which are the great centres of disease, are at the same time the great nurseries and fortresses of crime. The mind suffers in these cases with the body. Wesley was well aware of the connexion when he said, — Cleanliness was next to Godliness. That criminality can be abolished by sanitary reform, or by any one measure, is, alas! a vain expectation: but great hopes of a diminution may be rested on any system which shall destroy the existing strongholds of vice, as the merchant cities destroyed those of the robber barons. The history of the world has always been affected by the external circumstances in which its inhabitants have been placed.   A spirit of freedom—a determination not to be absorbed into any of the great aggregates which form the leading empires of the world — a chivalrous and warlike character, have generally distinguished the inhabitants of inaccessible districts.   Thus the same natural cause has produced similar moral traits, in places otherwise so unlike each other as the mountains of Switzerland and Dalecarlia, the bushy labyrinths of La Vendée, and the swamps of Holland.   If, therefore, we artificially create physical anomalies in our cities, we must expect to find a people assimilated to them; and so we have the city mountaineers of the Lawn Market, and the amphibious squatters in the Goose Dubs, or the Angel Meadow of Manchester — a race as rugged according to their own peculiarities, as those whose mountains lift them to the storm.   Their spirit of independence, to be sure, is a defiance of all laws human and divine; their enthusiasm is the zealous pursuit of every vice in whose service the skill of civilisation can pander to the appetites of barbarism; their chivalry is in the mutual bond to help each other's wickedness; and their warlike spirit is developed in a constant battle with the law.   And yet we are inclined to believe that, to a very great extent, society might be cleared of these wretches by the mere removal of their natural strongholds, — as a district relieves itself from panthers and rattlesnakes by clearing a jungle.

Such an object, we have already said, would be well worthy of a sacrifice by the middle and upper classes.   But we believe that the operation would, in the end, be better described as a good investment.   Like the draining and clearing of land, it would speedily more than repay itself in plentiful fruit.   Nor would that fruit be an unsubstantial and visionary one, in the vague return of increased public health and improved morality.   It would represent itself in hard cash, according to an account in which the tax for sanitary reform should be set down as a cheap forestalment of poor-rates, prison assessments, and taxes to support the administration of criminal justice.

It is in vain to expect that the wide operations necessary for the accomplishment of measures so comprehensive, can ever be efficiently conducted through purely local movements.   Whoever may transact the actual business, there must be somewhere a suggesting and directing skill of the highest order.   Let us just glance at the physical ravages on Nature effected by the rapid rise of a great manufacturing town, and think whether it is at all likely that such a creation should ever be willing or able, of itself, to supply a remedy for the mischief it has done.   In a valley between undulating grassy hills, dotted with trees, runs a clear brook, sedgy here and rocky there, whose speckled trout show the purity of its waters. The passing traveller, or indolent lounger, acknowledges the grateful influence of un-contaminated air, of pleasant sounds, and sweet smells — and sighs to think how sadly a large portion of his fellow men are cut off from such enjoyments? Let us suppose him returning to the spot twenty years afterwards, while in the mean time some manufacturing or trading facilities have brought about the sudden erection of a considerable town in the cheerful valley. The dense darkness of a smoky atmosphere now covers every thing. There is not a green leaf or blade to be seen, save some hemloc and nettles flourishing in neglected courtyards. The surface of the soil is everywhere saturated with putrescent filth. Of the human beings brought to the spot by the temptation of high wages, a large portion live in dens, damp, dark, and pestiferous. With the pristine tastes and habits enjoyed by them, when they first came there, they would have preferred to occupy fitting human habitations had they been able to obtain them; but now they are assimilated to their abodes. The stream that once ran clattering on, is sluggish with every variety of suspended ordure, and black as ink; the bubbling escape of poisonous gases is a dismal mockery of the leaping of the trout. The parched citizens are panting for water, while the surrounding moors, from want of drainage, are soaked in wet; and the impurities that would enrich the cold damp soil, are making havoc of the lives of the people. Let us hope that such a spot has yet another revolution to go through — that the stream will again run pure, though its banks be more artificially ornamented than of old, — that open spaces fresh and green may greet the wearied labourer's eyes, and tempt his children to healthy pastimes away from the gutter and the dung-heap, — that trees may cast their shade, as in former times, in summer evenings, over pleasant groups who have learned to prefer the sounds and sights of Nature to those of the gin-palace. That such revolutions may be made, we have actual experience in the improvements which have taken place in the parks and open spaces near the portions of our great cities occupied by the aristocracy. ' If the most fashionable parts of ' the Capital,' says Mr. Macaulay, ' could be placed before us such ' as they then were (in the reign of Charles II.), we should be ' disgusted by their squalid appearance, and poisoned by their ' noisome atmosphere. In Covent Garden a filthy and noisy ' market was held close to the dwellings of the great. Fruit-' women screamed, carters fought, cabbage-stalks and rotten ' apples accumulated in heaps at the thresholds of the Countess ' of Berkshire and of the Bishop of Durham. . . . St. James's ' Square was a receptacle for all the offal and cinders, for all the ' dead cats and dead dogs of Westminster. At one time a

' cudgel-player kept the ring there.   At another time an impu-
' dent squatter settled himself there, and built a shed for rubbish
' under the windows of the gilded saloons, in which the first
' magnates of the realm — Norfolks, Ormonds, Kents, and Pem-
' brokes — gave banquets and balls.   It was not till these
' nuisances had lasted through a whole generation, and till
' much had been written about them, that the inhabitants applied
' to parliament for permission to put up rails and to plant trees.'

The progress of true civilisation indeed, is best marked, we
should say, by the facility with which men may crowd together
into large city communities, without suffering from the confusion
and the pollution which such accumulations would naturally
create.   Art is here employed to bring us back to Nature ;
and, with the conveniences and pleasures of intercourse, to give
us no small portion of the personal independence, and the
freedom from offensive sights and associations, which pursue the
dweller in the desert.   The children reared round the Regent's
Park are heirs of all the civilisation of the greatest city in the
world, and can hold converse with Nature in meadows, trees,
and flowers, — and in the very wild beasts that are the terror
of the savage !   But far different are the children of St. Giles
and Angel Meadow :   Even for them however, we trust, a better
day is dawning ; and what the aristocracy have done for themselves, satisfactorily shows how far human ingenuity and perseverance have it in their power to discard the dregs of progress
and preserve its benefits alone.

But that communities which have grown up in degradation will never be able, unassisted, to emancipate themselves
from this servitude, is almost self-evident.   Left to themselves
they will remain as they are ; nor do the paltry attempts which
some corporations, under the fear of the Cholera, and of the
exposures to which they have been subjected by the promoters
of sanitary reform, have made to relieve themselves from
the scandal of their position, afford much ground for reliance
on municipal efforts.   Whatever *hands* may do the local work,
there must be wise and able *heads* to suggest, and sometimes
to command.   The advantages of having, in relation to such a
matter, a central body, with at least one mind wholly devoted
to the great object in view, and with continual access to the most
enlightened intellects, both at home and abroad, are too great
to be perceived at once, or easily estimated.   The ' Report on
' Quarantine,' which has been translated into French and
Italian, and is rapidly passing over the globe, was but the first
year's fruit of the Board of Health ; and it bids fair to set commerce free from one of its most vexatious and most costly
trammels ; nay, more — if its views be sound, as we cannot

help believing that they are—it teaches the beneficent doctrine, that it is by kindness and good offices, not by isolation or flight, that we may best protect ourselves from the great scourges of mankind. From such a body only can we hope for comprehensive projects for public works,—uniform, effective, and economical. It is very clear that the persevering and searching intelligence, which has predominated in all inquiries and suggestions as to the public health, is finding its way towards a great discovery, which will do as much to change the aspect and condition of our towns as gas or pavements. We refer to the plans now ripening for the removal of the impurities of great cities, and their distribution over the soil as manure,—by operations which will strip them, not only of their noxious but even of their offensive character. Thus we may hope, that what has hitherto disgusted the senses, brutalised the minds, and shortened the days of the dwellers in great cities, may become a most needful help to our suffering agriculture. From the same authority there doubtless will proceed arrangements for communicating supplies of water through crowded communities, in a form far more abundant, economical, and complete, than either trading companies or local corporations have yet dreamed of.

For reasons to be afterwards more fully stated, we consider it right that such a board should be immediately connected with the Government. We believe that some not unnatural jealousy has been felt by the medical profession as to the constitution of the present board; but we cannot regret the circumstance that its chief operative leader is not a physician. It is very necessary that such a department should have the best scientific council and assistance that the country can afford, and the debt which it owes to the recent services of Dr. Southwood Smith, Dr. Sutherland, and other physicians, cannot well be overrated; but, on the other hand, it seems indispensable that an administrative body, coming in contact with constitutional rights and responsibilities, should have another kind of leadership. To balance the heroism and disinterestedness, for which we most willingly give them credit, the medical body have some defects, especially in their jealousies and prejudices. It is difficult to get them to countenance anything inconsistent with what they have long seen and practised; and they would certainly not be so ready as laymen to give way to the collective wisdom of their own brethren. We firmly believe, in short, that the first physicians in the country will more frankly communicate to such a board as the present, their individual convictions, than to any convocation of their professional brethren; and that the board will more candidly weigh and more cheerfully adopt their views. The value of unprofessional superintendence—

the same class of persons who are to execute arrangements never being entirely the same as those who devise them — has been evinced in the management of the Admiralty. It has been appositely remarked, that Nelson would never have obtained high command from a board of old admirals. Nor is it uninstructive to remember that, though they have liberally responded to it, the idea of sanitary reform on the scale which we are now considering, did not *originate* within the medical profession: And, in truth, the constant direction of the faculties to the cure of actual disease does not seem likely to leave much observation to devote to the study of its external causes.

But the chief difficulty with which all general efforts for the preservation of the public health have to contend, is the cry against centralisation. People say that we are departing from the foundations of the free institutions of our Saxon ancestors, — when in reality we are strengthening and expanding them. It should be remembered, that a Government board means a board responsible to Parliament. A central board in this country, directing and helping local authorities, is, therefore, as different from a central official administration in the other great States of Europe, as a Representative Government is from a Despotism.

We are quite alive to the great importance of the people in general becoming acquainted, through the local management of their own affairs, with the efficient mechanism of a representative system; and have often expressed the opinion, that it is chiefly in such matters that our nation has shown that aptness for order and system, in which the impulsive people of France, and the graver, but more theoretic people of Germany, appear to be deficient. But we believe these practical qualities to be inherent in the nature of our people; and do not think they require to be factitiously encouraged, to the detriment of the public business, by leaving that to be done by local representative bodies, which can be better done by official functionaries, — responsible to the country, and morally, as well as legally, bound to give the public real and efficient service, in return for the trust reposed in them, and the salaries with which they are paid. There is, indeed, only a certain amount of business that can be expected to be gratuitously done by local representative bodies; and it is quite possible, in the midst of a national fervour in favour of local action, to overtask these capabilities. It is worth while also to bear in mind, that municipal corporations, although their character was considerably raised by the measures which about fifteen years ago widened their basis, do not now hold the important and critical position, which they had at one time to maintain, as the protectors of the people against the power of a great feudal aristocracy. They may still be useful for the transaction of some kinds of business; but they are no longer necessary for the safety of our liberties.

Such being their position at present, we may, without disrespect to great constitutional authorities, examine whether they perform their actual functions either effectively or economically; a question which should be viewed in connexion with the opinion, that local representative management is, as a principle, so very valuable to the country at large, that it is worth being paid for in the form of a considerable addition to our taxation. There can be no doubt that a large per-centage on our fiscal burdens must be attributed to taxation by means of local bodies; but we confess that we have a partiality towards this branch of the public expenditure, were it only more economically applied: And we believe that such a supervision as the Board of Health exercises over local boards, will tend eminently to produce this result; without, in the least degree, injuring the efficacy of these bodies, — and with a great saving to the community, of expenses which local boards would generally incur; though more from ignorance than intention.

It is in truth a fond hallucination that local elective bodies are now practically responsible to their fellow-citizens, whose money they dispose of, and whose service they profess to have at heart. No people, we verily believe, having the interests of their fellow-creatures in their hands, are generally more callous, more confident in their official station, more scornful of valuable counsel, and less amenable to ministerial or legal responsibility, than the great majority of these elective bodies. We fear, indeed, that there are very few cases in which the constituencies take a sufficiently active interest as vacancies occur, — unless when some accident surrounds the election with a partisan or a personal excitement. There is accordingly, little scrutiny into the character and motives of the individuals, who desire to become members of them; and the whole management of their often very important concerns is apt to fall into the hands of men neither respected by, nor known to, the people — of whom, notwithstanding, they are held to be the representatives. And we think we can explain the efficient cause of this. Even in this country, where public virtue is at a higher point, and where there is a greater willingness than in most others, to make personal sacrifices for the general interest, there is only a certain per-centage of available and really valuable gratuitous service ready to be given by respectable persons to the public. But that limited fund of service has, of late years, been very largely drawn upon, by railway and other joint-stock companies; and, of course, there is a comparatively smaller quantity of it now left for purposes purely municipal. The constituencies, in short, do not generally bestir themselves to look out good men for these offices : and, if they were looked for, they would not now be found in sufficient numbers — for purely gratuitous services.

It must be remembered, at the same time, that local powers do not now rise into existence as they probably did of old, by purely local and spontaneous movements. All new authorities, whether representative or administrative, are, in these days, brought into existence only by the national legislature. The local boards of health in England are created through the intermediate agency of a responsible administrative power created by the same national legislature; and are, wherever they supersede the operation of local acts, subject to the sanction of Parliament, applied by a public general statute. Now the only question of public interest obviously is, whether the system pursued in passing local statutes, or that under which these local boards are erected through the ministerial intervention of the General Board of Health, is best calculated to promote the interest and the wishes of the local constituencies, and most likely to subject the persons who tax their fellow-citizens and spend their money, to a real responsibility ? Until a very late period local acts, — conferring great powers on individuals, interfering with property, sanctioning taxation, and involving, in almost every shape and shade, the most important public interests, were passed without any inquiry being made beyond the precincts of St. Stephen's ; and we believe that the present system, under which such acts are preceded by local investigation, is an improvement for which the public are indebted to the chief promoter of the Public Health Act. Certain notices, indeed, were appointed to be given in assigned newspapers but they were generally expressed in technical terms intelligible only to legal practitioners, who often founded a valuable interest in supporting or in opposing the measures so announced. Plans were also deposited in certain places; but they were rarely seen by the bulk of the population, or examined by any one, except the attornies who sought out good cases for opposition or claims of compensation. The bulk of the population, in short, seldom knew any thing about the local act, until they were assessed to pay high rates for defective works and for legal expenses, — to an amount often as great as the cost of the works themselves. The parliamentary costs of a water bill for Liverpool amounted to 20,000*l.*, — a sum that it is said would have paid for the effectual drainage of nine thousand of the worst-conditioned houses in that city. In the much smaller town of Dundee, 30,000*l.* were expended in a parliamentary battle between the projectors of a general system of supplying water to the community, and the proprietors of some wells who objected to being taxed for the convenience and health of the public : And we believe the opposition was so truly formidable, that after an act embodying something like a compromise between the contending parties had been passed, the profession of a water-vender was still a common one in the streets of that crowded, filthy, and unhealthy town.

Now, in the machinery by which the Board of Health brings local boards into existence, there is a far fuller security for all parties being heard and made acquainted with the objects in view. The inquiry is conducted in the town itself. Due notice is given, and the inspector attends and takes evidence publicly. He is not unfrequently examined and cross-examined by those who are to be the ratepayers ; who may possibly, from old experience of high rates and worthless services, have doubts and jealousies to be appeased. When the inspector has made his own local examination, he submits his report to the General Board, who direct its local publication in such a manner that all who are interested may have access to it, — and indeed the local editors generally find it worth their while to reprint and publish it in a cheap form. In the report the changes proposed to be made are distinctly set forth ; and notice is given that during a month suggestions or objections will be received. If any matter of fact is challenged, or any point left obscure, another examination is made ; and generally all local doubt or opposition is silenced before the measure, embodied in a provisional order, is finally submitted by the Board to Parliament. The expense of these operations is, we believe, usually not more than one fifth of the average expense of an unopposed local statute — such as those numerous police acts, which display every variety of local prejudice and legislative blunder. The system has as many advantages over the old one, as uniformity, skill, and anxious attention have over legal complexity and diversity, carelessness and selfishness. The remark on the state of unrevolutionised France, that the traveller changed laws as often as he changed horses, was becoming oppressively applicable in this country ; where every town was obtaining its separate police act, — each as unlike its neighbours as jealousy and divergency of tastes could make it, — each large enough to form a national code, and each profusely scattering penalties around it, among a public notoriously ignorant whether they were obeying its injunctions or neglecting them.

It is therefore precisely in the system ignorantly called irresponsible centralisation, that we see the country's security for a real and vital responsibility, diffusing itself through the whole system—both central and local. Without doubt a general board, not immediately responsible to Parliament, would exercise a power little under the influence of public opinion, and too apt to be abused. But *local* irresponsible boards would be liable to the same objection. If they are an object of really great interest to the people, and create party-divisions and competition, the minority is ruthlessly trampled down by the majority. But more commonly the public apathy leaves the management of the whole in the hands of a few self-interested men, who have their own reasons for seeking office and managing the public business. Inquiries into misconduct, and attempts to eradicate fixed abuses, have ever been in such cases hard, tedious, and depressing tasks. But when at the head of the whole department there is, as in the present instance, a cabinet minister, liable to be questioned in Parliament, the responsibility to the country is complete and instantaneous. Let a single damaging case be made out,—let even papers be moved for which there is reluctance to give, or a question be asked that is awkwardly answered,—the whole system quivers with alarm, and the charge passes through to its destination, though originating in the humblest department of a local board, like an electric shock. Thus the General Board, if it be a centre of power, is also a centre—and a very sensitive centre—of responsibility. But we must always remember that its proper functions are, not the practical enforcement of sanitary rules, but the creation and embodiment of the local boards, and the imparting to them assistance and advice in the performance of their duties. If an individual, or a parochial board, should have made any great discovery in practical sanitary arrangements, it would be a toilsome task to persuade every local body of its efficacy. But as responsibility is ramified from the centre, so is light and knowledge. Ere the Cholera had approached our shores, the Board of Health, after tracing with sedulous vigilance its footsteps through every part of the world, and concentrating all that had been seen and known regarding it by the most skilful and sagacious men in all countries, were able to devise precautionary arrangements having the effect of arresting the progress of the pestilence. In the face both of the great experience and of the skilful deduction from that experience which were thus put before the public, and of which other European nations are now gladly taking advantage, many corporate bodies, in their self-conceit, chose to adopt totally different views, and to let the people die in thousands. They showed in this what was to have been hoped for from their unaided local efforts; but it was one of the advantages of the new system that their conduct has been exposed, and recorded as a warning for the future. Indeed, the thousand ways in which a body of competent and able men, with the great resources of the science of the nation at their dis-

posal, may impart knowledge, both of the existence of evils and
of their probable remedies, cannot well be estimated or even
conjectured. The sanitary condition of the mercantile navy —
a subject in which the British public might well be supposed to
take an interest — has been for the first time announced to the
public by the Board of Health. It has been shown by them
that many of our ships are moveable cellars, — as ripe fever-
nests as any of the Liverpool cellars, — and as urgently standing in need of amendment.

Another great service likely to be performed by such a Board
is at the same time the source of animosity towards it. On the
matter of sanitary reform, the interests of individuals and of
classes will often be at variance with those of the public, which
it will be the duty of the Board to protect. With attornies
seeking popularity and business, — with dethroned local
authorities, — and especially with owners of small and unwholesome houses, whose profits are enlarged by the degradation
of the people, — whoever seeks to enforce a Public Health Act
must lay his account with waging incessant war. The Board of
Health have, in their General Report, thus announced their
views and intentions on this matter : —

' Considering the provisions made for the satisfaction of the ratepayers with the application of the act, we should hesitate to recommend the enforcement of its provisions against the general and
deliberate wishes of the inhabitants of any town, when the intended
measures were placed fully and fairly before them. But in the face
of proved facts of preventible evils under which the great bulk of the
population of a town may be suffering, we should be cautious in
accepting as the real expression of opinion, declarations against
remedies, unless under scrutinies and precautions, such as experience
has suggested in relation to the guises assumed by such interests as
those above indicated.* We should not accept as expositions of the
aversion of " the people," or of the unwillingness of the town, declarations which we know to be got up on ignorant or false representations
by the owners of the worst conditioned tenements, in respect to which
it may be requisite to adopt compulsory measures, or by local functionaries whose powers it may be necessary to supersede ; or by one
local party in the mere spirit of opposition against the measure which
may happen to have been initiated by persons belonging to another,
or to no local party whatsoever.' (P. 67.)

It is painful to think that it is among those middle classes
where we otherwise find the best citizens of the State, that
opposition to sanitary reform has chiefly shown itself, and is
likely to continue. But we do not hesitate to say that their

---

* Viz., those of small house proprietors, who get themselves represented in the elected managing bodies, to suit their own interests.

228

opposition to it is generally as selfish as it is barbarous. There is unfortunately a sensitiveness against meddling with the *abuses* as well as the *uses* of property in this country, which seems to drive the comfortable classes frantic when anything can be called or made to appear an infringement on absolute and sometimes offensive rights, — and then compassion, justice, and the still small voice of reason will appeal to it, as to other frenzies, in vain. But let the middle classes be cautious, and be at the trouble to understand the question. If they now run their eye over society from its summit to its base, they will see that the one great remaining and most dangerous gap is where the middle class ends and the working class begins. It were well that this gap, like the others that have been but are no more, should be filled up, or smoothed over; and that can only be done when the humblest classes shall have shaken off a portion of the debasement which now hangs about them: Or the wealth which is retained through a selfish refusal to co-operate in this good cause, may in the end be found not so secure, as all who love the advancement of civilisation, as well as the security of property, must ever wish to see it.

ART. III.—1. *First and Second Reports of the Commissioners
for enquiring into the State of Large Towns and Populous
Districts.* London: 1844 and 1845.

2. *First, Second, and Third Reports of the Metropolitan Sanitary
Commission.* London: 1847 and 1848.

3. *Historical and Statistical Account of the Present System
of supplying the Metropolis with Water.* By JOSEPH
FLETCHER, Esq. Journal of the Statistical Society of
London. June, 1845.

4. *Supply of Water to London from the River Thames at
Henley.* London: 1849.

OLD STOW has preserved a tract written in the reign of
Henry II., by Fitz-Stephen, Thomas a Beckett's secretary,
in which he gives an account of London at that time, and thus
affords us the means of comparing ourselves with our ancestors.
As a point worthy of notice, he records that ' the only plagues of
' London are immoderate drinking of idle fellows, and often fires.'
This statement we fear is as true now as it was then. He
further asserts, with a gallantry worthy of his Norman blood, that
the city dames were very Sabines in chastity; ' Urbis matronæ
'ipsæ Sabinæ sunt.' Though not Normans, and speaking from
our own limited personal knowledge, we will be bold to declare
that this statement also is as true now as it was then. But
when he goes on to say ' there are also about London, on the
'north of the suburbs, choice fountains of water, sweet, whole-
'some, and clear, streaming forth among the glistening pebble
'stones,' our hearts fail us, and we have no courage to pursue
the comparison any farther. It may, however, not be altogether
useless, if we place before our readers a sketch of the actual
condition of London in respect of its supply of water, tracing
the measures which have brought it into its present difficulty,
and indicating the direction in which the remedy lies.

In the time of the Conqueror, says Stow, 'This city of Lon-
'don was watered (besides the famous river of Thames on the
'south part) with the River of Wells, as it was then called, on
'the west—with a water called Wallbrook running through the
'midst of the city, severing the heart thereof.' Then they had

Holy Well, Clement's Well, and Clerke's Well *, besides the
' Horse poole' in Smithfield ' sometime a great water,' and
another near the parish church of St. Giles's without Cripple-
gate.   Langbourne Water was a ' great stream' breaking out
of the ground in Fenchurch Street, and running down Lombard
Street to the Thames.   There were also private wells; 'and
' after this manner was the city then served with sweet and fresh
' water.'

But in process of time, ' the number of citizens being mightily
' increased, they were forced to seek sweet water abroad;' and
having turned their eyes to the remote district of Tyburn, one
Gilbert Sanford, at the personal request of King Henry III.,
granted permission to the citizens to take water from thence in
leaden pipes, for the supply of ' the great conduit in West
' Cheap builded in the year 1285.'   In 1438, the Corporation,
under the same pressure, went to Highbury; next year to the
Abbot of Westminster's springs at Paddington, and even to
Hackney and Islington.   In the next century, about 1568,
having exhausted all the supplies within their reach, they
raised water by machinery from the Thames to a conduit on
Dowgate hill.   We recommend to the consideration of the
Lord Mayor and Corporation of London the way in which
their predecessors attended to the supply of water to the city.

' On the 18th September, 1562, the Lord Mayor (Harper),
' aldermen, and many worshipful persons, and divers of the
' masters and wardens of the twelve companies, rid to the Con-
' duit Heads for to see them, after the old custom ; and afore
' dinner they hunted the hare, and killed her, and thence to
' dinner at the head of the Conduit.   And after dinner they
' went to hunting the fox: there was a great cry for a mile,
' and at length the hounds killed him at the end of St. Giles's.
' Great hallowing at his death, and blowing of hornes; and
' thence the Lord Mayor, with all his company, rode through
' London to his place in Lombard Street.'

In 1582, Peter Morrice, a Dutchman, raised water by a
wheel from the Thames at London Bridge, and conveyed it by

---

* St. Clement's Well was close to Clement's Inn.   Clerke's Well,
or Clerkenwell, was near Clerkenwell Church.   The church was
named from the well, and the well took its name from the parish
clerks in London ; ' who, of old time, were accustomed there yearly
' to assemble, and to play some large history of Holy Scripture.'   In
1409 these much-enduring men played, at the Skinner's Well, a play
which *lasted eight days:* and no wonder, for ' *it was of matter from*
' *the Creation of the World!*'   A large history, indeed.

small pipes to the houses — the greatest improvement in the distribution of water that had yet been made. In the beginning of the seventeenth century, the city of London formed the really creditable project of bringing water to London from the Chadwell and Amwell springs, twenty-one miles off in Hertfordshire. Their conceptions had however exceeded their energy, and the scheme would have failed, at all events for a time, but for the accidental union in one man of three conditions which command success. Sir Hugh Middleton, a citizen of London and a goldsmith (a trade in those days almost invariably connected with money dealing and financial operations), had been engaged in extensive mining transactions in Wales. In these occupations he had realised an immense fortune, and had acquired an unusual amount of practical engineering knowledge ; to which qualifications he added the rarer one of invincible resolution. Wealth, skill, and determination form in combination a power which accomplishes apparent impossibilities. He offered singly to bear the burden which was too heavy for the city of London, and successfully achieved what he had so boldly undertaken. On the 29th of September, 1613, the New River flowed into the town. At first it appeared that the Corporation had made a good bargain : for thirty years the dividends were not more than 5*l.* per share; Sir Hugh, who had embarked his whole fortune in the scheme, sold his shares and died, comparatively speaking, a poor man. King Charles inherited from King James half the stock of the Company, and sold it for 500*l.* a year. But the practical monopoly of supplying a growing city with one of the primary necessities of life must sooner or later be profitable, and the dividends have gradually risen from 5*l.* to 617*l.* per share. Such are the results to an individual of undertaking a speculation offering a prospective rather than an immediate profit, and to a city of sacrificing the future to the present, and permitting the privilege of supplying its inhabitants with water to pass into the hands of a trading company.

The example set by the Corporation was gradually followed, and water companies appeared in the other districts. On the south of the Thames, the Southwark Company was established about the middle of the last century, the Lambeth Company in 1785, and the Vauxhall Company in 1805. On the north bank, the New River Company, the Chelsea Company (formed in 1703), and some smaller companies, supplied the whole of the town up to 1810; but then the East London, West Middlesex, and Grand Junction Companies sprang up ; and, after a desperate competition, the larger companies absorbed the smaller, and partitioned out the metropolis among themselves.

One half of the population of London, who live to the east of a line drawn from Charing Cross, by Tottenham Court Road, to the Hampstead Road, are supplied from the small Chadwell spring in Hertfordshire, and from the river Lea, with water which, though unfiltered, has deposited much of its sediment in settling reservoirs. The rest of London is 'supplied from the Thames at various points between Waterloo Bridge and Kew Bridge at Brentford; the river being ponded back by the tide as far as Teddington Lock, nineteen miles above London Bridge, and the tide itself flowing back above the highest point whence any of the companies draw water. The West Middlesex and the Lambeth Companies give the unfiltered water of the Thames,—the others filter it more or less perfectly.

Of the two great uses of water, drinking and cleanliness, the latter is nearly as important as the former, and requires a vastly greater quantity : and as, in a town, whatever is to be removed from a house must also be carried beyond the limits of the town, the difficulty increases as the town increases. The expense of doing this by labour is so great, that, practically, in a large town, almost all that is not removed by some cheap process is not removed at all. The cheapest mode of removing matter is by suspending it in solution in a moving current ; and it has been happily provided that the greater part of the refuse and filth of a town answers to the required condition, and may be mechanically suspended in water. No town, therefore, can be considered properly supplied with water unless the quality is wholesome, the quantity sufficient to sweep away all impurities beyond its utmost limit, and the mode of distribution such that no individual is left out; for though people will go to water to quench their thirst, water must be brought to them, or they will neglect cleanliness.

It is now our business to show how far these results have been obtained in London, where water has been for more than two centuries an article of trade. And, first, as to quality. The eastern half of London is supplied from the river Lea, with some assistance from the Chadwell spring. Passing over the objectionable character of the open channel of the New River, we would ask our readers to inspect, on any large map, the district of which the Lea receives the immediate drainage. It is one of the most populous in all England. The town of Tottenham alone contains 9000 inhabitants. It is the line of the great north road ; and, for twenty miles, the chain of towns and villages is almost unbroken. The Lea was so palpably objectionable, that it was only resorted to, out of necessity, when the Hertfordshire springs had failed. Moreover, it is becoming worse every day, from the rapid increase of the population on its banks; indeed, only one source of supply worse than itself could be found, and *that* has been selected by the other companies. The rest of London, as we have said, is supplied by them from the Thames within the tideway. The real meaning of such a statement is this. The refuse and dirt from two millions of individuals, — the enormous accumulation of waste and dead animal and vegetable matter, — the blood and offal of slaughter-houses, — the outpourings from gas-works, dye-works, breweries, distilleries, glue-works, bone-works, tanneries, chemical and other works, — and a thousand nameless pollutions, — all find their way into the Thames. The mixture is next washed backwards and forwards by the tide; and, having been thoroughly stirred up and finely comminuted by the unceasing splash of 298 steamboats, is then pumped up for the use of the wealthiest city in the world!

Twenty years ago, a Royal Commission reported that the Thames, when free from extraneous matter, may fairly be called pure; but, ' as it approaches the metropolis, it becomes loaded ' with a quantity of filth which renders it disgusting to the senses, ' and improper to be employed in the preparation of food.' They expressed, in gentle phrase, their opinion, that this water ' can- ' not, even when clarified by filtration, be pronounced entirely ' free from the suspicion of general insalubrity.' We should think not, indeed; for filtration only removes the mechanical, leaving unaffected the mineral, vegetable, and animal impurities. They also thought that ' there were no grounds for ' assuming the probability of any improvement in the state of ' the water drawn from the London district;' more especially as it had been considerably deteriorated within the ten years previous. We heartily concur in this also; and, so far from dreaming of improvement, we conceive we have something very like a mathematical demonstration that what was bad then is abominable now, and will be intolerable ten years hence. It was said that fish had deserted the London waters; and that even Dutch eels, when placed in it, gave up their miserable lives. We believe this was an exaggeration; at least, when on a visit to a friend who has the happiness of residing in the dominions of the Grand Junction Company, we ourselves found a very lively shrimp in our water bottle. But when we read that there are 141 public sewers between London and Battersea bridges, — that Richmond, Isleworth, Brentford, Mortlake, Chiswick, and Hammersmith furnish 68 more, — and that the whole of their contents are received into the Thames, and returned by the reflux of the tide, — we perceive a state of things which renders exaggeration truly superfluous.

Bad as this water is, it is made very much worse by an arrangement which is in operation all over London, and is the direct result of the principle of trade. To avoid what, in the language of the water companies, is called *wasting* water, — though it is a strange term for washing away filth, — the supply is *intermittent*, necessitating the use of cisterns. The rich use large leaden tanks; the rest of the inhabitants — that is, nine tenths of the whole population — use the best substitute they can afford to purchase, from a wine pipe holding 130 gallons, down to a butter tub which costs a shilling. All the water brought to London is full of organic matter, and, therefore, always ready to reproduce vegetable or animal life. Any one may convince himself of this by letting water stand in his water bottle for a few days, when he will find the bottom of the bottle beginning to show a covering of vegetation. Generally, however, this experiment is carried on in the tank, out of sight. The process of vegetation is invariably accompanied by the breeding of insects. Professor Clark says, that animalcules abound in the waters of all the London companies. Once, out of curiosity, he counted the number of insects visible to the naked eye in a gallon, and found them to be 450. The real number was, he says, of course much greater. The specimen did not strike an eye accustomed to the London waters as at all unusual; and the Professor, prudently enough, ' made no ob-' servations as to the smaller creatures visible only by the micro-' scope.' But if such is the condition of water taken from the cistern of a gentleman's house, what is likely to be that from the half-rotten, dirty, uncovered butts and tubs of the poorer classes, — carpeted with a layer of soot, dust, and dirt, — into which insects scramble, and at the bottom of which swallows, young birds, rats, and cats are not unfrequently found?

But whatever may be the evils arising from impurity in the quality, those caused by a deficiency in quantity, and an intermittent distribution, are infinitely more deplorable. We are not now speaking of the houses of the rich, where, by large tanks and scientific appliances, much that is offensive to the senses may be removed; but of the houses where the millions live, — men whose wages vary from twelve to eighteen shillings a week, and whose lot chains them to particular localities. The first cost of laying pipes to inferior tenements is something: the water company, true to the commercial principle, throws the burden and risk on the landlord; the landlord, who lives in a good house elsewhere, throws it on the tenant; the tenant, being only a tenant, of course refuses to expend money for the benefit of the landlord, and water is not laid on. Closets require cisterns raised six feet from the ground; but these then become subject to an extra charge for ' high service,' and so the whole apparatus is dispensed with. Though without a system of drains a large supply of water is rather injurious than otherwise, yet without a plentiful supply there can be no drainage at all; and therefore, when water is not brought to these houses, refuse of all descriptions remains unremoved, accumulating in and around the houses, in the courts, in back yards, in cellars, and in cesspools. The most vivid imagination cannot adequately conceive the consequences of this; and if we were to transcribe the evidence which has been collected upon this branch of the subject, our readers would turn from the page with loathing. Little do the rich know of the state of their poorer neighbours, or of the masses of filth and misery from which they are separated only by a party wall. Behind some of the best streets in London scenes may be witnessed at which humanity shudders.

In populous districts it is common for eighteen or twenty houses to be built round a court: at one end is a water-cock, the water being turned on three times a week, and sometimes for half an hour on Sundays also. Those who can then attend fill a bucket or butter tub, and carry it to their rooms; those who, from any cause, cannot attend at the proper moment, go without water for the next two days.

Sometimes the cock is out of order, or the landlord has fallen into arrear with the water rent and the supply been in consequence cut off, and twenty families are deprived of all means of cleanliness. The husbands being away at their work, the wives must fetch the water, and they are often physically unable to carry it up stairs; — thence comes *economy* of water; and what that implies Dr. Toynbee tells us. Water, already filthy from having been used to wash clothes, is used over and over again for the same purpose : children are left dirty, greens are put into the pot without being washed, and the smallest possible quantity is used in cooking. Having to attend three children ill with scrofulous affections of the eyes and throat, he found them all rarely washed and in an extremely filthy condition, because the mother, once in respectable circumstances, was so far advanced in pregnancy as to be unable to go up and down stairs. Often, after dressing a patient, he could get no water in the room, sometimes not in the house. What were called clean towels were so offensive from having been washed in dirty water as to be unfit for use. He continually visited houses where the smell was unbearable, but the windows were never opened on account of the still more pestilential effluvium without. Within a district supplied by the New River Company, in the court and yards outside the houses was a mass of putrid, fermenting filth, and the subsoil was saturated with offensive matter till it could take up no more. In such a locality, the houses, the inmates, and everything around them became unavoidably 'horribly filthy.'

There is a most fatal and certain connexion between physical uncleanliness and moral pollution: the condition of a population becomes invariably assimilated to that of their habitations. There can be no sight more painful than that of a healthy, rosy, active countrywoman brought to one of these dwellings. For a time there is a desperate exertion to keep the place clean; several times in the forenoon is the pavement in the front of the house washed, but as often does the oozing filth creep along the stones, and she feels at length that her labour is in vain. The noxious exhalations infuse their poison into her system, and her energies droop. Then she becomes sick, or the supply has been cut off, or she has missed her turn, or her little store of water has been upset or stolen, and, cleanliness becoming impossible, she gets accustomed to its absence, and gradually sinks into the ways of her neighbours. The art of concealing dirt is substituted for the habit of cleanliness; she becomes a dirty, debilitated slattern, followed by sickly, scrofulous, feverish children; and she falls through successive stages of degradation, till, physical wretchedness having done its worst, she reaches the lowest of all, that in which she has ceased to complain. The fate of the children is, if possible, more heart-breaking. All idea of sobriety, all notion of self-respect, all sense of modesty, all instinct of decency is nipped in the bud: they congregate in masses, and mix with the worst vagrants. At last some dreadful fever forces on the notice of the public the existence of their squalid dens of misery; such as those in the Saffron Hill district, — where twenty-five people were found living in a room sixteen feet square,—where a man and his wife and four children, occupying one room, took in seven lodgers, — and where one house contained a hundred and twenty-six people, and only six or seven beds. These people save nothing, but invariably spend all they earn in drink; and with that precocious depravity too surely evinced by human beings when herded together like beasts, the young of both sexes live together from the ages of twelve and thirteen years.

It is right that these things should be made known — it is well that they should be considered. We have commission after commission to inquire — we have one pestilence after

another to warn us that the destroying angel is at hand: we
wait for twenty years, weighing in a balance the interests of
water companies, the contingent losses of millers, the hardness
of water from a well, and the impurity of water from the river;
and in the meantime tens of thousands of our citizens are
dragged down morally and socially by all manner of filth and
wretchedness, and hurried through a degraded and miserable
existence to an untimely end.   While our discussions go on,
they are dropping into their graves.   The worst water in the
Thames would be an unspeakable blessing to the denizens of
Red Lion Court.   We fill our gaols with felons, and we have
City Missions, and put our trust in education; but the influences
of filth are stronger than the policeman, the schoolmaster, and
the preacher; and we ought, by this time, to have learned that
the very foundation of moral training in a London tenement is a
pipe of wholesome water from the top to the bottom of the house.

But then the cost of an altered system!   Few will ask that
question who have steadily contemplated the cost of the present
system.   We would entreat our readers just to glance at the
evidence of Dr. Southwood Smith, physician to the London
Fever Hospital, and of Mr. Toynbee, surgeon of the St. George's
and St. James's Dispensary, and visitor for the Westminster
General Dispensary.

Fever is beyond all comparison the disease of adult life, and,
more than any other, depends upon causes within our own control: at least those forms of it, which arise from the decomposition of animal and vegetable matter.   A short period is merci-
fully given to us before putrefaction begins, within which we may
remove the evil; but when that period has expired, poisonous
gases are generated, and the seed of fever sown.   In many places
in London, on account of the want of water and proper drains,
this removal is not at all, and in others very tardily, effected:
we have therefore localities from which fever is never absent, —
these are the centres whence sickness is always emanating, —
the ever-burning matches by which the flames of disease are
re-lighted.   And the social and moral evils of fever, its pauper-
ising effects, and prodigious expense, whether in a public or
private view, are not easily described: for much as we are
alarmed by cholera, the returns show that in any one year fever
kills as many as cholera.

The rate of mortality in the east of London is double that in
the west.   To persons accustomed to the study of medical
statistics, this simple statement would be sufficient; they would
at once see the depth of misery which it indicates.   But to
others we must place it in a more familiar light.   Out of every

two persons who die in the east of London, one perishes from preventible causes. From twenty to thirty thousand of the labouring population of London are killed every year by causes which, if we chose, we might expel by a current of water. Though we do not take these persons out of their houses and murder them, we do the same thing in effect,—we neglect them in their poisonous homes, and leave them there to a lingering but a certain death.

The peculiar evil of fever is, that it seizes upon the labouring classes especially, and at the most valuable period of their existence. Those attacked between the ages of 20 and 30 years are equal in number to those attacked at all other ages put together. At that time of life the working classes are generally married, and have children to support; so that not only heads of families are most liable to this malady, but are most liable at that precise period of life when they have a young family entirely dependent upon their exertions. Females, too, seem to be more susceptible of this disease, perhaps are more constantly exposed to its causes, than males; and when smitten by it, they can neither nurse their children, nor attend to any one of those duties, which unless a working man's wife personally discharges, the house becomes a scene of disorder and distress.

The indirect effects of sickness are, moreover, far more hurtful, though less observable, than the direct effects of mortal disease. Those who merely suffer from fever are about twelve times as many as those who perish. The poison arising from animal or vegetable decomposition acts as a sedative; it lowers the tone, unstrings the nerves, and brings on physical languor and mental apathy. Persons affected by it become unfit for, and have a hatred of, labour. There is no expedient they will not seek in order to escape from toil. Under this depression, and as a relief from a peculiar inward *sinking* feeling, they have a craving for the stimulus of ardent spirits to an extent inconceivable by persons in happier circumstances; it amounts to a passion, and these debilitated beings, are unable to control it. The same poison, by deranging and weakening the digestive organs, produces complaints of a scrofulous and consumptive character, generally accompanied by a feverish and nervous irritability, constantly urging them to the unrestrained gratification of their appetites; and so the process of degradation goes forward. The effort to struggle against the surrounding mass of filth and wretchedness, is given up in sheer hopelessness, and the man's best energies are sapped by the irresistible poison, even while he is endeavouring to resist its influence. The class of workmen that in other places drink nothing but water, in London drink anything but water, so bad is it. The labourer comes home tired, and is glad to escape from the dirt and discomfort — the poisonous atmosphere of his home — to a pothouse.   In the morning there is no water to make him a cup of coffee, — again he is driven to the beer-shop; overpowered by the internal craving and external temptations, he inevitably becomes a drunkard, and, in time, unequal to hard work.   Soon the comforts of life are gone; then its decencies are neglected; the moral feelings, one after the other, are broken down before the most sordid appetites, alike ungovernable and insatiable: he is crushed by drunkenness, profligacy, and poverty, and sinks from one stage of vice and misery to another, till the intellectual faculties become dimmed, all moral and religious feeling expires, the domestic affections are destroyed, all regard for law or property is lost, and hope is quenched in desperate wretchedness: so that at last, owing to these withering causes, families have been found, even in London, huddling together like animals, the very instincts of humanity obliterated, and, like the brutes, relieving every want, and gratifying every passion in the full view of the community.

These are the reasons why the districts of filth are not only the districts of fever, scrofula, consumption, and cholera, but also of crime.   Habits are early formed of idleness and dishonesty — of brutality, inexpressible profligacy, and sensual indulgence; and here are educated those irreclaimable malefactors, the constitution of whose minds is a constant grief and, indeed, enigma.   Their wickedness we are prepared for, but we are not prepared for their callous insensibility to all the ordinary motives which influence human beings, for their unaccountable and uncontrollable irritability, for their recklessness akin to that of a wild beast, and for that distorted intellectual acuteness resembling more the dull cunning of a madman than the reason of a man.

The numerous deaths of an unhealthy district have a bad moral effect.   They harden the heart.   The expense, trouble, and anxiety arising from a sickly family often make the wretched parents regard their offspring as a burden, and their death as a happy release from a miserable existence.   But it is not with impunity that the natural affections are destroyed.   The transition from this state of mind to that which looks upon children's burial clubs as a source of profit, is too often found an easy one.

It has been said that an excessive rate of mortality is one of the appointed means by which evils work out their own cure, and an over-numerous population is thinned.   With a Christian philanthropist this argument, even if true, would have no weight. But it is more to our present purpose to remark that it has no foundation in fact.   An extreme mortality, caused by the morbific influences arising from the want of cleanliness, has hardly any effect in decreasing the numbers of the population; it only renders them weak and wretched. The worse their condition, the earlier they marry. These influences do not diminish fecundity; there is reason to suspect they increase it: and it is beyond a doubt that the greater the mortality among children, the more numerous are the births. Grown-up men and women are replaced by the more youthful; and this rapid substitution of the young and helpless for adults is doubly injurious: it diminishes the productive power of the country, while it accelerates the increase of the population. It entails a frightful expenditure, besides being a social calamity, and, as far as it is preventible, a national sin.

The expense of doctors' bills to the poor is far greater than is supposed. Many a workman receiving 20*s.* a-week pays, not only proportionably, but actually, more for medicine than a gentleman with 1000*l.* a-year. The cases of families brought on the parish by preventible sickness are innumerable. The sickness of a scrofulous child will cost from 4*l.* to 10*l.*; its burial 2*l.* to 4*l.* A confinement costs 4*l.* or 5*l.*; and numerous as these are, the miscarriages are still more numerous. We had selected, but are compelled to omit, the detailed cases of individuals who, though receiving regular wages of 20*s.* and 25*s.* a-week, became utter paupers solely from the expense of confinements, miscarriages, medicines, and undertakers' bills. Dr. Toynbee visited one hundred families, and found 212 of the members actually suffering from disease; there had been 251 deaths and funerals, and a corresponding amount of sickness; 350 members of these 100 families were dependent children, whose average age was little more than ten years. It is terrible to contemplate the amount of social misery caused, and the expense entailed upon the public, by the removal of *heads* of families from such a community as this. A little saving in sickness would pay a heavy water-rate. The comparison is not the less certain because the actual result cannot be stated in figures. Sickness and pauperism are inseparable, and the parish, in the long run, must pay for the sick labourer's rent, food, clothing, for medical attendance on him during his life, for his funeral at his death, and for the support of his wife and family after he is dead. To give some idea of the money cost of our present system, by which the preventible disease of fever is perpetuated, we may mention that the *extra* expense from *fever cases* in the Bethnal Green and Whitechapel Unions was at the rate of 2467*l.* a year. In 1843 the London Fever Hospital received 500 fever cases in four months, and, during a considerable portion of the time, thirty or forty applications a-day were refused, from want of room. When an inquiry was made by twenty metropolitan unions to ascertain what proportion of those receiving parochial relief were suffering from fever, it was found in the district of St. George's, Southwark, that out of 1467 persons receiving parochial relief, 1276 were ill with fever. After the cholera appeared last summer, Peahen Court, a little court off Bishopsgate Street, had sent to the parish of St. Ethelburga by the 29th of August, one cholera widow and twelve cholera orphans. It was calculated that they would cost the parish 420*l.*, and that the court might have been put in order, and probably all sickness prevented, for 30*l.* But, not to weary our readers, we will only refer to the official statement of the proportion of deaths from cholera in the thirteen weeks ending the 15th Sept. 1849. Since Cholera is in truth a health inspector, who speaks through his interpreter, the Registrar-General, in a language which reaches all ears, and points out with terrible distinctness and unfailing accuracy those districts which are not only occasionally the regions of death, but at all times the nurseries of disease.

PARISHES.	Proportion of Deaths from Cholera to every 10,000 of the Population.
Country District - Hampstead - - -	8
London north of the Thames : ⎰ St. James's, Westminster -	12
Marylebone - - -	15
Holborn - - - -	28
Shoreditch - - -	65
Bethnal Green - - -	75
London south of the Thames : ⎰ Lambeth - - - -	97
St. Saviour - - -	141
St. George - - -	142
St. Olave - - - -	151
Bermondsey - - -	163
Rotherhithe - - -	225

Now compare the extremes, Hampstead and Rotherhithe. At the latter, out of 225 persons, 217 have died from preventible causes ; there are 28 times the number of deaths that there are at Hampstead, 28 times the cases of sickness, 28 times the number and cost of funerals, 28 times the doctors' bills, and 28 times as many widows and helpless children to be supported by somebody. We must also remember that this is not the case of an epidemic scourging one locality and sparing another, but the index of what is going on at all times, and will continue to go on till the end of time, unless, by an abundant supply of water, we wash away the causes of those diseases which are silently but incessantly wasting away the health, the morals, and the wealth of the community.

Eminent physicians declare that the existing amount of sickness and mortality may be reduced one half; and to show that this is no vague exaggeration, we will quote the case of Windmill Court, in Rosemary Lane, described by Mr. Liddle, the medical officer of the Whitechapel union. It was dirty, undrained, and ill-supplied with water: he had to visit it two or three times a day for fever cases, and in seven months attended forty-one new cases of sickness in that one court. It was afterwards flagged, drained, and supplied with water; and Mr. Liddle tells the result. 'In the last four or five months I have ' had but two cases;' and the rents were so much better paid that the landlord was thought to have *profited* by the improvements, which he had executed at his own expense. A current of water had in fact swept away nineteen twentieths of the sickness. This is fullly corroborated by the experience of Harebrain Court, Cooper's Court, and other places. In Nottingham, in 1832, there were 1100 cases of cholera, of which 289 were fatal. After the disease had passed off, the town was supplied with water, and other sanitary measures adopted with such effect that when, in 1849, the cholera appeared a second time, there were only eight cases, of which six were fatal. And it appears that between the healthy and unhealthy districts of that town there is a difference of sixty per cent. in the average duration of human life. So that when we hear complaints of the quality of the water in London, and agree that it would be well to have a jet seventy feet high instead of the dumb waiters in Trafalgar Square, to have a magnificent fountain in the Temple, and cascades in the royal gardens, with abundance of water for cleansing the streets and extinguishing fires, we contend that,— although the water companies should accomplish all this to-morrow — the great and crying evil of the present system would, notwithstanding, be in no way lessened. It is not the convenience of the rich, but the necessities of the poor, that call upon us for instant legislation, under penalties so heavy and responsibilities so awful. The richer classes are in some degree able to protect themselves; but the masses, the millions who live by the sweat of their brow, these men are helpless. Whatever else we do, we do nothing, unless we give them plenty of water for the purposes of cleanliness. This is the main object; and we trust and believe that all

interests which stand as obstacles in the way will be made to
bend or break. To those who watch with admiration, mingled
with awe, the growth of the immense influence of the daily
press, the course generally taken by it on sanitary and economical questions affecting the interests of the poor, is a source of
unfeigned satisfaction and thankfulness, as well as a pledge of
success. It is to the honour and safety of the nation, when
journals like ' The Times' and ' Morning Chronicle,' and ' Daily
' News,' at once the exponents and guides of public opinion, in
their several quarters, take up these questions, and advocate the
cause of the poor with sound good sense and infinite perseverance,
research, and talent.

It may be asked, is this object attainable? Is it *possible* to
obtain anywhere a daily supply of sixty or a hundred millions
of gallons of pure water? The answer involves a consideration
of the topographical and geological position of London.

London is situated upon the lower tertiary or eocene formation; the upper stratum is a tenacious clay, the next is desig-
nated plastic clay, and is composed of argillaceous deposit and
beds of sand; these rest upon the chalk, a formation from 300
to 500 feet in thickness, not lying horizontally, but rising up
all round like the sides of a basin, and coming to the surface at
the Surrey and Chiltern hills. The water which falls upon and
percolates through the edges of the porous chalk, is arrested at
the bottom of the basin by a layer of gault or impermeable clay,
and accumulates there until the whole stratum becomes charged
with water; and the rim of the chalk basin being higher than
the strata which it contains, the water, whenever the opportunity is given by a sufficiently deep well or hole, has a tendency,
from the hydrostatic pressure, to rise through the superin-
cumbent beds to its natural level above the surface of the
ground. The wells are of three classes: the first are shallow,
and furnish an absolutely poisonous water, impregnated with
the leakage from gas pipes, the soakage from cesspools, and the
drainage from graveyards; the second reach the sandy water-
bearing beds of the plastic clay, and generally produce water
full of ferruginous and other impurities, and sometimes contaminated by the deep cesspools; the third class are sunk into
the chalk, and supply clear and good, though hard, water.

It was once imagined that an inexhaustible supply might be
obtained from the wells in the chalk; but that idea is now
exploded, — or nearly so; we make the reservation out of respect
to Mr. Tabberner, — the increased number of deep wells having
already diminished the quantity in the subterraneous reservoir.
Each new well lowers the level of the water in its neighbour: in

one brewer's well the water level has fallen ninety-three feet; Calvert & Co., and Barclay & Co., have restricted themselves to the use of their wells on alternate days; the Artesian wells at Brentford, at the Horticultural Gardens, and at the Bishop of London's gardens at Fulham, no longer overflow; the well constructed by the New River Company, near the New Road, is a failure; at the Pentonville Prison the average water-level has sunk twelve feet in seven years; and on the whole it seems that the water-level in the deep wells of London has been sinking for the last twenty-five years at the rate of two feet per annum. A project was started in 1840, and has been again revived, of obtaining a supply from wells in the chalk district near Watford; but the engineer at that time recommended farther inquiry, and the amount sought to be obtained is totally inadequate to the purposes now under consideration.

We are therefore compelled to turn our minds from water under the surface to the upper or river drainage — that is, to the Thames, or some of its affluents. Objections have been raised against river water, because every river receives a certain amount of urban and agricultural drainage. This is true; but we cannot go to ' the seven wells' at Cheltenham; and at every successive mile of its course the Thames receives some description of drainage. To supply London with perfectly pure water is, apparently, an impossibility. Purity then becomes a question of degree. The first requisite is a very large supply; the second, that it shall be as pure as circumstances will admit. We therefore reject the Lea and the Brent because they receive a very unusual amount of drainage; the Colne for the same reason and on account of its paper mills, which pollute water more than any other manufacture; the Wey on engineering grounds; the Wandle, Verulam, and similar minor tributaries, as being insufficient; and the Thames itself, below Maidenhead, because, emerging from the hills, it there enters into the rich basin of the London clay, and receives the drainage of the innumerable hamlets, villages, and towns which stud its banks. On the other hand the most fastidious have never sought to go beyond Oxford; and thus the discussion has practically been narrowed to one point — whether the supply should come from above or below Reading — from Mapledurham, or from Henley. Those who support the Mapledurham scheme do so on the ground that they avoid the drainage of Reading; the others argue that this objection may be removed, and, at all events, is more than compensated by the accession, below Mapledurham, of water from two tributaries, the Kennet and the Loddon, one fifty-three, the other twenty-four, miles long, — and both of very unusual purity, in consequence of traversing thinly inhabited chalk districts, containing much down land, little cultivated, and chiefly appropriated to sheep farming.   On the Kennet we believe there are only two or three mills by which the quality of the water can be affected.   After heavy showers also, as there is little surface drainage in a chalk district, in which the rain sinks into the ground and is filtered before it breaks out in a stream, the Kennet remains almost as pure as before, while the Thames is *comparatively* turbid, having received a large amount of surface drainage from the Oxford clay.   Whatever be the respective merits of these schemes, it cannot be denied that in this locality the Thames will afford a daily supply of 100,000,000 of gallons of water, sufficiently pure for all the ordinary purposes of life.   Lucretius, in the passage beginning,

> ' pereunt imbres, ubi eos pater æther
> In gremium matris Terræ precipitavit :
> At nitidæ surgunt fruges, ramique virescunt
> Arboribus ;'

describes, in his exquisite language, the showers perishing as they sink into the earth, and yet becoming the origin of the green foliage of the woods, and of the shining produce of the fields, the food of man and of beast.   The rain that descends upon the Wiltshire downs may be made to minister to a higher end, if we compel it to rise again amidst the tenements of the London workmen, and contribute to their health, their happiness, and their morals.

It is of importance, also, to observe that in no direction can London be approached by an aqueduct so easily as from the direction of Maidenhead.   The unexampled facilities afforded by the level valley of the Thames have been taken advantage of for the construction of canals and railways ; and the promoters of the Henley on Thames project assert that, if an aqueduct was carried westward from Paddington, without aiming at any objects but cheapness of construction and a suitable inclination for the current of water, it would strike the Thames at Henley Reach.   Whether this be the case or not, it is clearly desirable that the main reservoir of London should be as high as possible above the town, provided it be not higher than the average level of the ground along which the aqueduct is to pass, and that the water should flow into it by the force of gravitation alone, without requiring to be elevated by mechanical means, or checked in its current by locks.   Should the main reservoir not command the whole of London, it will be cheaper to form an additional reservoir at the required height, and pump water into it, than to bring in the whole quantity at the maximum elevation.

It cannot be disputed that, if we divert perhaps one third of the Thames at Reading in order to pour it through the sewers of London, we shall affect the corn and paper mills on the river. But this water power, once of great consequence, as being the only mechanical power in the vicinity of London, is yet subject to interruption from floods, frosts, and droughts, and is daily falling in value before the steadiness and certainty of steam power; and the cost of substituting steam for water power to every mill between London and Reading would not amount to any sum worth noticing. The preservation of the navigation is more serious. But whatever may be its importance, we do not hesitate to say that it sinks into insignificance before the other interests involved in this question. We are bound to look the difficulty in the face, and to carefully consider every suggestion, which holds out a prospect of removing it; but if no means can be found, perfectly adequate or perfectly unobjectionable, let us not shrink from a decision. On one side is our money, on the other our life; here is our commerce, there is our happiness. Is water given to us primarily to be a medium of traffic, or because it is a necessary of existence? Shall we use the railway and pay a shilling or two per ton extra, or shall we keep to the river and have an extra pestilence every fifteen years? Shall we empty our barges, or shall we fill our churchyards?

But the report of Messrs. Walker and Leach, the engineers of the Thames Navigation Committee, demonstrates that the difficulty is very far from insurmountable. The Thames, in that part of its course, flows in *reaches:* the depth of a river depends not alone upon the volume of water, but on the rapidity of the current, and the inclination of its surface; and the same skill which has carried canals over the most irregular and broken countries may, by locks and dams judiciously placed, not only maintain, but improve the navigation of the Thames, and that, too, without any inordinate expense.

The English, more than any nation of ancient or modern times, have adhered to the rule of carrying on their great undertakings upon the principle of trade, trusting to the boundless energy of private enterprise. Our lighthouses, our national bank, and our Indian empire, show the singular power and flexibility of this principle; but they also show the circumstances in which it fails, and by which the mere trading company is converted virtually into a department of the Government. Whenever a government has attempted to direct commercial enterprise and enter into a fair competition for its rewards, it has failed. On the other hand, whenever competition has been destroyed, and a practical monopoly established, the quickening impulse of the commercial principle seems to die away, and, in one form or other, Government control takes its place. There can be no competition in lighting the seas; and, lighthouses having in fact ceased to be private speculations, the Trinity Board is virtually under the control of the Government. The Bank of England only retains its exclusive privileges because it acknowledges its duties to the public to be paramount even to the interests of its shareholders, and by a judicious deference to the wishes of the Executive. The trade with India has passed into private hands, and the empire which our merchants won is ruled by a responsible minister. Wherever the principle of trade fails or ends in a monopoly, or wherever the discharge of a public duty is superadded to and supersedes the pursuit of private profit, the English people will trust none but a responsible body. A tendency to combination, in order to extinguish competition, is inseparable from that class of enterprises in which the amount of receipts is measured by the requirements of a specific locality, and where a large capital is necessarily sunk irrecoverably in the first instance. Competition between coaches, where the primary outlay is but small, may arise and die, and arise again perpetually; but between water companies, gas companies, or railways, whatever turns the scale at all will turn the whole trade. So that the struggle is for life or death, and no sacrifice is too great to crush a rival utterly. The consequence is, as Mr. Stephenson tersely expressed it, where combination is possible, competition is impossible.

Water companies show as clearly as any other instance the truth of this maxim. There never was a fairer area or greater scope for competition than the city of London, — the largest, the most populous, the most luxurious, and the wealthiest city in the world, and familiarised, by the bent of the national mind, to the encouragement of joint enterprise. Up to the beginning of the present century there was no competition; but when the East London, the West Middlesex, and the Grand Junction Companies arose in 1810, so violent a struggle ensued, that in four years all the companies were on the verge of ruin. In 1815 and 1817 they coalesced and partitioned the metropolis north of the Thames among them: since that date there has been no competition whatsoever; and we are never likely to see it again. The companies south of the Thames were under certain restrictions until 1834; but when these were removed, a competition broke out, which raged in full force from 1839 to 1842, and then died its natural death by combination. This contest stands pre-eminent in ruinous absurdity. There were in some streets three distinct sets of pipes, with separate sets of persons to attend to each. Capricious customers were constantly changing from one to the other, and the pavement was torn up daily. The plumber's bills for removing the pipes from one main to another were of course enormous. So sharp was the practice, that sometimes the pipes were put to the wrong main, and one company sent in the bill for water which its opponent had unconsciously supplied. The Vauxhall Company spent in one street 2400*l.* in pipes, and had in return the barren satisfaction of drawing from the Southwark Company tenants to the extent of 81*l.* The directors abused each other on paper, and the workmen actually fought in the streets. The famous war between Modena and Bologna, on account of the 'rape of 'the bucket,' was renewed in Southwark; and had the imaginative Tassoni lived in our days, he would have called to the inhabitants

> 'Vedrai, s' al cantar mio porgi l'orecchia,
> Elena trasformarsi in una Secchia.'

But no one good, — not even a good poem, as in the tuneful land of Italy, — resulted from this competition. The object of the companies was not to improve the water supply, but to ruin each other; the struggle was to get the custom of the rich, — none of them cared for the poor. The districts which were supposed likely to yield a good return had treble sets of pipes, and their streets perpetually broken up and rendered impassable; while others were left without water for domestic purposes and protection from fire. Water drawn from near Waterloo Bridge was supplied without even being filtered, although the sum annually expended in *useless* plumbing, paving, and canvassing, would have been more than sufficient for all that was wanted. While the companies under this process of mutual attrition were fast grinding their capital away, the sum paid by the public in water rents would have produced a dividend of *ten per cent.* upon the capital really requisite to provide them with an abundant supply of water. On both banks of the Thames, the coalition of the companies was followed by an augmentation of the water rates, beginning with 25 per cent. additional, and an extra charge for high service. The revenue has of course been enlarged in proportion; between 1821 and 1828 it increased, on the north side of the Thames alone, 44,000*l.* a year: in twenty years the total water rents have risen from 162,000*l.* to 370,000*l.* per annum.

Though competition, under these circumstances, does no good

to any one, the risk of competition, however remote, has a real effect in maintaining a costly and inefficient system. True economy in the distribution of water is obtained by a large outlay at first; but the possibility of losing the first outlay altogether, leads trading companies to reverse this principle, to save the first cost which falls upon them, and to swell the current charges which are paid by the public. The laying on of water to a fourth class house in London costs individuals about 4*l.* Neither the water company, the builder, nor the tenant will risk this first outlay, and consequently too often nothing is done; though all agree that if the first expense was borne by a public fund, and repaid with interest by a rate upon the property, the improvement would be readily adopted. Such economy is there in good *primary* general arrangements, that in Nottingham this same sum of 4*l.* per house has been found sufficient for all the outlay necessary to pump water from the Trent, to filter it, to convey it to the town, and to distribute it, at constant high pressure and in unlimited quantity, to every habitation.

The various improvements adopted by the water companies so far from arising from the principle of trade, are due solely to a threat of its being abandoned. The augmentation of rates consequent on the unholy alliance of 1817, produced a storm, which eventually burst in 1821, in the form of a Parliamentary inquiry, and taught the companies the danger of stimulating the public to seek an effectual remedy. Again, in 1828, a cry was raised against the quality of the water. Unhappily, in the conduct of this accusation the amount of truth contained in it was overlaid by great exaggerations; besides which, the Committee to whom the inquiry was entrusted, was not very judiciously handled, and symptoms of jobbing and favouritism appeared. The companies were not slow in availing themselves of the advantages thus placed in their hands: they exposed the errors of their adversaries; they brought up chemists and engineers, whose clear, cool evidence told well against the angry misrepresentations of their accusers. The Committee lost weight, — the Government refused to interfere, — and finally the companies, thankful at having weathered the gale, vowed amendment: some resorted to a purer source of supply, and others promised settling reservoirs and filtering beds. The cholera of 1832 produced in 1834 another Committee, but with no particular result. A scheme proposed by Mr. Telford broke down at once, not without some discredit to the author. Another Committee, in 1840, proved equally useless. While the public was relying on the expression of public opinion, and the effect of competition, the companies had ceased to care for either, knowing that the only real remedy had not yet been thought of. They out-argued their opponents, puzzled the Committee, and left them to waste their time in investigating a variety of empirical projects. The Committee separated without reporting; and with this impotent conclusion ended the last effort at legislative interference, — leaving London in the hands of a water confederation. No man has redress against increased rates ; no man can enforce attention to his complaints ; and no man, we suppose, is rash enough to dream of actual resistance to an antagonist who can ' cut off his water supply.'

We say that the principle of trade is not applicable to the supply of water to the metropolis, not only because it produces an irresponsible practical monopoly, but because it is necessarily inadequate to the purpose. It is admitted that water rents cannot be collected from weekly tenants. For the companies to retail this necessary of life to the very poor, does not *pay;* though it would pay if the first cost was charged on the property, and the interest and current expenses included in the rent paid to the landlord. The companies therefore leave them unsupplied. We do not blame them for this,—it could not, and never will be, otherwise. But the mere fact, that a vast number of houses in London have no water supplied to them, (the Report of the Health of London Association in 1847 puts the number at 70,000 : in the New River district the number of persons unsupplied was stated by the Health of Towns Commissioners to be 300,000,) is a positive proof that this principle does not accomplish what we require.

Mr. Babbage remarked, with great truth, how difficult it was for people to contend with monopolists who have tact enough to make some slight concessions when the public wrath begins to rise above ' the growling point.' Since 1817, the water companies have raised their rates and their dividends, and enormously augmented their revenues, — they have outlived two pestilences, — they have been subjected to four formal inquiries, in two of which the public mind was violently excited, and have come out of the ordeal stronger than before. Against the assaults of internal competition and external interference, they have been triumphantly successful. In this success lies, we think, the germ of their annihilation. On two points the public mind is in the course of being slowly made up; and the conclusion will be maintained all the more firmly, because it is formed against the national instincts. One is, that the principle of trade, applied under the most favourable circumstances, has failed to supply London with water as it ought to be supplied, and has failed most where most required, viz. in the poor and densely populated districts. The other is, that it is in vain to hope for anything better for the future from the companies themselves, through any pressure, legislative or other, which can be brought to bear against them. The conclusion is inevitable,—a different principle must be adopted : if there must be a monopoly, and no doubt there must, let it be placed in the hands of the Government, or some public body responsible to the consumers.

The constitution of such a body deserves careful consideration. Its duties must extend to the drains of London. It is not at first an unnatural idea that the supply of water *to* a house and its removal *from* it, are such different services that they might be entrusted to different functionaries. But the mains and the sewers are merely vehicles for the moving power of the water, and all three are parts of one system and require the nicest adjustment to each other. Besides, the house drainage is considered to be three times as important as the sewer or street drainage, and is inseparably connected with the distribution of water—so that a line cannot be drawn anywhere with advantage; for whoever is answerable for the main sewers ought to have jurisdiction over the house drains, the pipes communicating with the mains, and the mains themselves up to the reservoir. If a distinction must be made somewhere, it ought to be at the discharging orifice of the reservoir ; but we would prefer to concentrate responsibility on a single body, and that when complaints are made, the public should not be shuffled from one Board to another, — from those who distribute the water to those who merely convey it to London.

It would appear that as the funds for these purposes will be provided by the rate-payers, and the services of the Board chiefly devoted to supplying the wants of rate-payers, so the nomination of its members should proceed from them also. But we dread a Board whose members should have owed their election to their political bias or to their activity in canvassing ; and when we see the working of parochial elections, and how often private interest and political combinations interfere with the public benefit, and how slight is the real responsibility of the elected, we believe that the great body of rate-payers, who after all would probably take no share in the choice, would be better pleased to devolve the responsibility of selection upon the Government. But it is a question for the inhabitants of London to decide : our only desire is to have a body with elevated views and amenable to public opinion.

We must say a few words as to expense ; and we purposely avoid estimates, because there are broad facts stronger than any

estimates. The water rents paid in London amount to 370,000*l.*
a year, and allowing 44 per cent. for current expenses, we have
a net revenue of 200,000*l.* a year, which would raise and finally
extinguish an outlay of 4,000,000*l.* The citizens defray also
the expense of communication pipes, cisterns, &c. equal, as the
engineers tell us, to the whole capital of the water companies;
that is to say, as much capital is expended by the inhabitants
in bringing water on the intermittent principle from the street
to the house, as by the water companies in bringing it from the
river to the street. We will, however, not call this more than
one million. The repairs of these pipes are very expensive,
two thirds of the labour being actually consumed in *useless*
journeys, besides the waste from inexperienced workmen and
bad work. Mr. Hawksley says that one half of this expense
would be saved by the system of constant supply; and that in
Nottingham, on the principle of constant pressure, one man and
a boy can attend to 8000 houses, and keep all the works of distribution in perfect repair. Then there is the cost of removal
of filth calculated at 20*s.* per house annually, and London
contains 300,000 houses; so that the sum actually paid away
every year in London represents a capital of at least *seven
millions;* and this, without charging anything for fire insurance
and sickness, the expense of which latter item should be
reckoned in millions rather than thousands.

When we come to compare one city with another, we see at
once that the cost per house of distribution will be greater in a
large city than in a small one, but the first cost of an aqueduct
will be smaller. There is no city in the world on which the cost
of an aqueduct would fall so lightly as on London, in consequence of its immense size and its position in a level valley.
Taking the scale of outlay for all purposes, from the experience
of Nottingham, 4*l.* a house, it will give 1,200,000*l.* If we make
full allowance and double that sum, we shall still only reach
an amount represented by one third of our present annual
expenditure. With the example of a small town such as
Greenock or Nottingham, of larger towns such as Glasgow and
New York, and with such a wide margin for error, we want no
nice estimates to add force to our assertion, that an unlimited
amount of water might be poured into London for less money
than it now pays for a limited and bad supply, and that the most
extravagant proceeding just now would be — to do nothing.

Some apprehension has been caused by the idea that the
water companies would claim enormous sums as compensation.
Compensation for what?

We entirely disagree with those who seek to raise a clamour
against the water companies. We should be glad to find that

after all they have not broken their promises, have not given us
bad water, have not augmented the rates, have not neglected the
poor, and that the calculations which prove their dividends bad,
deserve the praise of honesty rather than ingenuity. Even if
disappointed in this, we would not be over zealous in blaming
men for having human infirmities, but conclude that these
trading companies have only followed the law of their creation.
On the whole, perhaps, the inhabitants of London have been
served better than they had any right to anticipate. If praise
or blame is to be administered, we think the praise should be
given to the companies for not having given 'another turn to
'the screw,' and the blame to those whose short-sighted incapacity
led them to trust the screw into any hands but their own. But
this is a matter, not of praise or blame, but of money; nor to
be determined on philanthropical or ethical, but on commercial
principles. The agreement between the companies and the
public is of the simplest character, beyond the wit of man to
mystify. On the one hand, the companies proposed to risk their
capital in the hope and on the chance that they would obtain
remunerative dividends. On the other, the public were ready
to submit their convenience, even their necessities, to the pleasure of an irresponsible body, to pay a large extra sum annually
in the shape of profits to the trader, and all simply to keep their
hands unfettered, and *not* to risk their capital. The existence
of half these companies demonstrates that no one has a vested
interest in the right of supplying water to London or any part
of it. Sir W. Clay, chairman of three of the companies, says,
quite fairly, ' to private parties the supply of water is a com-
' mercial enterprise : they have a right to look for rates which
' will not only pay current interest on the capital expended, *but*
' *as much larger a return as will be a compensation for the risk*
' *incurred.*' Precisely so : but to repudiate the risks — one of
them being this very chance of keeping up a virtual monopoly
— and in the same breath claim it as the foundation of vested
rights, could have occurred only to the London water companies,

> ' Those pagod things of sceptred sway,
> With fronts of Brass, and feet of Clay.'

Who offered to risk their money? The water companies. Who
received the dividends? The water companies. Who claim the
profits? The water companies. Who is to bear the losses?
The public will, — if they pay compensation on resumption.

There is no class in the community but has a deep interest in
the proper settlement of this water question. To the tradesman
it comes directly home as a matter of business. When an
epidemic breaks out, the wealthy escape to healthier localities :
few Londoners will dispute that 1849 was a bad season, and that

little money comes across the counter when the Registrar General returns three thousand deaths a week. Landlords are affected by the non-payment of their rents. It is an axiom among builders that rent is best got from healthy houses, and all agree that the poor pay as honestly as any other class, so long as they have the means. Mr. Little, a builder, says that three fifths of his losses of rent from his tenants, who are working men, are caused by sickness — principally fevers and those debilitating illnesses which, arising from want of cleanliness, and bad drainage, fall under the head of preventible. It might be thought that the landlord's interest would of itself lead him to remedy this; but there are often divided interests, which do not and cannot act simultaneously, and the profit would be divided among many, while the first outlay would be borne by one. In these cases the difficulty can be removed by the law alone. No house should be allowed to be inhabited unless it be provided with the appliances of cleanliness. No man has a right to erect a nuisance: and the public has clearly as good a right and as great an interest in enforcing cleanliness to prevent the outburst of an epidemic, as in requiring party walls to prevent the spread of fire ; to forbid the sale of putrid water, as well as of putrid meat. The first cost of what is necessary for the public health should be borne by the public, and the amount replaced by an annual rate upon the property.

Whatever increases the necessary expenditure of the workman increases by so much the cost of the produce of his labour, and is therefore a tax upon the consumer, whatever his position in life; besides which, the richer classes are often affected by circumstances from which they fancy themselves exempt. Albion Terrace, in the Wandsworth Road, consists of seventeen houses, and is occupied by persons in easy circumstances. Last August the spring from which they obtained water became contaminated with the leakage from a cesspool, and produced a disease which in a short time destroyed forty or fifty people in that one terrace. And the same thing may happen to any spring in London, such is the state of the subsoil. At Battersea, the spring used by a baker was poisoned in the same way, and for a long time the deleterious mixture was kneaded up in the dough, and sent round to his customers. Shocking as these things are, they are part of the great law which binds the rich and the poor together. It is well for us that our natural selfishness, hardened by the self-indulgence of wealth, should, at times, be rudely shaken, and aroused by our fears, if not by our sense of duty, — that we should be reminded that our destinies are inextricably mingled with those of the poorest and most degraded of our fellow countrymen, — that we have, after all, a common humanity; and that property,—which all consider the main, and some the sole end of society,—has its duties, as well as its rights.

None are free from this law. The statesman, in the pride of conscious power, while by the magic of his words he bends the assembled Commons to his will, is the prey of an influence subtler than his own. When the strong excitement of the hour has passed away, the unstrung nerves, the feverish pulse, the throbbing head, may warn him, when it is too late, that a heavy vapour from the pestilential courts of Westminster had glided into the presence of the rulers of the land, and had been busy at its appointed work. Even in that rich and glorious chamber where the Queen meets the Peers of England, and where the genius of Barry, prodigal of decoration, has exhausted art in combining all that can enchant the eye and intoxicate the imagination, even there, some spectator more inquisitive and thoughtful than the rest, may have learned that under that very building passes a huge sewer, which is fast becoming an enormous cesspool, and in whose capacious recesses are fermenting the deadly gases, which, when encountered in their intensity*, kill with the suddenness of a stroke of lightning, but which more ordinarily float in the atmosphere, visiting the palace as well as the cottage, and bearing the seeds of disease upon their wings. It was a wisdom beyond man's wisdom which bade us remember that we have the poor always with us. The labouring classes ought to be the stay and strength of our country,—but neglect, though it will not dissolve the connexion which fastens the upper to the lower ranks of society, and is indeed a union for better for worse, may make our fate that which was inflicted by Mezentius, and link us to a festering mass of rottenness and corruption.

But there are higher principles of action than our riches or our health. We have already said, that this is quite as much a question of public morals. An eye-witness, speaking in September, 1849, says that in Bermondsey there is an open sewer into which all the house drains go. Houses are built over it, and it receives all the filth from them: the liquid puddle is of the colour of strong green tea. And this is what the inhabitants *drink!* Unable at first to credit the evidence of his senses, he questioned the people. They said ' they were obliged to drink the ' ditch without they could beg or thieve a pailful of water;' and a wretched mother added, ' neither I nor my children know what ' health is; but what can we do,— we must live where our bread ' is.' We would seriously ask how much longer these things are to go on in a Christian city? and what greater proof we need

---

* This was the case of the Pimlico sewer.

of the insufficiency of the principle of trade? Can we wonder that these people fly to the pothouse to quench their thirst? that, when they are thus led into temptation, intemperance works their degradation and becomes their curse? or that they have small respect for the legislation which is blind to the wants of the poor, but Argus-eyed to protect the speculations of the rich? If it were the will of Providence that Bermondsey should be fourteen times as unhealthy and miserable as St. James's, we should bow to the decrees of Omnipotence. But if it arises from the ways of man, shall we suit our words to our actions, and say, ' The rated annual value of London is ten millions —
' property is a sacred thing — we dare not trust it to the prin-
' ciple of trade — Government must interfere, and we will gladly
' pay the police-rate. But life is quite another matter; Go-
' vernments are sadly given to jobbing, — we pay enough in
' rates already; the principle of trade is good enough here —
' every man for himself; there is plenty of water for those who
' are able to buy it — let poor people drink at the sewers — who
' cares whether they live or die?'

What has been done by other towns may be done by London. At Aberdeen the water supply is managed most satisfactorily by a public body, the Police Commissioners. The constant pressure system has been adopted with infinite advantage by Preston, Nottingham, Greenock, Paisley, Ayr, Glasgow, Tavistock, Bristol, Newcastle, Philadelphia, and New York. The Thames gives an abundant supply; and an aqueduct thirty miles long is a trifling work compared to a railway. At Nottingham 5000 poor tenements are supplied with an unlimited quantity of filtered water in every house for a penny per week each, and this leaves a profit to the parties furnishing the supply. Whatever, too, is done now, should be done effectually, for nothing is so expensive as to do work twice over; — and the rapidity at which London is increasing is prodigious. It appears by a return laid before Parliament by the Commissioners of Police, that in the metropolitan district, in the ten years ending 1st January, 1849, there were built 64,058 new houses, making 200 miles of new streets, and that the increase of population was 325,904 persons. For five centuries London has been outgrowing its supply of water, and its annual augmentations are now far greater than ever. If we would legislate usefully for the future, we must not overlook the experience of the past. London may yet contain four millions of inhabitants, so that a cramped scheme must be a bad one; *magnitude* is a main element of success.

The shameful condition of our great capital in this respect is now fully before the public; and the credit of England is, we think, involved in the course which we shall at last deliberately take. Whatever our provincial cities may do, it will be disgraceful to the nation if in our very metropolis we are surpassed in the arrangements for securing health and common decency, not only by the young republics of the New World, but even by the ancient empires of the Old. We boast of our wealth, our freedom, our science, our powers of combined exertion, our sense of comfort, and our love of cleanliness; we glory in our civilisation, but our glory becomes our shame, if still we are last in the race of humanity. The city of New York has expended 2,500,000*l.* on the Croton Water Works. An aqueduct forty miles long, and carried over the most formidable engineering difficulties, brings a daily supply of sixty millions of gallons for 400,000 inhabitants. This is an exertion of which our Transatlantic brethren may well be proud; it is a great work, and in a good cause, and we honour them for it. To form a just conception of it, we must consider the probability of the citizens of London, under a system of universal suffrage, taxing themselves to the extent of twelve millions and a half of our money in order to command a daily supply of 300 millions of gallons of water. Napoleon, the greatest administrative genius of modern times, proposed to supply Paris daily with 35 millions of gallons, brought by the Canal de l'Ourcq, from a distance of sixty miles. The scheme was postponed,—so that when the cholera appeared in 1832, a thousand persons sometimes perished in a single day; until the Parisian commissioners said, that in boundless terror and despair, the inhabitants fled precipitately from a city which they believed to be about to become their tomb. The capital of Eastern Europe has enormous cisterns; one of them, the reservoir of the 'thousand and one columns,' is calculated by Andreossi to be capable of holding a supply for Constantinople for sixty days. Carthage was supplied by an aqueduct forty miles long. Going farther back still, we find Solomon, the wisest of mankind, bearing testimony to the real duties of a government by building an aqueduct at Bethlehem to convey water from his *pools* or reservoirs to Jerusalem; and having thrown an arch or covering over his cistern, the Royal Poet draws a happy illustration from his own work, and (Cant. iv. 12.) compares his spouse to 'a garden inclosed, a 'spring shut up, a fountain sealed.'

But, beyond all other nations, the Roman people, that great race, the elevation of whose conceptions, and the granite firmness of whose character fitted them to become the masters of mankind,—and whose laws, whose combined and prolonged efforts, and lofty far-seeing policy seem rather the result of instinct than the slow product of human experience and observation, recognised the importance of a due supply of water. Our difficulties, physical, social, and pecuniary, are as nothing compared to theirs: but the difference is still greater in our wills. We need not mention the sewers of their kings. Three hundred years before the Christian era the first aqueduct was made: before the republic ceased there were 800 baths in the city. After that, the emperors built those gigantic *thermæ* which are still the wonder of the world for their magnitude and scientific construction. The baths of Diocletian could accommodate 18,000 persons at once.

There is reason to believe that in Rome every house had its fountain: nor was a dwelling considered fit to receive a tenant, however poor, unless it was provided with a supply of water. Pliny, with natural triumph, asserts ' that if any person con- ' sidered the abundance of water conveyed to the public for ' baths, fishponds, private houses, fountains, gardens, villas, ' over arches, through mountains, and across valleys filled up, ' he would acknowledge that nothing was ever more wonderful.' And well did the Roman energy justify this claim; for at one time the Imperial City contained 1300 reservoirs, into which the twenty mighty aqueducts that spanned the broad Campagna, poured a daily supply of fifty millions of cubic feet, or three hundred and twenty-five millions of gallons, of water.

It is vain to talk of freedom and civilisation, and vaunt of our Constitution as combining liberty with order, and sheltering our citizens alike from the bolts of autocratic tyranny and the storms of popular license, when we see our poor dying in pestilential courts; fighting in our streets, round a dribbling stand pipe, for the first element of cleanliness and health; or drinking, from the sewers of Bermondsey, worse than ' the gilded puddle which ' beasts would cough at:' and when we know that it would have been better for them if, we will not presume to say, they had never been born, but if they had been born the slaves of a Roman despot, or made good their way among a flight of emigrants to the munificent charity of New York.

Appius Claudius — who, about three hundred years before the Christian era, was censor and afterwards consul of Rome — was one of those remarkable men who impress on their age the stamp of their own minds. Greedy of power, and unscrupulous in the mode of acquiring it, he yet wielded it as became a statesman of the true Roman type. A fearless political reformer, he extended the franchise, and introduced into the Senate — until then a purely patrician assembly — a number of the sons of freedmen, hitherto despised by those haughty nobles as the sons of nobody. As clear-sighted in his administrative and sanitary, as he was bold in his political, measures, he constructed the famous Appian Way from Rome to Capua, and the still more famous Appian Aqueduct, which brought water, from a distance of eight miles, for the poor citizens who had hitherto used the water of the Tiber, and inhabited the low district of the Circus, — the Bermondsey of Rome. It was said at the time that these undertakings exhausted the revenues of the city; but the statesman knew that in such works lie the secret springs of national wealth. The rising tide of prosperity soon replenished the treasury; and the unbounded ambition of Appius Claudius, though neither forgotten nor forgiven, will never be so favourably judged of, as when we read that by his exertions Rome was supplied with water, and when we find the historian, scorning our favourite principle of trade, emphatically calling upon his readers to remark that the first aqueduct of Rome was built for the benefit of the *poor*.

It may be fancy, but it seems to us that a cycle of above two thousand years has brought round, in Great Britain, a train of somewhat analogous circumstances. We, too, have seen the leaders of the people force their way to official power, extend the franchise, and invigorate our too patrician Legislative Assembly with a portion of the more popular element. More fortunate than the Roman consul, we have seen the reform withstand conservative reaction, and, like a breakwater, guard the edifice of our monarchy from the flood of anarchy and communism which deluged Europe and broke over the continental thrones. We have seen a network of five thousand miles of iron roads spread over our islands with an expenditure of labour, science, and money which makes even Roman roads seem but the playthings of children. These, too, are said to have exhausted our resources; but they are a storehouse of national wealth. We trust that some of our statesmen will complete the parallel; and that they who have won a name in history as political reformers, and struck the last fetters from our commercial system, will, like unto Appius Claudius except in his ambition, achieve the higher glory of bringing health and cleanliness to the dwellings of the poor.

This is the true glory which outlives all other, and shines with undying lustre from generation to generation, — imparting to its works something of its own immortality, and, in some degree, rescuing them from that ruin which overtakes the ordinary monuments of historical tradition or mere magnificence. The Tomb of Moses is unknown; but the traveller slakes his thirst at the Well of Jacob. The gorgeous palace of the wisest and wealthiest of monarchs, with its cedar, and gold, and ivory, — even the great Temple of Jerusalem, hallowed by the visible glory of the Deity himself, — are gone; but Solomon's reservoirs are as perfect as ever.   Of the ancient architecture of the Holy City not one stone is left upon another; but the Pool of Bethesda commands the pilgrim's reverence at the present day. The columns of Persepolis are mouldering into dust; but its cisterns and aqueducts remain to challenge our admiration.   The Golden House of Nero is a mass of ruins; but the Aqua Claudia still pours into Rome its limpid stream.   The Temple of the Sun at Tadmor in the wilderness, has fallen; but its fountain sparkles as freshly in his rays as when thousands of worshippers thronged the lofty colonnades.   It may be that London will share the fate of Babylon, and nothing be left to mark its site save confused mounds of crumbling brickwork.   But the works of Nature are imperishable.   The Thames will continue to flow as it does now.   And if any work of Art should still rise over the deep ocean of Time, we may well believe that it will be neither a palace nor a temple, but some vast aqueduct or reservoir: and if any name should still flash through the mist of antiquity, it will probably be that of the man who, in his day, sought the happiness of his fellow-men rather than their glory, and linked his memory to some great work of national utility and benevolence.

ART. V. — 1. *Report of the General Board of Health on the Epidemic Cholera of* 1848 *and* 1849. Presented to both Houses of Parliament by command of Her Majesty. London: 1850.

2. *General Board of Health Report on Quarantine.* Presented to both Houses of Parliament by command of Her Majesty. London: 1849.

THOSE great modern innovators, the steam-boat and the railway, fix attention upon all the impediments which obstruct the progress of the traveller, or check the free commercial intercourse of nations. Of these none is more conspicuous, none more vexatious, than quarantine; while the successful invasions of every country in Europe and America by Asiatic cholera, despite all the opposition presented by quarantine laws, lazarettos, and *cordons sanitaires*, have given to the whole civilised world, in our own day, a very significant intimation of the impotence of those laws to resist the incursions of epidemic disease. And our Chancellor of the Exchequer himself, in his manifesto of June 2nd, has proclaimed that ' the spirit of the ' age tends to free intercourse; and no statesman can disregard ' with impunity the genius of the epoch in which he lives.'

The system of quarantine is to be vindicated or condemned by *facts*, of the truth or falsehood of which every shrewd man of the world is as competent a judge, and upon which, if true, he is as capable of reasoning correctly as if he were a member of the medical profession. Nay, without adopting the sarcasm of the great anatomist, that ' the ancients endeavoured to make ' physic a science and failed; the moderns have made it a trade ' and succeeded,' we must not forget that, in this country, the office of the physician is not to prevent but to cure disease; and that, accordingly, the art of preserving health and preventing disease is taught in no regular course of lectures at any of the great schools of medicine in the United Kingdom. Experience, indeed, teaches us that professional men are not the most fortunate advocates of professional reforms. For a quarter of a century we have witnessed successive Chancery reformers, and professional commissions of inquiry, labouring in unsuccessful attempts to remove the inveterate abuses of our Courts of Equity; they made demonstrations, indeed, and skirmished with the outposts; and new judges were created, and new courts were opened: but it was not until the administration of Lord John Russell appointed a commission, which included among its members two unprofessional men of vigorous minds, great sagacity, and extensive knowledge, whose feelings and sympathies were all with the client and against the system, that the stronghold of injustice and chicane was forced to capitulate, and the gigantic abuses of the Master's Office were surrendered. So has it happened with the question under consideration; successive governments have followed with undeviating uniformity the notable precedent established by a celebrated club, of which it is recorded that the venerable members having occasion to complain of the quality of their wine and of the size of the measures in which it was served to them, appointed a committee to investigate the grievance and devise a remedy, of which committee they nominated the landlord of the tavern where they held their meetings to be the chairman. and his waiters to be the members. In like manner, the most unfortunate circumstance connected with the investigation of questions respecting the origin and prevention of epidemic diseases, is, that governments have been in the habit of relying implicitly on the authority and advice of persons employed in quarantine departments; although it is manifest that the official instincts, the prejudices, and the self-interest of such persons utterly disqualify them from giving a sound opinion on the subject. Nor are instances wanting, even in recent times, where a Report, in which loose statements of events in remote places are so manipulated as to present a plausible *primâ facie* case of an epidemic having been imported through disregard of the principles of quarantine, has gained for its author the patronage of that department, and some mark of distinction, or some lucrative preferment in the public service.

This subject, however, being now happily emancipated from the trammels of a purely professional question, is no longer to be discussed upon merely technical grounds; and the time having arrived when it cannot fail to receive at the hands of statesmen and legislators that attention which its importance entitles it to demand, we shall endeavour to present the case fairly before our readers upon its practical merits, and to disabuse the public of some of those professional fallacies upon which has been constructed a system not less repugnant to the dictates of humanity than injurious to the interests of commerce—a system utterly powerless to arrest the progress of epidemic disease, but most powerful to multiply its victims and aggravate its horrors. The constitution of the General Board of Health, whose Reports upon Quarantine have drawn our attention to this subject, has been highly favourable to an enlightened, disinterested, and searching investigation of the question; for, while medical science was ably represented there, the majority of its members, being unprofessional, had nothing to unlearn; unfettered by the traditions of the schools, and unbiassed by professional prejudices, their feelings and sympathies were naturally with the patient and against the unchristian edict which said to him — ' Thou art sick, and we visit thee not; thou art in prison, and we ' come not unto thee.' And, accordingly, their Reports present a favourable contrast to most of the disquisitions on the subject so long as it was monopolised by medical writers, whose treatises commonly betray a lamentable ignorance of the most obvious rules of evidence, and a want of inclination or of ability to analyse the testimony by which statements of occurrences at distant places are supported. Loose general assertions by igno-rant or interested people, and vague hearsay rumours, which no court of justice would listen to for an instant in any question involving property of the most inconsiderable amount, are by an unreasoning credulity, which is perfectly incomprehensible in members of a learned profession, accepted without investigation or inquiry as indisputable facts, and are published and argued upon as conclusively proving the truth of doctrines upon which the health and the lives of whole communities depend. We have therefore perused with less surprise than shame the advice which, so recently as the year 1831, was addressed to the Executive Government by the most eminent physicians of London; and which was adopted by the Privy Council, and proclaimed to the public by Order in Council on the 20th of October in that year, when the steady march of epidemic cholera from Asia over the continent of Europe towards our own shores, warned us of the approaching danger at the same time that it demonstrated the utter futility of quarantine regulations, by overleaping every barrier which had been interposed to stop its progress, even in countries whose governments could command all the machinery necessary to execute such despotic regulations with all the rigour and precision of military discipline. The recommendations of this venerable body, true to the traditionary lessons taught in the schools, and blind to the lessons of experience taught by the events which were passing around them, proved that practically medical science had in this respect made no progress for upwards of two centuries; for they actually revived, and even surpassed, the barbarous counsels which prevailed in the days of King James the First, who inaugurated his reign in England by an ' Act for the charitable ' Relief and ordering of Persons infected with the Plague,' whereby, after reciting that ' persons infected being commanded ' to keep their houses, or otherwise separate themselves from ' company, do notwithstanding very dangerously and disorderly ' misdemean themselves,' it was enacted, ' that if any person in- ' fected, or being in an infected house, shall be commanded to ' keep his house and shall disobey, offering and attempting to ' break out and go abroad or to resist; and going abroad and ' resisting such keepers and watchmen as should be appointed ' to keep them in, it should be lawful for the watchmen, &c. ' with violence to enforce them to keep their houses, and if any ' hurt come by such enforcement to the disobedient persons, the ' keepers, watchmen, and their assistants shall not be impeached ' therefore.'* The Rules and Regulations, bearing date, College of Physicians, October 20th, 1831, ' for the purpose of prevent-

---

* Stat. 1 Jac. 1. c. 31. ss. 1. and 6.

' ing the introduction and spreading of the disease called cholera
' morbus in the United Kingdom,' not only fully adopted the
principle of this arbitrary statute, but sought to extend the
application of its principle to whole communities instead of confining it to individual cases. They were signed Henry Halford, President of the Board; and the Board comprised the
following members:—Dr. Maton; Dr. Turner; Dr. Warren;
Dr. MacMichael; Dr. Holland; Dr. Seymour (Secretary); Dr.
Sir James MacGrigor, Director of the Medical Department of
the Army; Dr. Sir William Burnett, Director of the Medical
Department of the Navy; Dr. Sir William Pym, Superintendent-General of Quarantine; together with the Controller
of the Navy, and the Deputy Chairman of the Board of Customs. After declaring that ' the measures of external precau-
' tion for preventing the introduction of the cholera morbus BY
' A RIGOROUS QUARANTINE HAVE HITHERTO BEEN FOUND
' EFFECTUAL,' these learned persons proceed to enunciate certain arbitrary regulations, founded upon this bold but incautious
assumption, which are too numerous and minute to be given in
detail; but we shall select some of the more vigorous measures
which were proposed by them to the Executive Government
for adoption; and which were ordered by the Privy Council to
be ' published in the " Gazette," and circulated in all the prin-
' cipal ports, creeks, and other stations of the United Kingdom,
' with a view that all persons may be made acquainted there-
' with and conform themselves thereto.' They claim a close
affinity to the legislation of the olden time.

' To carry into effect the separation of the sick from the healthy, it
would be very expedient that one or more houses should be kept in
view in each town, or its neighbourhood, as places to which every
case of the disease, as soon as detected, might be removed, provided
the family of the affected person consent to such removal; and in
case of refusal, a conspicuous mark (" SICK ") should be placed in
front of the house, to warn persons that it is in Quarantine; and even
when persons with the disease shall have been removed, and the
house shall have been purified, the word " CAUTION " should be
substituted, as denoting suspicion of the disease; and the inhabitants
of such house should not be at liberty to move out, or communicate
with other persons, until, by the authority of the local board, the
mark shall have been removed.'

' It is recommended, that those who may fall victims to this most
formidable disease should be buried in a detached ground in the vicinity of the house that may have been selected for the reception of
cholera patients. By this regulation it is intended to confine as much
as possible every source of infection to one spot; on the same principle, all persons who may be employed in the removal of the sick

from their own houses, as well as all those who may attend upon
cholera patients in the capacity of nurses, should live apart from the
rest of the community.'

' Wherever objections arise to the removal of the sick from the
healthy, or other causes exist to render such a step not advisable, the
same prospect of success in extinguishing the seeds of the pestilence
cannot be expected. Much, however, may be done, even in these
difficult circumstances, by following the same principles of prudence,
and by avoiding all unnecessary communication with the public out
of doors; all articles of food or other necessaries required by the
family should be placed in front of the house, and received by one of
the inhabitants of the house after the person delivering them shall
have retired. Until the time during which the contagion of cholera
lies dormant in the human frame has been more accurately ascertained, it will be necessary, for the sake of perfect security, that convalescents from the disease, and those who have had any communication with them, should be kept under observation for a period of not
less than twenty days.'

' All intercourse with any infected town and the neighbouring
country must be prevented by the best means within the power of the
magistrates, who will have to make regulations for the supply of provisions.'

This regulation calls to mind the exploit commemorated by
Milton ' of that gallant man who thought to pound up the
' crows by shutting his park gate.'

' OTHER MEASURES OF A MORE COERCIVE NATURE MAY BE RENDERED
EXPEDIENT FOR THE COMMON SAFETY, if unfortunately so fatal a disease
should ever show itself in this country in the terrific way in which it
has appeared in various parts of Europe; AND IT MAY BECOME NECES-
SARY TO DRAW TROOPS OR A STRONG BODY OF POLICE AROUND INFECTED
PLACES, SO AS UTTERLY TO EXCLUDE THE INHABITANTS FROM ALL
INTERCOURSE WITH THE COUNTRY; AND WE FEEL SURE THAT WHAT IS
DEMANDED FOR THE COMMON SAFETY OF THE STATE WILL ALWAYS BE.
ACQUIESCED IN WITH A WILLING SUBMISSION TO THE NECESSITY WHICH
IMPOSES IT.'

That regulations, such as these, which are alike contemptible
in the eyes of science and opposed to every sound principle of
legislation, should be advocated by superintendents of quarantine and their hangers-on, would excite no surprise; but that
they should have been deliberately promulgated by a body of
English physicians, among whom, besides the President of the
College himself, were some of the most eminent of their day, is
a phenomenon worthy to be recorded by the historian who
marks the scientific progress of a nation.

The state of mind which admitted of incredulity respecting
the influence of local causes in the propagation of this class of
diseases, was of course incompatible with an appreciation of the

true value of such preventive measures as are founded on a
knowledge of that influence.   No sooner, however, was the
Order in Council published which contained such outrages upon
common sense and common humanity, as actually to contemplate
the drawing ' troops or a strong body of police around infected
' places'—Liverpool, Manchester, Leeds, Hull, Bristol, Sunderland, or London itself, for instance —' so as utterly to ex-
' clude the inhabitants from all intercourse with the country,'
than its reception showed that, if ignorant of nothing else, its
authors were profoundly ignorant of the state and the strength
of public opinion in their own country.   They were quickly
convinced, that laws, which might have been ' acquiesced in
' with a willing submission' in the reign of King James the
First, were simply impossible in the reign of King William the
Fourth.   Accordingly, the subject being more fully and more
closely investigated, the opinions were revised and the recommendations considerably modified.   In less than a month, the
public were assured, by a circular issued from the Council
Office on the 14th of November, 1831, that ' with regard to
' precautions as to intercourse with suspected, or really infected
' persons or places, the Board are confident that good sense and
' good feeling will not only point out but *morally* establish, *as*
' *far as may be practicable*, the necessity of avoiding such com-
' munication as may endanger the lives of thousands.   But they
' STRONGLY DEPRECATE ALL MEASURES OF COERCION FOP
' THIS PURPOSE WHICH, WHEN TRIED UPON THE CONTI
' NENT, HAVE BEEN INVARIABLY PRODUCTIVE OF EVIL.'
But so capricious is the exercise of arbitrary power, and so
reluctant is poor human nature to withdraw altogether from
error which has become habitual, that the measures which had
been abandoned on shore as ' invariably productive of evil,' were,
by a disgraceful inconsistency, retained on the water, where they
could be enforced without encountering the universal opposition
of the public at large.   Thus at the very same time that the
intercourse of Sunderland and Seaham with all other parts of
Great Britain, by land was perfectly free and uninterrupted, so
that even the attendants upon the sick and the dying might and
did remove to any part of the country by land without let or
hindrance, intercourse by sea was interdicted; and the very
colliers arriving in the Thames were subjected to a rigid quarantine of fifteen days, from which the day and night coaches,
with their full complement of passengers, were altogether exempted.   Such were the counsels which prevailed during the
cholera epidemic of 1831-2.   ' At that time,' as is justly remarked in the First Report of the Metropolitan Sanitary Com-

missioners*, 'not only had no knowledge been acquired by
' experience of the true character of this disease, but nothing
' was known of the real condition of the classes which proved
' to be its first and easy victims, nor of the state of the locali-
' ties in which they lived. The metropolis of the poor has
' nothing in common with the metropolis of the rich, and as the
' map of London exhibits no trace of the lanes and alleys of the
' poor, so the very names of these places would at that time
' have sounded as strange to the inhabitants of our great
' thoroughfares and squares as the names of the streets of a
' foreign country.' But the very ignorance and incapacity
which were manifested on the occasion of that epidemic, coupled
with the opportunities which its outbreak in different places
afforded to intelligent people for observing facts with their own
eyes — particularly among the classes and in the localities where
the mortality was greatest — shook their faith in the vulgar
error of contagion, and caused them to look elsewhere for the
true sources of pestilence. Public attention, so long abused by
idle fables of epidemic fevers imported from abroad into low
lodging-houses in the foul clothes of seafaring men frequenting
those hotbeds of disease, was at length awakened to the pestilential condition of the districts themselves in which such lodging-
houses are situate; where diarrhœa and scarlet fever are ever
present to sacrifice youth, typhus manhood, and where, when
that epidemic influence prevailed, cholera invariably found its
victims of every age. The epidemic, however, having spent
itself, subsided; nor were the public taught, by any overt act
or even by any proposal of reform, to believe that the learned
persons themselves, to whom the guardianship of their health
had been confided, had turned the knowledge which they might
have acquired during the progress of the disease, to any practical account: they still clung to the doctrine that diseases are
imported and spread by contagion: no antiquated opinions were
retracted; nor were any remedial measures suggested founded
on the hypothesis that the low sanitary condition of a population — as bad drainage, ill-ventilated and overcrowded dwellings,
offensive sewers, unwholesome water, and the thousand other
kindred abominations which afflict the poor — could exercise
any perceptible influence in producing and fostering epidemic
diseases. ' But quarantine pays no regard to these conditions.
' Blindly intent on accomplishing an impossible object, it over-
' looks the circumstances on which the existence and extension
' of disease really depend; and after the experience of centuries

---

* P. 6.

' has shown the inutility of the securities it offers, it still pro-
' poses to go on reposing implicit confidence in them and in
' them only.' (*Report on Quarantine*, p. 16.) It was not until
six years afterwards, namely, in 1838, that men's minds were
strongly directed to these local influences. In that year the
deplorable sanitary condition of large masses of the population
in London was forcibly described by Dr. Southwood Smith,
in a Report to the Poor Law Commissioners on the physical
causes of sickness and mortality to which the poor are particularly exposed, and which are capable of removal by sanitary
regulation. This and similar Reports by Dr. Arnott and Dr.
Kay (now Sir J. Kay Shuttleworth) on the same subject, were
published by the Poor Law Commissioners in their Reports of
1838 and 1839. The facts disclosed by these Reports necessarily attracted the notice of Parliament, and on the motion of
Mr. Slaney, the late very useful member for Shrewsbury, a
Select Committee was appointed by the House of Commons in
1840, to inquire into the circumstances affecting the health of
the inhabitants of large towns and populous districts, with a
view to improved sanitary regulations for their benefit.

The subject had now acquired such importance that by special
direction of the Home Secretary the Secretary to the Poor Law
Board was, in 1842, instructed to report fully upon the sanitary
condition of the whole labouring population of Great Britain.
His carefully revised and elaborate Report justly produced a
powerful impression on the minds of all thinking men, and had
great influence in preparing the way for sanitary legislation : it
was followed in 1844 by the appointment of Commissioners to
inquire into the present state of large towns and populous districts, and the causes of disease among the inhabitants ; and in
1847, by the appointment of Commissioners for inquiring
whether any and what special means may be requisite for the
improvement of the health of the metropolis. The frightful
disclosures contained in these several reports, and particularly in
the valuable report of the Metropolitan Sanitary Commissioners,
proved that all these classes of epidemic or zymotic diseases invariably prevailed in the same localities, ravaged the same classes,
and were dependent for their severity and extension upon the
same sanitary conditions. A general conviction followed, when
the cholera epidemic of 1848-9 was impending over us, that the
preservation of the public health by removing the local causes of
pestilence was one of the duties of Government which had been
too long neglected. At the end of the Session of 1848 the
Public Health Act, and the Nuisances Removal and Diseases
Prevention Act (which had been introduced by Lord Carlisle)

were placed on the Statute Book; and a General Board of Health was constituted to administer their provisions. But, unfortunately, this favourable opportunity for revising the Quarantine Laws, and for placing the whole sanitary administration of the country in the hands of one efficient and responsible body, was lost.

When this new Board was appointed, comprising as it did the names of men who, having been most active in conducting the previous inquiries, were, by long study and accurate observation, completely masters of the subject in all its details, their attention was diverted from the duties which in ordinary times would have devolved upon them, by finding themselves forced to grapple with the epidemic of 1848, now threatening to spread itself over the country. Happily the knowledge acquired in their previous inquiries enabled them to encounter with promptitude, vigour, and success the difficulties of the crisis. They knew both the places where and the classes among which the disease would inevitably appear, if it appeared at all; they warned the local authorities of the dangers which menaced them; taught them to estimate the exigence of the moment, and the value of that moment well employed; instructed them in the means of averting these outbreaks, and if such means should be neglected, and the outbreak should occur, taught them how it could be suppressed. The complete success which attended the adoption of the measures recommended is shown in the Report on Cholera, as exemplified in the Metropolis, in Glasgow, in Bristol, in Dumfries, in Paisley, and in other places. The result at the same time furnished absolute demonstration of the soundness of the principles upon which the Board was acting. While they were engaged in these useful labours, and endeavouring to instruct the people in the true causes of these outbreaks, and in the true means of preventing them, another department of the executive made known its existence by placing in quarantine all ships, British and foreign, coming from Hamburgh or any other suspected port; and these needless severities were continued until the cholera, with its customary disregard for the orders placing it in quarantine, made its appearance in different parts of the United Kingdom. As was anticipated and predicted, it returned to the same countries, to the same cities and towns, and even to the same streets, houses, and rooms, which it ravaged in 1832. It is true that many places were attacked in the recent epidemic which had escaped in the former; but very few indeed that suffered then, escaped now, except in some few instances in which sanitary improvements had in the meantime been effected. In some instances

it reappeared on the very spot on which it first broke out
sixteen years before. The first case which occurred in the
town of Leith, in 1848, took place in the same house and
within a few feet of the very spot from whence the epidemic of
1832 commenced its course. On its reappearance in the town
of Pollokshaws, it snatched its first victim from the same room
and the very bed in which it broke out in 1832. Its first
appearance in Bermondsey was close to the same ditch near
which the earliest fatal cases occurred in 1832. At Oxford, in
1849, as in 1832, the first case occurred in the county jail.
This return to its .former haunts has been observed in innumerable other places. The same has been the case abroad. At
Gröningen, in Holland, the disease in 1832 attacked in the
better part of the city only two houses, and the epidemic made
its first reappearance in these two identical houses in the visitation of 1848. In numerous instances medical officers, who
had attended to the conditions which influence its localisation,
pointed out, before its return, the particular courts and houses
on which it would seize. ' Before cholera appeared in the
' district,' says the medical officer of the Whitechapel Union,
speaking of a small court in the hamlet, ' I predicted that this
' would be one of its strongholds.' Eighteen cases occurred in
it. Before cholera appeared in the district, the medical officer
of Uxbridge stated that if it should visit that town it would be
certain to break out in a particular house, to the dangerous condition of which he called the attention of the local authorities.
The first cases that occurred broke out in that identical house.
In a place called Swain's Lane, in the healthy village of Highgate, near London, there is a spot where the medical officer felt
so confident that the disease would make its appearance, that he
repeatedly represented to the authorities the danger of allowing
the place to remain in its existing condition, but in vain. In
two houses on this spot, six attacks and four deaths took place ;
yet there was no other appearance of the disease, during the
whole epidemic, in any other part of the village, containing
3000 inhabitants.* ' Before the appearance of the disease in
' this country,' say the Board of Health, ' we warned the local
' authorities that the seats of the approaching pestilence would
' be the usual haunts of other epidemics.' This conviction was
founded on evidence to which subsequent experience gave the
force of demonstration; for, as the Board had anticipated and
predicted, the usual haunts of typhus and diarrhœa in ordinary
seasons actually became, when the epidemic influence aggra-

---

* Report on Epidemic Cholera, pp. 18, 19.

vated the form of these diseases, and for the time banished almost every other form of disease, the chief abiding places of cholera.

We will not weary our readers with the instances cited from Bethnal Green, from Rosemary Lane, Whitechapel, from Plymouth, from Manchester, from Barnard Castle, from Doncaster, from Wolverhampton, from Alnwick and Canongate, from Gainsborough, Burslem, Nantwich, Clitheroe, Penzance and elsewhere, which establish the fact beyond the possibility of doubt.

The disease often attacked definite spots in the districts which it invaded, confining its ravages to particular streets, the adjoining streets escaping; and even to one side of a street, scarcely a single case occurring on the opposite side. Thus at Rotherhithe, in a street where numerous deaths occurred, the attacks were almost entirely confined to one side of the street, occupied by several respectable private families, the disease appearing in only one house on the other side. ' The disease,' says the medical officer of the parish, ' passed right through and ' across several of the streets like a cannon ball.' At Bedford two streets are named as having each suffered on one side severely, the other nearly escaping. At Bristol, and in several other towns, the same fact was observed, and it has been noticed in foreign cities, particularly at St. Petersburgh. In this respect, also, cholera bears a marked resemblance to typhus, yellow fever, and plague. While the pestilence thus passed over adjoining spots, it sometimes attacked places in groups; that is, it seized on a certain number of courts, alleys, or streets, decimated their inhabitants, then ceased, and broke out in a similar manner, often at the opposite extremity of the district, occasionally returning again, after an interval, to the first locality. In this manner the occurrence of six, eight, or even more deaths was not uncommon in a particular house; but such a house did not form a centre from which the disease spread to neighbouring houses, and thence over the district. On the contrary, simultaneously with the attack in this particular house, or as soon as the work of death had been accomplished in it, the disease reappeared at a considerable distance, the intervening houses escaping. The history of its progress from Asia to Europe, and through the several countries of Europe, shows that it advanced not by a strictly continuous, progressive, and uninterrupted course; but that at one time it sprang at a single bound over a vast tract of country, while at another time its course was retrograde. Its progress through a city was similar, there being in general no regular continuity in its course, but its progress consisting in a succession of local outbreaks. Hence in the course of the house-to-house visitation, which will be described hereafter, the disease having disappeared from one district, the medical staff were obliged to follow it to another, and thence to a third, and so on from district to district till the whole local epidemic seizure was at an end.

This law of the disease, that it spreads not by continuity of time or place, but occurs at irregular periods, and extends by a succession of local outbreaks, is decisive proof that it is propagated not by the contact of one infected person with another, but by a general influence operating on particular localities and persons, according to certain localising conditions and predisposing causes. We have not space to detail the horrible particulars, contained in the Report on Cholera, of the localising conditions and predisposing causes which existed in the spots where the epidemic raged with its greatest virulence. The effects of over-crowded, ill-constructed, and badly ventilated dwellings were evidenced by the outbreak of cholera in the workhouse at Taunton, where in the course of one week 60 of the inmates were swept away; in the lodging of the hop pickers at East Farleigh, near Maidstone, where the inmates were so huddled together that each individual had for respiration about 50 cubic feet of air, and where in a population of about 1000, within four days of the first seizure there occurred upwards of 200 cases of diarrhœa, 97 of developed cholera, and 47 deaths. Precisely similar was the onslaught of cholera on the pauper children at Tooting. But the most striking effects of over-crowding are seen in climates where the conditions of disease are the most intense, as in India, where in the native town of Kurrachee, consisting of ill-ventilated mud hovels, 1 inhabitant in 10 died of cholera: whereas of the same class of persons inhabiting the Bazaar, which was well constructed and ventilated, the proportion of deaths was only 1 in 30; while in the over-crowded jail at Hyderabad, of 400 prisoners 96 were cut off in 48 hours.

The baleful effects of an atmosphere contaminated by the emanations arising from filth accumulated in and about dwellings are now so universally acknowledged that we pass over the instances in which such localities are proved to have been the foci of epidemic disease. Such were — manufactories of artificial manure; the noxious animal effluvia emanating from bone-boiling establishments; offensive sewers and piggeries; grave-yards; foul canals and ditches; want of drains, bad drains, and sewers unskilfully constructed; unwholesome water; and all the impurities which pervade those parts of any town where sanitary measures are neglected, or, as too frequently happens, are so badly carried into effect as to increase the evil they are intended to remedy.   The evidence which traced the disease to these causes is complete and incontrovertible.   But the case does not rest here.   As we have shown that where sanitary precautions are neglected, there epidemic diseases will prevail, we shall proceed to complete the demonstration by showing that the converse is equally well established, and that where sanitary measures have been applied, there epidemic diseases will be avoided. Large groups of people who were living, during the whole course of the epidemic, in the localities where it was raging, and who belonged to the classes that were the chief sufferers, altogether escaped.

' Among the most remarkable of these exemptions were the establishments provided in the metropolis for lodging the poorer classes, founded for the express purpose of proving the influence of sanitary arrangement in preventing excessive sickness, and improving the physical well-being of the inhabitants.

' In George Street, Bloomsbury, and Charles and King Streets, Drury Lane, there are establishments for lodging single men, in which, though the sanitary arrangements are by no means perfect, the inmates are exempt to a considerable extent from the evils of bad drainage, accumulations of filth, over-crowding, and personal uncleanliness.

' These houses contain 210 inmates, among whom, with one exception, there was no case of cholera, the exception being an old man of intemperate habits, who rarely tasted animal food.   All the other inmates escaped.   It is remarkable that in George Street there were ten and in Charles Street two cases of diarrhœa, thus demonstrating that the epidemic influence was upon them, but that the improved sanitary conditions under which they were placed enabled them to resist it.   In the house in King Street there was no case either of cholera or diarrhœa.

' In the Lower Pentonville Road there is a group of buildings consisting of 24 houses, containing between 80 and 90 inhabitants. Here the sanitary conditions are upon the whole better than those of the establishments in Bloomsbury and Drury Lane, and the inmates of these houses enjoyed a complete immunity both from cholera and diarrhœa.

' In the Old Pancras Road is situated a large structure, called " Metropolitan Buildings," which is let out as separate tenements to families.   It contains upwards of 500 inmates, of whom about 350 are children.   This building is well drained, is kept clean, and an abundant and constant supply of water and other conveniences are provided for the inmates.   Though the structural arrangements of this building admit of considerable improvement, yet its sanitary condition is far superior to that commonly found in the dwellings of the poor.   A corresponding improvement has taken place in the health of its inmates. Taking the full period of its occupancy, its total mortality as compared with the general mortality of the metropolis, has been diminished one half, and as compared with the mortality of the worst parts of the metropolis it has been diminished two-thirds; while its infant mortality, the most delicate test of the healthfulness of a place, has been at least five times less than that of some parts of the metropolis. From its remarkable exemption from disease in general, and especially from the zymotic class of disease, notwithstanding it contained so large a proportion of infants, a confident hope was entertained that it would escape any visitation from cholera: and that hope was realised, for not a single case of cholera occurred among its inmates, and only seven cases of diarrhœa, although at a distance of between 300 and 400 yards from the building there were three deaths from cholera in one house; in an adjoining court the disease was very prevalent and mortal; the whole neighbourhood was afflicted severely with diarrhœa; and in this parish, though at some distance from this particular spot, within a space of 200 feet in length 20 fatal cases of cholera occurred.

' On board the American ship " Eagle " a sudden and violent outbreak of cholera took place precisely similar to an outbreak in a village, or the localisation of the disease in the district of a town. Here the sufferers were exclusively steerage passengers. They were over-crowded, and had no proper ventilation. There were in all 250 of these passengers, of whom a large proportion were attacked with diarrhœa, 21 with developed cholera, and 13 died. The cabin of this ship was large, commodious, clean, and well ventilated; and while the epidemic was raging in such close proximity to them, the passengers in this better conditioned part of the ship enjoyed a complete exemption not only from cholera but even from diarrhœa.

' In the Model Prison, at Pentonville, in the structure and arrangement of which important sanitary improvements have been introduced, out of an average of 465 prisoners, there was no attack of cholera and very little diarrhœa.

' Giltspur and Newgate prisons enjoyed, the former a complete, and the latter all but a complete, exemption from the disease, though situated in a district which suffered with extraordinary severity from the epidemic.

In the House of Correction, Cold Bath Fields, in the epidemic of 1832, when the number of prisoners was 1,148, there occurred 319 cases of premonitory diarrhœa, 207 of developed cholera, and 45 deaths. At that time the drainage of the prison was defective, the sewers, which were dry-built, without mortar, had in places fallen in, and were choked with soil; and, owing to the defective structure of the drains, their contents were not carried off. Subsequently the whole sewerage of the prison was rebuilt, and, on a late examination of it, was found to be in good order. The ventilation had been improved, and a small open fire, placed in each of the day rooms, appears to have operated beneficially, by preventing cold and dampness. In the late epidemic, among 1100 prisoners, there was not a single case of cholera, and only a few cases of diarrhœa, which, by prompt attention, were prevented from passing into the developed form of the disease.

' Bridewell Prison, in 1832, is described as having been in a most filthy state, the dirt on the walls being merely covered with lime-wash, so that when a thorough purification took place the walls were found coated with filth to the depth of two inches; three prisoners were allowed to occupy a single cell, no attention was paid to personal cleanliness, and there was a deficiency of medical superintendence. In the epidemic of that period 12 of the prisoners were attacked with cholera, and four died. The prison is now kept clean, personal clean-liness is enforced, only one inmate is allowed in a cell, and the pri-soners are under strict medical superintendence. In the late epidemic cholera raged on all sides of this prison, in houses closely contiguous, separated only by a narrow court; yet, among 90 prisoners, no case of cholera occurred, and only one case of diarrhœa, though fresh pri-soners were daily brought in of the lowest class, and in the greatest state of filth.

' Attention has already been directed to the violent outbreak of cholera in the workhouse of Taunton, in which only 68 cubic feet of space was allowed to each child. In the county jail, situated in the same town, the space allowed to each prisoner ranges from 819 to 935 cubic feet; each cell is perfectly ventilated, and an equable temperature is maintained through the twenty-four hours. Every prisoner has an unlimited water supply, and personal cleanliness is strictly observed. The inmates of the jail, being thus surrounded by the appliances of health, escaped without experiencing the slightest touch of the epidemic; while,—and the contrast will excite not only the attention of the philanthropist, but also that of the statesman,—of the 276 in-mates of the workhouse, no fewer than 60, or nearly 22 per cent. of the whole number, died of cholera within one week, and nearly all the survivors suffered to a greater or less extent from cholera or diarrhœa.

' Proceeding from the jail and the workhouse to the lunatic asylum, we find that Bethlem contains, on an average, 400 inmates. During the late epidemic no case of cholera occurred in this establishment, which enjoyed a similar exemption in 1832. Yet cholera prevailed extensively and severely within a hundred yards of the building. Mr. Granger states, —

' " Some years ago a particular gallery attracted the attention of " the authorities, in consequence of the inmates suffering from fever " and diarrhœa. This was the more unexpected, because the gallery " was one of the most favourably situated in the whole establishment; " it was lofty, very airy, and not at all crowded, and the patients " were of the healthiest class. Upon examination it was ascertained " that, owing to some defect in the water-closet, a leakage of the soil " had taken place beneath the floor. This was corrected; the sick-" ness ceased, and this gallery has ever since continued as healthy as " any part of the Institution."

' From the report of the resident medical officer of the asylum at Hanwell, it appears that no case of fever has occurred in that institution, containing 961 inmates since his appointment—a period of four years, and that he has been unable to find any record of such an attack for a much longer time.   There is unmistakable evidence that during the late epidemic this institution was not exempt from its influence, for 140 females were attacked with diarrhœa, 17 in one night, together with one nurse, all in the same ward, the diarrhœa being attended by great exhaustion, but none of these cases passed into the developed form of the disease, and no case of cholera occurred.

'We are next conducted to the great hospitals of the metropolis. In St. Bartholomew's Hospital, for example, 478 cases of cholera were admitted into some detached wards.   The average number of ordinary patients is 500, and there are upwards of 100 female attendants; out of this large number of nurses not a single case of cholera occurred.   It is stated that great attention is paid to the sanitary condition of the establishment, and that in the year preceding the late epidemic the sum of 2000*l.* was expended in improving the drainage of the hospital, which is represented as being now in a very efficient state.

'Similar exemptions are described as resulting from improvements recently introduced into St. Thomas's Hospital and Middlesex Hospital.

'Dr. Sutherland, after giving an abstract of the localising causes in the various cities and towns under his inspection, and pointing out the circumstances under which certain portions of them were exempted from cholera, sums up the result of his experience as follows:—

'"In every district which it attacked its ravages were most fatal
" where the sanitary conditions were the worst.   It took a smaller
" number from amongst those who lived in healthier localities; and,
" as a general rule, it may be stated, that those parts of our cities and
" towns which careful observation would pronounce as likely to be
" the most healthy, escaped almost entirely.   The epidemic was no
" respecter of classes, but was a great respecter of localities—rich
" and poor suffered alike or escaped alike, according as they lived in
" the observance or violation of the laws of their physical well-
" being."'

Even when the exemption was not (as in the preceding examples) complete, numerous instances occurred in various parts of Great Britain in which marked benefit was experienced from even minor sanitary improvements.   But we should abuse the indulgence of our readers by pursuing this branch of the subject further.

In every European city, as well as in the United States of America, the pestilence gave distinct warning of its approach, and intimated, by signs not to be mistaken, the severity of the impending attack.   An extraordinary prevalence and mortality of the classes of disease which have been observed usually to precede it foretold its approach and intensity: —

' At Moscow, at St. Petersburgh, and other Russian towns, its outbreak was preceded by a general prevalence of influenza and intermittent fever, the latter in many continental cities taking the place of typhus in this country. Diarrhœa also was generally prevalent before the actual outburst. At Berlin, intermittent fever, dysentery, but especially diarrhœa, were epidemic. The same diseases, but particularly intermittent fever, scarlet fever, and influenza were prevalent at Hamburgh. In London there had been during the preceding five years a progressive increase in the whole class of zymotic diseases, amounting to an excess above the average of 31 per cent.; while the mortality from typhus, which in 1846 considerably preponderated over that of 1845, was still higher in 1847, and exceeded in 1848, by several hundred deaths, the mortality of any preceding year. The deaths from scarlet fever were also greatly above the average; and such was the mortality from influenza, that in 1847 and 1848, almost as many at the earlier periods of life perished by this disease as by the more terrible epidemic that followed it; but the malady which all along continued its course with the most steady progress was that which was the most nearly allied in nature to the approaching epidemic, namely, diarrhœa; the deaths from this disease in the five years ending with 1848 amounting to 7580; whereas in the preceding five years they were only 2828; while taking separate years in this series, the deaths were in 1848 more than seven times greater than in 1839, and nearly five times greater than in 1841. All these circumstances indicated an epidemic force extending over the metropolis and steadily increasing, which justified the prediction of the Metropolitan Sanitary Commissioners — founded on their observation of the increased crowding of the population, its state of filth, its low sanitary condition, and the actual prevalence among the people of the diseases that precede and give warning of the approach of the pestilence, — that the impending epidemic would be more severe than that of 1832; and the event fully realised the prophecy.'

These facts attest the soundness of the conclusions to which the Board of Health are led in their Report on Quarantine : —

' But there is another consideration which alone appears sufficient to show that no reasonable confidence can be placed in quarantine as a means of protection against the introduction of pestilential diseases. Epidemics are in general really present in a country, and disorder the health of the people, before they are manifested in their peculiar and recognised forms. The significant signs by which their presence is declared are commonly called premonitory symptoms. These premonitory symptoms are more than warnings — they are indications of the actual presence of the disease — evidences that it has already commenced its work.

' It has long been observed that great epidemics are usually preceded by circumstances evidentiary of a change of condition in the health of the people, which is commonly regarded as constituting a predisposition or susceptibility to their influence some time before they make their decided and general attack. Thus it was observed by Sydenham, who has left a record of the epidemics that prevailed in London in the middle of the 17th century, for a successive period of sixteen years, including the time immediately before and after the great plague, that a remarkable change took place in the character of fevers and other diseases, approximating the general type of disease in several striking features to the distinguishing characteristics of the pestilence at hand, some months before that dreadful malady assumed its distinct and proper shape, which it did at last quite suddenly.

' A similar observation was made and recorded by Dr. Southwood Smith with reference to the type of fever in London six months before the visitation of cholera in 1832. During the six months immediately preceding the first appearance of cholera in this country, the character of fever in London so entirely changed, that typhus, which for a long series of years had been essentially an inflammatory disease, became a disease of debility, so closely resembling cholera, that the fever into which cholera patients commonly fell could not be distinguished from the primary fever found in the wards of the Fever Hospital when cholera was at its height, which had appeared there for the first time six months previously, but which has never disappeared since.

' Before the erection of quarantine as a barrier, therefore, the disease is already in the country busily in action, vitiating the blood of the most susceptible of the population, and preparing the way for its general outbreak.' (*Report on Quarantine,* pp. 12, 13.)

The cases of cholera in London in 1848 were among the first that appeared in Great Britain. The Board of Health had made the best provision, not only to prevent its extension, but also to watch its progress; and, aware of the importance of accurately observing the earliest cases of an epidemic, with a view to judge of its mode of propagation, they made arrangements for specially investigating on the spot every case that might occur the moment it was reported. Dr. Parkes, who had had much experience of the disease in India, was charged with this duty. The first undoubted case of Asiatic cholera occurred on Sept. 28.; from that day to the 10th of October there were in all 28 cases. Dr. Parkes's report gives the following results of the inquiries into them : —

' 1. These 28 cases occurred in 10 different localities.

' 2. These localities were not near each other, but were situated at remote distances.

' 3. In not a single instance, as far as could be traced, had the first person attacked in one locality been in contact or proximity with a person previously sick in another locality, and in some instances such contact or proximity was impossible.

' Thus the first case occurred (September 28th) at Horsleydown; two days afterwards (September 30th) two more cases occurred simultaneously, the one at Lambeth and the other at Chelsea; on the following day (October 1st) another case occurred in the City, in Harp Court, Fleet Street; the next day (October 2nd) a case occurred in the Justitia Hulk, at Woolwich; and three days afterwards (October 5th) the disease broke out simultaneously in the Dreadnought (hospital-ship) off Greenwich, and in Spitalfields.

' A convict was seized in the Justitia hulk at Woolwich on the 2nd of October, but the convicts at Woolwich, though they work in the dockyard, are watched by armed soldiers, and are allowed no intercourse whatever with other persons, while the Justitia herself lies about three miles below Greenwich, far apart from any other vessel except the convict hospital ship, no merchant vessel anchoring at this point of the river; so that, if cholera had been raging in Woolwich, and had been prevailing in the vessels in the Thames above Woolwich, the origin of cholera in the Justitia would not have been attributable to contagion. But there was no cholera in Woolwich, or in the merchant vessels in the Thames; and the only cases in London which were anterior in point of time to this in Woolwich were those at Horsleydown, seven or eight miles distant; Lambeth twelve or thirteen miles distant, Chelsea thirteen or fourteen miles distant, and Fleet Street ten or twelve miles distant. The occurrence of contact or proximity between these individuals and the convict at Woolwich may therefore be said to have been absolutely impossible.

' So again in the Dreadnought hospital-ship a man was attacked on the 5th October. The Dreadnought, as has been just stated, lies off Greenwich three or four miles distant from the Justitia, with which it holds no kind of communication; it is also many miles distant from Horsleydown, Lambeth, Chelsea, and Fleet Street. This man had been on board the hospital-ship under treatment for another complaint a month before his seizure; he could not therefore have been in contact or proximity with any of the nine cases which occurred previous to his attack, and no sailor arriving from any infected place had been admitted with any complaint whatever for some considerable time. "By permission of the officers," says Dr. Parkes, "I took the "opportunity of inspecting the admission book, and learned that no "sailor arriving in a ship from any port in or near which cholera was "or had been prevalent had been admitted for any complaint what- "ever for a considerable time. The disease therefore could not have "been brought on board by the clothes of some non-infected indi- "vidual arriving from an infected ship." '

At Glasgow the same results were obtained: —

' The parochial surgeon of the district in which cholera first broke out states, that no communication could be traced between the individuals first affected; and that 21 cases occurred under his own charge before he saw an example of two persons *consecutively* attacked in the same house or even in the same neighbourhood, that is, in the same street or lane. In 13 instances relatives lay in the same beds with the sick without being affected. In 9 cases children were suckled by women labouring under the disease, and yet not one of them was attacked.

' In numerous instances a person in sound health and living habitually in a pure atmosphere, on going into an infected locality and remaining there a short time, but without seeing or holding any intercourse with an infected person, imbibed the poison, went back into the country, and there sickened of the disease and died. In no instance that has come under our notice did such an individual communicate the disease to his nurse or to any member of his family, and in no case was his return followed by the spread of the disease in the neighbourhood.'

From the 15th to the 22d of October fifteen cases of cholera occurred among the convicts in Millbank Prison. The first was that of John Fisher, who had been there upwards of five months : he had no communication with any persons except the officer of his ward, the supervisor of his pentagon, the schoolmasters, the chaplains, and occasionally other prisoners of his own ward. None of these officers had been in any district where cholera prevailed; no prisoners had been received from Woolwich, and no stores from any place known to be infected. No prisoner in the same ward, or even on the same floor of the pentagon, was afterwards attacked, and the succeeding cases occurred for the most part in the most distant and separate parts of the building. In one instance two men occupying contiguous rooms were attacked, the one two days after the other ; but the two rooms did not communicate directly with each other, and the two men had no direct intercourse; but there were several other prisoners in the cells with them, none of whom were attacked.

' " In the Infirmary," says Dr. Baly, Medical Superintendent of the Prison " where there was the most chance of infection occurring, " since, although a special room is set apart for the cholera patients, " this room communicates with the other parts of the Infirmary, none " of the patients admitted for other diseases have been attacked with " cholera; and excepting the instances above referred to, the men " attacked with cholera in the pentagons have all been in different " wards, and where two cases have occurred in one pentagon this has " been even on different floors. In each of these cases it appears to " me there would be the same difficulty in accounting for the produc- " tion of the disease by contagion as in the case of Fisher. After an " unbiassed consideration of all the facts, therefore, I can but con- " clude that cholera has not shown itself to have a contagious cha- " racter in this prison."

' From the preceding evidence the conclusion is inevitable that the first cases of cholera in London, whether occurring in the metropolis generally or in particular establishments, did not originate and spread by contact or proximity of the infected with the uninfected. This observation is in accordance with the facts recorded with reference to plague by those who have had opportunities of observing the progress of this disease in the countries and cities in which it prevails as an epidemic, who state that on its outbreak the first cases are in like manner isolated ; that they appear in localities remote from each other ; and that there is no traceable communication between the persons first attacked.'—*Report on Quarantine*, p. 29.

' An attentive consideration of the course of the disease from nation to nation is not favourable to the view of its propagation by contact from person to person. But an inspection of the dates when the disease first made its appearance in the several towns and cities of this country is still more decisive against this opinion. For example, on its first outbreak in 1848 cases of it occurred, as reported to us, on the same day at Lasswade, near Edinburgh, Sunderland, and Hounslow ; on another day at Falkirk, Tynemouth, and Chelmsford ; on a third at Greenock, Preston Kirk, Monckland, Blantyre, Thornhill, and Cambridge, and the like instances might be multiplied to a great extent.

' In Dundee, Bristol, Liverpool, Hull, and every town in Great Britain in which the first cases were accurately observed, its invasion was similar ; so that this approach by isolated attacks, at considerable distances as to place, and intervals as to time, may be regarded as one of the laws of the epidemic. The popular notion that cholera is sudden in its invasion of a place or district, is as unfounded as the former prevalent opinion that it is sudden in its attack of the individual person. Experience has refuted both these opinions, and established the very opposite fact, namely, that, at least in this country, it is gradual and even slow in its approach. And the recognition of this law is of the highest importance in a practical point of view. These isolated cases occurring in any locality during the prevalence of a general epidemic constitution, are unequivocal and certain signs that an outbreak is impending over that place. They are warnings not to be mistaken, demanding the immediate and energetic adoption of preventive measures.'

From the facts—that this disease is not sudden in its attack, that it gives warning of its approach in time for the adoption of effectual means to arrest its progress, that even where its prevalence is most extensive its presence is confined to circumscribed localities, that in those very localities the mortality is restricted within an exceedingly narrow space, and that it seldom continues long at any one point, but attacks numbers of points in succession,—the practical inference was deduced that if those precious moments which intervene between the premonition and the attack were properly employed, the actual attack might be averted. Accordingly, a staff of qualified persons, consisting chiefly of medical students and young men commencing practice, was organised to make a house-to-house visitation in every locality in which the disease might break out, taking with them appropriate remedies for the premonitory stage, which they were instructed to administer on the spot. It was found that a large staff was not needed for this service, but that if those who undertook it devoted their whole time to the work, and performed it with the precision of a military movement, a small number of persons could visit every house in an infected locality once, twice, and even three times daily. This was actually done in every part of the kingdom visited by this plague where the advice of the General Board of Health was followed. The following are among some of the most remarkable results : —

1. The discovery of a number of dead bodies in the houses visited, the individuals having died of cholera without having received any medical assistance whatever. 2. The discovery of great numbers of cases of cholera in various stages of development, rapidly proceeding to a fatal termination, without medical assistance, or the slightest apprehension of danger on the part either of the sufferers or their friends. 3. The discovery of a vast number of cases of premonitory diarrhœa, without any medicine being taken, without any change being made in diet, without any thought of sickness, and much less without apprehension of the actual presence and positive commencement of a mortal malady. 4. A sudden increase in the number of applications at dispensaries for the supply of medicines, one special duty of the visitor being to direct all persons who might be taken ill after his visit to make instant application for aid to the nearest dispensary. 5. An immediate and progressive diminution in the number of developed cases of cholera. 6. An apparent increase in the number of the premonitory cases; premonitory diarrhœa taking the place of developed cholera. 7. A decided diminution in the number of fresh attacks. 8. A decided diminution in the mortality. 9. Sometimes a rapid cessation of the disease, and invariably a steady progress towards it. Thus, at Dumfries, with a population of 10,000, before the visitation system was commenced, 147, and before it was in full operation, 250 of the townspeople had perished. On the three first days during which the system was in partial use, the fresh attacks daily were respectively 37, 38, 23 ; and the deaths, 9, 6, 9 ; on the three succeeding days, when it was in full activity, the attacks diminished to 11, 14, 12, and the deaths to 7, 3, 6 ; and on the following three days the attacks sunk to 8, 4, 2, and the deaths to 6, 4, 5 ; in three days more the epidemic was at an end. At Charleston, a suburb of Paisley, when the system of visitation commenced, the fresh attacks amounted to 23 daily ; on the fourth day after the system was

in complete operation they fell to 3 daily, and in a few days more the pestilence ceased. At the small village of Nordelf, out of a population of 150 souls, there had occurred no fewer than 50 attacks of cholera. At this point the visitation system was introduced, after which only four new cases occurred, and these were saved. Out of the large and peculiarly predisposed population of Glasgow, 15,000 cases of premonitory diarrhœa were promptly brought under treatment; of these 1000 had already advanced to the stage of rice-water purging, yet out of this total number only 27 passed into developed cholera. The results were still more striking in the Parkhead district of the Barony Parish, Glasgow; where the system of visitation proved that the premonitory cases were to those of developed cholera in the proportion of 3000, 3300, 5900, and even 6000 per cent.; and where, tracking the pestilence by its invariable sign from street to street, and house to house, and room to room, it arrested its course, and prevented it from passing beyond the premonitory stage. The result was similar in the Metropolis, in Manchester, in Bristol, and other large towns. We forbear to give the details. It may suffice to state that the most earnest testimony is borne to the extraordinary efficacy of this mode of dealing with the pestilence from every place in which it was tried, and that it is now admitted by all — medical men and others — who have turned their attention to the results of this most important and instructive experience, — that if epidemic cholera should again break out in this country, the first duty of the Government and of local authorities will be to organise a plan for carrying this measure into prompt and efficient operation.

A most elaborate Report on Epidemic Cholera as it prevailed in the United States, in 1849–50, has been given to the world by Dr. James Wynne, Chairman of the Medical Department of the National Institute and Chairman of the First Committee of the Public Hygiene of the American Medical Association. The rise and progress of the disease in several different parts of the Union where it appeared are traced with minute accuracy; the first cases of seizure in each place are examined with the greatest care, and are found to have arisen among the same classes of persons, and in the same kind of places, while the mode of attack was the same, as in Great Britain. The haunts of the ordinary autumnal fever of the country supplied the epidemic with victims. In fact, we find in Dr. Wynne's Report a perfect counterpart of the history of the epidemic in Great Britain. Wherever the atmosphere was polluted by filth, foul drains, overcrowding, and the other local sources of pestilence, there the epidemic commenced and flourished, in the new country as in the old ; and it is most satisfactory to find that the same sanitary measures of precaution which we have shown to have averted the epidemic wherever they were adopted in Great Britain, are proved by Dr. Wynne to have been alike successful in the United States of America. His Report covers a large and diversified field, including New Orleans, Memphis, Nashville, St. Louis, Louisville, Cincinnati, Buffalo, New York, Albany, Newark, Philadelphia, Boston, Rhode Island, and Baltimore: it is more full and positive than the Report of the Irish Commissioners, and concludes thus : —

' In all these circumstances, the adjuncts in the production of cholera are found to maintain a striking resemblance to those which produce malarial diseases. If the question was propounded to me, After the collection of all these facts, can you tell what is the nature of the cause that produces cholera ? I should unhesitatingly reply that *I could not.* But I should give the same answer if I were interrogated concerning the nature of autumnal fever. It is true I might reply, in regard to fever, that it depended upon the presence of malaria. But what is malaria ? It is the decomposition, under certain known circumstances, of vegetable matter. These circumstances are the presence of air, heat, and moisture. Whenever these elements unite in due proportion, fever is produced, but if either be wanting, malaria is not generated. Hence during the cold of winter and the dryness of midsummer we have no fever, but with the decomposed vegetation of autumn, united with the heat and moisture of that season of the year, fevers prevail. Heat and moisture cannot produce fever ; it requires decomposed matter, uncleanliness, and filth. These are precisely the circumstances under which cholera makes its appearance, and the reader will have had frequent occasion to observe how much it is under the conjoint influence of elevated temperature and moisture, and how steadfastly it dwells among filth and uncleanliness.

' I do not assert that the cause of autumnal fever and cholera are identical, but I do aver that the whole history of the epidemic, as it prevailed in the United States, proves that it cannot exist in the absence of those conjoined elements known to produce fever ; and no facts more fully substantiate this position, than those connected with its prevalence at the Baltimore almshouse, and its absence in the city as an epidemic. No person will fail to recognise, in the filthy condition in which this establishment was kept, a sufficient cause for disease, and no one can doubt the influence it exercised over the spread of cholera in this immediate locality.

' If this position be fully substantiated, have we not the means in our own hands of arresting its desolating ravages ? Does not this disease present itself as a teacher as well as a scourge ? Every one must admit the justice of the following observations of Professor Caldwell : —

' " Cholera, though a fatal scourge to the world, will, through the " wise and beneficent dispensation under which we live, be productive " of consequences favourable alike to science and humanity. Besides " being instrumental in throwing much light on the practice of phy- " sic, it will prove highly influential in extinguishing the belief in " pestilential contagion, and bringing into disrepute the quarantine " and sanitary establishments that have hitherto existed."

' If these facts should prove to be true, and if they arouse the public authorities of large towns to the immense responsibility under which they hold their offices, these pages will not have been written in vain.'

Such was the pestilence — such the subtle morbific agencies which were to be counteracted by ordering vessels from Ham- burgh to perform quarantine in the Humber. The practical ill effects of that order drew forth a powerful remonstrance addressed by the Board of Health to the Privy Council*, on the 9th of November, 1848. Among other causes of just com- plaint, it appears that no provision was made for prompt medical attendance in case of sickness occurring on board vessels in quarantine. The roads where these vessels were stationed are distant eight miles from the port of Hull, where only was medi- cal assistance procurable.

' Considering the fearful rapidity with which cholera runs its course, it does appear to the Board to be a defect to place a number of persons who have been exposed to the cholera poison in a situation in which, even in the day-time, and under the most favourable cir- cumstances, they cannot be reached in less than three or four hours ; and under unfavourable circumstances, scarcely within six hours. The inspector of the river indeed says, — " it would, in general, be eight or " nine hours." But the difficulty and delay must be still greater, if any persons on board these vessels are seized suddenly during the night, which experience shows is the time when the subjects of this formidable disease are most commonly attacked.

' It appears to the Board, that if wayfarers, passengers, merchants, and foreigners are subjected to the anxieties of suspicion, the disad- vantage of confinement, and the inconvenience and loss of delay for

---

* Quarantine was introduced into this country by an Act passed in the ninth year of Queen Anne (9 Ann. c. 2.), on the appear- ance of the plague in the Baltic. The present law was passed in the reign of George IV. By a curious anomaly, the provisions of the Quarantine Act are administered, even in their minute details, by the Privy Council, acting, it is presumed, under the guidance of the Superintendent-General of Quarantine, who, with the other officers of Quarantine, however, is for the purposes of salary treated as be- longing to the Board of Customs and not to the Privy Council, whereby the establishment escapes the annual scrutiny of the House of Commons in voting the estimate of the Council Office.

the presumed safety of the public, justice requires that all practical precaution should be taken for lessening their danger, affording them assistance, and mitigating the evils of their unfortunate position.'

Several instances, indeed, occurred of persons leaving Hamburgh apparently in perfect health, who were seized with cholera on their passage to Hull; some of them being in a state of hopeless collapse, and others dead, on the arrival of the vessel at that port. Mr. Hardey, the Medical Superintendent of Quarantine at Hull, writes : —

' As I stated in my last, the two cases of Asiatic cholera to which I have been summoned on board these quarantine steamers have both been found in collapse when visited; whereas had they been at hand and early attended, they might probably have been relieved. The "Rob Roy" on Sunday had to break her quarantine ground, and steam to Hull Roads for assistance, but it was too late. She went down again after the death, and as I have heard nothing from her, I hope all continue well on board.

' The Board of Health would call the attention of their lordships to the anxiety and distress which would probably be excited in some of the passengers, on finding that this vessel had in vain broken her quarantine to obtain assistance, and that she had returned to the spot in which they had already experienced that all relief was hopeless.'

The letter from the Board of Health to the Privy Council is, in fact, an unanswerable exposure of the inutility and mischief of quarantine as administered on that occasion. Its statements have never been controverted. The actual working of the system is well exemplified, from his own personal experience, in the following letter from the Vice-Chairman of the General Steam Navigation Company : —

' Referring to the conversation had with reference to the quarantine regulations, to which ships coming from Hamburg have been subjected on their arrival in England, I beg to state that on my arrival at Hamburg on the 12th of October last, when returning from Schleswick, and with the intention of proceeding from that place direct to London the following night by the mail steamer, I learned that intelligence had reached Hamburg that on the 6th of October an order in London had been issued, "that all ships coming from Hamburg were to perform quarantine for six days, to be reckoned from the time of " departure ; but, were also, in case of any illness being on board, or " which came while lying in quarantine, to remain so, not only until " the party or parties were convalescent, but for six days more after " such convalescence," therefore making the quarantine almost for an indefinite period.

' On inquiry whether such an order had been issued, as it would very seriously impede the usual commercial intercourse, I found that such was really the case, and I found also that the same had created the greatest astonishment and surprise among officials, merchants, and captains; because, as they very justly said, that the cholera was in England, even in London; and the regulations as regards passengers were completely useless and vexatious, as those from Hamburg who had occasion to proceed to England were not compelled to go by sea, but had other routes open to them, the land route by Holland, as also the route by Belgium and France, and either of which would of course be taken by them, not being subject to any quarantine, nor suffering any inconvenience excepting that the journey would be much more troublesome, be twenty-four to thirty-six hours longer, and more expensive, but which was to be preferred to the annoyance of performing quarantine on board a ship, moored within sight of land, and surrounded by water and fogs sufficient to give those on board the ague, if not a worse disease.

' In order, therefore, to avoid all this, I, as well as several other individuals, proceeded by land through Hanover, Prussia, and Belgium to Ostend.

' I have also inquired of some of the captains of the Hamburg mail steamers during the period the quarantine regulations were lately enforced, whether any instructions had been received by them how to act, in case any serious case of illness or cholera had occurred while lying in quarantine, and if no instructions had been given, how they would have acted in case of such an occurrence either happening in the day or by night? It was admitted that in regard to such an occurrence they had been without instructions, and added, that if unfortunately such an occurrence had taken place, they would have hardly known how to have proceeded, as no communication with the shore was allowed ; perhaps, in the first instance, they would have probably administered a dose of cholera medicine which they have on board, and then have made a signal in the hope that the authorities would come to the ship; a person, therefore, before any assistance could come might be dead, or in such a state that there would be no hope of recovery.

' I believe I may, in conclusion, safely say, that withdrawing this useless regulation has given universal satisfaction, at least among mercantile and seafaring men, not because the one is thereby relieved from an inconvenience in travelling, or the other from imprisonment, but really on account of its utter inutility.'

' From these statements (and many similar representations have been made to the Board) it appears that even assuming the doctrine of contagion to be true, quarantine regulations are calculated to defeat their own object ; for neglect, inconvenience, delay, expense, and loss, all operate as so much bounty on misrepresentation, false swearing, and evasion.'

We have devoted so much time to the History of the Cholera Epidemic of 1848–9 because, of the three diseases which are the especial subjects of quarantine, viz., plague, yellow fever, and cholera, the last is the most personally interesting to the inhabitants of Great Britain, which it appears to be now steadily approaching in its former track*; and because the facts are less liable to distortion from having occurred in our own country, in very recent times, and before the eyes of hosts of living witnesses. The three diseases are of the same family, differing in external aspect, and in the internal organs which principally suffer, but agreeing in the following material points : —

' They are all fevers, they are all dependent upon certain atmospheric conditions, they all obey similar laws of diffusion, they all infest the same sort of localities, they all attack chiefly the same classes, and for the most part persons of the like ages; and their intensity is increased or diminished by the same sanitary and social conditions.

' The consideration of these common properties of pestilence, under whatever form or name it may occur, has led to the general conclusion that the true safeguards against pestilential diseases are not quarantine regulations, but sanitary measures — that is to say, measures which tend to prevent or remove certain conditions, without which pestilential diseases appear to be incapable of existing.

' The whole machinery of quarantine is based on the assumption that by an absolute interdiction of communication with the sick, either by the person or by infected articles, it can prevent the introduction of epidemic disease into an unaffected community.

---

* It has again begun in Persia, advanced to Russia, and visited Warsaw in a more terrible manner than ever ; there having been in that city nearly 6000 deaths, and according to the most recent advices half the attacked dying. From Warsaw it has spread to Dantzic and the neighbouring country, and at the same time advanced westward, having, according to the public papers, already reached Magdeburgh, about 150 miles from Hamburgh. In 1848 it was at Hamburgh in September, and in Edinburgh in October. In our own metropolis, as well as in many provincial towns, diarrhœa is now (September 9th) more epidemic than it was in 1848, before the actual appearance of the pestilence, and not a day passes without accounts being transmitted to the Board of Health of fatal cases of cholera, so exactly resembling Asiatic, that no difference is appreciable. Under these circumstances we are glad to perceive that the Government has appointed, as medical inspectors, to watch the progress of the disease both at home and abroad, and to make preparation for its outbreak should it occur, Dr. Sutherland and Mr. Grainger, who during the whole course of the last epidemic, ' more than any ' private practitioners, and more probably than any other public ser-' vants, were engaged in a personal and laborious examination of the ' conditions connected with the propagation of the disease, and in ' superintending in different towns in various parts of the kingdom, ' the application of the measures which, on the best consideration, ' were judged necessary to meet the most formidable attacks of the ' disease.' (*Report on Cholera*, p. 2.)

'But this assumption overlooks the essential condition on which epidemic disease depends, namely,—the presence of an epidemic atmosphere, without which it is now generally admitted that no contagion, whether imported or native, can cause a disease to spread epidemically. Allowing, therefore, to contagion all the influence which any one supposes it to possess, and to quarantine all the control over it which it claims, there remains the condition, the primary and essential condition, which confessedly it cannot reach, namely, the epidemic atmosphere.'

The letter to the Privy Council was followed in 1849 by a Report upon Quarantine, in which the facts bearing upon that subject are brought out with clearness, the arguments are logically deduced, and the whole question is investigated in the true spirit of philosophical inquiry. Although it did not excite in this country the attention which it deserved, yet on the continent of Europe, having been translated into French and Italian, it was extensively read, producing a powerful effect, especially in France, Austria, and Russia; and it appears to have materially accelerated the formation of a general congress, which the leading governments of Europe had for some years been earnestly labouring to convene, for the purpose of effecting a general revision of the practice of quarantine; accordingly in July 1851, at the invitation of France, a conference of representatives from different nations (*Conférence Sanitaire Internationale* *) assembled at Paris to consider this question. The countries sending representatives were Austria, France, Spain, Great Britain, Greece, Naples, Portugal, Rome, Russia, Sardinia, Turkey, and Tuscany.

The reasons for summoning this conference were ' the excessive and unnecessary severity of the Quarantine Laws in the ' Mediterranean, their inequality in different States, their arbi-

---

* During the fight on the Boulevards of the 4th December, 1851, amidst the roar of artillery and the fusillades of the infantry, the Conference was in Session, and refused either to accept the protection of guards or to discontinue its labours. While the battle was going on, the Conference was calmly discussing the great question of Sanitary Reform in the East, and the spread of civilisation and commerce among its inhabitants. It was at this meeting that it was decided to recommend the erection of the Boards of Health at Constantinople and Alexandria into Boards having special reference to the introduction of sanitary reforms over the whole extent of the Turkish Empire. The sanitary propositions were contained in a Report on the subject drawn up and signed by Dr. Sutherland.

This steady perseverance of the Conference, in its special work, drew forth the strongest expressions of thanks from the French Government.

' trary and irresponsible nature — the enormous losses they
' inflicted on commerce, which were estimated by the French
' authorities at 100 millions of francs for France alone — the
' strong doubts which have of late years been entertained by
' scientific men of the highest reputation as to the possibility
' of importing epidemic disease, and consequently as to the utility
' of quarantine, had begun to throw discredit on the system,
' while the inevitable march of events, the all-conquering power
' of steam, hastened the reconsideration of all its disadvantages
' — Steam would not much longer submit to lose the benefits of
' improved speed in transit from being placed under arrest by
' the health officer — Lastly the evident contradiction between
' the doctrines of quarantine and that necessity of intercourse
' which Providence is now, as it were, revealing and urging on
' the human race.   In the face of these reasons, it behoved us
' to demand of quarantine a justification of the faith that was
' in it.'

We are glad to perceive that towards the end of the last Session
of Parliament, Lord St. Germans, in a very able and statesman-
like speech, moved for the production of the proceedings of the
Conference.   From the debate on that motion, we learn that the
Conference agreed in the recognition of the great principle contended for in the Report on Quarantine — the substitution of
sanitary precautions for quarantine, coercion, and isolation.   This
is indeed substantially announced by the President of the *Conference* himself, M. David, who in presenting his Report said,
' In so far as concerns measures of Hygiene, they will be obli-
' gatory in all cases and against all diseases, for you have under-
' stood the importance of these measures, which at no distant
' date will render useless (*inutile*) by their efficacy all the
' other precautions, so onerous, which we are yet obliged to
' take against these destructive scourges, of which, without
' doubt, the civilisation of the 19th century will demand the
' reason.'

The Medico-Chirurgical Academy of Genoa has recently
given some account of the proceedings and main results of the
Conference.

We believe that the following is, so far as it goes, a correct
outline of the changes recommended : —

1. The equalisation of quarantine throughout the Mediterranean.

2. The reduction of the period of quarantine.

3. The total abolition of *suspected* bills of health, which would
sweep away the great majority of the quarantines at present
exacted.

4. The issuing of foul bills of health only on competent and responsible authority.

5. The immediate admission of clean bills of health to free pratique in every port.

6. The restriction of Quarantine to three diseases only, namely Cholera, Fellow Fever, and Plague.

7. The total abolition of the former distinction between susceptible and non-susceptible articles, — distinctions which filled volumes,—and the reduction of all articles to three classes:—

  a. Those which in time of disease must undergo quarantine and purification, namely, hides and skins, animal refuse, rags, wool, and silk.

  b. Those with reference to which quarantine and purification are optional, namely, cotton, hemp, and flax.

  c. All other substances, which go free.

8. That all steam boats carrying passengers should have a medical officer on board.

9. The responsibility of quarantine administrations.

10. The medical and other care of the sick in establishments properly adapted for their accommodation and treatment.

11. The reform of quarantine dues.

12. The application of measures of Hygiene against foul and infected ships and sea-ports, rather than quarantine against the country from which such ships may have taken their departure. It may be matter of surprise that with such views the *Conference* did not at once abolish quarantine. This, however, was impossible, because most of the members had specific instructions to the contrary, and there are unfortunately other and latent considerations connected with quarantine besides the mere question of the public health. All that could be done was to adopt sound principles as extensively as possible, to reduce quarantine to a minimum, and to equalise it over all the contracting States. These are reforms not to be rejected; commercially they are next in importance to Free Trade; sanatorially, thay are next in importance to the abolition of the cesspool and the cellar dwelling.

At this *Conference* Great Britain was represented by Dr. Sutherland, of the General Board of Health, and Sir Anthony Perrier, Her Majesty's Consul at Brest, who have discharged the duties confided to them with zeal, ability, and discretion, Lord Normandy being at the same time our ambassador at Paris, who not only in that capacity, but previously when holding the Seals of Secretary of State, had approved himself an active promoter of commercial freedom and sanitary reform. We anxiously look for the publication of the proceedings of the

Conference, and for the ratification of the international sanitary convention, to the construction of which its labours were directed; trusting that no sinister influences, no difficulties raised by quarantine departments, in matters of form where the principle cannot be impugned, no mere points of diplomatic etiquette, will be allowed to mar the success of a measure so conducive to the welfare, happiness, and harmony of the great European Family, and that the several Governments of Europe will disregard all the artifices by which quarantine seeks to prolong its baleful existence, at the expense of the health and commerce of the world. Having already achieved so many victories in the cause of commercial freedom, our own country has now a glorious opportunity — which it would be worse than foolish, it would be sinful, to neglect, — for vindicating her claim to the privilege of being foremost in the march of international sanitary reform.

Art. V.—1. *The History of Small-pox.* By James Moore, Member of the Royal College of Surgeons, &c. Longman. pp. 312.

2. *The History and Practice of Vaccination.* By James Moore. Callow. 1818. pp. 300.

FROM the commencement of our labours, with one or two exceptions, we have purposely abstained from medical disquisitions, under the impression that they occupy a more appropriate place in publications devoted especially to their admission. The question, however, which we now propose to canvass is one in which all men are not only interested, but upon which, with the evidence before them, all are competent to decide—a question too which annually involves the lives of nearly forty thousand individuals in the British islands alone, and the constitution and personal appearance of vast numbers besides. It is,—whether the recently proposed substitute for small-pox can establish its claims of being an effectual and safe preventive of that distemper? Until this question be finally decided, its agitation can never be out of time; but we have, perhaps, chosen the fittest of all periods for our remarks upon it, since the doubts of many as to the efficacy of vaccination, which had died away under the weight of evidence in its favour, have, by recent circumstances, been revived. At the moment in which we are writing, there are numberless parents suffering under the most cruel apprehensions lest their children should in after-life be obnoxious to one of the most formidable and fatal of all diseases. The vaccinated child, it is said, may resist the small-pox influence for a longer or shorter period, according to its peculiarity of constitutional temperament; but there is nevertheless a limit to this exemption, and the same

A A 2   small-

small-pox which cannot now be communicated even by inoculation, may, in after-life, spontaneously occur as the result of a prevailing infection. To enlarge, however, upon the importance of our present undertaking would be a waste of words; we shall therefore proceed to the business before us.

At the head of the present article we have placed the titles of two works, recently published by Mr. Moore,—the one on small-pox, and the other on vaccination—as it is conceived that a succinct history of the former will impart a somewhat more lively interest to the investigation of the merits of the latter.

It is in vain that we search the writings of the ancients for the description of any disease that can be recognised as small-pox, and the inference is therefore more than presumptive that the Greek and Roman fathers of medicine never saw the malady in question. The contrary position has, indeed, been maintained by those who can discern nothing in modern science of any kind which was not familiar in a different form to the ancients. Mr. Moore more judiciously assumes the ignorance of the Greek and Roman writers respecting it, on the ground of their utter silence on the subject. ' Erysipelas,' he says, ' erythema, lepra, herpes, and scrofula, are fully described by them; pimples, vesicles, and pustules, are also spoken of; but there is no account of a distemper clearly characterized, like the small-pox by the Arabians, though these were far inferior writers to Aretæus or Galen, or Celsus.'

Whence then the origin of small-pox? and whence its prevalence through the whole of the civilized world? Dr. Freind expresses his opinion that its seeds were first sown in Egypt. Dr. Mead supposed it to be of Æthiopian origin, and that from Æthiopia it extended itself into Arabia and Egypt. ' Hic igitur morbus mihi vera pestis sui generis esse videtur; quæ in Africa primum genita, præsertim in Æthiopia, quæ pars ejus intolerabiliter est torrida, in Arabiam deinde et Ægyptum (ut vastatrix illa populorum magna pestis) iis, quas diximus, modis delata est.'

Were there, however, nothing stronger against the hypotheses of these learned physicians than the circumstance of small-pox being, with respect to its prevalence, in a great measure independent of climate or local peculiarities, this in itself would be a sufficient refutation of their notions of its origin. The mistake of these writers as to the actual nature and probable production of this distemper seems to arise principally from their confounding the ideas of contagion and infection: thus, in the quotation from Mead, it is evident that he conceives the small-pox to be a species of plague, engendered by the nature of the Æthiopian atmosphere; but it is known that real plagues, the νοσημαία επιχωρια of Hippocrates, are incapable of being imparted, from one individual to another, in any

part

part of the world, whatever may be the nature of the soil, the climate, or the atmosphere, in which such communication is made.*

Notwithstanding then that our most distinct and accredited accounts of small-pox are to be found in the Arabian writers who flourished during the dark ages of European learning, it seems difficult to conceive the spontaneous origin of its virus in this, or indeed in any other part of the world; and we are naturally led to search for its existence in still more ancient records.

In the second chapter of his volume, Mr. Moore has endeavoured, and we think successfully, to prove, by the details handed down from the earliest Christian missionaries to China, that small-pox existed in that country ' from a very remote period;' and that even the artificial mode of communicating the distemper was known and practised by the Chinese many centuries antecedent to the diffusion of the poison through other regions of the globe.

' The missionaries (says our author) who were sent into China by the church of Rome, from their address and insinuation gained access to their historical records; and they have transmitted detailed accounts of the history of the Chinese, and of their knowledge in various branches of science. There is a memoir written upon small-pox by the missionaries at Pekin, the substance of which is extracted from Chinese medical books, and especially from a work published by the Imperial College of Medicine, for the instruction of the physicians of the empire. This book is entitled, Teou-tchin-fa, or a treatise from the heart on small-pox; which states that this disease was unknown in the very early ages, and did not appear till the dynasty of Tcheou, which was about 1122 years before Christ. The Chinese name for the malady is a singular one, Tai-tou, or venom from the mother's breast; and a description is given of the fever, the eruption of pustules, their increase, flattening, and crusting. In the same Chinese book there is also an account of a species of inoculation discovered seven centuries previously; but according to a tradition it had been invented in the dynasty of Long, that is, about 590 years after Christ. Father d'Entrecolles, the Jesuit, (continues our author,) mixes, in his correspondence from China, some information respecting the small-pox, which confirms the material part of the above information, for he notices having read some Chinese books which mention the small-pox as a disease of the earliest ages. He also describes a method of communicating the disease, which was occasionally used, and called *sowing the small-pox*: this was generally performed by planting some of the crusts up the nose, an operation which was approved of by some, but disapproved by most authors.'

---

* This indeed constitutes the great leading distinction between contagious and infectious diseases—that the one are independent of place and circumstance, the other not. A great deal has recently been said on the non-contagious nature of the plague, and it should seem, at least, probable, that this disorder is incapable of transference in the way that our quarantine laws suppose; but utterly to deny its infectious quality is to fly in the face of all fact, Plague is an infectious, but not, perhaps, properly a contagious distemper.

After

After every deduction from the accuracy of the records in question on the score of traditionary claims and conceits, there still remains a sufficiency of testimony to the fact that the Chinese had been familiar with the small-pox many centuries before the Arabian writers described it; and its early existence in Japan and Hindostan is likewise presumable from several striking particulars connected with Hindoo mythology and worship.

Assuming then the fact that Asia was acquainted with the disease in question long before its establishment in any part either of Africa or Europe, and very far antecedent even to the time of Hippocrates, it becomes a question of interest ' how it happened that the infection did not extend into Persia, and thence into Greece, long before the age of the last mentioned author.'

That a communication was established between Persia and India by the invasion of the latter country at a very early period is universally acknowledged; and it is also admitted that ' the rapacious invaders who went from Persia would of course be attacked by the diseases which prevailed in the countries they laid waste;' but, adds Mr. Moore, ' the numbers which perished, the time which was spent in so distant a warfare, and the extent of the deserts which were recrossed, appear to have secured their native country from being contaminated by the few survivors of those expeditions. With respect to the commercial intercourse subsequently established between the more western and the eastern countries, and the probability of diseased communication from that source, we are likewise to recollect the obstacles which in those times existed to ready communication, either by land or sea, from one part of the globe to another.'

Among the many traditionary fancies respecting the origin of small-pox, there is one which supposes it to have been first imparted to man by the camel: this notion probably took its rise from the circumstance that land commerce from Egypt to India was only practicable by means of this animal. But such kind of traffic was tedious and difficult, and it is conjectured that no person known to have the small-pox upon him would ever have been suffered to join himself to a caravan. Again, the tediousness of coasting voyages, the only ones then attempted, gave time for contagion to be extinguished, if by accident any of the sick were admitted into the homeward bound ships from the east.

Such are the explanations proposed by Mr. Moore and others of the exemption of Europe from small-pox for so long a time subsequent to its prevalence in the east; and these certainly appear the only plausible conjectures on the assumed fact. Yet when we recollect the extreme subtlety, and insinuating and transportable nature of the virus, it seems extraordinary that even such an interrupted

rupted and difficult commerce as was carried on at the time alluded to did not prove a medium of conveying the poison from China and Hindostan to the more western nations.

' If the Persians,' says Mr. Moore, ' had engaged early in maritime commerce, from their vicinity to India, they would probably have soon brought into their country the small-pox. But the ancient historians declare, that the Persians entertained an insuperable superstitious aversion to the sea; and Robertson asserts, that " no commercial intercourse seems to have been carried on by sea between Persia and India." The spirit of commerce, when once excited, is however active and persevering; and the European demand for the muslins, the silks, the spices, the pearls, and the diamonds of the east, perpetually augmented. To facilitate their transportation, a busy coasting trade spread on both sides of the peninsula of Hindostan to the islands eastward, to the kingdom of Siam, and even to China. The luxurious productions of these distant countries were thus brought to the most convenient harbours to be conveyed to Alexandria and diffused through the Roman empire. This lucrative trade was so tempting, that towards the beginning of the sixth century, the Persians began to surmount their aversion to maritime affairs, and their harbours were filled with trading vessels. They soon monopolized the silk`trade; for their vicinity to India gave them great advantages over the Egyptian merchants; *but it also augmented the danger of transporting the variolous contagion.* Indeed whatever attention might have been paid by the commanders of these merchant vessels, it was impossible that this calamity should have been avoided much longer; and as ships coming from India, both in their passage to the Persian Gulph, and to the Red Sea, *frequently touched at the Arabian ports, that country was peculiarly exposed, and there accordingly it was first observed.*'

Dr. Reiske, who was celebrated for his acquaintance with Arabian antiquities, in an inaugural Dissertation which he published in the year 1746, gave a translation of an Arabian manuscript found in the Leyden library, which dates the introduction of small-pox into Arabia in 572, the year that gave birth to Mahomet. Other testimonies seem to accord with the statement that it was at the siege of Mecca by Abrabah that the Arabians first became obnoxious to this pestilence.

The conquests of the false prophet, and the fanaticism of his followers, soon extended themselves far and wide; and, as may easily be conceived, the ravages of the new disease accompanied every where the track of the conquerors, who, in less than half a century, had established their dominion not only over Egypt and Syria, but a great part of Persia also. The contagion, however, was long prevented from finding its way into Europe, by the successful stand which the inhabitants of Constantinople made against the invaders. ' Thus the Mahometan empire was bounded by the Hellespont, and that entrance for the small-pox into Europe barred up.' This.

A A 4 indeed,

indeed, was done so effectually, that even in the tenth century we have it recorded by a resident physician in that city, (Nonus,) that neither the small-pox nor measles was known in Constantinople in his time.

It was not till the commencement of the eighth century, when the whole southern coasts of the Mediterranean had been subdued by the Arabians, that the contagion first visited Europe; and the landing of an army of Moors in Gibraltar and Spain, conducted by Julian, in order to revenge the outrage committed by Roderick on his daughter, is said to have been the means of introducing the disease in question into this quarter of the world.

' By this invasion,' says Mr. Moore, ' the small-pox must have been brought into Spain, and the victorious Saracens soon reached the Pyrenees. In the year 731, Abderame crossed these mountains, and inundated the southern provinces of France with an host of Saracens. They were opposed under the walls of Tours by Charles Martel, when Christians and Mahometans fought six days, indecisively, for victory. But in a closer combat on the seventh day, the impetuous yet slender Africans and Asiatics were crushed by the superior strength of the Germanic warriors. The Saracens and the Koran were repelled into Spain, but the small-pox and measles remained in France. No warlike efforts could drive off these infections; and the opportunities of diffusing them had at that time become innumerable. The Saracen fleets were triumphant in the Mediterranean; Sicily and Italy were frequently invaded; many cities of the coast were repeatedly captured, and Rome itself was menaced. It cannot be doubted that so much intercourse with Africa and Asia brought over these maladies, though no direct proof can be adduced. But the circumstantial evidence is sufficiently conclusive.'

It has been maintained by Mead, and since by Baron Dimsdale, that the small-pox was first brought into Europe by the crusaders; but besides that the historians of the holy wars take no notice of the Christian armies having suffered from that malady, it is very properly remarked by Mr. Moore, that the assumption is inconsistent with the fact that so early as the eleventh century treatises were published, both in Spain and Italy, upon the small-pox, as a well known and common malady. To the American continent the virus was conveyed by the Spaniards in their invasion of Hispaniola and Mexico, and thus did this destructive pestilence, commencing in Asia, successively visit Africa, Europe, and the New World.

We come now to the origin and progress of inoculation, or the practice of artificially communicating the virus, in order to render the disease of a less malignant kind and character. It is pretty generally known that this was introduced into England from Constantinople, but, from the extracts already given from Mr. Moore's publication, the artificial communication of the poison appears to

have

have been established in China long before even the disease itself was heard of in the Byzantine capital.

Inoculation, at whatever time it originated, was most probably founded upon the accidental observation of the comparatively mild nature of the distemper in some, when compared with other instances, for no reasoning *à-priori* would have conducted to the inference that by this mode of imparting the poison, the disease would be mitigated. Whether the suggestion or the discovery was first made by any of the faculty of medicine does not appear; as far as the imperfect accounts from Chinese records may be relied on, it seems to have been opposed very generally by the professed guardians of the public health.

' No account,' says Mr. Moore, ' is handed down of the origin of this custom; but the reverence in which agriculture is held by the Chinese, may have suggested the name (sowing the small-pox), and the usual manner of performing the operation. For they took a few dried small-pox crusts, as if they were seeds, and planted them in the nose. A bit of musk was added, in order to correct the virulence of the poison, and perhaps to perfume the crusts, and the whole was wrapped up in a little cotton to prevent its dropping out of the nostril. The crusts employed were always taken from a healthy person who had the small-pox favourably; and with the vain hope of mitigating their acrimony, they were sometimes kept in close jars for years, and at other times were fumigated with salutary plants. Some physicians beat the crusts into powder, and advised their patients to take a pinch of this snuff; and when they could not prevail upon them, they mixed it with water into a paste, and applied it in that form. In Hindostan, if tradition may be relied on, inoculation itself has been practised from remote antiquity. This practice was in the hands of a particular tribe of brahmins, who were delegated from various religious colleges, and who travelled through the provinces for that purpose. The natives were strictly enjoined to abstain during a month preparatory to the operation from milk and butter; and when the Arabians and Portugueze appeared in that country, they were prohibited from taking animal food also. Men were commonly inoculated on the arm; but the girls not liking to have their arms disfigured, chose that it should be done low on the shoulders. But whatever part was fixed upon, was well rubbed with a piece of cloth, which afterwards became a perquisite of the brahmin; he then made a few slight scratches on the skin with a sharp instrument, and took a bit of cotton, which had been soaked the preceding year in variolous matter, moistened it with a drop or two of the holy water of the Ganges, and bound it upon the punctures. During the whole of this ceremony, the brahmin always preserved a solemn countenance, and recited the prayers appointed in the Attharna Veda, to propitiate the goddess who superintends the small-pox. The brahmin then gave his instructions, which were religiously observed. In six hours the bandage was to be taken off, and the pledget to be allowed to drop spontaneously. Early next morning cold water was to be poured upon the patient's head and shoulders,

shoulders, and this was to be repeated till the fever came on. The ablution was then to be omitted; but as soon as the eruption appeared, it was to be resumed, and persevered in every morning and evening, till the crusts should fall off. Whenever the pustules should begin to change their colour, they were all to be opened with a fine pointed thorn. Confinement to the house was absolutely forbidden; the inoculated were to be freely exposed to every air that blew; but when the fever was upon them, they were sometimes permitted to be on a mat at the door. This regimen was to consist of the most refrigerating productions of the climate; as plantains, water-melons, their gruel made of rice or poppy-seeds, cold water and rice.'

Although it is not our design to engage in any practical discussion, it seems hardly possible to refrain from incidentally remarking the great superiority of these modes of treatment—a treatment founded on the dictates of nature—to those subsequently adopted by the Arabian and European physicians who forsook observation to follow hypothesis; and it is worthy notice that our modern improvements in the management of febrile and eruptive complaints consist mainly in permitting nature to follow its own course. We revert to ancient simplicity, and are therefore abundantly more successful than our immediate predecessors.

It has already been said that an obscurity hangs over the actual origin of this practice. In the opinion of some it commenced in the Arabian desarts, ' where neither physicians nor priests officiated ; the practice being monopolized by old women.' From *sowing* the small pox, it came in the course of time to be, and perhaps was originally, called *buying* the disease; which proceeded, it is said, from the circumstance of one child carrying to another a few dates, or raisins, the pretended price of the matter: this custom of buying the small-pox becoming general among the inferior classes along the African coast, at length found its way into Europe, and was even practised in some parts of our island.

Still, however, the faculty took no cognizance of any artificial method of communicating the poison, until the year 1703, when Dr. Emanuel Temoni Alpeck, who had graduated both at Padua and at Oxford, and who was then residing in Constantinople, was struck with the instances which he witnessed of the mitigated nature of the distemper when the virus was thus received into the human frame.*

A Venetian physician also, of the name of Pylarnus, had about the same time made the same observation of the success of the Turkish practice, of which, in 1715, he published a statement at Venice, in a tract entitled ' Nova et tuta variolas excitandi per

---

* Dr. Alpeck wrote an account of his observations to Dr. Woodward, by whom it was inserted in the Philosophical Transactions of the year 1714.

trans-

transplantationem methodus.' In the same year, too, Mr. Kennedy, an English surgeon, who had visited Turkey, endeavoured to excite professional attention to the advantages promised by the plan of engrafting, as he calls it, the small-pox.

It was, however, reserved for another coincidence in point both of time and circumstance, to be the means of rousing the members of the faculty from their apparent indisposition to investigate the merits of inoculation. Lady Mary Wortley Montague accompanied her husband as ambassador to the Ottoman court, and having observed with surprise that it was the custom in Constantinople for a set of old women to ' engraft' children with the small-pox every autumn, and moreover that the children thus infected had invariably a mild disease, she conceived the bold design of having her own son thus treated : this answered every expectation, and on her return to the British capital in 1722, she caused the same experiment to be made on her daughter, which was attended by the same happy results. Still, however, the profession hesitated to accept the proffered good, and notwithstanding that two princesses of the Royal family were successfully subjected to the same process under the influence of Lady Montague, the new practice went on at an exceedingly slow pace. As it was ascertained that the inoculated or ingrafted distemper was equally infectious with the disease when naturally acquired, it became a question in morals how far the individual who had his mind made up with regard to the eligibility of the practice, had a right thus to sow the seeds of the malady among others whose convictions were not in favour of inoculation, and who therefore refused its offers.

In process of time the question of inoculation came to be agitated with just the same virulence and party-spirit that have marked the modern controversy on the subject of vaccination, and it must be allowed to the impugners of the former, that they have a strong point in favour of their cause which the anti-vaccinists are without ; since, as we shall speedily see, inoculation has proved a private good at the expense of being a public evil. So successful was the opposition to the practice of engraftment at the times to which we are now alluding, that in spite of the high authority by which it was sanctioned, it fell both in this country and throughout Europe into general disuse, ' and there seemed little reason to imagine it would be revived.'

' When in this dormant state news was brought that multitudes of Indians in South America had been inoculated with as much success by Carmelite Friars, as the Asiatics had been by the Greek old women: a physician and surgeon also began in the year 1738 to inoculate in South Carolina; and only lost eight persons out of eight hundred. But a planter in St. Christopher's inoculated three hundred persons without
the

the loss of one. For it is singular that in those days all inoculations performed by private gentlemen, monks, and old women, were uniformly successful; and empirics afterwards were equally fortunate: none lost patients from inoculation except the regular members of the faculty. The American reports were so encouraging, that about the year 1740, the practice was revived by a few surgeons in Portsmouth, Chichester, Guilford, Petersfield, and Winchester; and gradually extended in the southern counties.'

Mead, too, took up his eloquent pen in the cause; and Mr. Moore tells us that his attributing the beauty of the Circassian women to the custom of inoculation which had obtained amongst them, had very considerable weight with the British ladies. The practice now very sensibly advanced among the higher circles, and for the accommodation of those in the lower walks of life, the Small-pox Hospital was erected in the year 1746. In 1754 the London College of Physicians gave their powerful sanction to the practice, by publishing a tract in its favour, and 'the press now groaned with works on inoculation, and with various plans of treatment.' These complicated modes of management, medicinal and otherwise, served, however, to bring the practice into discredit, which did not therefore become very generally diffused until its simplification and consequent improvement by a very conspicuous character in the Annals of Medicine.

'Daniel Sutton, (says Mr. Moore,) with his secret nostrums, propagated inoculation more in half a dozen years, than both the faculties of medicine and surgery, with the aid of the church, and the example of the court had been able to do in half a century. This man was the son of Robert Sutton, a surgeon at Debenham in Suffolk, and he and his brother assisted their father in his business. But after a time both sons left their father's house, and Daniel was content to serve as an assistant to a surgeon at Oxford. In the year 1763, he rejoined his father, and proposed to make some alterations in his plan of inoculation. These were condemned by the father as highly dangerous, yet Daniel was so confident as to make the experiment, and he found it successful. On this the father and son quarrelled, and the latter set off for Ingatestone, in Essex, where he set up as an empirical inoculator. He pretended to have discovered an infallible secret, and brought himself into public notice by the old and still successful trick of puffing hand-bills and boasting advertisements. Yet, in truth, his pretensions, though extravagant, were not without foundation; and in a short time such multitudes crowded to Ingatestone to be inoculated, that the town and neighbouring villages were filled with patients. It is much to be regretted, (adds our author,) that Sutton should have stooped to employ such unworthy devices; for his plan of treatment was greatly superior to that of any former practitioner; and had he followed the correct rules of open professional conduct, his name would have been recorded with honourable distinction. It appears, however, by the

analyses

analyses of his medicine and his own confession in his old age, that Daniel Sutton, in strictness, invented nothing, but judiciously combined remedies which had been found out independently by others. Sydenham had discovered the utility of exposing small-pox patients to the cool air, and of allowing them to drink cold water, but he did not venture to deviate so much from ordinary rules as to prescribe purgatives. Subsequent physicians had ascertained that great benefit arose from opening medicines, and particularly from mercurial purges; but in conformity to old theories, they at the same time confined their patients to bed, covered them warmly, and promoted perspiration. But Sutton had the sagacity to extract what was beneficial in both these plans, and to reject what was injurious. Almost every modern essay now recommended purgatives, and our reformer only made choice of the prescription which was most in vogue.'

We have introduced these remarks on Sutton's plans of treatment, merely in conformity with our wish to give as satisfactory an explanation as possible of the eventual success of inoculation; which now spread rapidly through almost the whole of Europe, with the exception of Spain. That country, as our author states, in the present case, profited by its sluggish indisposition to adopt the improvement of neighbouring nations; for after some partial and feeble attempts to introduce the practice, the endeavour was relinquished; and it is a notorious fact, and highly worthy of remark, that Spain has suffered incomparably less from small-pox than any other European state : the reason is sufficiently obvious; and the fact furnishes an equally obvious objection, as above hinted, against the practice of artificially disseminating a distemper so infectious, and so fatal. It is indeed beyond dispute that even the mortality from small-pox increased with the progress of inoculation, ' from the impossibility of prevailing upon the whole population to adopt medical counsel;' and of two estimates by two accredited physicians made of deaths from small-pox during the last thirty years of the preceding century, and laid before a committee of the House of Commons, 'the one stated the average numbers at 34,260, adding that he believed those deaths to be under the truth : the other physician made them amount to 36,000.'

' But this immense and *increasing* consumption of human lives, was not the sole evil produced by this distemper; for a considerable portion of the survivors were pitted and disfigured ; some lost one of their eyes, a few became totally blind, and others had their constitution impaired, and predisposed to a variety of complaints, which were productive of future distress, and sometimes of death.'

In this state, then, did things stand in reference to small-pox, natural and acquired, when the newly suggested substitute presented its claims to the consideration of mankind ; and the momentous business now devolves on us of investigating the legitimacy of these

these claims, or of ascertaining the grounds upon which such high pretensions are preferred.

Dr. Jenner (whose name requires no formal introduction) was originally employed in general practice in a district in Gloucestershire. It was in the year 1768 that he first heard the report of those sores which infested the teats of cows, and which infected the chapped hands of the milkers, being sometimes a preventive of small-pox ; and, in connexion with this report, it struck him as a remarkable fact, which came under his own cognizance, that many of the peasants whom he endeavoured to inoculate resisted the infection. Although these circumstances made at the time some impression on his mind, he did not systematically prosecute the investigation to which they ultimately led until after his return from London to establish himself at Berkeley. Then it was that he commenced the inquiry in earnest ; and in the relation which he has given of the progress of his labours in this very extraordinary pursuit, he informs us,

' That the disease (the cow-pox) had been known in the dairies from time immemorial, and a vague opinion prevailed that it was a preventive of small-pox. This opinion I found was comparatively new; for all the old farmers declared they had no such ideas in their early days, a circumstance which seemed easily accounted for, from my knowing the common people were very rarely inoculated for the small-pox, till that practice was become general, by the improved method introduced by the Suttons ; so that working people in the dairies were very seldom put to the test of the preventive power of the cow-pox.'

As Dr. Jenner proceeded with his inquiries, he found that several persons contracted the small-pox after they had been subjected to the disease from the cow ; and moreover that the medical practitioners in the neighbourhood ' all agreed in declaring, from experience, that the cow-pox was only an occasional, and a very uncertain preventive of small-pox.' These discoveries were certainly of a disheartening nature ; but, although they might damp the ardour of hope, they did not cause the abandonment of the pursuit. On further investigation he ascertained that the cow had occasionally several varieties of eruptions on her teat, all of which were indiscriminately named cow-pox when productive of sores on the hands of the milkers ; and it occurred to him as very probable that only one species of these eruptions possessed the preventive power ; and that this was the true explanation of the observed irregularity in point of effect. One obstacle thus appeared to be done away ; but lo ! another now presented itself, which by most persons would have been considered insuperable ;—' to his great mortification, Jenner found several examples of milkers who were seized with the small-pox, after having contracted sores on their hands from

the

the genuine cow-pox.' In spite even of this, our indefatigable investigator pursued his researches; and as it seemed to him inconsistent with the general uniformity of the laws of nature that this difference of susceptibility should so widely obtain, it occurred to him that the specific influence of the poison might not improbably vary with the progressive changes it underwent, after having been first secreted from the ulcerated surfaces of the cow's teat; and,

' after much investigation, he at length ascertained, that the milkers, who acquired the cow-pox from vesicles on the teats of the cows, while advancing to maturity, were secured from the small-pox; while those contaminated by cows, in an advanced period of the disease, remained susceptible of the small-pox. In fine, from a multitude of cases he was enabled to draw these conclusions, that the property of preventing the small-pox appertained only to one of those diseases which were vulgarly denominated the cow-pox; and that this power principally resided in the liquid secreted during the early stages of that disease.'*

With these exceptions then of a spurious matter in the one case, and of a matter taken at a wrong time in the other, Jenner conceived that he had made out the fact of cow-pox being a preventive of small-pox for life; for he exposed in various ways individuals, who had been the subjects of the former, to the latter infection, (after the lapse of fifteen, twenty-seven, and even fifty years,) and found that they resisted its influence.

Thus a clear way was opened for the important application of this singular discovery. May not this preventive be propagated from man to man, and thus supersede the small-pox virus? was the idea that suggested itself to the mind of the discoverer, a suggestion, which it is needless to say has been extensively acted on, and which has given rise to one of the most important problems ever proposed, viz. Is vaccination an actual, a permanent, a safe, and unobjectionable security against small-pox infection?

For a moment we will suppose its preventive efficacy to be admitted, in order to advert to a separate charge which has been adduced against its employment,—for the vaccine virus has been said to be a means of engendering foul humours, to lay the foundation

---

* Not with a desire to prejudice the case, but merely for the purpose of pointing out that analogy subsisting between the variolous and vaccine secretions, which is contended for by some writers, we subjoin the following extract from Mr. Moore, as a continuation of and comment upon the above quotation:—

' Jenner,' says Mr. Moore, ' perceived that these opinions corresponded with remarks that had been made on the small-pox, as the liquid most active for variolous inoculation is that which is first secreted; but the thick matter of pustules which have crusted, though it may excite local inflammation and suppuration, yet frequently fails of producing the real small-pox.'

of

of several chronic diseases, and to be therefore in the highest degree objectionable. This charge can only be substantiated by an appeal to facts; what then do these testify? Have chronic cutaneous eruptions (the disorders alleged to be the consequences of vaccination) recently been on the increase? All medical records and reports, presented to the world for the last twenty years, agree in the diminution rather than the augmentation, both of the number and severity of the complaints in question; and what may be considered as decisively to the point, is the following statement from a respectable surgeon to the Infirmary at Gloucester:—

‘ A more healthy description,’ says this gentleman, ‘ of human beings does not exist, nor one more free from chronic cutaneous impurities, than that which suffers most from cow-pox, by reason of their being employed in dairies; and the Gloucester Infirmary, one of the largest provincial hospitals, is situated in a county in which accidental cow-pox has been prevalent from time immemorial; many hundreds among the labouring people have had the cow-pox since the establishment of that institution, and that more severely than is generally the case in artificial vaccination, and yet not a single patient has applied to the Infirmary in half a century for the relief of any disease, local or constitutional, which he or she imputed, or pretended to trace to the cow-pox : and let it be repeated and remembered, that the artificial in no respect differs from the natural, except in being generally less virulent.’

This document, backed by the concurrent testimony of impartial and unprejudiced records from medical observers, that scrophulous and cutaneous affections are (as we have said) upon the decline, will, it is presumed, serve as a sufficient refutation of those partial and garbled statements which in the early stages of the controversy were made for the purpose of confirming the apprehensions of the timid, and giving strength to ungrounded prejudices. The question therefore of vaccine efficacy remains unincumbered by minor considerations, and it is now for us finally to observe upon the evidence by which the following proposition has been maintained, viz. that the vaccinated and the inoculated child stand upon precisely the same footing in respect of security against small-pox.

In spite of our professions of impartiality, we suspect that our readers have by this time set us down as determined defenders of the vaccine cause. We shall probably, therefore, excite some surprise by expressing it as our opinion, that the absolute truth of the above proposition does not appear to us to have been hitherto fairly established. It does, we confess, seem probable that there may be a shade of difference in the preventive efficacy of the vaccine and variolous virus; even this, however,

we

we must allow to the advocates of vaccination, has not been proved, and we hasten to adduce the evidence on either side.

Mr. Moore, who is a professed partizan of vaccination, argues for its identity as to effect on the ground of analogy, and contends that the exercise of the virus of only a partially preventive power would be an anomaly in nature. This argument is in itself forcible, and is managed by our author with considerable adroitness. It is needless, however, to remark, that it must fall powerless even out of Mr. Moore's hands unless backed by actual observation:— the preventive efficacy of vaccination is a question not of theory but of fact. That there have happened cases of small-pox of an indisputable nature, subsequently even to proper vaccination, no one can deny; but then it is urged that small-pox has likewise been known to occur twice to the same individual, and to have succeeded to inoculation in the same manner as it has to vaccination. The point, however, at issue is whether these anomalies are proportionately as frequent in the latter as in the former case; and, in determining this, Mr. Moore contends that the comparative estimates have not been made with due attention to every necessary particular.

' In making this estimate,' he says, ' an error has been committed by comparing the results of the *primary* practice of vaccination with those of the most approved state of variolous inoculation, forgetting that, when the latter operation was introduced, failures of every kind were far more frequent than of late, and that even the deaths amounted in early practice to one in fifty. In like manner, vaccination, on its first introduction, was so misconducted, that two children in a workhouse were actually destroyed by it, although, when skilfully practised, it is really less dangerous than opening a vein or cutting a corn. A multitude of lesser mistakes were then committed by the ablest men in the profession, who, deceived by analogy, imitated too nearly the plan of the small-pox inoculation; and many were not sufficiently aware either of the deterioration to which vaccine lymph is subject, or of the mischiefs which arise even when the lymph is pure from the vaccine process being interrupted or disturbed by violence, or by disease. The number of failures from all these sources of error in early practice has been considerable; it is therefore too soon at present to compute and compare the number of cases in which small-pox has occurred after inoculation and vaccination.'

We are not sure whether this be not rather too much in the spirit of a systematic advocate. Mr. Moore talks of failures from inoculation when first practised being one in fifty; but it ought to be recollected that such failures were rather referable to the mode of communicating and managing the disease, than to the occurrence of any second affection. Now the case is far different with vaccination; for ' although two children in a workhouse were actually de-

stroyed

stroyed by it,' these instances stand almost alone in the records of
the practice; and, however inefficiently the process may have been
performed by the several vaccinators who have undertaken the task
without being qualified for the office, we do not hear, excepting
from the most prejudiced and partial quarters, that any positive
injury was ever inflicted on the children thus ineffectually operated upon.

The best stand which the vaccinists can make on the ground of
comparative estimates, is that of the immense multitudes which
have undergone the process since the commencement of vaccination,
compared with those subjected to inoculation in the same number
of years from its primary establishment. When we hear of one
case after another, therefore, of small-pox subsequent to cow-pox,
it may be replied, that had as many children been inoculated, in
place of being vaccinated, the instances of failure would be equally
numerous. Whether such position would be correct can scarcely
be ascertained, since there is no register of the number of failures
in either case, and without it no actual calculation can be made.
We have, however, been just favoured with a document from the
Small-pox Hospital, which, in connection with the remarks that
accompany it, is highly favourable to the vaccine cause; and let it
be recollected that these remarks come from one who so far from
having been an enthusiast ab origine in the cause of cow-pox, has
been accused by his contemporaries of being a covert enemy to its
success.

' Every passing month,' says Dr. Adams, physician to the Institution
just named, ' serves to convince me of the absolutely preventive power
of vaccination when properly conducted. Not very long since, my observations led me to the inference that the efficacy of inoculation, when
compared with vaccination, or rather the probability of failures from
one and the other, stood at about the proportion of 1200 to 1000; but
I am now, to say the least, inclined to the inference, that both, when
properly managed, are *equally* efficacious; and that the instances of
failure we hear of, are either to be accounted for by the very large numbers that have been vaccinated, or by the process having been inefficiently performed.'

Such are the opinions of the principal officer, not of a *Vaccine*
establishment, but of the *Small-pox* Hospital, where, if in any
place, failures are likely to be heard and complained of. The document to which we have alluded, is a statement of the numbers
inoculated, vaccinated, and admitted with the natural small-pox
during the last seven years. The numbers inoculated, it will be
observed, are marked ' admitted;' since the laws of the institution require that those individuals, who are inoculated, shall not leave the
hospital till the fear of infection is over.

Admitted

	Admitted for Inoculation.	Vaccinated.	Admitted for natural Small-pox.
1811	86	1458	94
1812	82	1939	144
1813	50	1831	69
1814	35	1671	79
1815	30	2446	101
1816	37	2318	141
1817	42	3127	160

The reader who shall cast his eye over the above table will perceive that the numbers of vaccinated subjects have been very much increased during the three preceding years; and that the numbers of cases of natural small-pox have been likewise, during the same period, more numerous than before; the chances, then, of failure in both ways, that is, both from the increased prevalence of small-pox infection, and the increased number of vaccinated subjects must have been considerably multiplied; and yet we are told by the medical officers of the Institution, that such failures are decidedly and very materially upon the decrease; and let it be again remarked, that such statement comes from gentlemen whose minds, if they were likely to be biassed in any way, would rather bend towards the side of inoculation.

But, on the other hand, we hear of small-pox happening after vaccination in some institutions and districts in far greater numbers than would in all probability have been the case, had the individuals, instead of being vaccinated, been subject to inoculation. The children of Christ's Hospital, for instance, are under medical management of the most respectable kind; and the diseases happening in this institution are carefully recorded in quarterly reports. Now in these reports, ' Variola post vaccinationem' often occurs—a sequence which was not noticed, at least not recorded, when the boys were generally, as in former years, inoculated. We have further, another report from authority of an indisputable kind, stating, that in one small town and its immediate neighbourhood, fifty-four cases had been seen of small-pox subsequently to the vaccine disease. These, then, we repeat, and other testimonies more or less strongly to the same effect, are certainly calculated to make us pause before we set our hands to the proposition, that there is an absolute identity of preventive effect in genuine small-pox and genuine cow-pox.

Vaccination, however, has, we conceive, enough of positive evidence in its favour to meet all that has hitherto been advanced against it, either in the way of argument or fact. In the first place, it is to be observed, that with very little exception indeed, the cases of the variolous occurring after the vaccine affection, are of so mild and modified a nature as to be hardly worthy notice; and that

B B 2   even

even when such cases assume in the first stages somewhat of a malignant type, the unfavourable symptoms soon die away, and the period of danger in other variolous disorders becomes in these the period of convalescence. This, indeed, with the most trifling exception, is so much the case, that for our own parts we should witness with next to nothing of apprehension, small-pox breaking out among our own children, or the children of our relatives; and the strongest evidence that has hitherto been adduced against vaccination has never produced any solicitude in our minds that the children in whose welfare we are more immediately interested should be kept from small-pox exposure. Secondly, we may remark, that this kind of small-pox, thus modified and disarmed of all its malignity, has so many features of resemblance to those eruptions which are named chicken-pox, that it is fair to presume many supposed instances of the former have been in reality cases of the latter. This may easily be conceived, when we advert to the apprehensions of some, and we are concerned to state the apparent desire of others of meeting with facts adverse to the vaccine cause. Indeed, we scarcely hear now, as we were wont to do, of chicken-pox, but every eruption is put down to the head of small-pox after cow-pox.

But, thirdly, what shall we say to foreign reports in favour of the new practice? Amsterdam, it is affirmed, has not for a long time seen a single case of small-pox subsequent to vaccination; and in the year 1813, a report was published by the imperial institution of France, stating that 2,671,622 subjects had been properly vaccinated in France, of whom only *seven* had afterwards taken the small-pox! and it was added, that the well authenticated cases of persons taking the small-pox after variolous inoculation are proportionably far more numerous: and, indeed, reports of a similar nature reach this country from every part of the world in which the new practice has obtained—and where has it not obtained? It may be still urged that the immunity, after all, may be only for a time; but besides that this supposition violates the laws of all analogy, it is, in truth, contrary to the evidence of fact. Dr. Jenner, as we have already noticed, actually proved the impotency of the small-pox virus, as applied to individuals who had been subjected to the cow-pox fifty years before the experiment; and, let it be observed, as an important circumstance, that even natural cow-pox is imparted in the way of inoculation.

In conclusion, then, we would express it as our sincere and unbiassed conviction, that whether vaccination be or be not precisely the same as variolous inoculation, in regard to its preventive power over small-pox, it is demonstrably efficacious enough to justify its universal adoption; and that it deserves to be appreciated as one of the greatest blessings ever bestowed upon mankind by a
bene-

beneficent Providence. It is a mild substitute for a most malignant distemper; it is certainly not more influential in exciting latent complaints of the constitution, most probably much less só, than the old inoculation; and, to crown all, it does not sow the seeds among the community of a loathsome and devastating distemper !

On the merits of the treatises, the title-pages of which stand at the head of this article, we need say but little. The first of the volumes we have indeed tacitly expressed our approbation of, by the large use we have made of its contents. It is a most interesting,—we had almost said (notwithstanding that it is a treatise on small-pox) a fascinating work. The author has proved himself rich in resources and masterly in the management of them. Indeed, we have no hesitation in placing this performance of Mr. Moore among the few lasting monuments of medical literature. Sorry, however, are we to add, that the spirit of the partizan has, in the second volume, too much taken place of the mind of the liberal and learned historian; its composition, too, as a literary production, is, in all respects, inferior to the other. The author has been guilty in it of many offences, not merely against precision and taste, but against the most common principles of grammatical construction; and these become more conspicuous when contrasted with the chaste and classical style which pervades his History of Small-pox.

ART. XI.—1. *Researches into the Laws and Phenomena of Pestilence; including a Medical Sketch and Review of the Plague of London in 1665, and Remarks on Quarantine, &c.* By Thomas Hancock, M.D., &c. &c.   1821.

2. *A Treatise on the Plague, designed to prove it contagious from Facts collected during the Author's Residence in Malta when visited by that Malady in 1813; with Observations on*
its

its Prevention, Character and Treatment. By Sir Arthur
Brooke Faulkner, M.D., &c. &c.
3. *Results of an Investigation respecting epidemic and pestilential
Disease; including Researches in the Levant concerning the
Plague.* By Charles Maclean, M.D., &c. &c. 1818.
4. *Minutes of Evidence before the Select Committee appointed to
consider the Validity of the Doctrine of Contagion in Plague.*
5. *Miscellaneous Works of the late Robert Willan, M.D., &c. &c.
comprising an Inquiry into the Antiquity of the Small-pox,
Measles and Scarlet Fever, &c. &c.* Edited by Ashby Smith,
M.D., &c. &c. 1821.
6. *Historical Sketch of the Opinions entertained by Medical Men
respecting the Varieties and the Secondary Occurrence of
Small-pox; with Observations on the Nature and Extent of
the Security afforded by Vaccination against Attacks of that
Disease.* By John Thomson, M.D., &c. &c. 1822.

I N prosecuting inquiries relative to subjects on which the judgment, rather than the comprehension, is to be exercised, we
often find it difficult not only to avoid undue bias, but even to
know how far we are under the influence of a prejudice that has
perhaps been insensibly acquired, and has grown with our growth :
but there are other impediments to correct inference respecting
speculative truth than those arising from the above source—and,
some of them, of a nature exactly opposite; for the very apprehension of yielding with too much facility to generally admitted
dogmata may, and not unfrequently does, give rise to an unwar-
rantable and unseasonable scepticism.

The great discrepancy of sentiment that prevails on the con-
tested points of pestilence and plague, or rather on the manner
of their production and the laws that regulate their continuance
and spread, must in part, at least, be ascribed to this submissive
dependence upon prescriptive rule on the one hand, and the determination to disbelieve every thing that has obtained pretty
general credit, on the other. Thus, while one speculatist tells you
that a skein of silk may contain in its twinings poisonous matter,
sufficient, when let loose, to cause the sickness and death of
thousands ; another, with the same data before him, not only denies that the venom is thus transportable, but even stoutly contends for its non-existence, and maintains that the apprehensions
excited on the score of pestilential visits have no more foundation
in truth than nursery apparitions or monkish miracles !

' It is shown (says Dr. Maclean), by conclusions deduced from
undeniable premises, that it is impossible epidemic diseases
should ever depend upon contagion;' and he goes on to state that
' the prevalent notion of contagion being an inherent quality of
                                                pestilential

pestilential fever is absurdly derived from a popish rumour of
the sixteenth century;' while, on the other hand, one of the most
strenuous and able supporters of the opposite doctrine, Dr. Granville, maintains, ' that the disease called plague is never epidemic ;
that *it is independent of all influence of the atmosphere*; that it
commits its ravages when no possible cause of unhealthiness
exists, and is neither checked nor promoted by the south or north
winds, by the winter or summer, by an elevated or low situation.'

Between these extreme points, others take their stand at different distances; some of them more and some less readily admitting the principle of contagion as connected with plague, but all
denying its abstract power and independent essence.

Did these questions involve matter merely of curiosity, or
even were the interest they excite confined to the faculty of medicine, we should be justified in leaving them to the decision of the
medical journalists; but as inferences of a general and even
national concern depend upon the admission, or rejection, or
qualification of premises on the subject of pestilence, we have
considered this subject as properly falling within our own province, and shall proceed to canvass the particulars it embraces
somewhat at large, with a determination to present the arguments of the contagionists, anti-contagionists and moderates,
without any admixture of our own sentiments. It will soon,
indeed, be seen that we have opinions of our own, and that they
do not exactly coincide with those of any writer in the controversy; but, in propounding them, we will endeavour so to separate them from the deductions of others, that the reader shall be
furnished with a fair opportunity for the exercise of unfettered
comparison and unbiassed judgment.

The controversy, as we have just intimated, has been marked
by extremes of confident assertion, and occasionally, it is painful
to add, of intolerant dogmatism. In the list placed at the head
of the present Article will, however, be found some exceptions
to that dictatorial tone and that extravagant tenour of assumption which are not only at variance with the canons of legitimate reasoning, but even calculated to injure the cause they are
intended to serve.

To the volume of Dr. Hancock we are desirous of calling
especial notice, not with a view to invidious comparison, but as
being a comprehensive and candid investigation of the whole
question : the spirit of *system* may perhaps be occasionally seen
insinuating itself among the pages of this work ; and in the
remarks on another learned and candid writer (Sir Brooke Faulkner) we thought we detected a little too much leaning to favourite
inference ; but, upon the whole, we may confidently assert that
                                                                                    it

it has not often fallen to our lot to inspect the production of a
controversial author so free and fearless in its admissions, or so
candid and temperate in its conclusions, as that to which we
refer.

At first sight, the works of Willan and Thomson may appear
to have no direct connexion with the topic about to be discussed;
it will shortly, however, be perceived for what purpose they are
added to the list of volumes bearing upon the present controversy.

But it is time to proceed to the formal enunciation of the leading question : Are we right in supposing plague to be a specific
disease capable of being conveyed from one part of the world
to another, either by persons or goods, so as to render necessary restrictions upon indiscriminate intercourse ? In other words,
is pestilence a contagious and transportable, or is it merely an
infectious and local distemper ? Many minor points are, of
course, included in this interrogatory, which will be noticed as
we proceed.

Contagion ? Infection ? what is the precise import of these two
terms, which, it will be remarked, have been just employed in
some measure antithetically ; but which, in strict propriety, are not
perhaps open to this contrasted signification. Contagion indeed
implies contact and infection, although it does not express more
than the effect produced, yet necessarily supposes touch, upon
the principle that nothing in the material world can act but
where it is. The difference, then, rather hinges upon the *mode*
in which the communication or contact is brought about ; and an
infectious would be distinguished from a contagious disorder in
something like the following manner. A number of persons may
be assembled in a vitiated atmosphere, occasioned by something
emitted from the body of one or other of the individuals present ;
or by the mere confinement of the air itself, animal respiration
being a vitiating process ; or an exhalation peculiar to the place ;
if then, any of the persons so circumstanced become decidedly ill,
the induced sickness would be considered as a disease resulting
from infection. Now, take one of these subjects from the infectious atmosphere, place him where every thing, with the exception of his presence, is conducive to health, and then, if from
communicating with him, others fall into a disease which resembles
his, the morbid condition thus engendered would be considered
an absolute contagion. Even in this last instance however the
actual contact of bodies may not have taken place, and therefore
the terms employed to distinguish the two kinds of morbid being,
so far from elucidating, rather obscure the question.

And in our minds a great deal of the confusion which still
involves the controversy, arises out of what at first view might
seem

seem to render it more definite and precise, for authors have been
led to infer a distinction between contagious and infectious diseases
beyond the warranty of fact; and have thus imagined specific and
abstract differences in complaints, which are properly ascribable
to time, place, and circumstance. On this rock we believe it is
that both the advocates and oppugners of contagion in pestilential
maladies have split; each readily acknowledging, without sufficient reason, that some diseases are not only peculiar and absolute
in their origin, but that such peculiarity and absolute identity has
been preserved from their commencement to the present time.

The reasonings of Dr. Willan and Dr. Thomson (perhaps in
some measure unconsciously to themselves) seem to run counter
to the above notion of a disorder's transmission from age to age,
and from one country to another. It is supposed by most of
those who have given their thoughts to the subject, that the
small-pox and measles, or, as they are termed, the specific contagions, were unknown to the ancient physicians of Greece and
Rome, and that the Arabian writers were the first to observe and
record them. Dr. Willan has brought a great deal of learning to
the support of the opposite doctrine; if he does not quite succeed in establishing the point for which he contends, may not his
failure be partly at least referable to the principle now adverted
to? and may not the want of entire correspondence between the
ancient accounts of what our author supposes to be small-pox,
and the small-pox as it appears in this age and country, be attributable to the actual change effected by the lapse of time upon
a distemper which is still radically the same, or rather which sprang
from an identical source, but has had new features impressed upon
it by the hand of time? Did indeed this same small-pox, as some
contend that it does, arise, spread, decline, and disappear, without
apparent modification from external circumstances, our opinion
on its laws and limits would be very different; but this assuredly
is not the case. Do we not in fact find that the complaint is
now epidemic and general, now partial and infrequent; that it is
at one time mild, at another time severe, just as it happens with
those febrile derangements to which the anti-contagionist attaches
no specific notion? and are not these so many evidences of a susceptibility in the distemper, to modifications beyond the admission of the contagionist? It is a very curious fact, (pointed out
by Dr. Willan) that Aaron a physician and presbyter of Alexandria,
who wrote in the beginning of the seventh century, has arranged
the small-pox, measles, and pestilential bubo or carbuncle, as the
products of one specific contagion; and very long after his time
the two first diseases were considered identical—and were perhaps
actually so. But, further, it is a very remarkable circumstance,
that

that since vaccine inoculation has become general as a substitute
for small-pox, we scarcely ever see or hear of those eruptive disorders to which the term *varicella* or chicken-pox has been somewhat vaguely applied. The fact no one will dispute ; but opinion
does not seem quite so unanimous as to the explanation of which
the circumstance is susceptible. Dr. Thomson maintains, and
we think justly, that all varioloid diseases spring from one
source, and that the modified small-pox which so frequently
follows vaccination and the chicken-pox of former times are in
fact the same distemper, rendered different in their complexional
character by the present mild mode of inoculating—inoculating,
we say, for it would seem that even the genuine vaccine virus is
but a modification of the small-pox poison, disarmed greatly of
its noxious power by its having become the disease of a brute
animal.

It is worthy of remark, as bearing upon the present question,
that the nosology of one age and country is almost a sealed
volume to the student of diseases in distant times and places;
and this, among other reasons, is the cause why the study of
ancient authorities in medicine has fallen into comparative neglect.
Each succeeding period cannot however be imagined to create
new distempers, or to effect any thing further, than materially to
change the aspect, and modify the circumstances of the old ones;
but, then, this modification in the course of centuries comes to be
so considerable that scarcely any traces of the prime malady are
to be recognized. Even among ourselves, how various are the
shades of a disease which yet is nosologically regarded an identical
essence? this indeed is so proverbially the case, that many of our
modern free-thinkers in medicine make a mock altogether of
system, of classification, and of nomenclature as applied to
morbid states ; and even those who are less disposed to cast away
as scholastic rubbish every thing like rule and order in designating
distempers, cannot but admit the frequent fallacy of the best
nosological charts. In Dr. Bateman's recent, and in some respects excellent work on Cutaneous Affections, we find an abundance of error and self-contradiction to spring from the source to
which we now refer. For instance, we have *prurigo* and *psora*
marked out as not only differences in the same species, but as
absolute varieties of disorders in reference to the class to which
they belong ; and yet, it is admitted by the framer of the classification itself, that the former of these affections may pass insensibly into the latter; an admission which furnishes sufficient proof
that the scheme of arrangement is arbitrary, and in a great degree
inefficient.

There is another fact of importance as bearing upon the doctrine we now inculcate, namely, that a *degree* of disorder will sometimes result from exposure to specific affections, without the actual and absolute induction of the malady itself. Those who nurse children in small-pox having had the small-pox themselves are not unfrequently the subjects of a certain indisposition in consequence, which, neither in kind nor quantity, would be considered small-pox; and so on through the whole range of distempers to which the body is incident. In a word, a physical atmosphere may possess a sufficient quantity of contaminating influence without engendering absolute distemper.

Again: who has not made the observation, that since our soldiers in Egypt became the subjects of ophthalmia, inflammations and other disorders of the eyes, but still not actual ophthalmia, have been greatly on the increase? The Walcheren fever too, although owning a distinct and peculiar origin, frequently sowed its seeds in the constitution of individuals, the fruits of which, when ripened in this country, bore a different character from that which they would have assumed had the disease at once broke out among the Walcheren marshes. Such is the modifying power of time, place, and circumstance, evidenced even in phenomena that present themselves to our own observation; and it seems not unfair to suppose that the lapse of ages, the different habits of modern from ancient times, may make disease insensibly branch out into almost innumerable ramifications from a very few roots.

To assert that some species of sickness are not more independent, and less liable to change than others, would be obviously to fly in the face of fact; still, however, there is sufficient evidence in favour of the assumption, that even the most fixed and specific affections are gradually operated on, and ultimately converted in the way we have endeavoured to illustrate.

It may be thought that we have conceded considerably to the anti-contagionist in thus breaking down the artificial barriers by which morbid conditions have been separated; but so far are we from subscribing to that proposition which declares the incommunicability of distempers except in a very limited number and defined character, that we even conceive a power of transmission in maladies which some of the most decided supporters of contagion in plague do not generally admit. Colds, as they are called by a sort of metonymy, run in families. The wife that has nursed a consumptive husband often follows him to the grave—the victim of the same disease—and in many cases, as above intimated, the otherwise well receive a *measure* of sickness from being for a length of time near the ill, that cannot fairly be attributed to any other cause than a something emitted from the former and impregnating, so to say, the body of the latter. If

you

you ask for the proof of this, we reply by requesting you to point
out the actual matter in a palpable shape which gives the small-
pox, when it is not received by inoculation—this substance
equally eludes the ken of the experimentalist with all other disease-
creating agencies.

Upon the whole, then, we are of opinion, that the distinction
set up between contagious and pestilential disorders does not, in
truth, obtain to any thing like the extent commonly supposed;
and that the specific quality of *variola* itself is but different in
degree, not in kind, from the mere infection of plague. We
believe that both are occasionally spontaneous in their origin,*
more or less communicable in their nature—pass from individual
to individual in the same manner—and are susceptible of modification, in a different degree, we allow, but still in both cases to
an almost incalculable extent.

So much for our own sentiments respecting the laws of contagion and infection. We now proceed to a general but cursory
review of the authors who have recently written on the subject;
Dr. Maclean, Sir Brooke Faulkner, and Dr. Hancock—the first a
decided anti-contagionist,—the second as decided in his sentiments on the opposite side,—and the last, a believer certainly in
contagion, but who does not give to this power abstract qualities,
or conceive it to be the sole agent by which pestilence is generated and diffused.

It may be right, however, previously to say a few words respecting the opinions of our forefathers in medicine on the subject of pestilential influence, and the contagious qualities of
disease.

It is rather remarkable, that on this head the authority of the
ancients is somewhat slender. The great founder of the art never
once mentions contagion as a cause of disease, nor do we find this
source of disorder alluded to in the writings of Celsus, which is
curious, since these writings constitute a sort of summary of all
that was known and believed at the time they were composed.
This silence of the two greatest authorities among the ancients
has been seized on (as we hinted above) by Dr. Maclean, who
maintains that the belief in contagion is of modern origin; that

* We may be thought erroneous in talking of the *spontaneous* origin of small-pox ;
but certain it is, that this affection often make its appearance and disappearance quite
as unaccountably as other epidemic maladies ; nay, more so even than those epidemics
that are more obviously of local origin. The anti-contagionist will, perhaps, say, that
in these cases the seeds of the distemper have been made to germinate by the particular
circumstances of the district in which it breaks out and spreads; but in this he con-
cedes much to the opposite party, for the believer in specific contagion as applied to
plague and typhus, and yellow fever, accounts in the same way for the prevalence and
decline of the last mentioned maladies.

the

the ancients had no notion of diseases being thus propagated, and that the doctrine of such transmission was invented by Pope Paul III. in 1547, for the purpose of striking a panic among the fathers of the council of Trent, and to serve as a pretext for translating that council to Bologna.

Now it would not seem very likely that an ecclesiastic ruler should have recourse to a stratagem which implies the introduction of a novel belief respecting a medical dogma; and we should find much difficulty in giving credence to the hypothesis of Dr. Maclean, were there even no absolute authorities against its admission; but Dr. Maclean has not dealt fairly with the subject in concluding, from the silence of Hippocrates and Celsus on the question of contagion, that therefore the ancients did not recognize the fact of a disorder's communication by contact or fomes. Galen and Aretæus occasionally make use of expressions which imply the circumstance of contagion being an admitted principle. The former likens plague, in respect to its communicable qualities, with itch or inflammation of the eyes, συνδιαΐριβειν τοις λοιμωΐοισιν επισφαλες, απολαυσαι γαρ κινδυνος ωσπερ ψωρας τινος η οφθαλμιας, than which expressions nothing can be stronger to the point; and the latter even goes so far as to employ terms the very use of which supposes the belief to be prevalent that plague was of a contagious nature; ઠ μειον η λοιμῶ, says Aretæus, when treating of another disorder, the contagious properties of which he is desirous of illustrating.

That the ancient classics in medicine are generally without much allusion to the doctrine of contagion, may not improbably be attributed to their having thought it useless to discuss a matter so obvious in itself, and so freely admitted by all parties: in consonance with this opinion, we find more copious references to the subject by the historians and poets of antiquity, than by the strictly medical writers. We are told expressly by Dr. Willan, (we have not had an opportunity of referring to the work itself,) that ' Evagrius, in his Ecclesiastical History, proves himself well acquainted with the nature of contagion, and the operation of fomes; for he very correctly enumerates the various modes in which pestilential or contagious diseases are disseminated;' and this author, let it be observed, wrote just ten centuries prior to the time at which Dr. Maclean dates the first divulged notion on the subject of contagion, as applicable to epidemic and pestilential diseases.* We forbear to quote the ancient historians and

poets,

---

* Howel, as quoted by Freind, particularly alludes to the accounts given both by Evagrius and Procopius of the plague at Constantinople; and Freind himself mentions the representation given by Agathias, another of the Byzantine historians, in the
following

poets, since their allusions to the subject of pestilential contamination must be familiar to most of our readers ; and since those who deny that contagion was known to the ancients, might object to the authority of writings not strictly of a scientific cast, when used to establish a scientific principle. Certain it is, moreover, that the line of demarcation between infectious and contagious distempers is of modern origin ; but, if the course of reasoning into which we have briefly entered be correct, the ancients, by neglecting to recognize this proposed division, were not therefore farther than the moderns from the absolute truth.

We now proceed to give a brief summary of the views entertained on the subject of contagion by Dr. Maclean, Sir Brooke Faulkner, and Dr. Hancock—and we select these as representatives of many others, in order to avoid unnecessary repetition. It has already been stated why, in this general review, Dr. Hancock claims the most detailed notice.

The positions of Dr. Maclean, in reference to the subject under discussion, are briefly the following. Epidemic diseases, comprehending all the intermediate degrees of affection between the slightest catarrh and the most destructive pestilence, depend upon some change in the atmosphere, as their immediately exciting cause, the predisposition to be affected by such changes being referable to various combinations of heat, moisture, soil, situation, food, and water, corporeal labour, the passions, and motions of the mind; and in Christian communities (he adds) the belief in contagion contributes to the production of the morbid effect resulting from the above circumstances of predisposition and excitation.

' The effects of the action in its different degrees and modifications (says Dr. Maclean) of a power of diffusive and constant operation, which is the appropriate stimulus of the grand organ of respiration, and by which all the external parts of the body are perpetually pressed and enveloped, must necessarily be infinitely various. It is directly or indirectly the source of a great portion of all the maladies which afflict mankind. Its slighter consequences, which would not of themselves prove dangerous, frequently become the foundation of diseases which prove mortal; those which already exist, it aggravates, and renders some fatal which would otherwise terminate in recovery.

---

following manner. Having alluded to Procopius and Evagrius, Freind goes on to say, ' Et Agathias, qui secundam ejus invasionem describit, quæ Constantinopoli accidit A. D. 568, diserte ait, plerosque momento temporis obiisse, sicut a vehementi apoplexia ; et eos quibus maximæ natura vires suppeterent, quinto diei nunquam superfuisse. In Atheniensi autem, morbus ad septimum vel nonum diem ibat, qui quidem usitati erant mortis dies. *In eadem contaminati sunt, quicunque ad ægros accedebant ; in hoc vero, idem non obtigisse plane declaratur.*'

Here we have one of the highest authorities in medical literature for a distinct allusion to the principle of contagion having been made in the sixth century.

' *Popular*

' Popular tradition, then, seems justified in regarding common colds as
the foundation of almost all the ailments of mankind ; and the great father
of physic, in considering the air as the cause of almost every malady.

' The yellow fever of the West Indies, and of America, the fevers of
Bengal, Bencoolen, Batavia, Bulam, Cadiz, Gibraltar, Andalusia,
Malta, Walcheren, and Leghorn, &c. &c. &c. (for so the epidemics
which have occurred at these several places, have been most impro-
perly denominated) as well as every variety of remittent and intermittent fever, are all only modifications of one and the same disease, produced by modifications of the same cause, and yielding to modifications
of the same remedies.'

From this it will be seen that Dr. Maclean is a decided unbeliever in the specific nature of any of those maladies which come
under the denomination of plague ; and it is likewise sufficiently
evident, that he conceives each and every case of plague to be
contracted, not by communication or contact, not by a something
emitted from a sick person, and impregnating the well, not by
a peculiar poison, as in the case of small-pox, but by the influence
of atmospheric change assisted by several circumstances of predisposition ; and that he is sincere in his opinions would seem
sufficiently clear from the fact of his having voluntarily exposed
himself to the pest-houses of Constantinople, and freely communicated for hours and days together with their sick inmates.   Our
readers will be eager to inquire whether he came from these exposures unaffected by disease ? We have to reply, from the author's own statement, in the negative.   Dr. Maclean candidly con-
fesses that he was at length seized by the plague ; but not, he still
maintains, from the reception into his system of a specific virus,
not from touching or handling the sick, but from being subjected
to the malign influence of the plague *atmosphere,* the operation of
which was materially aided by the several circumstances of mental
agitation to which his duty exposed him.

It is matter of notoriety that pestilential distempers are in our
day comparatively unfrequent in the north of Europe ; and this
fact is taken hold of by Dr. Maclean for the purpose of proving
the indigenous and non-communicable nature of these maladies :
' the nations (he says) of the North generally have been advancing
in cultivation, while those of the Levant have been retrograding ;
some of them, however, have either been stationary, or made less
progress than others ; and accordingly we find the provinces of
Spain, some parts of Italy, the old Venetian provinces of Dalmatia, Istria, &c., many parts of Poland, and the Eastern fron-
tiers of the Austrian dominions, as Hungary and Transylvania,
little less liable to epidemic diseases than formerly ; not because
they are adjacent to Turkey, as has been inferred in conformity
with

with belief in contagion, but because they are in so backward a state of cultivation.'

In the Minutes of Evidence taken by the Select Committee, formed for the purpose of inquiring into the validity of the doctrine of contagion in plague, Dr. Maclean assigns the following ' additional reasons' for his belief that epidemic and pestilential diseases never depend upon contagion.

' Because the laws of epidemic and those of contagious diseases are not only different, but incompatible; and because pestilences observe exclusively the laws of epidemics, of which they are but the higher degrees. Because no adequate proof has ever, in any single instance, been adduced of the existence of contagion in pestilence. Because, had pestilential diseases been contagious, consequences must have followed which have not taken place. Being capable of affecting the same persons repeatedly, they would never cease where no precautions are employed, (and in such case no precaution could avail,) until communities were extinguished. Turkey would long ago have been a desert. Because the assumption resorted to by the anti-contagionist, " that to the effect of contagion a particular state of the atmosphere is necessary to produce the disease," is only in other words an acknowledgment that a particular state of the atmosphere is its real cause. Because for centuries before any intercourse direct or indirect was established between this country and the Levant, or rather as far back as history extends, pestilence was at least as frequent in England as in the sixteenth and seventeenth centuries, when our commercial intercourse with Turkey was considerable. Because when the free states of Italy traded both with the Levant and the north of Europe; when they were the carriers not only of the merchandize but of the troops of the principal powers of Christendom engaged in the crusades; and when they possessed Smyrna, Cyprus, Candia, Scio, Cephalonia, Caffa, and even Pera (a suburb of Constantinople); no apprehension was then entertained under a constant intercourse, of pestilence being propagated by infection, nor any precautions adopted by any nation for the prevention of such a calamity. Because during the century and a half which has elapsed since 1665, and in which there has been no plague in England, our commerce and intercourse with the Levant have been more extensive and more rapid than at any former period. Because there is no reason to believe that in modern times pestilences have undergone any revolution in respect either to their nature or to other causes, further than may depend upon the advancement or retrogradation of countries respectively in cultivation, civilization, or the arts of life; or upon an alteration in the seasons. . Because, as contagion where it does exist is sufficiently palpable (it did not require the evidence of inoculation to show that small-pox always depends upon that source, and never upon any other) if it were the cause of pestilence, its existence could not for thousands of years have remained concealed. It must have been discovered and demonstrated to the satisfaction of the world, by the ancient physicians; and could not

now

now have been a subject of controversy among their successors. Because no person has at any period of history been known to arrive in England from the Levant labouring under pestilence. Because no person employed in purifying goods in the lazarettos of England, or of Malta, has ever been known to be affected with pestilence, which could not have happened if contagion had existed in the goods; and because such goods could not be exempt from contagion in particular countries, if that were the cause of plague. Because, after three hundred thousand deaths from plague have happened in one season in Grand Cairo, two hundred thousand in Constantinople, and one hundred thousand in Smyrna, as we are told, has repeatedly occurred in those places, and the clothes of the dead have been worn by their surviving relatives, or sold in the bazars, and worn by the purchasers, the disease, instead of spreading wider and wider, as would have inevitably have happened if contagion were its cause, (since in that case it could not fail to be carried in the clothes,) has, on the contrary, regularly declined and ceased at the usual periods. Because in those countries in which the plague is supposed to be introduced by means of contagion, conveyed by travellers or goods, as Egypt, Asia Minor, and Syria, it never occurs epidemically, but at particular seasons; although in other seasons travellers and goods from places in which the disease prevails, continue equally to arrive. And because in other countries, as Persia, which maintain a similar uninterrupted intercourse with places liable to frequent attacks of the plague, that disease never occurs.'

We have thus presented to our readers the principal arguments and allegations of Dr. Maclean against the presumption that pestilence is regulated by laws that are influential in contagious distempers. We now proceed to the work of Sir Brooke Faulkner, in which the opposite doctrine is maintained. The opinion of this gentleman is, that plague may actually be transported both by persons and articles of merchandize, and that moreover it may be received by, and propagated among, a people resident in a place the air of which is no otherwise conducive to disease than in having received a taint from the specific virus by which the existence of the malady has from the first been occasioned. Sir Brooke Faulkner believes further that ' plague is communicated only by contact or close association with the person or thing infected.'

The circumstances connected with the introduction of the plague which prevailed at Malta in 1813, are those upon which Sir Brooke Faulkner principally rests his opinion; and in his treatise, the title of which stands at the head of the present article, he endeavours to prove that Malta, so far from being favourable to pestilential origin, enjoys great advantages in respect to climate, soil, and habits of the people. He then goes on to state that the arrival of the San Nicolo, which took place under
the

the following circumstances, was to all appearance the cause of the pestilence now adverted to.

' Two Turkey merchants shipped on board this vessel, at the port of Alexandria, a cargo of linen, flax, and leather, with some other articles. Part of the crew having died of the plague on their voyage to Malta, the vessel applied to the health department of the island on her arrival (the 28th of March) for admittance into port, previously using the precaution to notify her state, by hoisting a yellow flag with a black ball in the centre, this being the signal to indicate the actual existence of plague on board. Her application being acceded to, she was accordingly received into quarantine in the Marsachuchet harbour, within about a cable's length of several points of land and of the city of Valetta. The surviving part of the crew were taken into the Lazaretto, situated in a small island in the middle of the harbour. The captain of the San Nicolo and his servant sickened, in a day or two after their being received into the Lazaretto, and died, with indisputable symptoms of plague.'

In four or five days from this arrival the plague manifested itself in Valetta; and he considers the circumstance as next to demonstrative in favour of one event being the cause of the other. The first person attacked was the daughter of Salvatore Borg, a shoemaker, who died of what a Maltese physician considered a typhus fever. ' During the visit, however, our author observed on the chest of his patient, below the mammæ, two tumours which resembled carbuncles.' This was on the 19th of April. On the first of May the mother of this girl was attacked with fever, and complained of pain from a tumour in the groin. She died on the third. The husband was taken ill on the fourth, who had likewise affections of the groin and of the axilla. ' This man (says Sir Brooke Faulkner) continued to linger until the 12th of the month, when he died with unequivocal symptoms of plague.' A schoolmistress, in habits of intimacy with the family, is then attacked, and dies; afterwards a girl of the name of Grazia Pisani, who recovered after the bursting of a bubo: then Borg's father, and a second child of Borg; and, on the 17th, a relation of the schoolmistress, who had a carbuncle on the lower part of the back.

' Here then (says our author) we have traced the propagation of the disease from the first case in Valetta in eight distinct and well-authenticated instances, and all of them in a continuous line of communication with each other. The last six cases are given on the authority of medical reports published under the sanction of the government of Malta.'

The infection now became very general in consequence of unrestrained intercourse, and our author next pursues its progress into the Augustin convent, afterwards into the casals or inland

towns

towns and villages, and, finally, into the island of Gozo by a man
belonging to Casal Curmi.

'It rests upon respectable testimony (says Sir Brooke Faulkner)
that this person, previous to his removal into quarantine, found means
to conceal a box, containing wearing apparel, in the cottage where he
resided; and that at the expiration of his quarantine he re-entered his
cottage, out of which he took the box, and after paying a visit to Valetta, hired a boat and transported it to Gozo.'

Having remarked that the degree of severity which attended
the plague in the several casals of the island, was in the ratio of
their degree of communication with the sources of infection, our
author goes on to adduce evidence of an impure state of the atmosphere being insufficient to account for the generation of
plague. He tells us, that the fourteenth regiment were preserved
from the contagion by vigilance, although quartered in the most
infected part of Valetta; and that another regiment was infected,
notwithstanding it was stationed in the most healthy situation in
or about the place. How is it, he asks, that Valetta should have
been for a long period the *exclusive nidus* of pestilence, seeing
that there were villages and towns in the island, where every tangible cause of local impurity existed in a still greater degree, and
which places were known to be much more frequently unhealthful
than this city? Why were not those places visited in the first
instance? And, finally, is it consistent to suppose plague an atmospheric disease, when the island had been free from its visitation during a period of one hundred and thirty-seven years?

That plague does not universally affect is no proof, according
to Sir Brooke Faulkner, that it is not a communicable distemper, since non-susceptibility may exist to a great extent in
many individuals; and, that it arises and disappears at certain
determinate periods of the year, independently altogether of any
interference on the part of the police, is an assertion (he says) un-
supported by fact; 'as the disease is known to commence in the
same country under every diversity as to the seasons; in proof of
which we need go no farther than the last two plagues of Malta,
the former having commenced in the month of December, three
months previous to the time of its appearance in 1813.'

The doctrine which Dr. Hancock's volume is designed partly
to support, is, that 'while plague is destitute of that specific
something which is attributed to it by the hypercontagionist, its
virus is capable of being communicated from one individual to
another under certain circumstances; that although it is thus a
communicable distemper, it is capable of spontaneous origin, and
has much more reference to place and circumstances than many
are disposed to allow; that quarantine enactments are founded in
mistaken

mistaken views respecting the essence of pestilential visitation ; and that fevers generally have much less of specific peculiarity, than systematic authors for the most part ascribe to them.'

Dr. Mead, the most celebrated writer of his day on the subject of plague, is an advocate for contagion. This author, however, admits, and the concession is marked by Dr. Hancock as a matter of much moment, that ' it has never been known where the plague did not first begin among the poor,' ' that a corrupt state of the air attends all plagues,' and ' that fevers of extraordinary malignity are the usual forerunners of plague.' Dr. Russell, another writer of celebrity on pestilence, likewise, says Dr. Hancock, ' candidly admits, that quarantine and other regulations have often proved ineffectual in arresting the progress of plague—that it has frequently occurred insidiously when they have been rigidly enforced, and in a more extraordinary manner has ceased, when they have been entirely relaxed.' And although he too is a decided contagionist, there is scarcely any writer who has laid so much stress as Dr. Russell on what has been termed a pestilential constitution of the atmosphere.

But, says Dr. Hancock—

' Dr. Maclean adduces many specious arguments in support of his opinions. He has collected a number of interesting facts, and has brought together some useful general observations respecting the prevalence and decline of plague in different countries ; and it cannot be denied that he possessed many advantages, and had good opportunities of investigation, as he resided for some time in the Levant for the sole purpose of observing the nature and progress of this formidable disease. Yet I cannot perceive that he ever witnessed its devastations or its career when raging as a pestilence.

' When, however, Dr. Maclean's confidence in his own opinions led him so far, in the face of direct proof, as to brave the destroyer in his den, the pest-house at Constantinople; though we may applaud his resolution as well as his sincerity, and give him due credit for the ingenuity with which he seeks to explain the fact according to his hypothesis, we must, I think, reasonably doubt his principles, when we find that, by his own statement, he was attacked with this *non-contagious* malady on the fifth day after he entered that nursery of pestilence!'

In adverting to the work of Faulkner, he observes, that ' had as much pains been taken to procure further information respecting the concomitant circumstances of the period, as have been employed to establish a position which few are found to deny in a properly qualified sense, the volume would have proved more serviceable and important.'

' We have, indeed,' says Dr. Hancock, ' seriously to lament that most writers have attached themselves to this or that side of the argument so exclusively as to strain the simple bearing of facts to their own
hypothesis ;

hypothesis; to make a record only of these, and to keep out of view almost every circumstance of an opposite tendency. Hence what contrary statements, and marvellous, nay almost incredible, recitals do we find in authors, both ancient and modern, who have treated of this subject!'

' Contagion, according to some, has been locked up in holes, and caves, and chests; it has even made its hiding-place a spider's web, and at particular times, as by mere accident, has been released from its imprisonment to desolate the earth! According to others, comets and meteors, planetary conjunctions or appositions of baneful influences, volcanic eruptions and malignant blasts from the earth during its convulsions, have corrupted the air with pestilential steams for the destruction of the human species!

' *The first class have left us in ignorance by what laws the contagion ceased after its sources were so incalculably multiplied; and the last have not explained how a wide spreading evil like the vitiated air still left millions untouched.*

' And these two predicaments would seem to include the principal difficulties of the argument.

' One general fact should be noticed, that no people in the world have been willing to acknowledge their own country to be the first or indigenous seat of pestilence.

' Even Ethiopia, condemned beyond all others, the supposed nursery of plague from the time of Thucydides to Mead, where putrefaction is said to concoct and sublime its most deadly poisons, has its seasons and situations remarkable for salubrity, in which health cheers the native as well as the stranger; and authentic histories of that country by no means confirm the imaginary terrors of its climate; nor do they record any plague so fierce and destructive as what more temperate regions have often experienced. For those who have resided and travelled in Upper and Lower Egypt, as Alperius, Savary, Volney, and others, so far from admitting that plague is indigenous, gravely tell us of its importation from Constantinople and the coast of Syria.'

The plague which prevailed in London in the year 1665, is supposed by some to have been imported; by others it has been regarded as indigenous. Dr. Hancock has therefore thought it right to investigate the circumstances of this epidemic, to trace it through its progress, and occasionally compare it with others, as a general example illustrative of the laws by which pestilence seems to be governed. The points for consideration are, 1st, The adventitious circumstances connected with this plague. 2dly, Its progress from one part to another. 3dly, The character that it assumed at its commencement, height, and decline. 4thly, The persons and places that were exempt. 5thly, The facts deduced from the bills of mortality; and, 6thly, our author takes a summary review of the whole.

The adventitious circumstances were disease among cattle, a
crowded

crowded population, a long continued calm in the weather, and the appearance of common disorders under types different from those which they usually display. Quotations from the works of Sydenham, Hodges, Baynard, Hooke and Boyle, in proof of these statements, are introduced into the work which we are now reviewing. The author then proceeds to trace the progress of the plague as accurately as the records permit him. In the latter end of November or beginning of December, two men, said to be Frenchmen, died of the disease at the upper end of Drury Lane; about three weeks after another man died in the same house of the same distemper, and about six weeks after the last death another died in another house, in the same parish, in like manner. ' Now it was observed, and the fact, which the weekly bills of mortality place beyond a doubt, is very curious, that from the time the plague first began in St. Giles's, *the ordinary burials from other diseases increased considerably in number in that and all the adjacent parishes.'*

' It was not till the beginning of May, or five months after the supposed introduction of fomites into St. Giles's, that a case of death, or even of infection, was reported to have taken place within the walls of the city. This occurred in Bearbinder Lane. It was found on inquiry that this was a Frenchman, who, having lived in Long-Acre, near the infected houses, had removed for fear of the distemper, not knowing that he was already infected.'

In the second week in June four died within the city; and now, the weather having ' set in hot,' the mortality soon increased, and the disorder was particularly prevalent and fatal in St. Giles's. About the middle of the next month ' the disease, which had chiefly raged in the parishes of St. Giles, Andrew, Stephen, and towards Westminster, came to its height there, and began to travel eastward,' *always abating in one direction as it appeared more malignant in another.* It was about the 10th of September that the disorder came to its height, at which time more than 12,000 died in a week, though two thirds of the inhabitants of the metropolis had gone into the country. Not one house in twenty was uninfected, and ' it looked as if none would escape; but just then,' says the writer whom Dr. Hancock copies, ' it pleased God by his immediate hand to disarm this enemy. Nor was this by any new medicine, or new method of cure discovered; the disease was enervated and the contagion spent. Even the physicians themselves were surprized; wherever they visited they found their patients better.' It is worthy observation that before the number of infected decreased, the malignity of the distemper began to relax, so that now few died; and it is further remarkable that the chief sufferers were those who had recently

cently arrived from the country. The *nature* of the disorder, as it
is expressed by Hodges, having undergone a change, ' we were
now,' says the journalist, ' no more afraid to pass by a man with
a white cap upon his head, or a cloth wrapt round his neck, or
limping from sores in his groin—all of which were frightful to
the last degree but a week before.' Another curious circumstance
was, that the *disease did not visit the provinces till its rage
had been expended in the metropolis,* only one instance having occurred of the plague existing at the same time in London and the
country. The provincial town thus infected simultaneously with
the metropolis was Southampton, ' and it is very remarkable,'
says Dr. Hancock, ' that we should not have some authentic document to prove in what manner the disease was at so early a
period introduced into Southampton, if it was entirely dependent
on contagion for its propagation.'

Having thus discussed the general circumstances connected
with the last plague of this country, Dr. Hancock proceeds to remark on the time when pestilence usually appears, and the subjects it chiefly attacks. He states, and appeals for the truth of
his statement to the histories of several pestilential visitations,
that the poor are always the first subjects of the distemper, and
that the season of pestilence is mostly the latter end of spring. In
Egypt it is otherwise, and perhaps also in countries subject to a
malaria, or endemic marsh fever, where the autumnal months are
most sickly.

Pestilential visitations have been, our author affirms, for the
most part marked by general sicknesses; by a more than usual
number of insects; by blights, mildew, deaths among animals,
and many other indications of something in the atmosphere un-
friendly to the well-being of man. He has taken great pains to
cite authorities in proof of this affirmation, and the section of the
book in which these particulars are adverted to concludes in the
following manner.

' Thus we see that philosophers, poets, ancient historians, and physicians, speak as it were one language, and sound one note of warning ;
and even the sanction of Holy Writ may, without forced comment, be
applied in support of the general principle. *Whilst a single idea that
seems in its practical effects to exclude all other considerations—the dread of
foreign contagion—upon this point engrosses the concern of all the most enlightened statesmen of the most civilized countries in the world.*'

It has already been noticed that, even by the admission of
Mead, ' fevers of extraordinary malignity are the usual forerunners
of plague;' and this author (Mead) attributes this circumstance to
' that ill state of air which attends all plagues.' At times, however, it has been observed that at the approach of pestilence, even
before

before the distemper has actually manifested itself, other diseases become less general and fatal. Mertens, for example, states that the epidemic diseases which had raged for three years previous to the plague at Moscow, altogether vanished in the month of May, 1770; and in the spring of 1771 began the plague. Dr. Hancock supposes that something of this kind may have been the case in relation to Malta before the occurrence of the last plague in that island; and he thinks that, so far from the allowed fact making in favour of imported contagion, the very reverse is the legitimate conclusion.

' For by what combination of causes, it might be fairly asked, should the common prevailing diseases be banished as it were from a city or country at the very critical juncture when a disease of foreign growth, with which they have no natural connexion, is casually introduced amongst them? Do they hide their diminished heads, or flee away as from the presence of an unwelcome stranger?

' By what singular change in the elements of life should not only this effect take place, but a portion of unusual health be imparted to those whose peculiarity of constitutions enables them to resist the fury that is dealing destruction around them?'

That a few months bring to a period the most formidable of plagues in the generality of instances, although multitudes remain susceptible of contagion, is a presumptive evidence, Dr. Hancock thinks, in favour of the dependence of the malady upon atmospheric malignity; and, moreover, the progressiveness observed in its movements from place to place, to which allusion has already been made, seems inconsistent with the notion of a conveyed virus merely. It goes from the city to the country, from one country to another, ' and in each the disorder, modified however by various causes, passes through its several stages,' its decrease, like its increase, being moderate—its periods, too, being nearly the same in crowded, filthy and ill regulated cities, as in those where all the regulations of the strictest healthy police are enjoined and observed; proofs these that there is a power stronger than contagion to control its effects, and a power stronger than medicine to change the character of the disease.

' He, therefore, that, exclusively believing in a contagious virus, asserts medicine and police regulations can do all, and attributes the removal of pestilence solely to their means, may be as much in error as he who, convinced of a general contamination in the air, denies contagion, and believes a crowded or a scattered population would make no difference in the mortality; or that a filthy habitation would add nothing to the malignity of the distemper; and that, as the disease is from the air, it matters not whether he stands idly gazing on till it shall cease, or assists to remove a local nuisance out of the way.

' Hence it is clear there must be a proper medium between these
opposite

opposite views, which alone the cautious observer and the wise physician can pursue with safety.'

The circumstance of particular exemptions is strong in favour of something peculiar in the nature of pestilence beyond its contagious properties. In a plague at Bath no Italians, nor Germans, nor French became the subjects of the disease. And at Hafni, in Denmark, during a wide spreading pestilence, all strangers, as English, Dutch and Germans, escaped, notwithstanding they lived promiscuously in the infected habitations. The sweating sickness of 1485 attacked only Englishmen, who did not escape even by travelling into France or Flanders. Wilson says that in Egypt some of the villages were exempt from the plague, while the most neighbouring were desolated. This is so common, that the inhabitants particularize to Europeans those villages in their districts which, during the season, the plague has appeared in, yet do not themselves refuse to enter them.* And there are some instances of different liabilities not only from natural constitutions, but incidental and adventitious circumstances. Dr. Maclean lays considerable stress, as we have seen, on the dread of contagion, and he supposes the danger is lessened to the Turks in proportion to their exemption from such fears. On this particular our present writer remarks—

' It is a nice point to determine, putting humanity out of sight, whether a notion which tends to separate individuals from each other, and therefore to lessen the concentration of febrile miasmata, be not more likely to lead to security than an indiscriminate confidence or fatalism which crowds them together; and I cannot but suspect that if fear on the one side, and assurance on the other, exert any influence in predisposing to the disease, or exempting from its ravages, the disciples of Dr. Maclean would run the greatest risk.'

It will be inferred from what has already been advanced, that Dr. Hancock regards the allegation of imported contagion in the

---

* In Sir Robert Wilson's examination before the Committee of the House of Commons, we find the following striking fact, to which Dr. Hancock alludes, stated in reference to partial immunities. ' I would wish also to remark, that as we moved through the country the inhabitants pointed out to us particular villages that were infected with plague, and which plague did not extend out of those particular villages to any contiguous villages, although there was no precaution whatever used as to the communication with the inhabitants of the infected villages.' And a statement in Mr. Legh's Travels in Egypt contains a very pointed illustration of the different susceptibilities of different places :—' The plague in 1812 raged in Constantinople and throughout Asia Minor, yet, although the communication between this city and Alexandria was uninterrupted, the latter remained perfectly free from contagion. At the island of Scio, distant but a few hours sail from Smyrna, where the plague was raging with violence, and whence persons were daily arriving at the island, the British Consul observed " that he had no fear of infection being communicated from Smyrna; but (said he) should the plague declare itself at Alexandria, several hundred miles distant, we shall certainly have it at Scio." '
—*See our review of Legh's Travels.*

plague

plague of 1665 as more than doubtful. He devotes a considerable portion of one section of his work to point out that discrepancy in evidence relative to the supposed importation, which would render the matter exceedingly difficult of belief; but when we take into consideration the state of things external and internal *at the precise period when the imaginary visit was paid*, it would seem a strange coincidence for every thing thus to concur, in order to accomplish the dreadful purpose that was brought about.

It is a curious fact, that Oxford was exempt from the plague of 1665, while it raged in most parts of the kingdom besides, although the terms were kept in that place and ' the courts and both houses of parliament did there reside;' and it is further re-markable that at the same time that city was considered as more troubled than usual with small-pox. This exemption was attri-buted, and Dr. Hancock thinks justly, to the great care taken to ensure the cleanliness and constant draining of the place, and he seems to imply that the superiority of Oxford in reference to these particulars was equal to the counteraction of that condition of the atmosphere which was the cause of plague in other places, but that it had not sufficient controul over the elements to pre-vent the manifestation of consequent disorder in another shape.

Why, it has often been asked, has plague not appeared as an epidemic in London since the year 1665? This immunity some ascribe to the constant use of pit-coal, which, from its sulphure-ous quality, has proved an antidote; by others it is conceived that the steady operation of our quarantine laws has succeeded in preventing it. But Dr. Hancock is not a believer in either of these notions, for coals were in use long before, ' and no one can doubt that goods have often been landed in this country since, if not saturated with contagious effluvia, certainly deeply imbued with the air of infected cities. So that if any *seminium* from abroad could act as a leaven in gradually corrupting the air of our climate, it might as well be done perhaps by the pestilential air necessary to the diffusion as by the contagion itself.'

When the circumstances of this great town are compared and contrasted in respect of cleanliness and comfort with those under which it was at the time of the last plague, we shall not have to wonder, says Dr. Hancock, at its comparative insusceptibility also to formidable distempers; and he announces it as his opinion, that the plague has in fact been often in London since the period referred to, but from want of the nidus of filth, and the fostering circumstances of inattention or mismanagement the disease has never mounted higher in the scale of malignity than common contagious fever. ' If we look at the state of London in the middle of the seventeenth century, and compare it with the pre-

sent,

sent, we shall cease to wonder that it has become of late years
far more healthy. The mortality in 1697 was 20,970, whereas
in 1797 it was only 17,014;' and it will be found that the more
recent occurrence of plague in some of the larger cities of Europe, are fairly attributable to their defective condition in respect
of those particulars 'to which the present salubrity of London is
so largely indebted.

That we have not been defended against plague by the operation of quarantine establishments may be fairly inferred, Dr. Hancock conceives, from the remarkable fact, that none of the expurgators of goods in Great Britain at these establishments have
ever taken the plague since their origin ; and the same immunity
has been enjoyed by the establishments of other countries. The
commencement of the Marseilles plague has been alleged as
forming one of the exceptions to this immunity ;) but Dr. Hancock
denies that the rumoured importation of plague into Marseilles is
sufficiently entitled to credit in opposition to the general experience.
' If we consider,' says he, ' *where* it broke out, if we consider the
previous diseases in the city, the state of the famished poor, the
entire want of evidence as to any communication between the
Rue l'Escale and the suspected ships or lazarettos; if we take
into account that physicians on the spot would not at that time
admit the disease to be plague, we cannot possibly receive the
report as an axiom to build upon.' And how is it, asks our author, that the lazarettos have not preserved Cadiz and other towns
in the south of Europe? In these places indeed the fevers that go
under the denomination of plague, and are ascribed by many to
foreign importation, are so clearly characterized by indigenous
peculiarities, as to render their local origin almost a matter of
demonstration. Our author's opinion on the evidence to be deduced from quarantine is summed up in the following terms.

· Now if we ascertain that in some countries, where quarantine is
strictly enforced, pestilential diseases do notwithstanding find entrance;
that in others, where plague has raged before, under other circumstances, though carelessly administered, the disease has not made its
appearance for more than a century and a half; that in others, where
the regulations are entirely dispensed with, the disease exhibits itself
only occasionally, and obviously in connexion with a peculiar state of
indigenous circumstances, or extraordinary phenomena in the seasons,
&c.; that in others, where importation has been presumed, the fact, on
investigation, has always been so clouded with improbable conjectures
as to cause the most serious doubts of inquiring persons on the spot;
that at most of these establishments no well authenticated instance of
death in the frequently laborious and supposed hazardous employment
of expurgation has taken place; and that in every country where
plague has prevailed, circumstances of a particular nature, variously
modified,

modified, have existed, it should then appear that, in connexion with other views of the subject, a very comprehensive body of facts is within reach, for the impartial consideration of those whom quarantine may immediately concern.'

In another part of his work, Dr. Hancock more particularly dwells upon the necessary inefficiency of quarantine in preventing so subtle a principle as contagion from making good its lodgment on our shores, especially under the proverbial laxity in the administration of its enactments. ' No one doubts that many a bale of merchandize, both silk and cotton, from our regular intercourse with Turkey, must have been often introduced to this country during the long interval from the last appearance of the plague to the present time, brought directly from infected cities; I will not say infected, but touched by infected hands, and packed in infected air.—Therefore I cannot but subscribe to the conclusion of Dr. Heberden, that our exemption from plague is not so much to be attributed to any accidental absence of its exciting causes, as to our change of manners, our love of cleanliness and ventilation, which have produced amongst us, I do not say an incapability, but a great unaptness any longer to receive it. Any improvements which our quarantine laws may have undergone are by no means adequate to such an effect.'

The concluding chapter of Dr. Hancock's volume is composed of a few intimations respecting the want of specific character in some other diseases besides plague that are by many regarded as definite, and communicable distempers, such as the yellow fever of the western continent and islands, and the typhus of London. Because these are occasionally communicated from person to person, and perhaps by fomes, it is a mistake to conclude therefore that they are not often spontaneous and sporadic; our author likewise alludes to that principle, to which especial reference will be found in the first part of the present paper, viz. the extensive operation of external and adventitious circumstances upon the aspect and apparent nature of morbid affection. In the following extract the reader will perhaps perceive a similar intimation to that which we have ourselves given on the head of diseases assumed almost universally to be specific and permanent in their habits and relations. ' I am inclined to think the practice of inoculation, and still more that of classifying diseases, which depend on many causes, and are liable to many changes, as we do the stable and permanent characters of the subjects of natural history, have given an unscientific turn to our views both in regard to the origin of, and differences between, what are termed specific contagions, and what are not; and I suspect we

shall

shall have something to unlearn before we get into a proper train of investigation.'

In the Appendix he proposes to give a few particulars relative to the plagues of Morocco in 1799; of Malta in 1813, and of Noya in Naples in 1816. Jackson, from whom he takes the account of the first, alludes to the famine which had recently pervaded the country, ' and which was produced by the incredible devastation of the devouring locusts,' of the birds of the air flying away from the abodes of men, and of fear having an extraordinary effect in predisposing the body to receive the infection. In reference to the plague at Malta, Dr. Hancock attempts to point out some discrepancy in the statements with regard to its origin. The president of the college of physicians thinks ' it might have originated from the lazaretto, where persons from Alexandria had it.' Faulkner supposes it ' not improbable that some of Salvatore Borg's family, among whom it first appeared, might have got goods from the infected vessel.' Dr. Calvert, not satisfied with this report, gives the contagion a more aerial passage, and is strongly inclined to think that it travelled through the air from the lazaretto to Valetta, and lighted upon the daughter of Salvatore Borg.' But the people of the island, according to Dr. Granville, firmly believe that S. Borg, who was a shoemaker, had purchased some linen to line shoes from a Jew, *who had received it from* Alexandria. Tully too and Faulkner disagree in their accounts respecting the healthiness of the island; and from the statement of the former, that ' the more insidious the first commencement of a plague, the more destructive is its ultimate progress,' Dr. Hancock maintains that it is incomprehensible how such a law should be developed upon the plain principle of foreign contagion propagated by contact only. Again, says Dr. Hancock, there is an inconsistency in the assertion of Faulkner, that the disease had no reference to the air, when he accounts for its not being more rapidly diffused at first ' by *the state of the air,* and othier circumstances not *favouring* its contagious power in so great a degree as afterwards.' Further, the small island of Gozo, near Malta, was not visited till about eleven months after, and, what is singular, in the preceding plague of 1675, ' a considerable interval elapsed from the contamination of Valetta until that of Gozo:' and it is likewise very important to know, that *at this time, and a year previous, the plague was raging in different parts of the Levant.* In 1813 and 1814 it also raged on the banks of the Lepanto, on the shore of Albania and the neighbouring coast of the Morea, in Bucharest, Wallachia, Alexandria, &c. The whole range of coast from Albania to Spalatro, in the immediate

immediate neighbourhood of the Ionian islands, was in 1815 infected with plague to a great degree.

With respect to the Noya plague, it appears from the evidence of a writer in the Quarterly Journal of Foreign Medicine, that 1st, the disease was preceded by famine. 2d, it began among the poor. 3d, other diseases with which it might be confounded prevailed at the time. 4th, it was various in its appearance and not very contagious at the commencement. 5th, the south wind increased its spread. 6th, the individual who conveyed the smuggled goods was not affected. 7th, the nature of the disease was doubtful. 8th, it continued about six months, and then, like most of the plagues in that climate, ceased.

Granville and Tully are at variance with respect to the commencement of this plague. The former, on the authority of an official report, says, it *certainly* came from Dalmatia ; while the latter observes, that, ' although the source from whence it was introduced is still involved in obscurity, the most fastidious inquirer cannot oppose its foreign origin.'

Tully and Granville likewise disagree with respect to the introduction of pestilence at Corfu in 1815, one tracing it to the distribution of a number of skull-caps of red cloth left in the island by the captain of a vessel from Tunis ; the other to a large box deposited by a man of the name of Spiracchi in the house of his friend Potiti, which was opened after the lapse of more than a year by Potiti, Spiracchi not having returned. Dr. Hancock then refers to the omissions of Tully respecting the particular state of the weather, and the prevalence of indigenous maladies, and concludes the whole of his investigation by the following remarks,—

' Now what do all the uncommon circumstances stated in different parts of the volume relative to this event ; as of rains earlier than usual —of long drought and heat unnatural for the season of the year—of constant sirocco—of malignant fever in a marshy soil, raging amongst a miserable, and wretched, and ill-fed population—of unprecedented severity in the weather—of the ravages of pestilence following and giving place to remittent fever—of a sickly season setting in far earlier than usual, hurrying all alike into disease—what do these things mean, if they are not all connected in causation as well as in series ?

' It appears to me therefore, and I am far from credulous, and (but) earnest to discover the truth in this perplexing obscurity of fact and testimony, that he must be an infinitely greater sceptic who can disbelieve such a connection, than he who doubts the contradictory stories of Spiracchi's box and the skull-caps of red cloth from Tunis, brought into Corfu by stress of weather and distributed in Lefchimo.'

We have thus redeemed the pledge which we placed in the reader's hands. We have caused to pass in review before us the leading facts and most weighty arguments from which the doc-

trine

trine of specific contagion in plague is maintained by one, modified by another, and rejected by a third party; and we shall here limit ourselves to a remark or two on the contrasted statements of Sir Brooke Faulkner and Dr. Hancock; since the absolute verification of either one or the other of their assumptions might be supposed decisive of the question. Now, no one can deny that the testimony of such a writer as Sir Brooke Faulkner, founded as it is on a simple record of occurrences, constitutes a considerable weight of evidence in favour of imported contagion—nay, it is next to impossible to doubt the connection of the San Nicolo's arrival with the breaking out of pestilence on the island of Malta; and, upon the whole, we are called upon to give it as our unbiassed opinion, that a stronger case was never adduced in support of the principle for which its narrator contends.

It may, however, be permitted us to pause before we allow that an unqualified admission of all Sir Brooke Faulkner's data and inferences would absolutely establish the fact of an abstract, and, if we may so say, *uncircumstantial* power possessed by the contagious virus; and let the reader refer back to Dr. Hancock's intimations respecting the latitude of the island, the simultaneous existence of plague on some of the shores of the Levant and Mediterranean, and the probable condition of Malta itself in reference to its diseases, before he fully makes up his mind whether the arrival of the San Nicolo, under precisely similar circumstances, in the port of London or of Liverpool, would have been followed by the same results.* On this head we confess that we entertain considerable doubts, conceding, at the same time, that Sir Brooke Faulkner has placed a greater difficulty in the way of the anti-contagionist than before existed. Prior to the accounts of the Maltese pestilence, the circumstances connected with the appearance of plague at Moscow and Marseilles, constituted perhaps the greatest impediments to a reception of the anti-contagious creed; but still, in both these instances, a minute inquiry into particulars brings to light several considerable flaws in the evidence favouring absolute and abstract miasm; while the statements of Sir Brooke Faulkner do not appear, to say the least of them, quite so vulnerable. But, in whatever way we decide in reference to this particular, certain it is, that, on the other hand, Dr. Hancock has brought forward a vast body of testimony of the most unequivocal kind, illustrative of the proposition, that the origin, spread, and decline of pestilence has, for the most part, more re-

---

* Sir A. Brooke Faulkner admits that this very vessel was sent back to Alexandria with her infected cargo; and ' that none of the persons who navigated her back took the plague but arrived in perfect health;' and he believes that ' they who assisted in landing the cargo were not affected.'

ference

ference to the local peculiarities of the soil and climate in which it appears, than to any foreign importation; and that plague, if it be sometimes a contagious and transportable, is, for the most part, an indigenous or endemic distemper.

Let the fact be recollected as one of extreme importance, that pestilential disorders have been much on the decline since the advance of civilization, and that, for the most part, they only still prevail in countries and districts, where the habits of the people are such as are known to be conducive towards fanning contagious poison into malignant disease. ' It is remarkable' (says Sir John Pringle) ' how much the plague, pestilential fevers, putrid scurvies, and dysenteries have abated in Europe within the last century; a blessing which we can ascribe to no other second cause than to our improvement in every thing relating to cleanliness, and to the more general use of antiseptics.'

The remarkable exemption of Persia from the plague has been noticed by a great number of writers—remarkable, inasmuch as contiguous countries have been the greatest sufferers from pestilential visitations. For this exemption the Persians are obviously, in part at least, indebted to their peculiar habits, ' they are the most cleanly people in the world, many of them making it great part of their religion to remove filthiness and nuisances of every kind from all places about their cities or dwellings.' And, not to multiply instances of liabilities and exemptions in places and persons, we are warranted, it is conceived, in stating generally, that where lands are elevated, the climate temperate, and the soil dry, there pestilence of all kinds is of the least easy induction;—that, on the contrary, where the lands are low and swampy, the temperature hot, and the air at the same time humid;—there, more circumspection and care are required on the part of the inhabitants to counteract, by artificial means, endemic insalubrity;—and, during the last century, the greater part of Europe has been most happily and efficaciously acting upon this principle—swampy lands have been drained—waste marshes cultivated—filth removed from our cities—air made to circulate through our dwellings—superstitious apprehensions respecting pestilential visits considerably lessened—and (in consequence shall we say, without incurring the charge of assuming where we ought to prove?) the greater part of Europe, and our own country and cities in particular, instead of harbouring and fostering contagion into venomous, and permanent, and wide-spreading pestilence, have merely ' afforded a *short and niggardly entertainment* to the mildest form of contagious fever!'

Before we conclude, i tmay be expected that we should say a few words respecting the probable manner in which infectious

miasmata

miasmata are made to influence the frame. Is contagion absorbed occasionally through the surface of the body, or are the lungs its only inlet? The former is the opinion most generally received, and acted on, but it may be regarded as of questionable foundation. Some phisiologists indeed doubt whether, while the outer skin is whole and entire, it be at all permeable to the most minute and subtle matter from without; and whether every thing, both salutary and noxious, does not find its way into the system either through the lungs or the stomach? Lay, for example, the saliva of a rabid animal, the matter of small-pox, or that of vaccinia upon the skin merely, and you fail to inoculate with the diseases. It is necessary that the cuticle be abraded or punctured before the absorbents can receive the poison. But, on the other hand, it is urged that infectious effluvia, from their higher divisibility than the poisons referred to, may possess the power of penetrating through the scarf-skin and thus impregnate the body. In reply to this suggestion, others have urged the case of natural, as opposed to inoculated small-pox. Here we find the disease taken from secreted matter is as impalpable, and most probably in as minute form, as when sickness is the result of other infections; and yet this material, when it is concentrated into a tangible existence, and thus most probably possessed of higher power, must be made to enter the body by puncture or scarification. Neither does this poison affect as a contagious substance when received into the stomach. Dr. Rush informs us, that he gave a negro girl some variolous matter mixed with a dose of physic, and that no sensible effect was produced. It is, therefore, we repeat, highly probable, not however by any means certain, that the sole vehicle by which contagious or infectious influence operates upon the body is the lungs. This is not, of course, a matter of mere speculative curiosity; for, could it be certainly ascertained that the outer skin forms that barrier which we are inclined to believe it does, against the intrusion of a morbid poison, it would follow of course that there need be less scruple about handling the sick, and performing acts of sympathy and duties of humanity towards them, provided we carefully kept from immediately inhaling their breath; at all events, we believe, that those expedients are idle and fruitless to which recourse is had for the purpose of defending against impregnation by infectious miasmata, such as feeling the pulse through the medium of a cabbage-leaf, oiling the surface of the body, &c. and here, we may remark, that in our minds that notion is altogether ill-founded which attributes a preventive efficacy in cases of fever, to certain materials, such as camphor, and aromatic oils, and perfumes, which are, probably, all of them worse than nothing. The best, the only preservatives, are cleanliness and
ventilation,

ventilation, joined with a firm but not presumptuous confidence in the protecting power of Providence.

As a result of the whole inquiry the following corollaries appear to us to be pretty fairly made out—That all, or at least the greater part of morbid poisons are in some inscrutable way the produce of the clime and country in which they originally appear —that they are materially modified by time, and by the intercourse of nations, so much so, as in some cases to lose eventually their primary characteristics and habits—that some are much more permanent in respect of their specific peculiarities than others—but that *all* are, in a greater or less degree, subject to the modifying influence supposed—that those which are the most fixed, or the least changeable in their external habits and essential peculiarities, are the most easily conveyed from one country to another—but that there are few, if any, that may not be transported from the place which gave them birth, and transplanted into foreign soils; where, however, some will soon die away, or be changed into other forms and essences according to the natural tendencies or artificial habits of the new regions in which they have arrived, while others will retain for centuries a sufficient degree of peculiarity to mark their actual essence through all their variety of modification—that man can accomplish much towards mitigating the malign agency of contagious poisons—and that progress in the arts of civilization and improvements in polity have disarmed epidemics of a considerable portion of their power. Finally, it does not seem probable that the metropolis of England can ever receive from the shores of the Levant a sufficient measure of contagious miasmata to cause the existence or prevalence of positive plague—but, as some degree of uncertainty necessarily connects itself with our conclusions on subjects which, from their very nature, are insusceptible of absolute demonstration, it will be the part of a wise policy rather to err on the side of caution, than that of precipitancy or presumption. It is, however, to say the least, highly questionable whether laws framed for the purpose of preventing the intrusion of pestilence might not be much less restrictive, and expensive, and vexatious than they actually are, and at the same time equally, if not more, effective.

Art. VI.—1. *Facts and Observations respecting Intermittent Fevers, and the Exhalations which occasion them, collected chiefly on a Professional Mission to inquire and report on the Cause of the Sickness of the Army in Walcheren, in* 1809, *and to Northfleet, to report on the Expediency of establishing a Dock Yard and Naval Arsenal at that Place, in* 1810. *In* 'Select Dissertations on several Subjects of Medical Science.' By Sir Gilbert Blane, Bart. F.R.S. &c. &c. London. 1822. 8vo. pp. 398.

2. *De Regionibus Italiæ Aëre pernicioso contaminatis Observationum quas Munia Professoris ordinarii publici in celeberrimâ Universitate Berolinensi subiens Commilitonibus Prodromi instar ad Lectiones de Epidemiis et Contagiis habendas offert* Johannes Ferdinand Koreff, Dr. Med. et Chirurg. &c. &c. Berolini. 4to. pp. 37.

3. *Leçons sur les Épidémies et l'Hygiène Publique, faites à la Faculté de Médecine de Strasbourg.* Par Fr. Emm. Foderé, Professeur à cette Faculté. Tome premier. A Paris. 1822. 8vo. pp. 523.

4. *Recherches Historiques, Chimiques et Médicales sur l'Air Marécageux, Ouvrage Couronné par l'Académie Royale des Sciences de Lyon.* Par J. S. E. Julia, Professeur de Chimie Médicale, &c. &c. Paris. 1823. 8vo. pp. 155.

FEW of our readers, perhaps, are ignorant that the exhalations from marshy lands under certain circumstances give occasion to a variety of disorders, the principal of which are intermittent and remittent fevers. So extensive indeed is the influence of such exhalations, that it has been affirmed as a general truth, that the great difference of one country from another, in point of salubrity, consists in the greater or less proportion of that soil, which produces noxious effluvia. In England, the counties most subject to ague and to its grand exciting cause, the marsh mi-

asma,

asma, are Essex, Cambridgeshire, Lincolnshire, and the East
Riding of Yorkshire, although we are glad to see, from the last
population abstract, that the disease is by no means so rife as it
was formerly, owing in a great measure to the more extensive
draining of the soil.

Respecting the nature of marsh effluvia we are unfortunately
very much in the dark; their chemical components have never
yet been discovered, nor are they likely to be so; every eudiome-
trical experiment hitherto instituted having furnished the same
constituent principles, and the same quantity of them as
are contained in common atmospheric air. M. Julia, who has
paid considerable attention to chemical analysis, has sixty times
subjected to trial the air of the marshes of Cercle, near Narbonne;
of the pond of Pudre, near Sigéan; of Salces and Salanque, in
Roussillon; of Capestang, not far from Béziers; and of the different marshes on the coast of Cette; and has constantly obtained the like results. Various speculations have been indulged
regarding their nature; by some they have been pronounced to
be azote, and by others, carbonic acid gas, hydrogen, carburetted
hydrogen, and sulphuretted hydrogen; but all these suppositions have been proved to be unsatisfactory, and we still remain,
as we have just observed, in utter ignorance of their composition. One particular, however, seems tolerably evident, that
they are somewhat heavier than pure atmospheric air, as those
who live in elevated situations are less exposed to them (except
where such situations are the *foci* of the miasmata) than the inhabitants of plains: this observation will only apply, when the
atmosphere is undisturbed by winds; as there are numerous
proofs of the noxious effects of mal'aria upon the inhabitants of
mountainous districts, where they have been situated under the
lee of marshy lands. In the mission of Sir Gilbert Blane to
Northfleet in 1810, he observed a somewhat strange anomaly in
the action of the marsh miasmata, viz. that the inhabitants of
those places which were situated on a level with the marsh
whence the miasmata emanated were by no means subject to intermittent fever, whilst it was extremely prevalent on the adjacent
hills. The spot upon which it was proposed to form the dockyard and arsenal is a marsh of about 700 acres. On the banks
of the river, both above and below it, is a soil of a similar description, but not immediately adjoining it on either side; for
higher up the river lies the village of Green Hithe, which rests
on a chalky bottom, rising to within a few inches of the surface, and forming a projecting point of the chalky hills which
compose the adjacent country; and lower down, on the bank
of the river, there is a similar intervention of chalk, where the
                                                        village

village of Northfleet stands: both these villages are nearly on a level with the marsh, yet intermittent fevers are almost unknown at either of them, whilst they are extremely prevalent on the hills in the vicinity. This fact Sir Gilbert found to be analogous to others, which he learned in the course of his inquiries at that period. Dr. Maton informed him, that, in the neighbourhood of Weymouth, although there is stagnating water near the sea, pro·ducing intermittents, these disorders are not known in the dry districts on each side, on a level with the water, but they prevail on the adjacent hills. The way in which Sir Gilbert accounts for these phenomena is perhaps as probable as any.

' It is known to every one, ever so little acquainted with the operations of nature, and indeed the common phenomena of clouds and rain render it obvious to the most ordinary observer, that water recently exhaled from the surface of the earth, has a tendency to ascend, and being lifted over parts on the same level, impinges on the neighbouring heights. There is reason to believe, that impure and unwholesome particles in general are attracted by watery vapours, for it is remarkable, that, in case of fogs, offensive smells are perceived, which, in a dry state of the air, were fixed and quiescent. Though pure humidity, therefore, is innocuous, it may prove pernicious as a vehicle of unwholesome volatile matter. In like manner, the poisonous principle of marshes, whatever it is, being engendered by moist soils, will naturally adhere to the watery vapours, and ascend with them.'—p. 112.

From what has been observed, it may be easily understood that the inhabitants of the ground floor of any habitation may be more exposed to the noxious effects of marshy exhalations than those who occupy the upper stories. This circumstance is more especially observable at night; during the day, the emanations, through the heat of the sun, are carried up and diffused in the atmosphere, along with the watery vapours; whilst at night, a refrigeration of the air takes place, the aqueous evaporation no longer goes on, but, on the contrary, a copious precipitation occurs, and the miasmata, owing to their greater specific gravity, are detained at the surface of the ground. Dr. James Clark has given a striking instance of this, in his ' *Medical Notes on Climate, Diseases, Hospitals, and Medical Schools in France, Italy, and Switzerland,*' (a work which we strongly recommend to the valetudinarian, who may have been recommended to visit the South of Europe under the delusive hope that he may by that means be enabled to *escape* the winter,) which was communicated to him by Professor Brera, whilst attending the clinical wards of the hospital at Padua. The wall of that wing of the building where these wards are situated is washed by a branch of the sluggish Brenta, and it frequently happened that

the

the windows of them, (which were about sixteen feet above the surface of the water,) having been carelessly left open, until too late an hour, several of the patients were attacked with intermittent fevers, in some instances of the pernicious kind. This never occurred in the women's wards, which are immediately over those of the men, though there is no reason to believe that more care was taken in shutting the windows of those than of the former. It was likewise remarked at Walcheren that those who slept in the upper stories of houses were less liable to the disease, and had it in a milder form, than those who slept on the ground floors. The testimony of the natives was in favour of this observation. Dr. Ferguson, one of the principal medical officers of the army in St. Domingo in the late war, has remarked, that two-thirds more men were taken ill on the ground floors than on the upper stories.

It seems pretty clearly established that marsh miasma is only capable of acting with virulence sufficient to produce fever, within a certain distance, which distance must of necessity vary according as the exhalations are more or less virulent. In Zealand, they are more noxious than in England; the intermittents in the former country being more violent, untractable, and fatal, than those which occur in the fenny counties in the eastern parts of our own island. In that country they appear to be less virulent than in several parts of southern France and Italy, to which we shall have occasion to allude, whilst in tropical climates they would seem to extend farther and to be still more malignant than in the last-mentioned places. According to Sir Gilbert Blane, not only the crews of the ships in the road of Flushing were entirely free from the endemic of Walcheren, but also the guard-ships which were stationed in the narrow channel between Flushing and Beveland, the width of which is about 6,000 feet; and although some of the ships lay much nearer to one shore than to the other, there was no instance of any of the men or officers being taken ill with the same disorder as that with which the troops on shore were affected; whilst ships at the distance of 3,000 feet and even farther from swampy shores in the West Indies were affected by the noxious exhalations: the same thing is said to occur in the India ships in the channel leading to Calcutta. The increased heat of the atmosphere may account for the greater intensity and malignity of these exhalations within the tropics. On this subject, the Baron de Humboldt has observed, that the farm of Eucero, situated above Vera Cruz, is a stranger to the insalubrity which reigns over the whole coast; the elevation of this farm is 3,045 feet, and it forms the highest limit of the yellow fever. M. Rigaud de l'Isle has also endeavoured, by

some

some observations made in the neighbourhood of Rome, to fix the point at which the marsh effluvia are innoxious; this he considers to vary from 682 to 1006 feet above the level of the situation whence they emanate.

From the foregoing observations of Sir Gilbert Blane respecting the distance at which the miasma of Zealand was proved to be innoxious, or, at least, to fail in producing a similar fever to that which was raging on shore, as well as from those of the Baron de Humboldt and of M. Rigaud de l'Isle, our readers will imagine with what feelings of astonishment we perused the subsequent observations in a late Journal of our northern brethren. We scarcely believe it possible that the writer can have been serious when he penned the following passage :—

' It is commonly held that it (the miasma) cannot travel far from the place of its production; a fallacy often leading to very pernicious consequences. But the east wind has the power of transporting it to considerable distances; and we have little doubt ourselves, that whenever it occurs in this city,' (Edinburgh, we presume,) ' where it now is rare, the *poison is transported from Holland!* The east wind, which blows from Essex towards London, invariably carries it on, even for many miles, as all susceptible persons experience; and that this is not a mechanical consequence of the motion of the air, is certain, since the western winds do not transport it in the opposite direction. Nor will the east wind produce it, except in cases where it blows over countries subject to the mal'aria; a proof that the poison is present, and that the effect is not a property of the wind itself.'—No. lxxii. p. 542.

Our readers will readily see the utter futility of this opinion. In order to support the first part of the theory, (which by the bye appears to be almost unintelligible,) the miasmata must be borne aloft on the wings of Eurus, or rather of Notus, to a distance of some hundreds of miles across the ocean, must pass over several inhabited districts without molesting them; (for we have no account of the inhabitants of other places being doomed to be attacked by it at the same time with the devoted citizens of Edinburgh;) and single out the Scotch metropolis for the scene of its devastations; a supposition perfectly contradicted by the observation of Sir Gilbert Blane respecting the distance at which the Dutch mal'aria becomes innoxious, and as ridiculous as it is unphilosophical. The same observations will apply to the assertion of the critic regarding the mal'aria, which is said to be ' generated abundantly in St. James's Park.' That exhalations do take place there as well as in almost every other situation, to a greater or less degree, far be it from us to deny; but that they are there generated in abundance sufficient to exert any marked influence on the healths of those who inhabit situations in the greatest proximity to the place where they are supposed to emanate, is, to

say

say the least of it, very problematical : upon still less foundation
do we consider the following *minute* description of the line of
march of the mal'aria to rest.

' We have said that it (the mal'aria) is generated abundantly in St.
James's Park, and thence it spreads even to Bridge-street and White-
hall. Nay, in making use of the most delicate miasmometer (if we may
coin such a word) that we ever possessed, an officer who had suffered
at Walcheren, we have found it reaching up St. James's Street even to
Bruton Street, although the rise of ground is here considerable, and
the whole space from the nearest water is crowded with houses. After
this, we need scarcely remark, that, at the east end of London, it reaches
all through Finsbury division and Whitechapel, and is even brought up
at the back of the Strand along the course of the river. We shall hereafter see that it is in the same manner spreading, and that very rapidly,
through the city of Rome.'

We should not have considered the preceding reveries worthy
of notice, were it not that the minute and categorical manner in
which the progress of this ' airy phantom' has been described
might—

———— ' draw on some better natures
To run in that vile line'—

and induce a belief that such a focus of disease is really in existence. In spite, however, of all these mischievous assertions,
principally founded on the information obtained from this animated ' *miasmometer*,' who seems to have taken a pleasure in
administering pretty largely to the credulity of the Reviewer, we
can affirm, from an intimate acquaintance with the medical topo-
graphy not only of the western but of the eastern districts referred
to, that in the whole line of march which has been ascribed to it,
and even in situations most in proximity to the western focus of
this ' fitful pest,' there is no sensible evidence of the presence of
such a deleterious agent—that these very situations are as healthy
as others more remote, and that some of them are even remarkable
for their salubrity, and the longevity of the inhabitants ; thus, in
one street in the immediate neighbourhood of St. James's Park,
situated to the westward of this very canal—

' from whose humid soil and wat'ry reign
Eternal vapours rise'—

and consequently exposed to the pestiferous exhalations, were
any such in existence, during the domination of an eastern blast ;
they seem to take a delight in falsifying the visionary assertions
contained in that strange article. One gentleman, who had lived
for more than half a century in the street, died there lately at the
advanced age of eighty-two ; there are at present several sep-
tuagenarians in it, and a very old friend of our own has resided
there

there for the last five and twenty years, labouring under a pulmonary complaint nearly coeval with his existence. To any one acquainted with those districts where mal'aria is most prevalent, it is needless to state that the canal in St. James's Park is not the situation which gives rise to it in any ' abundance'; the water can never be said to be stagnant; and consequently, even during the summer heats, except under circumstances of great neglect, no decomposition can, in our opinion, ever take place to a sufficient extent for the production of epidemic disease. Those situations in which mal'aria is most virulent, are not countries deeply submersed in water, but those of a swampy nature, where the vegetable matter is capable of being reached by the solar heat, and of undergoing some sort of change, which causes the disengagement of the deleterious effluvia. Dr. Ferguson indeed seems to think that there is one only condition indispensable for the production of marsh poison, viz. the *paucity* of water, where it has previously and recently *abounded;* to this he considers there is no exception in climates of high temperature, and he thence infers, that the poison is produced at a highly advanced stage of the *drying* process : with the nature of the deleterious miasma, except that he is satisfied it does not arise from aqueous or vegetable *putrefaction,* singly or combined, Dr. Ferguson, like every other sensible writer who has treated the subject, expresses his thorough unacquaintance.

The mal'aria has been supposed by many to be the product of marshy districts only. There is every reason, however, to believe that it arises in places where the soil is dry and the ground elevated, particularly in volcanic districts: this is the case in the territory called the Maremma in Italy, a district which reaches from Leghorn to Terracina; it is a tract of country near the sea, varying in breadth, according to Chateauvieux, from thirty to forty miles, and being in length about one hundred and ninety-two geographical miles. The diseases produced by the mal'aria of this district are principally intermittent and remittent fevers, of which Professor Koreff has given some account in the second of the works before us. In consequence, however, of the richer inhabitants leaving this part of the country before the approach of the sickly season, but few opportunities have occurred for witnessing the diseases.

The miasmata do not appear to infect the inhabitants of the country in which they have their origin so readily or so virulently as strangers : thus the countrymen who come down in the harvest time into the Campagna, Modena, Ferrara, Bresse, &c. where the rice-grounds and marshy districts are principally situated, are most frequently attacked with the fever, even when the season is considered

sidered favourable by the natives. A similar observation was made at Walcheren; it was also remarked that strangers were variously affected according to the district whence they came—thus it was found that those of the British troops who were natives of mountainous countries and dry soils were more frequently affected than the natives of flat and moist districts. It was likewise well ascertained, that strangers, if they survived the first attacks, became afterwards much less liable to the endemic intermittent.

Art. IX.—1. *The Progress of Opinion on the Subject of Conta-gion.* By William Macmichael, M.D. 1825.
2. *Report from the Select Committee on the Doctrine of Contagion in the Plague.* 1819.
3. *Second Report from the Select Committee appointed to consider of the Means of Improving and Maintaining the foreign Trade of the Country. Quarantine.* 1824.

DE FOE thought the events of the plague in London, in 1665, so full of fearful interest, that he wove them into a fictitious narrative, which does not however exceed in the distressing nature of its details the representations handed down to us by eye-wit-nesses. Dr. Hodges, who remained on the spot when Sydenham fled, and who, by appointment of the government, visited the sick from morning to night for many months, was clearly not a man of strong intellect, but he has left us an account of what he saw and heard, which, although rhetorical and affected in style, it is im-possible to read without shuddering, and which we will not ex-tract, because we might be accused of desiring to interest the feelings of our readers in the opening of a most important inquiry, when it is and ought to be our intention only to appeal to their judgments. This scourge of the human race has been believed, by the most judicious physicians who have witnessed its ravages, to be communicated from person to person, that is, to be conta-gious. Quarantine laws were therefore instituted. ' *Before* this,' as Lord Holland has remarked, ' the plague frequently devastated every country in Europe; but *since* then its returns have been comparatively rare.' Before the year 1665, Sydenham remarked that the plague visited this country *only* once in forty or fifty years; since that calamitous year this happy land has known nothing of its ravages; and so many generations have lived and died in secu-rity, that the clause in the Litany which implores preservation ' from plague and pestilence,' has lost perhaps some of that intense earnestness with which it must once have pressed on the hearts of the congregation in prayer. In this blessed, yet dangerous ignorance of the public mind, certain persons have started up, who affirm that the wisest of their forefathers, and the most experienced of their contemporaries, have been, and are, all wrong upon the subject—that the plague is not conta-gious—that quarantine laws ought to be abolished; and the pub-lic, and even our legislators, seem inclined to believe them. In these critical circumstances it is a duty, which some one ought to perform, to give a true and faithful account of this moment-ous matter—to state the reasons which have satisfied the most competent judges that the plague is contagious—to expose the
ignorance

ignorance of those who are attempting to mislead the public, and the indiscretion of those who are inclined to believe them.

Some diseases become prevalent because their causes are so diffused as to affect many persons in the same place at the same time; other diseases become prevalent because the bodies of the sick give out a noxious material, which excites them in the bodies of the healthy. The former are called epidemic, the latter contagious diseases. The causes of epidemic diseases may be either deficient food, as in a general scarcity; or heat, or cold, or great vicissitudes from one to the other; or noxious states of the atmosphere, which are not perceptible by our senses, thermometers, or barometers. Some of these are understood, as marsh exhalations; others are involved in great obscurity. The human constitution is a delicate instrument, and can perceive qualities which our philosophical instruments and chemical tests do not enable us to detect.

The noxious matters produced by the bodies of the sick, which propagate contagious diseases from person to person, may be either something visible and substantial, as that formed in the pustules of small-pox, or the vesicles of the cow-pock; or something invisible, the existence of which is known only by its effects, as in the measles, the scarlet-fever, the hooping-cough.

The only way in which we can distinguish those diseases which are prevalent from an extensive cause acting at the same time on a number of people, from those diseases which are prevalent because they are communicated from person to person, is by certain circumstances in the mode of their diffusion. Now the circumstances by which we know that a disease is propagated by contagion, are these; 1st, that those persons are most liable to the disease who approach those affected with it, and that in proportion to the nearness of the approach; 2dly, that those who avoid intercourse with persons affected with the disease, generally or always escape it, and that in proportion to the care with which they avoid them; 3dly, that the disease is communicable from one to another by inoculation. If all these circumstances can be ascertained in the diffusion of a disease, and each with clearness and distinctness, we have all the evidence, which we can have, for believing that the disease is propagated by contagion. The proof is as complete as the nature of the subject admits. But the evidence for the belief that a disease is propagated by contagion, varies very much in degree in different cases; it may amount only to that which creates a strong suspicion—or it may amount to that which creates an absolute certainty. The most decisive single proof that a disease is contagious, is inoculation. Yet there are several diseases the con-

tagiousness

tagiousness of which is undoubted, notwithstanding the absence of this proof; as, for instance, the scarlet-fever and hooping-cough.

But there are occasions when it is necessary to act on the supposition that a disease is contagious, though the evidence for this opinion is far short of proof. The question is sometimes so difficult—life and health are so precious—and the precautions necessary to prevent the communication of the disease, if it should be contagious, comparatively such trifling evils; that a prudent physician will take care to be on the safe side, and use measures as if he was certain it was contagious, although to an indifferent person, weighing the evidence in the scales of mere speculation, it would appear only a bare possibility;—and here is the difference between a science, which makes its experiments on retorts and receivers, things of clay and glass, and a science, the subjects of which are flesh and blood, and health and life; that whereas in the former, the onus probandi lies on him who affirms the proposition, because the disbelief of it leads to no injurious consequence; in the latter, the onus probandi sometimes lies with him who denies it, because the disbelief would occasion the neglect of measures, which are harmless even if they be unnecessary, but the neglect of which may be fatal if they be essential.

Five-and-twenty years ago Dr. Wells published his belief that erysipelas was sometimes contagious. The following is one of several facts which led him to this opinion:—An elderly man died of erysipelas of the face. His nephew, who visited him during his illness, was soon afterwards attacked by, and died of, the same disease. The wife of the old man was seized with the same disease a few days after his death, and died in about a week. The landlady of the same house was next affected with it and then her nurse, who was sent to the workhouse, where she died. Dr. Wells mentioned his suspicion to several medical friends, among whom were Dr. Pitcairn and Dr. Baillie, and they related to him several circumstances which had led them to a similar opinion.

Lying-in women are subject to a disease called puerperal fever. In general it is of unfrequent occurrence, and out of large numbers scarcely one suffers from it. There are times, however, when this disease rages like an epidemic, and is very fatal. At these times circumstances sometimes occur which create a strong suspicion that the disorder may be communicated by a medical attendant or nurse from one lying-in woman to another. We give the following, out of many authentic instances. A surgeon practising midwifery in a populous town, opened the body of a woman who died of puerperal fever, and thereby contracted an offensive smell in his clothes: nevertheless, surgeon-like, he continued to wear

them

them, and to visit and deliver his patients in them. The first woman whom he attended after the dissection, was seized with, and died of, the same disease—the same happened to the second and the third. At length he was struck with the suspicion that puerperal fever might be contagious, and that he was carrying it from patient to patient in his offensive clothes;—he burnt them, and not another of his patients was affected.

These are incidents calculated to produce a deep impression on the minds of those who witness them, and to create a strong suspicion that these diseases are, under certain circumstances, contagious. Yet if such evidence as this be contrasted with incidents of an opposite kind, in which free communication has produced no such consequences, and be mixed up with the ordinary history of the diseases, the whole statement would produce little effect no indifferent persons—on cold judges like a committee of the House of Commons.

Few persons believe that consumption of the lungs is contagious; it is a question which requires for its solution long and well-used experience. A physician in early, and even in middle life, is an inadequate judge; but there are English physicians of the greatest experience, the highest eminence, and the least fanciful minds, who are convinced that this disease is sometimes communicated from a wife to a husband, or from a husband to a wife, during the long and close attendance which its lingering nature and strong affection sometimes occasion. It is an opinion, however, which he who entertains can never demonstrate to be true to him who rejects it; yet is it a reason for every precaution which does not interfere with the duties of the healthy to the sick.

In medicine, and all but the demonstrative sciences, there is often light enough to guide our conduct, when there is not enough to gratify our curiosity; and therefore it is that practical men are often compelled to act on evidence, which would sound unsatisfactory in the statement. There is no paradox in saying, that he who can give a striking reason for every measure which he adopts, is, for that very reason, a bad medical adviser; because he must neglect many which are necessary and useful, but the reasons for which at the outset are extremely obscure. We cannot give a stronger instance of the difference between the evidence which is required to satisfy incompetent judges, and that on which physicians are often obliged to act, than that which is detailed in Dr. P. M. Latham's excellent ' Account of the Disease lately prevalent at the General Penitentiary.'

Having thus considered the signs by which we distinguish a contagious disease—the different degrees of clearness with which these signs show themselves—and the necessity there often is to
act

act on the supposition that a disease is contagious, although the
evidence for it is far short of demonstration—we may now go on
to consider whether these signs are discoverable in the history of
the plague in a sufficient degree to make it proper for us to act
with respect to it on that supposition. Now whoever will carefully
examine the accounts of the plague transmitted to us by those
who have witnessed its ravages, will find ample evidence of
the following truths:—1st. That it is most liable to affect those
persons who approach patients affected with it, and that in
proportion to the nearness of the approach: 2dly, that those
who avoid all intercourse with persons affected with the plague,
generally escape the disease, and that in proportion to the care with
which they avoid it. There are few facts indeed in medical history
for which there is such a mass of evidence as these; or on which
the experience of past and present times is so uniform. The
most remarkable examples are afforded by the introduction of the
plague into countries which had long been free from it, in consequence of intercourse with places in which it was then raging.
The clearness with which this intercourse has been often traced
is truly wonderful, considering the many temptations which
travellers or mariners coming from countries infected with the
plague have to clandestine intercourse. Of such histories there
are so many on record, that the difficulty is which to select: we
will begin with the plague at Marseilles, in 1720.

For *seventy years* the plague had never visited this maritime
city, when, on the 25th May, 1720, a vessel sailed into the harbour, under the following circumstances: She had left Seyde, in
Syria, on the 31st of January, with a clean bill of health, but the
plague had broken out a few days after her departure, and she
had called at Tripoli, not far from Seyde, where she took in some
Turkish passengers. During the passage, one of the Turks died,
after an illness of a few days. Two sailors attempted to heave the
corpse overboard, but before they had time to do so, the captain
called them away, and ordered it to be done by the comrades of
the deceased. In the course of a few days the two sailors who
had touched the corpse fell sick, and speedily died. Soon after
this, two others of the crew, one the surgeon of the vessel,
who of course had attended the sick, were attacked with the
same symptoms, and died. These occurrences so alarmed the
captain, that he shut himself up in the poop during the rest of the
voyage. Three other sailors subsequently fell ill in the same way,
were put ashore at Leghorn, and died there; the physician and
surgeons of the infirmary certifying that their disease had been a
pestilential fever. The vessel arrived at Marseilles, and the crew
and cargo were landed at the lazzaretto. Soon afterwards, the
disease

disease (at first denied, but subsequently acknowledged to be the plague) attacked another of the crew—an officer put on board the vessel to superintend the quarantine—a boy belonging to the ship—two porters employed in unloading the merchandize—another porter similarly employed—three more porters employed about the merchandize—the priest who had administered the last sacrament to the sick—the surgeon of the lazzaretto—and his whole family.   Notwithstanding these events, the passengers, having performed a short quarantine of less than twenty days, were allowed to take up their quarters in the town, and to carry with them their clothes and packages.   There were anti-contagionists in those days at Marseilles, as there are now in England, and this conduct was the result of their advice.   When passengers after a voyage of nearly four months, and a quarantine of nearly three weeks, are at length let loose in a large city, their first employment is to roam about the streets; they have things to sell and to buy, and to see; they come in contact in the streets and in the shops with persons whom they think no more about, and who think no more about them.   It is not surprizing, therefore, that the exact traces of the disease should soon be lost, and that it should be often difficult, and even impossible, to follow it satisfactorily in every part of its progress.   Of its origin and early advances in the town, the following account is given by M. Bertrand, a resident physician at Marseilles at the time.

' What is certain, is, that the plague was on board the ship of Captain Chataud ; that it was communicated to the infirmary by the merchandize with which it was freighted ; and that one of the first who fell sick in the city, had been passenger in the ship, and had only quitted the infirmary a few days, with his clothes and merchandize ; and that among the very early victims of the distemper, were the family of a famous contraband trader, near the convent of the Carmes, and those of some other contraband traders, who resided in the Rue de l'Escale and its neighbourhood ; that the suburb adjoining the Infirmary was attacked nearly at the same time with the Rue de l'Escale.   I leave my readers to make the reflections naturally suggested by these facts.'

We pass over the terrific scenes which the subsequent progress of the plague occasioned in this ill-fated city; though they should be read by every one, if any such there be, who may have to legislate on this subject, and not be duly impressed with its fearful importance.   We will not represent in detail the early doubts and obstinate denials that the disease was the plague; the fears of the magistrates to alarm the people; the unwillingness of the people to believe; their terror at its first announcement, and, after a short and deceptive calm, their drunken joy and mad confidence; the contests between the physicians and the magistrates; the in-

sults

sults offered by the populace to the former; the scarcity of food; the bodies collected in the houses and in the streets, for want of persons to remove them; the fires lighted in the squares and market-places, and before the doors of every house, for the purpose of burning out the contagion, till the whole city was in a blaze; the flight of the people from the town; the immense graves; cart-loads of bodies tumbled into them in the utmost dis- order; the shops and public places closed, and the deserted streets; all these form a picture which bewilders the mind by the number and horror of the objects; the mere recapitulation of them produces a sensation of giddiness and sickness.

But out of this confusion, we must select one or two incidents from which an inference may be drawn.

The Hôtel Dieu contained between three and four hundred foundlings of both sexes, besides the proper officers and attend- ants.   At this hospital, a woman who had escaped from the Rue de l'Escale presented herself, stating that she was ill with a common fever.   She was taken in and conducted to her bed by two maid-servants of the house; the next day the two maid-ser- vants fell ill and died in a few hours.   The day after, the matron, who, according to the duty of her situation, had visited the patient, fell ill, and died almost as suddenly.   The disease spread with amazing rapidity; it destroyed all the children, together with every person belonging to the house—governors, confessors, physicians, surgeons, apothecaries, officers, servants; except about thirty, and even these took the infection, but ultimately recovered.

One of the greatest difficulties was the removal and interment of the dead.   At first, carts had been hired to carry them away, and beggars and vagabonds were employed in the service. These soon fell, and those who followed them in their offices, soon followed them in their fate.   The magistrates then applied to the officers of the gallies, praying for convicts to carry away the dead—this prayer was granted, and the convicts were promised their liberty if they survived.   The first supply amounted to 133; these perished in less than a week.   Another hundred were granted.   In the course of six days they were reduced to twelve; and thus in less than a fortnight, out of 233, 221 perished.

An official report, transmitted to the Regent, stated that the physicians and surgeons of Marseilles unanimously declared, ' that when one person in a family was attacked and died, the rest soon underwent the same fate, insomuch that there were instances of families entirely destroyed in that manner; and if any one of an infected family fled to another house, the contagion accompa- nied him, and proved fatal to the family where he had taken refuge.'

While

While these horrors were going on in the city, where intercourse was almost unrestrained, some places, in which precautions were used to prevent communication with the infected, escaped either in a great degree, or altogether. When the disease was admitted to be the plague, (and some useful time was lost before that admission was made) the gallies were detached from the shore, anchored in the middle of the port, and separated from the rest of the vessels by a barrier. There were two hospitals belonging to the gallies, one for the crews, the other for the convicts; the former was reserved for the infected, in case the disease should break out, the latter for patients under other diseases. There was a third or intermediate hospital, to which all doubtful cases were sent, until the nature of their disease manifested itself. The gallies were frequently visited by medical men, and on the slightest notice of indisposition, the patient was immediately removed to one of these hospitals. The plague, however, made its appearance, and continued in existence from the beginning of August to the beginning of March; the population of the gallies amounted to 10,000; yet 1,300 persons only were attacked, and about half recovered. We will not speculate on the many modes in which the precautions against intercourse with infected persons may have been evaded, though the particular instance has escaped detection; but we point our readers' attention to the singular difference between the numbers who took the disorder under one system on land, and under another at sea.

A certificate, given by the Bishop of Marseilles, states that ' the plague has not penetrated into the religious communities, who have had no communication with persons abroad, and who have used the precautions necessary to protect them.' Another, given by the first sheriff of Marseilles, states that ' the families which were shut up and had not communicated abroad, particularly the nunneries, had been protected from this scourge; which was introduced into some of them by communications with strange persons.'

Before the commencement of this plague, which certain physicians now call a *modification* of the typhus, the population of Marseilles was estimated at 90,000 persons. Of these, 40,000 perished; but it spread to Aix, Toulon, and various other places in Provence, and destroyed in all more than 80,000 persons. If the foregoing narrative does not satisfactorily prove that the disease was propagated from person to person, we know not what will. The contagiousness of the measles, scarlet-fever, and hooping-cough, certainly does not rest upon stronger evidence; and it will become impossible to prove any disease to be conta-

gious

gious, excepting those which are capable of being communicated by inoculation.

The next plague, which we propose to notice, was that which visited Moscow in the year 1771, and of which a short but lucid history was given by Dr. de Mertens, a physician practising in that city, at the time of the visitation. The plague had not appeared at Moscow for *more than a century and a half*. In 1769 war commenced between the Russians and the Turks; the next year the plague appeared in Wallachia and Moldavia, and many Russians died of it in the city of Yassy. The following summer it entered Poland, and was conveyed to Kiow, where it carried off 4,000 people. At first all communication was cut off between that city and Moscow, and guards were stationed in the great roads. A colonel, attended by two soldiers, set off from Choczin where the plague was raging. The colonel died on the road, but the two soldiers pursued their way, arrived at Moscow, were taken ill at the military hospital, and died soon after their arrival. This was in November, 1770. Towards the end of this month the Demonstrator of Anatomy at this hospital was attacked by a putrid petechial fever of which he died on the third day. The male attendants of the hospital lived with their families in two chambers separated from the others. In one of these one person after another, to the number of eleven, fell ill with a putrid disease attended by petechiæ, and in some by bubos and carbuncles; most of them died between the third and the fifth day. The same disease attacked the attendants who resided in the other chamber. On the 22d December an official statement was made of these facts, and ten physicians, out of eleven, pronounced the disease to be the plague. The hospital, which was placed without the city, was closed, and a military guard interrupted all communication from without; the patients affected with the pestilence, together with their wives and children, were separated from the rest, and the clothes and moveables of those who had died of the disease, and those who were still ill with it, were burnt. The weather became intensely cold, and the traces of contagion being lost in the hospital and in the city, the people passed from a cautious fear to fearless security. The communications with the hospital were re-opened in February, but on the 11th of March, the physicians were again convoked, when Dr. Yagelsky stated that in a large building, a manufactory of military clothing, situated in the centre of the city, and where 3,000 individuals were employed, eight persons had been attacked with symptoms similar to those observed in the patients at the military hospital three months before; that is, with petechiæ, carbuncles, and bubos. The work-people likewise declared, that at the

the beginning of January, a woman who had a tumour in the cheek had gone to the home of one of the work-people who was her relation—that since this time the disease had spread in the manufactory, and 117 persons had died of it. The manufactory was closed and guarded; nevertheless several of the work-people escaped by the windows the following night. We pass over the precautions used to prevent the spreading of the disease, and its abatement—the relaxation of precautions, and the recurrence of the disease. Towards the end of July the mortality amounted to 200 daily—by the middle of August to 400—towards the end of the same month to 600—at the beginning of September to 700—some days afterwards to 800, and at length to 1,000. On the evening of the 5th of September the populace rose, broke open the hospitals, put an end to the quarantine, and restored the religious ceremonies used for the sick—the images of saints were carried with great pomp to the sick, and kissed by every one successively; the people, according to ancient custom, embraced the dead, and buried them within the city, declaring that human precautions were odious to the divinity—they hunted down the poor physicians, broke their furniture and sacked their houses. This riot lasted only a few days, but it was followed by an addition of two or three hundred to the daily mortality—almost all the priests perished. In October the disease began to decline, and at length ceased together with the year. The total mortality was estimated at more than 80,000 persons, exclusive of that in the towns and villages to which it had spread, which cannot have been less than 20,000. These places, however, suffered much less, because the inhabitants, taught by the miserable example of Moscow, readily permitted precautions to be used. Criminals were employed to bury the dead, and when these perished, the poor were hired to do it. To each were given a cloak, gloves, and mask of oil-cloth, and they were directed never to touch a corpse with naked hands, but they paid no attention to this advice. Most of them became ill about the fourth or fifth day, and great numbers perished. The plague committed its greatest ravages among the poor; the nobles, gentlemen, and merchants generally escaping. ' It was communicated,' says Dr. Mertens, ' only by the touch of infected persons or clothes; when we visited the sick we approached them within the distance of a foot, using no other precaution than this, never to touch their bodies, clothes, or beds.' The physicians, who only inspected the patients, generally escaped the disease; but of the surgeons, who were obliged to touch them, two died in the city, and a number of assistant-surgeons in the hospitals. While the disease was raging in the city, the Foundling Hospital afforded a signal example of the salutary effects of seclusion. It contained

1,000 children, and 400 adults. All communication with the people was cut off, and the plague never penetrated within the building. One night four attendants and as many soldiers escaped from the hospital. These, on their return, were attacked by the disease, but they were separated from the rest of the house, and it spread no farther. Compare the fate of this establishment with that of the Foundling Hospital at Marseilles; the contrast of the two cases is one of the most striking circumstances on record.

The last plague which we shall notice is that of Malta in the year 1813, of which the history has been given by Dr. Calvert in the Medico-Chirurgical Transactions, and by Sir Brook Faulkner, both of them eye-witnesses. Valetta had not been visited by the plague *for* 137 *years*, when a vessel, called the San Nicolo, having left Alexandria where the plague was prevalent, arrived at Malta on the 29th of March, 1813. During the voyage, two of the crew had died of a rapid disease, one with a black tumour on his neck. In consequence of these deaths the hatches were shut down, and the crew kept on deck during the rest of the voyage. Upon the arrival of the vessel, the crew were sent ashore to the lazzaretto, the captain and his servant being separated from the rest. The day after, the captain was seized with head-ache, giddiness, and other symptoms of the plague, and died in thirty-six hours. His servant, who had assisted the two sick men during the voyage, was seized with similar symptoms, and died in the same length of time. These circumstances created considerable alarm in Valetta, but the rest of the crew continuing well, and the San Nicolo having returned to Alexandria with a new crew, the apprehensions of the Maltese soon subsided. On the 19th of April, however, a Maltese physician was taken to visit a child of the name of Borg, which had been ill for five or six days, and was dying with a carbuncle on his breast. On the 1st of May he was sent for to see the mother of the dead child, who was ill with fever and a painful tumour in the groin; she was pregnant; on the third day of her illness she was seized with premature labour, delivered of a seven months' child, which died directly, and died herself the next morning with another tumour in the other groin. During the illness of the mother, another of her children was taken ill, but recovered. On the 4th of May, Borg, the father of the family, was seized with fever, attended by glandular swellings in the axilla and groin. The physician now reported these circumstances to the deputation of health. Borg, his whole family, and those who were known to have communicated with them, were removed to the lazzaretto. The courts of justice, the theatre, and the public places were shut up, and the city was inspected by physicians. When Borg's wife was in labour,

bour, a midwife, who lived in another part of Valetta where there was no appearance of the plague, was sent for to attend her. She came, and having delivered her patient, returned to her home. Several days having passed without her appearance, one of her kinsmen went to her house and knocked at the door for some time, but no one answered. At length he broke it open, went in, and discovered her on her knees by her bed-side. She did not move, and on shaking her, he found that she was dead. It seems as if the poor creature, feeling the approach of death, had sought refuge in prayer, and had died in the very act and attitude. When the body was sent to the hospital, plague spots were found upon it. Her kinsman, on making this discovery, immediately ran to the committee of health, and stated what he had seen, on which he was not allowed to return to his family, but was sent to the lazzaretto, where, on the 17th of May, he was seized with the plague, and died in twenty-four hours. A girl, who was accustomed to sleep in the midwife's house, was taken ill with fever and glandular enlargements. Borg and his father died; another of his children became ill with it but recovered. Thus far the disease had been confined to the crew of the vessel which came from Alexandria, and to Borg's family and those who had communicated with them; but soon afterwards the disease began to appear in the town of Valetta. At first the medical men contended that it was not the plague—the people kept their sickness secret, for fear of being removed to the lazzaretto, clamoured against the precautions, and did all they could to thwart them. The disease spread not only through Valetta, Floriana, and the adjoining towns, but to many villages.

Whilst the plague was raging in Malta, the efficacy of strict seclusion was exhibited in some striking instances, as at Marseilles, and Moscow. The Augustine convent stands in an airy part of Valetta, near the top of one of the main streets, much above the level of the sea and the greater part of the city, and in a clean and open neighbourhood—its interior accommodations are spacious and airy. When the plague first broke out in Valetta, the strictest precautions were used by the inhabitants of this convent to prevent all communication with the town. At length, however, a servant, contrary to the regulations, went into a part of the town where the disease prevailed, and purchased clothes which were supposed to be infected. Soon after his return he confessed what he had done, on which he was immediately shut up, together with one of the brotherhood who volunteered to attend him. Both of them were taken ill and died of the disease, but no other person in the convent suffered. When the plague was at Malta in 1675, Cavallino, who described it,

states

states that all public establishments which cautiously shunned intercourse with the community enjoyed perfect exemption from the disease; as did the prisons and monasteries, besides all the vessels in the harbour. In the late plague it was the same—the hospital of St. John of Jerusalem, the prison, and several public offices, and private houses, which early adopted and steadily kept up a rigid system of insulation, were not less fortunate.

In a large building in the town, the ground floor was divided into seven separate apartments, occupied by as many Maltese families, while the upper stories were used as a military hospital for patients affected with common diseases. While the plague was raging in Malta, it penetrated into the ground floor, destroyed the inhabitants of four of these apartments, and in the other three, two only of each family escaped. While this was going on below, the sick tenants of the upper stories were shut in—all communication was cut off—and every individual among them escaped the disease, although it was raging in the habitations round about the hospital, and penetrating from the lower to the upper stories. Dr. Greaves, whose house was within a few feet of the hospital, and on whose authority this fact is stated, related it to Dr. M'Lean when he was at Valetta, and led him over the hospital; but no mention has been made of it by this *impartial* historian.

Thus (to return for a moment to the commencement of the plague) we find it attacking, first two sailors in a vessel which had come from a city where the plague was prevailing; and next, after her arrival, the captain of the same vessel, together with his servant—then the family of Borg, nominally a shoemaker, but really a smuggler—his children, his wife, himself, and his father—the midwife who attended his wife, whilst she was ill with the plague—a young woman who slept in her house—a kinsman who entered her chamber and touched her body—the child of the master of a wine-house near the quarantine harbour, where many persons resorted, and among others the servants of the Health Office who guarded the San Nicolo in the harbour—some of the guards of the San Nicolo themselves, with whom Borg the smuggler had frequent dealings. Whilst the plague was attacking successively the above-mentioned persons, it appears, by official statements, that there were no other individuals affected with it in any other part of Malta. Is the reader unsatisfied with this evidence? That there was any communication between the crew of the San Nicolo and the family of Borg there is no decisive and specific proof, nothing but a rumour that a piece of cloth had been conveyed from the vessel to Borg's house. Great stress has been laid on this; and the belief that the San Nicolo communicated the plague to Malta, in spite of this defect in the
chain

chain of evidence, has been loudly scoffed at as unphilosophical credulity. What evidence are we to expect under such circumstances as these? The parties, be it remembered, are a crew under quarantine, and a cunning smuggler—both under penal restrictions which they daily and hourly, but of course secretly, elude by all sorts of frauds and falsehoods. What other evidence, we repeat, of communication between such people so circumstanced are we to expect, unless the Devil on Two Sticks had been employed as a spy, and from his lofty station at night had actually seen the piece of cloth conveyed from the San Nicolo into the boat, from the boat to the shore, from the shore over every inch of ground, till it arrived at Borg's house, and then observed the unfolding of the cloth, and the escape of the contagious vapour? As this is a point of considerable importance, because the same defect in the chain of evidence which is here complained of, will be found in the other histories of the plague which we have laid before our readers, we shall run the risk of tiring them with a few remarks.

We have always understood it to be sound philosophy to require no more evidence, in any case, than the best in degree, and the whole in quantity, which the nature of the proposition, and the circumstances, under which it is presented for examination, render possible to be given. Now suppose that a vessel with the plague among its crew arrives in the Thames, and comes up the river. There is a rumour, but no proof of communication with the shore; however a week afterwards the disease breaks out in the contiguous neighbourhood, in the house of a smuggler and in an ale-house frequented by sailors; and after spreading among the relations and friends of the first sufferers, as well as those who have had casual communication with them, is found in London, where it has not been for 160 years, gets into the houses of deluding doctors and deluded legislators, and carries off thousands and tens of thousands of the inhabitants; if such a calamity were speedily to follow the arrival of a vessel under such circumstances, who would doubt that the disease had been communicated from the vessel to the metropolis, because he could not track every footstep that it had taken; because, in other words, he could not do that, which common sense would inform any unbiassed person the lapse of a single week, a single day or hour, in carelessness and unsuspicion, would make it impossible to do? But although the case may strike us more by being brought nearer home, it is not really stronger than the introduction of the plague into Malta; for Malta had been free from it almost as long as London has. Let not the people of London hug themselves in their long im-

munity;

munity; Malta had been free for 137 years, and Moscow for nearly 170.

The plague at Malta, in 1813, either arose as an epidemic, from a noxious state of the air, or it was introduced by contagion imported by the San Nicolo. Now granting that there is some difficulty to be overcome in either supposition; which is the greater; to believe, that the crew of the San Nicolo had communication with the family in which the plague first appeared in Valetta, with which family the captain was intimate, although this communication cannot be proved; or that the air of Valetta, which had continued free from plague for nearly a century and a half, should on a sudden assume a pestilential condition and that by an accidental coincidence, about a week after the San Nicolo sailed into the harbour with the plague on board? To find a difficulty in believing the former, but none in believing the latter, is indeed to strain at a gnat and to swallow a camel.

The foregoing accounts afford ample proof of the two propositions which we set out by stating; and, consequently, that the plague is communicable from person to person; but they form not one-twentieth part of the evidence to this effect. It is impossible, in the space allotted to us, to do justice to this part of the subject. We might now content ourselves with stating, that every competent person who had had opportunity of observing this tremendous malady, had come to the conclusion that it was contagious, and that there had been fewer dissentient voices than might have been expected, considering the nature of the subject and the wanderings of the human intellect; but as general statements produce little impression, we shall trouble our readers with a few instances.

Doctor Murdoch Mackenzie resided at Constantinople and Smyrna for twenty years, in the middle of the last century. During this time scarcely a year passed in which there was not some appearance of the plague in one or both of these cities. In 1751 it broke out at Constantinople, raged with great violence, and carried off, as it was estimated, 150,000 people. His observations on this disease he communicated from time to time, by letters, to Dr. Clephane and Dr. Mead, which were read before the Royal Society, and are published in the 47th volume of the Philosophical Transactions. The following extract from these letters will show the facts which he observed, and the opinions which he formed on the causes of the plague:—

' I can't see any other apparent cause of the virulency of the disease, this year, beside the occasion of greater communication. In the months of February, March, April, and May last, the distemper was so strong at Cairo,

Cairo, as appears by letters from the English consul there, that no doors
were opened for three months. In the mean time there arrived here, in
May last, four ships loaden with Cairo goods; which goods and men
being landed, spread the infection over all the city at once, after which
one conveyed it to another, by contact. In the village where we
lived, there died only sixty persons of the plague. The French ambassador's palace, next door to us, in the village, was infected; because five
of his people went at midnight to a bawdy-house, where the father
Demetry, the mother, and daughter at the same time had the plague,
and died of it afterwards, all three; so that two of his excellency's servants were infected by them, one of whom died, and the other recovered, and is still living, after taking a vomit, some doses of the bark
mixed with snake-root and Venice treacle, by my advice. We found
this last time, and upon all such occasions, that whoever kept their doors
shut, ran no risk, even if the plague were in the next house; and the
contact was easily traced in all the accidents which happened among the
Franks. Comte Castellane had, for three years running, persons attacked in the same room, in the months of July and August, notwithstanding all possible precaution used in cleansing the room, and even
white-washing it. At last, by my own advice to his excellency,
grounded upon the above theory, he built a slight counter-wall; since
which there has been no accident in that room, now five years ago. I
could give so many such examples as delassare valeant Fabium.'

Orræus, who was physician to Catherine, empress of Russia,
and sent to advise during the plagues at Yassy and Moscow,
states, that the most common mode of contracting the disease
was by contact. Samoclowitz, surgeon to the military hospital
at Moscow, who had also extensive experience of the plague in
Poland, Moldavia, and Wallachia, before he witnessed its tremendous ravages in Moscow, says, in the preface to his Mémoire
sur la Peste, ' it is certain that the plague is developed and propagated only by contact.' All the assistant-surgeons who were
employed under him, (fifteen in number,) took the disease, and
all died excepting three; while the physicians, who walked
among the sick without touching them, generally escaped. When
Mr. Howard, in the year 1785, went abroad to visit the principal
lazzarettos in France and Italy, he carried with him a set of
questions concerning the plague, drawn up by Drs. Aikin and
Jebb, which were to be submitted to the most experienced practitioners in the places which he visited. When he returned, Dr.
Aikin methodized and abridged the answers, and the result is
given in the celebrated work on the lazzarettos of Europe. We
have no room for it, and yet it deserves to be read by all those
who are in search of information on the subject. ' They all,' says
Mr. Howard, ' in the most explicit manner concur in representing
the plague as a contagious disease, communicated by near approach to, or actual contact with infected persons or things.'

During

During the *late* war (as we used to call it) in Egypt, now a quarter of a century ago, the medical officers of both the French and English armies had ample opportunities of observing the plague, and they almost unanimously came to the conclusion, that it was a contagious disease. Dr. Edward Bancroft, a man of unquestionable learning and talent, yet prone enough to dissent from received opinions, accompanied the British army during part of the Egyptian campaign. His testimony is particularly important, because, by his essay on the yellow fever, which he believes not to be contagious, he had shown himself fully prepared to adopt a similar opinion about the plague, if he had met with sufficient proofs of it: he thus expresses himself:

‘ The facts which prove the necessity of actual contact with some infected person or thing to communicate the plague, are so numerous, and many of them so notorious, that it must be unnecessary for me to enter upon a detail of them, after what Dr. Russel and others have published, and after the experience of the British army in Egypt, which invariably demonstrated this necessity, by showing that all those who avoided contact, invariably escaped the disease, whilst those who did otherwise in suitable conditions, were very generally infected. Nor was there, so far as I have been able to discover, any instance, in the French Egyptian army, of a communication of the disease without contact, though the physicians to that army, who have written on the subject, do not, I believe, positively assert the impossibility of such communication.’

Mr., now Sir James M‘Grigor, surgeon to the Indian army in Egypt, during the Egyptian campaign, in his medical sketches of that expedition, gives the following account of the arrangements at the pest-houses, and their result:

‘ In the pest-houses of the army thirteen medical gentlemen did duty, who in the Indian army might be said to have had the post of honour. They were Mr. Thomas, Mr. Price, Mr. Rice, Dr. Wayte, Mr. Grysadalé, Mr. Adrian, Mr. O'Farrel, Mr. Whyte, Mr. Dyson, Mr. Anglé, Mr. Moss, Dr. Buchan, and Dr. Henderson. In order to take from our medical gentlemen, in the pest-houses, some of the most dangerous part of the duty, it was my wish to procure some of the Greek doctors of the country to reside in the pest-houses, to feel the pulses there, draw blood, open and dress bubos, &c. The most diligent search was made for those people, and very high pay was promised to them, but we could tempt none of them to live in our pest-houses: a plain proof of the opinion which they entertain of the contagious nature of the disease. The thirteen gentlemen first mentioned, were those only that were directly in the way of contagion, for it became their duty to come into contact with the infected, and seven of them caught the infection, and four died. To the atmosphere of the disease, all the medical gentlemen of the army were exposed, as they saw and examined the cases in the first instance; but, except from actual contact, there never appeared to be any danger.’

The medical officers of the French army came to similar conclusions.

·clusions. Desgenettes, chief physician to the French army in Egypt, in his ' Histoire Médicale de l'Armée d'Orient,' thus sums up his opinion on the subject of the plague :

' The plague is evidently contagious, but the conditions of the transmission of this contagion are not more exactly known than its specific nature. The dead body has not appeared to transmit it—the animal body in a heated state, and still more in a state of febrile moisture, has appeared to communicate it more easily ; the contagion has been known to cease in passing from one river to another of the Nile; a simple trench made before a camp has been known to stop its ravages; and on observations of this kind is founded the useful insulation of the Franks, the practice of which has been sufficiently detailed by different travellers.'

Baron Larré, the principal surgeon to the French army, and the distinguished author of the Memoirs of Military Surgery, states a similar opinion :

' But however strong,' says he, ' may have been these affections, (moral,) their effects cannot be compared to those which resulted from the communication of the healthy with the sick, or to the effects of contact with contaminated objects. We may be convinced of this truth, by the ravages which the plague made in the year 9, (1801,) among the Fatalist Mussulmen; * * * it were to be wished that, on the first days of the invasion of the plague, its true character had been presented to the army. This would have diminished the number of victims, instead of which the soldier, imbued with the opinion which was at first propagated, that this disease was not pestilential, did not hesitate to seize and wear the effects of his companions dead of the plague. The pestilential germ developed itself in these individuals, who often sunk under the same fate. It was only when they had gained a perfect knowledge of this disease, that many preserved themselves by the precautions which were indicated.'

Dr. Sotira, another of the physicians of the French army in Egypt, relates the following striking circumstance :

' In the seventh year of the French republic, about eighty medical officers died of the plague. In consequence of this mortality, an order was issued to employ Turkish barbers in the pest-houses, to dress the patients, and to undertake all the medical treatment which required actual contact. The result was, that during the next two years, only twelve of the medical officers died of the plague, but half the Turkish barbers caught it.'

Thus far we have drawn our information from medical men, eye-witnesses of the facts which they relate. But as there are many persons whimsical enough to think that medical men are the worst judges, and that the less a man knows on a subject, the more likely is he to come to a right conclusion about it, we will give them the experience and the opinion of the late Sir Thomas Maitland, who witnessed the rise, progress, and cessation of four

different

different plagues in the Mediterranean; those of Malta, Gozo,
Corfu, and Cephalonia.   In a letter to Lord Bathurst, dated
Corfu, April, 1819, which is published at length in the Morning
Herald of June 29th, 1825, and is remarkable for its practical good sense and manly spirit, he states it as his firm opinion,
that the plague is taken only by contact.   ' I have invariably
found, (says he) that preventing contact, stops the disease, and
that so long as contact is permitted, it uniformly increases.   If
the absence of contact stops the plague, the allowing of contact
must be the cause of it.'   On this belief he acted in organizing
measures for the suppression of the disease.   Although Sir
Thomas Maitland was bred neither as a logician, nor as a physician, it would be difficult for the former to reason better, or for
the latter to act more skilfully.   In the system of police by which
he invariably succeeded in suppressing the plague,

' the exclusive object of the troops was to prevent contact; every
family was shut up in their own houses, fed at their own doors, and sent to
the lazzaretto the moment the disease appeared. The soldiers employed
in this service scarcely ever contracted the disease.   In the few instances
that occurred, and they were extremely few, it was uniformly observed,
of each soldier that took the plague, that he was loose in his conduct,
and neglectful of the necessary precautions. Those, on the contrary,
who attended to these precautions, never took it.   They were sent into
several villages, many of them with streets but a few feet wide; they
did the severest night-duties of all kinds, in these villages ; they lived
in exactly the same atmosphere as the inhabitants, yet they never caught
the disease, though it was raging in the villages; they were stationed
within a yard or two of camps and hospitals in which the plague was
raging with great violence, and they never caught it ; and lastly, they
were exposed to all those hard duties, which in all infectious diseases are
known to give a pre-disposition to the most violent and fatal type of the
prevailing disease, and yet they never caught the plague.'

We pause for want of room, not for want of matter; for we
have not produced one twentieth part of the trustworthy evidence
on record.   On this part of the subject there is a perfect glut
of proof, in examining which the mind gets so enured to the most
decisive facts, that its sense of evidence becomes blunted, and it
often puts aside proofs, as feeble and inconclusive, which, on any
other occasion, would strike with instantaneous conviction.   But
enough has been said under this head, we trust, to make out our two
first propositions; namely, that those persons are most liable to the
plague, who approach those affected with it, and that those generally
escape the disease, who avoid those affected with it.   This is enough
to prove that it is communicable from person to person : we have
no other proof of the contagiousness of hooping cough, scarlet-
fever, and, in the experience of the present generation, of measles.
But

But we shall proceed to the third test of a contagious disease, inoculation, and inquire whether the plague can be communicated artificially, like the small-pox and cow-pox. Under this head we must not expect very abundant evidence. People consent to the inoculation of small-pox, because they can generally have it only once in their lives, and because, by so doing, they substitute a disease which is fatal only once in five hundred cases, for a disease which is fatal in one case out of four. There are not the same temptations to submit to the inoculation of the plague; for, even if experience should prove that inoculation diminished the fatal force of the plague as much as it diminishes that of small-pox, it would not afford security from subsequent attacks. We must not expect, therefore, that many persons should have been so rash as voluntarily to inflict this disease on themselves. But a few such there have been, and we proceed to relate their experiments.

During the campaign in Egypt, in 1801, the French troops were much depressed by their dread of the plague. To convince them that their alarms were unreasonable, Desgenettes attempted to inoculate himself with the disease, but to secure himself from the danger of the experiment, he washed the part with soap and water; we will give his own account of this experiment, from the failure of which such erroneous inferences have been drawn:—

‘ It was to restore the spirits and exhausted courage of the army, that, in the middle of the hospital, I dipped a lancet in the pus of a bubo belonging to a convalescent patient, and made a slight puncture in the groin and in the neighbourhood of the axilla, without using any other precaution than washing myself with soap and water. I had, for more than three weeks, two little points of inflammation, corresponding to the two punctures, and they were still very tender, when on my return from Acre, I bathed in the presence of the army, in the bath of Césarée. This incomplete experiment, of which I have been obliged to give some details, because of the noise it made, proves little, and does not refute the transmission of contagion, demonstrated by a thousand examples.’

Soon after this, Dr. Whyte, a medical officer in the English army, hearing that Desgenettes had made the experiment with impunity, but not hearing of the precaution which he had used, repeated the former, without the latter, in the pest house at El Hammed, on the 2d January, 1802. He was an anti-contagionist, and wished to verify his doctrine by showing that the disease could not be communicated by inoculation. The experiment and the result are thus related in a letter from Mr. Rice, then doing duty in the pest house at El Hammed, to Mr., now Sir James M‘Grigor:—

‘ Dr. Whyte came here last night, January 2d, 1802 : soon after he came in, he rubbed some matter, from the bubo of a woman, on the
inside

inside of his thighs. The next morning he inoculated himself, in the wrists, with a lancet, with matter taken from the running bubo of a sepoy.'

In subsequent letters Mr. Rice states, that ' Dr. Whyte continued in good health on the 5th, and all day on the 6th till the evening, when he was attacked with rigors and other febrile symptoms.' He continued to have shiverings, succeeded by heat and perspiration, much affection of the head, tremor of the limbs, a dry black tongue, great thirst; a full, hard, irregular pulse; great debility and great anxiety. ' He still persisted that the disease was not the plague, and would not allow his groin or arm-pits to be examined.' He became delirious on the 8th, and died on the 9th, in the afternoon.

Dr. Valli was an Italian physician, who resided for some time in Turkey. He distinguished himself by a work on the plague, and has since, we believe, died of yellow fever, to investigate which he went to the West Indies. During his residence at Constantinople, he is known to have made experiments on the inoculation of the plague, and in the Journal de Médecine, for May, 1811, we find the following statement, which the editor says he received from one of his correspondents. Valli diluted the pestilential matter with small-pock matter, or with the gastric juice of frogs, or with oil. This compound he called his pommade. If a Mussulman came to consult him for an ophthalmia, he ordered him some of his pommade, to rub upon his eyelids: if another came, complaining of pain in the bowels, he ordered some of his pommade, to rub upon his belly. In this way he gave the disease to thirty persons. These facts M. Valli is said to have communicated to the Medical Society at Geneva, ' and doubtless,' says the reporter, ' he *will one day publish them in detail!*' Valli, however, never did publish them, probably ashamed of the result; for it is said that these experiments went to such a mischievous extent, that the Turkish government at length interfered, arrested the pharmacopolist who vended the pommade, burnt his drugs, and cut off his head.

We have now made out our three propositions; the two first by overwhelming evidence; and the last, by all the evidence which the nature of the proposition would lead us to expect, and of which the least that can be said is, that it furnishes strong ground for belief. We pause, therefore, and ask, whether there is not sufficient reason for believing that the plague is contagious, to justify us in acting upon this supposition—to make it unjustifiable to act upon any other. Considering the terrific nature of this disease, one would suppose that the bare possibility of its being contagious would induce us to act on that supposition,

and

and that men would lay down as a maxim, ' Take it for granted
that it is contagious, till you are certain that it is not.' But when
we consider the immense mass of evidence for the foregoing propositions, the clearness and distinctness with which they are made
out, the small number of dissentient voices, and the tremendous
importance of the stake at issue, one would suppose it impossible
that there should be men not merely incredulous enough to dissent
from this opinion, but mad enough to wish to act on their dissent.
Yet such is the fact.

' However indisputable the fact of the plague being contagious may be
deemed by modern physicians, it may be remarked, that it has been
strongly opposed as often as the subject of quarantine has fallen under
the deliberation of the legislature ; and the public, at such times, have
been constantly pestered by an inundation of pamphlets, which, without
advancing any thing new, merely retailed arguments which have long
before been refuted.'

These are the words of Dr. Patrick Russell, physician to the
British factory at Aleppo, about the year 1760, so applicable to
the present state of things, that they might seem to have been
written to-day and with express reference to it. The Levant
Company, finding the quarantine laws inconvenient, resolved,
a few years ago, to take a medical opinion upon the necessity of the
restrictions which they imposed. They accordingly selected and
sent to Constantinople a physician of the name of M'Lean, a
gentleman well suited to their purpose, who, although he knew
nothing of the disease by experience, was thoroughly convinced
that it was not contagious, and consequently that the restrictions
were as unnecessary as they were inconvenient. Going out with
these previous opinions, which we suppose we must not presume
to call prejudices, he found an experience of *seventeen days* sufficient to satisfy his mind, and he has ever since been incessantly
active in propagating his belief. Zeal and activity are the virtues
of a sect, and Dr. M'Lean with his few followers are entitled to
the praise of possessing them; in the shape of petitions to parliament, articles in reviews, paragraphs in newspapers,* and
speeches in parliament, they have kept their view of the subject
incessantly before the public; and the result has been, that the

* It is amusing to notice the things on this subject produced in the daily papers.
The Morning Chronicle for September 7th, of this year, which is now lying before
us, contains an account of a sitting of the Royal Academy of Sciences at Paris, in
which a M. Lassis, an unbeliever in the contagiousness of the plague, is represented
as saying that ' he denied the existence of contagion in every species of disease
excepting only the measles and siphylis.'! Then the small-pox and cow-pox are not
contagious,—diseases which we can propagate at will, by the point of a lancet, with
matter which we can see and feel! Where will the folly of man stop?

legislature has been prevailed upon to reconsider the quarantine laws, and ultimately to consent to a modification of them.

We proceed therefore to inquire what reasons have been discovered sufficiently weighty to set aside the experience of so many generations, and so many witnesses, together with all the inferences and precautions to which they have led. These reasons are to be found in Dr. M'Lean's work ' on Epidemic and Pestilential Diseases,' in his evidence before a Committee of the House of Commons, and in a dissertation on the subject by a writer in the Westminster Review.*

By way of introduction to the discussion it is first laid down that, on the question of contagion, medical men are the worst judges, and that the best are ' men of general science, whose minds are accustomed to weigh evidence,' but who are unacquainted with, and *consequently* unprejudiced on the subject. The only reason given for this remarkable but very convenient proposition is, that the students of medicine are the slaves of authority, which in after-life, as physicians, they seldom outgrow; but if it be common for the student to be oppressed by the authority of eminent teachers, we shall presently see that it is not impossible for the ignorant to be deceived by the mistatements of plausible reasoners. The question of contagion, like every other, requires two qualifications in those who are to pronounce a judgment upon it; a knowledge of the whole truth as to matters of fact, and a capability of reasoning rightly upon that knowledge:—it requires also something more—a knowledge of the whole truth as to matters of fact on certain analogous medical questions, as well as the reasonings upon which points once disputed in them have been finally settled; in order to compare the difficulties so settled, with difficulties still remaining in the way of any positive theory of contagion. It is obvious that men of science who know nothing of medicine can possess only one of these three qualifications; and a sufficient reason why they must be incompetent judges, is, that although they can appreciate what is neat in point of statement, and plausible or even accurate in point of reasoning, they are no judges whatever of what is true in point of fact. Hence, when they listen to a man who is little scrupulous about the accuracy of his facts, they are entirely at his mercy. It requires no great sagacity to perceive that the real motive for this appeal to those who are not physicians is, not because they are likely to be the best judges, but the most docile listeners— because they are less likely to detect the errors of their teachers.

---

* See Nos. V. and VI.

It

It is easy to argue triumphantly about law with a physician, about physic with a lawyer, about theology with either—in short, on any subject with any person who knows nothing about it.

From this introduction we pass to the first argument produced to prove that the plague is not contagious, which is, that it is not governed by the laws of contagious, but of epidemic diseases. This argument, which is announced with great parade, explained most elaborately, and referred to again and again, as the corner-stone of the system, is an attempt to lay down the laws by which contagious, and those by which epidemic diseases are governed, and then, having ascertained by what laws the plague is governed, to deduce whether it is epidemic or contagious. This is amazingly well suited to take in the ' men of general science,' the minds ' accustomed to weigh evidence,' for it has a logical air which they can readily appreciate, whilst it reposes upon facts of which they are entirely ignorant. If the reader will take the trouble to compress and comprehend it, he will find that it comes to this :— Contagious diseases (as small-pox, measles, and scarlet fever) are very uniform in their symptoms and duration—affect a person only once in his life—the patient under them is not subject to relapses, and they may be propagated at all times and seasons. On the contrary, epidemic diseases are very irregular in their symptoms and length—appear and disappear at certain times of the year—are most prevalent in certain countries, or even neighbourhoods—may affect a person repeatedly in life, and the sufferer is liable to relapses. Now, as the plague is very irregular in its symptoms and length—appears and disappears at certain seasons—is most prevalent in certain countries and even neighbourhoods—can affect a person repeatedly—and as relapses occur to the patient—as the plague has all these qualities in common with epidemic diseases, it is plain that it must be an epidemic and not a contagious disease. Now the first sophism discoverable in this argument is, that the contagious or non-contagious nature of a disease is here made a question of inference to be determined by reasoning, which in truth is a question of fact to be determined by experience. Let any man who has the smallest pretensions to understanding say *which* is the right mode of discovering whether or not a disease is contagious —to find out that it is uniform in its symptoms and progress— that it affects a person only once in life—that when convalescent he is not liable to relapse—and thence to *infer* that it is contagious—or to go among the sick, to observe and watch the way in which it spreads, and thus to *ascertain* whether it was contagious. When Gall first broached his craniological doctrines in Germany, they were ridiculed on the stage—a master is represented hiring his servants according to the shape of their skulls—he feels their

heads.—finds the bumps which constitute a good servant—infers
that they are sober, honest, and industrious—hires them *without
characters*, and in the end finds them drones, profligates, and
thieves.   Now the mode of proceeding, which in this instance
was only an imagined absurdity, is absolutely practised by Dr.
M'Lean and his followers in judging of the contagiousness of
diseases.

But not only is the question resolved by reasoning which ought
to be resolved by experience, but even in the conduct of the reasoning there is a fresh sophism or rather blunder.   One class of
contagious diseases, the eruptive fevers, is assumed to be the only
class—its laws are described, and every disease which is not
governed by them is inferred not to be contagious; whereas the
question at issue is, whether the eruptive fevers are the only contagious fevers.   If to determine whether negroes were human
beings, we were to take a particular people, as Europeans, and,
describing among their qualities a fair complexion, were to infer
that because negroes were not fair they were not human, would
not this be begging the question? yet this is precisely the line
we adopt when, in a dispute what are contagious fevers, we take
the eruptive fevers as the only examples.

Another argument against the contagiousness of the plague is,
that it breaks out at a certain season, lasts for a certain time, and
then subsides and remains dormant till the favourable season returns.   On the other hand we are told, that ' contagious diseases
can be propagated at any time, and among any number of persons'—
' That a disease depending upon a specific contagion must prevail
alike in all seasons, in a pure as well as in an impure atmosphere,
amongst the rich as readily as amongst the poor; and that the only
influence of these adventitious circumstances would be to render
the disease more or less severe.'   We could not produce a stronger
instance how unsafe it is to trust these discussions into the hands
of those who are ignorant of medicine; for no well educated physician could ever have penned such a statement, and no competent
judge could ever for a moment have listened to it.

Take the diseases which are unquestionably contagious:—What
is the fact with hydrophobia?   Sometimes it is so rare, and excites so little attention, that dogs run about without restraint, and
the public almost forget that there is such a disease.   At other
times it is so prevalent, and the bite of dogs is so often followed
by this terrific disease in man, that the public are kept in perpetual
alarm; the walls are placarded with orders to tie up the dogs,
and their appearance in the streets occasions the timid to fly, and
the mischievous to follow them with stones and clubs.   As the
contagion is always in existence, and the animals susceptible to it
                                                        always

always alive, whence comes it that it is more active and diffusive at one time than at another? It is plain that, beside the specific contagion, there is a diffused cause which renders the disease more communicable at one time than at another. Whether it is a peculiar condition of the atmosphere, as is commonly believed, and if so, how it acts, whether by rendering the poison more active, or the bodies of animals more susceptible to it, it is unnecessary for our present purpose to inquire. It is enough to know that hydrophobia, which ' depends on a specific contagion,' is not ' propagated equally at all times,' and does not ' prevail alike in all seasons.' The same fact may be stated, and the same inference may be drawn with regard to the hooping-cough. Parents well know that at one time it is almost a forgotten disease, at another time they can scarcely go into a family without coming in contact with it; and experienced physicians know that it generally prevails in cold damp seasons, as the end of autumn and winter, and is little heard of in the warm dry days of summer. Measles are generally most rife in spring and disappear in summer.

' The scarlet fever,' says Sydenham, ' though it may happen at any time, yet it most commonly comes at the latter end of summer.' ' The measles of 1670,' says the same distinguished physician, ' began *very early*, that is, at the beginning of January, and, increasing daily, came to their height in March ; afterwards they gradually decreased, and were quite extinguished in the following July.'

With regard to the small-pox and cow-pox, it is necessary to distinguish between the artificial and the natural propagation of contagious diseases. It is quite true that contagious diseases, which are propagated by inoculation, can, generally speaking, be propagated in this way ' at any time, and among any number of persons;' but leave them to be propagated in the natural way, and it is quite notorious that they spread readily at one time, and scarcely at all at another. The small-pox has been so much restrained, first, by the introduction of inoculation, and secondly, by that of vaccination, that experimentally we of the present day know little of its natural course ; but before the introduction of the one, and the discovery of the other, the small-pox used to lie dormant—then appear—rage for a time—and then subside—like epidemic diseases. Sydenham, who lived before the time of inoculation and vaccination, describes the small-pox as at one time appearing rarely, or not at all; then beginning to show itself at the approach of the vernal equinox ; spreading more and more every day, becoming epidemic about autumn, abating on the coming on of winter, returning again in the following spring, and prevailing till checked by the subsequent winter. The accounts

which

which this admirable physician gives of the small-pox in different years read exactly like accounts of an epidemic disease.

Boerhaave, speaking of the same disease, says, ' this disorder is generally epidemical, beginning early in the spring, increasing in summer, abating in autumn, ceasing almost entirely the following winter, to return in the spring, and reign again in the same order.' Van Swieten, who, though a commentator on Boerhaave, wrote from experience, after describing Sydenham's account of the rise, progress, and subsidence of small-pox, adds, ' I have seen many variolous epidemic constitutions, and they agreed in most things with the observations of Sydenham.' Sydenham, Boerhaave and Van Swieten saw the small-pox before in ulation was introduced, when it was propagated in the natural way, and we see that it used to run its course just like epidemic diseases.

Sydenham lived and was practising in London in the year 1665. He saw something of the dreadful plague of that year, and he had frequent opportunities of seeing the small-pox propagate itself in the natural way. Now it is curious, that so far from there being any striking difference between the progress of the plague, and the progress of contagious diseases, as the anti-con-tagionists assert, he selects these two as strikingly similar in their mode of appearing and disappearing.

' That such a disposition or texture happens to the mass of the air as occasions various diseases at different times is manifest to every one that but considers, that one and the same disease kills an infinite number of men at some certain seasons, and at another time seizes only here and there a man, and goes no farther ; and this is very apparent in the small-pox, especially in the plague, the argument of this chapter.

When Dr. Jenner first disclosed his discovery of vaccination, and every body was anxious to verify it by experiment, the London physicians could procure no matter, because, as they were told, the disease was extinct.

' Unfortunately,' says Dr. Woodville, (the physician to the Small-pox hospital,) ' at the time Dr. Jenner's publication appeared, no cow-pox matter could be procured, for the disease had then become extinct, nor was it expected to return till the spring, the period at which it usually affects the cows. Towards the latter end of January last, I was informed that the cow-pox had appeared among several of the milch cows kept in Gray's Inn Lane, and about four fifths of them were eventually infected.'

This circumstance is not peculiar to London; in Germany the cow-pox is apparently so extinct at one time, and so prevalent at another, that it is the belief of scientific men that it is newly ori-ginated; and Pilger, a veterinary surgeon, who is good authority for the purpose for which we cite him, says, ' that in Russia the
disease

disease arises among the cattle when they are driven from Kasan to Moscow.'*

It appears, therefore, that contagious diseases prevail much at one time and little at another, and, consequently, that two things are requisite for their ready propagation; the one, the contagious matter itself, the other, a diffused cause, supposed to be a state of the atmosphere favourable to its action. Let it never be forgotten, that this is the case with diseases unquestionably and notoriously contagious, and therefore that when it is found to be the case with the plague it can be no objection to the belief of its being also contagious. Are the anti-contagionists ignorant of these facts? In this, and other instances which we shall have occasion to notice, the error is so extraordinary, that it is really difficult to refer it to ignorance; ignorance so dense is almost incredible. But we go on.

The anti-contagionists, describing epidemic diseases, say,

' People are attacked, not in proportion as the inhabitants of the affected mix with those of the unaffected places ; but, in proportion as the inhabitants of unaffected expose themselves to the *air* of affected places. The visits of the sick to unaffected places is [are] followed by no increase of disease ; the visits of the inhabitants of an unaffected, to an affected place, is [are] attended with a certain increase of sickness. On their removal from a noxious to a pure air, the sick often rapidly recover ; but they do not communicate the disease to the inhabitants of a pure atmosphere ; in the history of all the epidemics which have ever prevailed, in all parts of the earth, there is not on record a single example of the communication of the disease from the sick to the healthy in a pure atmosphere.'—*West. Rev.* No. V. p. 145.

Here are, put only in several forms, two propositions : First, that when the people of healthy districts visit the affected districts, they take the disease not from the sick, but from the air. Secondly, that when the sick move from an affected to a healthy district, they speedily recover, and do not give the disease to others. Let us take these propositions, and try them in their application to the plague. If those who come out of a healthy into an affected district, took the disease not from the sick, but from the air, then those who avoided the sick, would be as liable to the disease as those who approached and touched them. Is this the fact with the plague? so notoriously the contrary, that all modern observers have come to the conclusion that absolute contact, either with infected persons or infected clothes, is necessary for the communication of the disease. Hence the security of those who, while the plague is raging, shut themselves up in the very town in which it is raging, and avoid all intercourse with the sick. Why did the

---

* Handbuch der Veterinäwissenschaft.

religious

religious communities at Marseilles, which practised this seclusion, escape? Why did the Foundling Hospital at Moscow, which was strictly shut up, escape, while the Foundling Hospital at Marseilles, which admitted a patient with the plague, was swept of its population? Why at Malta, in 1813, was the plague kept out of the Military Hospital, although it was raging in the ground floor, while in the houses in the immediate neighbourhood, the disease was not only getting access to the ground floors, but climbing to the very garrets? Why did the French medical officers in Egypt die in crowds, whilst they dressed the patients, and as soon as the task of touching and dressing them was put upon the Turkish barbers, why was the mortality transferred from the surgeons to the barbers? Why did the troops, employed by Sir Thomas Maitland to suppress the plague at Malta, escape the disease, although they were, not only in the same district, but in the same streets in which it was raging? In short, for we might have saved ourselves this recitation of facts, why is the practice of seclusion, or shutting up, as it is called, practised by the European factories in places liable to the plague, an effectual preventive of the disease? If it is said that those persons keep aloof in the healthy districts, then are the healthy and sick districts often separated by a distance only of a few feet—then is the definition of a healthy district, a place in which the healthy shut themselves up?—then is a man able to plant himself in the midst of a sick district, draw round him a magic wand, and say to the noxious atmosphere, so far shalt thou come, and no farther? Moses's out-stretched hand had not more power over the waters of the Red Sea, than is here attributed to human volition over a contaminated atmosphere.

Now for the second proposition, that

' the visits of the sick to unaffected places is [are] followed by no increase of disease. In the history of all the epidemics which have ever prevailed in all parts of the earth, there is not on record a single example of the communication of the disease from the sick to the healthy in a pure atmosphere.'

Our readers will bear in mind that the writer's own description of a pure atmosphere is, the atmosphere of unaffected places; otherwise, if, when the visits of the sick to unaffected places are followed by.the propagation of the disease, that fact be taken as a proof of the impurity of the atmosphere, it would be reasoning in a circle—a mere juggle, instead of an argument. Now, taking the proposition in this sense, a more daring and outrageous misstatement was never penned. Excepting only places where the disease is endemic, nearly all the plagues which have ever devastated the world, have followed the visits of the sick to unaffected places—the only difficulty in producing ' a single example,' is
the

the difficulty of choosing among a multitude. The plague of Malta, in 1813, followed the visit of the sick, in the San Nicolo from Alexandria, an affected place, to Malta, an unaffected place, unaffected for 137 years. The plague at Gozo followed a visit from Valetta, an affected place, to Gozo, an unaffected place — an elevated, little island, only a few miles long. The plague at Marseilles, in 1720, followed the visits of the sick from Seyde in Syria, and from Tripoli, affected places, to Marseilles, an unaffected place, unaffected for more than half a century. The plague of Moscow, in 1771, followed the visit of the sick from Choczin, an affected place, to Moscow, an unaffected place, unaffected for more than a century and a half. So far from being in want of a single instance, we have no room for the number which press on us; but we will give one which may serve better than any on a larger scale, and in more populous districts, because no stress can be laid on the impurity of the air. When the plague was raging in London, in the year 1665, the visit, not of the sick, but of the clothes of the sick from London, an affected place, to a village on the Peak of Derbyshire, an unaffected place, was followed by the appearance of the disease in the pure air of that remote and elevated spot. Dr. Macmichael has given a full account of this striking fact in his very interesting Pamphlet; but we find the following short mention of it by Mr. Howard, in his account of the principal lazzarettos of Europe.

‘ When the plague raged in London, in the year 1665, the infection was conveyed by means of a parcel of clothes to the remote village of Eyam near Tidewell, in the Peak of Derbyshire. In this place it broke out in September, 1665, and continued its ravages upwards of a year, when 260 of the inhabitants had died of it. The worthy rector, Mr. Mompesson, whose name may rank with those of Cardinal Borromeo of Milan, and the good Bishop of Marseilles, at its breaking out, resolved not to quit his parishioners, but used every argument to prevail with his wife to leave the infected spot. She, however, refused to forsake her husband, and is supposed to have died of the plague. They sent away their children. Mr. Mompesson constantly employed himself during the dreadful visitation, in his pastoral office, and preached to his flock in a field where nature had formed a sort of alcove in a rock, which place still retains the appellation of a church. He survived, and the entries in the parish register relative to this calamity are in his hand-writing. In the fields surrounding the town are many remains denoting the places where tents were pitched ; and tombs are still existing of large families entirely swept away by this devouring pestilence.’—p. 24.*

The

---

* The anti-contagionists have been in the habit of affirming that the plague had never penetrated into Arabia. We have received the following communication from Dr. Benjamin Babington, who came over land from India, and, in whom the soundest sense, and the most cautious observation, are hereditary qualifications. It bears immediately on this part of the subject.—‘The plague had never been in Arabia till the

middle

The statement then is utterly false; but that is not all; it is equally inconclusive; if we were to admit that the removal of the sick to places unaffected with the plague is often followed by speedy recovery, and by no spread of the disorder, we should only admit what is true with regard to diseases unquestionably contagious, as the small-pox. Van Swieten, who saw the small-pox when it was propagated only in the natural way, writes thus :

'I have sometimes observed large towns to be free from the small-pox, whilst it raged epidemically in the neighbouring villages ; and, on the contrary, some large towns universally visited by the complaint, whilst the villages in the neighbourhood remained in health, though the inhabitants of both mixed daily with each other. I also perfectly remember, that I once removed two patients of mine from a place where the small-pox raged to a large town, without propagating the contagion there; and many excellent physicians, with whom I have cultivated a friendly commerce with respect to medical knowledge, testify, that they have observed the same thing.'

A similar fact is mentioned by Sir John Pringle, in his Account of Diseases of the Army, where it is stated that ' the small-pox, being carried into a camp by some new raised recruits, quickly disappeared without becoming general, although it is notorious that other camp-diseases are but too apt quickly to spread themselves.' Again, the late and learned Dr. Odier, in a letter from Geneva to Dr. Haggarth, says,

' we have frequently inoculated at Geneva a great number of children in the years during which the small-pox was not epidemic ; these children have gone out every day, even after the eruption had broken out ; they have been in the streets, and in the public walks ; they have communicated freely with other children susceptible of the infection, and, not only the small-pox did not spread, but there did not occur, to my knowledge, any distinct instance of the communication of the disease from one individual to another in the streets or promenades.'

When Sir James M'Grigor was at Bombay, the small-pox was raging in the houses contiguous to the barracks, yet not one adult or child in the regiment was affected by it. In Africa, when the Harmattan blows, no contagion is active, not even that by inoculation of the small-pox.

We pass on to an observation which deserves more attention, be-

middle of 1815, when Mahomed Ali Pasha of Egypt, sent his troops across the desert into Arabia on an expedition against the Wahabees. On this occasion it visited Yambo and Jedda, and crept down the coast as low as Gamfada. Each of these towns lost nearly half its population. When I was at Milo, in the end of 1815, a vessel came into the port having one person on board ill with the plague. This vessel was ordered by the Greek authorities to quit the harbour. She put into Mitylene, where those in command being less cautious, allowed the sailors to land, several of whom had by this time become infected. The disease immediately afterwards broke out among the Islanders, and many fell victims to it.'

cause

cause it is not founded in mistatement; it is this: that the plague, when raging violently, sometimes suddenly abates at the very time when the supposed sources of infection, contaminated persons, or contaminated things, are most numerous. In the great plague of London, in 1665, Sydenham states, that ' the number of deaths which had increased to some thousands in one week in August, decreased and almost stopped at the latter end of November.' It must be obvious to the thoughtful reader, that this circumstance, on which so much stress is laid, is only another instance of a general accident of contagious diseases which we have already weighed and considered, viz. that they are propagated readily at one time and with difficulty at another. This has generally been explained by the supposed existence or non-existence of some quality in the atmosphere favourable to the propagation; if the atmosphere can suddenly assume such a quality, it is easy to understand how it may as suddenly lose it. If some changes are capable of increasing, other changes may be capable of diminishing the prevalence of a disease. There is no more mystery in the sudden diminution than there is in the sudden increase in the number of the sick, and there is no mystery in either to one who duly considers that two things are required for the ready diffusion of a contagious disease; the one, the contagious matter or effluvium; the other, a particular state of the atmosphere favourable to its action.

Other circumstances may contribute to the decline of contagious diseases. A man must have had little experience in medicine who does not know that some persons are more susceptible of disease than others. When a contagious disease first breaks out, it of course seizes the most susceptible subjects—they are the tinder, which take fire readily and burn rapidly. The disease spreads easily and widely as long as this combustible matter is abundant, but as soon as it is consumed the fire burns dimly, and at length goes out. Something too may depend on this, that the contagion may lose its pungency by passing through many individuals, and at length wear out. The vaccine matter fresh from the cow produces a more painful disorder than after it has passed for some time through the human subject by inoculation; and if vaccination be now less effectual than formerly as a preventive of small-pox, it may be because we have neglected too long to vaccinate with matter taken immediately from the animal. When siphylis was first brought from America to Europe, it was so virulent and so terrible, that we can hardly recognize in the descriptions left of it by our ancestors, the comparatively mild and tractable disease of the present day.

The last argument of the anti-contagionists which we think entitled to any notice, is the circumstance, that when the plague is
prevalent,

prevalent, so many persons are exposed to the contagion without being affected. This argument is founded upon the supposition, that because almost every body is susceptible to the contagion of small-pox, measles, and scarlet fever, therefore almost every body must be susceptible to the contagion of the plague if it be contagious; in other words, that the laws which govern the eruptive contagious fevers must be the same as govern all contagious fevers. This argument we have already destroyed, by observing that it takes for granted the very point in dispute, that the eruptive contagious fevers are the only contagious fevers. If because many who are exposed to the contagion of the plague escape it, we are to infer that the exposure is not the cause of the plague in those who take it, let us see to what conclusions we shall arrive. Of those who are bitten by a rabid animal, many are not affected by hydrophobia; therefore the bite of a rabid animal is not the cause of hydrophobia. Of those exposed to a cold and variable season, many are not affected with pulmonary inflammations; therefore cold and variable weather is not the cause of pulmonary inflammations. Of those oppressed by the intense heat of the season, many are not seized with the cholera; therefore a hot season is not the cause of cholera. But a truce to this—the causes of disease are not things which invariably produce them, but which produce them sufficiently often to leave no doubt that they are to be considered their causes. Every body is susceptible to small-pox, measles, and scarlet fever; but then, having had them once, he never has them again. Many people are not susceptible, at least for a time, to the plague; but then, having had it once, they may have it repeatedly—singleness of attack is a compensation for universal susceptibility—frequent insusceptibility is a compensation for the liability to repeated attacks. Nature, or rather Providence, abounds in these compensations.

We might now leave the subject, but there are a few statements of the anti-contagionists which it will be useful to notice, not as important in themselves, but as showing the structure of the minds of those who advance them, how little they are to be trusted even in the statement of a fact, and how unfit they are as guides on so momentous a subject. A writer in Blackwood's Magazine, alluding to the anonymous expositor of Dr. M'Lean's whims, says, ' it is true I know *nothing of the subject,* but the Article appears to me to be *quite conclusive.*' It is impossible to put it more happily—the exposition does appear quite conclusive to one who knows nothing of the subject. The most potent arguments are facts, and when the teacher cares little, and the student is totally ignorant, whether they are accurate or no, the business of conviction is an easy task. An instance or two will show what we mean.   ' The

'The small-pox secretes a contagious matter which is contained in its pustules—the measles secretes a contagious matter which is contained *in its vesicles.* Apply a portion of the fluid contained in the pustules of the one and *the vesicles of the other* to a healthy person, it will excite in the latter the same train of symptoms as existed in the individual in whom the contagious matter was secreted.'—*West. Rev.* No. V. p. 138. And again—' the small-pox is never without its pustules, the measles is never without its vesicles.'—*Ibid.* p. 139.

The writer has good reason for his distaste for medical authorities, and his preference of men of general science for his judges; for here is a fact, one of the main pillars of his argument, which such judges would receive without suspicion, but which every medical man on earth knows to be utterly false. The truth is, that though vesicles *sometimes* occur during the progress of measles, they are by no means the essential or characteristic eruption of the disease; the characteristic eruption of measles is a rash, containing no matter to inoculate with, and no one ever thought of producing the measles ' by applying a portion of the fluid contained in its vesicles.' Dr. Francis Home, of Edinburgh, who, in the year 1759, attempted to inoculate the measles, expressly says, ' there was no matter,' and therefore he was obliged to employ the blood. Again,

' Were epidemic diseases really propagated by contagion, it could not possibly be a matter of controversy; the facts establishing the truth would be so clear, so numerous, so overwhelming, as to place it beyond all question. *No one can doubt, no one ever did doubt, that the small-pox is contagious.* This alone must be sufficient to decide the matter in the judgment of every philosophical mind.'—*Ibid.* p. 147.

Now we beg leave to inform the ' philosophical minds' to whom an appeal is here made, that some one did doubt that the small-pox was contagious; no less a person than the greatest physician England ever produced, Sydenham. He saw the small-pox when its natural mode of diffusion was not interrupted by inoculation or vaccination, as it now is, and yet this great man had no suspicion that it was contagious. In his time a belief in the non-contagiousness of small-pox was not only the medical, but the popular opinion. Gadbury, the astrologer, in his ' London's Deliverance Predicted,' published in the year 1665, says, ' I say then, it (the plague) ought not to be deemed infectious at all, at least not more infectious than *small-pox,* scurvy, pleurisy, ague, gout.'

Mistatements, however, of the kind which we have just noticed, are not matter of surprize, for the argument is not addressed to medical men; it appeals from their judgment to that of men of general science acquainted with the laws of evidence. We come now to a different class, and we suspect that for the future even a
knowledge

knowledge of the laws of evidence may be found an inconvenient qualification in the men of science who are to decide the question. For example we are told that

' it is the custom in Turkey for the relations of those who died of the plague, to wear the clothes of the deceased, or to sell them at the public bazaar; they are never destroyed, they are invariably either worn by the relatives or sold at the public market ; *there is no instance on record of the disease being communicated by these means.* The persons who deal in the clothes are not infected, the persons who wear them remain free from the disease.'—*West. Rev.* No. V. p. 160.

A naturalist who had affirmed that domesticated hogs were infested with a species of vermin which did not infest wild hogs, was asked how he knew it; whether he had combed all the wild hogs in the world? So we may ask whether the anti-contagionists have traced all the old clothes which are worn by the relatives or sold at the bazaar ?

When Dr. M'Lean was examined before the Committee on contagion, he said,

' I used to walk into the city of Constantinople, even after I had the disease, and go through the thickest of the people, visiting the coffee-houses and other frequented places ; nor was the disease by that means propagated.'

How does he know? did he inquire into the fate of all the people whom he had jostled in the streets, and sat by in the coffee-houses ?

If we admit the fact that many people are exposed to the clothes of the sick without catching the disease, it proves no more than the fact that many are exposed to the sick themselves without catching it; and this we have already considered. It is not even of this value to the anti-contagionists, till they have satisfied inquirers on a few preliminary points in each case, which seem to have escaped them as of no importance. Were the clothes of the dead worn during their illness? Were they worn during that stage of the disease which is infectious? To what extent have they been exposed to the air since the death of their owner? A lancet dipped in vaccine matter kept for a few days in the pocket, and then used for vaccination, with all the advantages of intentional immersion in the contagious fluid, and careful insertion under the skin in the act of vaccination, is more likely to fail than to succeed in giving the disease; and hence the importance of bringing together the person to be vaccinated with the person from whom he is to be vaccinated, and performing the operation with fresh matter.

So much for the evidence in support of this sweeping statement that ' there is no instance on record of the communication of the
disease

disease by these means;' and now let us hear a little evidence against it.

' It is a notion,' says Dr. Russell, ' prevalent at Aleppo, that a plague cannot subsist in the city any considerable time without being imparted to the Jews. Many of that nation are employed as brokers and pedlars in most parts of the town, and numbers who deal in old clothes daily pass through the streets, purchasing their wares from all ranks of people. In this manner it is supposed the distemper is transported to the Jewish district.'

And again, says Dr. Russell,

' *if substances tainted by the sick should be conveyed into secluded retreats, and persons happen to be seized with the distemper,* can it be ascribed not to contagion, but to terror? and *the instances here alluded to are not the creation of fancy, but strictly consonant to repeated experience in Turkey.*

In another place Dr. Russell says,

' I met with *many* instances of the disease being communicated by coverlids, carpets, and apparel purchased from infected houses.

Dr. Pugnet, who was with the French army in Egypt, states that at Jaffa, an apothecary dying of the plague, his neck-handkerchiefs were divided among, and worn by, fourteen persons: *all these* were seized with the plague, and had bubos in their necks.

The anti-contagionists assert that the plague never was in Holland, although the Dutch have no quarantine laws. That singular but laborious writer Noah Webster has collected accounts of no less than fourteen plagues which ravaged Flanders and Holland at various periods, in one of which, at Delft, in the year 1557, the dead bodies were so numerous that the people fought for the coffins. As to the absence of quarantine laws, if this were true, how happens it that, as soon as England only relaxes her's, and thereby approaches the state of law said to exist in Holland, the several powers of the Mediterranean turn round upon her, and compel every vessel from her ports to perform quarantine before entering their ports?—a conduct which they do not observe towards the vessels of Holland, which undergo no quarantine at all. On inquiring of the Dutch authorities in this country, we learn that the Dutch have quarantine laws, but that, when a vessel arrives from the Levant with a clean bill of health, they are not always strictly enforced. Dr. Granville, who seems to have taken much pains to ascertain the fact, gives the following as the result of his inquiries, in his letter on this subject to the Chancellor of the Exchequer. The Dutch trade in the Mediterranean, in former times, suffered much from the Algerine cruizers; in consequence of which the Dutch merchantmen trading in the Mediterranean were, from the early ages of the Republic, directed to assemble at
Leghorn,

Leghorn, from which port they sailed under convoy to Holland. This arrangement leads to considerable detention at Leghorn, which, although originally intended as a security against pirates, served in point of fact the purpose of a quarantine, Leghorn being, as is well known, the port of all others in which the quarantine regulations were the most perfect, and most rigidly observed. In addition to this, whenever any Dutch vessel quitted a port where the plague was raging, the Dutch consul at that port refused her a ' *passe-port de mer*,' without which she was not safe in sailing through the Mediterranean, nor was she admitted into Holland.

It would be an endless task to go through what may be called the collateral absurdities in the reasoning of the anti-contagionists —yet we must mention one or two instances. Thus it is said that the doctrine of contagion is selfish and inhuman, and prevents the due performance of the duties of the healthy to the sick; while the doctrine of epidemic diseases remedies the evil. Yet the same persons say,

' People are attacked (with the plague) in proportion as the inhabitants of unaffected expose themselves to the air of affected places. The visits of the inhabitants of an unaffected to an affected place is [are] attended with a *certain* increase of sickness.'—*West. Rev.* No. V. p. 145.

Is it possible that they should not see that their objection applies more strongly against this doctrine than against that of contagion; for if the latter teaches us to avoid the *sick*, the former teaches us to avoid the *very air* which surrounds the sick. The latter says *only*, do not touch a patient affected with the plague, or the clothes which he has worn; you may go within a certain distance of him—observe his symptoms—prescribe for him—carry him medicine and refreshment. But the latter says, if you go into the chamber, or the house, or the very neighbourhood in which the disease is raging, you expose yourself to danger.

Another absurdity is, that the doctrine of contagion was a popish trick, and never heard of before the year 1547, when it was invented by Pope Paul III. as an excuse for removing the Council of Trent to Bologna. Two learned foreigners, Dr. C. F. H. Mark and Dr. Omodei, of Milan, have just published most satisfactory refutations of this statement. That of the former is entitled Origines Contagii; that of the latter is contained in the twenty-second volume of the Milan Annals of Medicine: of both an elaborate analysis is given in the Edinburgh Medical Journal. It was hardly necessary to expend so much talent and learning, as these gentlemen have displayed, upon a notion unworthy of serious refutation. As far back as Thucydides and Aristotle, through a long succession of historians and poets

down

down to Boccaccio, the notion is traced that pestilential diseases are contracted by communication with the sick. Dr. M'Lean is a little sore on this subject, and he has a curious mode of defending himself. When reminded in the Committee of Boccaccio's account of the plague at Florence in 1348, in which the healthy are represented as flying from the sick, to avoid catching the disease, he says,

' It is necessary to ascertain the precise date of its being printed, in order to appreciate the authenticity of the doctrines as being those of the writer, or as being introduced by interpolation of editors or commentators.'

What must be the condition of that man's mind who could suspect interpolation on such a subject?

When Dr. M'Lean was examined by the Committee on the doctrine of contagion, he told them that his opinions were founded on an experience of *seventeen days;* but requested them ' to recollect how little the value of experience might be commensurate with its duration—that the plague was generally fatal in nine cases out of ten—but that he could cure it in *four cases out of five.* When asked to what extent he had tried this triumphant mode of treatment, he said upon *one* patient, and that was himself. When reminded that Dr. Whyte had inoculated himself with the plague, and had died of it, he said ' that he took it' *by a coincidence.* When told that the Turks, who used no precautions to avoid the plague, suffer much more from it than the Christians, who avoid it, he said that he did *not believe it, because he did not see the grounds for it.* When asked upon what grounds he concluded that the Turks and Mahometans suffered less than the Christians, he said, *not from actual observation,* but from *the nature of things, and because there was no evidence to the contrary.* He said, he would not believe that a person had the small-pox twice, even if he were to witness it; *he should distrust the evidence of his own eyes.* When asked at what periods of the year the plague at Moscow in 1771 had prevailed and declined, he answered, that his impression was that it began *at the usual epidemic season in northern latitudes, and ceased at the usual time.* Being thereupon asked what he called the epidemic season at Moscow, he rejoined that it was the same, or nearly the same, as in this country, *judging from the pestilence in* 1771. So that the plague at Moscow was epidemic because it raged at the epidemic season; and that was the epidemic season, because the plague raged at that time; there is no circle in Euclid, which it would be more difficult to square than this. He denied that Thucydides describes the plague at Athens as contagious; it is true that this is in express defiance not only of that author's positive assertion, but of some

details,

details, occasioned by the contagious nature of the disorder; we infer, indeed, from Dr. M'Lean's cautiously worded answer that he would find a difficulty in reading the original; probably, however, he knows Latin, and as he professes to have formed his opinion from a *comparison of interpretations*, we would ask him whether he has ever stumbled on rather a spirited and yet faithful translation of that part of Thucydides by Lucretius; or, if his Latinity be confined to the Pharmacopeia, whether he ever looked at the best English translation by one Thomas Hobbes of Malmsbury. These were a few of the precious statements with which Dr. M'Lean favoured the Contagion Committee, and we know not which to wonder at most, the mind of the man who uttered them, or the patience of the Committee who could listen to them. This gentleman has been described by an enlightened member of parliament, as one of those extraordinary persons who will be pointed out by the finger of the future historian! History has two fingers, which she employs for different purposes in pointing out individuals to the notice of their fellow-men; which of the two she will use, if ever she happen to notice Dr. M'Lean, we will not venture to predict. Judging by his writings and his actions we conclude that he is a man of great self-confidence, zeal, and perseverance; these qualities, when combined with ability, judgment, and knowledge, form the improvers of science, the master-spirits of their age, the benefactors of their species; but when combined, as they often are, with wrong-headedness, and a heap of inaccurate and ill-digested knowledge, they form very absurd, and often very mischievous men. Every age affords examples of both; the latter are not uncommonly mistaken for the former; but time corrects the blunder.

We are tired of refuting errors and exposing absurdities which would require no refutation nor exposure if those, who are to decide, were well acquainted with the facts of the question. We call on our legislators, however, before they consent to abolish the system of quarantine, to pause and reflect on the tremendous importance of the stake; to consider that these barriers were built up by our experienced ancestors, and that we have no experience, who are about to pull them down; that the experienced powers of the Mediterranean behold with astonishment the opinions which have been broached in England on the subject, and in consequence of the relaxations to which our government has already consented, have refused to admit our vessels into their ports without a previous quarantine. We beg them to remember how often, in their own families, they act on the supposition of contagion when the evidence amounts only to a probability; and we entreat them to legislate for the nation on the same principles of wise and
humane

humane caution which they observe in the regulation of their own establishments. If in the details of the present amended system there be any thing vexatious or unnecessarily dilatory, and we are far from saying that there is nothing such, let it receive a still farther consideration, and any remedy be applied, which may appear to be adequate and proper; but we earnestly hope that no individual inconvenience, nor any ingenious speculations, however strongly the one may be pressed, or however plausibly the other stated, will induce our legislature to abandon the *principle* of quarantine, or introduce any system founded on the belief that the plague is not a contagious disease.

Dr. M'Lean must excuse the freedom with which we have examined his theory, his arguments, and his pretensions. We have written nothing in personal ill will against a man of whom we know nothing except on this question; but this is too important a matter to allow us to weigh any pain, which we may unavoidably inflict on him, against the cause of the public and of truth. His hobby, or his delusion, be it which it may, is not a harmless one, and he must not be indulged in it. We remember, a few years since, a newspaper story, with which, as not an inapt illustration of his proceedings, we will conclude. An odd fellow, a chemist, appeared before the Lord Mayor, begging leave to show experimentally, that detonating balls were quite harmless ; and drew half a pound of gunpowder out of his pocket, in which he meant to explode the balls; the Lord Mayor exclaimed loudly against the experiment; but at length, on his earnest entreaty and strong assurances, permitted him to try it with a small quantity of powder. To the chemist's utter discomfiture the powder exploded, he protesting that it *ought not* to have done so.

If parliament will but enact the part of the yielding Lord Mayor, the plague will not be slow to represent, very adequately, that of the detonating balls; Dr. M'Lean cannot indeed, like the chemist, limit the quantity of his gunpowder, but he will protest most solemnly and most consolingly over the dead and the dying, that the disease *ought not* to have spread amongst them.

ART. XII.—*A Letter to Sir Henry Halford, Bart. President of the College of Physicians, proposing a Method of inoculating the Small-pox which deprives it of all its Danger, but preserves all its Power of preventing a second Attack.* By R. Ferguson, M. D. Member of the College of Physicians of London and Edinburgh. 1825.

ABOUT twenty years ago, when it was proposed to purify the medical profession from quackery and ignorance by legislative enactments, the late Dr. Gregory of Edinburgh published a letter on the subject, in which he remarked that ' England is a free country, and the freedom which every free-born Englishman chiefly values, is the freedom of doing what is foolish and wrong and going to the devil his own way.' This is strikingly exemplified in the present state of vaccination in Great Britain, compared with its state in other countries of Europe. In the latter, general vaccination was ordered by government; no one who had had neither cow-pox nor small-pox could be confirmed, put to school, apprenticed, or married. Small-pox inoculation was prohibited; if it appeared in any house, that house was put under quarantine; and in one territory no person with small-pox was allowed to enter it. By such means the mortality from this disease in 1818 had been prodigiously lessened. In Copenhagen, it had been reduced from 5500 during 12 years to 158 during 16 years. In Prussia, it had been reduced from 40,000 annually to less than 3000; and in Berlin in 1819. only 25 persons died of this disease. In Bavaria only 5 persons died of small-pox in eleven years, and in the principality of Anspach it was completely exterminated. In England, on the other hand,—in England, the native country of this splendid and invaluable discovery, where every man acts on these subjects as he likes, crowds of the poor go unvaccinated; they are permitted not only to imbibe the small-pox themselves, but to go abroad and scatter the venom on those whom they meet. A few years ago it broke out in Norwich, and carried off more persons in one year, than had ever been destroyed in that city by any one disease, except the plague. A similar epidemic raged at Edinburgh; and last year it destroyed within one of 1300 persons in the London bills of mortality.

Before the introduction of inoculation, the small-pox was the most loathsome and fatal disease with which Great Britain was afflicted. It killed about one out of four of those whom it attacked, and left many of the survivors with blinded eyes, scarred faces, and ruined constitutions. When, therefore, inoculation was introduced into this island, it seemed a prodigious improvement; by this simple contrivance, especially after the

method

method had been improved by the Suttons, a disease which killed one out of four, was transmuted into a disease which killed only one in several hundreds. If this had been the only result, the benefit would have been unmingled, and great in a degree almost incredible, but it brought with it an evil still greater than the good; by perpetually keeping up a supply of the contagion, this disease, which had been propagated only at intervals before, was now propagated perpetually, far and wide, among those unprotected by inoculation; the annual mortality was greatly increased, and that, which all had hoped to find a blessing, turned out to be a national curse.

It is not surprizing, therefore, that when Jenner disclosed the wonderful truth, that the artificial production of a trifling and harmless disorder would impart a charmed life over which this loathsome disease should have no power, his discovery was soon hailed with enthusiasm by almost the whole medical profession. In the general exultation, its infallibility was over-rated; the advocates for vaccination affirmed that it was an infallible protection from the small-pox, and every instance of small-pox after cowpox was explained away. Such cases are now no longer to be denied. Patients have caught the small-pox who had been vaccinated by the most skilful vaccinators, even by Jenner himself, and it is generally acknowledged that out of a number of vaccinated persons, some do not resist the contagion of the small-pox.

The time has now arrived when all intemperate excitement on the subject is at an end. Vaccination has been tried on a vast scale for seven-and-twenty years, and we have a stock of experience whereon to determine (not with mathematical precision, yet with enough for the guidance of our conduct) to what extent vaccination has disappointed our expectations, and whether this disappointment is sufficient to induce us to abandon the practice altogether.

This general question resolves itself into two particular ones: 1st. What is the proportion of the vaccinated who are liable to the infection of small-pox; 2d. Do they suffer when infected as severely as those who have never been vaccinated, or is the small-pox in their case mitigated and converted into a harmless disease?

From the introduction of vaccination down to the present time, numerous instances have been recorded of an eruptive disease, similar to small-pox, in persons previously vaccinated. But though these records afford specimens of this occurrence, they throw no light on the question of its frequency; we pass them over, therefore, and select a few instances in which the security afforded by vaccination has been tried on a large scale, and the

first

first which we shall notice is a small-pox epidemic* which raged in Norwich in 1819, and which has been described by Mr. Cross, a well-informed and indefatigable surgeon of that city. The small-pox had been extinct in Norwich from 1813, to June, 1818, when a country girl, travelling from Yorkshire, caught it in a market-town through which she passed, and was taken ill soon after her arrival at Norwich. This girl was the innocent cause of the death of more than 500 persons; all of whom might have been saved if there had been a small-pox quarantine. For several months it crept from house to house like a spark of fire along a streak of gunpowder, but in February, 1819, it reached a charity school, a magazine of combustibles, and the explosion scattered firebrands all over the city. More than 3000 persons caught the disease; it proved fatal to 530; 43 were buried in one week, 156 in June, and 142 in July.—Now, there were in Norwich about 10,000 vaccinated persons exposed to the full rage of this very contagious and malignant small-pox. How did they stand it?

In 42 poor families, there were 91 persons who had been vaccinated at various periods from 1798 down to the commencement of this epidemic; these persons were continually in the same room, and many in the same bed, with those suffering small-pox; of these 91 persons, only two caught the small-pox. But besides those exposed to the contagion, several hundreds of the vaccinated were inoculated with small-pox. In one out of 40 or 50 there came out a slight eruption, which lasted only four or five days. Thus it appears that the proportion of vaccinated persons who were susceptible to the contagion was rather more than two out of every hundred. But when vaccinated persons caught the small-pox, what degree of severity did this disease assume? ' In no instance,' says Mr. Cross, 'has regular small-pox, as far as I have been able to ascertain, been produced. In about one in 40 or 50 a spurious eruption has appeared, in some presenting a few irregular pimples, in others resembling the small-pox; but I have not learnt that the latter have ever proceeded regularly, invariably drying up in four or five days, and never taking the course of regular small-pox.' ' Full-length small-pox in those who have been vaccinated,' continues Mr. Cross, ' has been so rare that I have not met with a single instance either in my own practice, or in my inquiries amongst the poor.' A few such cases, how-

* An *epidemic* is a *prevalent* disease, whether its prevalence arises from contagion, or from an unhealthy state of the air. In our last Number, under the article Plague, we consented to restrict this word to the latter class of diseases; this had been already done by the Anti-contagionists, and we were unwilling to waste time in a dispute about words when we have so heavy an account to settle with them about facts and reasonings.

ever,

ever, occurred under the care of some other surgeons. Six vaccinated persons caught the small-pox, which ran its full length, and two out of the six died. Those who were believed to have had small-pox formerly did not escape. Mr. Cross relates several instances in which the disease seized and ran its full length upon persons who were even *marked* by small-pox; and he gives at length the story of one patient who died; adding, ' such examples have been very frequent.' When the small-pox occurred in those who had had small-pox, it does not appear to have been rendered short and mild, as in those who had had cow-pox. The result of this Norwich epidemic, therefore, was as follows : of those persons who had neither had cow-pox nor small-pox, about 3000 caught the disease, and 530, that is more than one in six, died; of those who had previously had the small-pox, many caught it again, as severely as if they had never had it before, and one died ; of those who had been vaccinated, amounting to 10,000, rather more than two in every hundred were affected by the small-pox contagion, but it almost invariably produced a short and trifling disease. In only six instances did it occasion the full-length small-pox, and in two only did it terminate fatally—two instances out of 10,000!

In the 52d volume of Hufeland's Journal for 1821, Dr. Gittermann has described a small-pox epidemic which prevailed at Emden in 1819 and 1820. In an hospital in which there were 200 children, most of them vaccinated, 8 of the vaccinated either caught the small-pox, or took it by inoculation ; but it was that short and mild disease which is called modified small-pox. Here one in twenty-five took the abbreviated small-pox. In a letter from the island of St. Vincent, quoted by Dr. Thompson of Edinburgh in his ' Historical Sketch of the Opinions of Medical Men on the Secondary Occurrence of Small-pox,' (page 379,) the writer states that he had inoculated with the small-pox 130 negroes whom he had formerly vaccinated. Of these, six took the mild and abbreviated small-pox, that is, about one in 21.

We have here selected, out of a multitude of records, instances in which the vaccinated were exposed, under the most unfavourable circumstances, to singularly contagious epidemics, and in which the estimate of security is stated at the lowest. We could crowd our pages with statements on respectable authorities of many thousand persons who had undergone vaccination, and in which no individual had been known to have been subsequently affected by the small-pox.

During the years 1818 and 1819 the small-pox was epidemic in Edinburgh, Lanark, and other parts of Scotland, and an account of it has been published by Dr. John Thompson of Edinburgh, professor of military surgery in that university, a man whose ability, zeal, and learning are universally recognized. This account affords no information about the proportion of vaccinated persons who caught, and the proportion who resisted, the small-pox ; but it affords very valuable information about the degree of severity which the small-pox assumed when it attacked those who had been previously vaccinated. It was almost invariably an abbreviated and mild kind of small-pox, so exactly resembling chicken-pox, that Dr. Thompson believes them indistinguishable. ' In the characters,' says he, ' by which it has of late been supposed that chicken-pox may be distinguished from modified small-pox, observation leads me to place no confidence whatever.'

Dr. Thompson saw 836 cases of small-pox : of these 281 occurred in persons who had never had either small-pox or cowpox, and rather more than one-fourth of the number died ; 71 had already had small-pox, and of these two died ; 484 had been vaccinated, and of these one only died. The numerous cases of small-pox in persons who had already had it before, are very remarkable, and will teach the public that, although vaccination is not an infallible preservative against small-pox, neither is small-pox itself. Notwithstanding the numerous cases of small-pox in persons who had been vaccinated, it was so trifling a disease, that only one died out of nearly 500 ; ' results,' says Dr. Thompson, ' which evince the beneficial effects of vaccination in protecting the human constitution from the *dangers* of small-pox, and the great advantages which must ultimately arise from the universal adoption of this practice.' In another place, he remarks,

' It must now be universally allowed, that the protection which vaccination affords against the *fatality* of small-pox is at least equal, if not superior, to that which is afforded by having passed through the small-pox themselves, even in the natural way—a degree of security which, though it may not be absolute, is surely as great as can reasonably be expected of any human invention.' ' It has been impossible to see the general mildness of the varioloid epidemic in those who had undergone the process of vaccination, and the severity, malignity, and fatality of the same disease in the unvaccinated, and not to be convinced of the great and salutary powers of cow-pox in modifying small-pox in those who were afterwards affected with this disease. Proofs cannot be imagined more convincing and satisfactory of the efficacy of the practice of vaccination, and of the incalculable benefits bestowed upon mankind by its discoverer, than those I have had the pleasure of witnessing. It has been very agreeable, also, to observe, that the terrors at first excited by the occurrence of this varioloid epidemic in the families of those who had undergone cow-pock inoculation, have gradually given way in the

progress

progress of the disease; and that the comparison of small-pox in their modified and unmodified forms has often forced a conviction of the advantages of cow-pock inoculation upon the minds even of the most ignorant and prejudiced, and induced them to seek protection for themselves and their offspring in a practice which they had formerly neglected or despised.'

Last year (1825) the small-pox was singularly prevalent and fatal in London. Before the discovery of vaccination, the average annual mortality of twenty years within the London bills, from small-pox, was 1809 persons. This had been gradually diminishing since the introduction of vaccination, until in 1818 it was reduced as low as 421. Last year no fewer than 1299 persons died of small-pox, within the London bills of mortality; 419 cases of small-pox were admitted into the Small-Pox Hospital; of these, 263 occurred in persons who had neither had small-pox nor cow-pox, and 107 died; that is about 41 out of each 100, an enormous mortality; two had already had small-pox, and one of the two died; 147 were supposed to have previously had the cow-pox; of these 122 had the disease in a mild and abbreviated form, technically called the modified small-pox; in 25 it ran its full length, and in 12 of these it terminated fatally. Thus, if we are to take it for granted that these 147 persons who declared that they had been vaccinated, really had had the cow-pox, nearly one in 12 died. But had these 12 persons really had the cow-pox in a perfect and satisfactory way?

' My rule,' says Dr. George Gregory, the physician to the Small-Pox Hospital, on whose authority this statement depends, ' my rule throughout the year was never to exclude any one from this class who could show a scar, or, failing in that criterion, who retained a *distinct recollection* of having undergone some kind of protecting process. In many of the unmodified and fatal cases just referred to, *the evidence of prior vaccination was very imperfect,* but in others the proofs of vaccination were distinct and undeniable.'

Thus, in five the scars are described as not perceptible, which means, we suppose, that they had no scars at all. In one the scar resembled that of a burn, and in two others it was small, and wanted the characteristic appearance. All of them had been vaccinated in the country.

In the cases of small-pox after cow-pox, which occur among the poor of this metropolis, the history of the previous vaccination, which is an essential part of the evidence, is often singularly unsatisfactory. A country bumpkin comes to town, catches the small-pox, goes into the hospital, says that he was vaccinated some years ago, and shows his arm, on which there is sometimes a large scar, sometimes a small one, and sometimes none at all. All that can be learnt is, that some village Æsculapius had pricked

his

his arm with a lancet, and has left a mark or no mark on the part, but nothing can be learnt of the progress of the disease.

That when the poor are vaccinated in numbers, many of them pass through the disease in a way not to be relied on, is not a matter of conjecture. When the small-pox was raging in Norwich, in 1819, Mr. Cross vaccinated 500 persons; of these 28 had the disease in an unsatisfactory way, either from the vesicles being broken, or from their appearance deviating from that of ordinary cow-pox; 35 did not take the disease; and 24 either never returned after they had been vaccinated to show the progress of the disease, or ceased to attend after the first few days; so that Mr. Cross had no opportunity of ascertaining whether the vaccination had been complete. It is not, therefore, a probable conjecture, but an absolute certainty, that when a multitude of the poor are vaccinated, there are many cases in which there is no evidence of the perfection of the vaccination. It may have been perfect, it may have been imperfect, but it is impossible to determine either the one way or the other. We are far from referring all the cases of small-pox after cow-pox to imperfect vaccination, yet we cannot resist quoting Mr. Cross's pointed remark, that the number of vaccinated persons in regard to whom there is no evidence whether they had the disease satisfactorily or not, is *as great* as the number of persons who have the small-pox after cow-pox.

From the facts and calculations which we have laid before our readers, and the multiplication of which would be attended by no equivalent advantage, the following inferences may be safely drawn: 1st. That vaccination in a vast proportion of cases affords complete security against the contagion of small-pox: 2dly. That in a small proportion varying under different circumstances, but at the highest not to be estimated at more than one in 20, vaccinated persons do not resist the contagion altogether,—but resist it so far as to suffer none of its dangers, having its violence diminished, its length curtailed, and converted into a short, mild, and trifling disease : 3dly. That out of numerous cases in which small-pox occurs after cow-pox, the small-pox is sometimes undiminished in length and violence, and sometimes even terminates fatally; but that these cases—trifling even if compared with those in which the small-pox is abbreviated—when contrasted with the number of vaccinated who resist the contagion altogether, dwindle down to a number scarcely worth calculation.

It has been remarked, even by medical men, as surprizing and inexplicable that small-pox after cow-pox is now more frequent than formerly, and that it most commonly occurs in persons who
have

have been vaccinated several years. Where is the mystery? More vaccinated persons take the small-pox now than formerly, because there are more vaccinated persons to take it. From the discovery of vaccination to the present time their numbers have been augmenting; for although death would every year subtract some, vaccination would every year add a vast many more. That it has been gradually spreading over a larger surface of the population, and encroaching upon that which is unprotected from the small-pox, is obvious by comparing the mortality from small-pox in London during the first ten years after vaccination, and the mortality from the same disease during the second ten years. The former amounted to 13,690, the latter only to 8729, and in the year 1818 it was reduced as low as 421. Again, more persons catch the small-pox among those whose vaccination is old than among those whose vaccination is recent—because the former are far more numerous than the latter. The old are the gatherings of many years, the new the gatherings of only a few. This is not conjecture. When the small-pox raged in Norwich in 1819, the recent vaccinations were about one-tenth of the whole, nine-tenths being from three years old to more than twenty. In this instance, too, the proportion of recent vaccinations was unnaturally swelled, as the panic produced by the epidemic occasioned numbers to be vaccinated who would have neglected this precaution under ordinary circumstances.

It is a prevalent notion that vaccination affords protection only for a time; that its influence gradually wears out; and some have pretended to state how many years it lasts with undiminished force, how many years it gradually decays, and in how many it ceases altogether, leaving the constitution open to the inroads of small-pox. However probable this opinion may at first sight appear, on more attentive consideration it will be found not even probable, for it is contrary to analogy, as far as we have any; in all other instances in which a disease destroys the susceptibility to a repetition of it, it destroys it through life. The influence of small-pox, scarlet fever, measles, hooping-cough, which leaves the constitution insusceptible to a recurrence of these diseases, never wears out; we do not find that in these instances the patient is secure for so many years, less secure for so many more, and at length as susceptible to a repetition of these diseases as if he never had them. A few persons, it is true, take these diseases twice, but these are only the very rare exceptions to the general rule. But the notion is contradicted by experience; if it were true, ought we not to find that, in all the instances in which small-pox occurred after cow-pox, it occurred several years from the date of vaccination, and that the far greater

N N 3 number

number of such cases lay among those whose vaccination was the oldest? Is this the fact? No. We find instances of small-pox after cow-pox at all periods, from a few months after vaccination up to many years; and on the contrary, grown-up women who were vaccinated on the first introduction of the practice, nursing their children for the small-pox, without catching it themselves.

To *prove* that the protecting power of vaccination lasts only a few years, would be the hardest stone that has been thrown at the name of Jenner; but hitherto the charge has not been proved. That small-pox after cow-pox is more common now than formerly, and among those who have been vaccinated many years than among those who have been vaccinated a few, for the reasons we have already stated, proves nothing. If among a number vaccinated lately and an equal number vaccinated long ago, a far larger proportion of the latter caught the small-pox than of the former, this would go to prove the fact; but no such case has ever been made out.

Let those who would abandon vaccination because it is not infallible, look the consequences of such conduct fairly in the face. Would they omit both inoculation and vaccination, and expose the nation unprotected to the natural small-pox, a disease which kills one-fourth of those who catch it, and disfigures the countenances, or ruins the health of a crowd of the survivors?—or would they return to small-pox inoculation, which renders the disease mild in those who are inoculated; but, by keeping up constant supplies of the contagion, spreads it continually among the uninoculated, and occasions a greater mortality than if inoculation was neglected?—or, lastly, will they continue vaccination, which affords perfect security from small-pox in an immense proportion of instances—when it does not prevent it, deprives it of its danger—and permits a severe or a fatal disease in only a few rare instances?

The importance of the general question has occupied us longer than we intended, and delayed our notice of the interesting pamphlet the title of which stands at the head of this Article. There are many persons whose prejudices against vaccination are utterly insurmountable; they dwell on the few instances which they have known of small-pox after cow-pox, and forget the many in which the latter has afforded complete protection from the former; they dwell on a few instances of inoculated small-pox which were mild and ended prosperously, and forget that even the inoculated disease sometimes occasions death, disfigurement, or ruined health. We advise these unreasonable persons to mix a little wisdom with their folly, and if they insist on inflicting the small-pox on their infants, to adopt the method

recom-

recommended by Dr. Ferguson in this pamphlet. If a person who has had neither cow-pox nor small-pox is first vaccinated, and a few days afterwards inoculated with the small-pox, the two diseases proceed together; but the cow-pox so completely curbs the small-pox as to deprive it of more than half its length and all its danger. Of this curious and important fact Dr. Ferguson proposes to take advantage;—his object is, by vaccinating a few days before inoculating with the small-pox, to generate a disease as mild as chicken-pox, and as capable of protecting the patient from subsequent small-pox as full-length small-pox itself. The plan, the way in which he learnt it, and the whole developement of the scheme betray an observing, thoughtful, and judicious mind.

The incident which first led him to this view of the subject is very striking. There were three children in a poor family, two boys a few years old, and one infant at the breast; the two boys caught the small-pox—the mother, fearing that the infant, from its tender age, would sink under this formidable disease, consented to have it vaccinated, but it had already imbibed the small-pox, of which the eruption came out a few days after vaccination. But although the cow-pox was too late altogether to prevent the small-pox, it effectually curbed its violence, rendering it so mild and short that it resembled chicken-pox, so that, although the infant had not sickened till some time *after* the two elder boys, it was quite well several days *before* they were convalescent.

' Reflecting,' says Dr. Ferguson, ' on these three cases, it was evident to me that that form of small-pox known by the name of the modified small-pox, or the varioloid disease, was the mildest. I thought then that if I could generate it artificially, I should produce a disease which would unite all the certainty of small-pox in defending the constitution from any subsequent attacks of this horrible malady with the mildness of the chicken-pox. I saw, too, that the experiment had already been made in the case of the infant, for it had been exposed to the contagion of the small-pox, and also to that of the cow-pox, and that the result was a mild form of disease.'

The proof that, when cow-pox and small-pox meet at the same time and in the same person, the former restrains the violence of the latter, and converts it into a disease as trifling as chicken-pox, is corroborated by numerous experiments accidentally made before the nature of the process was understood. When vaccination was first discovered, Dr. Woodville vaccinated 500 persons in the Small-Pox Hospital, and soon afterwards inoculated several of them with the small-pox. In many (about three-fifths) of these patients there came out an eruption resembling that of small-pox; most of them had no fever, and the eruption disappeared in a few days. The disease

thus

thus produced was so short and slight that Dr. Woodville took it for the effect of vaccination. It is now certain that these patients had caught the small-pox about the time when they were vaccinated, and that the eruption was that of small-pox restrained by cow-pox. A few years afterwards Dr. Willan published some similar observations, together with the true explanation. He found that if the small-pox was inoculated within a week after vaccination, the patient had an eruption of small-pox pustules; but that if the inoculation was delayed till the ninth day after vaccination it produced no effect.

Thus, the fact had been ascertained by numerous experiments, but it remained for Dr. Ferguson to employ it as a means of restraining the violence of small-pox ; and for this he deserves great credit. These little steps in thought are great steps in the progress of human power; even Jenner's discovery consisted only in employing that as an art which was already known by numerous accidental experiments.

Before adopting the scheme two questions will occur to the considerate reader—1st. Whether previous vaccination may be depended on for abbreviating and ameliorating small-pox?—2d. Whether this abbreviated small-pox secures the patient from subsequent small-pox, like small-pox in the ordinary form ? As to the first of these questions, the restraining efficacy of previous vaccination has been proved by ample experience. It rests not merely on the cases which have been witnessed by Dr. Ferguson, but on the experiments of Dr. Willan, and on the numerous cases which occurred to Dr. Woodville in the Small-pox Hospital. As to the second of these questions, we have all the evidence which the nature of the subject admits of. From the introduction of vaccination down to the present time, cases of abbreviated small-pox after cow-pox have been continually occurring ; every one of these is an instance of the disease which Dr. Ferguson proposes to generate, yet we do not remember to have heard of one which was ever followed by a subsequent attack of the disease.

When the small-pox is inoculated, medicines are used to prepare the constitution, and to diminish as much as possible the violence and danger of the disease; but for these objects there are no medicines equal to a previous vaccination.

We do not recommend Dr. Ferguson's scheme as a substitute for vaccination—there is this decisive reason against its general adoption, that, like common inoculation, it would keep up a perpetual supply of the small-pox contagion, and thus augment the mortality occasioned by the small-pox : but the large class of *extremely cautious* persons we have already alluded to, cannot find elsewhere a guide either so ingenious or so safe as this author.

ART. VIII.—*The London Gazette for* October 20th, 1831. *Rules and Regulations of the Privy Council concerning the Cholera.*

WE are obliged to recur to a very painful subject, in consequence of the impression left on our minds, by the perusal of these directions, that the government of this country neither have done, nor are doing, nor even as yet contemplate doing, what we conceive to be their duty in relation to that pestilence which hovers at our doors. A hundred and fifty years have elapsed since any such visitation occurred in this happy island, and men of all conditions had been lulled, through long security, into a practical disbelief that the like may occur again. We mean no reproach to the present ministers in particular, when we state the fact that they appear to us to have taken up the consideration of the subject too late, and to have at length entered upon it feebly. We cannot forget how narrowly the government of Lord Liverpool, but a few years ago, escaped being seduced by our anti-contagionist reasoners into the repeal of all our laws respecting the plague.

History records instances of pestilence in which the mortality has been as great as in the cholera—others, in which the suddenness of the transition from life to death has been as appalling—and perhaps some few, in which the agonies of death have been not less excruciating ; but no disease has ever before presented so fearful a combination of these three features—of extensive mortality—concentrated power of destruction—and exquisite anguish of suffering.

What has been done to meet this fatal contagion ? *One* Board of Health has been established, and it has issued *two* documents. The first of these (lithographed in July) was made up of recommendations totally inapplicable and impracticable in a society such as ours, and which, if enforced, must have burthened us with evils yet more intolerable than those of death by cholera. Our wives and daughters, in the event of illness, were to be torn from us and thrust into lazarhouses ; the rest of our families were to choose between the alternative of accompanying their sick kindred to the pest-house, or being placed, perhaps among the refuse of society, in a lazaretto, until time had shown that they might return to their own dwellings without danger to the public safety. Our houses, meantime, if the malady had visited them, were to be surrendered into the absolute keeping of ' Expurgators '—outcasts, probably, capable of, and tempted to every crime ! The government, we must suppose, have the merit of detecting—at their leisure—the absurdity of thus applying

plying to Great Britain the plague code of the *garrison of
Malta!* and hence certain important modifications of the Board's
original views, in the regulations of the 20th of October.
But this second document, however superior to the first is, still
far from being a satisfactory one. The *advice* it contains (for it
is but *advice*) is of so general a nature, and so loosely worded,
that we doubt if any individual has been thereby guided to frame
for himself and his household a more efficient system of prophy-
lactics than a very moderate exercise of unprofessional common
sense might have at once suggested. It may be said that the
Board have been deterred from going into details, by the dread of
exaggerating alarm; but we cannot shut our eyes to the equal
impolicy and inhumanity of being held back, under such circumstances, by such considerations. The fatal consequences of *ignorance* have been written black and strong in every history of pestilence. The amount of evil has always been in proportion to the
want of knowledge and preparation. Witness Marseilles, where,
in the language of an eye-witness, ' the rich found no protection
—the poor no aid ;' witness the massacres during the plague of
Messina—the fearful anarchy which has attended the footsteps of
this cholera throughout Persia—witness various towns of Hindostan, where the whole population rushed in despair into the country,
and leaving their own valuables to destruction, spread the pestilence far and wide about them—and the islands of the Indian
Ocean, where Europeans were butchered on the shore, in sight of
British ships and Spanish soldiery. We are, in fact, inclined to
attribute the diminishing mortality of cholera, as it has advanced
into comparatively civilized regions, much less to any considerable
mitigation of its virus, than to the superior arrangements as to hospitals and police, especially adopted in foresight of its eruption.

When we compare our own country with those European states
as yet ravaged by cholera, so far from finding grounds to justify
comparative neglect on the part either of government or of individuals here, we are constrained to arrive at a far different conclusion. Allowing all that can be asked for, as to the many points
in which we are favourably distinguished—especially the morality
and cleanliness characteristic of great classes not elsewhere so far
advanced—and the skilfulness of our medical men—we are still
forced to suspect, that on the whole, the balance may be struck
against us. We have great towns in a proportion prodigiously
beyond any other European empire—London with probably
1,500,000 inhabitants, Dublin with 400,000, Glasgow and
Manchester with 200,000 each—five cities all above 100,000—
Edinburgh, Liverpool, Birmingham, Bristol, and Cork—at least
fourteen, of from 30,000 to 60,000—and about thirty, ranging from
15,000

15,000 to 30,000   Our inland commerce and habits of life are such as to connect all parts of the country together in a style wholly un-exampled. The extent and rapidity of our means of conveyance have never been approached. Then our, in general circumstances, admirable policy of doing everything to excite competition, has ren-dered us dependent on each other—on individual arrangements and exertions, even for the necessaries of life, to a degree unheard of in any other kingdom. The proportion of the people imme-diately dependent on the government for support, in the shape of soldiery, &c., is as nothing ; and there is a corresponding deficiency of those magazines which almost everywhere else are at hand in case of a famine. Lastly, except in one or two places, we are more destitute of a *police* than any community in the world. Every historian of pestilence, from Thucydides to Jonnès, abounds in awful descriptions of the outburst of *crime* that ine-vitably attends such visitations ; and as it is obvious that this can only proceed from the suspension of usual occupations, it is need-ful to inquire what occupations are the most sure to be inter-rupted—and what nation can ever have had such reason for fear, in the prospect of such a calamity, as the one that possesses the most enormous proportion of manufacturers that the world has ever witnessed ?

Have the king's ministers endeavoured to bring home to their own minds the effects of a sudden paralyzation of commerce through every limb of our body politic ? Have they tried to cal-culate the consequences of prodigious masses of artisans—and in times like these too—being sunk at once to the depths of pauperism ? Have they considered the necessity of guarding us, in case of the evil coming upon us in its most frightful form, against the rapacity of monopolists as respects food and fuel ? Have they begun to think of public stores of *bread* (in all pestilences the mortality is fiercest among bakers ?) Have they begun to make arrangements as to hospitals ? Have they warned our medi-cal officers, naval and military, that their services may be called for at a moment's notice ? Have they considered what ought to be done as to the supply of our markets—the supply of medicine and medical skill to a population dislocated in all its joints, and stricken in all its resources—the regulations as to travellers, inns, and public conveyances of all kinds ? Have they even dreamed of the enormous burden of care that may within a week devolve on them as a cabinet ?

The country has a right to expect much from the government, and we are sure the country will give every support to the govern-ment if they do their duty, and act and order with the energy and precision which the case demands. When we reflect on the good
sense,

sense, and the good feeling, the activity, and the liberality, which form the most valuable of the national resources, we are satisfied that if ultimate blame shall attach anywhere, it will not be either to English communities as communities, or to English families as families.

Let us suppose that the malady breaks out in an English town—for example, Hull. That town ought not to be taken unprepared : it should already have made its arrangements—for example : 1. A board of health should have been formed. 2. The town should have been divided into districts, and a district board established in each. 3. An efficient body of police should have been organized ; including magistrates, medical officers, attendants on the sick—commissaries—conveyers and buriers of the dead—all prepared to be separated from the community. 4. Contracts should have been entered into, insuring supplies of food, fuel, &c., in case of alarm deranging the operations of the adjoining districts, and the towns-people being exposed to the rapacity of monopolists, which would imply temptation to violence and outrage. 5. The householders should have calculated on a very great addition to the poor-rates. 6. Hospitals for cholera should have been made ready, and the strictest measures adopted for keeping the existing hospitals free from the disease. 7. Burial places should have been inclosed, and furnished with store of *lime.* 8. Every thing should have been done to ensure a lavish abundance of water everywhere, and there should be *depôts* of medicine (including wine and brandy), and of lime and chloride of lime, easily accessible, and in every district of the town.

In consequence of the absence of such preparations, the ravages of the cholera in the Prussian capital have been, and continue to be, frightful. It has now established itself in the neighbouring towns, and also (though the government would fain conceal this) in the numerous barracks and camps and *cordons sanitaires* around Berlin. Every hour brings the intelligence of some valuable life lost to that country—we are extremely sorry to say, that we have just received accounts of the death of that amiable and learned physician, Dr. Becker, part of whose letter to Dr. Somerville was quoted in a preceding page of this Number. At Hamburg, on the contrary, the alarm seems to have been taken in better time. A gentleman who has just performed his quarantine, describes that town as it was a month ago, before the pestilence broke out : ' Every shop was shut—every banking-house—the principal people meeting everywhere to adopt measures—the magistrates indefatigable.' And throughout the German towns generally, things are *now* in a state of preparation, which ought, without loss of time, to be as

far

far as is possible imitated here.   At Frankfort-on-the-Maine, for example (we speak on the authority of a friend of ours, that has just arrived from that city), the arrangements are complete.   The roads are patrolled and strict quarantine enforced.   Each street has had, for some weeks past, its cholera committee, consisting of two or three of the chief inhabitants.   These gentlemen visit every house daily, to see that rooms are white-washed, decayed fruit, vegetables, filth of every kind removed, and that at least one slipper-bath of tin is kept ready to be filled with hot water, under every roof. Soup kitchens have been prepared in every district.   Very large supplies of medicines, and of provisions of all sorts, have been laid up.   The medical professors have had their districts allotted to them.   Bands of trustworthy persons have been sworn in to act as attendants on the sick.   (At Berlin, the servants of families often ran off, and left their afflicted superiors utterly destitute.)   Extensive hospitals have been erected in the fields, about a quarter of a mile out of the town ; and, in a word, every precaution that two skilful physicians, who had been sent to Warsaw, could suggest, has been adopted under their immediate inspection.

In Catholic countries, the monastic buildings and religious persons have always been of the greatest service on occasions of this description ; we have no such resources, and should therefore attend the more closely to the example of Protestant communities such as Frankfort.   We believe the regulations of that town have been judged worthy of adoption by the government of Holland, and that arrangements similar to those above described are now in rapid progress throughout the various towns and villages of that well governed country.

Meantime such families as mean to quit, in case of pestilence, the town in which they reside, ought to hold themselves in readiness for immediate flight ; and the civil power should be prepared to take charge of the houses and property which they are to leave behind them.   The opulent must be content to pay dearly for such protection, but they have a right to expect it.

In such cases the excitement and alarm at the first outburst are so great, that, after a few days, people are apt to follow into the opposite extreme of indifference.   We get accustomed to anything ; and the progress of the mischief being probably slower than fancy had pictured, every hour the impression gets fainter.   It is now that the vigilance of the police is most called for.   The people must be saved in spite of themselves.   The obtuseness and rashness of the lower orders, on such occasions, are such as none but an eye-witness will believe.   At Vienna, the proportion of mortality among the very highest orders has been extraordinary, and is accounted

for

for solely by the vast troops of ignorant domestics which swarm about the palaces of the Austrian nobility. All vagabonds, beggars, and old-clothesmen must disappear. The least semblance of a crowd must not be tolerated; and all public conveyances must be *open ones.* The cholera took seventeen days to advance one hundred and fifty fathoms in the Mauritius. If due exertions be made, the malady may be arrested and suppressed at this early stage.

When the terror revives,—when the indifference consequent on the first paroxysm of alarm gives way before the knowledge that the disease is indeed creeping on from quarter to quarter, from street to street, the desire to quit the town becomes general, and a new mass of difficulties must be grappled with. The more that go the better; but none must go unless they have the means of conveyance, and know whither they are going, or without the license of the district board; and they that do go must submit to travel under regulations of the strictest kind.

The stagnation of trade becomes, of course, more and more oppressive as the pestilence advances; and they who deal in articles of luxury would do well to secure their goods in time, in some part of their own premises, and consign the key to the civil power. In case the disease should ultimately break out in the family, their property may thus escape the fumigation necessarily enforced as to all merchandize with which the infected *may* have been in contact,—and which must in most cases be attended with great damage, in many ruinous.

There should, if possible, be lazarettoes out of town, to which families might, if they pleased, remove,—care being taken that families of the same class, as to manners, be placed together, and that families thus secluded shall abstain from all intercourse with the city. They who have seen out a week or two of the pestilence in any one place should remember that the visitation generally terminates in six weeks or two months, and on no account think of removing. And when the disease is fast disappearing, persons who have been secluded, either in such asylums or in their own houses, must put great restraint on their feelings, and not go out too soon. Such, when the pestilence is believed to have at last ceased its ravages, such is the delirium of joy, and such the impatience of curiosity, that too much vigilance cannot be recommended to the police in the last hours of their labour. Thousands rush into danger in the search of friends,—in the eager yearning to ascertain what link of life has been spared to them.

Finally, a most painful and thorough examination and purification of all infected houses must be enforced on the disappearance of the pest. Owing to the neglect of this, the disease soon reappeared

peared in Moscow,—and that great city endured its miseries for five months in place of two.

Knowing, as we do, the kind-heartedness of the English nobility and gentry, we can have no doubt that families, not themselves possessed of country houses, would find hospitable gates thrown open to them far and near; while the commons in the vicinity of London, and the numerous parks and pleasure grounds, would of course be at the service of parties disposed to encamp, under proper regulations, and the surveillance of the health police of the next town. Our readers will do well to turn to Russell's Narrative of the Plague at Aleppo, for a lively description of the manner in which certain Frank families encamped at a distance from the infected city, the perfect success of their precautions, and the occupations with which they diverted the period of their seclusion.

We shall now submit a few notes, drawn up for a private family, whom we suppose to have determined to remain in London during the prevalence of the cholera. They are, we well know, far from complete, but they may be of service, if it were but in stimulating persons better qualified than ourselves, to consider the matter in its details, and lay their views before the public.

1. To the utmost practicable extent disfurnish the house, removing to an outhouse, or at least locking up in a separate room, all carpets and hangings whatever, and all needless articles of clothing.

2. Get rid of all superfluous domestics; and take care that it shall be impossible for those that are retained to communicate with any one out of doors.

3. Strip entirely of furniture, except bedsteads, &c., one or two rooms for the infirmary,—the nearer the door, the more distant from the apartments of the healthy, and the airier, of course the better. To these alone must the physician and the police inspector have access.

4. Be provided, if possible, with the means and materials for washing and even for baking in-doors; with hot or vapour baths; wines (the best of which seem to be port and sherry); brandy; opium, in its solid and liquid state; calomel; mustard and lintseed meal; æther; some of the essential oils, as cajeput, peppermint, or cloves; and a case of lancets.

5. All windows should be opened and every room thoroughly aired several times a-day. Our fire-places are admirably adapted for ventilating as well as heating apartments; and in their use we have a great advantage over the northern nations, whose stove system has contributed much to the ravages of this pestilence, enabling its virulence to withstand even a Russian winter.

winter. Chloride of lime should be used to sprinkle all floors occasionally, and a small vase containing it should be in the rooms principally inhabited. Sudden changes of temperature should be avoided : hot days succeeded by cold nights have been found powerfully to predispose to infection.

6. All letters and supplies of food must be received from the police messengers and purveyors, with the precautions adopted in lazarettoes. They must be drawn up to a window of the first floor, by means of a rope having a yard of chain and an iron pail attached to it. Whatever is not injured by wet should be then plunged into a metal or earthen vessel filled with a weak solution of chloride of lime, or vinegar and water. Bread, flour, and anything that would be injured by moisture, should be exposed to the heat of an oven before handling. Papers must be fumigated thoroughly with sulphur.

7. That regimen which the individual has found best suited to his constitution should be adhered to; those who have been used to an active life of course diminishing the quantum of their food in proportion as they are debarred from exercise.* It being universally admitted that whatever disorders the stomach and bowels predisposes to the cholera,—all unripe fruits, watery vegetables, as melons, cucumbers, &c., and all sharp liquors, as cyder, &c., must be avoided The use of the weak acid beer of the Prussians (the weiss-bier) has been found extremely injurious; and the sale, both of that sort of beer and cyder, has been entirely prohibited at Frankfort. Wine should be used, but in moderation. The system should neither be lowered by unwonted abstemiousness, nor excited by any violent stimulus.

8. It is needless to say, that personal cleanliness, at all times of great, is now of vital importance. We need not point out the usefulness of baths. The whole body should be rubbed daily with soap and water, and afterwards sponged with vinegar. The sympathy existing between the functions of the skin and those of the intestinal canal are most intimate. Linen, especially bed-linen, cannot be changed too often.

Those who are obliged to go abroad during the prevalence of a pestilence, ought to know that furs are, of all articles of clothing, the most likely to catch and retain morbific exhalations; that woollen stuffs are more likely to do so than cottons, and cottons than silks. The furs and flannel-bands of the Russians and Poles

---

* The diminution of bodily exercise, provided the air be pure, is found much less injurious than might be supposed. Women, who take very little exercise, live longer than men.

are

are particularly condemned by all the physicians who have watched the pestilence among them. The greatest care should be taken to avoid cold or wet feet—for diarrhœa is the worst of the predisponents.

As we are ignorant whether the pestilential matter enters the healthy body through the pores of the skin, the lungs, or the alimentary canal, prudence requires that we should act as if it may enter by all of them. In many parts of Europe the attendants on cholera patients, and those who come into contact with the dead, use garments pitched over, or made of oilskin; and in former times, when the plague was here, physicians were obliged to wear such dresses, both because their own lives· were considered as of the highest value, and that they might be at once distinguished in the streets. A false shame, or falser courage, might prevent many from spontaneously adopting such precautions, who would be happy to obey an official regulation enforcing them. The physician should carry a phial of chloride with him wherever he goes. His hands, after touching a patient, should be carefully washed with soap and water, and then sponged with the solution of chloride. The attendants on the plague wear a double handkerchief, steeped in vinegar, over the lower part of the face. The following pastile has been recommended :

> Dried chloride of lime, 12 grains,
> Sugar   .   .   .   .   1 ounce,
> Gum tragacanth   .   20 grains.

This, being flavoured with some essential oil, should be made into lozenges of 18 or 20 grains, and one of them held in the mouth during the visit.

In conclusion, we must entreat the public not to be swayed by the nonsense daily poured out in the newspapers, by persons the least entitled to be heard on this subject. Your merchant, whose traffic is likely to be interrupted, converts himself for the nonce into *Medicus, Senex, Detector,* &c. &c., and hazards assertions of the most unblushing audacity. In spite of the fearful ravages of this pest in all the islands of the Indian Ocean, we are told that England is safe—for cholera never crosses seas. Another assures us, that, at all events, a sea-voyage must prodigiously diminish its virulence ;—and yet it was after a voyage of three thousand miles—something more than the passage from Hamburg!— that it carried off, by thousands, the inhabitants of Mauritius. A third is ready with his assertion, that no medical man or attendant on the sick has died of the disorder ; and this, in the face of the Madras Report, which records the death of thirteen medical men in that presidency, and the illness of twenty more—of the St. Petersburg Reports, which show that every tenth medical

man

man in that capital was attacked, and that a very large proportion died; although we know, that of the small number of medical men at Cronstadt, four died ; that in Astracan *all* the nurses
and almost all the doctors were attacked ; and that in Vienna, out
of the first one hundred deaths in the whole of that great capital,
three were medical men.

Much is said, or whispered, as to the impolicy of exciting
fear. We suspect that the influence of this passion in predisposing the body to contagion, has been exaggerated; but if
that were otherwise, which would be likely to produce the
more injurious effects,—the fear that *may* be excited now, or
that which must be excited in case of the sudden apparition
of this pestilence in the very bosom of our families ? The system
of discountenancing fear has been tried abundantly. *Before* the
plague appeared at Marseilles, a wise man gave two pieces of
advice to the magistracy of that town.—' Consider every sudden
death as suspicious—Despise the squabbles of physicians.' The
magistrates despised his advice, and fifty thousand of the inhabitants perished before the doctors admitted that the disease was
contagious. At Messina the same course was followed. No
precaution was adopted. All at once the pest was found raging,
and the populace rose in the frenzy of wrath and despair, and
glutted themselves with murder.

As to individuals, in our humble opinion, the manly discipline
of mind for impending danger, is to contemplate its coming, cal-
culate its effects, and prepare ; and we warn our rulers that if they
neglect those preparations which they alone can make, the responsibility they incur is solemn. The question of contagiousness
or non-contagiousness, having in prudence established the quarantine, they may safely leave to the physicians : the fact of the mortality of cholera, when it once reaches any country, is that which
ought now to occupy their minds and direct their measures.
This pest destroys here a sixth, there a fourth, and in a third town
a half of the population. When such things *are* going on in a
great town, what business is it that must not stop ? What art can
hinder thousands from being plunged into absolute want ? or who
will pause to ask whether the poison hovers in the air, or is transmitted from person to person ? The instinct is to avoid the place
—and it is all but uncontrollable. Nothing will induce any man
to remain, who has it in his power to remove, except the knowledge that the government has done its duty—that all precautions
have been adopted, and all pre-arrangements made. The more
rigorous the laws, and the more strictly they are enforced, the more
certainly will the government be pronounced a merciful one, at
the time by the intelligent, in the sequel by all.

Art. IV.—1. *First Annual Report of the Registrar-General of Births, Deaths, and Marriages.* 1839.

2. *Statistical Report on the Sickness, Mortality, and Invaliding among the Troops in the West Indies.* Prepared from the Records of the Army Medical Department and War-Office Returns. 1838.

3. *Ditto, ditto, for the United Kingdom, the Mediterranean, and British America.* 1839.

4. *Ditto, ditto, for Western Africa, St. Helena, the Cape of Good Hope, and the Mauritius.* 1840.

PARADOXICAL as it may appear, it is certain that a man's health, nay life, is nearly as much in the keeping of those of whom he knows nothing as in his own. Of the three influences mainly acting on it—himself, society, and external nature—the first bears on it most intensely, the second most covertly, the last most constantly. Moral culture may teach the individual so to curb his passions and appetites as to develop all the forces of his organisation in their most healthful scope, or its neglect may set them loose as the deadliest instruments of self-destruction.

The

The social system acts upon us not only through its fashions and customs, but by the power of government; and an ill considered impost indirectly affecting the food, the habitation, or the clothing of the community, shall send more to their graves than ever fell by sword or spear.   Climate is always so greatly ameliorated by civilisation that we may safely say that it forms no exception to the general fact, that all the sources enumerated as influencing life are greatly modifiable, so that, though we may not believe with M. Quetelet in the perfectibility of our race, we may yet be sure that all its numerous ills may be immeasurably lessened.   Nothing is truer than that the mortality of a kingdom is the best gauge of its happiness and prosperity.   Show us a community wallowing in vice, whether from the pamperings of luxury or the recklessness of poverty, and we will show you that there truly the wages of sin are death.   Point out the government legislating only for a financial return, regardless or ignorant of the indirect effects of their enactments, and we shall see that the pieces of silver have been the price of blood.   It is only by such large surveys as are contained in the parliamentary documents now before us that the state of the public health can be ascertained.   And admirably do these Reports show it.   Many a peccant and cankrous sore, eating into the core of the body politic, is there laid bare ;   and many an evil which would have remained latent until it had gathered strength to sweep like a pestilence over our land, is here detected and exposed to those who have the power at least to prevent it.

The Military Reports are the most valuable gift, as to the effects of climate, which ever has been made to medicine, and reflect the highest credit not only on Major Tulloch, under whose especial auspices they are produced, and on his assistant, Dr. Balfour, but on those offices, whatever they are, in which such minute particulars have been so accurately kept, as to allow, at a moment's notice, the production of such a mass of valuable results as we now have.   Other nations may have possessed an extent of territory equal to that of the British empire, but ours is the first which has put forth for the benefit of mankind so noble a monument as this.   Besides arranging and collecting the enormous mass of materials implied in the returns of the British army for twenty years, Major Tulloch has added a series of observations on the influence of heat, electricity, soil, culture, moisture, in a word, on the circumstances determining climate in all parts of the globe, which are models of industry and research, and invaluable as records.

The Report of the Registrar-general is the first of an annual series exhibiting the social state of England; and let us frankly own,

own, that whatever may be the objections to certain parts of the registration bills, this, the registration of deaths, ought to be retained. Politics and party should not be allowed to interfere with public health—and public health is not ascertainable nor remediable unless such a search into all which affects it is presented to the nation. We understand that though the original bill required the registration of deaths, it did not require that the causes of death should be mentioned; and *this* has, we believe, been the sole work of the registrar-general. To him we are also indebted for a new weekly bill of mortality for the metropolis, which is in every respect immeasurably superior to the old one. In the detail he has been ably assisted by Mr. Wm. Farr. We remark that an earnest pledge to further Mr. Lister's object has been put forth by the Colleges of Physicians and Surgeons, and by the Society of Apothecaries, together with an injunction to all members of their respective bodies over England to do the like; and on the whole, we rejoice to find that all classes, lay and clerical, have promptly answered the demands of the registrar-general in matters in which all are alike interested. In the abstract of deaths Mr. Lister has entered into minute details, exhibiting enumerations of the deaths of persons of each sex at every successive year of age; thus collecting a large mass of accurate particulars, which will apply with greater certainty to the purposes of insurance than those we had hitherto possessed. The discrepancies existing among sets of tables, hitherto serving as data in the enormous money transactions connected with life insurance and annuities, are, as exhibited in a late Parliamentary return, and excerpted in the registrar-general's report, quite shameful. Of course the value of Mr. Lister's returns will increase annually; and a mean, derived from quinquennial or decennial observations, will probably leave nothing on this head to be desired.

In the present report Mr. Lister has divided England into twenty-five districts, ' for the purpose of comparing town with country, agricultural with mining and manufacturing districts, elevated with low situations, the maritime with the inland,'—with the view of furnishing better material for the use of benefit and friendly societies;—the actuary for the national debt having stated in 1833 that the difference of mortality in different districts was utterly unknown, and that tables for the use of the poorer classes, in reference to sickness and mortality, could not at that time be constructed for want of accurate information. Considering how extensive and how necessary these systems of mutual support among the poor are, we agree with Mr. Lister in the
principle

principle of a division of England into well-marked districts, having common properties. We, however, are advocates for a minuter division than that which he has adopted. What everybody wishes to know is the mortality of his own town or village, and this in the main would, in spite of its minuteness, lead to the most practical results. The mortality of places called low or hilly is very various, and we shall show that the influence of locality is minute, so that two spots contiguous to each other yield by no means a similar ratio. Thus the mortality of London is one thing, but the mortality of its various parishes another; some of them being twice, thrice, or even four times that of others. We therefore would recommend the exhibition of the mortality of the various counties, towns, and parishes, as they are laid down in the map, as the most useful for all purposes, even for those of subsequent generalisation, such as the registrar-general has now offered. The labour all this implies, and the voluminousness of the result, should be no drawbacks to the attempt; while the advantage attendant on the exhibition of the relative salubrity of places instead of districts would infallibly and rapidly lead to the endeavour of ameliorating the worser. It is nobody's business to attempt to alter the physical condition of a county, though many a squire and many a clergyman does that of his village and cure, and would do so with greater unity of purpose and effect were its ills clearly laid before him. Of course we would not carry this minuteness of subdivision beyond a certain point. In most instances those living in the same parish might be assumed to be under similar influences; it might be advisable, where the parish is very extensive and consisting of several separate masses of population, to take each separately. We venture merely to throw out these remarks, being convinced that if these twenty-five larger subdivisions of England be reproduced from year to year, it will be difficult to disentangle the efficient causes of evil from the mass which smothers them, and the great practical benefits of registration will be reduced to speculation. The stimulus to action given by Mr. Lister's first report has arisen more from his special deductions than from his larger generalisation: thus it is the difference of mortality among the different *parishes* of London which has called forth the energies of the Bishop of London to investigate the condition of the poorer classes of his diocese. One other remark too we would make, and it is that the very valuable tables put forth by the registrar-general should be accompanied by a more copious and detailed commentary. Mr. Lister cannot place too low the indolence and incapacity of all classes as to technical knowledge; and independent

of

of this excuse for neglecting what is intrinsically of exceeding value, every one is desirous of knowing what deductions the collector himself makes from his own records, and what improvements he would suggest. It is true that this is a duty which involves much tact and much moral courage ; for it will give a handle to cavil ; but by doing so it invites discussion and awakens the attention of society : we are certain, from the amount of industry and talent displayed in this first report, that Mr. Lister need not fear a dishonest opponent—and an honest one might act as an adviser.

Prefacing the subject with such general observations and re-sults as are suggested by the perusal of a valuable letter addressed by Mr. Farr to the registrar-general, we shall confine ourselves to the consideration of the mortality in large towns—especially in the metropolis.

148,701 cases of disease have been grouped into certain classes of malady readily recognisable. The number of males who died were 75,159 ; the females 73,542. The deaths by epidemic diseases, which in all countries are among the most numerous, amounted to 32,537 : males suffered rather more by these than fe-males—small-pox, croup, thrush, diarrhœa, dysentery, and cholera affecting the former most ; while influenza and hooping-cough cut off most of the latter—typhus, scarlatina, erysipelas, and measles affected both sexes equally. In 1000 of both sexes rather more than 4 died of epidemic maladies ; but 3 out of the 4 were children who perished of the various eruptive fevers. Small-pox destroyed 5811 ; measles, 4732 ; hooping-cough, 3044 ; and scarlatina, 2520. The reigning maladies were small-pox and typhus ; the enormous proportion of deaths in one-half year for the former malady is, we think, rightly attributable to the care-lessness about vaccination, which operation among the poor is always postponed, and sometimes *sine die.* Of diseases of the nervous system there were 21,852, or 15 per cent. of the whole registered. 3 in 1000 living perish annually of this class of mala-dies—more females suffering from them than males. Apo-plexies attack the male more frequently than the female. 27 per cent. of all deaths are caused by diseases of the respiratory system. And here these miserable maladies attack both sexes alike ; so that 5 out of 1000 living perish annually ; and of those 5, 4 are from consumption, though here females are rather more subject to it than males. 4 in 1000 births are fatal to the mothers.

The contrast between the mortality of town and country is very striking.

Mr. Farr has compared the mortality of about seven millions of of persons, one-half of whom are located in towns, the other half in counties. The concentration of the population in cities doubles the deaths from the epidemic diseases and those of the nervous system. In counties compared with cities the deaths by convulsion are as 1 to 3 nearly; so also deaths by water on the brain : acute diseases of the lungs are in counties as compared to cities as 1 to $2\frac{1}{2}$ nearly.

The deaths from consumption are increased 39 per cent.— those from childbirth 71 per cent.—those from typhus 221 per cent. in cities as compared with counties.

Why is it thus? Are cities then necessarily the graves of our race, as Süssmilch called them ; or can the condition of their inhabitants be ameliorated? Mr. Farr ascribes the mortality to the insalubrity of the air in populous towns. No doubt this is, if not the sole, still a very marked cause of the sad superiority of death in cities. But there is the moral cause, the temptation to vice and indulgence, which can never be so rife in rural as in urban districts, and its influence is quite as great as that of ill ventilated dwellings, and ill paved and sunless streets. ' There is no reason,' says Mr. Farr, ' why health should be impaired by residence in 1 more than in 100 square miles, if means can be devised for supplying the 200,000 individuals located in the former space daily with the requisite quantity of pure air nd for removing the principal sources of poisonous exhalations.'

What these are let the following facts, taken from the valuable pamphlet of the member for Shrewsbury,* a especially from Drs. S. Smith and Arnott's letter, addressed to the Poor Law Commissioners, attest.

In the last half-century the social condition of the working classes has undergone an immense change, which has not been sufficiently looked to by the legislature. In 1790, the workers in towns to the labourers in the country were as one to two. In 1840 it is just the reverse, the workers being to the labourers as two to one. The proportion of manufacturers, miners, and artisans to agricultural labourers is for Staffordshire, three to one; Warwickshire, four to one; West Riding of Yorkshire, six to one; Lancashire, ten to one; Middlesex, twelve to one. This influx has in many towns been very badly lodged; while the fluctuations of trade and manufactures have thrown thousands suddenly out of employ. It is among the lower classes, especially among the Irish who have emigrated into the heart of our largest towns, that fevers are the rifest and most fatal. Before touching on the fevers of our metropolis, let us look at

---

* State of the Poorer Classes in Great Towns. By R. A. Slaney, Esq., M.P.

the

the dwellings of the poor in the larger provincial towns. Of 11,000 houses at Nottingham, 8000 are built back to back—(*Journal of Statistical Soc.*, Jan. 1840), that is, they are devoid of ventilation. At Liverpool there are 7862 inhabited cellars, described as dark, damp, dirty, and ill ventilated; they lodge one-seventh of the whole population, of whom 39,300 are of the working classes. There are besides 2270 courts, in which from two to six families reside, and few of these courts have more than one outlet. What a miserable disregard does this show of all that should constitute a healthful abode!—the absence of pure air and sunshine, the constant presence of damp and contaminated vapours. In Manchester, of 123,232 workers, 14,960 live in cellars. At Bury, one-third of the working classes are so badly off, that in 773 houses, one bed served four persons; in 207, there was one bed for five; and in 78, one bed for six persons.

In Bristol, forty-six per cent. of the working classes have but one room for a family.

Leeds, which the registrar-general finds a most unhealthy place, of 17,800 houses, has 13,600 under 10*l.* In the north-east ward, containing 15,400 of the working classes, or about a fifth of the whole population, three streets have sewers; twelve have them partly; thirty-eight have none; and the state of forty is *unknown*.

The miseries of Glasgow,* as described by Dr. Cowan, are almost incredible in a country which is sending its gold and its missionaries to the millions who need them less than the amalgam of 30,000 Irish and Highlanders that wallow in filth, crime, and wretchedness in the cellars and wynds of this great commercial city. From ten to twenty persons of both sexes lie huddled together, amid their rags and filth, on the floor, each night. The cellars are beer and spirit-shops. Multitudes of the younger girls, says Mr. Symmonds, applied to Capt. Millar, the head of the Glasgow police, to rescue them from these scenes, to which they were driven by sheer want. A year or two served to harden and hurry them, from drunkenness, vice, and disease, to an early grave. Dr. Cowan, in his Vital Statistics, says,—'In 1837, 21,800 persons had fever in Glasgow.' In London, the mortality in some of the parishes is four times that of others. Poverty need not be so embittered. Want of food is not the sole cause, for the agricultural labourer works as hard, and is as ill fed. It is the

---

* We regret that the work of Dr. Alison, on the Poor of Scotland, had not reached us in time to use his facts on the present occasion. It is one of the most interesting volumes that we ever perused, worthy of a consummate physician, and kind and tender-hearted friend of the poor.

impurity

impurity of the dwelling, and the contamination which ensues where vice is allowed to herd with want, that fills our towns with misery and disease.

A few facts from the report of Drs. S. Smith and Kay, to the Poor Law Commissioners, will show how London is affected. A circular was addressed to the medical officers of the Metropolitan Unions, for the purpose of ascertaining the number of paupers attacked by the four kinds of fever known in this country : 1, as intermittent; 2, synochus, or the common continued fever ; 3, typhus ; 4, scarlatina.

It appears that the total number of persons in the metropolitan districts, who received in and out-door parochial relief during the year ending in March, 1838, was 77,186 ; and of this number, no less than 13,972 were subjects of this one disease, of fever, or nearly a fifth; of these, 7017 suffered from synochus, and 5692 from typhus.

The returns show that these fevers are most fatal where they are the most prevalent. Thus, of the 5692 cases of typhus, spread over the twenty unions, 4002 alone occurred in the seven following ; viz., Whitechapel, Lambeth. Stepney, St. George the Martyr, Bethnal Green, Holborn, and St. George-in the-East ; leaving only 1692 for the thirteen other unions. In Whitechapel, out of a pauper population of 5856, 2400, or one-half, were subjects of fever. But in St. George the Martyr, 1276 cases of fever occurred among 1467 paupers, leaving 191 only unattacked. The seven districts above named are the main sources and seats of the fevers of the metropolis, a fact long ago attested by the records of the Fever Hospital. They yielded no less than 9228 out of the total number of 13,972 fever cases.

In these seven districts the mortality was 1 in 3·8, while it was only 1 in 8·5 in the thirteen other districts. In the former, 1 in 44 of the pauper population was attacked, and only 1 in 93 of the latter.

The total population of the seven fever districts was 407,384, one out of every eleven being a pauper. The thirteen other districts comprised a population of 443,845, of which one in ten were paupers.

Taking all the cases of fever of every kind, one in every eleven attacked died.

More than one-fifth, then, of those who receive parochial relief in London are attacked by fever ; and, from the tabular view of the ages of those so suffering, it appears that its victims are precisely those on whom the welfare of others is most dependent, viz., the heads of families.

There

There are two ways in which the miseries of the poor are visited on the rich—on their persons, and on their purses. Once generated in a severe form among the hovels of the paupers, fever spreads to the best-housed and best-fed. ' The registers,' says Mr. Farr, ' show this; they trace diseases from unhealthy to healthy quarters, and follow them from the centres of cities to the surrounding villages and remote dwellings.' (p. 116.) On this score alone, if man will not be linked to man by sympathy of feeling, most assuredly he shall be by the bonds of suffering and disease. On the other hand, the rich will find it the best economy to alleviate the physical evils of the poor; for a little expended by way of prevention will materially diminish the poor rates, which,' say the commissioners, ' are invariably greatly increased by epidemic seasons. How, indeed, can it be otherwise, when the wife and the children become the widow and the orphans, or when the hand of the sick father can no longer earn the daily pittance for his family?'

We find the causes of these evils, and their remedies, ably discussed by the Poor Law commissioners and by the registrar-general. The most competent observers are agreed as to the magnitude of the evil, and the necessity of immediate measures of alleviation.

' The mortality of cities in England and Wales is high, but it may be immeasurably reduced.'—*Registrar Gen. Rep.*, p. 113.

' We have eagerly availed ourselves of the opportunity of making the present report, to submit to your Lordship the urgent necessity of applying to the legislature for immediate measures for the removal of these constantly acting causes of death and destitution. All delay must be attended with extensive misery; and we would urge the consideration of this fact, that in a large proportion of the cases, the labouring classes, though aware of the surrounding causes of evil, have few or no means of avoiding them.'—*Fourth Report of Poor Law Commissioners*, p. 7.

Let us add, neither have the rich; so troublesome and expensive are the processes, and so complicated are the laws, respecting ' nuisances' as the gloss is, that he must be a bold man who will venture to stir in the matter. We believe that laws sufficiently stringent, and perhaps sufficiently comprehensive, exist, but the power of executing them is confided to so many different instruments of authority, that, practically, they are either a dead letter, or quickened now and then by the caprice of a parish demagogue, so as to inflict a greater nuisance than the one which they were instituted to remove.

England is the only European country which is devoid of a medical

medical police, and in which the public health has been allowed
to shift for itself. The sources of our national health are not to
be traced to any constant supervision of Government, for it has
almost invariably at all times allowed evils to become intolerable
before they have been removed. It is to the absence of war from
our shores—but especially to the enormous wealth which has
permitted the population, as a whole, to be better fed, clothed,
and lodged than that of any other nation—that we owe this blessing. At the end of the seventeenth, and beginning of the
eighteenth centuries, when climate and many other physical circumstances were what they now are, the mortality was just double
that of this day. It diminished as the people prospered. When,
therefore, it is urged that the diminished mortality of England, as
compared with that of other nations, is a proof of the efficiency of
our public sanatory measures, we rejoin that this mode of viewing
the question is false. The question is not by what indirect means
we are bettered, but by what direct—have we taken advantage of
our means of alleviating the pressure on the public health in the
same degree as other nations have of theirs, or not?* Let the
following rapid survey of the causes ' of destitution and death'
furnish the reply:

There are two classes of causes to which the maladies of the
poor are referable,—

1. Those depending on their habits, and, 2. those independent
of these.

Among the latter are—1. bad sewerage, open stagnant drains,
ditches, and waters, in which animal and vegetable substances are
allowed to turn putrid; 2. undrained marsh-lands; 3. accumulations of filth in the streets; 4. the situation of slaughter-houses
in densely populated districts, and the bad regulation of these
establishments; 5. want of ventilation in narrow streets.

The bad drainage of districts is mentioned by the medical officers of the metropolitan unions as among the chief causes of fever.
Camberwell and parts of Lambeth are particularised. Mr. Wagstaffe seems to have called the attention of the commissioners to
the state of the sewerage of the latter district; and we can bear
ample testimony to the mesh-work of filthy open ditches and
ponds of water which are still left untouched.

* Property is more protected here than health. In Russia, France, and Germany,
a set of men are appointed to superintend the public health, and to report on all
those causes which influence it. All measures, therefore, of individuals, whether
dictated by avarice or a selfish scorn of the community, or by ignorance, must be
made compatible with the public safety. It is to these countries we owe the entire
body of the modern science of forensic medicine, not a work on this important subject
having originated here, although latterly we have followed in their track.

The

The difficulties of a remedy may be appreciated, when it is seen that the omnipotent Poor Law Commissioners are referred—and apparently referred in vain—from the commissioners of sewers to the surveyors of highways, and from these to the trustees acting under the Watching and Lighting Act. Whatever may be the willingness of any or all of these bodies, the chance of clashing renders any of them slow to move. In the interim death is doing double work.

Mr. Appleton says, ' that in the neighbourhood of an open sewer, a river of filth, formerly known as the Fleet-ditch, emptying itself near Blackfriars-bridge, fever is rarely absent.' According to Mr. Tensh, 'fifteen out of twenty-four cases of severe typhus occurred in one locality in the Hackney Union, near a pool of stagnant water, in which decayed animal matter was detained.' Mr. Caleb Radford finds that ' every part of his district is healthy but two, in which accumulations of filth are allowed to remain. In their vicinity were twenty cases of fever.' Mr. Bowling, of Hammersmith, says, ' that after an experience of thirty years, at certain seasons of the year fever prevailed to a great extent, attributable to miasma arising from the stagnant water in a brick-field.' 104 cases of fever occurred in one year, which Mr. Bowling attributes to causes which might be removed by efficient drainage. Mr. Little says, ' that fever is most prevalent where there is insufficient ventilation. In Johnson's Change, Rosemary-lane, Goodman's-fields, consisting of twenty houses, fever exists in almost every one.' Dr. John Lynch particularises West-street, John-court, and Field-lane, in the vicinity of Snow-hill, as abounding in poverty, filth, and disease. There is the Fleet-ditch, with a number of slaughter-houses, to generate and keep up fever, in a district ' which is never,' he says, ' wholly free from it.'

' In a field behind Euston-square,' says Dr. Arnott, ' a mass of filth, compounded of the meeting of several open sewers and the refuse of extensive cowsheds, used to overflow and stagnate. A school of 150 female children in its neighbourhood were affected in various years variously. In one year thirty were seized with spasm and convulsion of the limbs, similar to those produced by certain poisons; in another as many were attacked by typhus; on the following ophthalmia raged. These drains have since been covered, and all these diseases have disappeared.'—p. 13.

Another instance is given from the same authority :—

' In a mews behind Bedford-square a stable had been let to a butcher, and a heap of offal and dung had been formed at the door. During the time of removal, a coachman's wife and three children sat at an open window nearly over the place, until driven away by the insufferable stench.

stench. Two of the children died within thirty-six hours, and the mother and other child narrowly escaped.'—p. 13.

Particular attention should be paid to the state of the several mews in London. If not for the sake of the human being, the argument will have weight with those who value their horses. The stench from the yard of one of the great job-masters at the back of Charles-street and Lansdowne House is insufferable during summer, arising from a tardy and inopportune removal of the putrid straw which is so readily and necessarily accumulated where so large a number of animals are kept. With regard to the effluvia from slaughter-houses, an abbatoir is sadly wanted out of the metropolis. It is stated by Mr. Youatt, the very intelligent veterinary surgeon, that the annual value of the sheep, cattle, &c., at Smithfield, is five millions sterling: every year there are brought up 1,200,000 sheep, 150.000 beasts, 22,000 calves, 60,000 pigs, 12 to 15,000 horses. The conveyance of the refu ›
is very often very imperfect, even in meat-markets; while, where a butcher takes a private shop, the smaller cattle are usually killed in the basement-floor of a tenement having very inadequate conveniences for such a trade.

With regard to the second class of causes of disease, or such as arise from the habits of the poor, they are perhaps more intense than the first: poverty and destitution bring in their train recklessness, filth, and misery—beyond what is imagined by the rich. We have seen in one small garret, the husband ill of typhus, a child laid across the sick man's bed, also ill; two others sleeping under the bed: the two window recesses let to two Irish lodgers at sixpence a-week, as resting-places for the night; the wife, a young healthy woman, lying in the same bed with her sick husband at night, and supporting the family by taking in washing, which was hung across the room to dry—the parish authorities forbidding the exposition of linen out of the windows.

One of the most urgent of this class of causes is ' the state of the lodging-houses of mendicants and vagrants, and of a certain class of the more needy Irish poor.'

Mr. Robert Hatfull, the medical officer for the Deptford district, quotes Mill-lane as having several lodging-houses, in which thirty or forty people are lodged for the night, ' itinerants of the lowest description,' ' clean or dirty,' ' sick or healthy :' ' eighty-two cases,' he adds, ' required my attention in one year.' It appears that the existing laws will not reach the lodging keepers, who defy the parish authorities.

Mr. Robert Moger, of the Highgate district of Hornsey, quotes one house, which not even the fine air of that place can purify. ' It is a lodging-house, which is inhabited by a great number of the

the lowest and most abandoned persons, chiefly Irish beggars. These people sleep three or more in a bed, which appears never to be changed or cleaned. Within the last year eleven cases of severe disease occurred in this house, and five died.'

Mr. Evans, of Blackman-street, Borough, has attended 500 pauper fever cases in nine months, attributable to intemperance, filth, and inefficient ventilation.

Mr. Byles, of Whitechapel, says that Essex-street and its numerous courts ' have been the general and almost constant abodes of fevers for years past.' One house, 6, Little Pearl-street, is an especial nuisance ; it is inhabited by twelve or four-teen families, and has scarcely been free from fever cases for many years past. As soon as the patient dies or is removed, the room is immediately let to new tenants. The drainage in the neighbourhood is very defective. Mr. Byles saw 600 cases of fever in one year out of the workhouses. His letter points out many valuable sanatory precautions.

Mr. Farr says that the poor Irish are keeping up, if not in-troducing, fevers into the heart of British cities. (*Vital Statistics,* p. 528.) The three ports by which they enter this island are Bristol, Liverpool, and Glasgow. We find that more than one-third of the cases treated at the Glasgow Infirmary are fever cases. It is known that more than one-sixth of the population of Glasgow are Irish. Dr. Symmonds, of Bristol, mentions that thirty Irish slept in a room 20 feet by 16 feet ; that cholera was ' hovering over us ;' seven became corpses in a few hours.

We observe that Liverpool exhibits the highest mortality in the class of contagious diseases and in typhus, and the lowest chance of attaining old age in all England, according to the Registrar-General's report. Whether the unfortunate victims are Irish, Scotch, or English, the circumstances inducing such poverty and its attendant evils are in fault : what are the remedies? Drs. Kay and Arnott give the following directions upon this im-portant subject, and we would press them as strongly as possible on the public attention :—

' The means of removing completely the noxious animal and vege-table matters brought to or produced in cities evidently are :—

' 1. A perfect system of sufficiently sloping drains or sewers, by which, from every house and street, all fluid refuse shall quickly depart by the action of gravitation alone ; the streets, alleys, courts, &c., being moreover well paved, so that the refuse may be easily distinguished and detached.

' 2. A plentiful supply of water to dilute and carry off all such refuse, and to allow of sufficient washing of streets, houses, clothes, and persons.

' 3. An effective service of scavengers to remove regularly the rubbish and

and impurities which water cannot carry away, and fit receptacles for such matters until removed.

' 4. Free ventilation by wide streets, open alleys, and well-constructed houses, to dilute and carry away all hurtful aëriform matters.

' 5. Keeping as distant as possible from the people the practice of all the arts and processes capable of producing malaria or tainting the air. Hence the situation of cattle-markets, slaughter-houses, cow-houses, tripe-shops, gas-factories, burying-grounds, and the like, should be determined by competent authorities.

' 6. Preventing the great crowding of the lodging-houses of the poor.'

With regard to the first and third, the benefit would be incalculable to Bethnal-green, Whitechapel, Lambeth, and the poorer parts of Westminster. In the two last-named districts open sewers and filthy stagnant waters abound: Bethnal-green is a swamp, says one of the reporters, hardly any part of which is drained; in rainy weather entire streets are under water. There is abundant evidence in these reports to show that, where these conditions exist, fevers arise, and when they are removed, fevers cease.

With regard to free ventilation, the Registrar-General's report is emphatic. There is no doubt that ample ventilation would dilute and remove the noxious influences of crowded cities. To attain this the Building Act should be amended, so as to have some reference to public as well as to individual profit—to prevent any one running up as many houses in any swamp as may answer his views of speculation.

Of late, great improvements have been introduced into the metropolis, in widening the streets and in making a better kind of building; but the direct advantage is to the rich, little or nothing has been done for the industrious poor; they must reside near where they can get employment; and the speculator, aware of this, cares little what the kind of house is which he offers as a habitation; what they are is known only to the parish officer, the conscientious clergyman, and the medical attendant, who, as these reports testify, have often fallen victims to the discharge of their duties.

'By no prudence or forethought,' says Dr. Southwood Smith, ' can the poor avoid the dreadful evils to which they are exposed : no returns can show the amount of suffering they have had to endure from causes of this kind during the last year.' Some approximation may be made, however, by the result that one-fifth of the pauper population were attacked by fever, or 14,000 out of 77,000. From this immense nucleus of disease and destitution the rest of the metropolis became infected, and fever spread from the hovel to the mansion. The year 1838 was a fever year ;
and

and the truth of these remarks was fatally attested by the crowded state of the only hospital in London which admits fever. A cry was raised for additional receptacles for the poor, and subscriptions entered into for the purpose. In workhouses and in the general hospitals, the malady broke out, and swept off, in not a few instances, patients, nurses, and practitioners. No wonder then that the Poor-Law Commissioners recommend fever houses to be attached to each parish so as to separate him who has the ills of poverty alone from him to whom is added the pressure of disease. The statistician, curious in death, notes that every ten minutes some one of the inhabitants of this huge metropolis dies. If the passing bell be heard for those whom neither rank, nor wealth, nor precious affections and sympathies can save from the strong clutch of the poor man's malady—if the manly strength of the father or the gentler virtues of the young mother have alike succumbed to the force of that disease which hurries them in a few short days from scenes of which they were the very life,—the best monument they can raise to their dead is to shield from these afflictions those who cannot shield themselves.

These remarks derive importance from the kind of habitations with which the new and aristocratic parts of the town are fringed. 'Many of these,' as Drs. Arnott and Kay remark, 'exhibit so complete a neglect of the most common precautions as can only be accounted for by the fact of the rapid increase of population, allowing the owners of such property to command tenants notwithstanding the absolute defect of sewerage and other arrangements necessary to ensure health.'

Not only should the poorer quarters of the town be opened up by large spaces, by the removal of closes and yards, but by a better system of ventilation in these houses. It may be regarded as certain, that whether the street be wide or narrow, the poor will congregate in denser masses than the rich. The chief element of thorough ventilation among the latter is the chimney fire; which renews the air of the rooms and house incessantly and rapidly. But this is precisely what the poor cannot command: the houses destined for this class should therefore be constructed with a more pronounced reference to ventilation than those of the other classes, equal to that employed in hospitals, workhouses, and in general in receptacles where many must be congregated in a small space.

How this suggestion is to be enforced, and how the minute directions of the Commissioners are to be complied with as regards compulsory measures in building, as to limiting the number of lodgers, as to the cleanliness to be enforced in the interior of houses, and as to similar matters, we do not pretend to decide.

The

The ignorance of some, the cupidity of others, the recklessness of misery, or the listlessness of despair, will second the feeling that the Englishman's home is not to be interfered with by any system of police : however there is the evil ably exposed, and there are the remedies suggested by those who have investigated it.

Let it be remembered, however, society has already done much to improve the health of our metropolis. It is, after all, the healthiest of the great capitals of Europe. The pure climate of Naples has little power over the filth, the misery, and vice of a population in which the annual mortality is 1 in 28, while with us 1 in 44 only dies in the year—in Vienna 1 in 22 ; in Paris 1 in 36; in Brussels 1 in 29; in Geneva 1 in 43; in Rome 1 in 24 ; in Madrid 1 in 35; in Amsterdam 1 in 25. As compared with these then, our land and our city are blessed ; but not with these must the comparison be made, but with ourselves, and we shall find that the great inequalities of health between the richer and poor sections of our population may be equalised by means which are within the grasp of a cautious legislation.

Art. VII.— *Report to Her Majesty's Principal Secretary of State for the Home Department, from the Poor Law Commissioners, on an Inquiry into the Sanitary Condition of the Labouring Population of Great Britain ; with Appendices.* Presented to both Houses of Parliament, by command of Her Majesty, July, 1842. 3 volumes, folio.

IN the winter of 1837 fever was unusually severe in Spitalfields, and alarm being thereby excited of a return of the cholera, the Poor Law Commissioners deemed it their duty to send thither Dr. Arnott, Dr. S. Smith, and Dr. Kay, to inquire as to the *removable causes of disease.* These accomplished physicians in their report, dated May 12, 1838, declared the chief causes to be bad drainage and bad ventilation. The Commissioners, without loss of time, represented to Lord John Russell ' the urgent necessity of applying to the legislature for immediate measures for the removal of those constantly acting causes of destitution and death. *All delays,*' said they, ' *must be attended with extensive misery ; in a large proportion of cases the labouring classes, though aware of the surrounding causes of evil, have few or no means of avoiding them, and little or no choice of their dwellings.*' But although much was said and done for the Hill Coolies and the blacks, no notice whatever was taken of this appeal ; until, towards the end of the session of 1839, our energetic diocesan the Bishop of London, in his place in the House of Lords, called the attention of the Government to the Report, and moved an address to Her Majesty, praying for an inquiry as to the extent to which the causes of disease—stated by the Poor Law Commissioners to prevail among the labouring classes of the metropolis—prevail also amongst the labouring classes in other parts of the kingdom. This address being carried, Lord John Russell directed the Poor Law Board to institute such an inquiry, and the Commissioners, in the month of November following, gave instructions accordingly to their Assistants. They likewise addressed letters to the several boards of guardians, as well as to their medical officers, requesting them severally to furnish answers to questions inclosed : besides which a circular letter to the dispensary-surgeons and medical practitioners, having been inclosed to the provosts of Scotch burghs, a resolution was passed by the College of Surgeons of Edinburgh, recommending that all members and licentiates of that body should give every aid to this inquiry. In due time, from a number of medical men, residing in different towns and districts of Scotland, as well as of England, very valuable reports were obtained.

As soon as this mass of MS. was collected in Somerset House, its bulk being evidently more than the Commissioners or Parliament could find leisure to examine, the Secretary of the Board was directed to digest it in detail, and, comparing its various statements with such authentic facts as he might obtain from other sources, to frame a report exhibiting the principal results of the whole investigation. From his own various and extensive personal inspections, from the information which had been forwarded to the Commissioners, from the documents of the medical officers, and from his examination of witnesses, Mr. Chadwick, after nearly two years' labour, succeeded in completing the remarkable Report now before us.

Before, however, we enter upon the first important chapter, we cannot refrain from observing how little the subject to which it particularly relates—namely, the purification by science of the air we breathe—has hitherto been deemed worthy of consideration.

It is true that through our main thoroughfares, such as Oxford Street, Holborn, Piccadilly, the Strand, Pall Mall, and St. James's Street, the atmosphere is enabled to flow with healthful celerity; but to most of these ethereal rivers are there not linked on either side, in the forms of courts, alleys, stable-yards, and culs-de-sac, a set of vile, stagnant ponds in which the heaven-born element remains ' in durance vile,' until, saturated with the impurities and sickness of its gaol, it flows into, mixes with, and pollutes the main streams we have described? And yet if the pavement of St. James's Street be but cleanly swept, those who saunter up and down it, as well as those who in red coats or brown ones sit indolently gazing at carriages (many of which, as they roll by, seem mechanically to make their heads nod) appear not to be aware that they are one and all inhaling stale, pent-up, corrupt air, which an ounce of science could have dispersed by circulation. Even the hollow square of the royal palace is made to retain its block of the stagnant fluid, while several others of our public buildings, like the office at the bottom of Downing Street, and like the numerous high ' dead ' walls inclosing property of the crown, &c., seem to have been purposely planned to act as tourniquets upon those veins and arteries which, if unobstructed, would give health and ruddiness to the population. Instead, however, of philosophizing any longer in the streets, we will invite our readers to enter with us for a moment into one of the splendid mansions of our metropolis; and, accordingly, ascending its spacious staircase, let us take up our position just in the doorway of the second of the suite of drawing-rooms, beyond which, the assemblage, being under high pressure, makes it evidently impossible for us to advance.

We here see before us, in a dense phalanx, figures of both

sexes,

sexes, amongst whom stand conspicuous persons of the highest rank, beauty, and wealth in Europe. Upon their education no expense has been spared—money has done all in its power to add to nature's choicest gifts the polish of art. Their dresses are importations from every country of the civilized world. The refreshments are delicacies which it has required months, and in some cases even years, of unremitting attention to obtain. The splendid furniture has every comfort that ingenuity can devise. And yet within this painted sepulchre, what, we ask, is the analysis of the air we are breathing? That lofty duchess's head is sparkling with diamonds—that slight, lovely being leaning on her arm has the pearls of India wound around her brow — those statesmen and warriors are decorated with stars—the dense mass displays flowers, ribands, and ornaments of every colour in the rainbow; but among them all, is there, we ask, a single one who for a moment has thought of bringing with him the hogshead of air per hour necessary for his respiration? And if every guest present has neglected to do so, in what manner, it must be inquired, has the noble host provided for the demand? Alas! the massive, pictured walls around us, and richly-stuccoed and gilt ceiling over our heads, answer the question, and one has only to cast a glance at them to perceive that the 500 persons present are, like those in the Black-hole at Calcutta, conglomerated together in a hermetically-sealed box full of vitiated air.

Every minute 500 gallons of air pass into the lungs of those present, from whence, divested of its oxygen, it is exhaled in a morbid condition unfit for combustion or animal life—every respiration of each elegant guest, nay, even our own contemplative sigh, vitiates about sixteen cubic inches of the element; and yet, while every moment it is becoming more and more destructive to health—while the loveliest cheeks are gradually fading before us —while the constitutions of the young are evidently receiving an injury which not the wealth of Crœsus will be able to repay —what arrangements, we repeat, has the noble host made for repairing the damage he is creating? If foul air, like manure, could be carted away, and if good air, like fresh, clean straw, could be brought in its stead, surely one of the simplest luxuries which wealth could offer to society would be to effect this sanitary operation; and thus, instead of offering a set of lovely women ices and unwholesome refreshments, to spend the money these would cost in pouring upon their heads, necks, and shoulders a continual supply of that pure, fresh, exhilarating, oxygenous mixture which gives animation to their hearts, and colour to their cheeks. But is this expensive, troublesome, complicated, horse-and-cart mode of purifying the horrid atmosphere we are breathing necessary? No!

No! everybody present knows that outside the shutters and plate-glass windows of the rooms in which we are suffering, there is at this moment in waiting, not two inches from us, an overwhelming supply (which might be warmed) of pure air, just as desirous to rush in as the foul air we have been breathing and re-breathing is eager to rush out.

The laws of specific gravity ordained by nature are in attendance to ensure for us the performance of this double process—indeed so great is the supply of spare air in her laboratory, that the proportion of oxygen consumed by animated beings in a century is said not to exceed $\frac{1}{73886}$ of the whole atmosphere ; and yet, as though the demon of suicide had prevailed upon us to thwart these beneficent arrangements, we close our doors, bar our windows, stuff up by curtains and drapery every crevice, as if it were the particular privilege of wealth to feed its guests on foul air!

If any one of our readers who, like ourselves, may have grown out of patience at the long continuance of this barbarous custom, will take the trouble to put 500 beautiful little gold and silver fishes into a bladder of the filthiest water he can obtain, and then attaching a weight, throw the whole into a clear, crystal stream, he may justly say—aye, and he may grin as he says it—‘ *Behold an epitome of a London drawing-room!* ’ There is, to be sure, one difference :—the tiny creatures within the globule are as innocent of the foul suffering *they* endure as are those poor, lean, Neapolitan curs which almost every day throughout the year may be seen half choked by the rope that is dragging them reluctantly towards the Grotto del Cane, in order that one more inquisitive, good-humoured, ruddy-faced English family may see them forcibly suffocated in unwholesome gas.

In case, from the foregoing observations, it should become apparent that even among people of the highest rank, intelligence, and wealth, there has hitherto existed a lamentable neglect on a subject of such importance to them as the sanitary purification of the atmosphere in which they are living, it is reasonable to infer that if any one among us would make it his painful duty to penetrate into the courts, alleys, workshops, and residences of the lowest, of the most ignorant, and of the most destitute classes of our society, he would most surely detect a still greater disregard of scientific precautions, directly and flagrantly productive of misery and disease.

If, therefore, there was nothing at stake but the health, happiness, moral conduct, and condition of the labouring classes, the searching investigation unveiled in Mr. Chadwick's Report, coupled with the remedial measures submitted by him for con-
                                                                        sideration,

sideration, ought to win as well as claim our most serious attention ; but when we reflect that the air the labouring classes breathe
—the atmosphere which by nuisances they contaminate—is the
fluid in which rich and poor are equally immersed—that it is a commonwealth in which all are born, live, and die equal—it is undeniable that a sanitary inquiry into the condition, for instance,
of the ten thousand alleys, lanes, courts, &c., which London is
said to contain, becomes a subject in which every member of the
community is self-interested. Where nearly two millions of people
are existing together in one town, it is frightful to consider what
must be the result in disease, if every member should, even to a
small amount, be neglectful of cleanly habits. It is frightful also to
contemplate what injury we may receive not only from the living,
but from the 50,000 corpses which are annually interred in our
metropolis : indeed, no man who will visit our London churchyards can gaze for a moment at the black, cohesive soil, saturated
with putrid animal matter, which is daily to be seen turned up
for the faithless reception of new tenants, without feeling that the
purification of our great cities, and a watchful search throughout
the land we live in for every removable cause of disease, are
services which science should be proud to perform, which a
parental government should strenuously encourage, and which
parliament should deem its bounden duty to enforce.

If foul air and pure air were of different colours, we should very
soon learn to repel the one and invite the other, in which case
every house would be ventilated, and air-pipes, like gas-pipes and
water-pipes, would flow around us in all directions. Although,
however, we do not often see miasma, yet in travelling over the
surface of the globe, how evident are its baneful effects, and how
singularly identical are they with those patches of disease which
are to be met with, more or less, in every district in this country !
Let any one, after traversing the great oceans, contrast their
healthful climate with the low, swampy parts of India, with
the putrid woods of the Shangallah in Abyssinia, or with any part
of the western coast of Africa. In all these regions miasma
is either constantly or periodically generated by the corruption of
vegetable matter ; and the following description of the effects of
this virus on the white population of Sierra Leone is more or less
equally applicable to all :—

' Those who are not absolutely ill are always ailing; in fact, all the
white people seem to belong to a population of invalids. The sallow-
ness of their complexion, the listlessness of their looks, the attenuation
of their limbs, the instability of gait, and the feebleness of the whole
frame, that are so observable in this climate, are but too evident signs,
even where organic disease has not yet set in, that the disordered state
of

of the functions which goes under the name of impaired health exists, and in none is it more painfully evident than in the general appearance of the European women and children of this colony.' *

In corroboration of this statement, we may mention as a single example, that, out of 150 men of the 2nd West India regiment who in 1824 were sent to Cape Coast Castle, all, excepting one, were either dead or sent home invalided in three months. At the expiration of this time, Sir John Phillimore, arriving off the coast in command of the Thetis, sent on shore two midshipmen and fourteen men, to mount a gun on a height. The party slept there only a night, yet, in one fortnight, every individual excepting a black man was dead !

In the opposite continent of America, even in healthy parts, wherever the land has been wilfully flooded for the purpose of canal navigation, the trees all die, and as the passenger-barge winds its way by moonlight through these pale, barkless corpses, a green coating of vegetable matter, about as thick as a blanket, and very appropriately called by the inhabitants '*fever and ague*,' is seen writhing in folds before the prow.

Even in the most salubrious of the new settlements, where the air is dry, exhilarating, and the sky as blue as in Italy, the moment the virgin earth is turned up for the first time, the decomposition of vegetable matter brought to the surface invariably produces sickness ; and thus a whole family of little English children, with their teeth chattering from ague, have too often been found mourning in the wilderness, on an oasis, 'the garden and the grave' of their father who made it.

In like manner, in this country, it has been shown by abundant evidence that on whatever patches of land, especially in towns, vegetable or animal matter is allowed to putrify, *there* disease, more or less virulent, is engendered : indeed it has been repeatedly observed that the family of a particular house has continued for years to be constantly afflicted with the very languor and fever described by every African traveller, which at last has been ascertained to have been caused by the introduction into the immediate neighbourhood of a couple of square feet of Sierra Leone, or, in plainer terms, by a grated untrapped gulley-drain, from which there has been constantly arising a putrid gas ; and yet, instead of a few square feet, how many acres of Sierra Leone are, to our shame, existing at this moment in our metropolis in the shape of churchyards ! There is one burial-ground, now or very lately in use in London, which contains, under one acre of surface, 60,000 corpses ! There is in London a place where a crowd of young

---

* *Vide* Appendix to Report from the Select Committee on West Coast of Africa, ordered by the House of Commons to be printed, 5th August, 1842, p. 244.

children

children learn their lessons for six hours daily over a floor under which 12,000 dead bodies are festering ! *

Mr. Chadwick produces a tabular account of the mortality of England and Wales within the year 1838, caused by diseases which, he says, medical officers consider to be most powerfully influenced by the physical circumstances under which the population is placed; namely, the external and internal condition of their dwellings, drainage, and ventilation. It appears that the number of deaths in this category amounted to 56,461 : which Mr. Chadwick observes to be as if Westmoreland or Huntingdonshire were every year to be entirely depopulated. He adds :—

'that the annual slaughter in England and Wales from preventable causes of typhus, which attacks persons in the vigour of life, appears to be double the amount of what was suffered by the allied armies in the battle of Waterloo ;....that diseases which now prevail on land did, within the experience of persons still living, formerly prevail to a certain extent at sea, and have since been prevented by sanitary regulations; and that when they did so prevail in ships of war, the deaths from them were more than double in amount of the deaths in battle.'

But whatever may be the precise number per annum of our labouring population that actually *die* from diseases which are preventable, it is evident that it bears but a small proportion to the number of those who—although they have, as it is commonly termed, 'escaped from the attack'—have been subjected for a melancholy period to loss of labour from debility.

Mr. Chadwick, having endeavoured to define in general terms the aggregate extent and operation of the evils complained of, proceeds to consider them separately in detail. We cannot say that he shows much skill in the grouping and arranging of his facts and views : but in a work so meritorious, it would be hard to dwell upon minor defects; and our readers will not quarrel with us for taking the chapters as they stand.

I. *General condition of the residences of the labouring classes where disease is found to be the most prevalent.*

Here are detailed the varied forms in which disease, *attendant on removable circumstances,* has been found to pervade the population of rural villages and small towns, as well as of those commercial cities and densely-crowded manufacturing suburbs, in which pestilence has been supposed to have its chief and almost exclusive residence.

For instance—to begin with one of the prettiest towns in one of the most charming parts of England—Mr. Gilbert reports that, his attention having been excited by the high diet recommended to

---

* See Evidence taken before the Committee of the House of Commons on the Improvement of Towns, &c.—printed in 1842.

the

the guardians at *Tiverton,* in consequence of prevalent fever, he requested the medical officer of the union to accompany him through a certain district there. Even before reaching this locality, he was assailed by a small clearly proclaiming the presence of malaria: he found the ground marshy, the sewers all open, some of the houses surrounded by wide uncovered drains full of animal and vegetable refuse. The inhabitants were distinguishable from those of the other parts of the town by their sickly, miserable appearance: all he talked to either were or had been ill, and the whole community presented a melancholy picture. The local authorities had often endeavoured to compel the inhabitants to remove the nuisances and to cover the drains, but finding that, under the present state of the law, their powers were not sufficient, the evil had continued : medical officers were employed instead of the engineer; and, accordingly, ' comforts ' and ' high diet ' had been prescribed, instead of masonry and drainage.

Impressed with the fact, that, as there are specks in the sun, so in a large country like England there must unavoidably exist dirty places, which Mr. Chadwick or any searching inquisitor has the power, at his pleasure, to point out, we read with considerable caution a series of reports such as we have just quoted. We own, however, we were not a little startled at learning that royalty itself—but lately prevented from visiting Holyrood, or Brighton, on account of fever proceeding from miasma — has loathsome nuisances dangerous to the public health in its immediate neighbourhood even at Windsor !

Mr. Parker, after stating that there is no town in the counties of Buckingham, Oxford, and Berks in which the condition of the courts and back streets might not be materially improved by drainage, observes,—

' Windsor, from the contiguity of the palace, the wealth of the inhabitants, and the situation, might have been expected to be superior in this respect to any other provincial town. Of all the towns visited by me, Windsor is the worst beyond all comparison. From the gasworks at the end of George-street a double line of open, deep, black, and stagnant ditches extends to Clewer-lane. From these ditches an intolerable stench is perpetually rising, and produces fever of a severe character. Mr. Bailey, the relieving officer, considers the neighbourhood of Garden-court in almost the same condition. "There is a drain," he says, "running from the barracks into the Thames across the Long Walk. That drain is almost as offensive as the black ditches extending to Clewer-lane. The openings to the sewers in Windsor are exceedingly offensive in hot weather. The town is not well supplied with water, and the drainage is very defective." '

As snipes and wild fowl when they visit this country at once fly to our marshes and fens, so is it natural to suppose that the

cholera

cholera would, of its own accord, wherever it travelled, select for itself lodgings most congenial to its nature. The following glimpse of one of the places in which the disease first made its appearance deserves therefore attention. Mr. Atkinson, describing Gateshead, says of a person whom he found ill of the cholera—

' His lodgings were in a room of a miserable house situated in the very filthiest part of Pipewellgate, divided into six apartments, and occupied by different families, to the number of twenty-six persons in all. The room contained three wretched beds, with two persons sleeping in each : it measured about twelve feet in length and seven in breadth, and its greatest height would not admit of a person's standing erect : it received light from a small window, the sash of which was fixed. Two of the number lay ill of the cholera, and the rest appeared afraid of the admission of pure air, having carefully closed up the broken panes with plugs of old linen.'

Mr. Chadwick, however, states that the most wretched of the stationary population of which he had been able to obtain any account, or that he had ever beheld, was that in the wynds of Edinburgh and Glasgow. ' It might admit of dispute,' he observes, ' but on the whole, it appeared to us that both the structural arrangements and the condition of the population in Glasgow were the worst of any we had seen in any part of Great Britain.' Dr. Arnott, who perambulated the wynds of Glasgow, accompanied by Dr. Alison and Dr. Cowen, corroborates the above statement by details too offensive to be transcribed : suffice it to say that from one locality 754, of about 5000 cases of fever which occurred in the previous year, were carried to the hospitals. As a striking contrast to this result, Mr. Chadwick states that, when the kelp manufacture lately ceased on the western coast of Scotland, a vast population of the lowest class of people were thrown into extreme want—they suffered from cold, hunger, and despair—nevertheless, from their scattered habitations being surrounded by pure air, cases of fever did not arise among them.

We will conclude this branch of the investigation by a description of Inverness, copied from no less an authority than the report of its worthy chief magistrate.—' Inverness,' says the Provost, ' is a *nice* town, situated in a most beautiful country. . . . . . The people are, generally speaking, a *nice* people, but their sufferance of *nastiness* is past endurance.'

II. *Public arrangements external to the residences by which the sanitary condition of the labouring population is affected.*

This chapter Mr. Chadwick principally devotes to practical details as to drainage. But we must content ourselves with a few more specimens of his observed facts.

Dr.

Dr. Duncan doubts whether there is a single court in Liverpool which communicates with the street by an underground drain: having observed that sixty-three cases of fever had occurred in one year in Union Court, containing twelve houses, he visited it, and found the whole court inundated with fluid filth which had oozed through the walls from two adjacent cesspools. In one cellar, a well four feet deep, into which this stinking fluid was allowed to drain, was discovered below the bed where the *family* slept. It may be observed that there are 8000 inhabited cellars in Liverpool, containing from 35,000 to 40,000 inmates; and that of 2398 courts which were examined, 1705 were closed at one end so as to prevent ventilation.

' Until very lately,' says Mr. Burton, in his report on ' Edina, Scotia's darling seat,'

' the Cowgate, a long street running along the lowest level of a narrow valley, had only surface drains. The various alleys from the High Street and other elevated ground open into this street. In rainy weather they carried with them each its respective stream of filth, and thus the Cowgate bore the aspect of a gigantic sewer receiving its tributary drains. A committee of private gentlemen had the merit of making a spacious sewer 830 yards long in this street at a cost of 2000*l.*, collected by subscription. The utmost extent to which they received assistance from the police consisted in being vested with the authority of the Act as a protection from the interruption of private parties. During the operation they were nevertheless harassed by claims of damage for obstructing the causeway, and their minutes show that they experienced a series of interruptions from the neighbouring occupants, likely to discourage others from following their example.'

In a medical report on romantic Stirling, it is stated that the drains or sewers, *Scottice* 'sivers,' are all open; a few old men sweep the public streets from time to time, but sometimes the sweepings remain on the pavement many days; the refuse from the gaol, which contains on an average sixty-five persons, is floated down the 'sivers' every second or third day, emitting, during the whole of its progress, the most offensive odour; the slaughter-house being situated near the top of the town, the blood from it is also allowed to flow down the main street; and the sewers from the castle issue into an open field, polluting the atmosphere to a dreadful degree.

As a contrast to this wholesale account, the examination of Mr. T. Thomson, of Clitheroe, affords a striking proof how small, even in solitary houses, may exist the removable cause of disease. In the summer of 1839 some bad cases of fever occurring among a cluster of houses at Littlemoor, which had always been considered healthy, attention was drawn to the spot. An old half-choked drain was discovered, which was the cause of a shallow stagnant

stagnant fetid pool of a most disgusting nature. Measures were immediately taken to carry off this nuisance by a sewerage, and 'from the hour of the removal of the filth,' says Mr. Thomson, ' no fresh case of fever occurred.'

Portsmouth, which is built on a low portion of the marshy island of Portsea, was formerly extremely subject to intermittent fever : the town was paved in 1769, and, according to Sir Gilbert Blane, from that date this disorder no longer prevailed, whilst Kilsea, and the other parts of the island, retained their aguish disposition till 1793, when a drainage was made, which subdued its force there also.

In the same chapter we have many very instructive details as to the pecuniary results of removing the refuse of towns.

It appears from the evidence of Mr. Dark, of Paddington, a person of respectable character, who for many years has been a considerable contractor for scavengering, &c., that with the exception of coal-ashes (used for brick-making), lees, and a few other inconsiderable items, no refuse in London pays half the expense of removal by cartage beyond a radius of about six miles. ' *I have given away,*' says Mr. Dark, ' *thousands of loads of night-soil—we know not what to do with it!*'

When Mr. Chadwick visited Edinburgh with Dr. Arnott, they were both, without metaphor, ' led by the nose' to a certain stream properly enough called ' the Foul Burn,' from having been the aged receptacle of most of the sinks, drains, sivers, &c., of Auld Reekie. For a 'considerable time the character of this burn was repellent—and, accordingly avoided by poor as well as by rich, by young as well as by old, its contents flowed in mysterious solitude into the sea. Several years ago, however, some of the occupiers of the land in the immediate vicinity, instigated by self-interest, took the liberty of tapping this stream, in order to collect a portion of its contents into tanks for manure. The next step in the march of intellect was, by means of water, to irrigate the meadows from this source, in order to save the expense of cartage ; and thus, by degrees, 300 acres of meadow land, chiefly in the neighbourhood of the Palace of Holyrood, were fertilized from the contents of this common sewer : the result of which has been that some of these meadows are let at from 20*l.* to 30*l.* per acre ; indeed, in the year 1838, some were let at 38*l.* per acre, and in 1826 at 57*l.* Her Majesty's Government, however, being justly of opinion that this process is prejudicial to the healthiness of Holyrood House, and having accordingly directed legal process for the trial of the right of irrigation, the defendants now plead that the invalidation of their claim would deprive the city of the milk and butter of

3000 cows, and estimate the compensation which would be due to themselves at 150,000*l.*

About a quarter of a century ago we ourselves remember to have witnessed the process of a matrimonial alliance, such as we have described, between two parties, who from the beginning of time had always been shy enough of each other, namely, the very Foul Burn alluded to, and the Links or sand-hills on the sea-shore between Leith and Porto Bello. These hillocks, upon which nothing but a few stunted tufts of coarse grass had ever been seen to grow, and which for ages had been blown by the wind into a variety of fantastic forms, were one morning suddenly attacked by a band of workmen, who with spades and shovels were seen busily scattering the sand about them in all directions, while '*Are ye daft?*' was the repeated exclamation of the Mussulburgh fishwives, who, one after another, striding by with outstretched heads, swinging arms, and a creel full of cod on their inclined backs, could not contain their astonishment at seeing the dry region, which all their lives had been sterile, suddenly sub-jected to spade-husbandry. Indeed, when the mass was levelled, it was as barren and lifeless as the shingle of the sea; and con-tinued so during the formation of a network of arteries and veins which in the form of drains were imprinted over its surface. However, no sooner was this latter operation concluded, than— '*Oh whistle, and I 'll come to ye, my lad!*'—the produce of the Foul Burn, like Birnham wood coming to Dunsinane, majestic-ally made its appearance; in a few days the sand was verdant; and before the summer was over, it bore a dark-coloured, rank, luxuriant crop.

Our readers will probably have anticipated that the inference which Mr. Chadwick has drawn from this result, and from Mr. Dark's statement that he can find no sale for the refuse of London is, that the sewers of London, like those of Edinburgh, might be made to fertilize the land in their vicinity.

Mr. Chadwick states that, according to the scale of the value of that portion of the refuse of Edinburgh which has been ap-propriated to irrigation in the way described, the whole refuse of that city would produce an income of from 15,000*l.* to 20,000*l.* a year; while, according to the same scale of value, it appears that, in the city of London, refuse to the enormous value of nearly double what is now paid for the water of the metropolis is thrown away, principally into the Thames, and partly into recep-tacles in the districts of the poor, where it accumulates until it is removed at a great expense. Where the levels are not con-venient, Captain Vetch, of the Engineers, and other competent authorities recommend that the contents of the sewers should
be

be lifted by steam-power, as water is lifted in the drainage of the fens, and then be distributed in iron-pipes, in the same way as water is injected into the metropolis by the water-companies. Mr. Chadwick adds, that the estimated expense of this mode of cleansing and removal, as in the case of the conveyance of water into London, would not amount to a tenth part of the cost of cartage—and to show the practicability of the principle of re-moving refuse by water, he cites the following case :—The West Middlesex Water Company had almost concluded a contract for removing in the ordinary way about an acre of silt four feet deep, which in the course of eight or ten years had accumulated in their reservoir at Kensington, and accordingly 400*l.* was to be paid for this operation, which was to occupy three or four weeks. The bargain was all but sealed, when it was proposed by one of the officers that the silt should be mixed with water, stirred up, and in this liquid state washed away ; and this operation was successfully effected in three or four days, at an expense of only 40*l.* or 50*l.*

In small, moderate-sized, or even in large towns, *where the levels are favourable,* we are much inclined to believe that Mr. Chadwick's project of removing refuse by means of water might, to a limited extent, be successfully adopted for the purpose of irrigation. It is evident, however, that many previous arrange-ments would be necessary, and that, after all, many serious difficulties would be likely to occur—for it must always be re-collected that, in the case at Edinburgh, the burn being a safety-valve communicating with the sea, no accident or explosion can possibly occur—the farmer may therefore approach it or recede from it, may inject or reject its contents, at any hour, or for any period he may desire : whereas a covered sewer blindly administers all it possesses—without consideration, judgment, reflection, or mercy—its motto being 'Time and tide can wait for no man.' The supply of the manure and the demand for it might not therefore agree together for any length of time. Still, however, we can conceive arrangements which need not be de-scribed, by which this evil might be compensated, in which case there can be no doubt that an immense saving, especially that of cartage, would be effected—that the health of the town (in whose drains, constantly flushed clean by water, no refuse could remain) would be materially benefited—and that the produce of the land irrigated would abundantly increase.

But, although we are willing thus far to give Mr. Chadwick credit for his suggestion, and think it ought to be most seriously attended to in the case of our smaller towns, especially such as have considerable streams running through or near them, we

2 G 2

must

must say we consider his attempt to extend the theory to London by the application of the power of steam is preposterous in principle as well as in detail.

The first idea that naturally occurs is the enormous expense and incalculable inconvenience that would be attendant upon the condemnation of nearly the whole of the existing sewers of London, which at present run downwards into the Thames. We acknowledge it may not unfairly be replied, that the very same objection might have been raised against macadamizing our old-fashioned bumping pavement—against substituting wood for both —or against ruining our high-roads by the creation of railways. But admitting this first grave objection to be overruled : supposing for a moment that the old sewerage was destroyed, and that new subterranean works on completely different levels were constructed, there remain to be encountered difficulties above ground which we consider to be insurmountable.

It appears, from a parliamentary return lying before us, that the water pumped into London by the New River, Chelsea, West Middlesex, Grand Junction, East London, South London, Lambeth, and Southwark Water-Companies amounts to 4222 cubic feet per minute, day and night, throughout the year : of which quantity, considerably more than (say) one-half flows through waste-pipes, &c., into the sewers : and if, according to Mr. Chadwick's project, the refuse of the streets of London, instead of being swept up and carted away, as hitherto, were daily to be washed into the gulley-drains by a water-hose, the amount of water which the companies would be required to supply must be very considerably enlarged. To this menaced flood of water, if there be added the usual contents of the sewers, it at once appears how enormous would be the amount of the mixture to be daily ejected from the metropolis *viâ* the sewers; and if, from any accident to the engines, the lifting-power, pumps, or bucketed-wheels should suddenly be disabled, it is evident that a constipation of the sewerage must forthwith take place.

But there remains to be provided for a contingency infinitely more alarming. The area of London is, we believe, nearly 60 square miles : but, taking it only at 40 square miles, and estimating that during a thunder-storm and continued rain there might fall in the space of six hours* one inch of water : that quantity, on the surface last mentioned, would amount to 92,928,000 cubic feet of water, of which the greater portion would immediately go into the sewers. Now, when it is considered that the natural flow of the Coln river amounts only to about 6000 cubic feet per

---

* It appears, from the rain-gauge at Somerset House, that on Tuesday, the 30th of August last, nearly two inches of rain fell in two hours.

minute,

minute, that of the Exe to about 5000, and that of the Lea to about 5600, our readers will at once perceive what an overwhelming amount of fluid would within a very short space of time be added to the already enormous contents of the London sewers; and while the elements of heaven were raging over the venerable head of our metropolis—while the thunder was rolling—while the forked lightning was shivering from top to bottom one or two of our finest church-spires—and while the rain was reverberating from the pavement like myriads of fountains rising out of the ground— if at this sufficiently awful moment the tell tale wind were suddenly to inform us all that, Mr. Chadwick's 'infernal machines' having more work than they could perform, their neighbourhoods had become inundated; if the next blast were to announce to us that the main sewers were blowing up—and then, by evidence every moment becoming more and more insufferable, we were to learn that out of every gully-grate in the metropolis there was spouting up that which, like 'a legion of foul fiends,' no man could control; in short, if we were suddenly to find ourselves in danger of a pestilence, from which not even a cabinet council, hastily summoned for the purpose, could relieve us—we fear that this *Somerset* House '*Amendment Act*' would be a theme of general execration, and that the Poor Law Commissioners, as they plashed homewards through the streets on their respective ponies, would receive *vivâ voce* and oviform evidence that, like their sewers, they were in bad odour.

But admitting for a moment that Mr. Chadwick may be enabled to demonstrate that the contents of the London sewers, even with the extraordinary additions to them during rains and thunder-storms, could not equal the quantity of water which in many parts of England is at present raised in draining our fens; in short that, the power of steam being invincible, a sufficient number of pumps, or rather of bucketed-wheels (say 500 engines of 100-horse power each)* might be prepared to meet any contingency that could occur; yet we maintain that the amount of fluid-manure so lifted would be infinitely more than could possibly—we need not say *pleasantly*—be applied by irrigation—that the superabundance must go somewhere—and that, after all, the greater portion of the quantity lifted would inevitably find its way to the Thames, from which, by so much labour and expense, we had attempted to divert it.

The next topic handled is the severe privations which the labouring classes are subjected to from want of water, not only for

---

* In the Cornish engines it is supposed that each horse-power can raise 528 cubic feet of water per minute to a height of one foot.

ablution, house-cleaning, and sewerage, but for drinking and culinary purposes.   For instance, Mr. Mott states in his report on Manchester, that there, as elsewhere, it is the custom of owners of small cottage property in neighbourhoods where there are no pipes laid, to erect for a given number of houses a pump, which is frequently rented by one of the tenants, who taxes the rest for using it.   One poor woman told him that she was required to pay one shilling a month for permission to use this pump, while the water-companies were giving an abundant supply to houses like hers for six shillings a-year — exactly half the money.   In various Scotch towns the people have to go to public wells, the supply of which is so tardy, that crowds of women and children are obliged to 'wait their turns,' as it is called—indeed, these wells are sometimes frequented *throughout the whole night*.   In Edinburgh many have to travel to wells at a considerable distance, and afterwards to carry their *stoups* up five, six, or seven stories. But neither private nor public wells are always to be had.   In many places the poor are often obliged to collect water from ditches and ponds, so impure, that even horses that have not been accustomed to drink it are apt to suffer from it.   At Tranent some of the labourers use barrels drawn on carriages —others employ their children to bring it in small vessels ; and during the cholera, Dr. Scott Alison reports, it became so scarce, that the poor people went into the ploughed fields to collect the rain-water retained in depressions in the ground, and even in the prints made by horses' feet.

On the foregoing facts Mr. Chadwick justly observes,—

'Supplies of water obtained by the labour of fetching and carrying it in buckets do not answer the purpose of regular supplies brought into the house without such labour, and kept ready in cisterns.   The interposition of the labour of going out and bringing home water from a distance acts as an obstacle to the formation of better habits ; and in the actual condition of the lower classes, conveniences of this description must precede and form the habits.   Even with persons of a higher condition the habits are greatly dependent on the conveniences : it is observed that, when the supplies of water into houses of the middle class are cut off by the pipes being frozen, and it is necessary to send to a distance, the house-cleansings and washings are diminished ; and every presumption is afforded that if it were at all times, and in all weathers, requisite for them to send to a distance for water, their habits of household cleanliness would be deteriorated.   The whole family of the labouring man in the manufacturing towns rise early, before daylight in winter time, to go to their work ; they toil hard, and they return to their homes late at night : it is a serious inconvenience to them to have to fetch water from the pump or the river, on every occasion that it may be wanted, *whether in cold, in rain, or in snow*.   The minor comforts of
                                                                cleanliness

cleanliness are of course foregone, to avoid the immediate and greater discomforts of having to fetch the water.'

In our manufacturing towns (as we all know), those members of a family who are old enough to fetch water are thought strong enough to work: the mere value therefore of the time they expend at the pump is almost always more than the charge made by the companies for a regular and constant supply of water. For instance, in Glasgow the charge of supplying a labourer's tenement is five shillings a-year; in Manchester, six shillings; in London, ten shillings—for a tenement containing two families; for which sum two tons and a half of water per week may be obtained. Thus, for less than one penny farthing per week 135 pailfuls of water are taken into the house without the labour of fetching, without spilling, without being in the way, and yet in constant readiness for use : whereas, on the other hand, the cost to a labourer, or to any member of his family whose time can be employed in work, is very serious. In the Bath Union, a poor fellow, who had to fetch water from one of the public wells about a quarter of a mile from his house, quaintly observed to the Rev. Whitwell Elwin, ' *It's as valuable as strong beer !* '

At Paris, the usual cost of the filtered water, which is carried into the houses, is two sous per pailful, being at the rate of nine shillings per ton: while in London, the highest charge of any of the companies for sending the same quantity of water to any place within the range of their pipes, and delivering it at an average level of 100 feet, is sixpence per ton.

' The mode, however,' says Mr. Chadwick, ' of supplying water by private companies, *for the sake of a profit*, is not available for a population where the numbers are too small to defray the expense of obtaining a private Act of Parliament, or the expense of management by a board of directors, or to produce profits to shareholders....The Poor Law Commissioners have been urgently requested to allow the expense of procuring supplies for villages to be defrayed out of the poor's rates in England; but they could only express their regret that the law gave them no power to allow such a mode of obtaining the benefit sought.'

As regards the supply of water, we are clearly of opinion that a case for the necessity of legislative interference on the largest scale has been made out.

III.— *Circumstances chiefly in the internal economy and bad ventilation of places of work; workmen's lodging-houses, dwellings, and the domestic habits affecting the health of the labouring classes.*

In explaining the evils which arise from bad ventilation in places of work, Mr. Chadwick adduces first the case of the journeymen

neymen tailors, whose habits of life he was led to investigate from the number of early deaths observed to occur among them.

Thomas Brownlow, aged fifty-two, who had worked for Messrs. Stultze, Messrs. Allen, and in others of the largest establishments in London, stated that at Messrs. Allen's, in a room sixteen or eighteen yards long, and seven or eight yards wide, eighty men worked close together, knee to knee : in summer time the heat of these tailors and of their geese, or irons, raised the temperature twenty or thirty degrees ; after the candles were lighted, it became so insufferable that several of the young men from the country fainted ; during the season he had seen from 40*l.* to 50*l.* worth of work spoiled by the perspiration of the men ; in winter the atmosphere became still more unhealthy, with so depressing an effect that many could not stay out the hours ; too many, losing their appetite, took to drink as a stimulant—accordingly, at seven in the morning, gin was brought in, sometimes again at eleven, at three, at five, and after seven, when the shop was closed ; great numbers died of consumption. The average age of these workmen was about thirty-two, but in a hundred there were not ten men of fifty : lastly, when they died, no provision was made for their families, who, if they could not do for themselves, were obliged to go on the parish. Yet Messrs. Allen's wages at the time the witness refers to were 6*d.* an hour.

In a well-ventilated room, it is stated by different witnesses, journeymen tailors would be enabled to execute two hours more work per day ; they would do their twelve hours, whereas the utmost in a close, ill-ventilated room, is ten hours of work. Moreover, a man who had worked in these hot rooms from the age of twenty would not be as good a man at forty as another would be at fifty who had worked in well-aired shops in the country. The latter, in other words, would have gained ten years' labour, besides saving the money spent in gin.

Mr. Chadwick, therefore, calculates that, taking the average loss to a London tailor to be two hours per day for twenty years, and twelve hours for ten years, his total loss would amount to 50,000 hours of productive labour, which, at 6*d.* per hour, would have produced him 1250*l.* ; and this is 250*l.* less than was actually earned and saved by Philip Gray, who worked all his life as a journeyman tailor, and was remarkable for his cleanliness and neatness.

It appears that, of the registered causes of death of 233 persons entered during the year 1839, in the eastern and western unions of the metropolis, under the head ' tailor,' no less than 123 were from disease of the respiratory organs : ninety-two died of consumption ; in the whole number only twenty-nine died old.

' The

' The subscriptions,' says Mr. Chadwick, ' to the benevolent institution for the relief of the aged and infirm tailors by individual masters* in the metropolis appear to be large and liberal, and amount to upwards of 11,000*l.* ; yet it is to be observed, that if they or the men had been aware of the effects of vitiated atmospheres on the constitution and general strength, and of the means of ventilation, the practicable gain of money from the gain of labour by that sanitary measure could not have been less in one large shop, employing 200 men, than 100,000*l.* Independently of subscriptions of the whole trade, it would, during their working period of life, have been sufficient, with the enjoyment of greater health and comfort by every workman during the time of work, to have purchased him an annuity of 1*l.* per week for comfortable and respectable self-support during a period of superannuation, commencing soon after *fifty* years of age.

' The effects of bad ventilation, it need not be pointed out, are chiefly manifested in consumption, the disease by which the greatest slaughter is committed. The causes of fever are comparatively few and prominent, but they appear to have a concurrent effect in producing consumption.'

The results of good ventilation in the prevention or alleviation of disease are clearly manifested in our hospitals. In a badly-ventilated house—the lying-in hospital in Dublin—there died in four years 2944 children out of 7650 ; whereas, after this establishment was properly ventilated, the deaths in the same period, and out of a like number of children, amounted only to 279.

Glasgow supplies a striking example of the beneficial effects of ventilating a factory. In a range of buildings, called ' the Barracks,' 500 persons were collected. All attempts to induce them to ventilate their rooms failing, the consequence was that fever was scarcely ever absent. There were sometimes seven cases in a day ; and in the last two months of 1831 there were fifty-seven. On the recommendation of Mr. Fleming, a surgeon, a tube of two inches in diameter was fixed in the ceiling of each room : these tubes communicated with a large pipe, the end of which was inserted in the chimney of the factory furnace, which, by producing a strong draught, forced the inmates to breathe fresh air. The result of this simple contrivance was, that, during the ensuing eight years, fever was scarcely known in the place!

It would be a task infinitely more easy than pleasing to show the havoc annually created among the manufacturing masses by defective ventilation and overcrowding. We will, therefore, only observe that in the case of milliners and dressmakers in the metropolitan unions during the year 1839, as shown by the mor-

---

* Mr. Stultze, for instance, has subscribed 795*l.* in money ; is a yearly subscriber of twenty-five guineas ; has made a present to the ' Benevolent Institution for the Relief of Infirm Tailors' of ground worth about 1000*l.* ; and has besides undertaken to build thereon six houses for the reception of twenty poor pensioners.

tuary

tuary register, out of 52 deceased, 41 only had attained the age of 25; and the average age of 33, who had died of disease of the lungs, was 28. In short, there is too much reason to believe that among these poor workwomen, as in the case of the journeymen tailors, one-third at least of the healthful duration of adult life is sacrificed to our ignorance or neglect of ventilation. Alas, how little do the upper classes, who fancy that the cheque completely liquidates the account, reflect on the *real* cost of the beautiful dresses they wear!

As to ' *the want of separate apartments and the overcrowding of the private dwellings of the poor* '—a very small portion only of the evidence adduced will suffice. The clerk of the Ampthill Union states that a large proportion of the cottages in his district are so small, that it is impossible to keep up even the common decencies of life : in one cottage, containing only two rooms, there existed eleven individuals : the man, his wife, and four children (one a girl above fourteen, another a boy above twelve) slept in one of the rooms and in one bed—the rest slept all together in the room in which their cooking, working, and eating were performed. The medical officer of the Bicester Union has witnessed a father, a mother, three grown-up sons, a daughter, and a child, all lying at the same time with typhus fever in one small room. The medical officer of the Romsey Union states that he has known fourteen individuals of one family (among whom were a young man and young woman of eighteen and twenty years of age) together in a small room, the mother being in labour at the time.

The Rev. Dr. Gilly, whose able ' Appeal on behalf of the Border Peasantry' is cited in the report, describes a fine, tall Northumbrian peasant of about forty-five years of age, whose family, eleven in number, were disposed of as follows. In one bed he, his wife, a daughter of six, and a boy of four years had to sleep—a daughter of eighteen, a son of twelve, a son of ten, and a daughter of eight had a second bed—and in the third were three sons, aged twenty, sixteen, and fourteen.

The greatest instances of overcrowding appear, however, as may naturally be expected, at Glasgow, Manchester, Liverpool, &c. In Hull, a mother about fifty had to sleep with a son above twenty-one, a lodger being in the same room. In Manchester more than half-a-dozen instances were given of a man, his wife, and his wife's grown-up sister habitually occupying one bed! Mr. Baker, in his report on Leeds, states—' In the houses of the working classes, brothers and sisters, and lodgers of both sexes, are found occupying the same sleeping-room with the parents, and consequences occur which humanity shudders to contemplate.'

Our readers will probably by this time have arrived with us at the

the conclusion, that there exists no savage nation on earth in which more uncivilized or more brutalizing scenes could be witnessed than in the heart of this great country. Should, however, any doubts remain, we subjoin one short extract from the evidence of Dr. Scott Alison:—

' In many houses in and around Tranent, fowls roost on the rafters and on the tops of the bedsteads. The effluvia in these houses are offensive, and must prove very unwholesome. It is scarcely necessary to say that these houses are very filthy. They swarm likewise with fleas. Dogs live in the interior of the lowest houses, and must, of course, be opposed to cleanliness. I have seen horses in two houses in Tranent inhabiting the same apartment with numerous families. One was in Dow's Bounds. Several of the family were ill of typhus fever, and I remember *the horse stood at the back of the bed.* In this case the stench was dreadful. The father died of typhus on this occasion.'

Here is another very important piece of evidence:—

' A gentleman who has observed closely the condition of the work-people in the south of Cheshire and the north of Lancashire, men of similar race and education, working at the same description of work— namely, as cotton-spinners, mill-hands—and earning nearly the same amount of wages, states that the workmen of the north of Lancashire are obviously inferior to those in the south of Cheshire, in health and habits of personal cleanliness and general condition. The difference is traced mainly to the circumstance, that the labourers in the north of Lancashire inhabit stone houses of a description that absorb moisture, the dampness of which affects the health, and causes personal unclean- liness, induced by the difficulty of keeping a clean house.'

One consequence of the unwholesome workshops and houses in which the labouring classes are too often confined, is the dispo- sition it creates among them to dispel by drink that depressing effect on their nervous energies which is invariably the result of breathing impure air. In Dumfries, for example, where the cholera swept away one-eleventh of the population, Mr. Chad- wick inquired of the chief magistrate how many bakers' shops there were? 'Twelve,' was the answer. 'And how many whiskey-shops may your town possess?' The honest provost frankly replied, *'Seventy-nine!'* Another consequence is the rapid corruption, in such unwholesome places, of meat, bread, and other food, which, by preventing the poor from laying in any store, forces them to purchase their provisions on the most disad- vantageous terms.

' Here, then,' says Mr. Chadwick, ' we have from the one agent, a close and polluted atmosphere, two different sets of effects:—one set here noticed engendering improvidence, expense, and waste—the other, the depressing effects of external and internal miasma on the nervous system,

system, tending to incite to the habitual use of ardent spirits; both tending to precipitate this population into disease and misery.'

In lamenting over the picture, but too clearly delineated, of the demoralization and disorganization of our labouring classes, caused by the removal of those architectural barriers by which nature, even among savages, protects modesty and encourages decency, Mr. Chadwick maintains that no education as yet commonly given appears to have availed against such corrupting circumstances: dwelling, *per contrà*, on numerous instances of the moral improvement of a population apparently resulting from street-cleansing, land-draining, and improvements of the external and internal condition of their dwellings. We think it clear enough that it is mere mockery to talk of elevating by *education* classes whom we allow to be perpetually acted upon by physical circumstances of the deeply degrading tendency now sufficiently exposed. How striking are these words of Mr. Walker, the magistrate of the Thames Police Office! After deprecating the practice of building for the poor miserable hovels, instead of more comfortable and respectable, well-drained dwellings, he says,—

' From what I have observed, I am fully convinced that if shambles were built on any spot, and all who choose were allowed to occupy them, they would soon be occupied by a race lower than any yet known. I have often said, that if empty casks were placed along the streets of Whitechapel, in a few days each of them would have a tenant, and these tenants would keep up their kind, and prey upon the rest of the community. I am sure that, if such facilities were offered, there is no conceivable degradation to which portions of the species might not be reduced. Wherever there are empty houses which are not secured, they are soon tenanted by wretched objects, and these tenants continue so long as there is a harbour for them. Parish-officers and others come to me to aid them in clearing such places. I tell the police and the parish that there is no use in their watching these places; that they must board them up, if they would get rid of the occupants. If they will give the accommodation, they will get the occupants. If you will have marshes and stagnant waters, you will there have suitable animals ; and the only way of getting rid of them is by draining the marshes.'

Mr. Chadwick dwells on *domestic* mismanagement generally, as one great predisposing cause of disease. There is no doubt that the poor are in the habit of buying their tea, coffee, sugar, butter, cheese, bacon, and other articles, in small quantities from the hucksters, who, to cover bad debts, charge exorbitant prices. Destitution is often therefore caused by the wasteful misapplication of wages which, with habits of frugality, would prove to be sufficient; but the grand evil is, that every species of mismanagement promotes or ends in the gin and whiskey.

Every day ' intemperance' is talked of and preached against as the
cause

cause of fever, and of the prevalent mortality. We neglect, however, to reflect that it is the discomfort of the poor that drives them to drink. Rival pleasures might be encouraged, which would keep them sober ; but, alas, whiskey is declared to be *good* for damp and rheumatism, when drainage and a clean residence are really the physical remedies that should be prescribed.

IV. *Comparative chance of life in different classes of the community.*

There is no proverb more generally admitted than that ' Death is no respecter of persons.' Mr. Chadwick, however, has drawn from the mortuary registers a series of tabular returns, of which the following is a single specimen :—

No. of Deaths.	LIVERPOOL, 1840.	Average Age of Deceased.
137	Gentry and professional persons, &c. . .	35
1,738	Tradesmen and their families . . .	22
5,597	Labourers, mechanics, and servants, &c. .	15

—Again, it is an appalling fact, that, among the labouring classes in Manchester, more than fifty-seven out of every hundred die before they attain five years of age !—More than one-half of their progeny die within the fifth year of their birth; while one-fifth only of the children of the gentry die within the same period. In explanation of such a difference, Mr. Chadwick has annexed to his report plans of different towns, showing, by different tints, that the localities of the epidemic diseases which raged there are identical with the uncleansed and close streets and wards occupied by the poor.

Instead of actively searching for the causes which have been so fatally shortening as well as embittering the existence of our labouring classes, it has of late years been much the fashion among political economists—who clearly enough saw that this mortality, from whatever cause it was proceeding, did not affect *them*—to adopt the convenient theory that wars, plagues, pestilence, epidemic disorders, and accidents of every description, which cause premature deaths among the poor, are, if it could only be satisfactorily explained to them, a ' terrible corrective,' kindly ordained by Nature, in order to prevent population exceeding the means of subsistence. But Mr. Chadwick, standing forward as the advocate of Nature and of the poor, denies the Malthusian doctrine altogether, and produces tabular accounts taken from the bills of mortality of every county in England, which certainly appear to prove that the proportion of births to the population is greatest where there is the greatest mortality—and consequently that pestilence or excessive mortality does not diminish the sum total of population ! Our mismanage-

ment

ment produces disease, and that makes the gap which Nature immediately labours to fill up. Let us allow as largely as we choose for inconsiderate and reckless conduct in individuals— still, inasmuch as two things cannot occupy the same space at the same time, the young in almost every trade and profession of life must unavoidably defer marriage until their seniors vacate by death the places of trust and confidence which they have gradually attained. So long, therefore, as these places linger in the possession of the old, the increase of population is proportionably subdued; whereas, on the other hand, if, from avoidable or unavoidable disease, the duration of life be so shortened that those *loca tenentes,* who neither increase nor multiply, shall be either partly or wholly replaced by those of an age to do both, it evidently follows that this description of mortality must produce more births than deaths.

In fact, even the returns of the deaths, marriages, and births among the white population on the west coast of Africa demonstrate that, though the mortality there has been as frightful as we have described it, the births have exceeded it largely:—for instance, in the different districts of this pestilential abode the number of deaths (nine-tenths of which were of persons under forty years of age) amounted in 1839 to 241, while in the same year the number of baptisms was 464, and the number of marriages 542; indeed it seems natural that young people should become reckless of consequences, and regardless of the future, in a climate which, by the ravages it is daily creating, appears always to be relentlessly exclaiming to them, ' *To-morrow you die!*'

V. *Pecuniary burdens created by the neglect of sanitary measures.*

' To whatever extent,' says Mr. Chadwick, ' the probable duration of the life of the working man is diminished by noxious agencies, I repeat a truism in stating that to the same extent productive power is lost; and in the case of destitute widowhood and orphanage, burdens are created and cast, either on the industrious survivors belonging to the family, or on the contributors to the poor's-rates, during the whole of the period of the failure of such ability.'

It appears that the number of widows chargeable to the poor-rates in the year ending Lady-day, 1840, was 43,000, and that the total number of orphan children to whom relief was given was 112,000. Of these it is estimated that 27,000 cases of premature widowhood, and more than 100,000 of orphanage, might be traced to removable causes.

Take one pleasing example of a *cause removed* :—

' In one mine,' says Dr. Barham, ' the Dolcoath mine, in the parish of Camborne, in Cornwall, great attention is paid to obviate agencies injurious to the miners. Care is there taken in respect to ventilation

in

in the mines, and the men are healthier than in most other mines; there are more old miners. Care is taken for the prevention of accidents. Care is taken of the miners on quitting the mines : hence, instead of issuing on the bleak hill-side, and receiving beer in a shed, they issue from their underground labour into a warm room, where well-dried clothes are ready for them ; warm water, and even baths are supplied from the steam-furnace ; and a provision of hot beef-soup instead of beer is ready for them in another room. The honour of having made this change is stated to be due to the Right Hon. Lady Basset, on the suggestion of Dr. Carlyon. We may fairly attribute to the combination of beneficial arrangements just noticed that in Dolcoath, where 451 individuals are employed underground, only two have died within the last three years of miners' consumption; a statement which could not, I believe, be made with truth, nor be nearly approached, in respect of an equal number [of miners during the same term in any other Cornish district. The sick-club of the mine is comparatively rich, having a fund of 1500*l*.'

It appears to be the governing principle of Mr. Chadwick's report to demonstrate to the public that the welfare of the labouring poor is identical with that of all other classes—that whatever afflicts the former, sympathetically affects the latter—and consequently that whenever the poor are brought to an untimely grave by causes which are removable, the community in some way or other is sure to suffer retributive punishment for the neglect. For example—in corroboration of the evidence already adduced, he gives tabular returns, showing the difference in the proportions of ages between a depressed and unhealthy, and a comparatively vigorous population: by which it appears that, while in a hundred men of the former, there would not be two men beyond 60 years of age, not eight above 50, and not a fourth above 40— in the other population there would be fourteen beyond 60, twenty-seven beyond 50, or a clear majority of mature age. Now mark *one* consequence :—

' Whenever the adult population of a physically depressed district, such as Manchester, is brought out on any public occasion, the preponderance of youth in the crowd is apt to strike those who have seen assemblages of the working population in districts more favourably situated.

' In the course of some inquiries under the Constabulary Force Commission, reference was made to the meetings held by torchlight in the neighbourhood of Manchester. It was reported that the bulk consisted of mere boys, and that there were scarcely any men of mature age amongst them. Those of age and experience, it was stated, generally disapproved of the proceedings of the meetings, as injurious to the working classes themselves. These older men, we were assured by their employers, were above the influence of the anarchical fallacies which appeared to sway those wild and dangerous assemblages. The inquiry which arose upon such statements was how it happened that the men of
mature

mature age, feeling their own best interests injured by the proceedings
of the younger portion of the working classes—how they, the elders, did
not exercise a restraining influence upon their less-experienced fellow-
workmen?   On inquiring of the owner of some extensive manufacturing
property, on which between 1000 and 2000 persons were maintained at
wages yielding 40s. per week per family, whether he could rely on the
aid of the men of mature age for the protection of the capital which
furnished them the means of subsistence?—he stated he could rely on
them confidently;—but on ascertaining the numbers qualified for
service as special constables, the gloomy fact became apparent, that
the proportion of men of strength and of mature age for such service
were but as a small group against a large crowd, and that for any social
influence they were equally weak.   The disappearance by premature
deaths of the heads of families and the older workmen must practically
involve the necessity of supplying the lapse of staid influence amidst a
young population by one description or other of precautionary force.

‘ On expostulating on other occasions with middle-aged and experienced workmen on the folly, as well as the injustice of their trade
unions, the workmen of the class remonstrated with invariably dis-
claimed connexion with the proceedings, and showed that they abstained from attendance at the meetings.   The common expression
was, they would not attend to be borne down by “ mere boys,” who
were furious, and knew not what they were about.   The predominance
of a young and violent majority was general.

‘ In the metropolis the experience is similar.   The mobs against
which the police have to guard come from the most depressed districts ;
and the constant report of the superintendents is, that scarcely any old
men are to be seen amongst them.   In general they appear to consist
of persons between 16 and 25 years of age.   The mobs from such districts as Bethnal Green are proportionately conspicuous for a deficiency
of bodily strength, without, however, being from that cause proportionately the less dangerously mischievous.   I was informed by peace-officers
that the great havoc at Bristol was committed by mere boys.’

Since the publication of the Report alarming riots have occurred in the manufacturing districts; and our readers will
observe, from the following authentic details, which we have taken
some trouble to obtain, how singularly Mr. Chadwick’s statement has just been corroborated.

Ages of the Prisoners for Trial at the Special Commission in Cheshire,
Lancashire, and Staffordshire, October, 184 —

Below . . 16	.	. 13
16 and 26	.	. 316
26 and 36	.	. 154
Between 36 and 46	.	. 56
46 and 56	.	. 18
56 and 66	.	. 5
Above . . 66	.	. 3

565

This

This is enough—but it must be kept in mind that these prisoners were the *leaders;* their followers were probably much younger.

'The experience of the metropolitan police,' continues Mr. Chadwick, 'is similar as to the comparatively small proportion of force available for public service from such depressed districts. It is corroborative also of the evidence as to the physical deterioration of their population, as well as the disproportion in respect to age. Two out of every three of the candidates for admission to the police force itself are found defective in the physical qualifications. It is rare that any one of the candidates from Spitalfields, Whitechapel, or the districts where the mean duration of life is low, is found to possess the requisite physical qualifications for the force, which is chiefly recruited from the open districts at the outskirts of the town, or from Norfolk and Suffolk, and other agricultural counties.

' In general the juvenile delinquents, who come from the inferior districts of the towns, are conspicuously under-size. In a recent examination of juvenile delinquents at Parkhurst by Mr. Kay Shuttleworth, the great majority were found to be deficient in physical organization. An impression is often prevalent that the criminal population consists of persons of the greatest physical strength. Instances of criminals of great strength certainly do occur; but speaking from observation of the adult prisoners from the towns and the convicts in the hulks, they are in general below the average standard of height.'

He follows up these statements by some very curious details collected from the teachers of the pauper children at Norwood and elsewhere :—

' The intellects of the children of inferior physical organization are torpid; it is comparatively difficult to gain their attention or to sustain it; it requires much labour to irradiate the countenance with intelligence, and the irradiation is apt to be transient. As a class they are comparatively irritable and bad-tempered. The most experienced and zealous teachers are gladdened by the sight of well-grown healthy children, which presents to them better promise that their labours will be less difficult and more lasting and successful. On one occasion a comparison was made between the progress of two sets of children in Glasgow—the one set taken from the wynds and placed under the care of one of the most skilful and successful infant-school masters; the other a set of children from a more healthy town district, and of a better physical condition, placed under the care of a pupil of the master who had charge of the children from the wynds. After a trial for a sufficient time, the more experienced master acknowledged the comparative inferiority of his pupils, and his inability to keep them up to the pace of the better bodily-conditioned children.'

Our author pithily sums up the result.

' Noxious physical agencies, depressing the health and bodily condition of the population, act as obstacles to education and to moral

2 H   culture;

culture; in abridging the duration of adult life they check the growth of productive skill, and abridge the amount of social experience and steady moral habits : they substitute for a population that accumulates and preserves instruction, and is steadily progressive, a population young, inexperienced, ignorant, credulous, irritable, passionate, dangerous, having a perpetual tendency to moral as well as physical deterioration.'

VI. *Evidence of the effects of preventive measures in raising the standard of health and the chances of life.*

The results of measures which have lately been introduced into the navy and army, as well as into our prisons, offer indisputable evidence of the health attainable by simple means.   Mr. Chadwick declares that no descriptions given by Howard of the worst prisons he visited in England, come up to what appeared in every wynd of Edinburgh and Glasgow inspected by Dr. Arnott and himself.   Now on what principle can we defend our not applying to the benefit of the labouring poor, in as far as we can apply them, the measures which we know to have saved so many of our soldiers and sailors—which have therefore saved the nation such vast sums of money? Above all, what is to be said of the judgment of the community that makes prodigious efforts to improve the sanitary condition of its criminals, and apathetically neglects its poor ?

After giving us a mass of irresistible evidence as to the actual results of increased care in the case of soldiers and sailors and the inmates of jails, Mr. Chadwick proceeds to compare the expense to owners and tenants of the public drainage, cleansing, and supplies of water necessary for the maintenance of health, with the expense of sickness—the cost of the remedy with the cost of the disease.   His tables seem to prove that the cost of the application of his remedies to one-third (1,148,282) of the inhabited houses in England, Wales, and Scotland, would amount to 18,401,219*l.*   The annual instalment for repayment of this debt in thirty years would amount to 613,374*l.*; the annual interest, commuted at 5 per cent. on the outlay, charged as rent on the tenant, would be 583,644*l.*   Out of this sum, however, the cost of supplying every house with water, even at the highest charge made by the water companies, namely, 138 pailsful for 1¼*d.*, would, in fact, be a reduction of the existing expenditure of labour in fetching water; and many other similar reductions should be made from the account.   But, without lingering over such details, it may be at once stated that the experience of the effect of sanitary measures proves the possibility of the reduction of *sickness* in the worst districts to at least one-third of the existing amount; and sickness is no trifle in the mere calculation of pounds, shillings, and pence.

' The *immediate* cost,' says Mr. Chadwick, ' of sickness and loss of employment

employment falls differently in different parts of the country; but on whatsoever fund it does fall, it will be a gain to apply to the means of prevention that fund which is and must needs otherwise continue to be more largely applied to meet the charge of maintenance and remedies.

'Admitting, however, as a fact the misconception intended to be obviated, that the necessary expense of structural arrangements will be an immediate charge instead of an immediate means of relief to the labouring classes ;—in proof that they have, in ordinary times, not only the means of defraying increased public rates but increased rents, I refer to the fact that the amount expended in ardent spirits (exclusive of wines), tobacco, snuff, beer, &c., consumed chiefly by them, cannot be much less than from 45,000,000*l.* to 50,000,000*l.* per annum in the United Kingdom. By an estimate which I obtained from an eminent spirit-merchant of the cost to the consumer of the British spirits on which duty is paid, the annual expenditure on them alone, chiefly by the labouring classes, cannot be less than 24,000,000*l.* per annum. The cost of one dram per week would nearly defray the expense of the structural arrangements of drainage, &c., by which some of the strongest provocatives to the habit of drunkenness would be removed.'

These are most important statements. But still, let it be remembered, the labouring poor in our great towns cannot of themselves, as a class, improve essentially the condition of the localities which they occupy. The workman's location must be governed by his work—therefore the supply of house-room for him becomes almost inevitably a monopoly : he must not only take a lodging near his work, but he must take it as it is : he can neither lay on water, nor cause the removal of filth by drainage—in short, he has no more control over the external economy of his habitation than of the structure of the street in which it exists. But it is demonstrable that, if the employers of labour would but provide better accommodation for their labourers, they would receive in money and in money's worth—to speak of no higher considerations—a fair remuneration for their expenditure.

'We everywhere find,' says Mr. Chadwick, '(in contradiction to statements frequently made in popular declamations,) that the labourer gains by his connexion with large capital : in the instances presented in the course of this inquiry, of residences held from the employer, we find that the labourer gains by the expenditure for the external appearance of that which is known to be part of the property—an expenditure that is generally accompanied by corresponding internal comforts : he gains by all the surrounding advantages of good roads and drainage, and by more sustained and powerful care to maintain them : he gains by the closer proximity to his work attendant on such an arrangement ; and he thus avoids all the attacks of disease occasioned by exposure to wet and cold, and the additional fatigue in traversing long distances to and from his home to the place of work, in the damp of early morning or of nightfall. The exposure to weather after leaving the place of work

is

is one prolific cause of disease, especially to the young. When the home is near to the place of work, the labourer is enabled to take his dinner with his family instead of at the beer-shop. The wife and children gain by proximity to the employer's family, in motives to neatness and cleanliness, by their being known and being under observation : as a general rule, the whole economy of the cottages in bye-lanes and out-of-the-way places appears to be below those exposed to observation. In connexion with property or large capital, the labourer gains in the stability of employment, and the regularity of income incidental to operations on a large scale : there is a mutual benefit also in the wages for service being given in the shape of buildings or permanent and assured comforts; that is, in what would be the best application of wages, rather than wholly in money wages.'

We must refer to the Report itself for a long array of most pleasing examples of the practical truth of these statements. Not a few of the great master-manufacturers acknowledged to Mr. Chadwick that what they had done from motives of humanity had turned out, to their agreeable surprise, immensely advantageous to their own purses. But let us content ourselves with what is stated as to one particular source of evil, and the facility of cutting it off by a judicious employer. The example is from Leeds :—

' The effects,' says Mr. Fairburn, ' produced by payment at the public-house are to oblige the workman to drink. He is kept waiting in the public-house during a long time, varying from two to three hours, sometimes as much as five hours. The workman cannot remain in the house without drinking, even if he were alone, as he must make some return to the landlord for the use of the room. But the payment of a number of men occupies time in proportion to their numbers. We find that to pay our own men in the most rapid way requires from two to three hours. The assembled workmen, of course, stimulate each other to drink. Out of a hundred men, all of whom will, probably, have taken their quart of porter or ale, above a third will go home in a state of drunkenness—of drunkenness to the extent of imbecility. The evil is not confined to the men ; the destructive habit is propagated in their families. At each public-house a proportion of the poor women, their wives, attend. According to my own observation, full ten per cent. of the men have their wives and children in attendance at the public-house. The poor women have no other mode of getting money to market with on the Saturday night than attending at the public-house to get it from their husbands. They may have children whom they cannot leave at home, and these they bring with them. The wives are thus led to drink, and they and their children are made partakers of the scenes of drunkenness and riot ; for there are not unfrequently quarrels leading to fights between the workmen when intoxicated.

' It is only the inferior shopkeepers or hucksters who will sell on the Sunday morning, and they sell an inferior commodity at a higher price. Then the Sunday morning is thus occupied : the husband, and sometimes
times

times the wife, is kept in a state of feverish excitement by the previous night's debauch; they are kept in a state of filth and disorder; even the face is unwashed; no clean clothes are put on; and there is no church attendance, and no decency. Indeed, by the pressure of the wants created by habits of drinking, there is soon no means to purchase clean or respectable clothes, and lastly no desire to purchase them. The man, instead of cleaning himself, and appearing at church on the Sunday, or walking out with his-family on the Sunday afternoon in a respectable condition, remains at home in filth, and in a filthy hovel.

' The workman who has been absent from drunkenness comes to his work pale, emaciated, shattered, and unnerved. From my own observation in my own branch of manufacture, I should say that the quantity and quality of the work executed during the first day or so would be about one-fifth less than that obtainable from a steady and attentive workman. Another consideration for the master is the fact that such workmen, the most idle and dissolute, are the most discontented, and are always the foremost in mischievous strikes and combinations.'

Now what is Mr. Fairburn's prescription for these disorders? He sends a clerk into each room in his manufactory immediately after dinner-hour on Saturday to pay each man individually, who, by this simple arrangement, is not taken from his work half a minute. The master thus saves on an average an hour and a half's labour of 550 men, which amounts to 800 hours of labour per week; one great cause of non-attendance at church on the Sunday is abolished; and, lastly, not above four or five of his people arrive late at their work on Monday morning.

Let us turn for a moment to the rural regions. Out of many of Mr. Chadwick's witnesses, let us attend to one:—Charles Higgins, Esq., Chairman of the Bedford Union, thus describes the advantages which have arisen from an improved description of cottages in his vicinity:—

' The man sees his wife and family more comfortable than formerly; he has a better cottage and garden; he is stimulated to industry, and, as he rises in respectability of station, he *becomes aware* that he has a character to lose. Thus an important point is gained. Having acquired certain advantages, he is anxious to retain and improve them; he strives more to preserve his independence, and becomes a member of benefit, medical, and clothing societies; and frequently, besides this, lays up a certain sum, quarterly or half-yearly, in the savings-bank. Almost always attendant upon these advantages, we find the man sending his children to be regularly instructed in a Sunday, and, where possible, in a day school, and himself and family more constant in their attendance at some place of worship on the Lord's-day.

' A man who comes home to a poor, comfortless hovel after his day's labour, and sees all miserable around him, has his spirits more often depressed than excited by it. He feels that, do his best, he shall be miserable still, and is too apt to fly for a temporary refuge to the ale-
house

house or beer-shop. But give him the means of making himself comfortable by his own industry, and I am convinced by experience that, in
many cases, he will avail himself of it.'

Although, in the variegated picture of human life, one can
scarcely point out a more striking contrast than between a pale
drunken labourer zigzaggedly staggering by night from the ale-
house to his family, and a ruddy sober one rationally enjoying his
evening at home, yet it is not so very easy to analyse or enumerate
the invisible filaments which, acting all together like the strands
in a cable, have in the two cases produced such opposite results!

It is not the fresh air the ploughman has been inhaling all
day which, at the conclusion of his work, has irresistibly
brought him to his home; nor is it the appetite which healthy
labour has created—nor is it the joyous welcome of those rosy-
faced children who, following each other almost according to
their ages along the garden-path, have run to meet him at his
wicket-gate—nor is it the smiling countenance of his neatly-dressed
wife—nor the homely meal she has prepared for him—nor the
general cleanliness of his cottage, nor the ticking of his gaudy-
faced clock, nor the merry antics of his children's kitten, nor his
warm chimney-corner, nor the cheerful embers on his hearth——
no one of these tiny threads is strong enough to draw an able-
bodied labourer to his cottage; and yet, their united influence,
thoug still invisible to him, produces the happy result: in short,
fresh air creates health, and health happiness.

On the other hand, it is not the fountain of putrid air which all
day long has been steaming up from a small gulley-drain in front
of his shop that causes the workman to spend his evening at the
alehouse; nor is it the lassitude of his body or depression of
spirits produced by the want of ventilation in the building—nor is it
the dust he has been breathing there—nor is it the offensive open
drain that runs close under his own window—nor is it the sickly,
uncaptivating aspect of his care-worn wife—nor the neglected,
untidy appearance of his room—nor the emaciated countenances
of his poor children, who, as if they had lost the bloom of
modesty, are lying all huddled together in one bed—nor is it the
feverish thirst which assails him—nor is it that black, unwholesome board nailed by Parliament over the alehouse-door which
insists that the beer he desires is ' *to be drunk on the premises,*'
or, in other words, that he himself must be the pitcher that is to
carry it away—nor is it the abandoned immoral associates of both
sexes which this board has convened for him——no one of these
circumstances would be sufficient to estrange an honest workman
from his home; and yet, when they give ' a long pull, a strong
pull, and a pull all together,' the victim obeys their influence,

he

he knows not why, and, accordingly, however crooked may be his
path homewards, he, at all events, goes straight to the alehouse.

We have no desire to lecture on the old law which, in order to
save trouble and reflection, summarily prescribed punishment as the
natural cure for drunkenness. We trust, however, that the day
is fast approaching when the attention of our law-makers will
be directed to the prevention of the evil instead of its cure: for
if it be true that the sobriety of the labouring classes mainly depends upon sanitary arrangements on an extensive scale, which the
fiat of Parliament could instantaneously ordain, it certainly does
appear that, so long as this branch of legislation shall continue to be neglected, there is reason to doubt whether Parliament or the peasant be the most guilty of those cases of drunkenness which mainly proceed from a series of minute causes *not* removable by the latter.

Surely, Mr. Chadwick's main remedies—namely, efficient drainage, sewerage, and ablution of towns—come within the legitimate
province of the legislature. Surely, the interior arrangements he
proposes, such as the ventilation of all buildings in which a body
of workpeople are assembled, as well as due attention to a series
of other details conducive to their health, are, to say the least, as
much within the proper jurisdiction of parliament as the most humane mode of sweeping chimneys, or the proper thickness of party-
walls. The health of the nation being nearly synonymous with
its wealth, it is evident that the labouring power of the British
people is a machine which it is the duty as well as the interest of
the State to protect.

In France there has long existed a *Board of Health;* and whoever has read the Essays of Parent du Chatelet must know of
what vast benefits this institution has been productive. Many times
has a similar one been recommended and proposed here—but
there has always occurred some fatal hitch. We need not at
present enter on the discussion of the difficulties hitherto deemed
insurmountable. Meantime Mr. Chadwick thinks the machinery
of the Poor Law Commission might be rendered highly serviceable; and his practical proposal is, that in order to establish
throughout the country an efficient system of sanitary attention,
there should be appointed to each district two new superior
officers, a superintending Physician and a skilful Engineer.

Mr. Chadwick truly observes that the claim to relief on the
ground of destitution created by sickness already propels the medical officer of every union to the precise point where the evil is most
rife, and where the public intervention is most called for—namely,
to the interior of the abode of the sufferer: indeed, it appears that
in the metropolis during one year these officers were required to
visit

visit 14,000 residences of applicants for relief on account of fever alone. When it is considered that the number of medical officers attached to the new unions throughout the country amounts to 2300, it is evident what a searching professional inquiry these intelligent agents have power to make, and what opportunities they would have of recommending immediate attention to whatever physical causes of disease they might discover in their daily visits to the residences of the afflicted. It is equally obvious that the relieving officer of the union would, in the mere performance of his duty, be able to assist the medical officer in searching out removable causes of sickness, by reporting whatever he might deem worthy of attention.

In order, therefore, to carry out this reciprocal assistance, Mr. Chadwick proposes that the medical officers of the unions, whenever they visit the residences of the labouring classes, should be required, as an extra duty for which they should be properly remunerated, to examine, or order to be examined any physical and removable causes which may, in their opinion, have produced disease; and having done this, to make out a report, specifying any nuisances that may require immediate removal—which statement should then be given to the relieving officer, who should thereupon take measures for the removal of the nuisance at the expense of the owner of the tenement, unless he, upon notice being given to him, forthwith proceeds to direct its removal.

These preliminary arrangements being effected, the duty of the district physician would be to receive reports from the medical officers of the unions, and to give general supervision to their labours, so as to correct any error or neglect in their treatment of the destitute; to inspect from time to time the schools of the poor; and to visit in person also places of work and workmen's lodging-houses—in this last department advantageously superseding the sub-inspectors of factories.

'It would be found,' says Mr. Chadwick, 'that the appointment of a superior medical officer independent of private practice, to superintend these various duties, would be a measure of sound pecuniary economy. The experience of the navy and the army and the prisons may be referred to for exemplifications of the economy in money, as well as in health and life, of such an arrangement. A portion only of the saving from an expensive and oppressive collection of the local rates would abundantly suffice to ensure for the public protection against common evils the science of a district physician, as well as the science of a district engineer. Indeed, the money now spent in comparatively fragmentitious and unsystematized local medical service for the public, would, if combined as it might be without disturbance on the occurrence of vacancies, afford advantages at each step of the combination. We have in the same towns public medical officers as inspectors of prisons,
medical

medical officers for the inspection of lunatic asylums, medical officers of the new unions, medical inspectors of recruits, medical service for the granting certificates for children under the provisions of the Factory Act, medical service for the *post-mortem* examinations of bodies, the subject of coroners' inquests, which it appears from the mortuary registries of violent deaths in England amount to between 11,000 and 12,000 annually, for which a fee of a guinea each is given. These and other services are divided in such portions as only to afford remuneration in such sums as 40*l*., 50*l*., 60*l*., or 80*l*. each; and many smaller and few larger amounts.'

But after all that may justly be said in favour of medical assistance, Mr. Chadwick evidently considers that the chief physician of his sanitary system is the district engineer. We have many engineers at work—but no real good can be effected on a large scale unless there be *system* in the operations, and authority extending over more than this or that small object or locality.

'In the districts,' says Mr. Chadwick, 'where the greatest defects prevail, we find such an array of officers for the superintendence of public structures, as would lead to the *à priori* conclusion of a high degree of perfection in the work, from the apparent subdivision of labour in which it is distributed. In the same petty districts we have surveyors of sewers appointed by the commissioners of sewers, surveyors of turnpike-roads appointed by the trustees of the turnpike-trusts, surveyors of highways appointed by the inhabitants in vestry, or by district boards under the Highway Act; paid district surveyors appointed by the justices, surveyors of paving under local Acts, surveyors of building under the Building Act, surveyors of county-bridges, &c.

'The qualifications of a civil engineer involve the knowledge of the prices of the materials and labour used in construction, and also the preparation of surveys and the general qualifications for valuations, which are usually enhanced by the extent of the range of different descriptions of property with which the valuator is conversant. The public demands for the services of such officers as valuators are often as mischievously separated and distributed as the services for the construction and maintenance of public works. Thus we have often, within the same districts, one set of persons appointed for the execution of valuations and surveys for the levy of the poor-rates; another set for the surveys and valuations for the assessed-taxes; another for the land-tax; another for the highway-rates; another for the sewer-rates; another for the borough-rates; another for the church-rates; another for the county-rates, where parishes neglect to pay, or are unequally assessed, and for extra-parochial places; another for tithe commutation; and these services are generally badly rendered separately at an undue expense.'

On comparing the actual expense of the repairs of roads under a scientific management of the highways with the present cost, Mr. Chadwick estimates, that upwards of 500,000*l*. per annum might

might be saved on that branch of administration alone. In the collection of the county-rates, he considers that, by simple arrangements, 1000*l.* a-year might be saved in one county (Kent), sufficient for defraying the expense of constructing permanent drains for upwards of 500 tenements; and from a vast accumulation of similar data Mr. Chadwick states, as his deliberate opinion, that, by a consolidation of the collection of rates, enough might be saved from the collection of one local tax—the sewers-rate—to pay the expense of scientific officers throughout the country.

' Supposing,' he says, ' population and new buildings for their accommodation to proceed at the rate at which they have hitherto done in the boroughs, and supposing all the new houses to be only fourth-rate, the expense, at the ordinary rate of payment of surveyors' fees, would be about 30,000*l.* per annum for the new houses alone. Fees of half the amount required for every new building are allowed for every alteration of an old one, and the total expense of such structures would probably be near 50,000*l.* in the towns alone—an expense equal to the pay of the whole corps of Royal Engineers, or 240 men of science, for Great Britain and Ireland.

' But at the rate of increase of the population of Great Britain, to accommodate them, 59,000 new tenements are required, affording, if all that have equal need receive equal care, fees to the amount of no less than from 80,000*l.* to 100,000*l.* per annum. This would afford payment equal to that of the whole corps of sappers and miners, or nearly 1000 trained men, in addition to the corps of engineers.

' From a consideration of the science and skill now obtained for the public from these two corps for general service, some conception may be formed of the science and skill that might be obtained in appointments for local service, by pre-appointed securities for the possession of the like qualifications, but which are now thrown away in separate appointments at an enormous expense, where qualifications are entirely neglected.'

If, when our carriage is broken, we send for the coachmaker —if, when our chronometer stops, we send for the watchmaker, and so on,—it surely follows that when patches of fever are found vegetating in all directions around us—when pestilence of our own concocting, like an unwholesome mist, is rising out of the burial-grounds, courts, alleys, and *cul-de-sacs* of our towns, and out of the undrained portions of the country—and when every parish-purse throughout the kingdom is suffering from the unnatural number of widows and orphans, which, in consequence of these removable causes, it is obliged by law to maintain,—in short, when sanitary measures are at last proved to be necessary, —there can surely exist among reasonable men no doubt that the physician and the engineer are the head and the hand professionally

sionally most competent to undertake the cure. So long as we could affect to be ignorant of the evils that environ us, it was deemed unnecessary to send for either; but from the day of the publication of the evidence before us, this excuse, like a poisonous weed plucked from the ground, has been gradually withering.

Even if the amount of mischief by which we are surrounded were a fixed quantity, it surely ought to create among us very serious alarm; but, on the contrary, every day it is becoming more and more formidable. The sea-beaten shores of Great Britain remain unaltered—but the population within them is already increasing at the rate of 230,000 persons per annum. In the year, therefore, that has just closed, people enough to fill a whole county of the size of Worcestershire, or of the North riding of Yorkshire, have been poured upon us; and every progressive year the measure of increase will become larger.

What is to be the result of such an increasing addition to our population it is awful enough, under any circumstances, to contemplate; but if every living individual—' *de mortuis nil nisi bonum*'—be allowed to continue to pollute the air—our commonwealth—as much as he pleases; if pollution be allowed to continue to engender disease—disease, demoralization—and demoralization, mutiny and rebellion by a young mob—the punishment of our apathy and negligence, sooner than we expect it, may become, like that of Cain, *greater than we can bear.*

We cannot take leave of Mr. Chadwick without expressing our high sense of the energy with which he has conducted this all-important investigation, the benevolent feeling towards the poor and the suffering which has evidently animated and sustained him in his long labours, and the sagacity which distinguishes all his leading suggestions.

Art. V.—1. *Report of the General Board of Health on the Execution of the Nuisances Removal Act, and Public Health Act, up to July* 1849.

2. *Appendices to the Report of the General Board of Health on the Supply of Water to the Metropolis : videlicet, Appendix* 1. *Returns to the Queries addressed to the several Metropolitan Water Companies. Appendix* 2. *Engineering Reports and Evidence. Appendix* 3. *Medical, Chemical, Geological, and Miscellaneous Reports and Evidence.* 1850.

3. *Report of the Select Committee on Private Bills, with Minutes of Evidence thereon.* 1846.

4. *Subterranean Survey of the Metropolis.—Report on the Subterranean Condition of the Westminster District ; with a Pictorial Map.* By Henry Austin, Consulting Engineer, and Joseph Smith, Assistant Surveyor. 1849.

5. *Report on the Sanitary Condition of the City of London for the Year* 1849-50. By J. Simon, Esq., F.R.S., Medical Officer of Health to the City of London, and one of the Surgical Staff of St. Thomas's Hospital. 1850.

6. *The Laws of England relating to Public Health.* By J. Toulmin Smith, of Lincoln's Inn, Esq., Special Pleader. 1848.

IN a recent article we briefly traced the history of our London water-service through the five epochs of its gradual development; noting how its progress, during the last two centuries, has been impeded by the misfeasance of a corrupt Monopoly; and how this Monopoly has of late years been curbed in its turn by the growing force of the Sanitary Idea. Of that Idea we also rapidly sketched the progress—from its origin in the theoretic dogma of the *Preventibility of Disease,* to its embodiment in the practical formula of *Sanitary Consolidation.* Of these two fundamental propositions, standing to each other in the relation of Science to Art, or of ascertained Law to the means of its Technical fulfilment, the first is now, happily, too universally recognised to stand in need of further demonstration. The second principle, on the contrary, is still the subject of animated controversy in each of its two main bearings, Administrative and Structural; which, as their importance fully equals their obscurity, we propose to take up for present elucidation: examining, under the first head, the economical advantages of consolidated Sanitary *Jurisdiction;* and, under the second, the corresponding benefits of consolidated Sanitary *Works.* This exposition, succinct and familiar as we shall endeavour to make it, will yet, we trust, suffice to disprove the pretended analogy between

Sanitary

Sanitary Consolidation and the continental system of Centralization;
—to which it is, in fact, diametrically opposed. On the eve of a
great struggle for Sanitary Reform, against which parochial prejudices are diligently invoked, this demonstration will not, we think,
be inopportune : and though the main principles we seek to establish are of universal and permanent interest, we shall accommodate
our argument to the problems now pressing for immediate solution, by selecting our principal illustrations from the Water
question ;—so as to follow up our previous indications respecting
the quality and sources of water, by some remarks on its distribution and removal, on its applications industrial and sanitary,
and on the important question of its cost.

And first—to strike at once into the heart of the debate—let us
meet the charge of ' Centralization,' or the alleged tendency of
the new Sanitary system to supersede Local Self-government by
the arbitrary rule of a Metropolitan Board. To reduce this
question to its proper terms, we must begin by laying down a
well-marked preliminary distinction,—that, namely, which exists
between Local self-government, as it affects the *mass* of residents
in any district, and as it concerns the *functionaries*, often corrupt
and ignorant, by whom they are rated and ruled. Obviously,
wherever district rates are squandered by jobbing or incompetent
Local boards, the corrective intervention of a Central power, so
far from diminishing, may tend largely to increase, the *real* self-
governing power of the place, as measured by the control of the
population over the expenditure of their own funds. Just so the
gradual subjugation of the feudal barons by the imperial power,
and the suppression of such local privileges as those of ' pit and
gallows,' relieved provincial populations from an odious tyranny,
and procured them a large increase of local freedom : for which
(paradoxical as the assertion sounds) they were indebted to a development of Centralization. This distinction between *real* and
nominal Self-government—between the liberty of local communities, and the privileges of local functionaries—was perceived
ten centuries ago by King Alfred ; who stretched to the utmost
his prerogatives, in order to bring about the local enfranchisement of his subjects. Nay, his administrative expedient for this
purpose was actually borrowed from the Roman imperial centralization ; for he used to despatch Royal *Missi*, or Commissioners,
to the local jobbers of those days, with such peremptory messages
as this : ' I marvel at your insolence, who by God's gift and mine
have taken on yourselves the ministry and rank of wise men, but
have neglected the study of wisdom. Now, therefore, it is my
command that ye either give up at once the powers which ye enjoy,
or pay a much more devoted attention to the studies of wisdom.'

Nor

Nor did King Alfred confine himself to words; but occasionally impressed his precepts upon obdurate functionaries by hanging one or two of the more recalcitrant. Without staying to discuss how far this summary exercise of royal power was justified by the necessities of those rude times, we must frankly own ourselves indebted to this great king's centralizing vigour for the early development of our popular local freedom.

And this brings us to a second preliminary distinction, not less broadly marked than the first, nor less necessary to dispel the vulgar prejudice against so-called 'Sanitary Centralization.' Just as we have shown the local effect of the principle in question to be twofold, so now we have to exhibit as twofold its central manifestation. For, the imperial or central power has obviously two separate spheres of action—one general and permanent—the other particular and exceptional : the first embracing all the collective interests of the nation at large, but excluding the internal concerns of particular parishes ; while the second, still keeping in view the general interests of the nation, enters also on parochial ground, and interferes in the affairs of district populations, aggrieved by the misconduct of their local rulers. Those who are averse to Centralization in its first-mentioned general and permanent sphere, might as well demand at once a return to the heptarchy ; or claim for Marylebone and St. Pancras the right of declaring war against each other, or against France. Those, on the other hand, who repudiate the exceptional exercise of the central authority in its local sphere, evidently hold a less liberal doctrine than our own ; seeing that they would hinder the imperial government from complying with the prayer of district populations. Centralization is, in fact, equally legitimate in both cases, provided that in each its action be based on ascertained public requirement, national or provincial. It is only when these limitations are disregarded, when the exception becomes the rule, and when, in opposition to the public wish, the imperial power exercises by its nominees a direct and permanent sway over local affairs, that Centralization becomes excessive and obnoxious.

The term *Centralization* is in fact a double-edged word, susceptible of two interpretations ; and implying an exercise of power, in one sense wholesome, in the other odiously tyrannical. This dangerous ambiguity (like many others of the same sort) is fertile in sophisms and misconceptions, of which adroit advantage has been taken by parochial agitators, who denounce as *Centralization* (in its bad sense) the due regulation of their own misused powers, and the protection of the public interests against their private malversation. And herein we see also the equivocal source of the common but fallacious antithesis between
Centralization

Centralization and Self-government; forms of power which, rightly interpreted, are so far from being mutually repugnant and incompatible, that they are on the contrary necessary concomitants, developed *pari passu*, each as the corrective and counterpoise of the other.

We may elucidate this view by a simple illustration, drawn from the animal kingdom, and founded on the contrast presented by infusorial life, with the life and organization of Man :—(of Man, however—and we qualify the term to obviate possible misapprehension, by cursory readers, of this and some subsequent similar illustrations—of Man, considered in a purely physiological point of view, without reference to his higher spiritual endowments, which are beside the purpose of our present argument). The lowest forms of life are simple cells, or congeries of cells, equally deficient of individual organs and of collective unity. Cut these vesicular zoophytes into halves or quarters, and each portion lives. This diffuseness of the lowest infusorial life gives place, as we ascend the scale of being, to a twofold concentration: the one *local* and subordinate, determining the development of various organs, each well defined, self-centred, and working with spontaneous powers to a special end ; the other *central* and dominant, enforcing the harmonious co-operation of these manifold parts and their subservience to a collective unity. It is in Man, the highest type of life, that we find, at once, the most strongly pronounced unity of the whole organism, and also the greatest multiplicity, diversity, and individuality, of the constituent organs. And this concurrent expansion of the central and local vitality is not casual but necessary ; each being, obviously, the indispensable condition, as well as the inevitable consequence, of the other ; while in the well-balanced intensity of both we recognise alike the sign and the source of Man's organic supremacy. This counterpoised duality of individual life is repeated, on a vaster scale, in the social organism ; which is impelled to a similar double development, as well by blindly striving popular instinct, as by conscious philosophic statesmanship. And as, within the womb, the embryo Man springs at first from a mere nerveless cell, or simple Monad, which unfolds itself gradually, by simultaneous expansion of its local and central forces, into many-ganglioned, full-brained humanity ; so likewise does Society, during long ages of painful gestation, unfold progressively its double life, ganglionic and cerebral (or local and central), from primal anarchy to well-knit constitutional government. Civilization, indeed, is but the name we give to an intense manifestation of this double life, elevating while it complicates the organization of society, and exalting, by its reaction, the character

racter and conduct of individual man. And the idea of PROGRESS, when contemplated in the light of these physiological analogies, appears the very opposite of that Subversive Innovation with which it is often falsely identified, and stands revealed as neither more nor less than the CONSERVATIVE DEVELOPMENT OF ORDER.

These very expressions, indeed, *Order* and *Government*, if examined in a comprehensive spirit, yield a satisfactory disproval of the alleged repugnancy between centralized and local institutions. For all government, however narrow its sphere, implies a convergence and concentration of force, determining the subordination of minor to major interests, and of partial to collective rights. In that first degree of government, for instance, which a man is bound to exercise over himself, the passing impulse of each particular appetite and organ is subordinated to the permanent and collective interest of the whole organism ; which would be compromised by the unrestricted freedom of its several constituent members. So, again, in that second sphere of government which has its centre in the father of a family, each member's individual freewill finds its proper limit exactly at the point where further indulgence would compromise the interests of the entire household. And as individual self-government is but the first degree of centralized power, and paternal or family-government the second ; so likewise the district government of many households constituting a parish, or precinct,—the municipal government of many parishes and precincts, grouped within a town or borough—and the imperial government of many towns and provinces, forming a realm or kingdom,—are but ascending grades of the same progressive Centralization ; whereof even the last-named eminent degree still ranks below that loftiest supremacy, which, based on the general Law of Nations, and administered by their Diplomatic Representatives, subordinates the interests of particular States to the collective interests of Humanity. At each ascending step, we still find the power of a superior or more central organ maintaining order in a subordinate group, by regulating the mutual relations of all, and by correcting, when necessary, the internal irregularities of each. In the individual man, the *permanent* function of the great nervous centre is to keep the inferior organs in harmonious equipoise; while, by its *exceptional* curative interference, it also brings about the internal re-adjustment of any particular organ which may become deranged. So also it is the father's *permanent* function to maintain harmony among all his children ; and his *exceptional* duty to correct the aberrations of any particular child whose unaided freewill proves inadequate for its self-government. In like manner, it is the *permanent* office of parochial Boards, to maintain justice and

and fair play between household and household ; while they are
occasionally obliged, in consequence of private misrule, to restrain
or modify the internal government of particular domiciles.   And
to our judgment it seems clear, that the central state authority is
bound, by the same rule, not only to hold the balance even between
rival localities, but also, in each particular locality, to interfere
occasionally for the remedy of disorders caused by the misconduct
of the local power. Nor should we find it difficult, if it fell
within the scope of our present argument, to extend this analogy
to the highest international Centralization ; and to justify the
Supreme Diplomatic power, not merely in the exercise of its
permanent control over international relations, but also in its *occasional* curative intervention in the internal convulsions of particular states.   In all these cases, so widely different in aspect, so
profoundly identical in kind, the true object of government is to
increase the common enjoyment of *liberty*, by repressing the
reciprocal tyranny of *licence;* or, in other words, tó afford to each
individual governed a wider and steadier sphere of Freedom, by
restraining, in his neighbours as well as himself, the discordant
encroachments of fluctuating Caprice. The stringent application
of this principle, in each successive sphere of government, is
naturally distasteful to the erring subordinates corrected or restrained ; and, so considered, the protest of a Cabinet overthrown
by Diplomatic intervention, may differ from the clamour of a
Board superseded by Sanitary Consolidation, or even of a school-
boy under the paternal interdict, only in its wider echo, and its
graver form.

If, now, the question be raised, What degree of local mismanagement justifies the interference of the central power ? or
how, in any given case, is the need of such interference to be
determined ? the answer is obvious. The need of Central interference is evinced by the exact converse of that evidence which
suffices to prove the adequacy of Local Self-government : the
condition of the ruled furnishing, in both cases, the proper test ;
and manifest disorder calling for curative intervention, as plainly
as evident healthiness claims to be let alone. Just as a *complaint*
of the liver, transmitted in a message of pain along the nerves,
justifies the ganglionic nervous centre in determining towards it
a swifter supply of blood, or of nervous power, for its cure ; just
so the *complaint* of a parish or town, testified in a report of excessive mortality, or in a petition from the suffering inhabitants,
justifies the metropolitan sanitary centre in directing thither, by
the medium of a commissioner, the power necessary to abate its
disorder. Again, and further, just as this curative invasion of
the liver may be justified not only by its own complaint, but by
the

the complaint of neighbouring organs impeded in their action by
the liver's disorder; just so may the remedial interference of
a central authority with any house in a town, or any town in a
realm, be justified not only by complaints from inhabitants of the
disordered place, but also by detriment accruing to the residents
in its vicinity.

So close, indeed, is the analogy between the two organisms, individual and social, that in both cases the remedy becomes worse
than the disease when central interference is premature or excessive; so as to supersede, instead of regulating and restoring, the
normal action of the disordered part. A country whose provincial
towns should be permanently subject to the direct control of a
central sanitary board, ruling by local nominees irresponsible to
the ratepayers, would be in the exact condition of an individual,
whose local organs of digestion, &c., instead of working spontaneously, should be habitually urged to præternatural activity by
the administration of stimulating drugs. In both these cases (as
indeed in all others) excess is followed by equivalent privation;
and the unnatural tension, kept up for a time by undue excitement, induces, in the social as in the individual organs, a state
of ultimate torpor and debility. From Centralization in this
obnoxious sense our Sanitary Consolidation differs as much as
the occasional use of tonics or aperients differs from habitual
gin-drinking, or from Mr. Morrison's daily purge.

These distinctions have been clearly kept in view by the
framers of that admirable sanitary code, the Public Health Act
of 1848; an act which embodies the main principles laid down
by Sir Robert Peel's Commission of Inquiry into the means
of improving the Health of Towns;—and which will remain, we
believe, an imperishable monument of that great statesman's far-
reaching sagacity. This masterly enactment, while it places the
general sanitary interests of the country under the care of a Metropolitan Board (the pretext of the anti-centralization cry), also
recognises the principle of Local Self-government, by the simultaneous institution of District boards, elected by the ratepayers,
to whom they are consequently responsible, and liable to central
interference only in one of two cases: first, on an appeal or petition, emanating from the district itself, and signed by not less
than one-tenth of the ratepayers; secondly, on a duly certified
district mortality exceeding the high annual rate of 23 in 1000.
Even, indeed, when the regulating power of the Central authority
is thus called forth, either by the express prayer of a suffering
district, or by a mortality prejudicial to society at large, its
operation is surrounded by official delays and restrictions, designed to afford time for local deliberation, and popular concurrence

currence in the remedies proposed. Thus, before the solicited
inspection can be accorded under this Act, fourteen days' notice
must be given by newspaper and mural advertisement within
the district. The inspector, thus announced, is bound on
his arrival to hold an open court for the reception of evidence, against, as well as for, the proposed sanitary improvements. His report, based on this evidence, and on a personal
survey of the place, must next be published and circulated
amongst the inhabitants ; and to this official statement of his
intended measures he is bound to add a detailed account of their
cost, and a notice inviting the criticisms and suggestions of all
parties concerned. After this ample preliminary investigation
on the spot, the central board is empowered to issue a ' provisional order,' sanctioning the Inspector's plans, as modified by
local amendment. But (so jealously is ' centralization ' counter-
checked) this order itself must be sent down and circulated in the
district, for the reconsideration of the ratepayers ; on whom it
does not become finally binding, till sanctioned by the Privy
Council, or by Parliament.

With this open and eminently *popular* procedure, so falsely
stigmatized as Centralization, compare the old system of obtaining
local acts, under which Paving boards, Sewer commissions, and
other such district authorities have been hitherto created, and
empowered to levy rates. Drawn up usually by some district
attorney, desirous of sharing the expected patronage and pelf,
the local bill was advertised only in legal form, suited for none
but professional apprehension, and escaping the attention of the
public at large. This imperfect announcement was not followed
by impartial and open inquiry on the spot. There was no
scheme of improvement, emanating from the metropolitan focus
of sanitary experience, and overhauled by provincial mother-
wit ;—no cross-examination of the projector by adverse ratepayers ;—rarely any opposition but that of interested proprietors,
calculating on compromise and compensation ; nor any evidence
except that of witnesses brought up at great cost to the metropolis, for examination before parliamentary committees, unskilled
in questions of sanitary engineering, and giving but a languid
attention to debates, in their eyes petty and parochial. Evidently
this procedure, expensive as it was to the district ratepayers (so
expensive that a single local act has been known to cost 20,000*l.*),
conferred on the imperial legislature a virtual Centralization, in
the highest degree inconvenient and oppressive.

It thus turns out that the charge of Centralization, so far
from holding good against the sanitary reformers, applies in
point of fact to their assailants—the partizans of those antiquated
forms

forms of procedure which Sanitary Consolidation is designed to supersede.

And along with the main charge of Centralization fall also to the ground its several offshoots and corollaries ;—as, for example, that the new sanitary organization trammels and damps *Individual Energy* ; restricts the play of *Free Competition* ; and supersedes that economical *Division of Labour* which is the very basis of our industrial system. These allegations are not only untrue— they are the very reverse of the truth : the effect of the Health Act being, in fact, to reinforce and develope the very principles which it is here declared to violate. It discourages, no doubt, that disastrous kind of Competition in which rival Water and Gas Companies are wont to engage ; and which implies the wasteful employment of double capital, and double works, with double costs of management and maintenance, in the same limited field of supply ; besides involving ruinous parliamentary conflicts, which end invariably in coalitions against the public, so as to throw ultimately on the consumer the whole burden of these reckless expenses. But, while firmly maintaining the principle that one set, and one only, of sanitary works should be allowed in each area of sanitary jurisdiction, the Health Act encourages legitimate competition by enjoining on local boards the execution by contract, on public tender, of their proposed improvements. So anxious, indeed, were the framers of this Act to call into the field all available enterprise and energy, that they have expressly prohibited local boards from accepting any contract for works above the value of 100*l*., until ten days after the advertised invitation of tenders. Thus the competition of individuals and of companies, instead of being wasted as of old in internecine wars, is brought to bear once for all at the outset ; so as to secure to the public minimum charges, while guaranteeing individual or associated contractors in the enjoyment of the stipulated profits.

And while thus affording a new and most productive field for individual energy, Sanitary Consolidation also promotes, instead of obstructing as its adversaries pretend, the economical *Division of Labour*. It is true, no doubt, that Sanitary Consolidation tends to supersede the incoherent operations of the bricklayers, plumbers, and carpenters, who now 'divide' amongst them our Sanitary works ; and who have saddled us with a labyrinth of waterpipes and drains, utterly unsuited, in shape, size, and material, to each other and to their conjoint functions. But there is nothing in the principle of Consolidation to prevent the sanitary works of a district, though *planned* as a comprehensive whole, from being parcelled out for *execution* amongst the local traders and craftsmen ;

to

to each of whom may be assigned that portion of the work which falls within his special competence. In point of fact this is the invariable result of Sanitary Consolidation; which, by the vast scope and unity of the schemes it begets, facilitates their executive subdivision: just as, in a well-ordered factory, the multitude and high discipline of the operatives permits the economical 'division of labour' to be carried to else unattainable limits. The more, indeed, in any branch of industry, the functions of the workers are specialised, the more essential does it become that their efforts be also 'convergent;' every fresh subdivision of the total work involving evidently, as the condition of its success, a stricter unity of collective management. The common 'division' of Sanitary labour among individuals and companies, working without concert each to a special and separate end, issues in such incongruous productions as would result from the random manufacture of pins' heads and shanks, or of watch springs, wheels, and escapements, without any reference to each other.

But when driven from these, their main positions, the champions of the anti-centralization cry fall back on two or three subsidiary pleas, sufficiently plausible to deserve, in this place, cursory examination. For example, though constrained to acknowledge that the principle of self-government is fully recognised in that clause of the Health Act which prescribes, as the condition of its enforcement in any district, a petition emanating from the district itself, they object to the petition of a *minority* being admitted to sanction the central interference, in spite of the indifference or hostility of the *majority*. And they protest, if possible loudlier still, against those clauses of the Act which authorize central intervention in local affairs, for the purpose of protecting against possible infringement the interests of reversioners and absentees. Reduced to their simplest terms, and coupled together in a single expression, the two charges amount to this—that the Health Act imposes on the Central authority the duty of protecting the Weak against the Strong. The wisdom and justice of such a provision stand approved, we think, by the same broad analogies which have elucidated our foregoing argument. In the individual frame, local *complaint* justifies central interference for its relief, though what we have called 'the message of pain' proceed from only one circumscribed spot; and though the major part of the disordered organ protest (so to speak), by nausea, against the remedies imposed. So again, in the household, the weakest child's complaint claims redress at the upright father's hands, in spite of the indifference, or opposition, of the majority in his little realm. Nay, our parochial adversaries themselves use the powers conferred on them by the 66th clause of the Act to abate the congestion of
overcrowded

overcrowded lodging-houses, without waiting the concurrence of a *majority* of the inmates to sanction their remedial intervention. In presence of a rule thus universal, it is, we think, for our antagonists to show why the grievance of a Minority should be ignored, or its redress denounced as obnoxious ' centralization,' at that point only of the ascending scale, when the oppression complained of is that of a parish board, and the aid invoked that of the authority next above it.   For our part, we are content to rest the right of Minorities, in this last case, on its analogy with the undisputed claim of the weak to protection, in every other sphere of government.

And, in thus extending to our public polity that generous rule of private morals, which measures the duty of the strong by the helplessness of the weak, we virtually sanction Central intervention in behalf of those silent suppliants for care—the absent and the yet unborn.   While, therefore, the Health Act, by authorising the distribution of sanitary improvement-costs over terms of years, very properly relieves present occupants, and owners of terminable interests, from payments which, if levied at once, would be tantamount to confiscation; it also, with equal propriety, subjects this local distributive power to a central check, lest the present generation of ratepayers should make it a means of shifting from their own to their successors' shoulders an undue proportion of the fiscal burden which should be jointly borne.   It is for this reason that local boards, elected by the ratepayers of the day, and naturally disposed to favour the immediate interests which they represent, are bound, by the 119th clause of the Act, to obtain the sanction of the General Board of Health, before raising loans for Sanitary purposes on mortgage of improvement-rates, spread, as above described, over terms of years.   This restriction shuts the door against a mass of 'jobs' in which local boards would else probably be tempted to engage, to the present profit of themselves, or their friends, but to the grievous detriment of the next generation. Society owes, we think, to its unborn members, this protection against the cupidity of the living; and the supreme intervention by which the rights of posterity are thus guaranteed, cannot, in our judgment, be justly stigmatized as 'Centralization' in its obnoxious sense.

One other plea, however, affords a refuge to the impugners of Sanitary Consolidation, when driven to their last entrenchments. They take up their position as champions of Private Property; whose 'sacred rights' they declare to be infringed by the application of the new Sanitary dogma.   They denounce, for example, as inquisitorial and un-English, the sanitary inspection of private domiciles; and they protest against the legislative enforcement of house-drainage as an unconstitutional interference with proprietary privileges. Whether a cesspool under a house be a nuisance or not, is a question, they contend, for the householder himself to decide. From the recognised axiom that Every Englishman's house is his Castle, they infer that its invasion, on any pretence whatever, is Centralization in its most despotic form: nor do they admit any difference in this respect between the basement of the castle and the floors above—between the Englishman's drain and his dining-room.

The reader will at once perceive the applicability of our previous rejoinder to this auxiliary plea; and we refrain from wearying him with a formal demonstration that each man's right of private property, like his freedom of individual will, ends exactly at the point where its further extension would infringe on the similar rights of others. Naturalists tell us that in a beehive the movements of each little builder's feet tend to model the plastic wax in a circular form around him; and that it is the similar exertions of the surrounding artificers, acting in a contrary direction, that reduce each cell to the hexagonal form. Just so, in human societies, each individual's share of the collective power resulting from co-operation, is purchased (and cheaply purchased too) by a partial sacrifice of personal independence, compressed on all sides by the contrary development of like rights—equally expansive, and similarly restrained. So that any bee in the social hive who seeks to widen his hexagon into a sphere, finds himself immediately opposed by the six neighbours whose respective lodgings would be narrowed by such an encroachment. This principle, embodied in the well-known maxim of our common law, *Sic utere tuo ut alienum non lædas*, establishes a broad distinction between the dining-room and the cesspool or drain, as subject-matters of private property. For, in using the first, a man can hardly annoy his neighbour; whereas in using the second, or in neglecting the third, he pollutes his neighbour's air as well as his own. This distinction was clearly understood—and acted on—so early as the fourteenth century. For, in 1320, we find a complaint laid before Parliament by the inhabitants of Smithfield against the butchers in that neighbourhood, for digging wells or pits 'without the King's licence' to receive the offal of their slaughtered beasts; which malpractice the mayor and corporation of London were thereupon directed to restrain. Here again, therefore, as before, the *soi-disant* champions of private right prove to be really its rudest assailants; trespassing on the liberties of others while denouncing the infringement of their own; and practising the very despotism of which they complain.

A striking

A striking example of individual tyranny practised in the name of ' property's sacred rights,' will bear out these assertions ; and justify, we think, to average common sense, the value of the central counterpoise afforded by sanitary consolidation.

About a mile and a half from a certain Scotch town stands an old corn-mill, the original owner of which dammed up a small stream to turn his wheel. The surrounding country, to the extent of nearly twenty square miles, has its drainage obstructed by this mill-dam ; which causes periodical inundations, whereby extensive hay-crops are destroyed. The injury thus occasioned has amounted in the course of years to many thousands sterling ; while the mill whence all the evil springs only produces 25*l.* per annum. A proposal, made by the neighbouring proprietors, to purchase the removal of the dam, by payment in full of the annual rental derived from the mill, was stubbornly resisted by the owner—an ignorant man, standing on his ' private rights,' and caring apparently more for his mill than for the prosperity of the surrounding population. His decision, whether founded on whim or speculation, could not, it was found, be overruled without a special Act of Parliament, which funds were not forthcoming to obtain : and he has continued, year after year, inflicting loss of rent on the owners of the water-logged land, loss of produce and profit on the farmers, loss of wages on the labourer, and on all (himself included) hazard of marsh-fever from the poisonous miasmata left behind by the swollen waters in their subsidence. The restriction by imperial power of such ' private rights ' as these, whether exercised in town or country, cannot we maintain be justly stigmatized as excessive or unconstitutional Centralization. Nay, the justice of our new Sanitary code stands herein most conspicuously approved,—that whilst, as we have before seen, it protects oppressed Minorities against the dominion of the mass, it defends also, with equally scrupulous concern, the interests of Majorities, when in their turn oppressed by the tyranny of individual caprice.

For, indeed, just as our modern Political System accounts the Weak and the Strong to be equal in the eye of Civil law ; just so does our new Sanitary Code regard the Few and the Many as equal in the presence of Natural Law ; overruling, in virtue of that supreme authority, all irregular manifestations of human *arbitrium*, however strongly fortified by the concurrence of numbers, or by the sanction of immemorial usage. It is, indeed, this principle (hitherto vaguely felt, perhaps, rather than rigorously defined) which mainly distinguishes the Sanitary Movement from other less determinate forms of progress. Based on determinate physical

2 H 2   laws,

laws, which have compelled, by the terrible consequences of their infringement, the universal recognition of scientific men, the Sanitary evolution pursues its course independently of unenlightened Will, whether opposed to it by units, or by majorities of the population. Political movements, on the contrary, originating as they do not in ascertained *law*, but in fluctuating and controvertible *opinion*, depend essentially on the public *will*, manifested either by present numerical preponderance, or by old usage implying the concurrence of successive majorities in time past. Hence premature Political Centralization is abhorrent to a free people, who see in it the mere substitution of the will of the few for the will of the many ; while Sanitary consolidation becomes more popular the better it is understood, because it replaces all arbitrary will whatsoever (whether that of the many themselves, or of the few), by Natural Law : which substitution, *Lex pro arbitrio*, is instinctively felt by the mass of the people to lie at the very root of their progressive enfranchisement.

If now, quitting the theoretic for the practical point of view, and passing from the study of principles to that of results, we proceed to compare the actual working of the old and new forms of procedure, we shall establish, by evidence of the most positive kind, the superiority of Sanitary Consolidation.

It was in the year 1846 that public attention was first strongly directed, by the evidence taken before the Commons' Committee on private bills, to the extreme incoherency of the old local administrative system, and to its *previously unsuspected centralizing tendency*. It then, for the first time, became generally known that the Imperial Parliament passes, every year, a larger number of private and local than of public bills ; the measures of the former class enacted from the date of the Union to 1845 inclusive numbering 9200, while the general statutes carried during the same period amounted only to 5300. The Committee reported strongly against the virtual centralization which thus cast upon the imperial legislature so vast a burden of strictly local investigations ; and they recommended a consolidation of the laws affecting local interests as the proper remedy for this state of things.* Some years previously, indeed, it had come out before the Committee on Municipal Reform, that the local government of the corporate towns in England and Wales was carried on under no less than 700 acts, not only at variance with each other, but in many cases utterly inconsistent with the general laws of the country. Nay more, each individual town was found to be governed under a series of voluminous and conflicting Acts,

* See Report of the Select Committee on Private Bills, p. iv.

numbering

numbering frequently several scores, utterly defying popular apprehension, perplexing the magistrates, and baffling the acumen (while filling the pockets) of the very lawyers themselves.

Liverpool, for example, was found to be governed under no less than sixty local Acts—some antiquated and dormant—some amended and partially repealed—others, on the contrary, confirmed and extended, by their successors ; so that each new question, as it arose, involved laborious research, and led to costly litigations, ending often in the discovery of some preposterous ambiguity or contradiction, equally vexatious to both the parties. Under these incoherent statutes, grafted on the ancient common law, five or six independent local authorities had grown up in Liverpool, ruling fragmentary districts with divided powers, and mutually obstructing each other's functions. Thus, the Corporation of Liverpool controlled by three Committees the departments of Public Health, of Scavenging, and of Fire Police; but had no authority over water-supply, sewerage, and paving, which were administered by the Commissioners of Sewers. Of the water-service itself, so much as related to domestic supply was separated from the supply for extinguishing fires and watering streets, and was abandoned to the interested management of two antagonist trading companies. To complete this strange confusion, an outlying district called Toxteth Park was governed by independent commissioners of its own ; who, within their little realm, exercised collectively all the powers, dispersed, in Liverpool itself, amongst half a dozen conflicting boards. The further this sort of investigation was pushed, the more anomalies came to light. It appeared, amongst other things, that though the sewerage and paving of *courts* fell under the control of the Health Committee, the sewerage and paving of *streets* appertained to the Commissioners of Sewers; while *neither* board had any authority to compel the drainage of private houses, whether in courts or streets. Nay, by an almost incredible blunder of the legislature, power had been conferred on one set of commissioners to interdict the drainage of private dwellings into the sewers under their control; so that they could enforce on the inhabitants the retention, in stagnant cesspools, of the very refuse which sewers are provided to remove;—and this, notwithstanding the remonstrances of the Cleansing Committee, and the still stronger protests of the Committee of Health. The Fire-committee were crippled by an equally perverse severance of functions naturally allied ; the water brought into the town expressly for the extinction of conflagrations being, strange to say, withdrawn from their control, and confided to the Sewer-department. Hence, doubtless, the frequency of such calamities as that recorded by Mr. Rushton, the stipendiary magistrate ;

magistrate ; who told the Committee that Mr. Gladstone (the mayor
of Liverpool) as well as himself, had seen a hundred thousand
pounds' worth of property consumed by fire, for want of timely
water-supplies.   Of the administrative chaos resulting from this
medley of incongruous jurisdictions some idea may be formed from
the fact, that, while the *surface* of the streets belonged to the Surveyors of Highways, the *soil* beneath was vested in the Corporation ; so that before an area could be widened, or a branch water-
pipe laid on, two separate bodies had to be petitioned—one for
leave to take up the kerbstone, the other for permission to dig
below it.   'Hence,' said Mr. Rushton, 'double expenses of
all sorts ; double establishments and sets of officials ; surveyors,
engineers, clerks, lawyers, and all sorts of people in duplicate.'
Such a pass, indeed, had this random legislation reached, that the
same proceeding which, under one Act, was a fineable offence,
was expressly authorised under another, 'passed in the very same
session of parliament, and sanctioned by the Royal assent within
a few weeks of its companion.' *   So again, two exactly similar
thefts, committed at two points of Liverpool within a stone's
throw of each other, subjected the offenders to two widely different measures of punishment : one culprit rendering himself
liable to two months' imprisonment at the utmost ; while the
other,-falling within the range of a different district law, incurred
three months' incarceration, with the severe addition of *hard
labour*.   In some parts of Liverpool, again, it was found that a
citizen, owing arrears of rates, becomes liable under three different Acts to three summonses, three warrants, and three levies—
with all their accumulated costs.   Of these vexatious anomalies
the mass of the population could only, as Mr. Rushton stated,
'acquire a painful and expensive knowledge, by penal informa-

---

* This statement seems so incredible that we think it well to obviate any possible
scepticism on the reader's part by citing Mr. Rushton's evidence on the subject *ipsis-
simis verbis*. 'There are,' says he, 'Acts now in force in the town of Liverpool
which give one set of powers to the Commissioners of Highways, and another set of
powers [for the same purposes] to the Corporate body. The Commissioners of Highways are empowered, under one Act, to prohibit the projection of a certain portion of
a public building more than six inches on the foot-walk, under a penalty for each
offence. The Corporation are empowered, under the other Act, to permit the obstruction on certain conditions of assent being previously obtained. The Justices are empowered to enforce both those laws. On a recent occasion the Commissioners of
Highways laid an information against an inhabitant for an infraction of *their* law.
They clearly sustained their case, and I called on the inhabitant to justify his conduct,
or to state what he had to say why a penalty of 5*l*. should not be enforced against him.
He answered by producing an Act of Parliament, and showing that he had obtained
the assent therein mentioned, and was therefore justified in making the projection, for
the making of which the Commissioners of Highways sought to punish him. These
Acts were both passed in the same session of Parliament ; they both received the Royal
assent within a few weeks, and contained both those powers, applying to the same
town.'—*Minutes of Evidence taken before the Committee on Private Bills*, p. 2.

tions ;—of which no less than 11,000 had been laid against them during the previous year' (1845).

Nor was Liverpool put forward as an exceptional case. Its local arrangements were selected for description, as a fair type of the municipal organization prevalent in all the cities of this realm. Birmingham, for example, was found to be governed by no less than eight local Powers, employing eight separate sets of officers ; and acting with such utter want of concert that while one Board (the Birmingham Commissioners) had expended large sums of money to keep the town-sewage out of the river Rea, another Board (the Edgbaston Surveyors) had built a sewer for the express purpose of turning their refuse into that stream. From similar incoherencies arose doubts and disputations as to the apportionment of cleansing-costs, pending which filth was suffered to accumulate, soaking the ground with hideous overflows, which neither party would interfere to prevent. So keenly alive are the people of Birmingham to these crying evils, that they have for ten years past (as Mr. Bray, the town-clerk, states) been struggling to obtain a consolidated government ; with which view they last year petitioned in due form for the application of the Health Act to their town.

Equally pitiable, and still more curious, is the sanitary *morcellement* of Nottingham, as exhibited in the official reports. The sewage jurisdiction, in this town, falls short of the natural drainage area ; so that the inhabitants have no power over the outfalls of their own sewers. An obstruction in one of these outfalls, happening recently to concur with heavy rains, occasioned so severe an inundation that, in the lower levels of the town, the water rose two feet high in the houses ; depositing in its recession two inches of fœtid mud upon the floors. The terrified inhabitants of course besieged the parish officers who ruled over the obstructed sewer, with earnest entreaties for its clearance. But those worthies turned a deaf ear to their solicitations. They not only declined to abate the nuisance, but denied its existence ; and refused even to have the sewer examined. Upon this the town authorities, very properly sacrificing municipal etiquette, and arbitrary rules, to laws and requirements of a higher order, made an incursion into the outlying parish at the head of a troop of labourers—took possession of the obstructed sewer by a sort of *coup de main*—broke it open *vi et armis*—and cleared a passage for the pent-up waters.

This general want of concert, degenerating occasionally into open warfare, is bad and barbarous enough ; but it is not the worst defect of our Local Administrative system. Its powers are reduced, by extreme subdivision, to so petty a scope as rather to deter

deter than to attract the ambition of educated men. Theoretically, the conduct of local affairs should devolve on the wealthiest and ablest ratepayers: in other words, on those who, contributing most largely to the local funds, are most interested in securing their judicious expenditure—and who, by their superior knowledge and influence, are marked out as natural leaders of the community. Practically, however, such men shrink from engaging in parochial squabbles; and gladly suffer the paltry powers of half a dozen clashing boards to fall into the hands of an inferior class. This is especially remarkable in the largest towns, whose ' merchant princes' abdicate their legitimate sway over affairs of vast *collective* importance, because of their *subdivided* insignificance. Hence the low tone and narrow views of our existing local boards; hence the public indifference to their petty proceedings; hence also obscurity, parent of ' jobs;' and hence the coalition of active cupidity with inertial ignorance, in obstinate resistance to Sanitary Reform.

All these facts are matters of notoriety. Every one knows that owners of ill-conditioned tenements take local office, expressly to defeat measures within whose scope their own neglected property would fall. It is a matter of course for tradesmen to get themselves elected, or to procure the nomination of their friends, with a view to lucrative parish contracts, or to secure clerkships, &c., for their children. And each, so soon as his private ends are gained, shakes off by resignation his share of public responsibility for extravagant or defective works. Fluctuating thus, and unpaid, so as to be practically as irresponsible as they are interested and ignorant, these little knots of men nevertheless despatch offhand, at occasional meetings, held in snatched intervals of private business, sanitary problems involving the health of vast populations; and almost baffling by their extreme complexity the *unintermittent* study of the ablest engineers.

Nor have these blind leaders of the blind pieced out the defects of their own knowledge by the science of competent assistants. On the contrary, they have usually chosen their surveyors from a class of persons as uninstructed as themselves. In the country, ' ditch-caster's foremen,'—in the towns, ' decayed builders,' or ' artificers whose knowledge extends only to common bricklaying and carpentry,' are commonly appointed surveyors to the Sewer-Commissioners. In one important district an illiterate tinman is surveyor, with a salary of 150*l.* a year—just thrice the pay of a serjeant of sappers and miners, instructed in geometry, drawing, and mensuration, and engaged in taking levels for the Ordnance Survey. In another large urban district, the commissioners advertised for a surveyor ' understanding the use of the spirit level;'
a novel

a novel demand, which is reported to have 'astonished' the candidates (mostly common house-builders); though several 'began to learn' the use of the instrument, by way of qualifying themselves for the appointment! No wonder that the office-charges, dinner expenses, &c., of such administrative bodies as these have often equalled, and sometimes exceeded (in one instance by 200 per cent.!) the beneficial outlay upon works. No wonder that, in one sewage division, the tavern bills alone, in twenty years, had run up to 7935*l.*!

Such, five years since, was the state of our boasted Local Self-government in the provinces; and such, with some partial and scattered improvements, it remains to the present day. It was in the midst of this administrative anarchy that the Asiatic Plague of 1848 suddenly descended on our shores; and proved, with the stern logic of 70,000 deaths, the weakness of a 'divided house.' While rival Boards bickered, the Pestilence ravaged the population. 'In Dumfries,' says Dr. Sutherland, '147 persons were stricken down [out of a population of 10,000] without an effort to save them. Precious time was wasted in petty squabbles; and the town has been clothed in mourning in consequence.' Immediately, however, on the adoption of Dr. Sutherland's well organized preventive measures, the mortality fell from 38 to 11 per diem; which striking decrease continued uninterruptedly, till, on the fourteenth day, the plague was entirely stayed. Like want of concert everywhere prevailed; and everywhere with like disastrous results. In town after town the Inspectors found five or six independent authorities, shifting responsibility on one another's shoulders, and each refusing to recognise any rival power as supreme. 'Even where these separate authorities manifested a fair and liberal desire to coöperate, they necessarily lost much time in serving notices on each other, and in framing expositions of the motives of their mutual requests :' so that when a preventive machinery was at last brought to bear, the officers often discovered, in their first round, the corpses of many cholera-smitten wretches (50, in Glasgow alone, for example!)—who had died in their hovels without medical aid, or spiritual consolation; without so much as a cup of water to cool their raging thirst; or a hand to straighten their cramp-gnarled limbs; or decently to close, when dead, their staring eyes.

Nor was the administrative aggravation of this great public calamity confined to the provinces. London, the centre of our boasted civilization, presented if possible a spectacle of confusion still worse confounded. The Newspapers teemed with appalling disclosures of the miseries endured by the plague-smitten poor, and of the ignorance and apathy of the Parish Boards. The City

Guardians,

454   *Sanitary Consolidation—*

Guardians, in particular, made common cause with the graveyard
and slaughterhouse owners; who, in the face of an increasing
mortality, ' held fast to the abominations by which they had their
wealth,'* and continued ' under the veil of congenial obscurity
their loathsome and pestiferous practices.'† As for their loudly
asserted energy, forecast, and sanitary skill, they were with
weighty facts thus crushingly disproved:—

' In April, 1847, when an epidemic typhus broke out, and ravaged
the country with rapidly increasing violence, till at last, in the autumn,
it produced for several weeks fourfold the ordinary mortality, what
measures of sanitary reform were adopted by the parish officers?
What steps did they take to purge the air of those exhalations which
are the recognised vehicle of typhoid poison?

' When, in the eleven weeks from November 20, 1847, to February
5, 1848, there died in London upwards of 6000 persons above the
average number—an excess greater than the entire mortality produced
by pestilential cholera during the whole 21 weeks of its prevalence in
1832—what were the operations of the parish officers? What lesson
did they learn from this frightful mortality? What steps did they take
to secure us against its return?

' When the febrile influenza—that forecast shadow of Pestilence,
which preceded the Black death in the fourteenth century, the Great
Plague of London in the seventeenth, and the first terrible invasion of
Cholera in our own day—appeared with fearful significance two au-
tumns ago, and slew in a single month (December) 1000 of the inhabitants of London, where were the vaunted energy and sanitary skill of
the parochial officers?

' When, in the following spring, the Asiatic pestilence itself, following its sure precursor, came travelling rapidly towards us across the
continent, pursuing its old track, haunting its old lairs—entering even,
in many places, the *very same houses* which it attacked before—where
were our parochial strategists? What scheme of operations did they
plan, while there was yet time, to keep the Destroyer from our shores,
or to defeat and expel him when he came?

' The parochial officers did nothing—absolutely nothing. They left
the graveyards festering—the cesspools seething—the barrels of blood
steaming in the underground shambles—the great mounds of scutch
putrefying in the Bermondsey glue-yards. They left us all—the poor
in his squalor, and the rich in his fancied security—to be smitten una-
wares. And when at last it came, and the people were perishing by
thousands, and the Medical Officer urged, month after month, on the
parochial authorities, that the plague could only be combated *in the
homes of the poor*, by an organized army of preventive inspectors, what
did the parochial authorities do? They rejected the medical officer's
counsel—they scouted his warnings—they even mutilated his reports;
and only in the fifteenth week of a mortality unparalleled for two centuries, did they consent to the nomination of the domiciliary inspectors

---

    * Times, Sept. 15, 1849.   † Ibid.

—who,

—*who, in their very first round, discovered the corpses of six persons dead without medical aid !'**

We would not, however, be understood to lay on the parish authorities, *as individuals,* the whole blame of these fearful calamities ; which on the contrary we mainly attribute to the want of that Administrative Consolidation for which we are contending. Many individual functionaries, to our knowledge, struggled manfully against the grim Invader, and found their most strenuous efforts baffled by the state of the local law. The incumbent of Christ's Church, Regent's Park, for example, found himself, for all practical purposes, actually unacquainted with the law *of his own parish*—and the Board of Health, when applied to for information as to the requisite procedure for bringing about its cleansing and drainage, proved to be *as much in the dark as himself !* We record, as a curiosity, the main paragraph of their official reply:—

' At present no public maps are known to exist by which the areas of the metropolitan local jurisdictions could in such cases be correctly ascertained. There appear to be upwards of 120 local Acts for the denser portions of the metropolis, and 80 distinct local jurisdictions, many of which coincide neither with parish, nor union, nor police district, nor any other recognised division. Even single streets are divided, often longitudinally, and paved and cleansed at different times under different jurisdictions. In the parish of St. Pancras, where you reside, there are no less than 16 separate paving boards, acting under 29 Acts of Parliament, all of which would require to be consulted before an opinion could be pronounced as to what it might be practicable to do for the effectual cleansing of your parish as a whole.'

Take, as an instance of the cruel sufferings endured in times thus ' out of joint,' the case of a poor working man, in another parish, who lost both his children by cholera, owing to a nuisance of which (as he told Mr. Payne the coroner) he had only complained to his landlord, ' because he did not know the state of the law in his district, nor the proper authority to petition.' He had indeed, on the seizure of his second child, described the nuisance to a Policeman, who reported it to his Serjeant, who reported it to the Inspector, who reported it to the Commissioner of Police, who reported it to the Commissioners of Sewers ; who finally ordered its removal. But the poor child, meanwhile, had died ; a third had also perished ; and two more had sickened, and lay in the blue collapse.

We need not, however, refer to exceptional periods for examples of the social ills resulting from our defective local institutions. Pestilence is but the acute paroxysm of a disorder, of

---

* Times, Sept. 26, 1849.

which

which Pauperism is the chronic form. Both social maladies come of a common stock ; and, though diversely blossomed, have their roots in the same corrupted soil. A row of squalid houses left drainless by contending parish boards, is as prolific a nursery of paupers, as of fever-patients. 'From one of these filthy abodes,' says Mr. Hollins, ' I have often traced a respectable operative's gradual descent to the workhouse.' A six weeks' fever caught from some fœtid ditch or cesspool, first involves the poor man in difficulty ; his rent falls into arrear ; his goods are distrained ; he rises from his sick bed, disheartened as well as enfeebled ; and after struggling vainly against a load of debt, he ultimately sinks with his family into hopeless Pauperism.

All this misery and degradation are in the strictest sense PRE-VENTIBLE. A Consolidated local government, having the power and the will to grapple in good earnest with the Drain-god TYPHUS, might cast him out, and stay his obscene breath within five years ; so staunching too the noisome fountain-heads of Pestilence and Pauperism.

And these sources of Pauperism and Pestilence, be it remembered, are also the Swallow-holes of rates. Every relieving officer can point, with his finger, to the exact courts and lanes whither the streams of out-relief flow and disappear. 'The low lanes around the pier,' says Mr. Davis, the relieving officer at Dover—'the mass of wretched cottages called Manger's rents— the old workhouse ground,' and several other such filthy places, ' continually haunted by fever and smallpox, are the main absorbents of the 3400*l.* annually spent in relief at Dover.' We shall presently see that for less than half the capital corresponding to this annual rate, the sanitary regeneration of these fever-nests might be accomplished ; and their sickly, degraded inmates transformed into a healthy, self-supporting population.

But here another objection is interposed by the adversaries of Sanitary Reform. Granting, they say, for argument's sake, the alleged remissness of individual householders, and parish boards, what proof have you that your consolidated administration will work any better? Government 'jobs' are proverbial, and official management is invariably beaten by individual enterprise, whenever the two are fairly pitted against each other. Look for example at the government ships and steamers — notoriously inferior at all points to the produce of private yards, and as notoriously more expensive. The sure way to have sewers as badly built as frigates, and waterworks as expensively managed as docks, would be to establish a central sanitary *bureau,* like the Department of *Ponts et Chaussées* in France.

This objection is so curiously mixed of truth and error, and the

the deceptive compound passes current, on so many occasions, with so many cursory inquirers, that its succinct refutation may serve to elucidate, not this debate only, but many others of the same sort, hitherto obscured by the same sophism.

The sophism consists in the choice of a particular service, unsuited by its nature for official performance, as the criterion whereby to estimate the relative merits of private and public administration — of dispersed and consolidated works; and in drawing a general conclusion from this partial and one-sided comparison.

The public dockyards are, doubtless, expensively managed establishments: but their cost and comparative inefficiency depend on this obviously *special* cause — that the cumbrous machinery of a Board is here employed on a manufacturing business, *within individual competence.* The private shipbuilder, who is director, secretary, engineer, &c., all in one, can always compete with success against an admiralty board, or even a joint-stock company. But this is evidently no proof that a public department, or a joint-stock directorate, may not be indispensable forms of administration for affairs *beyond individual competence.* The alleged dockyard extravagance (taking it for argument's sake as proved) would but convict the Government, at worst, of an error in judgment, in building, rather than buying, the ships required for the public service. In point of fact, the Government knows very well that our public docks are carried on at a loss; and it thinks proper to maintain them nevertheless. It maintains them, not as commercially profitable, but as politically advantageous, for the assurance of speedy armament in case of sudden war. For the same reason the Lords of the Admiralty retain a permanent staff of shipwrights, for many of whom, in time of peace, they with difficulty find employment; counting their annual cost insignificant in comparison with the possible loss which might result to the country, from a dearth of well-trained labour, in the event of unexpected hostilities. With the policy of these views and arrangements (a much vexed and fairly debateable question) we are not now concerned. Our present object is merely to show, once for all, that no conclusion can be drawn from the case of the docks, against the propriety of Government intervention in affairs *beyond* private or parochial competence.

If, now, we are called on for an example of such affairs, to set against the case of the ships, we may cite the maintenance of the public roads;—notoriously mismanaged under the piecemeal system of the Turnpike trusts; and as notoriously improved and cheapened, wherever those trusts have given place to consolidated official administration. The old Turnpike Trusts,

1116

1116 in number, with usually 100 members at least to each
trust, have covered the country with 22,000 miles of highways,
'of which,' says Sir H. Parnell, 'there is scarcely one not extremely defective in all the qualities of a perfect road.' These
scattered Trusts, according to the Road Commissioners' report,
have employed 1300 surveyors, being ten times the requisite
number, with a proportionate excess of treasurers and clerks—in
all 3555 officers! Their *management* expenses alone have
averaged 10*l.* per mile per annum!—being, on the lowest estimate,
from five to seven times the cost of consolidated management.
On very imperfect repairs they have spent no less than 51*l.* per
mile per annum; and by these, and other such monstrous extra-
vagances, they have burdened the country with a road debt of
9,000,000*l.*—which is said to be still on the increase. This
waste, however, has been promptly checked in the local Trusts
round London, by their recent consolidation under the Metropolitan Roads Commission; which has already paid off the
accumulated debts, at the same time largely reducing the tolls,
and very much improving the condition of the roads.

So again, the recent consolidation of the old District Sewer
Commissions, which formerly divided London amongst them,
jobbing and peculating at their ease, has resulted in a reduction
of no less than 43 per cent. in *management-costs alone.* The
Westminster district, under the old régime, paid its surveying
staff, for services of a fragmentary and imperfect kind, salaries
amounting to 6000*l.* a year; a charge reduced by consolidation
to 4700*l.*, concurrently with a great improvement in the character
and efficiency of the staff. The superior *tone* of the consolidated
Commission was significantly indicated at their very first meeting;
when the old system of dining together at the public cost was
discontinued by a formal resolution; and when, as the noble
chairman declared in his opening address, 'they felt it their
ungracious duty to disallow, as illegal, dinner-bills to the amount
of 186*l.*, run up by their predecessors during the last two months
of their continuance in office.' *

Applying these simple facts and reasonings to the case of the
London Water Companies, we may easily compute the saving
that would accrue to the ratepayers, from the consolidation of
their nine independent Directorates into one central Metropolitan
Commission. We should have, instead of nine salaried boards,
one board; instead of nine engineers, one engineer; instead of nine
secretaries, one secretary; and so on through the whole list of
superfluous officers. Several of the chief functionaries, whom

---

* Lord Morpeth's Charge to the Jury, April 6, 1848.

consolidation

consolidation would supersede, are in the receipt of no less than 2000*l.* per annum each ; and it appears from the computations of the Board of Health, that in the single item of salaries a saving of 15,000*l.* a-year would be secured to the ratepayers by the new arrangements. Again, by consolidating the collection of the water-rates with that of the assessed taxes, the present ' collector's poundage ' of 9*d.* in the pound might be reduced to 3*d.* (the poundage of the assessed-tax gatherer) ; which would knock off· another 10,000*l.* per annum. So that 25,000*l.* per annum might be saved to the metropolitan ratepayers in *management* and *collection* costs *alone*, by breaking up the Water Monopoly.

The Monopolists, however, are not easily convinced of the saving to be effected by their superannuation. They fight their ground backward inch by inch ; and, though driven to admit the advantages of consolidation in the management of roads and sewers, they challenge us to prove its applicability to the administration of Waterworks.

This challenge we cheerfully accept.

Up to the year 1842 the South-Metropolitan districts were supplied with water by two rival Companies, called respectively the Southwark and the Vauxhall ; whose gross receipts (added together) were then 28,000*l.* per annum ; and their working expenses 18,500*l.* per annum. In 1842 the competition ceased ; and the two Companies were shortly afterwards consolidated under the able management of Sir W. Clay ; who, while he has raised their gross rental to 38,000*l.* per annum, has at the same time reduced their working expenses to 12,500*l.* per annum. We refrain from weakening, by any comment, the force of this simple collocation of figures.

Sir W. Clay, indeed, who represents a considerable section of the Metropolitan Water-trade, has been unable, in the face of these facts, to deny the saving which would accrue to the London public from a general consolidation of the waterworks. Nay, Mr. Quick, engineer to the companies which Sir W. Clay directs, estimates this saving at no less than 65,000*l.* per annum, or upwards of 15 per cent. on the gross annual metropolitan water-rental (431,898*l.*). It is even rumoured that several of the companies—at their wit's end apparently for a line of tactics—have, within the last few days, adopted this very saving as the basis of a scheme, which they are urging the Government to sanction, for combining their nine establishments into one Colossal Monopoly. They are making, it is said, all the fair professions usual on such occasions ; promising pure water, constant supply, high service free of charge, and considerably diminished rates. But these identical promises were made forty years ago by Sir W. Clay's own company (the Grand Junction)

tion) at its first starting, *before* it had made good its position. *After* its footing was gained, this company abandoned every one of its pledges; distributing 'puddle,' pumped opposite the mouth of the Ranelagh sewer; withdrawing the constant supply, so as to saddle its tenants with a collective outlay of about 50,000*l.* on cisterns; and making high pressure the subject of a rate, exceeding at least twenty-fold the actual cost of the service. With these scandalous breaches of faith still fresh in their memory, the inhabitants of London will hardly, we think, be again cajoled by the blandishments of these gift-bringing Greeks; nor open their gates to a new monopolist ' Junction,' still grander than its ' Grand' predecessor. Monstrous, indeed, as such a Coalition would be, considered as a privileged Trading Corporation, it would fall very far short of that comprehensive Consolidation which constitutes our most pressing sanitary need. Its tendency, in point of fact, would be to perpetuate the existing fragmentary régime, by maintaining the present administrative severance of the Water-supply from the Sewers-department and other connected sanitary services; a separation of which we have already pointed out the dangerous and burdensome consequences. But these immediate evils, grave as they would undoubtedly be, shrink into insignificance when compared with those which would result from the creation of a new Vested Interest on a gigantic scale, to thwart and trammel, probably for generations to come, the course of sanitary improvement. Such a partial consolidation (like all half-measures) would aggravate many preventible evils, while letting slip much attainable good; and we can but regard so preposterous a scheme in one of two lights—either as the wild inspiration of a Monopoly *in extremis;* or as a speculation, at once audacious and adroit, on the eventualities of a period of political embarrassment. We venture, however, to predict, that whatever other principles may have been compromised, and whatever other measures emasculated, in consequence of the present deplorable crisis, the Sanitary Movement will pursue its career, unparalyzed by any such Mezentian alliance with a Monopoly virtually defunct.

Our antagonists, however, have another arrow in their quiver; it is their last and their sharpest—and they launch it against us with a sounding string.

Granting, they say, for argument's sake, all your preceding allegations; and accepting, for the provinces, your sanitary consolidation in all its comprehensive integrity; your *Metropolitan* case breaks down, nevertheless, on a constitutional point of paramount importance. For you seek to deprive the citizens of London of an electoral franchise secured by

your

your own Health Act to provincial ratepayers. Everywhere but in the metropolis, the local boards, whether consolidated or not, are elected by the ratepayers, who are thus enabled to control by their votes the expenditure of their funds. In London alone you have intrusted the administration of the roads and the sewers, and you would now hand over the consolidated waterworks, *to Commissioners nominated by the Crown.* These Royal Commissions are a direct infringement of the great constitutional principle which entitles the British taxpayer to have a voice, through his representative, in the disposal of the revenue to which he contributes. If, then, we *must* have sanitary consolidation in London, let the new government at least be put on a constitutional footing, such as that laid down in the Health Act itself. Let us have no royal nominees to reign over us, and to level rates on us without our consent ; but give us a central municipal board, composed of delegates from all the metropolitan parishes ; a board as supreme in the local affairs of London, and as independent of royal control, as the local boards of Liverpool and Birmingham are, in their respective jurisdictions, independent and supreme.

This, we believe, is a full and fair statement of the main objection urged by the Parish-party against the proposed administration of our public works by Commissioners acting under the authority of the Crown, and responsible to the ratepayers only through parliament. It is a very plausible objection, we admit, and, if sound, would be a very grave one. We shall therefore rapidly but carefully examine each of the two great questions which it raises ; first, namely, the question of constitutional theory ; and, secondly, that of practical advantage.

To the constitutional argument we reply, that this metropolis, the seat of our Government, and the centre of our mighty empire, cannot be considered a mere *locality*, in the sense in which that term is applicable to a provincial town. The interests of London are eminently *national;* and every British citizen is more or less directly concerned in the prosperity of the British metropolis. Its noble monuments and institutions reflect a lustre on the empire at large ; and its sanitary *opprobria*—such as the Smithfield offal—the tidal ditches of Bermondsey—and the crimson kennels of Whitechapel—not only injure and disgrace the particular parishes in which they occur, but discredit London in the eyes of England, and England herself in the eyes of Europe and of the world.

The parishes of London stand, therefore, in an exceptional position ; and their sanitary well-being claims the solicitude, not merely of their respective guardians, but òf Parliament, and of the Crown. On these grounds we hold it in the strictest sense legitimate and constitutional that the future sanitary rulers of the metropolis should be responsible to the ratepayers *through parliament.* Indeed, this partial sacrifice of parochial independence to public requirements of a wider scope, is amply compensated for the citizens of London by the exceptional advantages of their position. The collective forces of the empire, converging in London, as in a central focus, invest it with a grandeur and importance by which its inhabitants are dignified and enriched. These benefits, conferred by the nation on London, involve, as their constitutional equivalent, a responsibility on the part of London towards the nation, in all that concerns the honour of the metropolis. This double responsibility, local and national, is admirably adjusted by the administrative expedient of a metropolitan commission, not *exclusively* controlled, either by the London parishes, or by the nation at large, but answerable to the representatives of *both* in parliament.

Consider, on the other hand, the grave constitutional inconveniences that would result from the adoption of the Parish-party's plan; the creation, to wit, of a sort of Municipal Parliament, composed of delegates from the 176 metropolitan parishes, governing the local affairs of London, and invested with power to deliberate and act independently of the Queen's ministers. Weigh well the political influence which such a body would acquire; ruling, as it would, over a population, and disposing of patronage, equal to those of a middle-class state. Bear in mind that London, within its area of 115 square miles, contains $2\frac{1}{4}$ million souls— a population exceeding that of Denmark, which covers 16,000 square miles; while the assessed property of the metropolis amounts to 12,186,000*l.*--exceeding by nearly a third the assessed property of all Scotland. A new corporate power, founded on a basis at once so colossal and so compact, would become in the strictest sense an *imperium in imperio.* Even the existing City Corporation, which governs only a seventeenth of the population of London, only a fifteenth of its houses, and only a twelfth of its property, carries with it a political *prestige* and influence which the Queen's ministers are chary of affronting. Multiply now this power, in imagination, 12, 15, or 17 times, and judge of the quasi-imperial dignity which would appertain to a consolidated common council, representing the entire population and property of the metropolis. Is it not evident that such a municipal parliament, placed side by side with the imperial legislature, would tend to uncentre the balance of national and local powers, and might, in periods of political excitement, exert a most inconvenient and unconstitutional pressure on the counsels of the Queen's Government?

This

This political antagonism, the inevitable consequence of creating in London a municipal power, *at once consolidated and representative*, would involve evils largely outweighing any that could result from the issue of a Metropolitan Commission of Works, framed on existing models, and subject to constitutional checks proportioned to its wider range of power. Here again, therefore, as before, we feel justified in turning the tables on our antagonists; and in charging their proposal with the unconstitutional tendency so vehemently imputed to our own.

Experience, and the recorded manifestations of public opinion, concur with the foregoing theoretical considerations to justify these views; and to exhibit the projected municipal parliament not merely as an unconstitutional innovation, but as an innovation likely to prove unpopular.

In 1828, when all London rose *en masse* against the intolerable tyranny of the Water Companies, the demand of the population, led on that occasion by Sir F. Burdett, was—not for a board of parish delegates—but for a Government Commission to supersede the Monopolists in the administration of the Waterworks.

More recently, the Metropolitan Roads Commission, already referred to, was issued; and, though responsible to the ratepayers only through parliament, its operation has been both successful and popular.

The Metropolitan Improvement Commission, appointed by Government, and responsible to the ratepayers only through parliament, was granted in compliance with popular demand; and has worked to public satisfaction.

The issue of the Metropolitan Sanitary Commission, similarly nominated and responsible, was received as a highly popular measure; and its reports elicited universal approbation.

Equally popular was the great measure of consolidation, which united under the control of a general Commission, appointed by Government, and responsible to parliament, the Metropolitan District Courts of Sewers. The subsequent unpopularity, and final dissolution of this Commission, will be recognised as a strong corroboration of our views, when it is considered that the Board was rendered unworkable, and ultimately broken up, by a well-meant but most unsuccessful attempt to give it a popular character, *by an infusion of parochial representatives.* The defective information, the jealousies, and the vestry-toned speeches of these delegates, so obstructed the labours of the competent and working members of the Board, that the business came at last to a standstill; and it was found necessary to dissolve and recast the Commission, *excluding the parochial members.* The remodelled Commission, though reduced to less than half its former number, still

2 ɪ 2   proved

proved inconveniently large, and would have gained in promptitude of action, and in popularity, by a yet further reduction.

The reversal of the inquiry corroborates these conclusions. For we do not find the existing representative boards in the metropolis either successful or popular in their administration of public works.

The Common Council, for instance, is an elective body intrusted (*inter alia*) with the management of the city sewers; in respect of which they are quite as unpopular as the old district Courts of Sewers used to be in their several localities.

As for the parochial Boards of Guardians, their apathy and niggardliness during the Asiatic pestilence met with universal reprobation. The course they took on the Extramural-burial Question was equally unpopular. Nor can any instance be cited from the records of parochial representative administration, of a success and popularity equal to that achieved by the Government Commission of Metropolitan roads.

The proposed new parliament of parochial delegates would be but a colossal Board of Guardians, or a dilated Common Council; more mischievously powerful as an organ of political passions, but equally incompetent to superintend the complex sanitary organization of a great city. Like the provincial boards described in a foregoing page, this parish parliament would be composed chiefly of tradesmen, unskilled in the problems of sanitary engineering. Numbering at least 176 members, who would meet only from time to time in the intervals of their business, and could give to the difficult questions before them only an intermittent and cursory attention, this unpaid, fluctuating, heterogeneous assemblage could not, in the nature of things, succeed; but, like the parochial portion of the late Sewers Commission, it would make speeches, instead of doing work. Its vaunted responsibility to the ratepayers would be so weakened by subdivision and discontinuity, as to be rather nominal than real. On the parish hustings, indeed, political motives would have more weight than sanitary considerations; and even with respect to these latter, a pledge to resist present rates would find more favour with the crowd than the most comprehensive plan for reducing future *filth-costs* by well judged immediate applications of capital. Nor would hustings pledges, in the new any more than in the old corporation, guarantee the ratepayers against jobbing and peculation. Owners of ill-conditioned tenements, and others having private interests to serve, would still be, as candidates the nimblest canvassers, and as members the most assiduous attendants. Under such influences, extravagant expenditure would alternate with equally extravagant parsimony; and the costly errors of the old regime (monumentally embodied

embodied in the city sewers) would be extended over the whole metropolis. The ratepayers would discover too late, that, in accepting this new representative administration instead of an ordinary crown-appointed Commission, they had lost the substance of responsibility in grasping at its shadowy semblance.

For, a substantive responsibility does really attach, in spite of all contrary asseverations, to crown-appointed Commissioners; and a Board of Metropolitan Sanitary Works would be subject to a controlling 'pressure from without,' of which experience enables us to appreciate the efficacy. First, Government would be responsible to public opinion, national as well as metropolitan, for the choice of the Commissioners named. Secondly, the Commissioners themselves, being few in number (half-a-dozen at most) and suitably paid for their service, would feel themselves *severally* as well as jointly liable to be called on for an account of their stewardship. Thirdly, as Government functionaries, holding office only during good behaviour, they would be amenable to the surveillance of Parliament; whose watchful jealousy of such boards was exemplified last session in the searching questions addressed, night after night, to the noble chairman of the Commissioners of Sewers. And this salutary surveillance of parliament would be reinforced out of doors by the still sterner vigilance of the Press; which recently proved its power over inefficient Government boards, by enforcing the dissolution and reconstruction of the Metropolitan Sewers Commission. Its inferior influence, on the other hand, against the abuses of an independent representative body, such as the Common Council, stands apparent in the case of Smithfield, so long attacked in vain by the united forces of the London press. Like another Troy, this citadel of filth has stood a ten years' siege; and its sturdy garrison, led by their chieftains in the Common Council—the Hectors and Memnons of intramural muck—so far from thinking of surrender, are engaged, at this moment, in fortifying their defences. The bolts of the Thunderer, terrible to Cabinets, have fallen quenched amidst the mud of the Corporation sheep-pens. Vainly, as yet, have the serpents of Apollo wreathed themselves around the body of Mr. Lowman Taylor; and vainly have they hissed into the ears of Hicks their threatful denunciations. The modern Cassandra, robed in the Broad Sheet, has clamoured without avail at the gates of St. Bartholomew; and her iron lips, still glowing with the kisses of the God, have filled the seething market-place with unheeded prophecies of pestilence and death. In those dismal Vaticinations ourselves have timely joined; foreshadowing in many a darkened page the coming gloom of pestilence; and, with almost tedious importunity, conjuring the Corporation to put away the unclean thing.

thing. Of the apathy which ignored our warnings the disastrous consequences are but too well remembered in many a decimated household. It is against the perpetuation on a vaster scale of such a Power as this, which sacrificed London to save Smithfield, and succumbed to the Plague while defying the Press, that we now raise our voice. The Defenders of the Filth, corporate and parochial, have ruled London long enough; the late pestilence revealed their incapacity, and proved our need of abler sanitary guidance. Metaphor apart, we want henceforth a compact board of sanitary rulers, appointed for their special skill, giving their undivided attention *de die in diem* to the business of their office, and amenable, in case of error, to the threefold censure of the Parliament, the Press, and the Public. Can it, we ask, be for one moment doubted that we should thus secure, along with superior prudence in counsel, and greater promptitude in action, a more *real* responsibility to the ratepayers, practically manifested in cheaper and more efficient works, than has ever resulted, or can reasonably be hoped, from the system of parish-delegation for which Mr. Toulmin Smith and his followers contend?

The principal arguments on either side of this momentous question hang now, we think, poised fairly (and in no doubtful scales) before the reader's eyes. One plea, however, still remains to add; and one so weighty as alone might turn the beam. It is on the side of the Crown-appointed, as against the parochial administration; and consists in the power of the London ratepayers, acting through their representatives in parliament, to impose on a Government Commission, at the period of its appointment, any guarantees and restrictions which they (the ratepayers) see fit. No hustings-pledge binds your parish-delegate to economy, so stringently as the Government Commissioner is bound by a restrictive clause in the Act which constitutes his title. By such a clause, for example, we would bind our new Consolidated Commission of Metropolitan Sanitary Works *in no case to increase* any rates now payable for water-supply, drainage, and the like; while, on the other hand, we would leave them unrestricted freedom to bring about all possible *reductions* in existing charges. By another definite proviso, we would settle a maximum average rate, *not exceeding the present average rate*, at which districts hitherto without water-supply, drainage, and the like, should be entitled to those sanitary services. By a third clause, stringently worded, we would extend to the metropolis that provision of the Health Act which fixes 2*d.* per house per week as the fair average price for a domestic supply of water in provincial towns; and on those terms we would legally entitle every London householder to claim an average supply, delivered at high pressure on the constant

stant system. So again, to secure for the ratepayers the full advantages of competition, and to hinder interference with private enterprise, as well as to guard against the possibility of 'jobs,' we would prohibit the Commissioners, by a stringent clause, from undertaking themselves the construction of works; whereof, contrariwise, we would bind them to submit the execution to public competition, on open tender, with proper securities for repair and maintenance, according to the principle laid down in the Health Act, and set forth in the foregoing pages. In short, by a series of provisos such as these, we would enforce on the Commissioners, and ensure to the ratepayers, every economy in expenditure, and every improvement in works, which the latest experience, up to the date of the Act, had proved to be attainable.

Such, compendiously stated, are the main features of Sanitary Consolidation, considered from the administrative point of view. We have endeavoured to trace its philosophical as well as its practical bearings; its relations to Self-government, provincial and metropolitan; its well marked opposition to continental 'Centralization' (in the obnoxious sense of that term); and its impartial adaptation to the rival rights of majorities and minorities, of populations and individuals, of actual and reversionary proprietors—of the living generation and of the yet unborn. We have severally examined, and endeavoured to refute, the principal objections raised against it by the opponents of sanitary reform ; especially disproving its alleged incompatibility with free competition, individual enterprise, private property, and the division of labour. We have compared it with other systems of administration and forms of procedure, ancient and modern, parliamentary and parochial, commercial and corporate. And we have endeavoured to justify, by a wide range of testimony, and an extensive induction of facts, our conviction of its economical superiority.

If, now, we pass from the Administrative to the Structural point of view, we shall find the evils of the existing *morcellement,* and the advantages of the proposed Consolidation, still more strikingly evinced.

Whoever has stood by the great Steam-pump of a London Waterwork, and listened to the throbbing of its heavy valves, and felt, at each dull beat, the rhythmic water-pulse of the iron aorta under his feet, must have been struck with the resemblance of the potent engine to a colossal Heart. It may not, however, have occurred to him that London is in this respect what Naturalists would call a monstrosity ; having no less than nine such hearts scattered at random through its giant frame. These it would be the first effect of Structural Consolidation to replace with one great central

central heart of ninefold power.   It appears from the engineering evidence taken by the Board of Health that by such a central engine, constructed on the plan of the Cornish mining steam-pumps, 388 tons of water (87,000 gallons) might be raised 100 feet high at a working-cost of *one shilling* : and that the whole daily supply of the metropolis (forty-four million gallons) might be raised to the same height for 25*l*.   The saving in pumping and establishment costs, which would result from this first and simplest structural centralization, are estimated at no less than 28,000*l*. per annum ; every farthing of which would be so much clear gain to the London water-consumers.   A single example will suffice to illustrate the economy which would accrue to individual consumers from this concentration of works, coupled with the abolition of the monopolist water-trade ; which measures charges, not by the cost of service, but by the consumer's need, and ' *squeezability.*'   Many of our readers are reminded quarterly of the extra charge, 1*l*. per annum, made by several London water companies for the supply of a closet on an upper floor.   Now this service, performed by a centralized establishment, would only involve an extra pumping-cost of *one farthing and a fraction per annum*, or a total extra cost, including all charges, of 6½*d*. per annum ; showing a difference of 3692 per cent. in favour of Structural Consolidation.

Follow, now, this pulsating current—the life's blood of the social organism—in its subterranean course through the diminishing branches of the distributary ducts, till at last it flows through a half-inch capillary into the consumer's house.   What becomes of it here ?   How is it stored for use ?   What channels are provided for its efflux, when done with, out of the house, and out of the town ?

These are questions which the water-merchants never ask themselves ; and which, under the existing fragmentary regime, they could not, if they would, resolve.   So vast a quantity of water is daily pumped into London, as would convert St. James's Park into a lake 2½ feet deep : but the household storage of this prodigious mass is reckoned a private affair for each inhabitant to settle with his plumber ; its discharge from our houses is left to the jobbing bricklayer's or builder's contrivance ; and its conveyance out of the town is the special concern of a separate Commission *ad hoc*.   The case of a sick man, who had intrusted his arterial system to the care of one set of doctors, his veins to a rival clique, and the intervening capillaries to a third, would aptly represent, in this respect, the condition of our poor patient, the Metropolis.

If, indeed, engaging in a new sort of Comparative Anatomy, and
practising

practising dissection on a colossal scale, we could with some great scalpel cut across a London street, and bring the severed extremity into direct comparison with the corresponding surface of an amputated arm or leg, two things would chiefly strike us; first, namely, the general structural analogy of the two limbs, individual and social; and secondly, the extreme deformity of the latter.

Look first at the surface of the stump left by amputation of a human limb. You observe the cut ends of two channels, and of a white chord, lying close to each other, and to the bone. One of the channels is that through which the blood flows, bright and pure, to the limb; the other is that which carries it away turbid and darkened with the refuse of the vital action: and as it is thus their function to convey the same stream in opposite directions, the two channels are of nearly equal size. The accompanying white chord is the nerve.

Turn next to the cut surface of amputated Holborn or Cheapside. Here also you observe the severed extremities of artery, vein, and nerve; but scattered far apart from each other, and monstrously disproportionate in size. The water-main, a foot or so in diameter, and about a yard below the surface, is completely filled with its arterial stream. But the venous conduit, buried far below, is at least twenty times as big; and of its wastefully redundant area, the turbid return-stream, even when swollen by the heaviest rains on record, never occupies more than five or six per cent. As for the nerve (of which more hereafter), it is represented by a fibrous mass of Electric wires, each insulated by a gutta percha integument, and the whole enclosed within an iron tube (or neurilema) lying separately entrenched beside the footpath.

Consider, now, the saving which would result to us, if, taking a lesson from Nature, we were to approximate and harmonise these scattered and incongruous works. First, we should have one trench only to dig, instead of three. And the cost of digging and removing the earth at about 1s. per cubic yard, and of taking up and reinstating the pavement at about 1s. 6d. per superficial yard, constitutes ordinarily from one-fourth to one-half the total cost of subterranean pipeage.

' I have before me,' says Mr. Chadwick, in his evidence before the Committee on Private Bills, 'an estimate of draining some 1200 or 1300 houses, and the amount of the estimated expense is 5000l.; of this sum 2000l. is for earthwork—for digging to make the sewers, and digging for the house-drains: all which money, or at least a large proportion of it, would have to be expended over again, in digging to lay down water-pipes separately. So that, by consolidating the two works, and laying both down at once, you save a great proportion of the expense of earthworks, besides avoiding the double disturbance of the residents and repeated obstructions of the streets.'

Keeping

Keeping this statement before us, and leaving out of the question (for the present) what we have called the *nerve*-tubes, we may easily conceive how vast the sums must be which have been squandered in London on double earthworks for drainage and water-service; and how great a saving, under this single head, may still be effected by Structural Consolidation in the districts remaining to be drained and piped. Some detailed estimates, elucidating this point, will find their appropriate place in a future page; our present object being but to sketch in outline the salient features of the subject.

Amongst these stands prominently forward the great economy attainable by the reduction of the venous conduits or sewers, now so monstrously dilated, to juster proportion with the arterial mains which they accompany. In some of the old sewage districts, small courts, containing only six houses, are drained by vaulted conduits no less than 4 feet high by 2½ feet wide; whilst recent experiments have shown that a little pipe, 4 inches in diameter, amply suffices to carry off the sewage of such a place. Nay, in a trial work, superintended by Mr. Morris under the direction of the late Metropolitan Sewer Commission, 150 houses were found to be perfectly well drained by a single earthenware pipe 6 inches in diameter. Some comparative trial works, devised for the elucidation of the same point, and conducted by Messrs. Hall and Lovick under the direction of the same Commission, were still more strikingly conclusive.

Mr. Hall experimented on a sewer in Upper George Street, Edgeware Road, measuring 5½ feet high by 3½ feet wide, and receiving, by several tributary conduits, the whole drainage of about 44 acres. This great vein Mr. Hall proceeded to tie, as Magendie might tie a rabbit's. For this purpose he chose a point, only 560 feet above the mouth of the conduit; and where, consequently, its current was swollen by the collateral streams from the whole area drained. Here he built a brick wall across the sewer; leaving only a hole 1 foot in diameter for the passage of the stream. From this hole a pipe, 1 foot in diameter, was carried to the outlet; a distance, as we have said, of 560 feet. This portion, therefore, of the old vein, was virtually replaced by a new one, of less than a twentieth the former size, and about as big as an ordinary arterial water-main. The results of this experiment were capital, and very curious. The original sewer had—like all its monstrous tribe—been wont to accumulate deposits, which were only partially kept under by incessant flushing. But in this twelve-inch pipe no deposit whatever took place; a result attributable, of course, to the increased velocity of its closelier pent stream. This, indeed, ran 4½ times faster in the little conduit than

than in the large one; so that broken stones of several ounces
weight each, when put in at the top of the pipe, were heard
rattling along it, and speedily issued at the other end. Nay,
when the pipe was flowing about half full, two brickbats,
weighing 1¾ lbs. each, were carried through its whole length, and
emitted with such force from its mouth, as to strike the man who
was watching for them a blow on the legs, which he declared to
be painful. And a live rat, put in on the same occasion, came
out at the lower end in so headlong a fashion, as proved him to
have lost all control over his own motions.

Nor were Mr. Lovick's experiments less instructive. They
took place in a flat-bottomed sewer, 3 feet wide by 5 feet high,
draining 1200 houses, and accumulating no less than 6000 cubic
feet of foul deposit per month. Here was laid down a pipe of
15 inches diameter; through which, by an intercepting wall, the
whole of the sewage was made to flow. This pipe, like Mr.
Hall's, transmitted the stream far more swiftly and freely than
the great sewer which it replaced had done; and its own scour
sufficed to keep it free from deposit. Such tubes, we learn from
the engineering estimates before us, may be laid down for less
than a fifth the cost of ordinary brick-sewers built on the old
'Roman grandeur' principle. Nay, the mere cost of flushing
these latter amounts in many districts to 29*l.* per mile per annum;
whilst the total construction-cost of the self-flushing tubular
sewers, if distributed over 20 years, would barely amount to 20*l.*
per mile per annum. Even in the comparatively well-managed
Holborn and Finsbury district the flushing-costs amount to
17*l.* 5*s.* per mile per annum: so that, striking a fair average between the higher and the lower figure, we may venture broadly to
assert that *London might be drained* (de novo) *on the tubular, or
physiological system, not only without levying fresh rates on the
inhabitants, but with a direct and immediate diminution of existing
charges.*

These are but cursory indications; yet they will give the
reader some idea of the advantage which would result from a
Structural Consolidation, tending to approximate and adapt to
each other the main veins and arteries of London, at present
so absurdly incongruous.

Push now the dissection a little farther. Carry the scalpel
through the house itself, and lay open with a widened gash the
ultimate capillaries of the urban circulating system. A whole
series of new disorders and deformities are thus at once revealed.

First appear two great tumours—one (so to speak) *aneurismal,*
on the influx pipe, or artery; the other *varicose,* on the efflux
channel,

channel, or vein. These two abnormal dilatations, named respectively Cistern and Cesspool, are companion evils ; or rather companion forms of one great evil....STAGNANCY—parent of sanitary ills. In these receptacles of sediment and filth are bred the deadliest of the poisons which taint the earth we tread on, the water we drink, and the air we breathe. They are a sort of abscesses in our social system ; and their evacuation and removal is the most pressing duty of the sanitary surgeon.

Another disorder, analogous in kind and consequence, consists in the abnormal dilatation of the venous capillary, or house-drain, not only as compared to its arterial companion (the water-pipe), but also relatively to the main vein, or public sewer,—monstrous as we have just shown this to be. For your ordinary private-house drain is very commonly a foot in diameter ; and large enough, therefore, to carry off the sewage of 44 acres, according to Mr. Hall's experiments ; or of 1200 houses, according to Mr. Lovick's results. The minimum size of house-drains permitted by the Building Act is 9 inches diameter ; and the collective sectional area of these private drains in London equals, on a low estimate, fivefold the sectional area of the Thames at Waterloo Bridge during high water. To keep these capillaries full and flowing would take a river above 1000 feet wide by 100 feet deep, running at the rate of two miles per hour : whereas the actual water-supply of the metropolis—all that really passes through them—would scarcely keep a brook 9 feet wide by 3 deep, flowing at the same rate. The consequence is that our house-drains, lacking water to scour them, get choked with a pitchy coagulum—like the stagnant blood in a cholera-patient's veins.

But the material of these conduits is not less strikingly incongruous and absurd than their bulk. The water-pipe and cistern are of lead—which is converted by oxydation into a poison, possessing the frightful power to paralyse different parts of the body successively : so as first to destroy the peristaltic action of the bowels—then to palsy the wrists—and finally to disorganise the brain itself. The corrosion by which this poison is produced, takes place so rapidly,—especially with such hard water, and such impure lead, as are in use in the metropolis,—that cistern-bottoms weighing 8 lbs. to the foot are sometimes eaten through in two years, and very commonly in four or five. Under some circumstances the corroded matter is taken up by the water in clear solution ; in other cases it lies, as an insoluble precipitate, at the bottom of the cistern—or sticks in carbuncular masses to its sides : and we have known it to rise, with other impurities,
and

and float as an iridescent scum on the surface of the water.* There is probably, at this moment, not a leaden cistern in London which is free from poison in one or other of these conditions; poison above, poison below, or poison round about ; poison invisibly dissolved in the water, poison visibly suspended in it as a milky cloud, or poison glittering in the scum upon its surface. We have seen leaden water-pipes completely honeycombed, and eaten into holes by hard water transmitted through them ; nay, we can cite individual cases of lead-poisoning from this cause, within the district of the New River Company. Under consolidated arrangements, tubes of glass, earthenware, glazed iron, or other incorrodible material, would at once be adopted instead of these leaden conduits ; which, independently of their poisonous quality, are actually *costlier* and less durable than either of the above-named substitutes. Let us add, in anticipation of the cry of ' impracticability ' ever at the tongue's tip of the sticklers for routine, that glass service-pipes, experimentally fitted in a London house, have worked well under high pressure for twelve months past ; and that the town of Maestricht, on the Meuse, in Holland, is supplied with gas through 6-inch tubes of glass, which, though laid down three years since beneath the streets, have not only stood the ordinary traffic, but have borne without fracture the passage of heavy artillery, dragged over them repeatedly at their manufacturer's instance, to place the question of their strength beyond a doubt. We are happy to learn that this application of glass, which Sir Robert Peel predicted some years since in taking off the excise on this material, is at present engaging the attention of our principal glass-manufacturers in the north; so that in this particular also the late minister's forecast bids fair to be justified by the event.

But for ludicrous incongruity between its structure and its function, the house-drain, if possible, outdoes even the water-pipe. Though it is essential that these channels should be water-and-air-tight, they are yet built of bricks, so porous that each will absorb about a pint of water ; and so small that a thousand of them, with a thousand chinks between, go to the making of an ordinary house-drain. The chinks, no doubt, are stopped ; but in a rude fashion ; and with so soft a mortar, as readily gives way (like the bricks themselves) before the teeth of the rats. Hence fluid-leakage into the soil beneath, and gaseous exhalation into the air above ;—pernicious damp dilapidating the foundations of the house, and poisonous miasmata undermining

---

* We owe our knowledge of this most important fact to Mr. Noad, the chemist, who obtained an abundant precipitate of lead from the scum of water contained in a leaden cistern at Clapham.

the

the health of its inmates. Beside evils of such magnitude as these, it may seem almost puerile to notice the annoyance of the pilfering rodentia admitted through these sieve-like drains into our larders. Yet this is no light evil in the aggregate. It is computed that the wholesome food, which the rats of London consume or spoil, would suffice for the nourishment of several thousand men. Their multitude is at once the measure, and the reproof, of the foulness of our social organism; which is infested by these vermin, as the unclean individual is by other parasitic swarms—equally nimble and equally loathsome.

But we are not at the end of the anomalies, disclosed by this new sort of dissection, and manifesting our urgent need of Structural Consolidation. Every one knows that water is chiefly consumed, and sewage produced, in the offices at the *back* of our houses; whereas the water-mains and sewers are, with a strange perversity, laid down *before* them, in the middle of the street, some 60 or 80 feet from our back-offices. Hence four important evils. First, the capillaries, arterial and venous, of each house, must be 60 or 80 feet long (more or less)—instead of 10 or 15 feet, which would suffice were our sewers and water-mains laid in the rear. Under this single item, therefore, *five-sixths of our expense would be knocked off at one blow by Structural Consolidation.* Secondly, the branch-drain, in order to reach the sewer in the street, must pass beneath the house which it relieves; whereas to reach a postern sewer it would pass beneath the back-yard only, and its exhalations would ascend, not into the house, but into the open air. Thirdly, a front-drain, 60 or 80 feet long, can rarely have a good fall, so as to ensure a rapid and free discharge; whereas, with the shorter back-drain, we should command a five-fold slope, affording proportionally swifter and more certain evacuation. Lastly, with drains under our houses and sewers under our streets, we are subject to frequent invasions of workmen; who tear up our kitchen-floors to repair the private ducts; and obstruct our streets with great trenches, and barricades of paving-stones, to operate on the public conduits: from which grievous annoyances the postern system would deliver us for ever, only imposing on us, in their stead, the comparatively trifling evil of an occasional incursion into our back-yards.

Of these four evils (all, be it observed, preventible by Structural Consolidation), the second is by far the worst; as many of our readers know, probably, by experience, and as others may gather from the following anecdote, for the accuracy of which we can vouch :—

A gentleman of distinction, occupying an elegant mansion in one of the principal streets in London, found his abode so haunted by by unpleasant smells that he at length made up his mind to abandon it. So far his case was commonplace enough. But the circumstance which especially provoked and perplexed our friend was, that the stench invariably arose in greatest strength, *whenever he gave a party.* He had, of course, caused the drain of his house to be opened, and search to be made for any obstruction or lodgement of foul matter within it. But nothing of the sort was found; nor could any of the builders, consulted on the case, explain the mysterious aggravation of the nuisance precisely on those occasions when the gentleman's friends were assembled around him, and his house was swept and garnished for their reception. It seemed as if some malignant agency were at work underground for his especial vexation and discomfiture. At last, when he was on the very point of giving up the house, a builder, more sagacious than the rest, traced the strange evil to its physical cause. The house-drain, which ran beneath the kitchens, had become leaky, through the fall of mortar from between the bricks, and the gnawing of holes by the rats. Whenever a party was given, more fires than usual were lighted in the house; while the windows and doors were kept shut for the exclusion of cold and noise. The upward draught of air through the chimneys being thus increased, while the ordinary channels of indraught were diminished, a stronger suction-power naturally took effect on the column of foul gas within the drain; and this gas, as it streamed upward into the house, was replaced by fresh supplies from the common sewer—of which, therefore, in simple fact, this house (like many others in London) was virtually a mere recess.

And here we cannot refrain from interposing a remark on the error of those who regard Sanitary Reform as a purely philanthropic movement, deserving support as useful to the poor, but little if at all affecting the personal welfare of the rich and great. Many hundreds of the aristocratic residents in Belgravia, and of the merchant-princes in the City, are undergoing, more or less consciously, the baneful influence of such noxious exhalations as we have just described. The 17 million cubic feet of decaying residuum, now lying a subterranean chaos under London, debilitate us all, without exception; and injure rich and poor more equally than is commonly supposed. It appears, indeed, from that most appalling revelation, the Report of the late Subterranean Survey, that Belgrave and Eaton Squares, as well as the whole splendid neighbourhood of Hyde-Park Gardens, stand over sewers 'abounding with the foulest deposit, in many cases stopping up the house-drains, and emitting the most disgusting effluvium;' and that the more ancient sewers of Cavendish, Bryanstone, Manchester, and Portman Squares, are in such a state of rottenness and

and decay that there is no security for their standing from day to
day, and that even the attempt to evacuate them, by flushing,
' might bring some of them down altogether ;'—while, curious to
tell, ' the only little spot in the whole Westminster district, of
which the sewers are at all in a satisfactory condition, is SEVEN
DIALS !'

Nor is our gracious Queen herself, in her sumptuous palaces,
exempt from the pressure of these universal evils, nor less directly
interested than the meanest of her subjects in the question of
Structural Consolidation. Windsor Castle, indeed, was lately ascertained to stand over a complete labyrinth of leaky drains and cesspools, which, through a thousand unsuspected chinks gnawn by
those Secret Poisoners—the Rats, poured forth the ' vapours which
have strength to kill' into the gilded banquet-halls above. The
basement floors of Buckingham Palace, some years ago, were so
riddled by these little Subterranean Traitors, that two eminent
savans, who were called in to suggest a remedy for the resulting
stench, found her Majesty's apartments, so to speak, ventilated
through the common sewer.

We read in the Chronicles of old Asser the monk, King Alfred's
friend and tutor, that our great monarch was led to strike out
his remarkable invention, the horn lantern, by the flickering of
his graduated clock-candles, whose unprotected flame swayed to
and fro in the wind ' that blew in through the chinks of his
palace.' And in contrasting this barn-like gustiness of King Alfred's
dwelling with the snugness of our modern mansions, we are apt to
indulge in a self-complacent smile at the rude architecture of that
semi-barbarous age. Is it, however, quite certain, after all, that
our own condition justifies this disdain? Is it quite certain that
centuries hence, when Windsor Castle is an ivied ruin, and the
bats flit by moonlight through Buckingham House, Posterity will
not smile, in its turn, at the vaunted luxury of our royal palaces—
exposed, by subterranean crannies, to far more noisome blasts than
ever visited, through lateral chinks, King Alfred's primitive
abode ?

These questions, however, it is not ours to solve—nor even here
to ponder. They will have served their end, if they remind our
more exalted readers of their inevitable share, as well in the burdens of our epoch, as in the duty of struggling for their removal :
which how to set about, and with what prospect of advantage,
comes next in order to be shown. How may we best accomplish,
at what cost in capital, and with what annual saving, the abolition
of cisterns and cesspools ; the substitution of back drainage and
water-supply for the present mains and sewers beneath the street ;
the adoption of a constant and unlimited supply through pipes
kept

kept full at high pressure, instead of the intermittent or tank-filling system, to which the water-monopolists so stubbornly adhere; and, finally, the exchange of our tumid barrel-drains of brick, for short, small tubes, of well-burnt vitreous earthenware, carried *from*, not *through*, our houses?

These being all plain questions of feet and inches, and of pounds shillings and pence, the best way of settling them is evidently to select a fair average block of houses, in an average locality; and then, rule in hand, with plan and builder's price-book before us, to work out the precise saving which would result to each householder from the adoption of the combined and simplified works under consideration.

Such an average block, comprising 282 houses, and covering 9 acres of ground, exists at Hanway Yard, Oxford Street. It forms a compact square mass, or *insula* to borrow a term from the Romans, favourably situated for sanitary engineering, with a sewer on either side, at sufficient depth to afford the requisite outfall. Mr. Cresy, assistant surveyor to the late Sewers Commission, inspected this block, and ascertained the existence of house-drains and cesspools occupying collectively about 8500 superficial feet, or one-fifth of an acre—being just a forty-fifth part of the entire area. The whole of this subterranean network was loaded with decaying matter, which had also oozed into the soil around; and from this vast evaporating surface arose an effluvium by which the houses were all more or less offensively infected. The mass of earth requiring excavation, in the *separate* execution of drainage and water-works for these houses, was ascertained, by careful measurement, to be 10,256 cubic yards; and the extent of pavement requiring to be lifted and replaced was 1400 superficial yards :—costing together (at 1s. 1d. per yard for the digging, &c., and 1s. 6d. per yard for the paving) 726l. 13s. 6d.—half which, or 363l. 6s. 9d., represents the saving in earthwork attainable, in this case, by the joint execution of the two works.* It further appeared that the cost of draining these houses on the old plan, and fitting them with cisterns, &c., on the intermittent system, averaged 22l. 3s. 2d. per house; whereas the cost of the improved back-drainage through stoneware tubes, and of water-pipeage on the constant principle, without cisterns, averaged only 4l. 17s. 7d. per house.

Take another example, selected from a superior class of houses,

---

* The saving would, in fact, be greater; for the prices cited in the text for digging, paving, &c., are such as jobbing contractors have obtained under the old régime, but which would be largely reduced under the new. We have, however, adopted Mr. Cresy's figures as they stand, to show *separately* the economy attainable by the diminution of earthwork, without reference to a financial advantage due to other than the *Structural* reforms at present under review.

and equally conclusive in favour of the new plan of Postern drainage over the old Street-sewer system. Great George Street, Westminster, contains 44 large houses, drained by brick barrel-drains running under the premises from back to front into the common sewer, which passes down the middle of the street. These brick drains were measured by Mr. Grant, one of the surveyors to the Metropolitan Sewers Commission, who found their collective length to be 3686 feet, and their total cost, on a low estimate, 910*l*. 19*s*.—or 20*l*. 14*s*. 1*d*. per house. The collective length, and the cost, of tubular back-drains for these same houses, were respectively 1544 feet, and 83*l*. 11*s*. 10*d*.—or 1*l*. 18*s*. per house. The comparison, it will be observed, is in this case made between the drains alone, without reference to water-service and other connected apparatus.

Vast, however, as the saving is, and striking the improvement, thus attainable in average cases, still greater economies result from the application of the improved works in fouler and more neglected districts. Nay, paradoxical as the assertion may seem, the improved drains are not only cheaper than bad drains, but cheaper even than *no drains at all*.

For proof of this we must explore one of the plague-spots of the metropolis; such an one, for example, as exists in the parish of St. Giles, and is commonly known as the ' Rookery.'

In this dismal place, 95 small houses, crowded on an acre and a tenth of ground, lodge every night a huddled swarm of 2850 human beings ! It does not fall within our present scope to dwell on the obscenity and crime engendered by this brutal herding of a promiscuous and fluctuating multitude, comprising males and females, children and adults, the innocent and the depraved, pressed together, by night, in a way which renders privacy impossible, and breaks down every barrier to lust. Our business lies, not with the palpable outgrowth of this misery, but with its deeply-planted roots ; and for these roots we must grope underground. We must probe the horrible pits of festering putrescence, of which one (for example) is described by Mr. Gotto * as ' situated in the back yard of No. 10, Carrier Street, having its brim 12 inches above the level of the house-floor, and covering the yard with its black overflow, which, spreading to the wall, soaks into the adjacent premises.' We must contemplate, without shrinking, the loathsome spectacle of ' one resort, common to 5 houses containing about 150 persons'—and of ' a narrow passage, between high walls, 4 feet apart, covered with deposits which diffuse through the premises a sickening stench, till the dustman comes at morning to remove them.' We must note the scanty water-

----

* Report by Mr. Gotto, June 15, 1849.

supply—

supply—in one place doled out ' through a pipe in a cellar occupied by 15 persons;' further on, begged, pailful by pailful, from the neighbouring chandler, who turns this strange almsgiving to account by laying an extra halfpenny on each loaf of bread supplied to his mendicant customers. And we must take into account the ' masses of ashes and filth' thrown from the windows into the streets, for lack of dustbins, and rotting there amidst stagnant pools of slop, which drains are wanting to remove.

Count, now, the cost of this frightful squalor, and compare it with the cost of cleanliness. Weigh against each other the expense of good drains, and the expense of no drains at all. Bear in mind that these foul accumulations *must*, after all, somehow or another, be kept down. The total mass of filth in the ' Rookery' does not *increase* from year to year, but, large as it is, remains fixed at an average quantity. The annual addition is, therefore, in point of fact, annually removed; and the task of its extrusion is not diminished one jot by what may be called the *floating balance* of refuse always remaining on hand. By what power then, and by what vehicle, is this carrying business performed? Where drains and water-pipes exist, the vehicle is *water*, and the power that of *steam*, by which the water is raised and delivered. But in the absence of pipes and water, the work must be done by *cartage*, and by the power of *horses* and *men*. Tube-drainage is therefore cheaper than cesspool-drainage, for the same reason, and in the same degree, that steam-woven calico is cheaper than hand-made lace. The filth and the finery are both costly, because they both absorb human toil; the cleanliness and the calico are alike economical, because they are alike products of steam-power. The principle is plain enough; and it is plainly borne out by the ascertained facts of this case. Most of the cesspools in the Rookery hold about two cart-loads, and require emptying every five or six weeks, at a cost of 7*s.* per load. One such cesspool was stated to accommodate ten houses, and to require emptying once a month, at an annual cost (including candles and beer for the unhappy men who are condemned to the needless degradation of this odious pursuit) amounting to 10*l.*—or 1*l.* per house per annum. In still more crowded houses the cost is 2*l.* 2*s.* per house per annum; and there is one house in which this charge amounts to no less than 4*l.* per annum. Striking an average of these costs, together with those of the slovenly scavenging, and the miserably deficient water-supply, it appears that what we may call the *squalor-costs* of the Rookery amount altogether to about 4*l.* per house per annum.

Now, an Improvement-rate of 1*l.* 15*s.* per house per annum, payable during twenty-two years, would reimburse, with interest,

2 K 2   the

the capital requisite for the laying down of public sewers and water-mains in the Rookery, for levelling the pavement of the streets and yards, for emptying and filling up all the cesspools, and for fitting each house with a tubular drain, a suitable soil-pan apparatus, a dust-bin, and a set of pipes conveying an un-limited supply of water at constant pressure, to every floor.

Independently, therefore, of the pecuniary burdens indirectly resulting from filth, by reason of the disease, orphanage, &c., to which it leads, we have here a direct money-charge of 2*l.* 5*s.* per house, as the annual excess of the cost of filth over the cost of cleanliness. Or, to reduce the expression to its simplest and most technical form, this difference of charge per house per annum, represents, in the case before us, the superior economy of steam-and-water-power, over hand-labour-and-cartage, as means of urban defecation.

But will these 4-inch tubular drains really work? are they not liable to stoppages? are they not too small to carry off the water of occasional storms, in addition to the ordinary house-drainage? To these very fair and pertinent questions let facts afford their equally fair and pertinent reply.

In 1848, Mr. Grant, the surveyor, drained five houses through one 4-inch pipe, which has worked perfectly, without stoppages, ever since. Some months afterwards he laid down similar drains for a number of houses at Exeter; and notably for one block of 130 houses; which have all acted well, notwithstanding a com-paratively scanty supply of water.

In 1849, Mr. Morris, the surveyor of Poplar, drained several courts with 4-inch tubes, each carrying away the refuse of six houses; and these drains, like Mr. Grant's, have since worked, and are still working, perfectly well.

In the same year, an outbreak of epidemic fever, in the cloisters of Westminster Abbey, induced the Dean and Chapter to con-sent to a similar subterranean revolution in that heretofore stink-ing quarter. On opening the ground a hideous sight was dis-closed. A series of cesspools, barrel-drains, and brick sewers, were found, so large and so crammed with stagnant filth that no less than 500 loads were taken from a single portion of the net-work, serving only 15 houses! The sewer at one part measured 7 feet wide—at another part 17 feet high! Under the West-minster School the soil stood 9 feet deep: a pleasant reflection for parents who have had sons, paling over their books, day after day, amidst the fumes of that pestiferous gulf. The area of the 15 houses, the School, the Chapter-house, &c., with the con-nected grounds, was about two acres; the evaporating surface of subterranean filth was 4800 square feet—or about 5½ per cent. of the

the whole area. This mass of abomination was at once swept away by Messrs. Austin and Lovick ; who replaced the old stagnant drains and cesspools with 3000 feet of tubular mains, submains, and capillaries, measuring respectively 9, 6, and 4 inches in diameter. These drains work perfectly; the immemorial stench has ceased ; and the inhabitants have ever since enjoyed an unaccustomed exemption from sickness. The Dean of Westminster, in a letter to the Commissioners, says, ' I beg to report that the success of the entire new pipe-drainage laid down in St. Peter's College has, during the last twelve months, been complete. The Clerk of the Works has examined every closet once a week, and entered his written report on a book laid every Wednesday before the Dean and Chapter ; and not one case of failure or imperfect working has occurred.'

As for the discharge of storm-water through these 3 and 4-inch house-drains, this much-vexed question was experimentally determined by Mr. Medworth, acting under the directions of the late Metropolitan Commissioners of Sewers. Mr. Medworth ascertained that a 4-inch drain-pipe, 50 feet long, laid with a fall of 1 in 120 (or 5 inches higher at its upper than at its lower end) discharged 100 gallons of water (equal to 24 hours' supply of sewage from a house) in one minute and a half. One-sixteenth of sand, mixed with the water, was freely discharged by the sweep of the current. As the heaviest rainfall known in this country does not deliver more than one gallon on each square foot per hour, such a pipe would discharge the storm-water of 4000 square feet. And even this abundant discharge was more than doubled by increasing the declivity of the pipe to 1 in 60. As for the velocity of the current in these pipes, its rate was found to be four miles an hour, even with so slight a fall as 1 in 240 : so that refuse, thus discharged at any given moment from the Post-Office, would, within 45 minutes, be already beyond the three miles' radius ; and, within 2 hours, be far beyond the utmost limits of the metropolis.

It would be wasting words to insist on the impossibility of attaining these admirable results except by combined operations, including private as well as public works, planned as a systematic whole, and executed at contract prices, determined by open tender, in accordance with the principles of Sanitary Consolidation. It is found practically impossible to bring about the drainage even of a single block of houses by the agency of the several occupiers or owners ; who, though served with compulsory orders to this effect, prefer the risk of disobedience, to the costs and difficulties involved in the single-handed execution of the task imposed. 'One man,' says Mr. Cresy, ' will perhaps begin ;
but

but his next neighbour will demur ; and another, as has actually occurred in my experience, will request to delay the works, until he shall have communicated with his landlord in the West Indies.' Evidently, we might as well call on each citizen to provide his own watchman, or to organise his share of the army and navy, as to plan and execute his private modicum of the general drainage and water system of the metropolis.

It is, indeed, curious to note the hidden relations between private and public cleanliness ; relations, not merely connecting the defecation of our own dwellings with that of London at large ; but even making our personal ablutions, and the general scavenging of the town, part and parcel of the same operation. We are prepared to establish, by facts which will be found irrefragable, that no citizen of London can keep his own skin decently clean, in the absence of Sanitary Consolidation.

The 300,000 houses of London are interspaced by a street-surface, averaging about 44 square yards per house, and therefore measuring collectively about 13¼ million square yards, of which a large proportion is paved with granite. Upwards of 200,000 pairs of wheels, aided by a considerably larger number of iron-shod horses' feet, are constantly grinding this granite to powder : which powder is mixed with from 2 to 10 cartloads of horse-droppings per mile of street per diem,* besides an unknown quantity of the sooty deposits discharged from half a million smoking chimneys. In wet weather these several materials are beaten up into the thin, black, gruel-like compound, known as London-mud ; of which the watery and gaseous parts evaporate, during sunshine, into the air we breathe ; while the solid particles dry into a subtle dust, whirled up in clouds by the wind and by the horses' feet. These dust-clouds are deposited on our clothes and furniture ; on our skins, our lips, and on the air-tubes of our lungs. The close stable-like smell, and *flavour*, of the London air, the rapid soiling of our hands, our linen, and the hangings of our moos, bear ample witness to the reality of this evil ; of which every London citizen may find a further and most significant indication in the *dark* hue of the particles deposited by the dust-laden air in its passage through the nasal respiratory channels. To state this matter plainly, and without mincing words,—there is not at this moment a man in London, however scrupulously cleanly, nor a woman, however sensitively delicate, whose skin, and clothes, and nostrils, are not *of necessity* more or less loaded

---

* This estimate is based partly on the results of experimental cleansings carried on for several months in that part of Regent-street which extends from the Circus to the Quadrant, and partly on the working of the street-sweeping machines in the City. The data are extremely imperfect—but a proportionately wide margin has been allowed in the computation, which we believe to be an under-estimate.

with

with a compound of powdered granite, soot, and a still more nauseous substance. The particles which *to-day* fly in clouds before the scavenger's broom, fly *to-morrow* in clouds before the parlour-maid's brush, and *next day* darken the water in our toilet-basins, or are wrung by the laundress from our calico and cambric.

Precisely, therefore, as we have already seen that the two modes of urban defecation (by cesspool-cartage, and by sewer-flow) are but the same task, performed by *human labour* in one case, and by *steam-power* in the other; precisely so it now appears that our private dustings and detergent operations in London (so far as they exceed the ablutionary average of the country) are but the costly substitution of private *hand-labour* for *steam-power* scavenging, by which the same filth might be economically and effectually removed.

This is no exaggerated statement, dressed up for effect. It appears from experiments instituted by Mr. Lovick that a jet of water from a well-charged main, made to play through a hose and nozzle upon the pavement, will rapidly and thoroughly cleanse the streets, with an expenditure of one gallon of water per square yard of carriage-way, and half a gallon per square yard of foot-path: or about 11 million gallons for the total street area of the metropolis. Mr. Lee, of Sheffield, having at command a stronger hydraulic pressure, performed the same work with a third less water, and in a third less time. The stones, thus washed, shine out as white as if they were just laid; and the cost of thus brightening up the Strand every day would come (on Mr. Lovick's estimate) to 3*d.* per house per week; or with the higher pressure employed by Mr. Lee, (and proposed for adoption in the metropolis,) to 1*d.* per house per week. The jet, when directed upward in the form of spray, was found to wash, cool, and sensibly to freshen the air; acting, indeed, as a *moveable fountain.* The cleansing of the same surface by hand-sweeping, and cartage, proved incomparably less effectual, and nearly six-fold dearer. As for the cost of removing the same soil, *after* its settlement (though partial only) on the furniture, clothing, and persons, of the Strand-residents, it is approximatively represented by the difference between town and country washing-bills; and if this difference be taken as only 6*d.* per individual per week, it gives a balance of 5000 per cent. in favour of steam-power cleansing; —an economy, be it observed, wholly independent of the further incalculable saving in wear-and-tear of furniture and dress, in health, strength, doctors' bills, &c., which would result from this substitution of public for private cleansing, by means of Structural Consolidation.

The

The more closely, indeed, we study the financial bearings of this momentous question, the more clearly we perceive the error (already noted) of those who regard Sanitary Reform as a mere matter of charity,—the harmless hobby of a few philanthropic dilettanti, but utterly beside the 'main chance,' and indifferent to its sturdy poursuivants.   Consider, for example, the evidence of practical men on the Fire-risks of the metropolis ;—on their enormous aggravation by the present condition of the water-service ; and on the vast annual saving in premiums of insurance, which would accrue under this single head to the citizens, from the Structural Consolidation for which we contend.

It appears from the valuable evidence laid before the Board of Health by Mr. Braidwood, Superintendant of the Fire Brigade, and by Mr. Baddeley, Secretary to the Society for the Protection of Life from Fire, that 838 fires happened in London during 1849, ' *of which two-thirds would have been stopped at once had there been means of applying water immediately.*'   Mr. Braidwood, in referring to the chances of escape on these occasions, states, that assistance, ' to be of any use, must generally be rendered within five minutes after the alarm is given.'   The average time, however, which elapses before the first engine can be procured and got in play, is stated by Mr. Baddeley to be 23 minutes ; more than four times Mr. Braidwood's maximum.   Even when the first engine arrives, and is set to work, it can only furnish one jet, of about an inch in diameter ; which 26 men, toiling hard at the pumps, can only throw 50 feet high.   Under the proposed new constant-pressure system, the effective force of half a dozen such engines, manned by 156 men, will be maintained, day and night, before every house in London, ready to act within two minutes from the first alarm.   For the police will only have to screw the hoses to the fire-plugs, and half a dozen powerful jets will at once rise simultaneously into the air, ready for instant direction on the burning edifice.   These arrangements are already adopted at Preston ; where, indeed, the millowners carry high-pressure water-pipes into their warehouses, with a fire-plug and hose on every floor.   The cost of these precautionary measures is only about 2l. 2s. per warehouse per annum.   And the resulting security is so complete, that several millowners now dispense with insurances which formerly cost them 500l. per annum, and upwards, each.   Similar arrangements have been recently adopted in Liverpool ; with a saving, in the first year (as Mr. Newland, the town surveyor, informs us) of 25,000l. in insurance premiums alone.   In Hamburgh also, we learn from Mr. Lindley (who superintended the rebuilding of the town, after the late disastrous conflagration), that ' the power of eight engines may be anywhere applied in two
minutes,

minutes, the mere time required to screw on the hose; and thus have been promptly extinguished, *in every case*, repeated fires which, under the delay of the old system, might have occasioned extensive conflagrations.' In New York, again, the losses by fire have been diminished *one half*, and the premiums of insurance *one quarter*, since the high-pressure water-service has come into use; and it is but reasonable, we think, to believe that a similar organization of our London water-service would result in a proportionate abatement of our risks, and of the insurance charges we have to pay.

With many of our great manufacturers and merchants, however, the mitigation of these exceptional disasters, and the prospect of these contingent and ulterior economies, will weigh less in favour of the consolidated régime, than the direct and immediate reduction it will effect in the rates now levied on them by an extortionate Monopoly. We have been at some pains to compute the amount of this reduction; and we present the following figures as a close approximation to the truth.

The East London Water Company has 247 large manufacturing customers, whose united annual consumption amounts to 266 million gallons; for which their collective payment is 12,000*l.* per annum, being at the rate of 11*d.* per 1000 gallons. Now, the Nottingham charge per 1000 gallons, delivered on the constant system, is only 3*d.*; and this, with a larger consumption and improved arrangements, would be susceptible of further reduction, in London, to about 1¾*d.*;* at which rate the East London large consumers would pay collectively only 2000*l.* instead of 12,000*l.* per annum. Any individual manufacturer, therefore, on whom the monopolists now levy 300*l.* per annum for a supply of hard river water from the Lea, would, under the new arrangements, obtain the same quantity of superior Farnham water, for less than 50*l.* per annum; clearing thus 250*l.* a year, as his share in the profits of Sanitary Consolidation.

And here we may mention, as especially interesting the manufacturing class, a new industrial application of pipe-water cheaply delivered at high pressure from a centralized pumping establishment. We refer to the applicability of such water as a Motive Power for driving machinery. It has already been stated that 388 tons of water can be pumped 100 feet high at a working cost of 1*s.*; and the whole cost of delivering this water through pipes, taken as averaging 1¾*d.* per 1000 gallons, or rather less

---

* Our calculations lead us to believe that a very small fraction over 1½*d.* per 1000 gallons will prove a sufficient price for water in London, under the consolidated arrangements in view. The figure given in the text must therefore be taken as a moderate estimate of the economy to be anticipated; an estimate adopted from prudential motives, and in the desire to err, if at all, on the safe side.

than

than one farthing and three quarters per ton, would amount to 12*s*. 8½*d*. Now, the head of water thus raised at the central establishment, will of course exert its hydraulic pressure on the water in all the pipes throughout London ; constituting thus a mechanical force available at any point of the entire network, and capable of being turned on or off by means of an ordinary tap. It is easy to calculate the cost, and effective value, of this new motive power. 388 tons of steam-raised water will, in descending through 100 feet, raise the same weight of corn, coal, or any other commodity, to an equal height, in equal time ; proper allowance being made for loss by friction. Assuming this and other abatements to raise the cost of this new lifting power to one halfpenny per ton per 100 feet, it will still enable us to unload and warehouse merchandise with an economy, relatively to the cost of human haulage, which we leave to the appreciation of our commercial readers.

Steam-power itself, indeed, cannot be generated in small quantities by individual manufacturers, so cheaply as it might be procured from the vast boilers of a Centralized Pumping establishment, through the medium of the water-pipes. Small steam-engines of one or two horse-power, employed for driving light machinery, or for doing intermittent work, require as constant and as costly attendance as engines of tenfold size ; and they might be replaced, with great advantage, by a motive force involving no cost in wages, creating no smoke nor dirt, and shut off when not wanted, so as to preclude the possibility of waste. Cranes, indeed, contrived to work by water-power, are already employed, though under great disadvantages, in London. Printing-presses are economically driven by pipe-water power in the United States. Coffee-mills, packing-presses, smiths' bellows, chaff-cutters, bean-crushers, and mechanical ventilators, are a few among many examples that might be cited, of light machines capable of being economically worked by this new form of power.

These new industrial applications of steam-pumped pipe-water suggest as their obvious corollary, the employment of the same power for the abatement of Domestic Drudgery. Without laying undue stress upon a benefit as yet prospective, we cannot, consistently with our public duty, pass over in silence a probable result, so pregnant with important consequences. The Steam-engine has worked a revolution in the great Mining operations, and in several of the Agricultural processes, by which the raw materials of wealth are raised from the surface, or fetched up out of the bowels of the earth. Still more completely has Steam-power transformed the Manufacturing processes which adapt these raw materials to our use, and the Distributive machinery by which they are transported over land and sea to the consumer's abode. But

But here, hitherto, Steam-power has stopped short. It has lent no aid, as yet, to the legions of domestic drudges incessantly engaged in keeping household property fit for use. Vast as is the collective amount, and burdensome the cost, of human labour day by day absorbed in raising coals and other household stores—in washing walls and floors—in blacking shoes, cleansing kitchen utensils, and polishing innumerable forms of wood and metal—no portion of these repugnant tasks is yet performed by steam ; though they are all eminently suited, by their monotonous simplicity, for mechanical execution. And yet it is beyond doubt that the daily care and cleansing of our household goods usually involve a larger aggregate expenditure than the original purchase of the articles. The *cleansing-costs* of a plate or knife, for instance, reckoned in wages paid for servants' time, will in the course of a dozen years exceed, tenfold and more, the few pence or shillings originally paid for the utensil. Of the total labour expended on boots and saucepans, from the period of their first construction to that of their final decay, the shoeblack gives probably a larger share than the shoemaker, and the kitchen-wench more than the tinman. Now, the mechanical appliances for relieving domestics of the more toilsome portions of this household drudgery are ready contrived to our hands. All sorts of rotatory brushes, polishers, and cleansing apparatus, are advantageously employed in our factories ; and would be available for domestic use, *if we had a cheap motive power to work them.* This final condition—the only link required to complete the necessary chain—will be supplied by a Structural Centralization, enabling us to employ pipe-water as a Vehicle for the distribution of Steam-power, in retail quantities, to private domiciles. And though we would carefully guard ourselves against being supposed to advance these eventualities, however probable, in support of an argument too firmly based on ascertained facts to need any such speculative corroboration, we are free to declare our belief that the introduction of Steam-power into private households (coupled with the before-described replacement of much private cleansing, by public steam-jet scavenging, &c.) will at no distant date as thoroughly transform our Domestic economy, as it has already transformed our Mining, Manufacturing, and Commercial systems. And when it is considered that of the metropolitan population nearly 8 per cent. are domestic servants; while the grand total (1,165,223) entered as such in the last census is the largest return under any one head—exceeding nearly fourfold the whole number (302,376) employed in the cotton manufacture, and nearly fortyfold the whole number (29,497) employed in the iron manufacture—it will be admitted, we think, that this Domestic Revolution is likely to rank amongst the
most

most signal of the benefits flowing directly or collaterally from the principle of Sanitary Consolidation.

But we number, doubtless, among our readers, especially among those of the fair sex, some who understand little, and care less, about mechanical improvements ; who, like Madame de Staël, *adorent l'inutile;* and, with Göthe, encourage the Beautiful—relying on the Useful to encourage itself. To all such we would respectfully point out the favourable reaction which Sanitary Consolidation will have on the fine arts :—the impulse, for example, which every successive abatement of filth must give to the decoration, exterior and interior, of our now dingy habitations; the prolonged preservation, by the same means, of the priceless relics of ancient art—now rapidly obscured by sooty deposits, and imperilled by their periodical removal ; and, finally, the multiplication throughout our cities of cascades and fountains—those most living and poetical of all urban embellishments. When copious streams of water can be poured foaming down the mimic rocks, or thrown up, sparkling, high into the sultry air, at the cost of about 4*s.* per 100 tons, what park in London need lack its waterfall—what square or open space remain without its elegant *jet d'eau ?* Already, in imagination, we see their graceful columns, rising translucent from the sculptured bronze ; their sun-lit summits crested with cool spray, and sparkling with iridescent light ; each drop one moment poised, a flashing prism — then falling back, a silver-frosted curve, with liquid cadence on the ringing marble. Nor will these delightful harmonies of form and light and colour, of liquid melody and living motion, be accessible to us as heretofore only in our public promenades. Few residents in the suburbs, possessing gardens, or in the heart of the town, having conservatories attached to their dwellings, will think it needful to debar themselves the luxury of a private fountain, when a half-inch jet, 30 feet high, may be kept playing for 2*d.* an hour—scarcely more than the burning-cost of an ordinary Argand lamp.

And now, from these pictures of prospective enjoyment, let us turn for a moment to the contrasted spectacle of that which is passing around us. With these sparkling fountains of a Centralized system let us compare Monopolist waterfalls, and the cascades of the Fragmentary régime. Taken collectively, they form a vaster torrent, these metropolitan cascades of ours, than the reader probably suspects : for it has been ascertained, by accurate gaugings, that they consume thirty million gallons of water per diem, or more than TWO-THIRDS of the whole supply daily pumped into London. Where, then, are they—these copious cataracts ? What unknown squares or Fortunate Fields do they adorn ? Where foams our London *Trevi ?* Where sparkles our

fountain-

fountain-crowned Viminal Hill? What cloven rock, gushing beneath the rod of a marble Moses, pours forth for us its ' happy waters' ?

Alas ! these precious streams, available for so many purposes of use and luxury, run squandered in the sewers. 1181 public standcocks dribbling to waste in squalid lanes and courts—a hundred times as many overflow-pipes from waterbutts and cisterns —such are the unseen vents through which TWO-THIRDS of our recklessly managed water-supply are suffered to leak away. London, to resume our old metaphor, lies bleeding at a hundred thousand wounds ; and from its iron arteries gush out, each day, TWO-THIRDS of the vital stream.

The exhaustion which this frightful hæmorrhage entails on our social system may be easily conceived. We forbear to paint the dismal condition of those on whom this culpable waste inflicts entire destitution of the first necessary of life, and who are actually reduced to beg their daily jugful from door to door. The cruelty of the Standcock system to some thirty or forty thousand of the labouring poor, and the cost thereby entailed upon society at large, fall more within our present scope to reckon. The computation is but too easy. Conceive thirty thousand poor creatures (chiefly women), whose time and strength are all their property, condemned each day to fetch, pailful by pailful, from the public tap, their thirty thousand several supplies ; and these to drag, up toilsome staircases, to the upper floors of their respective dwellings. Bear in mind that, by our centralized pumping establishment, the whole of this water (say 60,000 gallons) might be delivered, at high pressure, on every floor, for about 9*s.* ; and with this charge compare the cost, in time equivalent to money, imposed on these unfortunates by the standcock delivery. If her daily water-task cost each poor woman only ten minutes' time, and a proportionate amount of working strength, evidently the collective daily expenditure of the whole 30,000 amounts to 300,000 minutes, or 500 working days—worth, at the low average wage of 1*s.* per diem, 25*l.* ; which is, therefore, the actual present cost of a service capable of being profitably done, by Steam-power, for 9*s.* Even at the rate of 6*d.* per diem—the lowest wage, we believe, allotted to the worst paid needlewoman—Society loses upwards of 2700 per cent. by every minute diverted from productive needlework to this painful water-drudgery.

Here we are content to stop. We will leave them flowing side by side—the Standcocks of the old régime in their costly squalor—the Fountains of the new in their inexpensive beauty. Comment would but weaken the vividness of this simple contrast : which may fitly close a portion of our argument, destined, as the

reader

reader will remember, to prove, by its influence on Sanitary *structures*, the value of that regenerating principle, which we had already appreciated in its effect on Sanitary *administration*. From the point now reached the reader may survey, at a glance, the general plan of this second part of our argument; and review, as at the close of the first, our principal conclusions. For as, in a former article, we took up our station in the midst of the Gathering-grounds, and showed the reader (so to speak) as much of the subject as could be surveyed from the top of Farnham hill; so, on the present occasion, we have stood with him in the centre of the Metropolis, and, dissecting-knife in hand, have laid bare, branch by branch, its colossal circulating system. Each stroke of the scalpel has helped, we think, to justify the analogies which, at the outset of our argument, we ventured to trace between the Individual and the Collective organism. At each point of the inquiry we have found our best economy to lie in a vigilant observance of Nature's laws; and in a close, though not a servile imitation of her admirable patterns. Studying thus what may be called the Anatomy and Physiology of Towns, we have been led to approve the unitary centralization of structures at present dispersed and fragmentary, and the harmonization of organs hitherto utterly discordant. Thus, step by step, we have been brought to perceive that one great heart, or centralized Waterwork, is better than nine little scattered ones; that water-mains and sewers should be proportioned to each other, like the companion-vessels of a limb; and, generally, that our urban vascular system should be so constructed and disposed, as to fulfil its functions with the greatest economy of material, and the least possible liability to obstruction. Reduced to their practical expression, these principles went to show the superiority, at all points, of small postern sewers to the great tunnels now built beneath our streets. Pushing forward our dissection from these main trunks to the capillaries, arterial and venous, of each separate house, and referring again to the corresponding structures of the human body, we found no natural precedent for those companion-forms of stagnancy—the Cistern and the Cesspool; which we accordingly marked, as abnormal tumours, for immediate excision: while a very brief analysis, of the same kind, decided us against poisonous lead and porous brick as materials for branch water-pipes and drains. Bringing these physiological views to the test of engineering experience, we set forth the heavy charges entailed on us by the old circulating system of London, and cited a series of experiments and computations to prove at once the economy and the efficiency of the new. Amongst other unexpected results, this comparison forced on us the conclusion that our old sewers might be abandoned

and

and London drained *de novo*, not only without levying new rates, but with a positive reduction of existing rates, swelled as they are by the enormous flushing-costs of the present defective structures. Finally, in our anxiety to bring these advantages home in a tangible form to every class of our readers, we showed how the proposed consolidation would have for its effect to abate the risks of fire, and the costs of insurance; to promote and cheapen public and personal cleanliness; to extend, by the provision of a distributive vehicle, the applications of steam-power—available, henceforth, not only for industrial but also for domestic use; to embellish with cascades and fountains not only our public squares, but also our private dwellings; and, lastly, to relieve the labouring poor from a needless drudgery, wrongful to themselves, and burdensome (like Wrong in every form) to Society at large.

From these details, severally minute, though broad in their collective scope, we would willingly return with the indulgent reader to the philosophical ground whence we started together; and, rising to a higher point of view, study with him the true import and ulterior tendency of the Sanitary Movement, its relations to the higher political life of Society, and its rank among those characteristic developments, which distinguish modern from ancient civilization. But in the few lines and moments remaining at our present disposal, we could scarcely propound, much less develope, these vast and pregnant themes; which therefore for the present we forego:—content if, at the point which our argument has reached, we have in any degree fortified the reader's judgment as to the distinctions between *real* and *nominal* Self-government, between *wholesome* and *obnoxious* Centralization, between *substantive* and *shadowy* Responsibility; distinctions which, once clearly apprehended, can scarcely leave a doubt between the rival claims of a Grand Junction Trading Monopoly, a Metropolitan Parish Parliament, and a Board of Crown-appointed Commissioners, to the future sanitary government of London. It is, indeed, obvious that the responsibility, avowedly wanting in the first body, and but nominally attaching to the second, would be really and availably inherent in the third:—unfluctuating as its composition would be; its members few, paid, and removable; its labours continuous; its errors subject to the triple censure of the Parliament, the Press, and the Public; and its duty and interest concurring with the clauses of a stringent Act, to maintain it in steadfast allegiance to the great principles of Sanitary Consolidation.

As for those admirable principles themselves, we should indeed rejoice if we could inspire the reader, at parting, with our own profound conviction of their truth, and earnest solicitude for their prevalence. From whatever point of view, indeed,

deed, we contemplate the luminous Code in which they are embodied, we find it still pregnant with incalculable good, to ourselves as well as to our successors. We find it strengthening the double basis, local and central, of our well-poised constitutional government, by a *simultaneous* expansion of municipal and imperial institutions. Concurrently with this development of our collective or social life, we find it prolonging the term, and enhancing the enjoyment, of our individual existence, by bringing its material conditions into closer conformity with Natural Law. Nor is it merely a physical emancipation which we find the Sanitary Movement thus gradually working out. Each alleviation of bodily disease and drudgery absolves also our nobler faculties from the reaction of a degrading bondage; and makes us at once fitter and freer for the pursuit of those high destinies which, albeit originating amidst the corruptions of the present, have their term in the brightness of futurity. To secure these inestimable advantages, what self-abnegations are we called upon to practise—what perils to encounter—what personal sacrifices to undergo? None,—absolutely none.   In the very lowest, as well as in the highest sense of the term, we shall be *gainers*, each and all of us, by the progress of Sanitary Reform : and our private interests, personal and pecuniary, are closely bound up in the success of a Cause, which might well inspire, and would worthily requite, the most heroic self-devotion.